MEANING IN ACTION

MEANING IN ACTION

INTERPRETATION AND DIALOGUE IN POLICY ANALYSIS

HENDRIK WAGENAAR

M.E.Sharpe
Armonk, New York
London, England

To Tesse and Nicolaas, inexhaustible sources of meaning

Library of Congress Cataloging-in-Publication Data

Wagenaar, H.
  Meaning in action : interpretation and dialogue in policy analysis / by Hendrik Wagenaar.
    p. cm.
  Includes bibliographical references and index.
  ISBN 978-0-7656-1788-0 (hardcover : alk. paper)—ISBN 978-0-7656-1789-7 (pbk. : alk. paper)
  1. Policy sciences. 2. Policy sciences—Methodology. I. Title.

H97.W334 2011
320.6—dc22   2010040049

Printed in the United States of America

The paper used in this publication meets the minimum requirements of
American National Standard for Information Sciences
Permanence of Paper for Printed Library Materials,
ANSI Z 39.48-1984.

♾

EB (c)	10	9	8	7	6	5	4	3	2	1
EB (p)	10	9	8	7	6	5	4	3	2	1

CONTENTS

PREFACE

Late in 2004, in a bar in Copenhagen, Frank Fischer asked me to contribute a chapter on interpretive policy analysis to his *Handbook of Public Policy Analysis* (Fischer, Miller, & Sidney, 2007; Wagenaar, 2007b). When a few months later I began working on the chapter, I wrote, somewhat to my surprise, eighty pages in less than a week. Central to this early draft was the insight—now the organizing principle of this book—that the concept of meaning as it figured in the various approaches to interpretive policy analysis was plural, and that it showed three distinct "faces," each grounded in widely different philosophical assumptions, working methods, and topical preferences. Clearly, this was far too much material for a chapter, and I began to entertain the idea of expanding it into a book.

The rush of material was the result of my experience teaching interpretive policy analysis in a series of master seminars at the University of Amsterdam. For several years Maarten Hajer and I had taught a successful seminar in the run-up to and the wake of our volume *Deliberative Policy Analysis* (2003). This had given me a feel for the bewilderment and struggles of students who were disappointed by empiricist-instrumentalist policy analysis and wanted to apply interpretive approaches to understanding policy issues. As it was difficult to find good teaching material (most books being too parochial, too specialized, or too abstract), I concluded that there was room for a book that provided a reasoned overview of interpretive approaches.

I have incurred debts to many people during the writing of this book. First, of course, Frank Fischer, tireless promoter of interpretive approaches in policy analysis, in our many shared ventures in this area. Without the opportunity he gave me to articulate my teaching experiences, this book would probably not have been written. Then my good friend and colleague Guy Adams, who, over dinner in our kitchen, stimulated me to write this book in the best possible way: by getting me in touch with Harry Briggs from M.E. Sharpe. Then, the participants of an exciting book workshop (a fringe event of the Second International Conference on Interpretive Policy Analysis in Amsterdam) at which Jason Glynos and David Howarth's book *Logics of Critical Explanation in Social and Political Theory* (2007) and an early draft of my book were discussed. This workshop gave me two things that are indispensable in the relatively early stages of a large project: a perspective on how to situate my book in the field of other books, and a sympathetic reception by a knowledgeable audience that communicates that the project is viable. There were too many people there to thank each of them personally. I single out Jason and David for their, as always, critical, incisive, and supportive commentary. Their suggestions for additional readings kept me busy for months but eventually strengthened the argument of this book. I also single out Thomas Schwandt, who regrettably was prevented by illness from attending the workshop and the conference, but took the trouble to write up his notes on reading the draft. An early version of chapter 8 originated in a panel on dialogical approaches in policy analysis at the aforesaid conference. John Forester's comments greatly improved the paper that resulted from that panel (Wagenaar, 2008).

A special word of thanks goes to Robert Weiss. In the 1980s he was my mentor in the art and craft of qualitative interviewing and data analysis. A number of years ago we began to articulate our insights about doing and teaching grounded theory. For various reasons we did not manage to finish the paper, but chunks of it found their way into chapter 9 of this book. I suggested that he coauthor the chapter, but he generously left the honors to me. It will be obvious that I am deeply indebted to Bob. Without him I would be a lesser researcher and writer.

I am immensely grateful to the students in my and Maarten Hajer's Amsterdam seminar on deliberative policy analysis. With their curiosity and critical engagement they gently forced me to present my material as clearly and accessibly as possible. They also taught me to avoid unnecessary abstractions and to demonstrate general principles in the presentation of concrete cases. I hope I heeded their lessons. Later, in a methods workshop at the University of Essex and a Ph.D. seminar at Roskilde University, I had the good fortune to repeat the experience with an (almost) finished draft of the book. Even at this late stage, the generous critical spirit of the participants was very helpful in inducing some important final changes to the manuscript. I thank Aletta Norval and Eva Sørensen for inviting me to these seminars. I also thank Steven Griggs for making it possible for me to present parts of the book at the Institute of Local Government Studies at the University of Birmingham.

This book was long in the making. It would have been considerably longer if not for the practical support of a number of people. I am indebted to Peter van der Voort, librarian of the Netherlands Institute for the Study of Crime and Law Enforcement, for his tireless efforts to procure every book or article that I requested, no matter how exotic, within hours. I thank my in-laws, Josef and Gerda Prainsack. In their beautiful house in Feldkirchen, Carinthia, they provided the ideal writing retreat whenever I needed it. The time I spent there was the most productive and pleasant of the years that I worked on this book. I thank our office manager at the Centre for Governance Studies of Leiden University, Pam de Groot, for her editing efforts in the last phase of the book. She is the kind of intelligent, careful editor that every writer dreams of. I express my special gratitude to Elizabeth Granda Parker and Angela Piliouras of M.E. Sharpe, who gently nudged my almost-English toward a clear and more attractive text. I also thank Harry Briggs of M.E. Sharpe for his boundless patience and gracious encouragement when I had to inform him of yet another postponement of the delivery of the manuscript.

Finally, my loving thanks to my wife, Barbara Prainsack, whose infectious enthusiasm for this book from its earliest stages has sustained me throughout the long labor of writing and rewriting. We spent many hours discussing innumerable parts of the manuscript. Her critical spirit and good judgment are present in every sentence of this book.

PART 1

POLICY INTERPRETATIONS

Theory and Applications

1

INTRODUCTION

Interpretation in Policy Analysis

WHAT IS INTERPRETIVE POLICY ANALYSIS?

As good a definition as any is the following: "Interpretive approaches to political studies focus on meanings that shape actions and institutions, and the ways in which they do so" (Bevir and Rhodes, 2004, 130). This comes close to being a standard definition of interpretive policy analysis in that it contains all the necessary elements: political actions, institutions, meaning, and the reality-shaping power of meaning. Meanings are not just representations of people's beliefs and sentiments about political phenomena; they fashion these phenomena.

On the surface, giving shape to actions and institutions sounds innocent enough, and I imagine that few people will take issue with this description of the interpretive approach to policy analysis. It suggests that to study public policy it is sometimes useful to look beyond overt acts of political behavior such as voting or expressing a preference for party X or proposal Y. To understand, for example, why a particular policy fails to bring about its intended effects, or why people resist the reconstruction of their neighborhood, it may be important to gauge what that policy or neighborhood means to those people, what impact a change in one or the other has on their lives and their community. To this effect it is necessary to employ different methods than the standardized survey instrument or the quasi-experimental research design. We need methods that allow us to record and analyze the original language in which people express their feelings, beliefs, ideals, fears, and desires, in relation to themselves, their neighborhood, their community, or the impact of a particular public policy. Such methods have been available for many decades, of course. Qualitative research interviews, ethnographic observation, and the inductive generation of mid-level grounded theory from the rich data that such methods yield have provided researchers with invaluable insights into the experiential aspects of, for example, structural unemployment among black men (Liebow, 1967 [2003]), life in a youth gang (Whyte, 1943 [1993]), homelessness (Wiseman, 1979), or chronic mental illness (Estroff, 1981). Such studies explained, for example, why service programs for alcoholic homeless men or the chronically mentally ill are often less effective, or effective in a different way, than providers had hoped for.

It all comes down, it seems, to matching the method to the question. If we want a reliable estimate of how a political phenomenon is distributed in a population or the extent to which it is statistically associated with another phenomenon, we employ quantitative, empiricist research methods. If, on the other hand, we want to get an understanding of what a policy means to the people who are affected by it, how they experience the concerted efforts of a state agency to improve their lives, we employ interpretive research methods.

If only it were this simple. In fact, those who are attracted to an interpretive approach to policy analysis quickly run into a number of obstacles that stand in the way of an easy intellectual and practical grasp of the field.

THE PROGRAMMATIC NATURE OF INTERPRETIVE POLICY ANALYSIS

First, interpretive policy analysis is not *just* a method or family of methods, something you take off the shelf to answer a particular research question. If anything, it is more like a doctrine, a tenet. I don't mean this pejoratively, but in the technical sense of a set of more or less warranted beliefs about how to act; in this case, how to address a number of epistemological and methodological problems in the social sciences in a fitting manner. Doctrines deal with ought questions. You can muster good, even compelling, reasons for them, but in the end it is your argument against their argument, and there is no guarantee that you will be able to persuade the other (Hood & Jackson, 1991). Most interpretive analysts do not satisfy themselves with the modest claim that values, beliefs, and feelings are important political phenomena in their own right, well worth paying attention to if one desires to understand the formulation and implementation of public policy. In fact—as the definition by Bevir and Rhodes made clear—almost all interpretive analysts operate on the stronger philosophical claim that meaning does not merely put a particular affective or evaluative gloss on things, but that it is somehow *constitutive* of political actions, governing institutions, and public policies.

Constitutive is a concept that is simultaneously controversial and trite. It is trite in that it, and its synonyms "constructed" (with or without the prefix "socially") and "contingent," have become so pervasive in interpretive social science that they tend to function as shibboleths, symbolic markers that signal that you speak the right language and belong to the *initiated*. (Insert "created" or "made" for "constructed," or "happenstance" for "contingent," and you get a feel for the ritualistic, coded quality of these terms. This plain-speaking language conveys the same ideas, but sounds much less interesting.) It is controversial because it glosses over a slew of philosophical and practical difficulties that are usually more hinted at than explicated. I will discuss some of these later in this book (particularly chapter 7), but I want to mention here one point that is especially relevant to the subject of interpretation in policy analysis.

The word "constituted" contains a weak and a strong claim (see also Schwandt, 2000). The weak claim is as in the Bevir and Rhodes statement and consists of two parts: (1) all sorts of social influences shape how people understand, experience, and feel about any given social phenomenon; and (2) the "meaning" that people attach to social phenomena in turn influences the structure and functioning of common categories of social analysis such as institutions, social practices, and public policies. Meaning influences people's behavior. For example, upon coming into office in 1997, the British Labour Party faced an administrative landscape that was fragmented and hollowed out by years of market-driven, conservative administration. Labour wanted to restore the traditional role of the state as provider of security and basic services to those in need, but at the same time take seriously the neoliberal critique that found inefficiency, welfare dependency, fiscal irresponsibility, and lack of competitiveness when the state took that role. This is the "meaning" that Labour attached to public administration upon coming into office. Its reaction was to modernize governance by creating outcome-focused, problem-driven administrative strategies that aimed at including citizens and other social actors in policy making by designing programs of "joined up" government (Bevir & Rhodes, 2003; Newman, 2001). This form of interpretivism is an important program in policy analysis. One could call it a sophisticated institutional analysis that includes beliefs and values (Scott, 2007). But it is not particularly novel or eyebrow-raising. It doesn't challenge any deep-seated experience of reality.[1]

The strong claim also starts with part 1, but differs on part 2. Instead of stating that meaning influences institutions, practices, and policies that form the categories and objects of social analysis, it holds that meaning brings them into being. Buried in this is an epistemological and moral program. For example, mental illness is sometimes seen as "socially constructed" (Coulter, 1979). What is implied is a moral-analytical program that goes somewhat like this: there is no such thing as an immutable social object we can call "mental illness." Whenever we speak of mental illness we impose a particular interpretation on a particular slice of behavior. That interpretation is driven by a hidden power configuration, and by bringing this configuration to light the analyst opens up the possibility of more benign or humane interpretations of the same behavior.[2] This is a simplified reading, and there are many variants of it that I will discuss in due course, but what I want to draw out here are the moral aims of the strong claim. By engaging in constructivist work under the strong claim, you engage—implicitly or explicitly—in an emancipatory endeavor. One does not go without the other. Under the strong claim there is no morally neutral constructivist work. The purpose is to unmask, to reveal what is hidden (Hacking, 1999, 53). My purpose at this point is not more than to raise awareness of the programmatic quality that is intrinsic to constructivist talk. Attention should not go just to the rightness or justifiability of constructivist explanations, but also to the social goals that the analyst wants to achieve with them.

THE NORMATIVE DIMENSION OF INTERPRETIVE POLICY ANALYSIS

Policy analysis is a moral activity. This is a self-evident statement, but value issues make analysts, both of the empiricist and interpretivist stripe, uneasy. So, before we describe how both camps deal with the moral character of policy analysis, let's first unpack the role of values in public policy.

The official line, espoused by Lasswell, one of the founding fathers of the discipline, is that policy analysis is a normative discipline in the service of spreading democracy in the world and defending it against the threat of tyranny (Lasswell, 1951). The motto of the journal *Policy Sciences,* the torchbearer of Lasswell's program, is: "integrating knowledge and practice to advance human dignity for all." This is an important statement, but most practitioners of the trade will consider it peripheral to their daily work and the kind of pious statement that one disperses at official occasions. In practice the choices of the analyst are much more mundane, driven by the exigencies of organizational reality. Here is an authoritative definition of everyday policy analysis: "[P]olicy analysis is a process of multidisciplinary inquiry designed to create, critically assess, and communicate information that is useful in understanding and improving policies" (Dunn, 2004, 1–2). And Dunn goes on to say that policy analysis aspires to generate knowledge that is relevant to the various stages of the policy-making process, from problem structuring, to policy implementation, to the evaluation of public policy. He concludes that the methodology of policy analysis is "based on scientific methods," but in the end "policy analysis also rests on art, craft, and persuasion." (2004, 2). "Critically assess," "useful," "improving," "art," "craft, "persuasion"—do I need to go on? Values shape the myriad unrecognized practical judgments that go into everyday analytical work: framing a problem, formulating a questionnaire, analyzing data, drawing conclusions, shaping arguments, presenting the report. Value judgments cannot be avoided. They extend to every aspect of the work of professional policy analysis. Just how to deal with the value dimension of policy analysis, however, is not so clear.

Perhaps those who still are reluctant to accept the normative dimensions of policy analysis will be persuaded by the following example from Dunn's widely read textbook, *Public Policy Analysis: An Introduction* (2004). Dunn argues that policy analysis has an important role to play in "policy structuring." In fact, in policy analysis "methods of problem structuring take priority over methods of problem solving." The reason is that "lower-level questions" of problem solving assume that the analyst has a clear understanding of what the problem is. Dunn illustrates this with the problem of industrial pollution: "Lower-level questions about the net benefits . . . of alternative solutions for the control of industrial pollution already assume that industrial pollution is the problem." At the "next-higher level" of problem structuring the analyst "may well find that the most appropriate formulation of the problem is closely related to the driving habits of Americans for whom gasoline and oil are comparatively cheap and heavily subsidized by the government" (72–73). No matter on which side of the issue analysts find themselves (for or against reducing air pollution by discouraging automobile use), each stance is, inescapably, a normative one.

There is nothing new here, but most policy analysts, particularly of the empiricist stripe, prefer to deny this inconvenient fact. They want it both ways: to be scientifically rational *and* to argue for a particular normative position. This conflict is resolved by sleight of hand. You relegate the value aspects to the periphery of the analytic process—to the formulation of the policy problem, where values enter unnoticed under the guise of policy goals, and to the recommendations at the end of the report. In the middle is the "objective" process of scientific research. Objectivity is guaranteed by an excessive focus on method. It is hoped that the value position that bookends the scientific analysis is carried by the allegedly rational research process. How do interpretive analysts deal with values in public policy? Much more directly and imaginatively. Values, or rather the inability of empiricist approaches to deal with values, formed the spearhead of the critical policy analysis movement of the mid-1970s (Rein, 1976; Taylor, [1967] 1985b; Tribe, 1972. The analysts of that movement rightly argued that values are not an add-on to the policy process, but are intrinsic to the very purpose and subject matter of the profession. Some critical analysts have translated this critique into imaginative programs of value-critical, interpretive policy analysis (Fischer, 1980; Rein, 1976; Stone, 1997).

The moral program that is implicit in the interpretive, constructivist approach should be highly relevant to the prospects of an interpretive form of policy analysis. Yet, the intrinsically normative nature of policy analysis raises difficult issues for the interpretive analyst. For, if the goal of policy analysis is to improve the quality and outcome of political decision making (Human Dignity for All!), then this goal extends by implication to whatever interpretive method the analyst applies in analyzing a specific policy. This then raises a number of further issues and challenges, such as the place and nature of knowledge in policy making, the practical, action-oriented nature of policy making, the position of the analyst in the institutional house of public policy making, the relation between policy making and democracy, and the relation of the analyst to the object of analysis. Clearly, these issues cannot be evaded by the stock phrase that policy analysis is an applied science, implying that the analyst is nothing more than a neutral scientific professional who supplies objective, academically credentialed knowledge to political decision makers. I will return to many of these issues in the final chapter of this book.

The opposite position, that the analyst is a critical voice for the downtrodden, outside the apparatus of government, I also consider somewhat of a cop out. Don't get me wrong: promoter of social justice and amplifier of the voice of the powerless are important roles for policy analysts to play (Forester, 1999b; Greenwood & Levin, 1998; Reardon, 2000). In chapter 8, "Dialogical Meaning," I will discuss a number of approaches in which the value of democratic equality is central to both the goal and the organization of the analytical work. But even in our decentered networks of governance, government institutions play a key role in public policy making, and if analysts want their critical analyses to have any influence with public officials, they eventually will have to converse with them (as is readily acknowledged in the dialogical approaches in chapter 8). In fact, as we will see in the next chapter, both conceptually and institutionally, interpretive analysis forms an integral part of the political-administrative institutions of liberal democracy. In addition, the origin of interpretive policy analysis as a critique of the hidden ideological quality of traditional analysis places a particular responsibility on the shoulders of interpretive analysts to live up to the critical, reflexive ambitions of their approach. One of the main arguments of this book, an argument that I will begin to develop in chapter 5, is that the design of interpretive policy analysis should not only reflect these circumstances, but address them head-on. Unraveling some of the thorny philosophical and ethical issues involved here is one of the purposes of this book.

FEAR AND BEWILDERMENT IN INTERPRETIVE POLICY ANALYSIS

This is not the last of the obstacles to grasping interpretive policy analysis. Even if we are comfortable with the normative, emancipatory stance of interpretive policy analysis, we still haven't reached dry ground. For, once we venture past the introductory pages of the standard text on interpretive social research, we suddenly find ourselves in an intellectual landscape that is downright bewildering. First, interpretive policy analysis is not one but many approaches. Labels such as frame analysis, ethnomethodology, discourse analysis (with subdivisions named after its various proponents: Foucault, Laclau and Mouffe, Potter, Fairclough, Gee), narrative analysis, genealogical analysis, hermeneutics (with or without the adjective "philosophical"), phenomenology, structuralism and poststructuralism, and practice theory indicate an enormous variety of approaches to interpretation in social research. In addition, these approaches differ not only with regard to the object or method of analysis, but also in their philosophical assumptions. These assumptions concern a range of epistemological and even ontological issues—the nature of political reality, the role of language in our grasp of the world, the place of values in the constitution of political reality, the meaning of meaning, the position of the interpretive analyst versus his object of analysis, the relation between acting and knowing, or the balance between structure (and determination) and agency (or freedom to act)—each one of which is enough to awe a professional philosopher, let alone the graduate student who feels attracted to interpretive approaches in policy analysis.

Then there is the writing. We write to communicate, not to impress, but many authors in the interpretive realm seem not to have taken this undergraduate maxim to heart. Obscurity and impenetrableness reign. The debates among interpretive theorists have generated their own vocabulary richly studded with exotic "isms" such as social constructivism (both strong and weak), interpretivism, meaning realism, holism, essentialism, foundationalism, and perspectivism. In addition, the language of interpretive social science is rife with well-worn phrases, such as that discourse "constitutes" a social phenomenon, or that X is "socially constructed," or that it makes sense to think of a policy as a "text" or "text analogue," which obscure more than they explain.

These are not merely academic issues. Years of teaching interpretive research to graduate students has convinced me that the pitfalls of interpretive analysis are many, and that an insufficient understanding of the varieties of interpretive analysis and their respective philosophical assumptions directly translates into deficient research designs. (I will return to this point in chapter 9.) This risk is aggravated by an, at first sight, curious dearth of texts that tell the interested reader how to go about actually *doing* interpretive analysis. The common format of a text on interpretive analysis is an elaborate exposition of its theoretical principles, usually in the form of a sustained critique of an opposing approach. Brief, carefully chosen, highly stylized examples must give the reader an impression of how the approach works in practice. But these are hardly the detailed exemplars that the novice needs, to begin to grasp how to engage in independent, productive practical work. How to do actual research with, for example, poststructuralist discourse analysis, or value-critical frame analysis, or critical discourse analysis is by and large left unstated.

It is little wonder then that students who venture onto the path of interpretive analysis soon find to their dismay that it is narrow and slippery. Here is a brief but representative sample of common errors: Many narrative analyses make little use of the specifically *narrative* qualities of the text to explain political phenomena, qualities such as the orchestrated interplay of text and audience through the strategic positioning of implicit meanings in the story, or the "inseparability of character, setting and action" that is so characteristic of storytelling (Bruner, 1986; Gee, 1985). In fact, in many such studies the reader can easily interchange the term "narrative" for "belief" or "exposition" without altering the semantic meaning of the text. Similarly, quite a few studies that purport to engage in discourse analysis are in fact nothing more than a simple content analysis of a series of newspaper clippings or policy reports. In such studies discourse is, de facto, nothing more than public debate. The specific quality of discourse analysis, namely its ability to account for the creation of social categories and objects by relating them to the largely implicit and self-evident body of social rules that enable them to stand out and be perceived as categories and objects (Howarth, 2000), is nowhere in sight. Also, few novice interpretive analysts have a good grasp of the complexities and exigencies of their position qua analyst. They assume, for example, that meaning simply exists out in the social world to be picked up by a detached researcher, instead of being painstakingly reconstructed in a dialogue with the subjects of analysis. Or that to declare yourself critical (by revealing the hidden ideological character of a certain "discourse") is enough to change the world. To be sure, bad research is not restricted to any particular scientific approach. My argument is merely that each interpretive approach raises its own particular challenges, which can only be met by a thorough understanding of the range of conceptual, methodological, and practical issues that, taken together, define the craft of interpretive research.

INTERPRETIVE POLICY ANALYSIS IS HARD TO DO

What makes interpretive policy analysis particularly difficult to execute is the interpenetration of method and theory. Or perhaps it is more precise to say that the relation between theory and the practice of analytic inquiry is densely layered and fraught with the kinds of elusive contextual judgments that elude formalization in research methods or protocols. To my mind the relation between theory and practice in interpretive analysis raises at least three important and related issues. First, each approach to interpretive analysis forms a theoretical and methodological whole, a "complete package," as Jørgensen and Phillips call it (2002, 4). The package contains ontological and epistemological assumptions, assumptions about society, power, and social identity, social and policy theories, a preference for certain types of questions over others, methodological guidelines, and a few exemplars of analysis. All of this is crystallized in a set of concepts that define the approach. The term "whole" indicates that all of these elements form a more or less integrated entity. Jørgensen and Phillips admonish researchers to combine packages by borrowing and combining elements from different approaches (they call this "multiperspectival" work [2002, 4]). I am less sanguine about that prospect. It is difficult enough to do good analytic work within a particular perspective. Moreover, the philosophical and theoretical assumptions of the different approaches tend to contradict, and in some cases even exclude, each other.

Second, the interpenetration of theory and analytical practice places a large burden on the analyst to find the proper balance between the two. This is precisely the point where much interpretive policy analysis goes off the rails. We already saw that, with some exceptions, the intellectual leaders of the field are strong on theory and weak on empirical application. It is little wonder, then, that over and over again I see student dissertations in which a truly interesting topic is hidden behind a wall of grand theorizing. A student can, for example, suggest a fascinating topic such as a comparative study of the proliferation of closed-circuit television cameras in various countries or the nature of return programs for immigrants and asylum seekers, and then smother the subject under mountains of turgid prose on poststructuralist discourse, Lacan's theory of the subject, the subject position as it is constituted by a particular order of discourse, or whatnot. In the meantime the real, flesh-and-blood world of closed-circuit television cameras or immigration policies has receded far behind the horizon. In my opinion the issue is at heart clear and simple. Interpretive policy analysis is always an interpretation *of* something: people acting, fighting, communicating, negotiating, experimenting, and so on. No amount of sophisticated philosophizing can alter that basic truth. After years of teaching, I have come to consider Intemperate Theorizing the single most common pitfall for graduate students of interpretive policy analysis.

Part of the problem is that the interpenetration of theory and method in interpretive policy analysis kicks the chair from under the usual methods text. The few methods books that do provide a manual of how to do interpretive analysis (see, for example, Charmaz, 2006, or Yanow, 2000) testify to this point. The novice analyst is instructed on how to collect data (interviews, participant observation, policy documents), how to safeguard their validity and precision, how to organize them for analysis, and finally how to analyze them. What is missing is the essential ingredient: the particular interpretive theory that defines the analytical problem, that drives the data collection, and that gives direction to the analysis. For example, those who engage in a governmentality approach to mental health policy, will, from the very start, work within the conceptual assumptions and social ontology of Foucauldian genealogy.[3] They will interview people, read policy documents, and engage in observation, but right from the start their perceptual and analytic gaze is steered by the assumptions of the governmentality approach. They will be sensitized to the way government agencies and professional organizations define the categories of understanding of mental health policy. They will be on the lookout for the practices and technologies with which these institutional actors impose a certain worldview upon society. They will then let their analysis of their data be guided by Foucault's conception of power as a dispersed, productive force. Had they opted instead for the critical discourse approach of Fairclough or the Bevir and Rhodes approach to policy interpretation, their study would, from its inception, have taken a different tack.[4] Clearly, in quantitative, empiricist research method and theory are also interconnected, but in a much more concealed, much less obvious, and easier to handle way. There, at least, one can have the illusion that one engages in "pure" method. In interpretive analysis, even this illusion is not available to the analyst. Interpretive inquiry without theory is like an airplane without lift. It never gets off the ground.

My answer to the interpenetration of theory and method in interpretive policy analysis, and to the pitfall of Intemperate Theorizing—and this is my third point—is similar to that of those other crusaders against grand theory, Glaser and Strauss. Although they were writing in a different age (1960s) and within a different discipline (sociology), their words still ring true in Interpretive Policy Analysis anno 2010: "[M]any of our teachers converted departments of sociology into mere repositories of 'great-man' theories and taught these theories with charismatic finality that students could seldom resist" (1967 [2006], 10). Or: "Verification of theory is the keynote of current sociology" (ibid.). Or: "[T]he adequacy of a theory for sociology today cannot be divorced from the process by which it is generated" (1967 [2006], 5). Their "cure" was not a repudiation of theory (their other bugbear was blind empiricism), but a recalibration of the notion of what theory is and can be within sociology. Theory was to be mid-level, substantive theory, and the task of the researcher was the "discovery" of such "grounded theory," "theory from data systematically obtained from social research" (1967 [2006], 2). One of the leitmotivs of this book is the appreciation of the empirical world in interpretive policy analysis. Clearly we cannot do without the conceptual insights of the great interpretive theorists, but the task of policy analysts is to contribute something intelligent to real world policy making, and that obliges them to pay attention to the everyday concerns of policy makers. One way of obtaining that balance between interpretive theory and the practice of policy making is grounded theory, which I conceive of as an ongoing dialogue between theory and the empirical world. In chapter 9 I will argue that, no matter our grand theoretical allegiance, grounded theory is the hot core, the key heuristic, of interpretive policy analysis.[5]

Because of its grounding in practical policy work, interpretive policy analysis is both contextual and situated. That is, it proceeds by immersing itself in the concrete problem-solving efforts of ordinary social actors. This makes interpretive policy analysis less a method than a praxis: an actionable approach to judgment, understanding, and problem solving, which is only partly captured—as any practice—by recourse to an explicit method. The upshot is that interpretive policy analysis is as much an art as a craft. This is a cliché of course, but I risk stating the obvious because of its real implications for the doing and teaching of interpretive analysis. One of the arguments throughout the book is that in able hands interpretive analysis is a powerful, exciting approach that often does not live up to its promise because of sloppy, careless execution. A quick analysis of some policy texts or the presentation of some stories of policy actors with the "real" meaning of the policy slapped on by the researcher are, alas, not uncommon in, at least, this author's experience. Also, too little attention is paid to the careful execution of the various elements of interpretive analysis, such as interviewing or empirically grounded, systematic inductive analysis. Again, in chapter 9 I will argue that skillful, systematic analysis lies at the heart of that dialogue among theory, the analyst's presumptions, and the empirical world that is, or should be, interpretive policy analysis.

PLAN OF THE BOOK

Chapter 2 presents the standard account of interpretive social science. I draw the customary contrast between causal and interpretive explanation and argue for the central place of intentions in the latter. However, I also argue that intentions are not subjective mental states, but publicly owned and therefore publicly verifiable statements. This has two momentous implications for interpretive analysis. First, to explain something in an interpretive way is to situate it in its proper context. And, second, we do this by carefully attending to the empirical world. My position in this book is that, without downplaying the importance of theory and conceptualizations, interpretive analysis requires detailed empirical research.

To introduce the variety of interpretive approaches, in chapter 3 I present four case studies of one policy problem: the provision of services to the mentally ill. The first is a standard empiricist study of a wicked problem, the explosive rise in readmissions after the onset of the deinstitutionalization of care for the chronically mentally ill in Chicago in the mid-1980s. The other three cases are three versions of interpretivism: qualitative policy research, a genealogical discourse analysis of the transformation of the psychiatric care system, and an action research type of study of a conflict between patients and professionals in a Dutch mental hospital.

The three interpretive takes are the upbeat for chapter 4, where I present the conceptual heart of the book—the three types of meaning: hermeneutic, discursive, and dialogical. By way of summing up I present what I call an actionable approach to interpretive policy analysis. I argue there that the problem of the ambiguous status of "social structure" in hermeneutic meaning stems from the representational nature of hermeneutic analysis. Knowing, in the representational view, is equivalent to making a pictorial, linguistic, or mathematical image of the thing to know. In opposition to this I follow the philosopher Ian Hacking in introducing interventionist approaches to knowing. We know by acting upon the world. The move toward interventionism is particularly pertinent to policy analysis. After all, policy analysis pretends to contribute to improving collective problem solving. The notion of action draws our attention to the ongoing, negotiated character of understanding and explanation. Within an actionable, interventionist approach meaning is the emergent outcome of the way human beings negotiate situations. One way that this book can be read is as an exploration of what an actionable approach to meaning implies for policy analysis.

In part 2 I give an overview of the bewildering variety of interpretive approaches. For each approach I discuss the theoretical underpinnings, as presented by its originators. I have always been impressed by Thomas Kuhn's observation that young natural scientists learn their trade by studying exemplars, concrete examples of how certain puzzles in the natural sciences have been put and solved by their more experienced peers. In the spirit of Kuhn I present exemplars of each of the approaches to interpretive policy analysis that I discuss in part 2. I conclude the description of each approach with a discussion of its strengths and weaknesses.

In chapter 5 I discuss three approaches to hermeneutic meaning. Hermeneuticists explain a puzzling or obscure phenomenon by situating it in a wider context. The three approaches are qualitative policy research, frame analysis (the early version of it; I discuss the later, more interactive version in chapter 8), and Bevir and Rhodes's interpreting governance. In chapter 6 I discuss discursive meaning. Discursive analysts see meaning as emerging from the interplay of the structural elements of language or discourse. Discursive meaning is at the heart of that large and confusing family of interpretive approaches that go by the name of discourse analysis. Again I discern three major approaches here. First is the genealogical analysis of Foucault, that towering giant of discourse analysis. Foucault also spawned an approach to political analysis that, because of its obvious relevance to policy analysis, I discuss separately: governmentality, or the analytics of government. Next I discuss poststructuralist political theory as developed by Laclau and Mouffe. Finally, I discuss critical discourse analysis as developed by Fairclough and others.

Before I turn to dialogical meaning I insert a chapter on the social construction of meaning. Constructionism is one of the most inflated concepts in interpretive policy analysis. However, it is not just a faddish concept. It touches upon some major issues in interpretivism, such as the malleability of (social) reality and the relation between language and reality. In chapter 7 I try to separate sense from nonsense in social constructionism. In chapter 8 I present dialogical approaches to meaning. Dialogical approaches are action oriented and argue that meaning emerges in the interactions between actors and between actors and the world. Here I discuss narrative analysis and a loosely grouped family of approaches that consider policy analysis as the interaction between analyst and stakeholders, such as action research, public policy mediation, and collaborative dialogue.

Part 3 consists of two chapters. Chapter 9 is a "methods" chapter, except that on the first page of this chapter I muster four arguments why methods thinking is not very useful. Instead I organize this chapter around heuristics, strategies of problem solving in designing and executing interpretive research projects. I argue here that grounded analysis of empirical data is the hot core of every interpretive approach of whatever stripe. In line with the position I staked out in this and the next chapter, no matter how intricate the theoretical artistry to which analysts subject their material, the beginning always consists of making sense of qualitative empirical data. Grounded theory is the master template for this analytical work. I walk the reader through the steps of grounded theory, taking pains to "ground" the discussion as much as possible in my own concrete experiences of doing interpretive policy analysis.

In the concluding chapter 10 I bring the discussion back to policy analysis proper. You could say that I raise the question in this chapter of the added value of interpretive policy analysis over traditional empiricist approaches. To nip in the bud any facile answers about the "obvious" value of science to policy making, I begin the chapter with presenting what one could call an ontology of the world of public policy. I describe the world of public policy as it looks from the perspective of the administrator and elected official. I enter this problem through the window of fit. Several scholars, myself included, have argued that interpretive approaches allegedly "fit" the world of public policy better than empiricist approaches. But what is meant by fit and how can we conceive of it in an interesting manner? Public policy, I argue, is above all action driven, aimed at acting on collective problems. Furthermore it is characterized by complexity, emergent time, and deep pluralism. I then discuss the fit of the four main approaches to policy analysis—empiricism and hermeneutic, discursive, and dialogical meaning—to the world thus described. I ask to what extent they help us to deal with the four characteristics of my policy "ontology," and to what extent they contribute to enlightenment (the most sophisticated claim of the contribution of knowledge to public policy) and aid-in-action (the claim of the forward-looking, rational, economistic approaches to policy analysis of the 1950s).

It will be no surprise that the results are nuanced. I argue that if we take seriously the messy problems that policy makers face, all approaches have their place in the sun. I illustrate this position in chapter 10 by asking what it means to be critical in interpretive policy analysis. All of the approaches that I discuss claim to be critical. Some even carry it even on their sleeve. I use an extensive study, *Democracy at Risk* (Macedo et al., 2005), to show the many ways in which different approaches to (interpretive) policy analysis can be critical. Finally, I bring interpretive policy analysis back to Lasswell's famous programmatic claim that the aim of the policy sciences is the furtherance of democracy, and I ask how interpretive policy analysis contributes to democracy.

READING GUIDE

This book can be read in different ways. Those who like to get an overview of the richness and variety of interpretive approaches in policy analysis can read chapters 3, 5, 6, and 8. Taken together these chapters present a fairly complete map of the family of interpretive approaches that are current in the policy sciences. Those who are interested in the philosophical-theoretical background of interpretive policy analysis can read chapters 2 and 4 and the first parts of chapters 5, 6, 8, and 10. If you want to get an idea of how to do interpretive policy analysis, read chapter 9 (and chapter 3 for some extended examples). Chapter 9 is not a methods chapter in the traditional sense of the word. As I explained before, I don't have much faith in methods books or courses. Instead I offer what I believe is the core heuristic of interpretive inquiry: the grounded analysis of qualitative data. Everything else, no matter how exotic an interpretive method, follows from that. Finally there is chapter 7. It discusses this much used, and abused, phrase: "the social construction of . . ." (and its corollary, "constituted"). It can be read as a corrective to sloppy constructivist talk in interpretive research. It can also be read as a bridge between the standard interpretive approaches and the dialogical approaches of chapter 8. Its message is that we do indeed construct our world, but this involves a whole lot more than mere talk.

NOTES

1. To be fair to Bevir and Rhodes, I will discuss the innovative aspects of their approach to policy interpretation in chapter 4.

2. This program may lead some analysts to debunk a particular category as a sham, as in *The Myth of Mental Illness* (Szasz, 1984).

3. In chapter 6 I discuss Foucault's approach to discourse analysis, including governmentality.

4. I discuss Fairclough's critical discourse analysis in chapter 6; policy interpretation according to Bevir and Rhodes in chapter 5.

5. In teaching interpretive policy analysis I find the challenge of method even more daunting than I describe it here. Instead of a dialogue between theory and method, in practice it turns out to be a conversation among three voices: the student's initial substantive hunches and preferences; the interpretive approach that might best provide an answer to that, usually rather unarticulated, choice of topic; and the craft of collecting and analyzing data. For students who are trained to keep problem, theory, and methods dutifully apart (as in separate chapters in their thesis), getting this conversation going is an almost insurmountable task. Also, it is not easy to master the fine points of a particular interpretive approach, such as Foucauldian discourse analysis or philosophical hermeneutics, as we will see in part 2. Yet, the quality of the analysis is commensurate with the level of such mastery. The originators of an approach were without exception engaged in a dialogue with different philosophical and theoretical traditions from which they wanted to distinguish themselves. To get it right, thus, requires some understanding of where these thinkers were coming from. Often, it is advisable to read commentators on the work of the originators, as they are able from an external perspective to clarify obtuse points. In addition, it is not enough to study the originators' theoretical statements to find out what they mean; one must also work through the applications of their thoughts. Ideally, such nuances and subtleties inform the application of an interpretive approach. Yet, there is a tendency to reify the approach, to boil it down to a few basic principles and the deft use of the proper jargon. However, abbreviated or vulgarized renditions of an approach will inevitably result in careless research.

2

THE TRADITIONAL APPROACH TO INTERPRETATION

Causal Versus Intentional Explanation

WHY IT IS IMPORTANT TO BE PHILOSOPHICALLY INFORMED IN INTERPRETIVE POLICY ANALYSIS?

An interpretive approach to policy analysis focuses on the meaning of actions and institutions. But what is meaning? The concept of meaning in the social sciences is notoriously difficult to grasp.[1] How do we conceive of explaining something in terms of meaning? What is the difference with causal explanation? Is meaning one concept or are there different conceptions of meaning? How, by what methods, do we register meaning? What is the relation between meaning and action? These questions will be the subject of this and the next two chapters. I will show that meaning is an elusive concept, with roots in complex philosophical issues. In fact, as I will argue, how one thinks about meaning cannot be seen apart from the stance one takes on a number of epistemological and philosophical assumptions—whether one is aware of this or not. There are a great number of approaches in interpretive policy analysis, each of which operates on a more or less distinct conception of meaning and, inter alia, on quite diverse positions on such issues as the nature of interpretive knowledge, the role of the individual in interpretation, or the justification of interpretive knowledge.

Is this important to the practicing interpretive researcher? Yes, to a certain extent. One of the key arguments of this book is that the philosophical grounding of the interpretive approach of choice—particularly its methods-in-use, as opposed to its professed methods—has large consequences for the analyst's de facto conception of the relation between policy analysis and public life.[2] I do not mean to say, of course, that policy analysts must be full-fledged philosophers to be good researchers. That would be as nonsensical as to require that chefs must be fully credentialed chemists to be good chefs.[3] Rather, I want to make a different point: while most interpretive researchers straddle different approaches in their daily research practice (a large dose of exegesis, a distinct preference for language analysis, some leftover empiricism, a hint of poststructuralist radical pluralism, perhaps a bit of *phronēsis*), whatever they do has epistemological and ontological consequences. And those consequences in turn determine the kind of knowledge they generate, the relation to their subject of inquiry, and the ethical theory-in-use they adhere to. Epistemology is intimately related to our political understanding of the world, as Hajer and I argued on another occasion (Hajer & Wagenaar, 2003). The upshot is that, to design an interpretive policy study, to translate a policy issue into a question that can be answered with interpretive methods, to collect reliable, meaningful data, to draw warranted conclusions from the interpretive analysis of data, to grasp the differences between interpretive methods—in short, to become an informed interpretive researcher—it is necessary to have at least a minimum of awareness of the underlying philosophical issues and how they inform the meaning of meaning.

CAUSAL AND INTENTIONAL EXPLANATION

Let us edge into the meaning of meaning with a simple example. How, in what terms, would we explain voting preferences? According to the empiricist conception of social science we would say that one or another factor "causes" voting preferences. However, to understand voting preferences, explanations in terms of a causal connection between an independent and a dependent variable don't make much sense. For example, to say that when I decline to vote for candidate A because I disagree with his position on abortion my behavior is "caused" by his position on abortion would be misleading. After all, despite his stand on abortion, I could still have decided to vote for him because I believe he is a better leader in times of crisis, or because he is the lesser of two evils, or because I feel affinity with his personality, or because I have been voting Republican or Democrat all my life and to do otherwise now just doesn't feel right, or because my father-in-law votes for him, et cetera, ad infinitum. Not only does the terminology of causation suggest an airtight level of determination that simply isn't warranted in the world of human action, but, more importantly, it is beside the point.[4] The very concepts that figure in the explanation—"voting," "disagreeing with a position on abortion," being a "strong leader"—are not mere behaviors but *action* concepts; that is, activities that are defined and constituted by an intrinsic intention (Fay, 1975, 71; Taylor, 1985a). Differently put, we, as voters and citizens of Western liberal states, grasp these concepts, and the associated behaviors, in terms of what they *mean* to us.

Formally stated—but this leaves a lot unsaid as we will see in chapters 3 and 4—philosophers agree that meanings are not causally but intentionally connected. An action is explained intentionally when we are able to specify the future state of affairs that requires the specific action (Elster, 1983; von Wright, 1971). The difference with causal explanation is in the different explananda. An example suggested by von Wright will make this clear. When an experimental psychologist stimulates the cortex of a monkey to elicit certain movements of the monkey's left arm, the language of intentions plays no role in the explanatory scheme. We could even say the electrical stimulation made the monkey wave its hand, but that would be irrelevant to the causal explanation of the arm movement as an effect of the stimulation. By saying that the electrical current to the cortex triggered certain neurological activities in certain nerve strata, which in turn made the muscles of the left arm contract so that the monkey lifted its arm, is to exhaustively explain the monkey's arm movement. By "exhaustively" I mean roughly that the electrical current is a necessary and/or sufficient condition for the occurrence of the monkey lifting its arm. To add that the electrical stimulation of the cortex made the monkey wave at us would be to ascribe something to the monkey that greatly and unwarrantedly transcends the explanatory scheme. What is explained is why parts of the monkey's body move under the causal influence of electrical stimulation of the cortex.

Now consider the following situation. At the time of this writing, a small controversy erupted in the Dutch media over a Moroccan-Dutch imam who, upon being introduced to the minister of immigration—who, a fact that is essential to this small drama, is a woman—refused to shake hands with her. The scene, including the minister's defiant reaction, was broadcast on television, and instantly a wave of indignation at the imam's rude behavior engulfed the media. To explain the imam's behavior in causal terms would do injustice to the situation. (However, this being a very orthodox imam, one could argue that for him the refusal to shake hands with a woman had reached a virtually nomothetic state.) In fact, in the days following the incident, various actors in the media, including the imam himself, stepped in to explain the refusal to shake hands. Experts on the Islam said, for example, that certain statements in the Koran prohibited the imam from touching a woman to whom he is not married. Far from being insulting, this behavior signified respect for the honor of the woman. This explanation gained support from an unexpected corner.

A spokeswoman from a Jewish organization explained that in some orthodox Jewish circles similar prohibitions on the mingling of the sexes prevailed. Critics of the imam maintained that in the context of secular Dutch society, his refusal to shake hands with a woman was insulting and demonstrated an inability or unwillingness to adapt to Dutch cultural values.

To summarize this small cultural drama involving the minister and the imam, the explanandum in this case is not some muscular movement, but an *action*. To call a particular behavior an action it needs to have an intention, or, as von Wright puts it, an *inner* aspect, which is behind the action, and some result that the action is supposed to bring about, or the *outer* aspect of the action (von Wright, 1971, 86). The inner and the outer aspect of action are welded together, for most of the time we act because we intend to bring about some result.[5] The result inheres in the intention.[6] For example, I hit the brakes of my car to prevent hitting a cyclist who suddenly appears in my headlights. Whether I succeed or not is immaterial to the explanation of my behavior. (Not to the fate of the cyclist, of course.) Even if I hit the cyclist, I will say: "But I tried to avoid him. I didn't intend to hit him." In other words, the whole sequence of behavior that runs from suddenly perceiving the cyclist, to hitting the brakes, to sighing with relief that I avoided hitting him is *explained* by my intention, not the result.[7] We cannot take the element of intention out of this sequence without robbing it of its sense. The physical movements alone—the muscles of my right-leg tensing so that they push the brake pedal, and the rest—are not even a necessary condition of the action of trying to avoid the cyclist, because there are other ways of doing that, such as swerving the car. Similarly, by taking the intention (not to violate the commands of the Koran) out of the explanatory scheme of the imam refusing to shake hands with the minister, we wouldn't be able to make sense of the situation. In fact, in this particular case, intentions literally bring the situation into being, from the expectation of shaking hands when officials meet, to refusing to acknowledge the minister's extended hand. The whole storm in a glass erupted at all because a social code exists that defines into being extending and accepting (or refusing) hands as the patterned activity we recognize as greeting (Geertz, 1973b).[8]

HOW NOT TO THINK ABOUT INTENTION

This is what we mean when we speak of actions having *meaning*. This is also the bare-bones formulation of how we understand meaningful action; how we acquire valid knowledge of it through intentional explanation. This approach to explanation in the social sciences, in which we explain social phenomena through uncovering the intentions of the actors involved, is called *interpretivism*. Interpretivism "may be defined as the view that comprehending human behavior, products and relationships consists solely in reconstructing the self-understandings of those engaged in creating or performing them" (Fay, 1996, 113). This is a broad definition. It states that interpretive explanations must "capture the conceptual distinctions and intentions of the agents involved" (Fay, 1996, 114). It does not mean that the actors necessarily have a conscious grasp of the conceptual distinctions involved. It only states that these must be available to them. I will discuss this important distinction in the next paragraph. But having said this, the definition of interpretivism leaves many questions open, some of which I will discuss in this section, and some in the next chapters. In this section I will begin with expanding on the role of intention in interpretive explanations.

The central point in interpretive explanation is that the units of analysis, the "brute" data of the social and policy sciences, are not hardwired into social reality, but require interpretation to make them "visible" at all.[9] As we saw, terms such as "voting," "marrying," or "negotiating" can only be inferred from the physical movements that carry them by assuming a particular purpose or intention that makes this particular movement or verbal utterance a case of voting, marrying, or negotiating. In the social sciences, observation requires interpretation.

Critics of interpretive social science infer from this that interpretive inquiry is, by inference, a subjective enterprise. I'm not quite sure what "subjective" means in this context, and there is in fact quite a lot of confusion about subjectivity in interpretive social science. According to the dictionary definition, "subjective" means "individualistic" (as in "resulting from the feelings or temperament of the subject, or person, thinking rather than the attributes of the object of thought") or "idealist" (as in "having to do with any of the elements in apprehension or apperception derived from the limitations of the mind rather than from reality independent of mind") (McKechnie, 1979). There is an approach to interpretation—phenomenology—that takes precisely these two meanings of "subjective" as its point of departure—and then struggles mightily to steer clear of them. (See chapter 4, where I will both show phenomenology's enduring influence and pervasiveness in contemporary interpretive social science, and discuss some of its limitations.) Here, I want to argue that there are two reasons why the evocation of the term "subjective" in relation to intention might be misleading. First, "subjective" suggests that intention is something that takes place within the mind, and can therefore only be grasped by mental processes.[10] Second, the acceptability of interpretive statements is as constrained by the empirical world, as is the acceptability of causal statements (Thomas 1979), but, I would add, constrained in a different way. Both objections to the term "subjective" hang together.

What, for example, does it mean when it is stated in a police report that "the suspect was placed under arrest because he intended to rape the victim"?[11] Given that the police officers felt quite justified about their decision to imprison the suspect (despite the circumstance, so common in situations of date rape, that the suspect vigorously denies that he intended to rape the victim, while the victim maintains that he raped her), this statement probably does not refer just to a mental state, which is only accessible to the suspect himself, and which only he can avow or deny. Intention has "no experiential essence," as the sociologist Coulter puts it in an essay that admirably succeeds in clearing away some of the confusions around the notion of intention. The word "intended" in the above phrase does not denote a subjective state of the suspect's mind that can only be reflected upon by the subject himself, or inferred, through empathic identification of an observer with his or her subject. The seemingly mentalistic word "intend" here refers as much to an observable action as does the seemingly objective word "rape" later in the sentence. As Coulter puts it:

> To learn the expression "I intend" is not to learn, miraculously, to assign a label to some introspected experience—for how could one be trained to make the correct identification of his introspected percept?—but consists, rather in learning how to perform what Austin termed a "commissive."[12] To declare [or disavow, as in my example] one's intention is to perform a specific sort of illocutionary act, which, like all such acts, require appropriate "felicity" conditions. Thus there is a clear and crucial connection between particular sorts of intentions and particular sorts of circumstances. . . . [A] description of an intention is a description of an action (an envisaged action), not of an experience. Avowals and ascriptions of intentions, then, are organized by, and gain their intelligibility from, not some mental divinations but from the particulars of public states of affairs. (1979, 40–41)

So where does this leave us? "People act on their beliefs and preferences," Bevir and Rhodes state, and add that therefore it is possible to explain human actions by referring to the relevant beliefs and preferences (Bevir and Rhodes, 2002). Yet, the beliefs and preferences that people hold are ever so many action concepts that derive their meaning from the way they function in a larger social system. Suddenly, only a few paragraphs into the subject of intention and interpretive explanation, it seems that we are the ones left standing in this game of interpretive musical chairs. We need subjective meaning to get access to meaning at all, yet subjective meaning is predicated on impersonal social-linguistic structures in which personal beliefs and preferences are embedded. So do we look left or right in crossing the perilous road of interpretive explanation?

SUBJECTIVE AND OBJECTIVE MEANING

It is customary in the philosophy of the social sciences to distinguish between subjective and objective meaning. Subjective meaning includes such entities as reasons, motives, and purposes, which are part of the actor's consciousness and which determine or describe the actor's actions (Thomas, 1979, 85). Subjective meanings form the self-understandings of the actors we study. For example, if we ask a welfare administrator, "Why did you spend so much time despite your excessive case load on getting this client a slot in a computer course?" the administrator will be able to state his or her reasons. (For example: It would help the client obtain skills for the job market. The client is motivated to get off welfare. The client is deferential and pleasant to work with.) The administrator provides reasons that convincingly explain the action.

The approach to interpretive social science that sees meaning as deriving from the intentions and reasons of an actor is called *intentionalism*. Intentionalism is thus a more restricted form of the general category of interpretivism. Those who believe that meaning is tied to the conscious intentions of actors will want to reconstruct the inner aspect of an action or event (as opposed to just observing its outer effects or manifestations) to establish, for example, that the arm movement is indeed a greeting and not to point at something or an attempt to hit me.

Yet, some of the "reasons" for an action are not necessarily available to the actors although they, undeniably, shape their actions. For example, when I negotiate a mortgage with my bank, part of my actions are influenced by the concepts, rules, and conventions that surround entering into a mortgage contract—or more precisely, that enable the activity of entering into a mortgage. These conventions, which are implicit in the activity of entering into a mortgage contract, are objective meanings. Objective meanings belong to the group or community. They are the basic assumptions and conceptualizations that make a particular activity possible; hence the term "constitutive" that is often associated with objective meaning. For example, to enter into a mortgage we need basic conceptions of property, loan, interest, contract, discounting the future, and individual responsibility. So, although I might describe my decision to enter into a mortgage contract in subjective terms (buying a house is cheaper than renting it, and allows me to leave some property to my children), the very notion of a mortgage presupposes the concepts described above. Fay calls these presuppositions "concepts we think with" (as opposed to the subjective "concepts we use in thinking" or "think about") (1996, 116). These presuppositional concepts are implicit; they lie under the surface of our conscious activities. Objective meanings do not explain an individual's actions but rather the meaning that a pattern of activity has in and for the larger culture. In this way Geertz famously interprets the cockfight in Bali as the enactment or display of the emotional vicissitudes of the Balinese status hierarchy (Geertz, 1973a). Although actors posses objective meanings in the sense that they have a more or less articulate grasp of the conceptual presuppositions that make a particular activity possible, most of these are implicit in that they are not part of the reason-giving of these actors. This observation is important for our larger argument about the interpretive analysis of public policy, because capturing objective meanings requires considerable interpretive work on the part of the analyst.

The notion of subjective meaning has generated a common epistemological misunderstanding, namely that the validation of explanation in the social sciences resides in the actors' conceptualizations. There is a strong and a weak version of this misunderstanding. The first is (mostly) wrong and the second one-sided, as I will show. The strong version of subjective epistemology states that the validity of the analyst's explanation depends upon it being couched in terms of the actor's conscious meanings. To explain something, then, is to reconstruct what meaning an actor ascribes to a particular situation. Thomas cites ascribes this position to Winch, and calls it "contextual interpretation." "To understand a situation we must come to view it in the actors' terms. We must grasp how the actors' meanings constitute the situation. . . . In hermeneutic terms, *verstehen*, the process of understanding the actors' viewpoint, is adequate as a methodology for the whole of social science" (Thomas, 1979, 81).[13] We will see in chapter 4 that one of the philosophical precursors of interpretive policy analysis, phenomenology, also adheres to the strong version of subjective meaning. To stay with Geertz's example of cockfighting in Bali, according to the strong version a valid explanation would not exceed what the actors would state as their reasons for engaging in cockfighting. This example already illustrates the weakness of this argument. First, different actors would probably state different reasons. By which criteria would we decide which are the "better" reasons (Thomas, 1979, 90)? These could only be criteria external to the actors' stated reasons. Second, actors could be mistaken or misled about what they think are the reasons for doing something. Think of someone with a neurotic personality who rationalizes self-destructive behavior, or of someone who is trapped in some form of "false consciousness." Granted, these are problematic concepts, but the idea that people can be misled about their own motives is common enough. And third, how important are subjective reasons, after all, for understanding a class of actions such as cockfighting? The beauty of Geertz's essay is that he carefully sketches the wider *context* of the phenomenon of cockfighting, finding his explanations in the way that cockfighting is both informed by and continually supports that wider context. The subjective reasons of individual actors have little bearing on this wider context, although the status hierarchy of which the cockfight is an expression is still "possessed" by the actors themselves, albeit implicitly (Fay, 1996, 117). Objective meaning, in other words.

The weak version of subjective epistemology states that the validity of an interpretation can only be assessed from within the mental and conceptual framework of the actors we study. So, if I were to study male-female relationships in Muslim communities in Western Europe, my explanations of the behaviors I observed should reflect the beliefs, ideas, and concepts of the Muslim community. To interpret them from, let's say, a Christian perspective would be unwarranted. This position is called *perspectivism*. Perspectivism is not only the basis of interpretive social science, it is also a dominant view in modern epistemology in general. Perspectivism states that whatever we perceive as facts are always facts *under a particular description* (Fay, 1996; Hawkesworth, 1988).[14] We always bring to a situation a prior vocabulary that suggests principles of significance on the basis of which we can organize our observations (Fay, 1996, 74). Without it, we simply would be unable to "see" anything at all. Stone provides an excellent example when she discusses how there is no such thing as an objective description of a calamity or a natural disaster. Policy actors always discuss these in terms of a moral-causal scheme that rides on ascriptions of blame and intentionality. For example, for the relevant government agency it makes a huge difference, morally and legally, if the train crash was caused by the momentary inattentiveness of the train driver or by structural problems with the tracks for which the agency is responsible. And, as the events surrounding Hurricane Katrina demonstrate, even natural disasters such as floods or hurricanes are interpreted in light of the presence or absence of timely and adequate government intervention.

Perspectivism—"a fairly innocuous philosophical position," as Fay calls it (1996, 77)—is by now the default setting in epistemology, both in the natural and in the social sciences. Also, perspectivism is a powerful analytic tool in policy analysis. I will give a more extended example shortly, but to understand behavior that at first appears to us as obscure or irrational by framing it in terms of the beliefs and customs of the actors themselves can be exhilarating and enlightening. In fact, we will discuss a whole approach to interpretive policy analysis—philosophical hermeneutics—the purpose of which is to arrive, through careful dialogue, at grasping the other's, at first alien, point of view (see chapter 4 and chapter 8). What is the problem with perspectivism, then? Perspectivism becomes a problem when it gets wedded to the idea of radical difference. In this case perspectivism transforms into *relativism,* the position that the rightness, truth, or reasonableness of a belief or practice can only be judged from within a particular conceptual framework, and that no independent criteria—such as human reason or compassion—exist at all to arrive at such judgments.

Relativism presupposes a basic incommensurability between beliefs or points of view. Incommensurability means that no common criterion or yardstick exists by which to assess two different objects or phenomena. Usually the conclusion that two things are incommensurable is accompanied by much hand wringing, as if we have reached a definitive dead end in our exchange of arguments. But it can be safely stated that incommensurability is in most cases neither as serious nor as final as it is made out to be. For example, to ask if a Bach cantata or a Beatles song is better is to ask a meaningless question, as no common yardstick exists by which to compare the two. Bach and the Beatles are incommensurable. But our world doesn't collapse after this conclusion, and many people happily include both in their musical preferences (Wagenaar 1999). Incommensurability becomes a bigger problem when it involves deep-seated value positions. The alleged incommensurability of Muslim and Western lifestyles is one of the reasons for the current acrimonious debate about Muslim "integration" in many Western European countries. The Muslim position on women, gay people, or religion in general is seen to have no common ground with the secular Western position on these issues. But how different are the positions of Muslim immigrants and the original residents, and how difficult is it really to reach common understanding?

"Relativism's biggest mistake," Fay argues, "is that difference requires a background of deep similarity" (1996, 82). Relativism "overemphasizes difference while failing to appreciate what is shared" (ibid.). The handshaking incident between the minister and the imam provides an example. Both parties probably would agree on such values as mutual courtesy, the fact that each religion dictates certain precepts (albeit different ones), the very notion of religion as a sacred value, and so on. On top of that the minister and the imam share a set of descriptive terms; whether they acknowledge it or not, they move about in the same world. They share a background of common beliefs, aspirations, concepts, and so on.[15] Perhaps this is why the Bach versus Beatles incommensurability doesn't really bother us: it is easy to agree that both wrote captivating music.

Must we conclude that subjective meaning is a waste of the researcher's time and that researchers who are worth their salt go for explanations in terms of objective meaning structures? That would be too fast. First, in policy analysis it is often advisable to try to see the world through the eyes of the target audience of a particular policy. One of the banes of public policy making is negative unintended consequences (Merton, 1936; Sieber, 1981; Wagenaar, 1995). More often than not, these result from an insufficient or biased understanding of the lives and world of the policy subjects. Reconstructing the subjective meaning that a particular policy has for its target audience, thereby revealing the practical and conceptual limitations of the policy, is an important task of interpretive policy analysis. In chapters 3 and 5 I will discuss several examples of this type of qualitative policy analysis.

Perhaps we should follow Geertz and simply say that the whole dichotomy of subjective and objective is misconceived. To insert "meaning" where he uses "culture," we would conclude that meaning, "though ideational, . . . does not exist in someone's head, though unphysical, . . . is not an occult entity" (1973b, 10). Geertz is perfectly right here, of course. It doesn't make sense to try to locate meaning ontologically in the mind or in some reified cultural or institutional pattern. Actions are meaningful in that they signify something, and the question is then: What does this particular action (a disavowal of rape; the refusal to shake hands) signify? Something larger than the particularity of that singular action is being said, something that exists before, and independently of, the individual who is acting. But that "something" is not some reified "deep structure" or some axiomatic set of rules; it is more a shared set of understandings that are linguistically and actionably inscribed in the world, and that are invoked, and, in an ongoing dialectical movement, sustained, whenever actors engage in a particular behavior, and whenever we "read" the symbolic meaning of that particular behavior. So perhaps this is the place to insert what may be Geertz's most often quoted statement on culture, the analysis of meaning, and the continuity of observation and explanation in interpretive analysis: "Hopping back and forth between the whole conceived through the parts that actualize it and the parts conceived through the whole that motivates them, we seek to turn them, by a sort of intellectual perpetual motion, into explications of one another" (1983, 69).

To close this digression on the nature of meaning in interpretive analysis—if its ambiguities and open endings can ever be laid to rest—I will conclude, and this is my second point, with a more practical, a more "hands-on" statement of methodological import. The dual nature of meaning implies that, whatever our research interest—for example, the intentions of mental patients who are negotiating the transformed social service landscape of a large U.S. city in the 1980s (Lewis et al., 1991; Wagenaar, 1987), or the emergence of the school as we know it from the confusing beginnings of the early Prussian state (T. Hunter, 1996), or the evaluation of a particular educational reform (Dunne, 1993; Schwandt, 2002)—our work begins with the careful and precise registering of the concrete behaviors of concrete actors. Now, these behaviors can have many different manifestations. They can be statements in interviews, observed activities, written statements in documents, both formal (reports, laws, position papers) and informal (letters, diaries). They can take the form of stories that people tell to explain their actions in particular circumstances. They can be our renderings (in research notes) of what we believe we have observed. They can be descriptions (part descriptive, part interpretive) of artifacts such as buildings or office spaces, or of performances or rituals. They can be carefully put together reconstructions of a developmental trajectory. Or, they can be a description of a long collaborative effort for social capital formation in a disadvantaged neighborhood. What ties all these different forms of registering behaviors together is that we regard them as the expressions of, the carriers of, social meaning. Behaviors are a window upon meaning; and, save the a priori imposition of theoretical schemes upon the research material (a practice that Glaser and Strauss derisively call "pseudo-verification"), there is no shortcut to the extrapolation of meaning from concrete, microscopic behavior. As Geertz puts it: "Behaviors must be attended to, and with some exactness, because it is through the flow of behavior—or more precisely social action—that cultural forms find articulation" (1973b, 17). The interpretive analyst acts on the assumption that the general is folded into the particular. The analogy here is with DNA. As DNA carries within itself the basis upon which a particular life form unfolds as a result of interactions of genetic and nongenetic factors, so the cultural life form in all its meaningful complexity emerges by individuals acting upon, in and with their environments.

This plea for the careful observation of behavior as the royal road to interpretive analysis must not be mistaken for a call for behaviorism (the expulsion of meaning by reducing the world to observable behavior). Interpretive analysis is empirical (as in pertaining to the world), not empiricist (as in there being terms whose meaning is directly given by reference to a prelinguistic reality). Two points must be kept in mind here. First, as we earlier saw, our registrations are themselves already interpretations of what we observe. We do not approach our research subjects as tabulae rasae. We preselect, we unknowingly accept our subjects' self-interpretations, we tacitly ascribe meanings to what we see, simply to be able to distinguish signal from noise, to make our objects of observation and analysis stand out from the context in which they are embedded. This makes for perilous navigating between the two traditionally distinct research activities of "observation" and "explanation," as the behavior as a natural fact and the same behavior as a theoretical category tend to get blurred (Geertz, 1993a, 15). Again there is no shortcut here. Through a painstaking and systematic process of imaginative induction, we transform our crude, earlier observations/ interpretations into better, higher-order, more enduring interpretations that somehow capture the meaning of what has transpired. By continually confronting our initial observations (understood here as interpretations of interpretations) with further and more divergent observations and explanations, we hope to arrive at an interpretation that makes what was initially opaque, in the final analysis (more) senseful. Interpretation rests on dialogue.[16]

But, as we saw earlier, this process of interpreting interpretations itself takes place in what one could call a semiotic public space; or, more precisely, is made possible at all by being suspended in this shared linguistic realm. If, to return to our earlier example, a detective weighs the evidence that will or will not lead to the conclusion that the suspect had the intention to rape the alleged victim, this process hinges on the public availability, and the possibility for public inspection of, such categories as "victim," "rape," and "consent" in the early twenty-first century Netherlands. All actors in this drama—victim, suspect, detective, and later district attorney, lawyer, judge—are bound by these pre-given cultural categories, and are unable to overstep the boundaries of these "concepts-in-use" (to use a famous phrase by Schön) on peril of being misunderstood in the best case and ostracized in the worst. A different way to put this is that data, judgments, and conclusions (and the warrants for the conclusions) in this social event are all situated. They make sense only within a particular context. The rape claim is predicated on a complex set of (mostly tacit) background knowledge about value systems surrounding gender, about the relation between men and women, about the set of conventions that guide the initiation of sexual contact, and more. Data, conclusions, and the grounds for those conclusions are constituted by the shared expectations, beliefs, values, routines, and practices of the members of a culture; "constitutive" indicating that the shared background knowledge "creates the very possibility of certain activities," and, I would add, certain categories (Searle, 1995, 27; see also Fay, 1975, 76; and Taylor, 1985a). This is the meaning of those oft-used words "public" and "transparent" here. Terms such as "rape," "sexual," "intending" (or "voting," "promising," "shaking hands") are publicly available. They are there for everyone to see. They are transparent in that:

> A description of an intention is a description of an action (an *envisaged* action), not of an experience. Avowals and ascriptions of intentions, then, are organized by, and gain their intelligibility from, not some mental divinations but from the particulars of public states of affairs. (Coulter, 1979, 41)[17]

Finally, it is in this multilayered, "fictitious" sense ("fictitious" as in holding a complex ensemble of background assumptions constant for the time being), that meaning, similar to causality, is inferred from observable phenomena, where the observations usually take place under especially arranged circumstances to abet the process of inference and to safeguard it against errors of judgment. It is also in this sense that there is little difference between the natural and the social sciences. Both are naturalistic in the sense that they operate on the assumption that there are "empirical constraints on the acceptability of [their] statements"; that they proceed by "testing of [their] statements against the world" (Thomas, 1979, 2). The differences that do exist between the natural and the social sciences are in the objects and means of observation, in the mode of inference to arrive at warranted conclusions, and in the type of warrants. Interpretive social science is, as much as any science, based on precise observation and registration of data (although these are, in the social sciences, "constructions of constructions"), on careful inference of what the data signify, and on the formulation of conclusions in such a way that their validity and good sense can be assessed by all knowledgeable members of the relevant community of practice, be they politicians, professors, or both—which, I guess, makes good interpretive policy analysis so difficult to pull off.

With this we have drifted far away from the formal standard description of interpretation as intentional explanation. Instead, we have concluded that to explain something in an interpretive manner is to situate it in its proper context. By grasping the context we make sense of whatever it is that needs to be made sense of. Some analysts prefer to couch interpretive explanation not in terms of intention, with its mentalist overtones, but of social rules. Fay, for example, says that actions mean something to someone because they "fall under some description which is socially recognizable as the description of that action because it involves reference to certain social rules" (1975, 75). But how do we understand the notion of "rules" here? Clearly not in an algorithmic way as binding prescriptions for acting. Rules can best be understood, we conclude, as shared understandings, shared conceptions and ways of doing, that structure and articulate the world in an attuned, recognizable way. Context again. The conclusion is unavoidable: interpretation is contextual. But this raises many questions concerning the nature of meaning, the way to arrive at interpretive knowing, and the grounds for trusting that knowing as right or justified. It is to these questions that I turn in the next two chapters.

NOTES

1. See, for example, Thomas: "There is no more confused area in the philosophy of social science than that of the problem of meaning" (1979, 74). Or Fay: "The interpretation of the meanings of actions, practices, and cultural objects is an extremely difficult and complicated enterprise" (1975, 115).

2. This is a key issue in policy analysis, as Torgerson (1995) rightly argues. Throughout history the relationship between politics, civil society, and science has been conceptualized in different ways. Torgerson observes that it is characteristic of the postwar era of technocratic policy analysis to assume a strict distinction between politics and policy analysis. Scientific policy analysis should be quarantined from the irrationality and passions of politics. The interpretive turn is an attempt to reconnect policy, science, and society.

3. Although, to extend the metaphor, a certain grasp of the chemistry of cooking certainly helps one to arrive in a reliable and predictable manner at well-cooked dishes. For a treatise on the everyday science of cooking that as instructive as it is entertaining, see This, 2007.

4. As we will see shortly, regularity and predictability of behavior are not the decisive point here. In the realm of human action, some reactions to behavioral stimuli are so predictable that they have an almost lawlike quality. Nevertheless we would still explain such actions as actions, that is, in intentional and contextual terms.

5. An action without intention is called a reflex (Von Wright, 1971, 87).

6. Outcomes which are not the result of our intentions are called, fate, chance, happenstance, or unintended consequences.

7. It is of course *appraised* by taking result, intention, and preceding conditions into account. If I had been speeding, for example, as can be causally inferred from the length of my brake marks, then my intention to brake will be appraised differently than if I had been abiding by the speed limit.

8. By consistently talking about intentional *explanation* I have stayed clear in this section of the well-known distinction between explanation and understanding. As Roth, a philosopher, summarizes this distinction,

it is one between "analyses conforming to the terms and laws of a causal-mechanistic idiom and analyses couched in the language of intentions and human significance." Then more specifically: "Explanations explain by subsuming specific cases under laws; understanding proceeds by making plain the rules and relations in which activities are embedded, and which give them their significance qua human actions" (1991, 179). According to this line of reasoning, reasons cannot count as explanations because they are insufficiently exhaustive and deterministic; "they lack the law-like relations to actions demanded by explanations" (Roth, 1991, 180). Roth rejects this distinction and argues for a type of explanation of human affairs that he dubs "narrative explanations" and that consists of an amalgam of explanation, interpretation, and action. Although I am sympathetic to almost everything in Roth's paper, I take a slightly different route in this chapter to arrive more or less at the same point. Although in the world of everyday affairs we acknowledge that reasons and intentions do not figure as exhaustive, final explanations of human actions, in many instances we see them as good enough *given the circumstances* and *for the time being.* "Good enough" then means that they throw light upon a formerly obscure or confusing situation in a persuasive manner *and* that they constitute sufficient ground for legitimate action. An intentional explanation thus needs to fuse understanding and warranted action. What legitimates us to say that despite the provisional nature of intentional explanation some action has been satisfactorily "explained" this way is that either the person or persons who provide the explanation are seen as competent actors, or the explanation has been jointly arrived at through a legitimate process of dialogue.

9. Compare Geertz's famous observation in anthropology: "[W]hat we call our data are really our own constructions of other people's constructions of what they and their compatriots are up to" (1973b, 9). Or Bevir and Rhodes's statement that interpretive analysis comes down to telling stories about other people's stories (2004, 133). In philosophy of science it is sometimes stated that the human sciences are "doubly interpretive" or "doubly hermeneutic." While the observations of the natural sciences are interpretive in the sense that they are theory laden, the objects of the human sciences are, as we saw, interpretations of interpretations because, as Taylor puts it, in a statement that has become classical, they deal with human beings who are already "self-interpreting animals" (Bohman et al., 1991, 5; Rouse, 1991, 44; Taylor, 1985a).

10. Often the term "subjective" is mentioned in conjunction with the method of *verstehen. Verstehen* refers to some special empathic identification of an observer with his or her subject (see Thomas, 1979, 81; and for his critique of *verstehen* as a method for the human sciences, 1979, 88–89).

11. The example is taken from Vera Haket's study of the treatment of rape in the Dutch judicial process (Haket, 2007).

12. "The whole point of a commissive is to commit the speaker to a certain course of action. Examples are: promise, covenant, contract, undertake, bind myself, give my word, am determined to, intend, declare my intention, mean to" and others (J.L. Austin, in Coulter, 1979, 163).

13. Winch actually argues for both subjective and objective meaning. He, both develops a Wittgensteinian, rule-based conception of social science, and argues for the primacy of actors' self-understandings. The latter position, notoriously, landed him in an extreme culturally relativist corner. My sense is that Winch's interpretive subjectivism is the result of his rhetorical zeal to defeat causal, empiricist social analysis (Thomas, 1979, 95; Winch, 1958, ch. 3).

14. Hawkesworth discusses perspectivism under the heading of presupposition theories of science. Presupposition theories "suggest that perception depends on a constellation of theoretical presuppositions that structure observation, accrediting particular stimuli as significant and specific configurations as meaningful" (1988, 49).

15. The philosopher Donald Davidson provided a formal renunciation of the relativist position that he called the Argument from Translation. The argument states that even in cases of extreme difference we are usually able to translate at least some of the other's position into our vocabulary so that we at a minimum know what the other is saying. But that implies that we share a similar background of beliefs, attitudes, linguistic skills, and so forth. See Fay, 1996, pp. 84–86 for a clear presentation of the Argument from Translation.

16. I will develop this point further in chapter 9.

17. Vice squad detectives have a keen awareness of the publicly available criteria for statements such as their suspects utter. Most of their work can be seen as collecting observations that make suspects' statements warranted or unwarranted according to criteria that experienced members of a culture share.

3

INTERLUDE

Meaning in Action

CONTEXTUAL MEANING: PUZZLES AND PERPLEXITIES

As we concluded in the preceding chapter, the general description of meaning as contextual leaves many questions unanswered. We have seen that, although meanings are objective in the sense of being precipitated in the linguistic and social conventions of a society, in a practical sense they also have a subjective element. Meanings are held by people, even if they are not always aware of the full import of those meanings, and a common way to access meanings is to simply ask people about them. For example, we could infer what the planned expansion of an airport means to the residents who live in its vicinity by asking them what they think and how they feel about it. But, this leaves the relation between meaning as a state of mind and meaning as social rules ambiguous. Is subjective meaning wholly determined by objective meaning? Are the beliefs and opinions of people who live near the airport the product of the social rules that constitute categories such as airport, airlines, and air travel, or do they have freedom to depart from the cognitive and behavioral molds of social rules? As we have seen, meanings should not be confused with belief. In many cases people do not have access to meaning, particularly not the kind of tacit, constitutive meaning that underlies social practices. To stay with the airport example, those same residents would have a hard time elucidating the tacit social rules that constitute the concept of "negotiating," although they probably would have no trouble engaging in this activity. Or, another analyst might argue, residents who enter into negotiations with airport authorities quite likely deceive themselves. If they only understood the grand collusion of airport authorities, airlines, governments, and professionals such as economists, which keeps certain alternatives off the political agenda and biases the information about airports, they wouldn't negotiate but would engage in political activism. And what are the implications of these issues for researching meaning? How do we register meaning, for example, if individuals don't have access to it or are deceived?

Also, how do we deal with conflicting meanings? Nothing is more common in policy analysis than to run into groups that have widely divergent beliefs, feelings, and attitudes about a particular policy measure. According to many political theorists deep pluralism is one of the basic characteristics of the political (Connolly, 2005; Dryzek, 1989; Mouffe, 2000). How do we decide between these meanings? Although we saw the error in relativism in the preceding chapter, practically speaking deep pluralism poses many obstacles to policy makers and analysts. More often than not they are caught in a controversy of perspectives, where "truth" is decided either by the assumptions one holds or by the position one has in the division of power. Or, to zoom in on the position of interpretive analysts, do they have to decide at all, or should their task only be to register all the different meaning perspectives in a particular policy field, in the hope that this will enlighten the contesting parties by creating "the conditions for mutual understanding" (Fay, 1975; Yanow, 2000)? How does mutual understanding relate to behavioral change? What is the relation between interpretation and change (Roth, 1991)?

25

And, finally, where is meaning located? It may be in the act or text or practice that we study, in which case explaining something in an interpretive manner is akin to reading the meaning in the act, text, or practice. Or it may be that meaning is by definition *for* someone, who is relative to an observer, in which case meaning is the product of an interaction between the interpreter and that which is interpreted.

In this and the following chapter I will address these and other issues around the meaning of meaning in interpretive analysis. Obviously meaning is not of one kind. In the vast literature on interpretive social science we encounter different conceptions of meaning. Not only subjective and objective meaning, but also different kinds of what I would like to call meaning-in-use. To avoid making the discussion overly abstract, I will present three extended examples of interpretation in policy analysis, all of which address the same issue: care for the chronically mentally ill. I will take some time to present my examples because it is only by following a case in a detailed manner that we get a feeling for the way that the analysts conceive of their particular version of interpretive policy analysis. This is in accord with the thrust of my argument. On the one hand, we will see that although each example captures what could be called the meaning of care for the mentally ill, the differences between the approaches are substantial. The approaches address different questions, they construct meaning in different ways, they use different methods, they evoke different theoretical assumptions, they have different ethical and critical implications, and they conceive differently of the role of the analyst. Without sliding into relativism, it is perhaps not an exaggeration to say that they evoke different, incomparable worlds. On the other hand, I do not want to overstate my case. We will see that the different kinds of meaning are also related; somewhat like the outspoken, unruly children of one close but animated family. The differences in meaning are real, but they are differences-in-use. They should not be seen as unassailable differences-on-paper. They assert themselves, they spring to life, when one practically engages in interpretive analysis. I will return to this in chapter 4. Be that as it may, at the end of this chapter only one conclusion remains: there is no single, unitary activity called interpretation in policy analysis. Interpretive policy analysis has different faces. The thrust of this book is to explore the consequences of this interpretive pluralism for interpretive policy analysis.

MEANING IN ACTION: THREE EXAMPLES OF INTERPRETIVE POLICY ANALYSIS

The Transformation of Psychiatric Care

Between about 1955 and 1985, in many developed countries a transformation of the care for the severely mentally ill took place. In the space of thirty years, the large-scale, custodial mental hospital was transformed from a free-standing facility of long-term care to a short-term facility in a network of ambulatory community care. This sea change in the position of the mental hospital was expressed in two sets of numbers. In the United States, the number of patients who resided in a mental hospital declined from over 500,000 in 1955 to 121,000 in 1982. Yet, in that last year, 344,000 additions (admissions, readmissions, and returns from leave) and 342,000 discontinuations (discharges and placements on leave) were registered in U.S. state mental hospitals. Not surprisingly, given these numbers, length of stay had also declined. Between 1970 and 1980, median length of stay in U.S. state and county hospitals went from 43 to 21 days. In that same period the number of treatment episodes for psychiatric care in general hospitals increased rapidly, surpassing that in traditional state hospitals by the end of the 1970s. However, all evidence indicated that general hospitals catered to a different, less impaired population than state hospitals (neurotic disorders and substance abuse, instead of poor, psychotic, or dangerous patients), suggesting that the growing importance of general hospitals in the provision of psychiatric care represents an expansion of, and not a substitution within, the mental health system (Wagenaar, 1987).

As with every large change in the functioning of once-stable institutions, a wide range of factors was at work here. The large-scale mental hospital had emerged in the middle of the nineteenth century as a model for the treatment of the severely mentally ill. Under the influence of an optimistic belief about the possibilities of the mental institution as a new, humane treatment technology for mental illness, many states began to construct large-scale mental institutions, often in idyllic pastoral surroundings (Rothman, 1971; Scull, 1979). At the end of the nineteenth century, under the influence of demographic change and the urbanization of American society, many of these institutions changed into the underfinanced and overcrowded "madhouses" that came to occupy an uneasy place in the nation's collective conscience (Grob, 1983). Beginning in the 1950s real reform of the mental institution came to be seen as a possibility. First, the discovery and rapid acceptance of psychotropic medication severed the link between the locus and the mode of treatment in psychiatry. While it was always necessary to hospitalize patients to provide psychiatric treatment—in fact the temporary removal of patients from their pathogenic environment was considered an essential element of the treatment—antipsychotic medication made it possible for psychiatrists to stabilize patients while they were living at home or in a community-based treatment facility. The success of lithium in controlling the violent mood swings of patients suffering from bipolar disorder made it a model of the hope and possibilities that psychotropic medication offered.

In addition, careful sociological studies that demonstrated that long-term hospitalization decreased patients' initiative and autonomy and increased their dependency on the institution (the so-called hospitalization syndrome) had eroded the legitimacy of long-term hospitalization. These studies demonstrated the severe iatrogenic effects of a prolonged stay in the mental hospital (called "institutionalization" in the United States and "institutional neurosis" in Britain). After a long period in the hospital patients began to suffer from apathy, lack of initiative, loss of interest in the outside world, resignation, and submissiveness (Miller, 1986, 22; Stanton & Schwartz, 1954). The mental hospital came to be seen as contributing to patients' illnesses, instead of curing them.

Third, mental patients, like ethnic minorities, women, and gay people, became the subject of legal and civil emancipation. In many countries, patients' rights activism, which in the United States took the form of litigation, shifted the emphasis in the commitment of mental patients from clinical to legal criteria. The decision to admit or discharge became, for all practical purposes, voluntary. The traditional segregation of the mental hospital from civil society broke down rapidly in the 1960s and 1970s when an array of legal aid attorneys, patient advocate committees, and accreditation and licensing boards began to monitor the quality of care and the implementation of due process in hospital-patient relations. The result was that the state hospital was drawn into a larger, variegated network of psychiatric care (Wagenaar, 1987, 11–12).

Under the influence of successful experiments in community treatment in the Netherlands, Britain, and Italy, progressive psychiatrists began to see it as both possible and desirable to keep patients in their own domestic and community environment for as long as possible. Promoted by psychologists and social workers, who saw an opportunity to break the hold of psychiatrists over the treatment of the mentally ill, these insights turned into the community mental health movement of the 1970s. According to its doctrine, a network of ambulatory care centers, carefully distributed over large population centers, were to provide most of the day-to-day treatment of the mentally ill, and coordinate whatever care these patients needed elsewhere. Only in episodic moments of severe psychotic breakdown would patients be admitted to a mental hospital, and then only until the psychotic episode had subsided and further treatment in the community was possible again.

Finally, the budding community mental health movement had the good luck to be launched in a favorable policy environment. In the United States in the early 1970s, many states were facing an expensive overhaul of their literally crumbling mental institutions. In most cases the buildings were almost a century old and needed to be either torn down and rebuilt from scratch or drastically renovated. Either way, the bill would come to hundreds of millions of dollars. Community mental health care presented itself as a win-win situation. It was a cheaper, more humane, and more effective mode of treatment of the severely mentally ill. Under the influence of these converging factors, the so-called deinstitutionalization movement took effect.

Very soon, however, it became clear that deinstitutionalization had been oversold. In the mid-1970s readmission figures in the United States had exploded. Between 1969 and 1975, the period in which many of the changes described above were fully instituted, the proportion of readmissions increased from 47.1 to 60.1 percent of total admissions; an increase that most observers found alarming. In combination with an explosive increase of admissions proper (from 185,500 in 1955 to over 400,000 in 1970), experts and policy makers felt that the problem of readmissions was out of control. Psychiatrists jumped to these numbers with a predictable "I-told-you-so" attitude, and argued that patients had to return to the hospital because they had been insufficiently treated. Angry commentaries in psychiatric journals began to point to what they saw as one of the uglier consequences of community mental health reform: an abandonment of the national responsibility for the severely mentally ill. The concern found a label—"the revolving door"—and a public problem had emerged that urgently needed reform. Community mental health adherents retorted by accusing psychiatrists of using disingenuous, self-serving arguments. If anything, the construction of community mental health facilities was behind schedule and the problem would be solved as soon as states constructed the centers they had promised.[1] It was in this overheated, acrimonious environment that a team of policy scholars at the Center for Urban studies at Northwestern University began a study of the deinstitutionalization of the severely mentally ill in Chicago. I had the good fortune to join the research team, headed by Dan Lewis, in 1985 to work on my doctoral dissertation.

The Revolving Door: The Conventional, Empiricist Approach to Understanding Mental Hospital Readmissions

From the start we took a sober look at the readmission problem. "Given a population with severe and often chronic illnesses, with few supports and little income, and an organization (the state hospital) whose mission is to return that group to the community as quickly as is clinically and morally possible," we wrote, "it is no wonder that two-thirds of the patient population will return to the hospital" (Lewis et al., 1991, 46, parentheses in original). We then proceeded to question two assumptions behind the deinstitutionalization movement, assumptions we labeled as "mental health exceptionalism" and "guild innovationism." The first is the belief that the mental illness is the primary cause of the rehospitalization, and the second is the belief that the way to reduce hospital recidivism is "to create a new clinical service that will do a better job of maintaining the person in the community" (ibid.). Unfortunately, we concluded, two decades of reform had not produced much convincing evidence that either assumption was warranted. We then set out to probe the correlates of readmission. Who is readmitted to the mental hospital?

To gain an understanding of hospital readmissions, the conventional approach is to do a descriptive statistical analysis. The aim is "to portray the population in terms of fundamental sociodemographic and patient treatment/status variables and to explore the bivariate relationships of those variables to outcome criteria" (ibid., 48). In the conventional, descriptive approach, readmissions are studied in the framework of previous admissions to the mental hospital. Within this framework an admission is seen as the culmination of a psychiatric career or illness episode (ibid., 47). "Reviewing a patient's previous admissions permits identification of the correlates of the number of previous admissions by simply working with the case records of the patients who have entered the state hospital. This kind of research is practical and efficient for it involves working with records that are usually on hand" (ibid.). However, the standard design, which relies on data that are collected retroactively, introduces a bias in the research. The sample consists of patients who both survive and continue to rely on the state hospital. It turned out that a method of sampling that used a panel that prospectively, longitudinally, charted which patients are readmitted in, let's say, a period of one year completely reversed the findings.

Thinking retroactively, the strongest predictor of previous admissions is age. Other significant predictors include marital status (married patients do not turn to the hospital as often as unmarried patients), sex (males use the hospital more frequently than females), legal status (voluntary patients have more episodes of prior admission), race (blacks are more likely to be readmitted), and diagnosis (schizophrenic patients are more often hospitalized than those in any other diagnostic category) (1991, 50–51). In short, readmissions are primarily a problem of an older, male, severely disturbed population. In the prospective panel the results are more or less reversed. As is to be expected, the number of previous admissions is an important predictor of subsequent readmissions. But the two strongest additional predictors are age (younger patients are more likely to be readmitted) and diagnosis (patients with the diagnosis character disorder have a higher chance of returning to the hospital). In other words, prospectively it is the younger, less disturbed patient who is more likely to be readmitted (1991, 55).

I will shortly probe the reasons for this remarkable finding, but I first want to draw out some implications regarding the status of the conventional approach to understanding the problem of mental hospital readmissions. As we saw, the central claim of the empiricist approach to the social sciences is "the objective explanation of social and political life through statistical correlations and causal laws that are empirically discovered" (Gibbons, 1987, 1). The notion of objectivity rests on the assumption that the data and their statistical or causal organization exist independently of the observer and the methods used to reveal them. Clearly, in our study of readmissions this key claim has been violated. By choosing another mode of sampling we literally reversed our findings. We had no a priori reason to use a particular method of sampling, except that we felt that the prospective approach was more useful for policy purposes. The panel could be tracked over time so that we could observe how the clinical and social factors that operate in the community affect the use of the state hospital. Differently put, the choice of method was dictated by the goals of the researchers and the convenience of data collection; it was not suggested by the ontological structure of the phenomenon under study. Nothing in the world out there suggested that one empirical method was to be preferred over another. If I put it in yet another, and less generous, way: despite the fact that we worked wholly within the empiricist framework, the values and biases of the researchers profoundly affected the data. Even when used carefully and diligently, the empiricist approach turned out to be vulnerable to the researchers' intentions.

A careful use of the empiricist approach is, thus, by no means a guarantee that the researcher attains the ideal of objective explanation. However, the problem runs deeper than the uncontrolled contamination of findings by the researcher's intentions. Data such as age, legal status, and psychodiagnosis are selected and produced by the state mental hospital. In other words, the readmission is wholly couched in conceptual and linguistic categories that represent the modus operandi and the institutional position of the state hospital. By using such data the researcher unwittingly privileges the perspective of the state mental hospital in understanding recidivism.

Despite their objective gloss, these data cannot but reflect the organizational goals and needs of the state hospital. They are intrinsic to these data. By sampling prospectively, on the other hand, we opened ourselves up to the perspective of the community, introducing the concerns of patients, their families, and their service providers, as they struggle to keep patients out of the hospital after release. My point is not that one perspective is to be preferred over the other, but that no matter how one cuts the cake, so-called objective data always represent a particular perspective. In the social sciences data can never be neutral in the sense of being independent of the observer. They are literally constituted by a particular perspective, and they surreptitiously "contain beliefs and expectations about what is correct, appropriate, or 'rational' behavior" (Bernstein, 1976, 104, quotation marks in original; see also Taylor, 1985b). One simply cannot escape perspectivism, neither in "soft" qualitative nor in "hard" quantitative data. This fundamental insight into the nature of data requires a different strategy of understanding, collecting, and handling data in the social sciences, one that uses the intrinsically perspectivist nature of social data in a productive way. I want to introduce what such an approach might look like, by presenting three different ways of understanding mental hospital readmissions.

Example 1: Virtual Institutions—A Qualitative Study of Mental Hospital Readmissions

Dissatisfied with the assumption that rehospitalizations could be exhaustively explained by psychiatric illness, we set out to explore the antecedents of hospital admissions more fully.[2] To this end we organized a qualitative study of readmissions. We didn't enter the study with a blank mind. A study of the sociological literature on mental illness had convinced us that the decision to hospitalize or discharge was strongly influenced by a series of factors that are tangential to the mental condition of the individual, such as availability of a partner or family, housing, insurance coverage, or the administrative policies of community centers (Lewis & Hugi, 1981; Wagenaar, 1987, 34–37). On the basis of these presuppositions we set up a sampling procedure that would allow us to explore the full range of factors that led to the readmission of formerly hospitalized patients living in the community. The sampling proceeded as follows: in a ten-week period those patients from the total sample of our study who were readmitted to two of the four Chicago state mental hospitals were approached by the interviewer. The purpose of the study was to reconstruct the pathway to the hospital. To this end, we asked each patient who was willing to be interviewed about his or her readmission if they would allow us to interview all those who were involved with the readmission or who were knowledgeable about it. Interviews were held as soon after the readmission as the clinical condition of the patient allowed. Interviews were held in the hospital, or, if the patient had already been released, in his or her place of residence. Interviews with non-patients were held in the setting where the person lived or worked. In this way I interviewed 17 patients and from 2 to 6 additional people (friends, family, and service providers both inside the hospital and in community-based facilities) about the most recent readmission (Lewis et al., 1991, 58; Wagenaar, 1987). The qualitative strategy I used was that of grounded theory (Glaser & Strauss, 1967 [2006]). The purpose of this approach is to develop midlevel, substantive theories to explain the data. Or, as Charmaz describes it:

> The "grounded" nature of this research strategy is three-fold: (1) researchers attend closely to the data (which amounts to "discoveries" for them when they study new topics or arenas), (2) their theoretical analyses build directly on their interpretation of processes within *those* data, and (3) they must ultimately compare their analyses with the extant literature and theory. (1990, 1165; parentheses and italics in original)

To escape the assumption that a readmission is the inevitable outcome of a failed or prematurely terminated treatment, I used a more general concept of trouble, involving both definitional and remedial components, to indicate the complex of factors that might result in a return to the hospital (Emerson & Messinger, 1977). An analysis of the readmission stories revealed that there were three kinds of trouble that preceded hospitalization: personal, family, and institutional. Each represented a distinct combination—a better word would be "interplay"—of symptoms, personal and interpersonal conflict, and service options (Lewis et al., 1991, 59; Wagenaar, 1987).

The label *personal trouble* applied to all those patients who were overwhelmed by painful or negative feelings. Often these patients were lonesome, isolated men, who had trouble relating to other people in a mutually satisfying manner. Their stories echo themes such as unemployment, poverty, loneliness, substance abuse, abandonment by family and friends, and loss of self-esteem and control. Quite regularly they are so overwhelmed by anxiety or depression that they fantasize about suicide. Their existence is downright precarious—financially, socially, and emotionally. They get by relying on public resources such as welfare, the community mental health center, and the state hospital. For them the state hospital provides respite from the relentless stresses of poverty and psychiatric illness. They know the formal and informal rules of getting admitted and thereby getting access to a clean bed, regular meals, cigarettes, and social contact with the other regulars at the ward. For a few days at least the hospital serves as a haven in a hostile world.

Not every readmission took place at the initiative of an individual who experienced overwhelming distress. In fact, most of the individuals in our sample returned to the hospital because someone else wanted them to be hospitalized. In those cases in which the patient had caused trouble for family or friends to the point that they felt that his or her behavior could no longer be tolerated, we labeled the pathway to the hospital *family trouble*. Most individuals who were admitted by their families had displayed bizarre or unusual behavior. But although persons around them considered their behavior puzzling or troublesome, the unusualness by itself was not necessarily considered a threat and was therefore an insufficient reason to trigger the readmission. In fact, over and over again I was struck by how much families were willing to endure from their loved ones. Only when the family member's behavior is interpreted as posing a serious threat to the family's personal safety, when the patient's behavior is grossly indecent or threatening to his or her own safety, or when the family's standing in the community is severely compromised, is remedial action undertaken, and then it is swift and decisive. Violence is usually the trigger that spurs families to contain the behavior of one of its members. Although most of these patients displayed an array of problems before their readmission, such as exaggerated suspicion, confusion, hearing voices, or utter neglect of personal hygiene, repeated violent behavior is the strongest stimulus for the family to start readmission procedures.

Personal and family troubles are two kinds of trouble that trigger rehospitalization. In the first instance, the individual evaluates his or her own situation and acts upon it; in the second the individual is evaluated and acted upon by others. In the second case the nature of the trouble is strongly dependent on the framework that others bring to the particular situation. The decisive influence of external frameworks to the definition of trouble applied in particular to those individuals who lived in community facilities that provide shelter and care. I labeled those pathways to the hospital *institutional trouble*. Dorothy's case is instructive here.[3] Dorothy lived in a homeless shelter. However, she was unable or unwilling to abide by the basic rule that the residents of the shelter actively work toward a resumption of their independence. In fact, by volunteering to do cleaning work and in general making herself agreeable to staff and fellow inmates, she made it clear that she would like to stay in the shelter. The shelter staff regarded her as a difficult case. To the shelter, Dorothy was a management problem, a threat to the shelter's organizational integrity.

As the counselor explained: "We tried to get her into work, a live-in housekeeper somewhere. She wouldn't do it. She kept thinking her main purpose was to clean here. . . . She tried so hard to please everybody, *but she couldn't do what we wanted her to do*, so she failed here" (italics added). The shelter staff then tried to transfer Dorothy, but discovered that they had very few options. She was turned down by another shelter and the shelters in Chicago were considered too violent and too dangerous for her. (The shelter Dorothy was in was located in a relatively affluent suburb.) This made the state hospital the only remaining alternative. It also made it necessary for the shelter staff to present Dorothy as someone in an acute psychiatric crisis. And this is exactly how she was perceived by the hospital staff, which said, "She was confused and delusional" (Wagenaar, 1987).

The picture of hospital recidivism that emerges from the qualitative study is very different from that in the regression analysis. The qualitative story is richer in detail, dynamic in its depiction of the process of readmission, and suggestive not only of the multitude of factors that impinge on the readmission process, but also of the different ways that these factors hang together. As Howard Becker says of this latter point, "The point [of qualitative, ethnographic research] is not to prove, beyond doubt, the existence of particular relationships so much as to describe a system of relationships, to show how things hang together in a web of mutual influence or support or interdependence or what have you, to describe the connections between the specifics the ethnographer knows by virtue of having been there" (1996, 56). The qualitative picture describes the point of view of the actors involved: the patients, the families and friends of patients, the community organizations that provide care and shelter to these patients, the staff at the hospital. In that sense the qualitative study reconstructs the meaning that readmissions have to the actors involved.

This can lead to a radically altered view of the readmission process. For example, instead of the received view that depicts patients as more or less passive victims of an overwhelming illness, the qualitative study showed that patients and other actors actively use their insiders' knowledge of the system to gain entrance to the hospital. Many patients knew the exact boundaries of a hospital's catchment area. They were familiar with the overt and hidden criteria for admission, the advantages of voluntary over involuntary admission, the number of days one could be admitted without losing one's eligibility for Social Security Income, and other practical know-how. Some patients, to gain entrance to the hospital, even presented their symptoms in a strategic manner. From the point of view of the actors in the mental health system:

> A readmission, given this analysis, is not a mistake or a failure. A readmission is a solution to a real problem. These problems are faced by the patient, his or her family, and the agencies charged with the patient's care. The solution, a readmission, follows from the options one perceives and the difficulties one is facing. The state hospital is the place to take someone who is mentally ill and needs help. There are few alternatives with people with little money. Agencies that are responsible for the care of the mentally ill person choose whom they serve. The problems the mentally ill and their families face are serious. Private agencies who serve state patients need the hospitals as a last resort when the problems arise. (Lewis et al., 1991, 76)

Carefully reconstructing the actors' point of view prevents the egregious error of ascribing to subjects experiences and intentions they don't have. Becker calls this "errors of attribution" and thinks they are commonplace in "studies of behavior foreign to the experience and lifestyle of conventional academic researchers" (1996, 59). This is particularly pertinent to policy analysis. Most policy programs are formulated for people with whom the policy maker has very little direct experience. Most policy programs rely on strong assumptions about the motivations and intentions of the subjects of these policies. Policy makers assume, for example, that a particular instrument will act as deterrent or an incentive or that people will act in a utility-maximizing manner when confronted with a particular choice, without much understanding of how the world is actually experienced by these actors (Stone, 1997). Qualitative analysis aims at understanding the meaning that the world has for a particular population. Its aim in this is not invariant truth but verisimilitude, the accurate rendering of the actors' point of view. (I develop this point further in chapter 5 when I discuss qualitative policy research.)

In addition to accurately describing the actors' point of view, we developed midlevel, substantive theories that purported to explain the data. As we saw in chapter 2, explaining in interpretive research does not mean that we subsume specific cases under invariant laws. Instead we clarify the social rules and practices in which the activities of the actors in our study are embedded (Roth, 1991, 179). Or, in the more formal terminology of the philosopher: we have explained readmissions not causally but intentionally by making a plausible connection between an act (to readmit X) and future condition (for example, to prevent X from harming his family) (von Wright, 1971, 83). Or, in more everyday, realistic terms: we have explained an action (to readmit X) when it becomes understandable or senseful by embedding it in the context of a larger life-form (getting by with psychiatric problems and little money in a large urban environment).

Example 2: Psychiatric Power

The qualitative study drew a picture of the way mental patients in a large metropolitan area dealt with the effects that a changing service system had on their lives. But, as an analysis of public policy, the qualitative study was limited. Deinstitutionalization was not confined to the Chicago area, the site of the study, or even the United States as a whole, but amounted, as we saw, to a complex transformation of the psychiatric care system that occurred in many developed countries between 1950 and 1990. In all of those countries the position of the large state mental hospital in the provision of care to the mentally ill was reconsidered. In addition other professionals, such as psychologists and social workers, began to encroach upon the terrain that traditionally had been the prerogative of hospital psychiatrists. In some countries, such as Britain, the Netherlands, and Italy, the first stirrings of these institutional changes were already visible before World War II. The move toward community-based psychiatric care seems to be one of those complex policy trends in which the boundaries between concerted action and social movement are fuzzy; that involve a multitude of actors in loosely organized communities of professionals, government officials, and other experts, without clear management from the center; and that are driven as much by doctrinal clashes and pet solutions as by any clear definition of the problem at hand (Kingdon, 2002). The sheer breadth of the movement toward community-based care for the mentally ill thus care raises wider questions about the origins and driving forces of this trend in public policy, questions that are not easily answered by a mode of interpretive explanation that exclusively focuses on the meaning that the state hospital has to a group of actors in one community. The explanation of the drive toward community care in the highly developed economies of the West is the subject of yet another approach to interpretive policy analysis, one that focuses on the power of psychiatry.

According to the standard history of psychiatry, one of the driving forces behind the deinstitutionalization movement was a sustained critique of professional psychiatry. Recurrent media exposés about the deplorable conditions inside the asylum, research about the hospitalization syndrome or "institutional neurosis," sociological labeling theory, anti-psychiatry, Rosenhan's famous study of hospital admissions that allegedly demonstrated the arbitrariness of psychiatric diagnosis, and sociological work on "incarceration" as a form of social control in the service of the state, all contributed to an erosion of the moral and professional legitimacy of the large, "Victorian" mental hospital. The main theme in these diverse criticisms of the mental institution is the power of professional psychiatry over various categories of distressed or deviant individuals. Psychiatry is depicted as a repressive force in the service of the state with the task of controlling and confining aberrant individuals. The pervasiveness of the theme of unchecked professional power in the critique of psychiatry invites a closer look at what precisely is meant by the power of psychiatry.

In a searching essay on "critiques of psychiatry," Miller summarizes this onslaught of criticism during most of the twentieth century under the headings institutional, theoretical, and legal critique (1986, 22–26). *Institutional critique* focused on the nature and functioning of the mental hospital. Its main thrust was sociological research on the adverse effects of the asylum. This included the damaging research on the "institutional neurosis" syndrome. At first institutional neurosis was thought to be a form of neglect, but later research demonstrated the pathogenic effects of prolonged hospitalization in even well-run mental hospitals (Stanton & Schwartz, 1954) Separately, Goffman's famous studies showed how the mental hospital could be viewed as a "total institution" that "exerted on behalf of society an absolute domination over the lives of those individuals who entered as patients." He questioned the very nature of madness as he showed how individuals were recruited into the moral career of mental patient by the internal workings of the mental hospital (Goffman, 1961; Ludwig & Farrelly, 1966; Miller, 1986, 22). Particularly damaging was Rosenhan's famous and prominently published study that showed that even perfectly normal volunteers were diagnosed as mental patients when they presented themselves to the admission office of a mental hospital (Rosenhan, 1973). These theoretical conclusions were given a boost by the widely popular movie *One Flew Over the Cuckoo's Nest* with its crude depiction of the mental hospital as a modern day concentration camp. The conclusion was that the nineteenth-century mental hospital was beyond reform. It was an institution of oppression and the arbitrary exertion of professional power over helpless individuals that not only failed to live up to its own therapeutic ideals, but was downright iatrogenic to those who were forced to live inside its walls.

The *theoretical critique* was concerned not so much with the institution, but with the profession that was associated with it: psychiatry and its somatic model of mental illness. This critique came in two forms, anti-psychiatry and theories of social control. Since its heyday in the 1960s, anti-psychiatry has fallen into disrepute. It is now criticized for attacking a straw man, by painting a picture of psychiatry as an instrument of repression with tools such as electroshocks and lobotomy at its disposal, whose sole purpose was to medicalize deviance in the service of a bourgeois society that was intrinsically hostile to the unadjusted. Moreover anti-psychiatry's denial of the underlying reality of the symptoms of mental disorder—by reducing these to merely the reaction of the individual of being labeled mentally ill (Scheff) or by inverting psychosis as a valuable and creative experience (Laing)—is with hindsight seen as downright naïve. Yet, Miller warns us that the value of the anti-psychiatry movement was that it provided us with a "view from the other side," that it reminded us of the "personal and experiential dimension of the mental patient" (1986, 28), thereby opening up the possibility of noninstitutional alternatives to psychiatric care.

Social control accounts of psychiatry cast their net much wider by criticizing the mental hospital as a practice of incarceration, which also includes the prison, the judicial apparatus, and the welfare system, and associated disciplines such as psychiatry, criminology, and social work (Cohen & Scull, 1983; Garland, 2002; Piven & Cloward, 1971; Scull, 1979). Social control arguments against psychiatry have four characteristics. First, psychiatry is one of a number of scientifically legitimated practices of controlling and disciplining deviant and marginal groups in society. Second, the need for this control is related to the socioeconomic production relations of capitalist society.

Third, psychiatry is one of the manifestations of the expanding role of the state in capitalist societies, particularly in regulating personal conduct that is unproductive, or that poses a threat to the efficient working of the production sector. Fourth, psychiatry exerts its controlling role through the medicalization of deviance. "By medicalizing deviance psychiatry establishes a consensus that we should *do* something about such ill-health, and a legitimacy that centers on the claim that this is in the interests of the sick person and of society" (Miller, 1986, 30; italics in original).

Finally, *legal critique* focused on the regulation of confinement in and admittance to the mental hospital. In the nineteenth century these issues had been widely discussed and the judiciary had appropriated an active role for itself in regulating psychiatric internment. Admittance to a psychiatric institution usually meant that the individual temporarily lost some of his or her constitutional rights for the period of hospitalization. In addition there was always the risk that people would be admitted for inappropriate reasons, with the attendant risk that the hospital would be used to confine unwanted or difficult groups (divorced women, the infirm elderly, immigrants, political dissidents) (Grob, 1983). In many instances the judiciary deferred the decision to admit to psychiatrists, but this was always within the context of legal oversight. As Miller concludes, the delegation of the power of admission to psychiatrists was never an unconditional one. "It was rather one that established that the boundary between the legal and medical regulation of asocial behaviors is potentially a fluid one" (1986, 19). In the 1960s, in the wake of the gradual inclusion of various hitherto peripheral social groups (blacks, women, sexual minorities) into the constitutional core of society (Janowitz, 1978; Wagenaar, 1987), the boundary between the legal and the medical regulation of mental disorder shifted once more. Movements for the emancipation of the mental patient sprang up everywhere, admittance was restricted to the point that it became almost impossible to admit someone against his or her will, and conditions in the hospital were monitored on a permanent basis independent from the influence of professional psychiatry. The legal emancipation of the mental patient was one more element in a climate in which the legitimacy of the mental hospital was ever more called into question.

So far, this has been a fairly straightforward, albeit complex, historical analysis of the decline of the mental institution and the emergence of community-based psychiatric care, a story that is largely fuelled by resistance against the power of psychiatry. However, this is not what Miller, and the other authors in the collection of which his essay is part, have in mind. Their aim is to restructure the concept of psychiatric power, and show how such a redefined notion of power gives rise to a different type of analysis. As Miller and Rose state their program:

> Such an analysis would not view power as some kind of monolithic and malign presence, to which we must oppose ourselves and which we must strive to abolish. Rather, it would analyse the power of psychiatry in terms of what it makes thinkable and possible, the new objectives to which it allows us to aspire, the new types of problems it allows us to conceive, the new types of solutions it inserts into our reality. This broadens the focus of analysis from a concentration upon medicine and the mental hospital to a consideration of the development of techniques of social regulation animated by psychiatric themes, the adjustment of institutional practices in the light of psychiatric considerations, and the instrumentalization of social relations in the service of psychiatric objectives—the minimization of mental pathology and the promotion of mental health. It also implies a different perspective from that common to most contemporary critiques of psychiatry. (1986, 2)

What are the elements of this "different perspective"? First, and foremost, is a different conception of power. The authors take their cue from Foucault here, in treating power not only as something negative and repressive but also as something creative, a social force that makes things possible, that shapes new aspirations and ideals, that brings ideas, images, and practices into being. (I will discuss Foucault's considerable contribution to interpretation in policy analysis in chapter 6.) In this generative way, power operates on such diverse phenomena as "modes of personal existence, forms of interventions in the lives of individuals, discursive practices, and specific social categories such as the 'mad,' the 'unhappy person,' the 'neurotic'" (Miller & Rose, 1986, 39). In relation to these phenomena power has a "productive and constitutive role." Individuals are not so much victims of repression, but instead the ways they understand and perceive themselves are brought into being "through the operation of power relations" (1986, 40). Second, the authors step away from the state, and its ancillaries, as the perspective of choice in political analysis. In their analysis the state is no longer the "exclusive focus of debate and explanation" (Miller, 1986, 33). Instead of psychiatry being a "sub-plot to a history of the controlling power of the state," the analysis focuses on the multiple "sites of operation of psychiatric expertise and knowledge" (1986, 38). This Foucauldian analysis of psychiatric power doesn't place the state in opposition to civil society. It operates instead on a broader, decentered conception of governance and self-regulation that includes both civil society and the various agencies, officials, and instruments of the state.

This dispersion of the workings of psychiatry also extends to the very concept of mental illness. Rather than taking mental illness as a self-evident category, it conceives of it more as a kind of focus, a focus that is "directed towards the different behavioural dimensions of personal life that have become objects of psychiatric knowledge and intervention" (Miller, 1986, 38). Psychiatry also involves the normal population; its theories, techniques, and vocabulary extend to various domains of social functioning such as the workplace, the school, childrearing, or marital relations. Finally, Miller and Rose employ a different policy theory, or more precisely, a different theory of governance, for how the state operates on society. Given the dispersed nature of psychiatric power, psychiatry "is not an institution that can be traced back to an originary strategist—the state, the economy, society's need for social control—rather, it operates within and through multiple and interlocking strategies of social regulation" (ibid.). In modern democratic societies the state doesn't so much decree and monitor as attempt to regulate the habits of the population through the internalization of personal norms and habits of healthy, appropriate, or "normal" living. Successful governance transforms the public into the private.

Although both can be branded as interpretive, on the face of it, Miller and Rose's analysis of the decline of the state hospital and the emergence of community psychiatric care differs in almost all respects from the qualitative study of rehospitalization in Chicago. Miller and Rose's analysis differs with regard to its object, its scope, its basic categories, and its underlying interpretive theory. Its focus is on power—in a thoroughly refashioned manner—and how it operates in society. It employs an unusual and intriguing theory of the state and of the way the state effectuates public policy. Finally, its focus is not on the countless activities from which the researcher hermeneutically derives the intersubjective meanings that inform and thus clarify those activities. Instead, the researcher's aim is to unearth the larger configurations of ideas, practices, artifacts, and doctrines that shape the texture of social reality as we recognize and experience it. These configurations are known by a variety of labels, but in the next chapter I will settle for the term *discourse*. Meaning in this approach is *discursive meaning*.

Example 3: Stories as Change Agents

Abma, a Dutch evaluation researcher, reports on what she calls "an experiment in narrative practice" in a Dutch mental hospital (Abma, 1997). The story revolves around a vocational rehabilitation project in which a rundown patient store on the premises is restored and redecorated by two patients. Initially it is a story of success in which two chronic patients regain self-confidence and a sense of mastery through improving and managing the store. The story comes to a dramatic end, however, when the two patients, who by then had a considerable emotional investment in "their" little shop, were transferred to another project to make room for other patients to work there. What from the point of view of the vocational rehabilitation counselors was business as usual (regular transfers of patients to other projects; the assessment that one of the patients was "too highly functioning" to work in the store and should really find something in the regular labor market) was a personal drama for the two patients. One of the patients (the "high functioning" one) was rehospitalized as a consequence; the other one found a new job himself.

Abma first reports on this incident in terms of the unequal power distribution between patients and professionals. Obviously the meaning that the two patients attached to the store differed appreciably from that of the professionals. It is the difference between, on the one hand, pride, accomplishment, reconnecting with a normal working life that preceded admission to the mental hospital, and on the other, the store as a practice site and temporary work project—the difference between "existential" and "functional" meaning (Abma, 1997, 23). She then continues by showing how the patients' meaning had no standing in the setting of the hospital. The patients' reactions were seen as emotional and chaotic. Whatever the patients said was interpreted as an expression of their illness. It also didn't help that they spoke the regional dialect, which underscored the patients' distance from the therapists. The professionals' language was abstract and systematic, full of professional jargon, and in high Dutch. Their version of the situation was seen, by themselves and the other professionals, as rational and self-evident. In the end the patients resigned themselves to the situation.

But this is not where the story ends. Abma shows how some of the professionals are aware that their routine solutions and instrumental language do not always accord with the world of the patients. In fact, some professionals express their suspicion that the patients' dependency and lack of initiative might be an unintended consequence of professional routines, the kind of resignation that was the result of the store incident. Their very clinical methods, which framed patients as sick and incompetent, created a corresponding self-image in the patients. Moreover, patients began to resist the standard therapeutic approach. The incident around the store was only one of several such incidents.

For example, Abma decided to organize a picnic in which patients and professionals would have a chance to meet each other in an open setting. She structured the meeting by inviting patients to tell a story about themselves and the vocational rehabilitation project. Not surprisingly, the patients' stories reveal that vocational rehabilitation is a process of personal struggle, of setbacks and successes, of self-doubt and the need for personalized support, of the gradual, painful acceptance of personal limitations, and of unexpected obstacles, such as faced by the illiterate patient who feared that he had to learn to read and write and at the same time was ashamed of his deficiency. Rehabilitation turned out to be a process that is full of ambivalences and contradictions. Sometimes patients wanted a time-out from the stresses of working, but then they resisted the suffocating pressure of group therapy. They wanted support and understanding from the professionals but they also wanted to be challenged. The professionals operated on a strict distinction between therapy and vocational rehabilitation, but the patients' stories eroded that distinction. Professional categories had little meaning for the patients.

The therapists experienced the patients' stories as confrontational. Initially they reacted defensively. Abma recorded one of the therapists saying, "If you're not careful, they might become psychotic." But they also admitted that the patients' stories revealed a world that they were largely unaware of. They realized that a gap existed between therapeutic jargon such as "deciding together" and the paternalistic reality of vocational rehabilitation as experienced by the patients. Perhaps they could give the patients more freedom to choose without fearing that psychosis is imminent. Perhaps they should try to find a better balance between the expressed need for security and support and the equally pressing need for independence and the freedom to make mistakes. These insights did not come spontaneously. Abma had the picnic participants retell one another's stories. She says, "Retelling the story made it possible to make connections and break through false dichotomies. By retelling someone else's story in your own words, that person was invited to distance himself temporarily from his own story" (1997, 28; translation by author).

Abma's report does not contain sufficient detail to trace what in the patients' accounts affected the interpretations and practices of the therapists, but in another publication she describes the conceptual background to her approach. Under the heading of "responsive evaluation" she notes that she is interested in the

> variety of meanings that actors attach to public policy. The goal is to arrive at a shared construction, but even if no consensus can be reached, an evaluation might result in an increased awareness of one's own constructions and a reconfiguration in the sense that one is more or better informed. To grasp meanings the evaluator must participate in the situation that is the object of research. The active participation of target groups is important because they have the experiential knowledge that the evaluator lacks. No less important is the fact that those affected by the policy have the right to exert influence on the study's findings because these will have real consequences for them. (1996, 66; by author)

This third example of interpretive policy analysis of care for the chronically mentally ill introduces yet another take on meaning. Where the qualitative study situated meaning in the personal experiences of the actors who populated the mental health service system and the study of psychiatric power situated meaning in large configurations of practice and language, the study of the troubles in the vocational rehabilitation program situated meaning in the dialogue between patients and therapists. What we witness is that meaning gradually emerged from the dynamics of interaction. Both parties tried to make sense of a conflict over a routine transfer of two patients. In struggling with this ordinary experience both parties became aware of the profound differences between the meanings they attached to a particular aspect of the program. However, initially the patients' position had less standing, as it was seen by the therapists as marred by mental illness and expressed in a deficient, highly personal, emotional language. Only the continued confrontation with the obvious failure of the official therapeutic program made some of the therapists aware that they had little understanding of the way patients experienced their programs. Not only did they begin to accept the value of the patients' understanding, but they also obtained a more inclusive understanding of the ambiguities and contradictions of vocational rehabilitation. This gradual broadening of their perspective was a painful process for the therapists. Dialogical meaning is about the joint creation of meaning, and the genuine attempt to overcome failures of communication between societal groups.

MEANING IS NOT OF ONE KIND

Several things stand out from the three examples. Despite the fact that the substantive area is the same for all three (public policy toward the chronically mentally ill in a changing service landscape), and despite the fact that all three examples profess to engage in interpretive research, the differences couldn't be larger. I'm not only thinking here of obvious differences, such as in the methods used, the subject matter, and the research question. I'm also thinking of such less obvious, but no less important, things as the scope of the study (from a case study of one mental hospital to a wide-ranging study of psychiatric institutional change in postwar Western society), or the position of the researcher vis-à-vis his or her topic (from the traditional, more or less neutral observer in the first example, to the critical analyst in the second, to the engaged change agent in the third). Also, there seem to be philosophical differences. Simply going by the examples, the qualitative study and the study of psychiatric power seem to operate on different conceptions of knowledge (naturalist versus constructionist), and different conceptions of meaning (subjective versus objective). Also, the power study and the study of change employ different conceptions of human agency (determinism versus freedom). And finally, the three examples give rise to different conceptions of policy change. While the first assumes a relatively straightforward enlightenment model (better knowledge leads to improved policy), the second seems to question the very possibility of enlightened concerted action. In contrast to this, the last study formulates an explicit model of change through a dialogue between policy makers and the groups affected by the policy. I don't want to belabor these points here, but the three examples seem to operate on different operational, epistemological, and perhaps even ontological assumptions. Yet the labels "interpretive policy analysis" and "meaning" accommodate all of this variety. Perhaps it is time to bring some order to this miscellany.

NOTES

1. This was before the numbers of homeless people, a considerable percentage of whom were chronically mentally ill, surged in large urban areas in the 1980s, demonstrating that the problem of deinstitutionalization ran deeper than just delayed spending (Jencks, 1995).

2. The material in this section is based on Wagenaar, 1987, and Lewis et al., 1991.

3. Names have been changed for reasons of anonymity.

4

THE THREE FACES OF MEANING

Some Philosophical Background to Interpretation

In this chapter I will distinguish three distinct types of meaning: hermeneutic, discursive, and dialogical. In the process I will give some philosophical background to interpretation. At the end of the chapter I will take a position on interpretation that will guide my discussion of interpretive policy analysis in the remainder of this book.

Although I think that the differences between types of interpretation are substantial (more than just an analytical tool) and, in light of the choices that a practicing policy analyst has to make, consequential, the borders are fuzzy. For example, hermeneutic meaning has, in its methodological execution, elements of on an ongoing dialogue with the object of analysis. Even as great a champion of discourse analysis as Foucault moved toward hermeneutics at the end of his life. Poststructuralist political theorists such as Bill Connolly and David Howarth, who work within the discursive tradition, also adhere to the kind of deep pluralism and the ensuing dialogue between adversaries that a pragmatist such as William James would applaud.[1] And narrative is impossible to catalogue altogether. Strictly speaking, narrative meaning derives from the interplay of its structural elements; it claims to guide action and in practice mostly is used hermeneutically. So, the three types of meaning I distinguish in this chapter are not preconceived, hardwired categories. Rather, the main dimension on which they are arranged is the analyst's approach to capturing meaning. (In the preceding chapter I called them differences in meaning-in-use.) By "approach" I mean the emphasis that the analyst places on certain aspects of the general interpretive framework that emerged out of the philosophies of Husserl, Heidegger, Dewey, Gadamer, and Wittgenstein. That general framework can be described as the loss of an absolute, realist foundation of knowledge—the naturalistic model of reality—because objects (both natural and social) are always embedded in "a communal background of intelligibility that preshapes how the world appears and who we are as agents" (Guignon, 1991, 84). The three approaches to meaning that I distinguish here are thus not intrinsic to meaning or intentional explanation. They result from the pragmatic choices that analysts make as soon as they apply the general interpretive framework to concrete questions in public policy.[2]

Hermeneutic meaning, then, focuses on the way individual agents move about in this background of understanding, on how they interpret themselves in light of it. The task of the hermeneutic researcher is to make the actions of individual agents intelligible against a backdrop of shared understandings and routines. *Discursive meaning* focuses on the large linguistic-practical frameworks, unnoticed by individual agents, that constitute the categories and objects of our everyday world. These frameworks act both as grids of possibilities (making certain practices and beliefs possible, natural, and self-evident) and conceptual horizons (by making other practices and beliefs incomprehensible, bizarre, or illegitimate). The focus of the researcher is on clarifying how these unnoticed grids historically emerge and how they constrain and enable, often in surreptitious ways, the individual agent. Finally, *dialogical meaning* focuses on the fundamentally social and practical nature of meaning. By "dialogical" I mean that meanings, although held by individual agents, "depend on the agency being shared" (Taylor, 1995c, 172). Individual agents become intelligible to themselves and to others by jointly engaging in practices that flow from an inarticulate background understanding—a shared world that is "always there" (Taylor, 1991, 308). The analyst's focus is on how meaning is constructed in the interaction between agents and between agents and the world in everyday situations.

In the average interpretive policy study there is considerable overlap (usually a large dose of hermeneutic exegesis, with a sprinkling of discourse analysis, and some reference to the notion of practice).[3] This is to be expected. Professional disciplines are complex crosscurrents of ideas and practices. The people working within them, often unbeknownst to themselves, dip into different intellectual founts as it suits their practical needs. When they write up what they did, they enhance the consistency of their work by siding with one or another approach to interpretation. For two reasons, I want to hold on to the conceptual purity of my three types, though. Analytically, I consider these approaches to meaning distinct because they are based on different, sometimes conflicting, philosophical assumptions. For example, the representational epistemology of hermeneutical exegesis disagrees with the actionable epistemology of a dialogical approach to meaning. But more important to the practicing analyst: different approaches to meaning function differently in interpretive analysis—addressing different questions, generating different types of analysis, evoking different knowledge claims, and leading to different conclusions. Different approaches to meaning lead you in quite different analytical and ethical directions. I hope to make that clear in the pages that follow. This brings me to my second purpose: pedagogy. As I said earlier, what interpretive analysts do often differs from what they say they do. One of the purposes of distinguishing these three kinds of meaning is to elucidate—call it highlight—the philosophical and practical implications of working within one or another of these three approaches to meaning. I believe that awareness of these differences will lead to better research. I also hope to make that clear in the pages that follow. The aim of this chapter—and the remainder of the book—is therefore is to map these different conceptions of meaning, and discuss their possibilities and limitations in interpretive analysis as they figure in the family of interpretive approaches to policy analysis.

HERMENEUTIC MEANING

The Phenomenological Legacy . . .

Most people have hermeneutic meaning in mind when they read that the purpose of the social sciences is the search for meaning. It is for all practical purposes the easiest way in to interpretive research (although to do it well, as with all interpretive research, is far from easy), and in the hands of experienced and sensitive practitioners it has the exhilarating effect of making insightful what before was impenetrable and obscure. To get an idea of what hermeneutic analysis can achieve in the hands of an acknowledged master, one only needs to read Geertz's classic essay "Deep Play: Notes on the Balinese Cockfight" (1973a), or some of the papers in the collection of studies on welfare and poverty edited by Danziger and Lin (2000). The hermeneutic approach to meaning has a long and venerable intellectual heritage in two important philosophical traditions: phenomenology and classical hermeneutics.[4] It offers an attractive alternative to empiricist or naturalist conceptions of the social sciences. And it offers a relatively clear methodological program (Charmaz, 2006; Soeffner, 2004; Yanow, 2000). Perhaps most important, hermeneutic meaning—clarifying a puzzling phenomenon by discovering its "real" or underlying meaning—is more or less the default setting in interpretive analysis. It is what many interpretive researchers end up doing, even when they claim to be doing other things. Hermeneutic meaning is also the position that the other two approaches to meaning explicitly challenge. It is for these reasons that I will spend some time clarifying the underlying philosophical assumptions of hermeneutic meaning and some of its problems and limitations.

Taking their cue from phenomenology, proponents of hermeneutic meaning take individual self-understandings as their point of departure. Against the empiricists' self-evident realism, phenomenologists are interested in the commonsense understandings of individuals as they argue that the social and normative order is rooted in these individual perceptions and interpretations (Mayrl, 1977, 265). For contemporary observers it is difficult to grasp the enormous impact that phenomenology, and its most important proponent, Husserl, had on the philosophical community, and very soon thereafter on the larger community of the human and social sciences. As Safranski, the German writer and famous biographer of Schopenhauer, Nietzsche, and Heidegger, observes: "When Edmund Husserl came to Freiburg in 1916, the fame of phenomenology had not yet spread beyond the confines of philosophers working in the field. Yet a few years later, during the first postwar years, this specialized subject turned into what was almost an ideological hope" (1998, 71)

Phenomenology is based on two connected assumptions—perhaps "exhortations" is the more accurate term—which, although they are not applied in a literal sense anymore today, still echo through the interpretive sciences. The first is the instruction to open oneself up for the pure perception, the bare phenomenon that is unencumbered by taken-for-granted routines:

> To open themselves thus to evidence, that was . . . what the phenomenologists wanted; their great ambition was to disregard anything that had until then been thought or said about the consciousness or the world. They were on the lookout for a new way of letting the things approach them, *without covering them up* with what they already knew. Reality should be given an opportunity to "show" itself. That which showed itself, and the way it showed itself, was called "the phenomenon" by the phenomenologists. (Safranski, 1998, 72; italics added)

The aim of phenomenology was to strip our observations of the world of what we already know and assume; to become aware of our inextricable involvement in the world; to relearn, in Safranski's happy phrase, the "real alphabet of perception" (1998, 72).[5] The way to go about this, and this is the second of Husserl's adumbrations, is to pay close attention to one's own consciousness. Thus, surprisingly, instead of a focus on the riches of the external world, phenomenology leads to introspection, but a closer inspection of what Husserl intended reveals the logic of this move. We grasp the world, phenomenologists argue, through our perceptions, and our perceptions appear to us as phenomena of consciousness. For example, we never see a tree as an isolated object, a thing-in-itself, but as something that appears in our consciousness encumbered with meaning—as something that gives shade on a hot summer day, that can be felled with an axe to sell the wood, an object of memory, or an object of systematic botanical classification. Consciousness is always consciousness *of* something. Our consciousness always relates to the world. That world is as much part of our consciousness as our consciousness is part of the world (Safranski, 1998, 74–75). In this way the distinction between the mind and the external world—so central in the naturalistic epistemology of scientism—disappears.[6] Phenomenology does not preach a new philosophical idealism—although in practice it threatens to end up there (Gorman, 1976; Gutting, 2001).

Before I delve any further into the philosophical intricacies of phenomenology, I want to draw out its legacy for contemporary interpretive research. That legacy can be summarized in three principles. First is the assumption that human actors grasp the world by constantly interpreting their own acts and those of others. This observation signals an inescapable fact of the human condition: the intelligibility of the world depends on ordinary, everyday understandings.[7] For example, Dilthey, one of the first philosophers to argue for the autonomy of the human sciences in opposition to the natural sciences, locates the "solid foundation" of social scientific research in inner experience, in the "facts of consciousness." "All science is empirical, experiential science," Dilthey argues, but experience derives its coherence and validity from the "structuring a priori of our consciousness" (Grondin, 1994). And as Prus, commenting on Dilthey, puts it:

> For Dilthey . . . the paramount reality is the world of Human Lived Experience. In contrast to those positivist social scientists who tend to dismiss human lived experience as subjective, epiphenomenal, or inconsequential, Dilthey observed that human reality could not exist other than through people's experiences of the world. (1996, 36; see also Gutting on the great French phenomenologist Merleau-Ponty, 2001, 186–87)

In the social sciences the everyday world of human experience occupies center stage; there simply is no way of getting around that.[8] Policy analysts may go to great lengths to come up with clever operationalizations of concepts such as race, mental illness, or social class to arrive at "objective" measurements of them, but to be able to grasp them as the concepts they are, we need these ordinary, taken-for-granted interpretations of that particular slice of the world in which the idea of race, mental illness, or social class makes sense. In the final analysis all scientific categories and operationalizations ride on everyday experience. Take the everyday experience out—if that would be possible at all—and the scientific concept would evaporate. It simply wouldn't make sense.[9] The elaborate conceptual structure of the social sciences (class, race, institutions, policy, structure, process, delinquency, psychiatric illness, state, democracy, etc.) exists only by the grace of our everyday experience. Commonsense interpretation is the bedrock of social science.

The second part of phenomenology's legacy has to do with the problem of how to move from grasping individual consciousness to an understanding of the intersubjective features of the world. Although phenomenology is as much a methodological program as an epistemological position, how to move from inner experience to an understanding of the world is far from obvious. Most treatises on phenomenology are exceedingly abstract, and what it entails in practice is not always clear. The problem resides in the fact that in their eagerness to escape the Cartesian dichotomy of mind versus world, with its implied causal order in which the world gives rise to perceptions and observations, phenomenologists fuse mind and world in one fundamental activity called "intending." This is not an easy idea to grasp. Intentionality means that objects somehow exist simultaneously inside the mind and outside the body. A large part of consciousness is always "beyond itself," and this is what enables us to perceive slices of the world as meaningful units. As Gorman puts it, "An individual, obviously possessing both a mind and body, is no longer seen as a whole, spatially enclosed unit. An essential element of this individual is beyond itself and uncircumscribable" (1976, 497). With the key concept of intentionality phenomenologists want to convey that the mind projects itself outward to grasp objects by ascribing meaning to them. The mind is not passively imprinted on by the world, but instead actively reaches out and "constructs" the world. The mind reaches outward to "meet" the world of which it is already conscious. Thus, "what exists, for Husserl, has its being in our conscious processes" (Gorman, 1976, 492). In this sense, self-conscious awareness is considered the ultimate foundation of knowledge.

If this sounds ambiguous, it is.[10] In a philosophy that gives epistemological primacy to consciousness, and considers self-conscious awareness the foundation of knowledge, the question of how exactly consciousness hooks up with the world becomes key if phenomenology is not to dissolve into philosophical idealism. Several solutions have been suggested to prevent this from happening. They all have in common that they project some form of transcendental meaning that informs subjective acts of consciousness and that takes us beyond individual experience.[11] Dilthey assumed, for example, that the fixed intersubjective structures of society are immediately intelligible to us once we have succeeded in carefully registering the mental imprint that our subjects of research leave on our consciousness (Grondin, 1994, 86).[12] For Husserl, the transcendental glue that held individual acts of consciousness together was a fundamental, a priori "eidetic" knowledge. This "pure" consciousness of the world could be grasped by an almost meditative approach to understanding.[13] Even Merleau-Ponty, probably the most worldly and least idealist of the phenomenologists, cannot extract himself from the mind-world dilemma. He rejects the idea of a transcendental subjectivity, a retreat into a "separate and entirely 'inner' world accessible only via special acts of introspection and intuition" (Gutting, 2001, 189). Instead of a privileged "eidetic" knowledge that somehow allows us to grasp the underlying phenomenal fields of everyday perceptions, Merleau-Ponty posited a subject that is always situated within the lived world, or, differently put, the "inextricable *unity* of world and consciousness with neither assimilated to the other" (Gutting, 2001, 188; italics in original). But to prevent the phenomenologically reflexive subject from becoming enmeshed in the "thickness" of everyday reality (and from being reduced to a "mere" sociologist), he proposes a generalized, largely linguistic, tacit "cogito" that makes perceptions and experiences possible. For all his insistence on keeping the richness of the embodied, experiential-phenomenal world inside phenomenological analysis and his unwillingness to succumb to an idealist foundationalism, because Merleau-Ponty never really explicated how this tacit cogito hooked individual consciousness to the world, we have to conclude that he also became ensnared in the mind-world dilemma. It is at this point, we will see shortly, that classical hermeneutics begins to inform the search for hermeneutic meaning.

Finally, phenomenologists in the Anglo-Saxon world, particularly the influential Alfred Schütz, have similarly grappled with the mind-world problem. As Schütz's solution is tremendously influential in interpretive social science, I discuss it at greater length here. In Schütz's formulations the emphasis shifted from the experience of the individual to the structures that are assumed to give rise to these individual experiences. As a recent text from the German-speaking world on the phenomenological basis of qualitative research, puts it:

> Life-world, in Edmund Husserl's sense, is the original domain, the obvious and unquestioned foundation both of all types of everyday acting and thinking and of all scientific theorizing and philosophizing. In its concrete manifestations it exists in all its countless varieties as the only real world of every individual person, of every *ego*. These variations are built on general immutable structures, the "realm of immediate evidence." Alfred Schütz adopted this idea of Husserl's and attempted to discover the most general essential features of the life-world, in respect of the particular problems of social as opposed to the natural sciences. The general aim of life-world analysis, oriented to the epistemological problems of the social sciences, is therefore to analyse the understanding of meaning comprehension by means of a formal description of invariable basic structures of the constitution of meaning *in the subjective consciousness of actors*. (Hitzler & Eberle, 2004, 67; italics in original)

According to Schütz, subjective experiences are by definition sociological in nature because they always refer to, and—a crucial addition—are made possible by, the intersubjective features of social reality. Differently put, an inevitable dialectical relationship exists between subjective and intersubjective experiences. They bring each other into being. But what does that oft-encountered and intellectually soothing phrase "bringing each other into being" actually entail? Above all it refers to an active process of perception. "Perception is seen not as a passive-receptive process of representation but as an active-constructive process of production" (Flick, 2003 89). But that is stating the obvious. Passive perception has been a straw man since the days of Hume. However, the idea of active perception becomes more interesting when its philosophical implications are spelled out. On the one hand, the production metaphor of individual perception leads to a commitment to one or another form of social constructivism. I deliberately hedge my bets here, as social constructivism is a diverse and contested epistemic (and epistemological) position (with weak and radical versions) to which I will return in more detail in chapter 7. On the other hand, a constructivist form of perception deals a death blow to the idea that we can verify our observations against a firm, uncontested foundation, be it brute, observer-independent facts, or "unassailable" structures, or "pure" experience. As we saw in chapter 2, all perception requires a prior vocabulary.[14]

The upshot is that the seemingly self-evident concept of "intersubjectivity" raises overwhelming practical, methodological issues. I will argue later in this chapter that interpretivism, the position that meaning is ultimately dependent upon the self-understandings of our subjects of analysis, is flawed. I will discuss different ways of going beyond interpretivism, and suggest a solution that is based on the notion of action and dialogue in interpretation. But first we need to further explore the phenomenological legacy in interpretive social science, and the important hermeneutic approach to interpretive policy analysis that it gave rise to.

The third insight that phenomenology bequeathed to the social sciences is almost an afterthought to the preceding two: the individual is the primary source of knowledge of the "life-world." This obviously follows from phenomenology's position that everyday understanding forms the epistemic foundation of the social sciences. This has translated into the methodological principle that the standard way to gain access to subjective meaning is by interviewing individuals or observing them in their natural habitat. This is what I did in the qualitative readmission study. I ventured into the ghetto and conducted unstructured qualitative interviews with patients and others in their own environment: at home, in fast food restaurants, in community centers, or in the hospital.[15] In this way I not only recorded individuals' stories about their struggle with mental disorder, but also picked up the incidental, tangential information (Becker, 1996, 65) that enabled me to see the material circumstances in which patients, family members, and service providers lived, worked, and received or provided services, thereby adding a measure of reality to stories that would otherwise remain abstract and detached. The purpose of all this was to obtain as accurate, dense, and precise a description of the world of these individuals as possible.

Taken together, the threefold legacy of phenomenology to the social sciences—ordinary subjective experiences are the bedrock of the social sciences; such subjective experiences both refer to and entail larger intersubjective meaning structures; and finally, the individual as the main entryway into social research—are common to all interpretive approaches. However, as we have seen so far, it is not at all clear in the original phenomenological program how we derive intersubjective structures from subjective experience. The original thinkers, dead set on staking out an autonomous epistemological position for the human sciences against the hegemony of the natural sciences, formulated a strong intentionalist program of interpretive explanation for the human sciences. However, by exclusively situating meaning in the mind of the individual, they painted themselves into an idealist corner: there was no consistent way to link the individual with the social. In fact, as we will see shortly, most of the different approaches to interpretive social science can be traced back to this key issue. But before we go into that, I need to discuss one important and common answer to phenomenology's methodological problem of intersubjectivity: classical hermeneutics.

...And Its Hermeneutic Ally

Geertz, in his classic paper on the interpretation of cultures, states that the analyst's task in the social sciences consists of clarifying the intersubjective meanings that form the foundation of social reality as the latter is expressed in the everyday behaviors of ordinary people. This is a common enough depiction of the interpretivist program to which Geertz has famously attached the epithet "thick description" (Geertz, 1973a). But mellifluous as it may sound, thick description raises several important conceptual-methodological issues.

The first has to do with the purpose of qualitative data collection. Becker puts it better than anyone else:

> There is something wrong with this [thick description] on the face of it. The object of any description is not to reproduce the object completely—why bother when we have the object already?—but rather to pick out its relevant aspects, details which can be abstracted from the totality of details that make it up so that we can answer some questions we have. (1996, 64)

As we saw earlier: perception is active. To see something, to make something stand out from the overwhelming mass of detail, we need a perspective, a point of view. This point of view is supplied by our prior beliefs and understandings, but also by our interests. Or, if we are researchers, by our research question and the preliminary assumptions that guide it. Prior interests are the great organizing principle in research. The preconceptions and beliefs they generate prestructure the otherwise inchoate mass of detail we enter. Every qualitative researcher must have had the disconcerting experience on entering a new social domain of being out at sea: Where on earth to begin? How to distinguish relevant from irrelevant data? How to make sense of what comes at us from all sides? How to see at all? To arrive at meaning through qualitative description thus implies that researchers bring their own interpretations to the field. By confronting our interpretations with those of the individuals we study we will arrive at the higher-order interpretations that we recognize or accept as "the meaning" of a social phenomenon. Observation is always continuous with analysis, or, as Geertz puts it:

> In the study of culture, analysis penetrates into the very body of the object—that is, *we begin with our own interpretations of what our informants are up to, or think they are up to and systematize those*—the line of . . . culture as a natural fact and . . . culture as theoretical entity tends to get blurred. (1973b, 15; italics in original)

So, the meaning that a social phenomenon has for an individual relies on the meaning that the researchers bring to the research situation. Wherever researchers see meaning they are, inevitably, looking into a mirror.

A common way of putting this is to say that the qualitative interpretive analyst *reconstructs* meaning. But what it is that we are reconstructing? The assumptions are that some collective understanding of a social phenomenon exists in the world that we study, that it is not immediately obvious to the outside observer, and that this collective understanding or meaning can be reconstructed by gaining access to the multiple individual subjective meanings that make up the aggregate collective understanding. We have some assurance that what we come up with is meaning as it appears to the actors involved because it is based on our methodical, thick descriptions of the research field. This approach to finding meaning has strong affinities with classical approaches to hermeneutics. Later I will introduce a different approach to hermeneutics (philosophical hermeneutics) that attempts to overcome some important limitations of classical hermeneutics, but for the moment it is important to grasp what classical hermeneutics entails.[16]

To make sense of a particular human action we have to go beyond subjective meaning and try to situate it in a larger context. For example, to understand why so many patients were rehospitalized after being discharged from the state hospital, I reconstructed the life-world of these patients. The vivid—I'm inclined to say compelling—picture of how these patients coped with the stresses of poverty, psychiatric illness, dead-end jobs, obtaining housing, a fragmented service system, and living with friends and family, made the reader somehow "understand" why so many of these patients returned to the hospital. The mental hospital was understood to be an important resource in the life of indigent mental patients. I take "understanding" here to mean something like sympathetic empathy, a state of mind that could be indicated by the statement "I probably would have done the same if I were in the situation these patients are in."[17] The framing of the state hospital as one resource among many to cope with the combination of poverty and mental disorder "makes sense" in this way. It makes a confused, contested situation more coherent. The rendering of state hospitals as resources for the indigent mentally disordered seems accurate, precise, and believable as it takes into account a rich, dense body of qualitative data (Becker, 1996, 67). Whether it is true is anybody's guess. Interpretive explanations do not deal in truth and falsity, but in plausibility— always under the provision that this particular explanation is not exhaustive and that at any time a better one might come up. But, for the moment, this one will do as an adequate understanding of a complex, open-ended and indeterminate policy situation.

Hermeneutics brings the smells and sounds of the world, a measure of objectivity if one wants, to the purely intentionalist account of meaning in phenomenology. Meaning is not just in the actors' conscious experiences. Instead, the hermeneutic analyst looks for the "intentionality that is contained within the act itself, not what is in the mind of the actor" (Fay, 1996, 140). And this requires that the analyst places the act in the wider context of the actor's social setting (ibid.). This approach to understanding intersubjective meaning draws upon the familiar notion of the hermeneutic circle. In order to understand the part (readmissions) the researcher must grasp the whole (the life of poor mental patients in an urban environment). By situating the original action in a wider context the effect is that what was initially puzzling has been clarified. The part obtains meaning from the whole and, vice versa, the whole is explained by the individual parts. The basic idea of hermeneutical interpretation is that the world is a relatively confined universe that contains a meaning, which, although it is obscured, can be found by "consideration of a passage in the light of the intent and form of the whole" (Bleicher, 1980). Hermeneutical explanation derives from textual exegesis, and indeed some interpretive analysts suggest that we think of the world as a text (Flick, 2003; Potter, 1996; Ricoeur, 1977; Yanow, 1996). Hermeneutics is the theory of interpretation whose purpose is to provide rules and methods for valid interpretation, where "valid" means the exclusion of arbitrariness (Grondin, 1994, 18). For example, the admonition to be accurate and precise in one's description of social reality to avoid "errors of attribution" (Becker, 1996, 58, 67) is an example of such a hermeneutic rule in qualitative inquiry. This to-ing and fro-ing between the part and the whole is captured in the famous metaphor of the hermeneutic circle. The concept of the hermeneutic circle simultaneously refers to a basic mode of commonsense understanding, to a method of analysis that is peculiar to the social sciences, and to a particular epistemological stance (Bernstein, 1976, 138). The latter requires some explanation.

The phenomenological spirit of privileging ordinary, everyday experiences in understanding and explaining society is complemented by the exegetic spirit of classical hermeneutics that searches for the coherent whole that animates the singular experiences.[18] In other words, hermeneutics bridges subjective and intersubjective meaning, and we will see in the next chapters that different policy scholars have found different ways of accomplishing this task. Working within the tradition of hermeneutic meaning, what they all have in common is that the analyst "objectifies" (i.e., stands over and against) that which is to be interpreted (Bernstein, 1976; see also Taylor, 2002, 127). In that sense, analysts remain external to the topic of their research, the people who are part of it, and the interpretive process they analyze. In fact, the epistemological requirements of good inquiry compel them to do so. In this sense also, the approach of the qualitative, hermeneutic analysts has a naturalistic, sometimes even objectivist, flavor—maybe not de jure, but certainly de facto, as we will see in chapter 5. For despite many statements to the contrary, in actual practice the hermeneutic analyst operates on the principle that meaning exists out there in the world and it can be recovered in an authoritative way by carefully following the methodological precepts of good interpretive research.[19]

This position is sometimes described as "meaning realism," or "the view that meanings are fixed entities that can be discovered and that exist independent of the observer" (Schwandt, 2000). Meaning realism is a theory-in-use. One infers it from the way that interpretive analysts actually engage in their task of understanding social reality. Meaning realism is a common feature of those versions of hermeneutic analysis that aim at exegesis, the elucidation of the meaning of texts. (This is why I called this type of meaning hermeneutic. But meaning realism also characterizes discursive approaches to meaning.) The method of exegesis revolves around two related premises: (1) that the interpreter and the object of interpretation are distinct, and (2) that the first is not involved with the latter. The second premise must be taken in an epistemological way. The analyst is not necessarily emotionally uninvolved, but remains at arm's length from the act of interpretation: "Thus, in interpretive traditions, the interpreter objectifies (i.e., stands over and against) that which is to be interpreted. And, in that sense, the interpreter remains unaffected by and external to the interpretive process" (Schwandt, 2000, 195). Sometimes this epistemological distance has a normative ring to it (to get involved would compromise the validity of the analysis); sometimes it is mere convenience (desk research is easier than spending months and months in the field trying to establish relations with the subjects of our analysis). To get the interpretive analysis started, analysts not only have to project an a priori, and in practice more or less distinct and monolithic, "meaning" in the world, the exact nature of which is to be discerned by them, but simultaneously to place themselves outside the process of meaning making (despite rather noncommittal statements that the analysts are part of the world they analyze) to function as an Archimedean point.

I do not intend the phrase "meaning realism" in a critical or pejorative way. When done well classical hermeneutic analysis can lead to wholly satisfying results. A talented, skilled analyst with experience in the field can come up with interpretations that are enlightening and senseful, as they combine the sympathetic understanding of the insider with the perspective of the outsider. In practice meaning realism entails that the analysts are on the lookout for bias that will distort the veracity of their picture of social reality. Interpretive analysts who work within the hermeneutic tradition often tend to emphasize the overriding importance of research methods. Again, the point is not that this is the wrong way of going about interpreting meaning, but that it is a way; one particular way of interpreting social reality with its own strengths and limitations, its own usefulness for particular research questions, its own epistemological and ontological assumptions. My point is also that there are alternative approaches to interpretive analysis that conceptualize meaning in different ways. To get at these alternative approaches I will first discuss some problems with the hermeneutic approach to interpreting meaning.

SOME PROBLEMS WITH EXPLAINING SOCIETY THROUGH
SUBJECTIVE MEANING

As we saw, the hermeneutic approach to the interpretation of social reality proceeds by capturing the subjective understandings of the individuals who move about in it. The analyst reconstructs the meaning of a particular phenomenon (psychiatric recidivism, for example) by finding out how the individuals who are involved in that phenomenon perceive, imagine, experience, and discuss it and placing those experiences in the wider context of the individuals' lives and social settings. Although this approach has an obvious appeal, there are suspicions about the validity of subjective meaning. The problem with the hermeneutical approach is the assumption that registering subjective experiences is a nonproblematic affair. Hermeneutic analysts proceed from the rather self-evident expectation that individuals have privileged access to their own subjective meaning. In fact, it is for this reason that we go to such lengths to obtain thick descriptions of the perceptions, feelings, and experiences of our subjects. We see these as personal attributes that can only be accessed by asking the individual. But what if the individual is not aware of some aspect of his or her world? What if he or she is misled, or for some reason has no access to experiences that are nevertheless there for others to see? And what if both subject *and* researcher are blind to certain dimensions of the world that the latter tries to understand through research? These are questions that far exceed the issue of proper method.

In general there are three ways in which individuals may misunderstand or fail to have access to their own experiences. First, people may be misled about their own beliefs or intentions. We are all familiar with situations in which someone's self-understanding seems at odds with another, deeper, more fundamental reality to which the individual is blind. The neurotic individual, who keeps repeating self-destructive behavior for reasons that others surmise but that he is unable to grasp, is one example. The complacency and the attendant rationalizations of whole groups of people in situations of obvious subjugation are another. In the first instance we say that the individual's unconscious or repressed impulses prevent him from understanding his situation properly. In the second we ascribe the lack of insight to ideology or brainwashing. To make the individual aware of the extent of his self-delusion in such instances is almost automatically an act of liberation, of emancipation. Even more pernicious is the situation in which both subject *and* analyst are in the dark. The annals of social science are littered with examples of such analysis, seen in the eyes of later generations as thoroughly misguided, if not downright evil.[20] The notorious rational analyses that guided the allocation of troops and aerial raids in the Vietnam War, or the widespread use of eugenics as a social technology by social democratic governments to control those considered racially inferior and sexually deviant in many European countries before World War II, are but two egregious examples out of many (Gerodetti, 2006; Mottier, 2008). With hindsight we describe such projects as misguided, caused by doctrinaire blindness, but we tend to forget that at the time they were not considered iniquitous or out of the ordinary. In fact, in many cases they were business as usual.

A second way in which people don't have immediate access to their experiences is in the case of objective meanings, the rules, concepts, and norms that are implicit in a practice and that make that practice possible. In chapter 2 I gave the example of entering into a mortgage contract. The notion of a mortgage rests on notions of property, loans, interest, contracts, discounting the future, and individual responsibility. These in turn are grounded in a particular conception of human relations and the autonomous nature of individuals (Taylor, 1985a, 32), and in a set of values that privilege property and money over loyalty and security. Now, when I undertake a mortgage, I am not aware of all these implicit meanings, but I understand the practical and semantic distinctions that these concepts and norms carve out in the world that I inhabit. I understand them to such an extent that I am capable of successfully negotiating and completing a mortgage contract. Although implicit, they are at least available to me.

There is a third category of experiences that are not available to me no matter how hard I try. These are the tacit, embodied competences that suffuse most of my actions. Think of bike riding. An experienced cyclist knows how to stay upright in a curve, but would be hard pressed to explain how he does it. Similarly, we are all competent conversationalists. That is, we all master the art of turn taking—picking up the subtle verbal and bodily cues that signal that it is our time to step in with a remark. However, none of us would ever be able to explain how exactly we do it. Even complex semantic skills, such as telling a senseful story in a complex, equivocal situation, rests on a remarkably subtle set of tacit skills in prosodically organizing the narrative while it is unfolding (Gee, 1985; Wagenaar and Hartendorp, 2000). Tacit, embodied, linguistically inscripted competences underlie all of our actions and practices, not just motor skills. The way we perceive and experience the world is as it is because we are embodied beings. We grasp the world by acting in it. Tacit, embodied competences literally make action or practice possible, yet they are completely inaccessible to us.

These situations, in which subjects and analysts are blind to some aspect of social-moral reality or don't have access to their skills or experiences, pose large epistemological and methodological problems to interpretive analysis. As Fay trenchantly puts it, on the one hand:

> social science in so far as it studies intentional phenomena intentionalistically described must be interpretive, and as such must be rooted in the distinctions and concepts of those it studies. Social science cannot simply ignore or replace the distinctions of its subjects with its own technical concepts. In this way, interpretivism is correct. (1996, 118–19)

On the other hand, if the reconstitution of the intersubjective basis of social reality proceeds through the recovery of subjective meanings, and the validity of subjective meanings is compromised in some situations, then the whole dialectical machinery by which the grasp of the whole through its parts and the parts through the whole runs into the ground. Perhaps the phenomenological legacy of privileging subjective self-understandings should be questioned. Fay again: "But because social scientists are thus bound in important ways to the concepts and terms of those they study, does this mean that they must understand others solely in their own terms?" (1996, 119).

The upshot is that there are limits to the hermeneutic project. We must somehow go beyond the self-understandings of the subjects we study without ignoring these altogether, as scholars working in the empiricist tradition are wont to do. In the next two sections I will explicate two ways to expand interpretive analysis by transcending individual self-understandings.

TWO ALTERNATIVE CONCEPTIONS OF MEANING

What does it mean to go beyond individual self-understandings in capturing or reconstructing meaning? Let's edge into this question by asking ourselves what constitutes a "flaw in self-understanding" from within the interpretive framework? That is, how can we conceptualize the idea of a flawed self-understanding without taking recourse in the realist, objectivist epistemology of empiricism? An interpretive claim that the beliefs of X are flawed rests, minimally, on two conceptual requirements: (1) the notion of a (necessarily limited) perspective, and (2) an outside interpreting observer. The notion of perspective makes it possible to imagine an alternative vantage point from which to comment on or criticize the views held by the actor.

The outside observer is the agent who provides the alternative perspective and engages in the activity of critically questioning the perspective of the original actor. The two alternative notions of interpretive analysis that are able to go beyond self-understandings both mobilize these two requirements, but they do it in wholly different ways. Let's first explore the two requirements separately.

One obvious way in which self-understanding is flawed is that it is inevitably, inescapably, partial. Our actions and self-understandings, as we have seen in the preceding section, are embedded in a vast environment of tacit understandings and dispositions. By "tacit" I mean that these understandings and dispositions are mostly unarticulated, and that we would find it difficult, if not impossible, to explicate large chunks of this background knowledge if asked (Polanyi, 1958; Taylor, 1995c, 173). The acquisition of this background knowledge is what it means to be socialized in a certain community. This insight, that everyday actions and understandings rest on a reservoir of unarticulated background knowledge, runs as a leitmotiv through the work of philosophers such as Heidegger, Wittgenstein, Dewey, Gadamer, Bourdieu, and Taylor, who inaugurated and articulated the transformation of social theory. With important nuances and differences, they all agree that (1) explicit understanding can only be partial, (2) meaning resides not in the individual experience of actors but in larger social configurations of which the actor is an integral part, (3) meaning emerges from *acting* upon concrete situations, and (4) meaning, in the sense of our actions exhibiting sensefulness, is created dynamically in an ongoing interaction among actors and between actors and larger social configurations. But while critics of subjective meaning agree on an alternative conception of meaning that has these four features, they disagree on the conceptualization of the key term "social configuration" and, as a consequence of this, about the nature of the meaning-forming interaction. In fact, it is precisely at these two points that an important juncture in interpretive theory can be seen, with one road leading to what I call a discursive, and another to what I call a dialogical, conception of meaning.

Before I elaborate on the differences between discursive and dialogical meaning, let me first be more precise about what they agree on. Those who aim to go beyond the play of beliefs, affects, and value dispositions of the individual argue that the inevitability of background knowledge relocates meaning from the subjective self-understandings of individuals to something "outside" individuals. If self-understanding relies on background knowledge and if that background knowledge is available to individuals but not fully articulable, it means that it must be something over and beyond individual subjectivity. Simply put, if the individual were to perish, the background knowledge would not perish with him. Now, where proponents of a discursive conception of meaning part ways with those of a dialogical bend is in their belief that the outside "something" must be seen as large, disembodied belief systems, institutionalized practices, a particular vocabulary, and the artifacts that go with these. Language is tricky here, for although discursive analysts all operate on the assumption that meaning is uncoupled from the individual's self-understanding, they disagree on how to conceptualize the nonsubjective carriers of meaning. The terminology ranges from "structures," "contexts," "practices," "field of discursivity," and *"dispositif"* to, simply, "discourse."

The hot core of all these concepts is that the individual's self-understanding and concomitant behavior are in one way or another influenced, dependent upon, shaped, or even determined by these wider discursive structures.[21] Discursive meaning is thoroughly *perspectivist,* as I discussed in chapter 2. It assumes that there is no ultimate foundation of human knowledge. In assessing the veracity of our knowledge of the social world we don't have recourse to a neutral court of arbitration such as brute facts, or "lived experience," or the power of the logical syllogism. Our understanding is inevitably shaped by a historically conditioned point of view.

DISCURSIVE MEANING

Perspectivism is shared by discursive and dialogical conceptions of meaning, but they draw almost diametrically opposed conclusions from it. Discursive conceptions of meaning are not satisfied with the weak notion of perspectivism as a generally accepted epistemological principle in the natural and social sciences that all perception operates under a particular description. Discursive approaches to meaning take perspectivism in the stronger sense of conceptual and practical frames that more or less exclude each other. (In chapter 6 I will explore in greater detail the qualifier "more or less" in this statement.) By relocating meaning formation to larger, sedimented meaning structures, discursive-meaning analysts reduce the role of individual agency. The discursive conception of meaning operates on a trope of captivity; individuals are locked into the larger meaning structures of their place and age. They are the apocryphal Platonic cave dwellers. Their perspective is irretrievably limited. They cannot see beyond the horizon of the discourses that surround them.

This metaphor, although correct in a general sense, is also misleading. It suggests that a world exists outside the cage—truth? undistorted meaning?—to which the individual, under certain circumstances, might have access. But this is not what the concept of discourse is about. It is meant to be exhaustive. Perspectivism is universal. The cage *is* the world, and whoever manages to venture outside the cage will find himself in yet another one.[22] In discursive analysis even truth is the product of perspective (Allen, 1993). Working within the tradition of what is trenchantly called a hermeneutics of suspicion, many discursive analysts tend to couple truth to the will to power. As Foucault, one of the foremost analysts in this tradition, tersely puts it, "What rules of right are implemented by the relations of power in the production of discourses of truth?" (Foucault, 1980a, 93) The result is that discursive perspectivism leads to relativism. The emergence of the community mental health movement is within a discursive framework not seen as an improvement upon the state hospital or an emancipation from oppressive professional practices and misguided ideas, but as yet another internally coherent set of beliefs, practices, values, and artifacts within psychiatric care (Miller & Rose, 1986, 3). In Platonic terms, the world is like a vast underground complex of interconnected caves with no possibility that one will ever find a tunnel to the surface, because there simply is no surface. The "outside" world is nothing but an image painted on the walls of one of the caves.

The transfer of meaning to larger discursive configurations has important consequences for the way that meaning formation is conceptualized. Meaning is seen as internal to discourse; not as something that is tacked on to the different elements of a discourse by these being processed through the filter of individual subjectivities. It emerges from the interaction of the elements of discourse: belief systems, practices, artifacts, narratives, linguistic routines. Discursive theorists tend to think of this interaction as an ongoing play of contrasts and consonances. Meaning becomes visible as a set of contours and demarcations that emerges from the reflection of social objects in their opposites. For example, Miller, in his essay on the historical emergence of the community mental health movement, comments that "Foucault has shown brilliantly how unreason becomes constituted as other and as knowable only from the side of reason" (1986, 41).

Discursive meaning is, thus, a depersonalized form of meaning. Individual agents are not expected to play much of a role in meaning formation. They are restricted to acting out the largely unconscious, taken-for-granted understandings that emerge from the interplay of larger social forces. This does not mean that subjective meaning does not exist. Obviously it does, but it cannot function as the foundation of a project of interpretive explanation as it can only be a derivation of the landscape of differences and congruencies that we recognize, to stick to our example, as the field of psychiatry and mental disorder. Discursive formations are self-referring. That is, meaning is not projected by individuals onto social objects, but the objects appear to the individual, who is endowed with a set of proper understandings, beliefs, dispositions, and values acquired during the formative phase of the discourse. For example, the meaning we attach to the mental illness of a family member is the result of the conditioning that follows from the historical emergence of psychiatry as a social institution, with its attendant professional language, its diagnostic routines, its practice of incarcerating mentally disordered individuals in large mental hospitals, its very distinguishing of certain people from the larger social body as "psychiatric patient[s]" (Foucault, 1979). Even our self-understanding as being a mother, father, someone with healthy living habits, a skilled lover, are the product of discourses, which are themselves "bearers of power" (Foucault, 1980a, 94). The discursive formation of professional psychiatry makes certain ways of seeing and doing possible and even "natural."

It follows from this that the task of the discursive analyst is, by implication, a critical one.[23] The discursive analyst does not stop at unearthing *what* social phenomena mean (in terms of the actors' self-understandings), but he also wants to know *why* they occurred (Fay, 1996, 119). The analyst is not satisfied with just unpacking the content of a particular worldview or social phenomenon, or even the objective meaning structures that make up that worldview or phenomenon. Our analyst would want to know *why* this worldview came into being in the first place. In terms of our example, he would be interested in the elements that make up, let's say, the discursive formation of community psychiatry, or the historical process by which community psychiatry came into being as an alternative to the asylum.

But as the emergence of a particular configuration of practices, understandings, and norms inevitably reflects the power distribution of an era, this kind of analysis is by nature critical. The goal of the discursive analyst is to unmask and to emancipate. The argument here goes as follows: discursive meaning structures are not the result of historical necessity, but, instead, of chance, fortuity—or, in the jargon of discourse analysis, are "historically contingent." The emergence of discourses is part happenstance, part purpose, and part convenience. Discourses are makeshift structures, put together by a wide range of social actors dispersed in place and time, who negotiate a particular practical challenge out of the ideational, institutional, and moral material that happens to be available at the time. But, as proponents of genealogical discourse analysis tend to emphasize, it could have been otherwise, but it isn't—and for a reason. A particular interpretation of social reality as it is embedded in and expressed by a complex matrix of institutions, beliefs, language, and practices can never be seen apart from the interests of certain groups in society. In other words, processes of power and domination are central. I don't want to sound overly deterministic here. One of the real contributions of discourse theory to social theory and policy analysis is a subtle conception of the dispersed and formative way that power operates in society, in which power itself is seen as an emerging discursive formation (Foucault, 1980a, 1980b). This decentered, formative notion of power is expressed in evocative phrases such as "governing from a distance" "self-regulation," and "power without an author." I will return to this in chapter 6.

Again, there are many important differences and nuances among the various approaches to discursive analysis, particularly in the importance that discursive analysts attach to the role of language, the relation they see between the discursive and the nondiscursive, the role they give to agency, and the way they deal with power. I will discuss these extensively in chapter 6. However, whatever variant of discursive meaning we encounter will have these two characteristics: a theory of meaning in which meaning emerges out of the differences and consonances of a discursive entity (story, discourse, *épistéme*), and a performative perspective on language. That is, meaning is not the intersubjective aggregate of the subjective understandings of individual actors. On the contrary, individual understanding is the product of a larger meaning structure that emerges out of the interplay of the elements of a discursive entity. In addition, language is not taken in its representative function as describing aspects of the external world, but instead in its generative function as bringing these aspects into being by enacting them. Language, in discursive analysis, is seen as action. Methodologically, discursive analysis focuses on supra-individual aspects of social life: belief systems, ideologies, institutions, traditions, and public policies. The general thrust of discursive analysis is to make the discursive structures that envelop us visible. Usually this takes one of the following two forms, or both: a synchronic (the architecture of the discourse) or diachronic (its historical development over time) analysis of the formation of discursive structures, or an analysis of the functioning of discourses in historical and contemporary social phenomena. The outcome of a discourse analysis is a reconstruction of how the basic categories of social reality, the problems and objects that are addressed by public policy, are themselves assembled by an assortment of social actors from a broad range of societal materials.

DIALOGICAL MEANING

As I said earlier, proponents of discursive and of dialogical meaning draw radically different conclusions about the nature of interpretation from the inevitable partiality of subjective understanding. Where the first see perspective as a cage, a self-contained universe, that determines every aspect of the individual's understanding of the world (including self-image and standards of truth), the second see it instead as a prerequisite for understanding (Grondin, 1994, 110). In grasping the world we are inescapably immersed in our own experiences and preconceptions, experiences and preconceptions that are linguistically determined, but without which we simply wouldn't be able to discern anything meaningful or relevant. Gadamer, one of the originators of the dialogical conception of meaning—he calls it philosophical hermeneutics—uses the metaphor of a horizon, a historically conditioned experiential space that guides our gaze onto the world, but also constrains and distorts our understanding of others. It is a condition of humanness that we cannot easily transcend this horizon. We cannot set aside our prejudices. But far from considering this a problem, being locked into a perspective is, in Gadamer's philosophy, a productive force.[24] Being locked into a perspective makes us see things, and particularly *wants* us to see things. In Gadamer's conception of hermeneutics, meaning does not reside in the phenomenon itself, to be dislodged by the analyst questioning others about their understanding of it. Instead meaning emerges when an observer begins to question the phenomenon from his particular position. Preconceived notions make certain things stand out in the world as interesting, important, urgent, or valuable. But we do not helplessly surrender to the constraints of perspective; our preconceptions can also be used to obtain a better understanding of others (and thereby of ourselves). Meaning is always "*for someone* such that it is *relative to an interpreter*" (Fay, 1996, 142; italics in original). In other words, in the discursive conception of meaning, meaning is relational.

Dialogical meaning, as articulated by Gadamer, represents a radically different conception of meaning. Both in the hermeneutic and discursive versions, meaning is considered a property of the object of analysis (Fay, 1996, 146). The position of the analyst here is that of a knower who gains knowledge *about* an object (the meaning of a particular human activity) (Schwandt, 2000, 194). The act of knowing here is unilateral and aimed at obtaining control of the object of analysis. The analyst "grasps" the meaning of the activity as if it resides out in the world for him to uncover. Meaning is "identified" (Yanow, 2000, 14), and to put it that way makes sense within the hermeneutic and discursive approach because the identification is based on the careful recording of the statements, stories, and practices of the research subjects. In the dialogical conception of meaning, on the other hand, meaning emerges only in relation to an interpreter. As a consequence, meanings change when an object or action meets a new interpreter, or more likely, community of interpreters. For example, the meaning of the French Revolution is different for British observers of the late eighteenth century than for those of the early twenty-first century. It means something else again for a community of European historians and again for a group of East Asian historians. But the reverse also holds true: the act of interpretation is not a neutral event that leaves the interpreter unaffected. In trying to grasp what an object means in relation to his own life and situation, the interpreter, inevitably, learns something about himself.[25] We can very well imagine that a Chinese historian might see aspects of his own country's history in a new light when he tries to grasp the ideals of the French Revolution. As Fay puts it:

> The interaction between a meaningful object and an interpretive community is not a one-off event. New interpretations will help to refashion the nature of the interpretive community and the newly re-fashioned interpretive community will undoubtedly come to re-interpret the meaning of the original object afresh. The result is a constantly evolving process of interchange in which both the meaning of the object and the nature of the interpretive community change. Here the hermeneutic circle is a spiral of reciprocity as new interpretations of past meaningful objects change the nature of the interpretive community to which they are related which in turn changes the interpretation of the meaningful objects, and so on indefinitely. (1996, 146)

But here a problem arises. As we are irredeemably locked inside our preconceptions while we try to discern the meaning that something has for us, what guarantee do we have that we will recognize the "truth" of the other at all? As we have no recourse to some neutral ground, as we cannot escape our "irreducible cultural variation" (Taylor, 2002, 129), how are we to distinguish those preconceptions that lead to misunderstanding, distortion, and self-deception from those that help us to critically reflect on them and see the other in a less distorted, more inclusive way? Are the hard-nosed discursive analysts right, after all, in being wary of individual understanding? Dialogical analysts are careful not to succumb to an unwarranted subjectivism by simply reading their own preconceptions into the object of analysis (Fay, 1996, 144). They argue that by engaging in a dialogue with the object of our understanding we are able to shed light on the nature of partiality in understanding. The first step in overcoming our preconceptions is self-critique; by confronting them with the object or person that we try to understand, in a way that allows the other to present itself "in all its otherness and thus [assert] its own truth against one's own fore-meaning" (Gadamer, in Grondin, 1994, 112). Dialogical analysts are careful to allow the object of analysis to speak to them. However, they are also aware that by confronting the object with our particular concerns and preconceptions, we elicit different dimensions of meaning from it. Through engaged interaction, meaning becomes more inclusive. In this sense, dialogue may overcome partiality. The catch is that, following from the nature of dialogue, this overcoming of partiality is itself partial, provisional, and fallible.

We began this section on transcending interpretivism by asking what it is to be partial. We are now in a position to give a fuller answer to that question and also to probe why it is central in understanding meaning.[26] By way of example, and to avoid undue abstraction, let's take a closer look at the archetypical administrative problem of applying a rule.[27] One of the simplest rules in the traffic code is the one that prohibits running a red light. The rationale for the rule—endangering other participants in traffic—is unchallenged in our society, and probably in any society where there is an abundance of traffic. And what makes it also attractive is that its violation can be easily and unequivocally detected, so easily, in fact, that in many places cameras do the job of noting that someone ran a red light. But how unproblematic, and by implication how fair, is the mechanical recording of the violation of the red-light rule? I might have compelling reasons to run a red light and take a calculated risk to endanger others and myself. For example, I might be bringing my aging father to the hospital because he had a heart attack. Or, I might want to intervene in a robbery in progress on the other side of the intersection. Or, I might not have a motive at all, but have been suddenly struck by a dizzy spell and run the red light before I recovered.

A standard solution to these objections is that we should refine the rule by including those exceptions that we deem fair or reasonable. But for two reasons that solution will not do. First, it is impossible to foresee all possible reasonable exceptions to the rule.[28] This is not just a practical point, but one that points to an existential impossibility of ever fully explaining ourselves. Projecting legitimate exceptions to the rule is, in the end, a self-defeating task. It implies that we would have a definitive answer to every exception that might come our way. That can be the case only if we have thought out in advance every possible motive or circumstance that may lead to an infraction of the rule, and that clearly defies credibility. In fact, to apply the rule in a fair and reasonable manner in concrete situations we don't need to work out in advance all its possible permutations. We understand the rule because we understand the kind of situation (intersections, heavy traffic, the effects of collisions, etc.) from which the need for such a rule emerged in the first place (Taylor, 1995c, 166–67). Differently put, we have practical experience with these kinds of situations that allows us to negotiate them in appropriate ways.

Second, the rule itself does not tell you how to apply it in concrete situations. The rule does not contain recognition rules that will tell the administrator how to connect the abstract world of the rule to the concrete life-world to which it has to be applied (Kagan, 1978). In the final analysis the administrator bases the establishment of a valid and acceptable connection between the rule and the real world on a calculated judgment. The centrality of practical judgment in fair and effective rule application suggests that we might be misguided about the nature of administrative rules; that we might mistake the surface phenomenon (the abstract rule) for the thing itself (the fair and effective ordering of a particular aspect of the collective world). As I put it in my essay on rule application:

> Rules are not instructions that tell the individual what to do. Instead they are repositories of the accrued experience of a community of people. In that sense they function as signposts in a practical-moral landscape, giving the individual a bearing, suggesting what fruitful and feasible direction to take, and providing standards to assess the direction finally taken. (Wagenaar, 2004, 654)

The point of this example is that this understanding of rules and the real-world situations from which the rules have emerged is never completely under our control. The proliferation of meanings and understandings that make up this background world is simply too large and too indeterminate to fully grasp. As Grondin puts it, "We are more subject to history than it can be subjected to consciousness" (1994, 114). To return to our initial question: what guarantee do we have that we recognize the "truth" of the other at all? The answer is: none. The implication of the irreducible partiality of our understanding is that we always run the risk of misunderstanding the other and being misunderstood (Taylor, 1995c, 167). The only way that we can hope to come to terms with the fallibility of our understanding is to engage in a dialogue. In philosophical hermeneutics the term "dialogue" is taken quite literally: it is seen as a mutual, reciprocal conversation aimed at clarifying misunderstandings and making us aware of the constraining effects of our prejudices. I would like to draw the concept of dialogue broader, however—as also involving practices—

"patterns of appropriate action" (Taylor, 1995c, 171)—that represent solutions to commonly recognized problems or issues. I will return to the concept of practice in the next section, so I restrict myself here to two remarks. Practices are not mere activities, not the private activities of individual actors, but instead are part of a "shared agency" (ibid.). To understand practices as senseful, feasible, and legitimate reactions to particular situations requires that they be part of a shared framework of understandings and actions. Practices seen in this way are dialogical in that they represent a meaningful give-and-take between our actions and their impact on the material and social world at which they are directed.

How does meaning emerge from dialogue? Meaning through dialogue is similar to coming to an understanding. Let me quote Taylor on this:

> The road to understanding others passes through the patient identification and undoing of those facets of our implicit understanding that distort the reality of the other. At a certain point, we may come to see that "opinions" have a different place in our life-form than in theirs, and we will then be able to grasp the place of beliefs in their life; we will be ready to allow this to be in its difference, undistorted by the assimilation to "opinions." This will happen when we allow ourselves to be challenged, interpellated by what is different in their lives, and this challenge will bring about two interconnected changes: we will see our peculiarity for the first time, as a formulated fact about us, and not simply a taken-for-granted feature of the human condition as such; and at the same time, we will perceive the corresponding feature of their life-form undistorted. These two changes are indissolubly linked; you cannot have one without the other. (Taylor, 2002, 132)

Dialogical meaning is, thus, a human condition, an awareness of the open-ended, fallible, and shared nature of our understanding of the world, and of our tentative, never-finished attempts at elucidating and overcoming the indissoluble partiality of our position in the world. But meaning is not the product of thinking, of "cogitation," as Wildavsky (1979) famously put it. In dialogical meaning, understanding is intimately tied to action. It emerges from the patterned activities we engage in when we grapple with concrete situations that present themselves to us as in need of being resolved. Meaning emerges from our interactions with others and with the world.

INTERPRETATION IN THE WORLD: TOWARD AN ACTIONABLE APPROACH TO INTERPRETIVE POLICY ANALYSIS

There are important loose ends regarding the place of interpretation in the world to be dealt with before we move on to the role of interpretation in policy analysis. One of the biggest, as we saw in our discussion of phenomenology, is the nature of the structural features of social reality. The ambiguous nature of social structure in phenomenology points to the core problem of interpretive analysis: how to connect individual consciousness with the world. A bugbear for phenomenologists, it spreads as an inkblot over all of interpretive analysis. It presents itself as the phenomenologist's conundrum of intentionality (how to relate inner experience to external social structure) the discourse analysts' dilemma of determinism (how to retain human agency within a discursive framework), the predilection of some hermeneuticists to reduce social reality to a text (but how do the words relate to the phenomenal world of sensations and impacts?), and the preference of many to call social reality "constructed" (but what about objects that exist independent of our representation of them?) (Searle, 1995). All these examples point to an inability within interpretivism to hook up individual consciousness with the world in a convincing manner.

One common solution to the phenomenologists' problem of social structures external to individual consciousness is to claim that they somehow emanate from the myriad activities of individual actors. However, when intersubjective social rules are contingent upon the individual's subjective grasp, when social settings are "self-organizing with respect to the intelligible [i.e., rational] character of its own appearances" (Garfinkel, 1967, 33), then no intelligible path is indicated by which we travel from individual experiences to the social world as we know it. For what is "self-organizing" if we want it to be more than a deus ex machina in a nineteenth-century stage comedy? To get around this problem social phenomenologists are therefore impelled, as we saw, to conjure up preexisting abstractions they call social rules or institutions. The fundamental question for research is then to explain how these "abstractions enter the daily lives of individuals" (Mayrl, 1977, 265). As Mayrl summarizes it:

> It [social phenomenology] shares with all phenomenological philosophy a fundamental ambivalence on the question of reality external to the solitary ego. The world, in this case society, is said to exist but not in any meaningful sense independent of individual consciousness. Therefore its role as a determinant of human activity becomes confused. The resolution of this confusion is found in the relegation of social facts to the status of abstractions built out of members' definitions. . . . Ultimately then, society exists in the individual mind as a factor which is constructed by, yet at the same time enters into, mental activity. (1977, 276)

Outside, yet inside. We keep going in circles. More importantly, it is hard to reconcile this formulation with the all-too-real pressures and stresses of the individuals, for example, in the qualitative readmission study. The phenomenological reliance on subjective meaning as the foundational units of the intersubjective world is confused, as it is unable to reconcile its exclusive focus on the individual as the source of social understanding with the all too real fact of the individual's exposure to the forces and resistances of worldly agency. Phenomenology posits a social science without society—to paraphrase Mayrl's trenchant summary of his critique of interpretive approaches that conceive of meaning as originating in individual experience.

One reason that the subjective-intersubjective issue in interpretive analysis is so intractable is that it is really two problems nested into one. The first is that the relation between subjective and objective meaning is asymmetrical. It is relatively easy to see how we get from objective to subjective meanings. Our personal reactions are influenced, informed, shaped by the larger social understandings into which we are socialized as members of a particular society. But the reverse relation is harder to conceptualize. It is not easy to see how the macrostructures derive from the micro-understandings; how the second aggregate into the first. The second is the problem of how to conceptualize structure or objective meaning. While structures or objective meanings are derivative of agency, of personal choices (after all, we do influence institutional rules and conventions), they transcend the realm of individual action. (They resist change, and remain after the individual has perished.) Objective meanings are hybrid entities, both *of* and *over* individuals. As we saw, there is a tendency among interpretive scholars to escape this uneasy straddling of individual agency and impersonal structure by occupying one of the poles of the hybrid: either pure agency or disembodied structure; either freedom or determinism. Perhaps there is a third, closely related problem looming under the surface: how to research the subjective-objective nexus? Or to be more precise: How do you research the pulsating, living connection between subjective agency and the more or less durable structures of social reality without simply asserting one or the other? How do you do justice to the subtle dialectic between the two?

Dialogical meaning, with its emphasis on acting, suggests a way out of this dilemma. Mind and world are disconnected because the problem is posed at a wholly representational level. "Eidetic knowledge" and "transcendental structures" that are mysteriously present in the mind, are hapless attempts to connect individual consciousness with external reality. "Discourse," "*epistème*," and "*dispositif*" are similarly partial attempts to do justice to the inevitable influence of external reality on the individual. Did I just mention reality? Yes. To avoid any suspicion that I have just lapsed into naïve realism I need to distinguish between representation and intervention.

A representation is an effigy of some slice of the world. To put it this way invites a series of questions and judgments about the relationship between the representation and the part of the world it depicts. Any thesaurus will suggest synonyms such as "likeness," "resemblance," or "similitude" and antonyms such as "misrepresentation," "distortion," or "falsification." Does this sound familiar? Yes, these are the epistemological criteria of empiricist and hermeneutic methodology: avoid bias, strive for precision and verisimilitude. It is one of the most stubborn of all cultural tropes, both of common sense and social science; one that analytical philosophers call the "correspondence theory of truth" (Allen, 1993, 9–10). Each representation has an exact match with a thing out there in the world.[29]

The above is naïve realism, of course. For one thing, it is hard to imagine how we have unfiltered, unalloyed access to brute natural reality (Allen, 1993, 132). Another way to put this is that all observations are theoretically loaded (Hawkesworth, 1998). Our observational "copies" of nature are not pictures of things, but rather pictures of pictures. Interpretations of interpretations, as Geertz would have it, which makes all talk of likeness or distortion particularly problematic. But this is not the way I want to go. I want to follow Ian Hacking in his argument that representation is not a mirror of reality, but reality is an attribute of representation (1983, 136).[30] This inversion of the taken-for-granted ordering of representation and reality is much less provocative than it sounds at first blush. It doesn't make the world less real, as we will see, but it does allow us to grapple with a few of the interpretivists' conundrums. To suggest that the concept of reality follows the practice of representation is to postulate an intrinsically loose coupling between theory and empirical reality. This is exactly the situation in which we find ourselves in the social sciences. The great issues of social science—poverty, crime, immigration, unemployment, inflation, social inequality, democratic participation, climate change—accommodate different, and often conflicting, theoretical explanations—or, to use our language, different systems of representation. Particularly so, as most "theories" in the social sciences are exceedingly complex constellations of empirical fact, causal explanation, interpretation, ontological speculation, and normative statements (Taylor, 1985b). Most of what is in there—state, process, institution, civil society, power—cannot be observed.[31] It will surprise nobody that in such situations there is no fact of the matter. "Reality," however we think of it, doesn't arbitrate here in any binding manner.

This is a more vexing problem than we, as sophisticated post-empiricist social scientists, tend to think. The problem is not that there are competing theories/representations, but that most of them do an equally decent job of explaining or making sense of the phenomenon at hand. In this way, social science threatens to turn into a battle of theories with few if any criteria to decide once and for all which one is "best." On the level of theories, social scientists are locked inside a world of representations, with no obvious exits (Hacking, 1983, 272).[32] I think that this is the situation in which the hermeneutic and discursive analysts find themselves. The mind/world dilemma cannot be resolved because it takes place exclusively inside the world of representations—in this particular case, representations with a decidedly ontological cast. Although concepts such as "eidetic knowledge" or "discourse" claim to refer to the world, they are at no point hooked up with it. The debate doesn't go anywhere because there is no "friction," no "rough ground," to give it sustained direction.[33]

Can it be otherwise? Yes. By moving from theory/representation to action. Because as soon as we act upon the world it will resist, talk back, defy our expectations. As soon as we intervene in the world, it bears upon us, it has an impact, with which we as humans have to grapple and to cope (Pickering, 1995, 6). *That* is reality, as it is undoubtedly experienced by the mental patients and professionals in the fragmented mental health service system in Chicago, or the patients and professionals who were engaged in the rehabilitation program in the Dutch mental hospital, or the policy makers who were confronted with an explosion of readmissions once they restricted access to mental hospitals under the doctrine of deinstitutionalization. We connect with the world through our actions. Or better, the world connects with us through our actions, whether we like it or not. To avoid any realist misunderstanding, this is not the kind of full-blown, God's-eye reality that we hope can arbitrate between the complex social science theories/representations that I mentioned above. I don't think we will ever reach the point that we can effectively decide between these complex representations. "Every test of a representation is just another representation," as Hacking puts it (1983, 273).[34] No, what I'm talking about is a more straightforward, experiential reality of the kind that states that the car is sitting in the driveway (Hacking, 1983, 145). There is no theory/explanation/representation here. Just a simple observation statement that few of us would want to challenge or deny.[35] After all, I can act upon the assertion about my car by turning the ignition key and driving off.

What I am referring to here is the difference between theories and entities. "The question about theories," says Hacking, "is whether they are true, or are true-and-false, or are candidates for truth, or aim at the truth. The question about entities is whether they exist" (1983, 27). To appreciate the difference between theories and entities we only have to think of different theoretical explanations of the same social phenomenon (unemployment, juvenile delinquency, democratic participation), each equally plausible, each supported by reams of empirical evidence. Moreover, sophisticated social scientists have no trouble living with multiple, incompatible theoretical explanations for the same phenomenon. No such ambiguity exists around entities. The car is in the driveway or not. The discharged mental patient is readmitted or not. Entities assert themselves as soon as we venture out into the world. They can only be ignored at one's own peril, as policy makers overwhelmed by the unintended consequences of their interventions have learned. My point is that action brings out that kind of incontrovertible reality.[36]

What I am arguing is that we move from a philosophy of representation to a philosophy of *intervention* (Hacking, 1983). By "intervention" I mean any activity that purposely aspires to change an aspect of the world. Sawing off a log of wood to make a table is an intervention. Building a bridge is an intervention. Meeting a patient every week in a psychotherapeutic encounter is an intervention. And reforming a mental health service system is an intervention. Interventions require some knowledge, some understanding, some reliable and useful representation of the world in which we intervene. Ian Hacking, who sensitized us to the importance of this distinction, puts it as follows: "We represent and we intervene. We represent in order to intervene, and we intervene in the light of representations" (1983, 97). But, as I hope to make clear in the second part of this book, the emphasis is always on actionable realism. On the necessity to engage purposefully and actively with the empirical world, the world of entities, when we engage in interpretive policy analysis. For empirical reality has a way of subverting our best laid plans and ideas once we act upon it. Or as Hacking succinctly puts it: "[I] think that reality has more to do with what we do in the world than with what we think about it" (1983, 17).

I will return to the actionable, interventionist approach to interpretation in chapters 8 and 10. I will then also connect intervention to the notion of policy, as policy making is an interventionist enterprise *pur sang*. For now, it suffices to say that the insertion of action into our conception of meaning opens a way out of the mind/world dilemma. In an interventionist approach to meaning the "structural" features of social reality are the emergent property of the interactions of individual actors. They are not so much the willed, deliberate outcome of human design (although design may very well have been the impetus that spurred the action), but the unintended consequence of the interactions of actors with each other and with the world. For example, the emergence of the community mental health movement was the contingent outcome of a series of loosely coupled and widely dispersed actions taken by an uncounted number of individuals. While purpose and agency are clearly discernable in, for example, the development of the first psychotropic drugs or the development of the Community Mental Health Services Act, the effects of these activities produced an environment, in the shape of new possibilities, challenges, or dilemmas, that presented itself to others as a preexisting structure. The notion of emergent property does justice both to the supra-individual character of social structures (individuals can change them but not quickly or in any which way; they keep existing even if the individual has disappeared), and to its genesis in individual purpose and action. Structure as emergent property has qualities distinct from, and irreducible to, to the qualities of the individual actions that produced them (McAnulla, 2006, 121). In this way, individuals produce structures but they do not choose them. As McAnulla puts it:

> Agents find themselves cast into material relationships, roles, or practices that they did not choose but which will subsequently condition their future actions. While agents have properties such as intentionality and rationality, structure may have properties such as "relative endurance, natural necessity and the possession of causal powers." Understood another way, the actions of individuals produce emergent properties (whether conceived as structure, discourse, tradition or culture) which can later serve to "act back" on people. (2006, 121; the quotations are from Archer, 1995)

Structure as emergent property respects its ontological difference from agency without uncoupling completely from it. In this way structure, while produced by human agency, nevertheless acts as its constraint or enablement (McAnulla, 2006, 122). Also, and here I already look forward to an issue that will come up in chapters 5 and 7, by conceptualizing structure as an emergent property of human action, implies that it is more than a text or a story. But first I will address the third problem: how to analyze subjective and objective meaning/structure and agency, without reneging on the subtle dialectic that brings each into being?

The notion of activity draws our attention to the ongoing, negotiated character of human living, one of the great themes of the philosophical pragmatists, in particular John Dewey. Understanding emerges in the course of acting upon a particular situation. Acting upon a situation at hand inevitably entails struggling with the resistances and "affordances" that the situation throws up (Burke, 1994; Cook, 2008). The acting harbors the dialectic between individual experience and social reality. As Prus puts it:

> Activity draws our attention to the matter of ongoing enterprise, to the constituent notions of defining, anticipating, invoking, encountering resistance, accomplishing, experiencing failure, reassessing and adjusting, on both interactive as well as more solitary behavioral levels. . . . While notions of intersubjectivity, particularized worldviews, reflectivity, activity, negotiated interchange, and relationships are all central to the ways in which the interactionists approach the study of human lived experience, so is the matter of process. Referring to the emergent or ongoing nature of group life, process is basic to an understanding of these other themes. Intersubjectivity (and the sharing of symbolic realities) is an ongoing process.

. . . The primary conceptual and methodological implication of this processual emphasis is this: since all aspects of group life take place in process terms or take their shape over time, *it is essential that the human condition be conceptualized and studied in manners that are actually mindful of the emergent nature of human lived experience.* (1996, 16, 17, 18; italics in original)

Interpretive analysis, thus, requires that the analyst is attentive to the action-oriented, interactive, and ongoing nature of meaning. Intention resides in the expectations with which we encounter a particular indeterminate situation. Meaning is the emergent outcome of the way human beings negotiate these situations. In this sense meaning is intrinsically open-ended and provisional. This insight considerably raises the methodological stakes of how to infer the social from the individual. For the central challenge of interpretive analysis can now be formulated as the design of methods that enable the analyst to register, in a reliable and valid manner, this give-and-take between the initial expectations and preconceptions of the individual subject and the way the world talks back to him. And to do this in a way that does justice to the fact that we, as analysts, cannot possibly extract ourselves from the situation of analysis, for the simple fact that we are as much part of this process of intersubjective understanding as are our subjects. Interpretive analysis requires active engagement. I will return to this insight in chapters 8, 9, and 10.

NOTES

1. I will discuss some of Connolly's Jamesian inspirations in chapter 10 where I explore ontological pluralism.

2. We will see that the distinctions within the general category of interpretive social science that I introduced in chapter 2, such as interpretivism, intentionalism, and subjective and objective meaning, are folded inside the three meaning types. Where necessary for purposes of clarification, I will discuss them in the light of my tripartite distinction of meaning types.

3. Hajer's oft-quoted study *The Politics of Environmental Discourse* (1995) is a good example. Although it uses the language of discourse analysis, it is better characterized as an example of framing, and thus of hermeneutic analysis. Nevertheless, it reaches out to the other two approaches to interpretation. In its emphasis on stories, and how these function to stabilize a complex policy field, it is dialogical in character. In its analysis of the way institutionalized practices form a deep structure of formative rules, it has discursive traits.

4. I take hermeneutics here as exegesis, as a method of systematically interpreting texts, of imposing an interpretation on a slice of social reality that already is. This could be called classical hermeneutics, as developed and practiced by Chladenius, Schleiermacher and Dilthey (Grondin, 1994). Classical hermeneutics should be distinguished from philosophical hermeneutics (as propagated by Gadamer), in which understanding is not so much a method but an essential mode of human experience, of finding one's way in the world. The third face of meaning, to which I will turn shortly, is informed by this later, more universalistic, version of hermeneutics.

5. In this way phenomenology takes a stance against realist, naturalist science. Empiricist science takes the phenomena it studies for granted, and fits them to an explanatory scheme of causality or probability. In doing this science bypasses the lived experience that makes these phenomena stand out as phenomena in the first place (Gutting, 2001, 186).

6. This active outer-directedness of the mind is captured in the concept of *intentionality.* The philosophical concept of intentionality should not be confused with the common meaning of "intentionality" as someone's motives or purpose. I will discuss philosophical intentionality later in this chapter.

7. We will see later that philosophical hermeneutics departs from the same assumption, but draws wholly different conclusions from it.

8. This theme, the epistemic primacy of lived experience, has traveled deeply into the domain of interpretive social science. It is central to the work of symbolic interactionists such as George Herbert Mead and Herbert Blumer, phenomenologists such as Alfred Schütz, social constructionists who are inspired by Schütz, such as Peter Berger and Thomas Luckmann, and ethnometodologists such as Harold Garfinkel.

This representative quote comes from Schütz: "The thought objects constructed by social scientists refer to, and are founded upon, thought objects constructed by the common-sense thought of man living in his everyday environment" (quoted in Flick, 2003, 90). A good overview of the way that this premise, and the second one, the intersubjective nature of lived experience, have disseminated through the social sciences is in Prus (1996).

9. That is probably why theoretical physicists use metaphors such as strings or black holes, to anchor their mathematically derived theoretical conjectures about the structure of the universe in commonsense understanding.

10. Phenomenology finally became ensnared in the ambiguities surrounding the concept of intentionality. But a similar and ultimately more fruitful notion—that we are part of a larger whole of background knowledge (Taylor), that all our thoughts and actions are embodied (Taylor), or that we are part of organism-world configurations (Dewey/Burke)—has been further developed both by pragmatism and philosophical hermeneutics. I will return to this at the end of this chapter.

11. "The phenomenological method of 'bracketing,' or *epoché,* in [Husserl's] treatment signified basically an attempt to unravel the meaningful core, or 'essence,' of phenomena as disclosed in (or 'constituted' by) a purified consciousness. In this respect his approach replicated the solipsistic dilemma of early language analysis and of much of traditional philosophy: to the extent that consciousness was presented as 'transcendental limit' of the world, the domain of intersubjective understanding and clarification of meaning was obliterated. In his later writings Husserl sought to overcome this dilemma by introducing the notion of the 'life-world,' or world of mundane experience, but the relationship between mundaneness and consciousness was never fully clarified" (Dallmayr & McCarthy, 1977, 9). As Gutting explains in his exemplary discussion of French phenomenology, similar problems bedeviled Merleau-Ponty's work (Gutting, 2001).

12. The logical consequence of this position was that psychology would be the master science from which all other human sciences derived. But, commenting on Dilthey's phenomenology, Grondin rhetorically asks, "Is a purely descriptive psychology possible, however?" He continues: "Dilthey replies that it is, for mental phenomena have an advantage over externals: they are immediately intelligible by means of inner experience. They can be conceived just as they are, that is, without the mediation of the senses, which are unavoidable in perceiving the external world. Through direct awareness of our inner experiences, a 'fixed structure (is) immediately and objectively given,' Dilthey asserts, and this provides the 'indubitable, universal foundation' of descriptive psychology. Because it is based on the certainty of direct inner experience, psychology acquires methodological significance. It becomes the foundation of the human sciences, as mathematics is of the natural sciences" (Grondin, 1994, 86).

However, a psychology of direct, pure experience as the epistemological foundation of the human sciences proved to be untenable. Grondin again: "The unsatisfactoriness of Dilthey's psychology of lived experience, thus methodologically presented, did not escape his contemporaries, and soon perhaps Dilthey himself perceived it. Two deficiencies are especially evident. First, it is doubtful that merely descriptive psychology (which in certain respects predates Husserl's idea of a phenomenology of inner experiences) really offers direct, hypothesis-free access to the coherent mental structures whose self-evidence to inner perception has been postulated. If these structures were in fact so self-evidently given, there would be no dissent about them within psychology. Second, Dilthey did not succeed in proposing a plausible connection between his new psychology and the concrete human sciences whose foundation he was supposed to be elucidating. Nowhere does he show how interpretive psychology could validate the objectivity of propositions in the human sciences. In these respects, too, Dilthey's project could not get beyond the merely programmatic stage" (1994, 76).

13. An illustration of this connection between detachment and purity of observation in Husserl's phenomenological "method" is the following statement by him as quoted in Safranski: "This universal validation . . . of all attitudes to the given objective world . . . does not therefore confront us with a Nothing. What we instead acquire, or, more clearly, what I, as a meditating person, acquire as a result is my pure life with all its experiences and all its pure meaning-units, the universe of phenomena in the meaning of phenomenology. The *epoché* . . . is—to put it another way—the radical and universal method by which I understand myself as a pure ego, and with my own pure consciousness-life, in which and through which the entire objective world exists for me, and in the way that it does exist for me" (1998, 76).

14. In their favor it must be said that social phenomenologists recognized this vexing problem and wrestled with it for decades. On the one hand, individual behavior is the basic building block of social reality. But human behavior must be *intentional* to be meaningful. "Meaning is '*a certain way of directing one's gaze at an item of one's own experience*'" as Bernstein quotes Alfred Schütz (1976, 143; italics in original). And later: "[M]eaning is merely an operation of intentionality" (ibid.). But, as we saw, meaningful action (a tautology in

the phenomenological framework) requires the presence of intersubjective meaning structures. The individual is always interpreting *something*. We choose interpretive schemes, as Bernstein says, but these schemes are not private, they are "essentially social or intersubjective" (1976, 145). These intersubjective interpretive schemes form a stock of commonly available commonsense knowledge that is "socially preformed." But then, revealingly, how this "preformative" process occurs "is an aspect of common-sense knowledge that Schütz did not explore in depth" (1976, 148).

15. This raises the exceedingly important and at the same time grossly underestimated issue of how to interview. Obviously, the quality of the interview is decisive for the quality of the data. I will touch upon this in chapter 5 and discuss it at length in chapter 9.

16. For the initiate the problem of getting a handle on interpretive social science is twofold: the difficulty of fixing the meaning of major concepts such as discourse, frame, or practice, and the bewildering—and often conflicting—number of labels (such as *objectivism, perspectivism, foundationalism, constructivism*) that indicate the finer shades and aspects of these major concepts. The concept of hermeneutics is no exception. (Grondin rightly says that "the word *hermeneutic* is afflicted by a vast amorphousness" (1994, 18). In its current usage, hermeneutics is usually applied to an approach that I describe later in this chapter under the heading "Dialogical Meaning." It is associated with the names Gadamer, Taylor, and Heidegger, and is usually designated by the phrase "philosophical hermeneutics." The term "hermeneutics" proper refers to a much broader range of philosophical approaches, however, such as (1) a philosophical development that involves most of nineteenth- and twentieth-century Continental philosophy such as phenomenology, existentialism, and philosophical hermeneutics (Grondin, 1994, 9); (2) a general theory or philosophy of the interpretation of meaning (Bleicher, 1980, 1; Grondin, 1994, 18); and, more narrowly, (3) a method of interpreting texts (sometimes labeled "classical hermeneutics"), where the emphasis is on delineating systematic methods that avoid arbitrary ascription of meaning (Grondin, 1994, 18). Perhaps it is easiest to find one's way in the nomenclature of interpretive approaches when one keeps in mind that the use of terminology does not so much reflect hard and fast distinctions in the landscape of interpretive approaches, but more the specific aims of the author. The author's use of a particular term indicates how he or she wants to carve up the conceptual space that has been entered. By using the term "hermeneutics" in this section on subjective meaning I want to distinguish a particular exegetic, objectivist approach to grasping meaning from two other, distinct approaches. In my usage the term "hermeneutics" comes closest to the second and third meanings given above. Given my purpose of elucidating different conceptions of meaning, it also includes qualitative research as well as the various phenomenological approaches to interpretation, where the aim is to demonstrate the "originary phenomenon of interpretation or understanding" (Grondin, 1994, 18). As I will make clear, these also display a similar exegetic and foundationalist stance. Whenever I refer to the more participative, dialogical forms of interpretation of Gadamer and Taylor, I will use the qualifier "philosophical."

17. See Abbott on explanation in ethnography: "We can envision what it is that they see themselves doing, and we can see what they are doing as reasonable, as something we would do if we were in their place. The field-worker has translated, however imperfectly, their world into one we find comprehensible. Typically, ethnography accomplishes this by providing detail, by showing ramifications, and by embedding the strange habits of unfamiliar people in the everyday habits of those same people and then connecting their everyday world with our own" (2004, 30–31). Prus speaks in this regard of "role-taking" and "sympathetic introspection" as the key heuristic moment in ethnographic research: "Ethnographic research requires an openness to the other. Indeed, it is only through 'role-taking' (Mead) and interpersonal inquiry (or what Cooley termed 'sympathetic introspection') that one may attempt to achieve intersubjectivity with 'the (human) other'" (1996, 22–23). I want to emphasize that one should not confuse sympathetic empathy with *Verstehen*. Verstehen is a "psychological process of identification" in which analysts "re-experience the thought processes which went through the minds of agents when they performed various actions" (Fay, 1996, 141. Fay speaks here of "re-enactment" as opposed to interpretation. But the drift of his argument is the same). Sympathetic empathy is an epistemological warrant for interpretation, in which we assess how convincingly we have situated an action in its larger social context.

18. The epistemological position of classical hermeneutics follows from its origins as a systematic method of the exegesis of ancient and biblical texts. Grondin, in his admirable historiography of hermeneutics, presents eighteenth-century scholar Johan Martin Chladenius as one of the first to develop a conception of hermeneutics that transcended the specialized scholastic approaches that were current up to then. According to Chladenius the task of the hermeneutic scholar is to clarify obscurity. In a remarkably prescient insight Chladenius saw obscurity in texts as resulting from insufficient background knowledge. This, he argued, was a universal problem for everyone who dealt with the interpretation of language: "A thought that has to be conveyed to

the reader by words often presupposes other conceptions without which it is not conceivable: if a reader is not already in possession of these conceptions, therefore, the words cannot effect the same result in him as in another reader who is thoroughly knowledgeable about these conceptions" (Chladenius, quoted in Grondin, 1994, 53). Interestingly, Chladenius conceived of hermeneutics not in analytical but in pedagogical terms. Interpretation was nothing more than adducing, presenting, and communicating (*auslegen*) the background concepts necessary to comprehend the texts. There is a lot more subtlety in Chladenius's viewpoints than this brief summary conveys, particularly in his thoroughly modern idea of the inevitability of viewpoint in interpretation, but it remains incontestable that his conception of hermeneutics remains firmly ensconced in eighteenth-century rationalism. It would take Kant, and Schleiermacher, to break up this mold and formulate a more modern version of hermeneutics.

The rationalists' belief was that the human mind could, by force of its reason, penetrate the natural and logical architecture of the world. Kant's insight was that, as this must apply to the input of our senses, the natural and logical order of the world is something that is preconstructed by the workings of an active mind that is prompted by sense impressions. The implication was that the brute order of things, the world-into-itself, was forever outside our reach (Grondin, 1994, 64).

Post-Kantian thought had two effects on hermeneutics. First, inevitably it placed the interpreting agent in a position of radical subjectivity. For, as an unbridgeable abyss had emerged between phenomena as they present themselves to us and the thing in itself that gives rise to the phenomena, the agent only had his fallible sense perceptions to go by as the starting point of his interpretive labor. But, second, hermeneutics found a new telos in that every text from then on was seen as receiving its sensefulness from an undisclosed, although possibly unreachable, whole (or spirit, as some scholars called it) that informed the text. Putting the two together places the interpretive scholar in the position that it his he, and he alone, who can enter into a dialogue with the text, bringing his own preconceptions to bear on it, and in the end deciding that enough is enough in the interpretation of this particular text. In other words, as Grondin observes, the nineteenth-century hermeneutic scholar was an inveterate romantic, an interpretive *Fliegende Holländer* who forever and in vain searched for the spirit of completeness and coherence that animated the text but, fatefully, knew that he would never quite attain it (Grondin, 1994, 63). It would take another century before scholars such as Heidegger, and in particular Gadamer, would free hermeneutics from its implicit romanticism and systematically articulate the further implications of radical subjectivism for the craft of interpretation.

19. A well-known approach to interpretive social science in the German-speaking world is even called "objective hermeneutics" (Reichertz, 2004, 290). To give an idea of what objective hermeneutics entails, I quote some key statements that are wholly in line with classical hermeneutics. First, "The procedure consists of first conceiving and fixing the social action in question as a text, in order subsequently to interpret it hermeneutically with regard to action-generating latent meaning structures" (ibid.). Then, from the originator of objective hermeneutics, Ulrich Oevermann: "This [the procedure] is simply because the meaning structures which are to be reconstructed can be ascertained by means of fundamentally definable rules and mechanisms of a basic algorithmic structure in a precisely testable and complete way in a protocol that is accessible at all times" (quoted in Reichertz, 2003, 290). And later: "An *objective reconstruction of objective structures* is understood as a limit that is reached through constant application of the canonical directives of objective hermeneutics" (ibid., italics in original). Finally, if the italicized "objective reconstruction of objective structures" is not persuasive enough, the text quotes Oevermann once more: "'[T]ruth' results from the correct epistemological procedure, since the correct treatment of text causes 'the thing to speak for itself'" (quoted in Reichertz, 2003, 292). Going by these quotes, objectivism is not so much a position as a sentiment. What objective hermeneutics demonstrates above all is that the romantic longing for a firm epistemic foundation to distinguish the scientific from the nonscientific is simply irresistible.

20. Think of Adams and Balfour's telling definition of administrative evil as happening when administrators, within their normal professional and administrative roles, engage in discriminating, hurtful, and ethically loathsome acts without being aware that they are doing anything wrong (Adams and Balfour, 2009).

21. As we will see in chapter 6, discursive analysts threaten to become ensnared in the mind-world dilemma backward, as it were. Where phenomenologists become trapped in the idealist prison of individual consciousness, discursive analysts must find ways to avoid crude determinism so that the individual retains a measure of freedom and agency within the discursive structure that contains him. Foucault's intellectual journey from a rigid structuralist to a proponent of an ethics of self-cultivation and individual resistance is testimony to this dilemma. I already draw attention here to Bevir and Rhodes's interesting, and utterly reasonable, solution to the mind-world dilemma in their version of interpretivism. I will discuss it in chapter 5.

22. Most discursive analysts operate on the assumption that a discursive perspective is contingent. The

particular shape and content of the discourse is itself not seen as inevitable. Discourse has a confiscatory power. To the individual who lives inside it, the discourse presents itself as natural and inevitable. The power of discourse is that it obliterates its own horizons. The critical thrust of discursive analysis is precisely to make the arbitrariness of the discourse visible and suggest new horizons, new aspirations and possibilities of living.

23. That doesn't mean that the other types of meaning are not critical. I will discuss the various forms of critique in interpretive policy analysis in chapter 10.

24. In fact, perspective, or historicity, is considered an ontological condition in philosophical hermeneutics. We only discern things because we have a dim, unarticulated pre-understanding or pre-involvement (the terminology is not crystal clear here) of objects and situations. Bleicher quotes Heidegger on this point: "The explication of what remains implicit, the appropriation of understanding in interpretation 'is always done under the guidance of a point of view, which fixes that with regard to which what is understood is to be interpreted. In every case understanding is grounded in something we see in advance—in a foresight (*Vorsicht*)'" (Bleicher, 1980, 102). Interpretation is, thus, not a singular act, that one can switch on and off, but an ongoing, largely unconscious, automatic mode of being. Hermeneutics is an existential condition.

25. The different meanings that the French revolution has for a history teacher and for his students (based on their different personal histories), and the way both are emotionally affected by it, is brilliantly and movingly depicted in Graham Swift's novel *Waterland*.

26. It is exactly in addressing these two questions that a number of important trends in twentieth-century philosophy and social theory converge. I'm thinking here of Wittgenstein's formulations of what it means to follow a rule, Dewey's notion of experience and its role in problem solving, Polanyi's concept of tacit knowledge, Hannah Arendt's political philosophy, Gadamer's philosophical hermeneutics, various strands of practice theory as exemplified in the work of Bourdieu, Schatzki, Lave, Wenger, and others, and Taylor's social humanist philosophy. What they have in common is a movement away from overly cognitive, intellectualist, and foundationalist conceptions of understanding. Instead, with different emphases, these thinkers argue that our grasp of the world is open-ended and driven by acting as much as thinking.

27. This section is based on my article "'Knowing' the Rules: Administrative Work as Practice" (Wagenaar, 2004).

28. It is for this reason that rule application is to a large extent left to the discretion of the administrator. It is by now a standard insight in public administration theory that administrative discretion is not only inevitable, given the complexity and indeterminacy of real-world administrative situations, but also a necessary prerequisite for fair and responsive rule application (Maynard-Moody and Musheno, 2003; Vinzant and Crothers, 1998).

29. This last sentence is a summary of three assumptions that together make up the correspondence theory of truth: (1) Nature takes priority over language, culture, or the effects of historical experience. Differently put: there is something hardwired in the world that exists independently of human beings. (2) Truth is a kind of sameness between what is said and what is out there. Truth is a copy of nature. (3) Signs, language, are derivative, secondary to the natural nonsigns they stand for (Allen, 1993, 9–10). Needless to say that all three of these assumptions of the correspondence theory have been challenged.

30. "The first peculiarly human invention is representation. Once there is a practice of representing, a second-order concept follows in train. This is the concept of reality, a concept which has content only when there are first-order representations. It will be protested that reality, or the world, was there before any representation or human language. Of course. But conceptualizing it as reality is secondary" (Hacking, 1983, 136). On the basis of an analysis of the use of the Greek verb "be" (*einai*), Allen comes to the similar conclusion that the projection of a noumenal Nature or Being is more or less a lexical accident. He cites Kahn, an expert on early Greek thought: "If we bear in mind the structures of the veridical use of the verb ["be"], we will easily see how the philosophers' interest in knowledge and truth, taken together with this use of 'to be,' immediately leads to the concept of Being as . . . the facts that make true statements true." Allen then concludes: "What began as a meaningless assimilation survived the Greek language as a metaphysician's platitude: Truths are true of what there is" (1993, 15).

31. Hacking: "With misleading brevity I shall use the term 'theoretical entity' as a portmanteau word for all that ragbag of stuff postulated by theories but which we cannot observe. That means among other things particles, fields, processes, structures, states and the like" (1983, 26).

32. See also Flyvbjerg here: "The social sciences do not evolve via scientific revolutions, as Kuhn says is the case for the natural sciences. Rather, as pointed out by Hubert Dreyfus, social sciences go through periods where various constellations of power and waves of intellectual fashion dominate, and where a change of one

period to another, which on the surface may resemble a paradigm shift, actually consists of the researchers within a given area abandoning a dying wave for a growing one, without there having occurred a collective accumulation of knowledge. Not paradigm shifts but rather style changes are what characterize social science: it is not a case of evolution but more of fashion" (2001, 30).

33. These are, of course, Wittgenstein's famous phrases for indicating that words do not work "outside the context of activities or gestures . . . that are intuitively understood" (Dunne, 1993, 65). Wittgenstein's full quote is: "We have got on slippery ice where there is no friction and so in a certain sense the conditions are ideal, but also, just because of that, we are unable to walk. We want to walk: so we need *friction*. Back to the rough ground!" (Wittgenstein, 1974, § 107, italics in original).

34. See Flyvbjerg (2001) for a different argument for the fundamental undecidability of social theory, an argument based on the primacy of phronesis, or situated judgment, in the social sciences. To avoid misunderstanding at this point: undecidability does not mean that we can't make intelligent statements about the relative quality of theoretical statements based on such criteria as explanatory inclusiveness, empirical fit, empathic fit, or narrative persuasiveness. My point is that the world that is the subject of these big theories/representations is itself too big to be captured exhaustively by any theory.

35. Hacking: "The representations of physics are entirely different from simple non-representational assertions about the location of my typewriter. There is a truth of the matter about the typewriter. In physics there is no final truth of the matter, only a barrage of more or less instructive representations" (1983, 145).

36. Philosophically, the matter is less clear-cut than I present it here. One can be a realist or an antirealist about theories and about entities. Or, one can circumvent such distinctions and call oneself a causalist by emphasizing the causal powers of things. Perhaps one can never get to the bottom of the concept of power, but can persuasively point to its causal effects in a particular situation. Or, one can believe in the reality of IQ, but lack even the most basic causal understanding of it (Hacking, 1983, 38–39). To complicate things even further, some philosophers use causality as the decisive criterion for attributing reality to things. I call electrons real because I can successfully predict what will happen by manipulating them in certain ways. To explore this in more depth would lead us away from the subject of this book. Moreover, within the range of positions in the philosophy of science, mine is pretty much middle-of-the-road. See Hacking (1983) or Cartwright (1983) for further discussions of these issues.

PART 2

VARIETIES OF INTERPRETATION
IN POLICY ANALYSIS

5

HERMENEUTIC MEANING

In this chapter I will discuss those approaches to interpretive policy analysis that fall within the classical hermeneutic tradition. I call them hermeneutic because they share two features that are characteristic of classical hermeneutics. The first is the deliberate aim to clarify what is muddled or obscure by looking for a particular meaning that is somehow "behind" the policy and that is, initially at least, hidden. The second is the phenomenological assumption that the experiences of policy actors are, if not the bedrock of understanding meaning in society, then at least a convenient entrance for discovering it. The hermeneutic approach to interpretive policy analysis is probably the most popular and the most frequently employed among policy scholars who prefer to work outside the traditional, empiricist tradition. It doesn't require a lot of theoretical baggage to get started, and in its emphasis on everyday understanding, it accords, as I discussed in chapter 4, with an intuitive understanding of interpretation and meaning. As I hope to show, in the hands of experienced analysts that popularity is warranted. Hermeneutic interpretation can be a sophisticated tool in understanding policy problems, with a clear and decisive added value over more traditional empiricist approaches to policy analysis. However, in less-experienced hands, it quickly deteriorates into arbitrarily ascribing preconceived "meanings" to events or actors, with not much more justification than the analyst's attitude of "because-I-say-so."

I will discuss three interpretive approaches that fall within this tradition: qualitative policy research, frame analysis, and the interpretation of governance. In each case I will follow this format: First, I will outline the main conceptual and methodological features of the approach. Then I will present an example that illustrates the application of the approach. The applications are important because they show how a particular approach holds up in the actual, concrete process of policy research and analysis. The applications show the approach-in-use, as opposed to its espoused version. I have tried to be generous in my choice of illustrative examples. That is, in each case I have selected examples that give a strong and persuasive impression of the particular interpretive approach in action. Also, I have attempted to find examples by someone other than the originators of the approach. To my mind, an approach is more viable and productive when it inspires strong work by followers who have learned about it largely through written sources. Finally, I will wrap up the presentation with a discussion of the strengths and weaknesses of the approach. In each case I will be particularly sensitive to differences between theory and practice. As I said in chapter 1, one of the problems of interpretive policy analysis is that its theoretical sophistication is not always matched by its methodological performance. Inspired by the subtleties and eloquence of their philosophical sponsors, interpretive approaches tend to promise more than they deliver. In this light it is important to assess how robust a particular method is in the context of real-world policy analysis.

QUALITATIVE POLICY RESEARCH

Exposition

It is sometimes overlooked that qualitative research is, in method, analytical thrust, and explanatory logic, a full-blooded interpretive approach. There is a rhetorical tendency among scholars writing in the interpretive tradition to depict the interpretive approach as a clean break with an alleged positivist past. Interpretive analysis then deals with meaning, where meaning is considered something wholly different from the naturalist, realist world that forms the subject of traditional, positivist approaches to social science. This rhetorical dissociation of "meaning" and the "naturalist world" receives an added thrust when the language of social constructionism is introduced.[1] In itself there is nothing wrong with this argument, but it tends to obscure that "meaning" is simply another term for explanations of qualitative material. Explanations, as I argued in chapter 2, not in terms of causality or functional patterns, but in terms of intentions. And, as I also argued in chapter 2, we arrive at intentional explanations by carefully attending to behaviors because (I am following Geertz at this point) it is through behaviors that meanings find their articulation. Thus, in practical, operational terms, interpretive analysis, of whatever stripe, proceeds through good qualitative research. I will pick up on this theme again in chapter 9.

Qualitative research has a long tradition in sociology and anthropology. Some of the best-known examples (Estroff, 1981; Liebow, 2003; Whyte, 1943 [1993]; Wiseman, 1979) succeed in imaginatively reconstructing the experiential world of the subjects of study. Although public policy is peripheral to these studies' aim, they nevertheless resonate with policy implications. For example, both Wiseman and Estroff studied the use of social services by specific marginal groups (homeless alcoholic men and chronic mental patients, respectively). Both found not only that for these groups the social service system had different functions than its designers and practitioners envisioned, but also that the way the target group used the services counteracted, and even undermined, the official goals of the system. However, these studies were not intended as policy studies, and although they provide a powerful commentary on the reigning approach to service delivery in their area of study, their relationship with policy making is indirect at best.

Nevertheless, in strictly quantitative terms, qualitative research is the method of choice for most policy researchers (at least in Europe)—also for many who would be genuinely surprised if someone pointed out that they are de facto working according to the precepts of a post-empiricist, interpretive epistemology. The standard qualitative policy study is a case study of a particular policy initiative, in which the case serves to "illustrate" a particular theoretical position. I deliberately put quotation marks around "illustrate" as it is not always clear what the function of the case is. Often, it must be feared, the suggestion is that the case is meant to "verify" an a priori theory. However, as the explanatory logic that leads from empirical data to more general conclusions is often left largely unspecified, such verification is usually of the kind that Glaser and Strauss disparagingly call "opportunistic," in that the study has at its conclusion "a tacked-on explanation taken from a logically deduced theory" (1967 [2006], 4). In fact, despite the ubiquity in policy analysis of a "quick-and-dirty" type of qualitative research, the place of qualitative research in policy analysis is far from self-evident. One analyst, commenting on the tensions that exist between the "mechanistic" logic of policy making and the hermeneutic logic of qualitative research, uses the term "precarious" to characterize the relation between the two, calling "its utility for policy-making . . . problematic" (Lin, 2000, 4). To make qualitative research work for the analysis of public policy requires careful consideration of the way that the hermeneutic logic of qualitative research can help illuminate the goals and effects of a particular policy. It is perhaps for this reason that, besides pockets of strong qualitative, ethnographic research (on such topics as poverty, crime, street-level bureaucracy, and, recently, policy networks), no widespread tradition of qualitative *policy* research exists.

Before I discuss how qualitative research can enlighten public policy, I need to discuss what I mean by it. For qualitative research to function as a strategy for exploring the subjective meanings of a particular "interpretive community," it is necessary that, both in its method of data gathering, and in its explanatory strategies, it is firmly rooted in empirical reality. Particularly the approach known as "grounded theory," with its admonition to inductively and systematically develop explanations of the data from the empirical material, is important in this respect. The purpose of grounded theory is to "build middle-ground theoretical frameworks that explain the collected data" (Charmaz, 1990, 509). The analytical steps of grounded theory—coding data, memo writing, and theoretical sampling (Charmaz, 1990; Glaser & Strauss, 1967 [2006])—are crucial in keeping the conclusions grounded in the data at all times. I will discuss grounded theory at greater length in chapter 9.

Coding and memo writing are key analytical moments in qualitative analysis. They form the hermeneutic element in qualitative research. Through coding and memo writing the researcher sets up an ongoing dialogue between data and (emerging) theory in which he carries "his thinking to its most logical (grounded in the data, not speculative) conclusions" (Glaser & Strauss, 1967 [2006], 107). One way to think about this dialogue between data and theory is as a constant search for meaning. Similar to the other approaches in this section, and in accordance with the precepts of classical hermeneutics, articulating meaning through qualitative analysis requires having—and developing—a conceptual context for particular items of data. To explain something in an interpretive manner is to situate it in its proper context I concluded in chapter 2. Any datum can be fit into an infinity of contexts but I'm concerned here with the context that emerges by immersion into the world that is the object of the study. In good qualitative work our interviews and observations get better over time; as a result of a patient and open exposure to the life-world of the subjects under study, more sophisticated theoretical explanations go hand in hand with a better, more practical grasp of the way the world works.

In one of the few methods texts that have been written expressly for interpretive policy analysis, it is easy to recognize the contextual logic of qualitative research (Yanow, 2000). Yanow aims for the reconstruction of the perspective of the groups that are involved and the wider context from which the policy derives its meaning. For example, in one key step in her approach to interpretive policy analysis, "identifying interpretive communities," Yanow suggests to the reader that relevant information may be found in written sources (newspapers, magazines, agency newsletters, annual reports, government documents, reports, etc.), oral sources (interviews with key actors), observation (of actions, interactions, and the material context in which the actors move about), and participation. As Yanow explains, "The interpretive policy analyst needs to build a context in which to access local knowledge. Knowing what specific object or piece of language has significance comes from situational familiarity—understanding what is important to stakeholders, to policy-relevant publics" (2000, 38). The actual process of analysis entails two steps: "(1) a daily sense making, out of which (2) puzzles emerge (events or acts or interactions that contradict what the analyst expected, or which he cannot make sense of, given what he knows at that moment, or which contradict one another)" (ibid.). In short, these are the same data sources and analytical steps that make up any good qualitative study.

So what is it then that makes qualitative research in a policy context "precarious"? In a splendid essay titled "Interpretive Research for Public Policy," Lin argues that the difficulty is in establishing a convincing connection between our observations in the field and their implications for policy tools that are "meant to change behavior" (2000, 4). Or, what Schön and Rein famously call the "normative leap" between research and action (Schön & Rein, 1994). The precariousness of this relationship resides in the wholly different external demands that impinge upon each of the two domains. Where policy is driven by the requirements of the political process, such as the need to show results, to be accountable for spending, or to pay heed to the reigning policy doctrine, research is shaped by standards of validity, precision, and acceptability to peers. David Laws, in an insightful reinterpretation of the research-for-policy literature, argues that these tensions pull research and policy in different directions that tend to lock them into separate domains (Laws, 2007).[2]

Within this perennial tension the potential gain of qualitative policy research over traditional survey research can be intuited but is not a given. Survey studies can establish a statistical association between a particular policy (for example, long-term welfare receipt, or de-institutionalization of mental patients) and a socially undesirable outcome (teenage pregnancy, or an explosion of readmissions to mental hospitals). However, an association is not an explanation. As Lin argues:

> For example, documenting an association between long-term welfare receipt and teenage childbirth does not establish why teenage childbirth is associated with long-term welfare receipt. The association might signal a lack of interest or desire to work, the lack of opportunity to acquire skills, a default position as the family baby-sitter for sisters and cousins who have children after they begin working, or numerous other possibilities. . . . [W]hich explanations merit investigation depends on the investigator's background and interests. If a researcher is not acquainted with a social milieu in which extended families pool incomes and provide services for each other, she is unlikely even to consider this explanation. (2000, 1–2)

Lin argues that familiarity with the world in which the "targets" of our policies and research live is essential for putting the analyst on the right track in tracing and explaining the effects of a particular policy. On the face of it, this is a provocative statement, which challenges the institutional distance between policy and practice. Usually, the institutional organization of policy making is such that those who formulate public policy are at a far remove from those who receive it. Interestingly enough this distance is reproduced in the methodological tactics of survey research (Throgmorton, 1993). The result of this institutionalized ignorance is far-reaching indeed:

> The policy implications of these problems are significant. Policy solutions based on inferences from observed behavior, as gathered in surveys and evaluations alone, will neglect dimensions that were not included in the data gathering. This can result in policies that fail or that have unanticipated consequences. Similarly, if explanations of behavior reflect the investigator's notions of plausibility, their "goodness of fit" depends on the investigator's knowledge of the groups in question. When this knowledge is incomplete, biased by class and racial assumptions or overly schematic, policy solutions based on the investigator's explanations will be mystifying at best, destructive at worst. (Lin, 2000, 2)

The potential gains of qualitative research for public policy are in principle considerable, but it is not easy to actually attain them. One common pitfall is that the very logic of qualitative research, with its emphasis on dense, multifaceted descriptions, pushes researchers toward infeasible recommendations. Early examples of qualitative policy research, as Lin describes, often ended in grandiose and impractical recommendations:

[I]nterpretive work does not analyze isolated causal relationships, which makes it hard to identify specific policy tools. The contextual, multidimensional character of interpretive work is antithetical to the creation of specific policy initiatives: the interrelationships described imply that every problem must be solved, in a coordinated fashion, before anything can improve. Thus early interpretive studies of poverty that illuminated the behavior and the perspectives of the urban poor often concluded that wholesale restructuring of an unfair economic system, the creation of new cultural models, and/or the political mobilization of ghetto communities would be required to improve the conditions of the poor. But even if it were, the gap between restructuring an economic system and specific policies to this end remains deep and wide. (2000, 4)

Productive use of qualitative research requires a careful welding of the interpretive, explanatory logic of hermeneutics to the practical logic of policy making. Perhaps the most important contribution of qualitative research to public policy is to bring the perspective of the target audience into view. Building upon its ability to articulate subjective meaning, qualitative policy research can give voice to otherwise excluded and marginalized groups. Not just for the sake of enhancing the democratic quality of the policy making process, important as that is in itself, but also for the more instrumental purpose of identifying biases and prejudices that prevent a more differentiated understanding of the policy problem. Familiarity with the life-world of policy subjects reveals issues that create obstacles for the policy but are unanticipated by policy makers (Lin, 2000, 5). For example, welfare-to-work programs in the Netherlands fail to reach "hard-core" welfare recipients. In a qualitative study of long-term welfare clients we discovered that the considerable psychological effort of adjusting to a life without perspective made it difficult for clients to mobilize themselves to wholeheartedly participate in work reintegration programs. The real pain of an anticipated failure led to various defensive attitudes that made it less likely that the client would succeed in coping with the efforts of identifying with the prospect of a new job and presenting oneself in a job interview (Balder, 2007). Good, qualitative research gives us insight into the way that policy subjects understand a policy in the context of their own life-world. In this way, qualitative research can lead to the reframing of a policy solution. If psychological adjustment is the problem, then reintegration programs that focus on improving work skills and giving the client access to labor market information are beside the point. Thus, the distinctive function of qualitative policy analysis is that of critical enlightenment (C.H. Weiss, 1979, 1980).

Examples

Low-Income Single Mothers in the United States

The aim of qualitative policy research is to reconstruct the subjective meaning of the subjects of a policy: their intentions, reasons, motives, and purposes as understood from within their life-world. In an environment of institutionalized ignorance this is in itself a critical act. The contrast with the official policy uncovers the stated and unstated assumptions and images that drive that policy. The studies in the volume *Coping with Poverty,* to which Lin's essay functions as an introduction, provide several good examples (Danziger & Lin, 2000). For example, welfare reform in the United States has "enshrined in law a vision of parenting that focuses primarily on economic provision" (Lin, 2000, 14). The Personal Responsibility and Work Opportunity Reconciliation Act (PRWORA) places time limits on the receipt of cash assistance and required the recipients of benefits to work or enroll in work-related programs. The purpose of the law is to promote responsible fatherhood and motherhood (ibid.). By exclusively focusing on work placement rates, shifts in benefit levels, or factors explaining time spent on and off welfare rolls, official evaluation studies of the program tend to replicate the assumptions that inform the policy. However, a carcful qualitative study of single mothers who were either on welfare or held jobs in the low end of the labor market revealed not only that these mothers' perspective on parenting involved a lot more than economic considerations, but that the welfare regulations confronted them with impossible dilemmas.

Kalil et al. interviewed twenty-three low-income single mothers in the state of Michigan about work, welfare, and parenthood (Kalil et al., 2000). Based on what they call an "inductive analysis" of these interviews, they describe the life-world of these women. First, like all working mothers, they had to balance the needs of children against the demands of employment. However, the interview makes clear that this challenge to negotiate multiple roles is particularly difficult for low-income single mothers, "who have limited income and experience stressful living conditions" (2000, 202). Moreover, because of their dependence on the harsh regulations of the welfare program, their decisions carry more serious consequences for themselves and their children, such as sanctions that lead to even further income reduction (2000, 203). Yet, as the study shows, this doesn't change the complex parenting situation that these single mothers faced. Kalil et al. identify "four dimensions of care-giving that together constitute these women's conception of child rearing" (ibid.). The authors describe these four dimensions as the need to provide material goods, the need to provide adequate health care for their children, the need to provide quality child care, and concerns about the amount of time they were able to spend with their children.

The study shows that all of these mothers expressed a commitment to work for its economic and personal rewards, but also were invested in their role as caregivers. Within each of the four dimensions identified, these mothers faced considerable stresses and dilemmas, and the study clearly shows how their assessment of their situation along any one of these dimensions influenced their choices regarding work and welfare—some of which seem irrational or irresponsible to the outside world. For example, the availability of quality child care was an absolute condition for these women to be able to work. Affordable, quality child care is barely available for low-income mothers. The state can sanction mothers for not working unless it has been determined that child care is unavailable. However, the state is not obliged to assist mothers in finding child care. The mothers in the study were understandably reluctant to place their children in the care of the low-quality providers that were generally available to them. Many resorted to their own parents or other family members to look after their children when they were at work. But this often led to clashes about parenting style or to discomfort about having to ask for help from people who had their own responsibilities and stresses to deal with. The choice between taking a low-paying job and having to pay for child care, or staying on welfare and being sanctioned for noncompliance, became a devil's dilemma: "Ironically, women's reluctance to choose a provider based on concerns about quality or safety could result in economic sanctions that could threaten children in other ways" (Kalil et al., 2000, 216).

The authors sum up what they consider to be the "policy-relevant issues" of their study with the following points: First, "that work does not pay from an economic perspective." Taking a job means losing food stamps and Medicaid, and the phasing out of savings. Particularly for women whose children had health issues, the risk was not worth taking. Second, "that women consider the combination of welfare and education their best long-term strategy for self-sufficiency." While these women recognized that they lacked the skills and credentials for employers to offer them a livable wage, the combination of work, parenting, and school proved for many to be an insurmountable obstacle. And third, "that women arrive at both of these conclusions in the context of their dual roles as workers and mothers." As the authors conclude, "[A] central point in our discussion with mothers about work, welfare and parenting is that regardless of the choice that each ultimately made (e.g., some combination of work, welfare, and school), each mother faced the reality that her choices regarding the balance between working and parenting were limited, not only because she had little economic power, but also because the welfare system offered her few options" (Kalil et al., 2000, 220–22).

Technology Transfer in Germany

Social distance brings out the critical enlightenment function. But an example from an entirely different policy domain—government funding for technology transfer in Germany—demonstrates that the critical strength of qualitative policy analysis remains intact when the players in the policy field have more intrinsic affinity (Hofmann, 1995). Distance is not only social but, as the example shows, also conceptual and practical. Like most advanced economies, Germany spends hundreds of millions of euros a year on basic research in universities and institutions known as *Technische Hochschule*. This policy rests on a set of powerful, more or less self-evident assumptions about science and technology. For example, that technology is the successful application by industry of the results of basic research conducted in universities. This basic research is developed by scientific communities that operate as autonomous groups and that generate new knowledge for its own sake. The quality of that knowledge is determined according to criteria internal to the discipline in question (Hofmann, 1995, 130). Technology develops by means of the "cascade" model whereby new scientific knowledge is translated into technology. The role of businesses is to adopt the scientific insights and to translate these into technological applications (1995, 139). However, given the autonomous character of the development of scientific knowledge, the links between the scientific and the business communities cannot be expected to emerge spontaneously. Government must vigorously stimulate and support such links through policies of technology transfer (1995, 130). Hofmann summarizes the assumptions that underlie national policies of technology transfer as follows: "First, [that] research institutions produce knowledge of direct relevance to the economy; second, that they hold an advantage over industry in terms of knowledge and skills; and third, that this repertoire of academic knowledge constitutes the foundation for the cooperation between firms and academic institutions." These assumptions can be encountered in almost "every policy statement concerning technology transfer" (1995, 131).

However, similar to the Israeli policy of establishing community centers as described by Yanow, the official policy formulation on technology transfer generated a number of anomalies. First, Hofmann found, business spent much more on research than universities did and the gap was widening (1995, 138). Second, a large number of evaluation studies showed that in terms of the creation of new businesses or the development of new products, the state's support of technology transfer had little or no effect (1995, 141). Hofmann's research revealed even deeper anomalies. The reasons that firms collaborated with universities—if they did at all—had little to do with "the standard logic of technology policy thinking" (1995, 132). Firms sought out universities because of convenience rather than strategic considerations: spatial proximity, personal links from earlier college days, personal trust in a particular researcher, and the proven success of earlier experiences (ibid.). Universities were seen as attractive because of the low price for their services, not for exclusivity. In fact, the majority of consultation and development services that universities provided could also be performed by private operators (1995, 137). And finally, universities were seen as providers of high-quality trainees in an informal labor market of academic institutions and businesses, thereby making the recruitment process more efficient (1995, 133).

From the point of view of the academic community, relationships with businesses were guided by equally "mundane and pragmatic considerations." Universities liked to maintain close links to the local business community to be able to provide training places for their students. Instead of pursuing independent, "pure" basic research, universities were mostly involved in commissioned projects and practical advice. Many university professors had acquired their practical experience in one of the local firms. In addition, Hofmann notices a widespread practice in which businesses donated written-down business equipment to university laboratories. Hofmann sees a wider practical rationality at work here:

> There is an enormous wealth gap between business and academic research in almost all application-oriented areas of technology. This means that academic institutions are confronted with the serious problem of keeping pace with the modernization efforts of the so-called "technology-takers." From the perspective of the academic researcher, many would find it difficult to continue their work without a steady supply of industrial funds. Indeed this applies not only to the provision of machinery and equipment, but even more to the generation of knowledge linked to their production and application. To be sure, such a perspective on business-science contacts pretty much sets technology policy theory on its head. While the technology policy world view postulates that new technological knowledge flows from the academic research lab to the firm, an increasing amount of this knowledge is transferred in the opposite direction. (1995, 138)

Hofmann notices that university-business relationships seldom had a deep impact on the firm. Such hoped-for effects as large-scale modernization or major transformations of product or production profiles had not occurred, and were not expected by the firms to occur. From the firms' point of view, cooperative relationships with universities were entered into because they increased the efficiency of existing production processes, not because they generated new technology. Hofmann concludes, "It helps to save time, money, and to avoid roundabout solutions, but typically within the framework of projects which would otherwise have been performed internally or in cooperation with other forms" (1995, 134).

Thus, instrumentally, the official policy of technology transfer was a failure. The impact of basic research from academic institutions on the development of new technologies was nil, as was its effect on the modernization of production processes. Yet, year after year, hundreds of millions of euros kept being poured into it. What is the explanation for this puzzle? Similar to what Yanow found in her Israeli community center study (Yanow, 1996), Hofmann sees the explanation as residing in the meaning of technology transfer to a particular community of policy actors. However, in a small but significant difference from Yanow, Hofmann adds that the persistence of the technology transfer policy in Germany came from the "plausibility and the inherent integrity of the underlying assumptions concerning technological development" (1995, 142). Hofmann adds a constructivist twist to Yanow's argument. To the architects of the official policy of technology transfer, the assumptions discussed earlier had the status of an "ontological axiom." This not only made the policy makers highly resistant to conflicting experiences. Indeed, the assumptions brought into being a reality of their own, a policy reality with its own inner logic, its own legitimacy, its own internal consistency, its own ability to shape relations among government, academia, and the business community, and its own criteria for success. (After all, German industrial technology has a stellar reputation.) In fact, the official policy of technology transfer must be seen as a coherent story that enabled policy makers to act in an exceedingly complex and baffling world. Without such a story, they would be completely rudderless.[3]

Commentary

Qualitative policy research is attractive as it combines clear methodological procedures with potentially powerful outcomes. Collections such as Danziger and Lin's book or the special issue of *Policy Sciences* mentioned above give a good overview of the different ways that qualitative policy interpretation is conducted in practice. Based on these different sources I discern two problems, however: (1) the temptation to engage in a restricted version of the qualitative research process, including the widespread tendency to consider public policy a text, and (2) the (almost) absence of political conflict and power in its analytic scheme.

Constricting the Qualitative Research Process

Qualitative research is demanding. It is time consuming, and requires effort and a good measure of tolerance for the inevitable ambiguities and frustrations that are part of the collection and analysis of qualitative data (Cerwonka and Malkki, 2007). Qualitative research also introduces an element of risk into the professional life of the researcher. Sometimes this is personal risk, as when one ventures into a dangerous area, such as a ghetto or the milieu of drug dealers, for ethnographic field observation. But there is also a more subtle risk, the risk that comes from the confrontation with beliefs, behavior, and life styles that are radically different from our own. Usually it takes considerable mental and emotional effort to understand such a distal perspective. It makes us vulnerable because it tends to challenge deep-seated beliefs and routines. Sustained confrontation with different life-worlds comes with what Taylor calls "identity costs." Not only are the voices of our research subjects an elliptical commentary on our own life-world; often they make it impossible to maintain the taken-for-granted acceptance of our everyday life that is the hallmark of a stable identity. Questioning assumptions is an open-ended process with unpredictable implications for one's understanding of self and others (Wagenaar, 2008).

For these reasons there is an understandable temptation to curtail the qualitative research process. One common way to do this is to restrict the sampling process. A frequent shortcut to sampling consists of the selection of only "safe" respondents such as administrators, professionals, or elected officials. Another tactic is to avoid risky environments by scheduling interviews in familiar settings such as professionals' offices. A third is to refrain from going the extra mile to locate and recruit marginal groups such as ethnic minorities, petty criminals, or members of youth gangs. In all of these cases, the data will be biased. Important perspectives are excluded from the interpretation of the policy domain, and researchers deny themselves the opportunities to pick up accidental observations that come with immersion in the milieu of the subjects.

Another, insidious, way to constrict the research process is by inadequate data collection. The data collection method of choice in qualitative policy analysis is the semi-structured qualitative interview. More than fifteen years of teaching qualitative interviewing to graduate students has left me with the conviction that most interviewing is of less than optimal quality. The purpose of the qualitative interview is to obtain data that are sufficiently rich to make analysis according to the inductive principles of grounded theory possible (Charmaz, 2006, 25). The logic is that of backward mapping: analysis dictates interviewing. Interview data should be detailed and concrete, and the interview must be conducted in such a manner that it allows for novelty and surprise. I will discuss interviewing at greater length in chapter 9.

A third way to curtail the qualitative research process is by not researching the full spectrum of behaviors, objects, and utterances in the field, and restricting oneself to written sources. As this is a common practice—if not a doctrine—in interpretive policy analysis, I will pay some attention to it here. Many interpretive analyses of public policy limit themselves to the study of policy texts: policy reports, newspaper articles, minutes of meetings, and the like. Convenience meets doctrine here. Clearly, it is easier to analyze policy documents at one's desk than to venture into the field to track down and interview hard to locate, recalcitrant, unpredictable subjects. In addition, this practice probably is furthered by the fact that academics are socialized as symbolic analysts who feel more at ease with words than with the hustle and bustle of real-world actors moving about in a social or political arena. This practice seems to be officially sanctioned by a number of prestigious authors, who have argued that social reality can fruitfully be seen as a text. For example, Winch argues that "social relations exist only in and through their ideas" and that "social interaction can more profitably be compared to the exchange of ideas in a conversation than to the interaction of forces in a physical system" (Winch, 1958, 123, 128).[4] The most widely quoted source of the language analogy is Ricoeur, who argues for an "objectification" of action "similar to the fixation which occurs in writing" (1977, 322).[5] The idea of acts as texts is picked up in policy analysis by Yanow when she says that "not only is legislative and other language a text that is interpreted by implementers and others, but those interpretations—in the form of implementing agency language, objects and acts—themselves become 'texts' that are 'read' by those actors and others" (2000, 17–18).[6]

It would exceed the boundaries of this chapter to thoroughly discuss linguistic reductionism in interpretive social science. Let me restrict myself to two comments that are relevant to interpretive policy analysis. First, even if the language analogy holds, to restrict one's research to written sources only is to commit a logical fallacy. Even if action can rightfully be considered analogous to written texts, this does not imply that one can reverse this proposition and claim that written texts are therefore similar to action. This is the logical error in Ricoeur's paradigm of text interpretation. No matter how you cut the cake, there is a difference between experience and texts, and, inter alia, between the meanings of experiences and of the texts describing these experiences. Or as Taylor puts it in his famous essay "Interpretation and the Sciences of Man," there is a difference between "experiential meaning" and "the semantic field of the terms characterizing these meanings" (Taylor, 1985a, 26). To distinguish the two obliges one to articulate their relationship, and this is precisely what Taylor does.[7] Language does not have an a priori priority over experience. If anything their relationship is circular or dialectical, with experience being shaped and maintained by language and vice versa. One can establish the meaning of actions, feelings, and human artifacts, just as one can establish the meaning of texts. As Geertz convincingly demonstrated, the interpretation of cultures still requires the careful study of behaviors, which can then be treated as inscriptions to be "read."

Perhaps the best way to treat the language analogy, and this is my second point, is precisely as that: an analogy, a heuristic metaphor. Similar to considering social reality as a system or a market, we can think of it for practical purposes as a text. The metaphorical analogue foregrounds elements in the object of analysis that might result in productive, interesting analysis. In the next chapter we will see how French structuralists have used the language analogy in analyzing society. However, employing language as a generative metaphor has the status of a hypothesis—not a doctrine. We use it as long as it generates interesting, insightful explanations of social reality. When the analogy has exhausted itself it is time to move on.

As a practical strategy of interpretive policy analysis, the text analogy carries methodological risks. An example is a paper by Chock on U.S. immigration policy. Chock restricts her analysis to transcripts of congressional hearings on immigration policy. In the first paragraph of her paper the key metaphor of immigrants as "populations" is introduced. The author wants to make the point that the seemingly biological, neutral population metaphor serves to obfuscate the race, gender, and class dimensions of immigration, and that that useful function helped it to become "hegemonic" in the U.S. discourse on immigration (1995, 165). In the remainder of the article the author presents evidence that ought to demonstrate the plausibility of this interpretation, but does not. Chock's interpretation is not necessarily implausible or wrong, but the reader can't see where it is coming from. Moreover, on closer inspection, snippets of congressional hearings that the author presents to support her case reveal the use of other metaphors (aliens, insects) that do allow direct reference to race, class, and gender. Despite the talk of "competing interpretive frameworks," the impression is that the analysis is front-loaded.

Insufficient Attention to Power

A second pitfall of qualitative policy analysis is that it pays insufficient attention to power and conflict. In general, for policy analysis to be appropriate for its intended use, it must be consonant with its political setting. This is not a "secondary consideration," as Dryzek rightly points out (1982, 310), for policy analysis differs from "basic" social science in that it is intended to be used in practical political settings. That setting, as I briefly mentioned in chapter 1 and will discuss at greater length in chapter 10, is characterized by interaction, power play, structural inequality, deep complexity, indeterminacy, dispersed decision making, lack of trust among actors, value pluralism, and a fundamental orientation to practice (Bohman, 1996; Dryzek, 1982, 1990; Forester, 1999b; Hajer and Wagenaar, 2003; D. Stone, 1997; Wagenaar and Cook, 2003). Power is not a dimension of public policy that the analyst can choose to include or ignore in his analysis. Instead, as I will argue in chapter 10, it is an intrinsic, constitutive part of all public policy—call it an ontology. Power differentials are at the heart of the categories that structure problem formulations, the way that policy alternatives are selected and prioritized, the choice of acceptable policy instruments, and so on. Even more important, power differentials determine which problems are *not* on the public agenda. The problem with power is that you can never escape its reach in policy analysis. Ignoring it means being implicated by it. This is the message that Foucault, as no other, drives home, as we will see in the next chapter.

Very little of this resonates in the examples of policy interpretation we have encountered in the preceding paragraphs. Qualitative policy research, as I have discussed it so far, is only implicitly critical; it reveals the biased or mistaken assumptions on which a particular policy (deinstitutionalization of the chronically mentally ill; welfare reform; technology transfer) is based. In other examples of policy interpretation the critical dimension is either absent (Yanow's study of community centers in Israel) or has a tacked-on quality (Chock [1995], uses a vocabulary of hegemony and domination, but hardly shows how power is exerted in U.S. immigration policy). Obviously, I do not say that qualitative policy analysis is useless because it does not address power head on. Revealing biases in policy assumptions without systematically laying bare the hidden power dimension of the social phenomenon has an obvious enlightening, critical function. It will not be too difficult for most readers to connect the dots. In the next chapter, however, we will see different examples of interpretive policy analysis that not only give power central stage in the analysis, but also introduce sophisticated conceptions of power to grasp the hidden, structural differentials in influence that characterize the world of public policy.

FRAME ANALYSIS

Exposition

Frame analysis is associated with Rein (and in later versions his long-time collaborator, Schön). It is a good example of the pragmatic nature of the tripartite distinction of meaning I introduced in chapter 4. While early versions of frame analysis, in their attempt to find the competing meaning perspectives that underlie a policy controversy, are hermeneutic, later formulations, with their emphasis on practice and the development of frames through contestation between policy actors, have a more dialogical character. In this chapter, I discuss early frame analysis.

For a proper understanding of the concept of frame and the aims of frame critical policy analysis, it is important to grasp its practical origins. The concept of frame was an answer to a number of concerns about real-world policy making and the ability of social science to inform or guide public decision making. Rein's affinity with the practical concerns of policy making (as is demonstrated by an important paper on the problems of program evaluation in concrete political settings which he coauthored with Robert Weiss [R.S. Weiss & Rein, 1970]) is probably related to his early career as a practicing professional in inner-city neighborhoods. Frames speak to the "relationship between reason and purpose," as Rein calls it (1976, 96). Epistemologically, frame analysis is an attempt to account for the central role of values and action in the world of policy making. For several reasons, frame analysis is an important and interesting interpretive method. First, it provides the analyst with a tool to go beyond the mere description of multiple meanings or stories and to engage in a *critical* analysis of the assumptions, beliefs, and aspirations to intervention that make up a particular policy proposal. Also, in contrast to most interpretive approaches that refer to continental hermeneutical or linguistic philosophies, frame analysis has always been informed by the American tradition of philosophical pragmatism. And, as I indicated above, frame analysis is interesting because over the years it has transformed itself from an interpretive method that is firmly within the hermeneutical tradition of finding meanings in the world of public policy (although with a pragmatist flavor), to a more deliberative form of policy interpretation in which meanings arise out of the mutual interaction of policy actors as well as their ongoing struggle with real-world problems.

In his first statement on frames, the 1976 book *Social Science and Public Policy,* Rein is very much concerned with the lack of impact that even excellent social science research had on policy making. In the wake of disappointing experiences with large public programs such as Head Start or the Negative Income Tax Experiment, he asks: Why, if everyone subscribes to the belief that the development of public policy should be guided by rational review, do we see so little of it? In fact, in the domain of social policy, an increase in scientific knowledge is not, even by the most generous standards, accompanied by a commensurate increase in our ability to design and change policy (1976, 97). And, to support his concern, he cites an Assistant Commissioner of Research for the Social Security Administration, who says, in utter frustration, "There is a growing recognition that much of the federally supported extramural research, particularly in the social sciences, has added little or nothing either to basic knowledge or to practical decision-making" (quoted in Rein, 1976, 97).[8] In his later work Rein became concerned with policy controversies. Disputes are endemic to the world of policy making. These disputes are often bitter, often deep, but some—think of current controversies in Europe over the integration of Muslim immigrants, or the reform of the health care system, or the way to deal with the problem of juvenile delinquency—distinguish themselves by their inability ever to be settled. They seem immune not just to reasonable argument, but also to facts and the outcomes of scientific research. One party in the dispute can come up with sheaves of data or research to support his position; the other party simply counters with other data and other research that seem to bolster his position. As Schön and Rein put it, "The policy disputes we call controversies are immune to resolution by appeal to facts. . . . [Such] disputes . . . tend to be intractable, enduring, and seldom finally resolved" (1994, 4).

Rein identifies three obstacles to the use of social science research in public policy making. The first two are democratic pluralism (there is no such thing as a homogeneous public interest;

there is only a heterogeneous collection of sectional interests) and the sheer complexity of social phenomena (causal laws are rare; the best we can hope for is to discover highly unstable and context-dependent regularities). But, even we if we acknowledge pluralism and complexity, we could, in principle, subscribe to a more modest utilization model: policy research could perhaps not guide policy, but could act as a "probe" that provides insights into the nature of social reality (1976, 103). However, this will not do either, because, and this is Rein's third point, information about complex events only makes sense when it is related to some framework of interpretation. Rein, thus, turns the usual sequence of knowledge leading to insight on its head. The starting points are priori insights that make it possible to know something in the first place. Rein calls these a priori insights frames (or, in 1976, under the then-fashionable influence of Kuhn's work, policy paradigms). It is worth quoting him on this:

> The term paradigm is used here to suggest a working model of why things are as they are, a problem-solving framework, which implies values and benefits but also procedures, habits of thought, and a view of how society functions. It often provides a guiding metaphor of how the world works which implies a general direction for intervention: it is more specific than an ideology or a system of beliefs but broader than a principle of intervention. The concept of the poverty cycle provides a working model of the causal interactions that are believed to result in poverty, a moral interpretation of the responsibility for intervening in this causal chain and a guide to the interventions that are therefore relevant and right. (1976, 103–4)

So, in Rein's view, the preliminary assumptions that we need to make sense of, to give meaning to, social reality involve a lot more than just a set of beliefs. They combine thought, valuation, action, and moral imperative in one more or less coherent framework of more or less self-evident understanding. And interestingly, as the quote suggests, causal relations are not deduced from the data—if that were possible at all—but imposed upon them beforehand through the guiding force of an a priori interpretive frame.

In a later paper, Rein returns to the frame concept and there puts full emphasis on the aspects of value and action (Rein, 1983a). He begins the paper by hitching on to an argument against the fact-value dichotomy by Putnam, the philosopher (H. Putnam, 1981a). This is interesting for various reasons. First, as I said earlier, contrary to most interpretive analysts who ground their understanding of meaning and interpretation in continental philosophy, Rein evokes Anglo-Saxon analytical philosophy as the theoretical foundation of his anti-essentialist approach to issues of meaning, truth, reality, and action. Rein follows Putnam closely when he argues (1) that we have no access to a "mind-independent, discourse independent" reality that is "really" out there (the by now well-known perspectivism argument); (2) that values are crucial in making sense of everyday reality, and that purpose is central to value;[9] (3) that action is also central to valuation and thinking;[10] (4) that even basic categories such as "truth" depend upon "standards of rational acceptability" that are themselves outside truth; and (5) that sense making and values have no meaning outside the everyday "common experience" of actors, or, as he later calls it, "the context of interpretation and action." On the basis of this argument Rein then concludes:

> Purpose and values are therefore absolutely essential to any inquiry into facts. While there is clearly a reality and while truthfulness consists in trying to behave so as not to deceive oneself or others, we cannot grasp reality independent of the categories of understanding we impose, and these categories depend upon our purposes and values. (1983a, 89)

Having said this, Rein then introduces theory. He sides with the perspectivist or presupposition theorists in agreeing that there are no brute facts.[11] On the basis of his pragmatist and perspectivist reading of the philosophy of social science literature, Rein concludes that facts, theory, value, and purpose are deeply interrelated—interpenetrated would be the better term—in making sense of everyday reality. This, he then argues, introduces an ineluctable element of contingency and indeterminacy in our world. We cannot ever aspire to one overriding, conclusive depiction of the world we live in. Rein moves toward a social constructionist position:

> Reality then consists in multiple descriptions: the bit, the event, the phenomenon—the experience we are trying to describe is itself many things. Hence, no single summary is ever adequate. The questions we ask of reality depend upon the perspective we take in approaching the phenomenon, and it is this perspective that shapes the categories we use to impose order and give meaning to reality. In this sense, then, we construe reality by the categories of understanding that we impose, the questions we ask, and the perspectives and purposes with which we approach our inquiry. However, this does not mean that we reject the facticity of the world and its underlying reality, even though facts are seldom so compelling that they repudiate and decisively refute our previously held interpretation of how the world is and ought to be put together. Hence, the factual aspects of our values and theories are seldom conclusive. We know that nothing we say about reality is definitive, authoritative, and fully settled. (1983a, 94)

When applied to issues of public policy, these arguments then require an "analytic concept that addresses the question of purpose and the action implications embedded in our theory" (1983a, 95). Such a concept is "frame," which is defined as a "structure of thought, of evidence, of action, and hence of interests and of values" (1983a, 96). Within this "structure," the elements are not only "internally related," but even "mutually constitutive of each other's identity." Frames explain deep controversies over what to do in the equivocal and unforgiving world of public action. I pause to emphasize the action dimension in Rein's frame concept. It is crucial to the concept of frame. (And it already points toward his later, dialogical version of the frame concept.) This is very clearly stated by the originator of the frame concept in policy analysis himself, when he says that "[b]oth the categories of description and the lines of investigation we pursue are shaped by our experience of trying to act on the world, and are limited by the sorts of actions we see as possible" (1983b, 221). He adds:

> I do not believe that the situation should be more like that of the positivist ideal; to define a problem as independent of the actions addressing it is to propose unattainable utopia[s] and to treat research as though it possessed some sort of timeless validity separate from the world of becoming, to which it should properly belong. The center of both fact and value is the world of action. (1983b, 222)

Nowadays the frame concept is used widely in interpretive policy talk. It is an idea in good currency. But usually the action implication has been bleached out of it. Frames have been domesticated to mere positions, points of view in a policy debate. I will return to this.

How is the frame concept applied in policy analysis? What does "value-critical policy analysis," as Rein calls it, amount to? Rein suggests the following three applications: First, *frame-criticism,* or the elucidation of the taken-for-granted assumptions of policies and the context that nourishes these assumptions. Next, *frame creation*, which consists of a systematic critique of a particular "framework of action" because of "its failure to deliver on its implicit moral promise," followed by the development of an alternative framework. And finally, *the redefinition and integration of frames* to make then compatible (1983a, 103–6). In general, he suggests, we recognize frames through their action implications. While theories may result in different actions, the reverse does not hold true. Once we have a prescription for action, we can identify the ensemble of beliefs, information, values, and aims that uniquely informs that particular action preference (1983a, 99).

The implications for understanding policy making that flow from this conception of frames are significant. First, frame analysis supposes a pluralistic universe; the world of policy is intrinsically contested, contingent, and indeterminate. (In its emphasis on contestation, frame analysis exhibits more "face validity" to the political setting to which it refers than does qualitative policy analysis.) No Archimedean point (facts, science, first principles, belief systems) exists from which we can ever hope to arbitrate policy conflicts. Facts, theories, values, and purposeful action are irrevocably interwoven to the point at which they mutually constitute each other. Hence, policy controversies are not disputes about data, but about the persuasiveness of the a priori interpretive perspectives that bring the policy into being. Data and knowledge generated by policy analysis have only a limited reach; they come to a stop at the conceptual and valuative borders of a policy frame. Frames operate on the principle of cognitive dissonance. Data that do not fit within the frame simply don't make sense to the adherents of the frame. They are considered irrelevant or otherwise neutralized through psychological denial.[12] Also it needs no comment that frames are extremely resistant to change, for, similar to policy stories, if you take a policy makers' frames away, you rob them of their only device with which to act upon the world. In addition, many frames are institutionalized, in the sense that they are collective, have owners who jealously guard them, and prop up professions and careers.[13]

Example

Although "frame" and "framing" have become standard terms in policy analysis, there are, interestingly enough, not many studies that consciously employ the concepts and methods of frame analysis to throw light upon a contested policy area. Rein himself has used frame analysis to good purpose in his analysis of conflicting goals and dilemmas of choice in U.S. poverty policy (Rein, 1983c). Although he doesn't use the actual terms, Gusfield's work on drinking and driving can be seen as an instance of frame analysis (Gusfield, 1984). A contemporary example can be found in the work of Hajer. Although he uses the language of discourse analysis, his concept of discourse coalition is more akin to a frame.

One of the most elaborate examples of frame analysis can be found in the work of Gamson, the sociologist. Gamson's work is important because he has made a concerted effort to develop the frame concept methodologically. A good example can be found in Gamson's analysis of the post–World War II debate on nuclear power in the United States (Gamson & Modigliani, 1989). Similar to Yanow, Gamson and Modigliani emphasize the symbolic aspect of public policy. They think of policies as symbolic contests over which interpretation will prevail in the political arena (1989, 2). To support this contention the authors introduce two key assumptions. First, the meaning that an issue, such as nuclear power, or policy, has for an individual has a certain organization and coherence. The authors call these meaning clusters "packages." Second, these "packages" are socially constructed. In a highly developed society such as ours, where most people do not have direct experience with many policy issues, the media play a central role in this construction process. But it is not just the media who are in the business of meaning formation. In most cases we see that frames or "packages" have institutional sponsors: organizations who have a vested interest in the issue, and who are in the business of promoting and protecting a frame.

A package consists of a core frame, the function of which is "to make sense of relevant events, suggesting what is at issue," and a number of "reasoning devices, that justify what should be done about it." Framing devices are: metaphors, exemplars, catchphrases, descriptions, and visual images. Reasoning devices are "roots" or causal analysis, "consequences," or a "particular type of effect," and "appeals to principle," or moral claims. It helps the fortunes of a package if it can be expressed in a "condensing symbol"; a particularly evocative metaphor, a catchphrase, or some striking visual symbol (Gamson & Modigliani, 1989, 3). Think, for example, of the powerful metaphor of war that has been attached to various aggressive efforts to eradicate societal problems (war on drugs, war on terror, war on cancer). This extensive definition of the frame concept has the considerable advantage that it suggests relatively clear-cut methods of empirical inquiry into issue packages. The authors describe in detail how they constructed a representative sample of four decades of media utterances on nuclear power. Subsequently they conducted a "systematic content analysis that uses standard coding and reliability techniques" such as the use of multiple independent coders and the calculation of interrater reliability (1989, 11).[14] Here is how the authors typify the frame or package they have labeled *Progress:*

> If the electric chair had been invented before the electric light, would we still be using kerosene lamps? There has always been resistance to technological progress by nervous Nellies who see only the problems and ignore the benefits. Resistance to nuclear energy development is the latest version of this irrational fear of progress and change, the expression of modern pastoralists and nuclear Luddites. Certainly nuclear energy development is not free of problems, but problems can be solved, as the history of technological progress shows. The failure to develop nuclear power will retard our economic growth and make us renege on our obligation to the poor and to future generations. If coercive utopians prevent us from moving ahead now with nuclear energy, the next generation is likely to be sitting around in the dark blaming the utilities for not doing something this generation's officials wouldn't let them do. (1989, 4)

Gamson and Modigliani see a policy field as being made up of a series of contesting packages. True to their assumptions, the authors conceive of this political pluralism in symbolic terms. For example, the wider culture constrains and affords the construction of packages. Packages are influenced by what the authors call "cultural resonances": "Certain packages have a natural advantage because their ideas and language resonate with larger cultural themes. Resonances increase the appeal of a package; they make it appear natural and familiar" (1989, 5).[15] For example, the progress package in the debate on nuclear power resonates with the deeply embedded ideal of technological progress. Also, diversity is not just the result of conflicting interests but of thematic contrast: "It is useful to think of themes dialectically. There is no theme without a countertheme. The theme is conventional and normative; the countertheme is adversarial and contentious" (1989, 6). Gamson and Modigliani capture the symbolic environment of a package with the term "issue culture." It is not always clear, though, if the issue culture refers to the embedding cultural environment or to the collection of conflicting packages that make up a particular policy dispute (1989, 3).

In addition to the cultural environment, a package is also influenced by sponsor activities and media practices. As the broad cultural themes in an environment remain largely constant, sponsors and the media are needed to explain how packages adapt to changing circumstances. Sponsors promote the careers of packages: "The sponsor of a package is typically an agent who is promoting some collective rather than personal agenda." For the progress package in nuclear power, public officials from the Atomic Energy Commission (later the Nuclear Regulatory Commission) acted as sponsors. Industry groups such as the Atomic Industrial Forum and the Edison Electric Institute were also important sponsors (1989, 7). Often sponsors have easy, routine access to the media, with the effect that the media often side with the dominant interpretation of a policy issue (ibid.). The result is that issue cultures have a kind of built-in inertia. Despite changing circumstances and external events, they are held in place by cultural anchors: cultural resonances, sponsor activities, and a successful fit with media norms and practices (1989, 9).

In the remainder of the paper the authors chart the vicissitudes of various packages through the events and debates surrounding nuclear power from the 1950s to the 1980s. For example, in the 1950s the progress package was hegemonic, but it had a dual structure. As the images of the unprecedented nuclear destruction of Hiroshima and Nagasaki in Japan were still fresh, beneficial applications of nuclear power had to be carefully kept separate from military applications. In fact, as the authors show, the progress frame was so unchallenged that a serious incident at the Fermi reactor outside Detroit went almost unnoticed in the media (1989, 14). From the late 1960s on the public debate on nuclear power suddenly expanded. Under the influence of the oil crisis of the early 1970s a second pro-nuclear package emerged that the authors label *Energy Independence.* Under the influence of the cold war and the proliferation of nuclear weapons, the nuclear dualism that characterized the progress package began to crumble. Moreover, growing concerns about the safety of nuclear reactors made people aware that the destructive power of a meltdown was similar to that of a nuclear bomb. Three anti-nuclear power packages came into being: *Soft Paths,* which propagated an environment-friendly, low-energy life style; *Public Accountability,* which focused on the industry's power to keep alternative energy sources off the political agenda; and *Not Cost Effective,* which argued that the large hidden costs of nuclear power altered its allegedly favorable cost-benefit balance (1989, 16).

The authors then chart the debate in the aftermath of the accidents at the Three Mile Island nuclear power plant in Pennsylvania in 1979 and at the nuclear power plant in Chernobyl, Ukraine, in 1986. They conclude, for example, that television coverage of protests provided ambiguous images, which can be interpreted in various ways depending on the frame one adheres to. Also, they show that the anti-nuclear-power frames are more sympathetically portrayed in the written press. And they argue that the media show controversy but fail to supply the frames from within which the protesters operate. The authors "discover" two new frames after the accidents. *Runaway* is a more fatalistic take on the debate that homes in on the theme of the intrinsic intractability of complex technologies and the near certainty of fatal unintended consequences. The second, *Devil's Bargain,* is more ambivalent and combines our society's dependence on the unlimited supply of cheap energy with the near certainty that we will have a terrible price to pay for this at some future moment (1989, 20, 25). Also, the authors show how packages adapt to changing circumstances. The progress package quickly incorporated arguments about the effectiveness of safety procedures that had prevented a meltdown after the Three Mile Island incident (1989, 21).

The purpose of Gamson and Modigliani's paper (1989) is to demonstrate that the outcomes of opinion polls on nuclear power are hard to understand, or even misleading, without an understanding of the underlying issue culture. They demonstrate this by bringing onto the stage an imaginary "member of the public, old enough to remember Hiroshima and the age of nuclear dualism, trying to make sense of the issue of nuclear power" (32). Back in the 1950s such a person would almost certainly have used a progress frame to understand nuclear power. But as she traveled through the 1970s and 1980s her understanding of the issue would change:

[H]er personal exposure to the issue culture through either the media or other discourses, her enduring predispositions, and her interpersonal interactions would all have played a role in the modification of her working schema on nuclear power. Many paths were possible, but the nature of the media discourse suggests that certain ones were especially likely . . . [W]e would hypothesize that many older people during this period began to conflate their pro-nuclear progress schema with runaway themes to produce some version of the ambivalent devils' bargain. (1989, 32, 33)

Opinion polls, with their tendency to fit everything into clearly delineated, dualistic pro/con schemata, would entirely miss such ambivalences and trajectories. Opinions are indicative of the meaning that citizens attach to issues. Those meanings, the authors argue, signify action-oriented beliefs. And these emerge as a reaction to events in the world, shaped by a particular, personalized, cultural background.

Commentary

The frame concept is useful in understanding the role of social science in the fundamentally contested world of policy making. Frame analysis is a sophisticated theory about the relationship between social science research and public policy making. It makes short shrift of simple-minded ideas about the linear, instrumental contribution that research should be able to make to policy. Instead frame analysis shows how the perspectivism that is inherent to both policy making and research shapes and limits their reciprocal relationship. Similar to qualitative policy research, frame analysis also helps to articulate the hidden value assumptions of the conflicting positions on such issues as such poverty, homelessness, pension reform, and affirmative action (Hawkesworth, 1988, ch. 5; Rein, 1983b; Schön & Rein, 1994). And, as one of the earliest attempts to bring values and action into the heart of policy analysis, it has been invaluable as a critique of instrumentalist, scientistic approaches to policy analysis. Yet, frame analysis raises several problems.

First, the concept of frame is frustratingly ambiguous. Despite Rein's eloquent conceptualizations and the elaborate methodological prescriptions in the Gamson and Modigliani paper, it is still unclear when to call a frame a frame. The frame concept does not contain recognition rules that unambiguously hook it into the world of policy contestation. This then raises the question, what is it exactly that the analysts identifies when he "finds" frames? Differently put, the epistemic status of frames is unclear. Are frames actually *in* social reality to be discovered and found by the analyst who uses the proper methods? Or are frames a conceptual shorthand for an interpretation *about* social reality; an interpretation we impose on an otherwise formless flow of events? (Fay, 1996 178, 190). The first position is called meaning realism, the second meaning constructivism.

Frame analysis, and by extension this applies in lesser or larger measure to all forms of policy interpretation based on hermeneutic meaning, tend to adopt a meaning realist position. *Meaning realism,* as we saw in chapter 4, is the position that "meanings are fixed entities that can be discovered and that exist independent of the interpreter" (Schwandt, 2000). For example, Gamson and Modigliani claim they identify "packages," but that is what they set out to find in the first place. Differently put, packages are pre-assumptions. There is nothing inherently wrong with that. In one important theory of meaning, as we saw in chapter 2, interpretations are "party dependent," as Taylor calls it (2002)—the product of the interaction of an interpreter with the interpreted and for that reason always closely tied to the goals, understandings, and beliefs of the interpreter. But this insight sits uneasily with the realist claim inherent in the frame/package concept, that the perspectives through which experience is interpreted are enduring. This is a widely shared assumption that also characterizes, for example, the advocacy coalition framework of Sabatier or the idea of tradition in Bevir and Rhodes's interpretivism. In fact, for concepts such as frames to do the work that they are supposed to do, they need to be enduring. It wouldn't make sense to explain the stubbornness of policy controversy if it was based on the quicksand of some ephemeral idea or presupposition that could be different tomorrow than it is today. Hence Gamson and Modigliani's decision to keep the package labels constant throughout thirty years of intense public debate of nuclear power and despite considerable changes in the argumentative composition of the packages. Hence, also, their decision to identify ever more new packages instead of, for example, considering some of them as adjustments of existing interpretive schemes. The unstated assumption of the need to identify frames or packages is that social reality is organized by means of orderly, stable, clearly identifiable meaning structures. Through the skillful application of method these meanings can be identified by the analyst. It is the exegetic impulse that characterizes classical, objective hermeneutics.

But one could also argue that the metaphors, images, and statements point to analytic predispositions of the interpreter. In line with Gamson and Modigliani's own argument that people's interpretations "are constantly revised and updated to accommodate new events" (1989, 2), the issue culture can be portrayed as much more open and fluid than it is in their paper. In fact, it is not so far-fetched to imagine someone who believes in scientific progress, but, under the influence of Chernobyl, has some unresolved doubts about nuclear safety, without the need to solidify this "ebb and flow" into solid perspectives. Even the common recourse to unchanging "core values" will not do, as values change color the moment that they are effectuated. A deep belief in technological progress "means" something else in the context of, let's say, the dissemination of the Internet, than in the realm of nuclear power.

In actual practice, the hermeneutic search for "frames" or "meaning" almost inevitably acquires a meaning realist character. This tendency is reinforced by the linguistic reductionism that slips into the methods for detecting frames. As the Gamson and Modigliani paper shows, frames are made up of linguistic and pictorial signs. This exegetic approach to frames denies the action dimension of framing. Clearly people interpret experience, and they do that from within a conceptual and valuative framework. However, the interpretations and understandings they arrive at are momentary, provisional resting places in the ongoing process of negotiating a particular slice of reality. Frames are closely tied to our acting in the world. This colors the nature of interpretation. We interpret in a landscape of action. Or, in the language of chapter 4, framing accompanies our intervening in the world. Our interpretations, and the perspectives that inform our interpretations, can be swayed by unforeseen external events, by encounters with others, by the way the world talks back after we act upon it, by reflecting on our own experiences, or all of the above. These interpretations have an ineluctable element of coming into being, of emerging, along an arrow of emerging time. And when they find linguistic expression, in statements, metaphors, catchphrases, or similes, we realize and actualize this process of coming into being (Schwandt, 2000, 198). Even more importantly, the way we identify perspectives depends in large measure upon the one who is doing the interpreting. Instead of frames being out there in the world, they emerge to a large extent from the interaction of interpreter and interpreted. Frames are relative to an interpreter (Fay, 1996, 142). Differently put, meaning is as much in the act of interpretation as it is in the object to be interpreted. The action dimension of frames pushes you into this position. This important insight is easily lost in some versions of frame analysis.[16]

I will briefly note two additional problems with frame analysis. The first regards the "critical" in "value-critical policy analysis." To criticize frames or policy positions requires some standard of judgment outside the interplay of frames. But this collides with the self-professed epistemology of frames. Frames are ways of world making. They provide the interpretive schemes that enable us to discern meaningful social phenomena in the first place. Differently put, there is no Archimedean, frame-independent point from which we can assess frames. (In practice, of course, the analyst tacitly assumes this position, keeping himself, in a meaning realist manner, apart from any of the frames he detects.) Although the articulation of the implicit presuppositions that inform policy positions is a critical act in itself (as we saw in our discussion of qualitative policy research), it is unclear what interpretive position he occupies. Unless he speaks from hidden assumptions himself, he simply cannot make any evaluative statements about frames.[17] Part of the problem, and this is my second point, is that frame analysis, similar to qualitative policy research, lacks a theory of power. While it can be critically important to "probe the categories of people's thoughts, examining where these thoughts come from, where they lead, and what ambiguities and inconsistencies they contain" (Rein, 1983a, 101), where these concern a hegemonic policy solution, frame analysis cannot reveal why a particular solution has become hegemonic in the first place.

Interestingly enough, in his later work with Schön, Rein is strongly aware of the "relativist trap" that exegetic frame analysis leads him into, and he puts the question of how to make informed, reasonable judgments of the plausibility of competing frames without fixed, foundational criteria, at the center of his analytic approach. Rein and Schön suggest a number of solutions that not only radically transform the aims and analytical thrust of frame analysis, but also give the pragmatist heritage a much more prominent position in the frame concept. In fact, as we will see, in its 1990s reformulation, frame analysis has become a dialogical approach to interpretive policy analysis.

A final comment. Frames and framing have become "an idea in good currency" in contemporary interpretive policy analysis. Many panels and workshops are devoted to frames. Perhaps it is better to speak of concept inflation, because it is often not clear what is meant by frames in these contexts. Frames, metaphors, narratives are all mentioned in one breath. What is left is the statement that positions and beliefs in public policy are relative to a perspective. Hardly a reason to pay the registration fee for the conference. It goes to show that concepts must be handled with care when they are used outside their original context. In the hands of its originator, frames were tied to a particular project: to explain intractable policy controversies. This gave the concept a particular content, particularly the focus on action. I do not want to argue that concepts cannot undergo changes. But these must follow from different projects, which in their turn shape the concept. In Rein's original formulation the action dimension was central to frames. In the later reformulation with Schön it became even more important. To my mind to take the action out of frames is like taking sexuality out of *Don Giovanni*. What we are left with is Salieri, not Mozart.

INTERPRETING GOVERNANCE

Exposition

Over the last decade the British political scientists Bevir and Rhodes have written a number of influential texts on interpretive political science. I discuss their approach because it has obvious relevance to policy interpretation. In contrast to qualitative policy research and frame analysis the Bevir and Rhodes approach is attuned to more contemporary conceptions of networked governance and rests on a more sophisticated philosophical foundation. In a short autobiographical note Bevir characterizes this approach as a "distinctive interpretive theory" that he developed from his work in the philosophy of intellectual history and subsequently applied "across the humanities and social sciences" (2006, 281). In their main text, *Interpreting British Governance* (2003), the authors position their approach in opposition to traditional political science by calling it anti-foundational (2003, 1). The basic categories of traditional political science (and the same applies to policy analysis) such as institutions, problems, programs, networks, power, or governance are reified, they argue.

Take the ubiquitous concept of institutions. In traditional political science institutions exhibit fixed operating procedures and rules that constrain and determine people's activities in pre-given, nonproblematical ways (2003, 63). However, as Bevir and Rhodes point out, in many analyses, institutions do not completely fix actions. There are national and local variations, unintended consequences abound, and culture is brought in to explain the differences. In other words, the concept of institutions (or for that matter, policy program, rule, or network) is "fatally ambiguous" (ibid.). For this reason, Bevir and Rhodes prefer to explain institutions as the contingent products of actors' ongoing actions, struggles, and negotiations. They summarize their decentered version of interpretivism as follows:

> To decentre governance is . . . to focus on the social construction of policy networks through the ability of individuals to create meaning. A decentred approach changes our view of governance. It encourages us to examine the ways in which individuals create, sustain and modify social life, institutions, and policies. It encourages us to recognize that institutional norms—or some logic of modernization—do not fix the actions of individuals. They arise from the beliefs individuals adopt against the background of traditions and in response to dilemmas. . . .
>
> [S]ince people confront these dilemmas in diverse traditions, there arises a political contest over what constitutes the nature of these failings and what should be done about them. . . . So any reform must be understood as the contingent product of a contest of meaning in action. . . . [A] decentred approach implies that governance arises from the bottom up. (2006b, 98–99)

As this quote shows, Bevir and Rhodes's "distinctive interpretive theory" centers on three concepts: *tradition, dilemma,* and *decenteredness.* (And a "sympathy for bottom-up inquiry." I come back to that [Bevir and Rhodes, 2006a, 3].) They argue the case for interpretation by stating two key assumptions: (1) people act on their beliefs and preferences, and (2) we cannot infer people's beliefs and preferences from objective facts about them (such as income level) or general assumptions (such as the rationality of human actors) (2003, 19). Taken together these two premises lead to the conclusion that we cannot get around interpretation in political science.

Bevir and Rhodes's version of interpretive policy analysis is theoretically perceptive in its awareness of the strengths and weaknesses of the family of interpretive approaches. In fact, it explicitly announces itself as a "third way" (my term) between hermeneutics and poststructuralism (2003, 31).[18] Although indebted to both of these approaches, it attempts to avoid some of the problems that the authors ascribe to both of them.[19] The authors are sympathetic to the decentered approach of poststructuralists such as Foucault, who see meaning as emerging from an almost randomly thrown together assemblage of practices, beliefs, and meanings that makes the very existence of certain social categories possible. To understand a social object or a particular behavior is to interpret it in the wider "discourse" that makes that object of behavior possible (2003, 23). However, they reject the poststructuralists' hostility toward the role of human agency in social affairs, which makes these approaches "come dangerously close to denying any scope to the subject and reason" (2003, 43). On the other hand, the authors also try to stay clear of the individualistic assumptions of classical hermeneutics. As they see it, hermeneutics departs from an epistemologically dubious subjectivity and essentialism (all-knowledgeable, autonomous subjects who "think and act according solely to their own reasons and commands" [2003, 32]), so that this approach can "come dangerously close to embodying an analysis of the subject as autonomous and an analysis of reason as pure and universal" (ibid.). They summarize their position by distinguishing between autonomy and agency. While autonomous individuals, "at least in principle," can act and think outside any context (I'm not sure how to imagine this), agents have freedom to act in novel ways but always situated within cultural and historical contexts that shape their thoughts and actions (Bevir and Rhodes, 2006a, 4).

Key to Bevir and Rhodes's third way of policy interpretation is the notion of decenteredness. This term may easily give rise to misunderstanding. Decenteredness does *not* refer to the currently much-discussed displacement of the policy process to networks of actors inside and outside the traditional realm of the state. While the emergence of the idea of policy networks is certainly the backdrop to their decentered approach, what they have in mind is a focus on practices of governance in which actors of all stripes understand issues and attempt to solve them by interpreting the situation at hand:

> While many political scientists have lost faith in the Westminster model of British Government, their alternative accounts of governance focus on the allegedly objective characteristics of policy networks and the oligopoly of the political marketplace. Their accounts stress topics such as power-dependence, the independence of networks, the relationship of policy outcomes to the size of networks, and the strategies by which the center might steer networks. To decentre governance is, in contrast to focus on the social construction of policy networks through the ability of individuals to create meanings. A decentred approach changes our view of governance. It encourages us to examine the ways in which individuals create, sustain, and modify social life, institutions and policies. It encourages us to recognize that institutional norms—or some logic of modernization—do not fix the actions of individuals. They arise from the beliefs that people adopt against the background of traditions and in response to dilemmas. (Bevir & Rhodes, 2006b, 98)

Decenteredness, thus, does not refer to the fragmentation of the policy arena. That would amount to a reification of policy networks. Instead, by calling governance decentered, Bevir and Rhodes refer to the differentiation of meaning, or to the "various contingent meanings informing the actions of the relevant individuals" (2003, 62).

Bevir and Rhodes introduce the concept of "tradition" to balance agency and determinism in understanding intention and meaning in the world of politics. The central place of tradition follows from their philosophical account of interpretive—or as Bevir calls it, "narrative"—explanation. An interpretive explanation, according to Bevir, "relates actions to the beliefs and desires that produce them" (2006, 286). The connections between belief, action, and the desire fulfilled by the action are conditioned by a particular social context or "tradition." We hold the beliefs we have and act upon them in a certain manner because we are immersed in a particular tradition. Bevir and Rhodes define a tradition as "a set of understandings someone receives during socialization" (2006a, 7). They prefer the concept of tradition over such related concepts as language, paradigm, or *epistéme* to emphasize the reciprocal relationship between social context and individual actors: although traditions shape the activities of individuals, in the end they are also the product of individual activity (Bevir, 2006, 288). As Bevir and Rhodes explain:

> [W]e do not imply that tradition is constitutive of the beliefs that people later come to hold or the actions they then perform. Instead, we see tradition mainly as a first influence on

people. The content of the tradition will appear in their later actions only if their situated agency has not led them to change it, and every part of it is, in principle, open to change. . . . [W]hen we stress situated agency, we suggest that social contexts only ever influence, as distinct from govern, the nature of individuals. We suggest that traditions are themselves products of situated agency. (2006a, 7–8)

For a tradition to be a tradition, it must be passed on from one generation to the next. It must express some minimal continuity that people can be socialized into. Also, not just any jumble of beliefs counts as a tradition. There must be some consistency, some coherence in the conceptual links between the beliefs (Bevir, 2006, 288; Bevir and Rhodes, 2006a, 9). Yet Bevir and Rhodes take pains not to reify tradition. (Whether they have succeeded in this we will see later.) Social scientists tend to think about tradition in an essentialist manner—as a fixed set of core beliefs that determines people's beliefs and actions.[20] Or, traditions are seen as existing independently of the beliefs and actions of people, waiting for people to discover and embrace them, like they would join a religion. Rather, according to Bevir and Rhodes, traditions are "contingent products of the way in which people develop specific beliefs, preferences and actions" (2003, 34). A tradition is not a cultural prison, but an "initial influence" on people that "colors their later actions." Traditions emerge from "local reasoning" and "micro-practices" (2003, 35). Whenever the situation calls for it, people may feel the need to alter traditions. Thus Bevir and Rhodes carefully balance intentionalism (in which meanings spring from the purposes and preferences of the actor) with a broader interpretivism (in which meanings are situated in the larger context of the actor's environment).

How do traditions change? They change because actors struggle with "dilemmas." Sometimes an external pressure, a challenge that is thrown up by some event, a particular moral understanding, or a new idea comes to stand in opposition to the traditional web of beliefs. Sticking to their nonessentialist program, the authors emphasize that dilemmas are not hardwired into reality: "A dilemma arises for an individual or institution when a new idea stands in opposition to existing beliefs or practices and so forces a reconsideration of these existing beliefs and associated traditions" (2003, 36). Dilemmas may arise from people's experiences, but this need not be the case. "Dilemmas can arise from both theoretical and moral reflection and from experiences of worldly pressures" (2003, 36). The point is that traditions and dilemmas are both defined in a constructionist way: "What matters, in other words, is the subjective, or more usually, inter-subjective understandings of political actors, not our academic accounts of real pressures in the world" (ibid.). Traditions, dilemmas, and local practices are mutually constitutive: "Because people confront these dilemmas in diverse traditions, there arises a political contest over what constitutes the nature of the failings and what should be done about them" (2003, 64). This then raises the issue of how the analyst "recognizes" dilemmas and traditions. I will return to that shortly.

Methodologically, Bevir and Rhodes propagate the ethnographic approach that scholars such as Geertz and Prus argue for so persuasively. Decentered studies of political phenomena require that we "build a multifaceted picture of how the several actors understand and construct" the phenomenon. We should not expect to find one overarching truth, but rather a fundamentally pluralistic world; a world made up of "narratives about how . . . people understand what they are doing in networks, where these understandings usually both overlap and conflict with one another" (2003, 66). Ethnographic research enables the analyst "to get below and behind the surface of official accounts by providing texture, depth, and nuance." It also allows interviewees to "explain the meaning of their actions, providing insights that can only come from the main characters involved in the story" (2006b, 101).

This multifaceted picture is constructed through "ethnographic studies of individual behaviour in everyday contexts" (2003, 77). However, interpretive analysis of governance should also include historical and comparative analysis. Ethnographic analysis alone fails to capture the force of tradition, either at a historical moment in time or in a particular culture. Bevir and Rhodes use a famous paper by the Danish policy analysts Bang and Sørensen, "The Everyday Maker," to argue for their more inclusive version of interpretive analysis (Bang & Sørensen, 1999). In this paper Bang and Sørensen claim to have detected a new kind of active citizen who operates outside the usual political or party categories. Based on ethnographic research in the Nørrebro district in Copenhagen, they find citizens who act in shifting alliances on concrete issues, sometimes with, but often independent of, government. Bevir and Rhodes draw two lessons from their critique of the Bang and Sørensen paper. First, they say that ethnographic analysis should not be restricted to bottom-up analysis. It should also include the various levels of administrators in the Copenhagen city government, elected officials, and other stakeholders such as housing corporations, hospitals, or schools. Not only will the experiences of these stakeholders differ from those of the citizens, but the stakeholders will also have an influence on the way that issues present themselves to the citizens and on the constraints and possibilities for dealing with these issues. In other words, there is no unified "true account of the issues in Nørrebro." Second, Bevir and Rhodes conclude, Bang and Sørensen's microanalysis of Nørrebro prevents them from seeing the activist reputation—call it tradition—of this district, even within a society that is itself famous for its tradition of high levels of citizen participation and consensual modes of conflict resolution in local governance networks.

The upshot is that in its emphasis on ethnographic research about the relevant policy actors, Bevir and Rhodes's methodological prescription shows remarkable similarities to qualitative policy analysis. (Although they also engage in historical analysis.) Where it differs is in its sophisticated philosophical rationale, and—yes—the disciplinary tradition in which they themselves work. Here is another example of the confluence of research and theory that I mentioned in chapter 1 as characteristic of interpretive analysis. Although qualitative policy analysts and researchers working in the Bevir and Rhodes tradition would on the surface engage in almost identical activities, their analysis, in its object of research, its leading questions, and its focus on data analysis, would, in all likelihood, be quite different, shaped as it is by different philosophical assumptions and disciplinary tradition. In contrast to qualitative policy analysis, Bevir and Rhodes focus on the traditional questions of political science: democratic governance in a context of institutions, rules, and political doctrine. To this traditional agenda they bring a sophisticated, interpretive approach that is wholly in tune with the pluralistic and fragmented character of contemporary government.

Finally, Bevir and Rhodes explicitly address the question of how their version of policy interpretation can contribute to policy advice. Their answer demonstrates sensitivity to the indeterministic implications of their notion of decenteredness. Traditional policy analysis, as embedded in the institutional framework of the liberal-democratic state, seeks to improve the ability to manage societal sectors. Institutions, markets, and networks are considered as fixed entities that can be manipulated by using the right policy instruments (2006b, 103). The ontological assumptions of the interpretive approach have effectively "undercut" the traditional managerial approach. The main reason seems to be that the key assumption of decenteredness introduces an ineluctable element of indeterminacy and happenstance into governance:

> Since traditions and practices are not fixed, we cannot know in advance how people will develop their beliefs and actions in response to a dilemma. Therefore, political scientists cannot predict how people will respond to a dilemma. . . . [A]ll they can offer are informed conjectures that seek to explain practices and actions by pointing to the conditional con-

nections between actions, beliefs, traditions, and dilemmas. Their conjectures are stories, understood as provisional narratives about possible futures. . . .

[W]hile statistics, models, and claims to expertise can have a place in such stories, we should not become too preoccupied with them. Instead, we should recognize that they too are narratives about how people have acted or will react given their beliefs and desires. No matter what rigour or expertise we bring to bear, all we can do is to tell a story and judge what the future might bring. (2006b, 103)

This is an important statement, although I disagree that telling stories is the only thing we can do in the face of the indeterminacy and deep pluralism of the world of public policy. In the chapters on discursive and dialogical meaning I will show that a much wider repertoire of strategies exists to harness the existential uncertainties that are thrown up by a pluralistic, dispersed policy field. However, in their willingness to take their interpretive approach beyond policy research, to address the practical-normative question of policy analysis head on, and to face up to the implications of their constructivist approach for traditional notions of policy making and policy advice, they again show themselves to be ahead of the interpretive pack. Bevir and Rhodes's approach to policy interpretation is an important addition to the family of interpretive approaches that has not yet yielded all of its possibilities yet. However, it is also suffers from a number of problems that, although they do not detract from the sophistication and richness of the authors' approach, should be taken seriously as they lead to a certain partiality in the analysis. These problems can all be traced to Bevir and Rhodes's unbending hermeneutic universalism; their position that whatever we experience must be the product of interpretation "all the way down" (2006a, 2); and their tendency, similar to the other two versions of hermeneutic policy interpretation, to "textualize" social reality. But let's first see how policy interpretation in the manner of Bevir and Rhodes holds up in its practical application.

Examples

Bevir and Rhodes provide various examples of their approach in their two main books. Illustrative for their approach is their treatment of the always-popular concept of governance. The traditional approach to networks, according to Bevir and Rhodes, is empiricist. Policy networks are described in the literature by their supposedly objective characteristics:

Current positivist approaches to governance . . . stress topics such as power-dependence, the independence of networks, the relationships of the size of networks to policy outcomes and the strategies by which the centre might steer networks. To decentre governance is, in contrast, to focus on the social construction of policy networks through the ability of individuals to create meaning. (2006a, 75)

The emergence of policy networks is usually explained by referring to some inexorable logic of modernization or changing institutional challenges (2006a, 85). Instead Bevir and Rhodes see governance as a much more diffuse concept that "arises from the bottom up": "Governance is a product of diverse practices that are themselves composed of multiple individuals acting on all sorts of conflicting beliefs which they have reached against the background of a range of traditions and in response to varied dilemmas" (2006a, 76).

Bevir and Rhodes discern four main narratives of British governance: intermediate institutions, networks of communities, reinventing the constitution, and joined-up government. These narratives correspond respectively with the Tory, Liberal, Whig, and Socialist traditions in British politics. The authors claim that the beliefs that make up these narratives are shared by academics and officials alike (2006a, 79). It would go too far to describe in detail all four of these versions of governance. So let's take a closer look at one of them: the socialist one. Governance, according to the socialist tradition, is a reaction both to the old Fabian, centralized, top-down, command-style bureaucracy and the New Right's forceful rejection of that style of government. In response to these challenges New Labour, in the 1980s, formulated a set of ideas and practices that came to be known as the Third Way. The Third Way was the response of social democratic parties in a number of countries to a complicated set of challenges. The Third Way was the "logo" for a new master narrative that signified "a reconfiguration of relationships between economy and state, public and private, government and people" (Newman, 2001). The political context of the Third Way consisted of the traumatic experience of stagflation (the combination of high inflation and high unemployment) in many Western countries in the 1970s, the unbridled growth of the public sector in combination with the belief that the state was overloaded, and the belief that the cradle-to-grave welfare state created dependency and a concomitant loss of personal initiative and community among its beneficiaries. These threats and challenges spurred the New Right revolution of U.S. president Reagan and British prime minister Thatcher with their emphasis on downsizing the state, monetarist and supply-side instead of Keynesian economic policy, and intense government reform.

The British version of the Third Way was, of course, influenced by specific national circumstances. As Newman phrases it:

> [T]he trajectories of reform in continental Western Europe and the UK showed important differences. The political context of the UK—the dominance of class politics, the rise of Thatcherism, the conflict between the state and the trade unions, and the long failure of Labour to gain electoral success—shaped Labour's attempt to forge a new political settlement. Here the Third Way can be viewed as an attempt to carve out a territory which distanced "new" from "old" Labour while rejecting the worst excesses of the neo-liberal politics of the "new right." (2001, 41)

New Labour hitches on to several of the New Right's ideas about effective government, such as an emphasis on individual choice and some features of new public management. However, it rejected the marketization of public services and instead opted for networks that enable public and private organizations to collaborate (Bevir & Rhodes, 2006a, 84). Bevir and Rhodes single out "trust" as the driving value behind the collaboration in the public sector. Trust signifies the recognition of the interdependence of individuals in our society, and the preference for collaboration instead of competition. The key term in the socialist version of governance is "joined-up government": "The term covers both horizontal joining-up between central departments and vertical joining-up between all the agencies involved in delivering services. . . . The state is an enabling partner that joins and steers flexible networks" (ibid.).

The conclusion is that "governance arises only as the differing constructions of several traditions." Starting in the 1970s, politicians began to react to the "dilemma of overload" by involving individuals in the process of governing. While conservative politicians appealed to individuals' role in the community, and liberals sought to involve them in markets, socialists saw individuals as participating in partnerships and networks (2006a, 85).

However, I want to present a study by Sullivan, a policy scholar, to illustrate what the British approach to interpretation can mean for policy analysis (Sullivan, 2007). Sullivan's study is about leadership in local government. As in many advanced democracies, the emergence of powerful new actors—such as housing corporations, large service-delivery agencies, and citizen associations—in addition to traditional political and corporate actors, has made governing in an urban environment exceedingly complex. Effectiveness in governing now hinges on the ability to collaborate "across boundaries" of interest, ethnicity, power, and belief (Sullivan & Skelcher, 2002). Sullivan argues that the situation of "governing through multiple modes and responding to the demands of diverse 'publics'" has generated a considerable interest in "appropriate forms of leadership." The standard image of leadership is that of "leaders" inducing, rousing, or summoning up followers. But how should leadership be defined in these dispersed governance situations, which are so characteristic of contemporary urban governance? According to Sullivan, in the "current environment" the standard leader-follower dynamic is reversed: "Now there is a need to begin with the identification of community needs and wants, to broker agreement where there is conflict and to facilitate collaboration with partners in achieving goals" (2007, 142). However, despite considerable government interest in local leadership as expressed in several reports and white papers, policy makers and scholars remained divided over the precise meaning of the concept.

The emphasis on local leadership in New Labour's Local Government Modernization Agenda (LGMA) provided an opportunity for Sullivan to study manifestations of leadership in local governance. Different articulations of local leadership circulated in the implementation of the LGMA. To identify these Sullivan explicitly evokes Bevir and Rhodes's interpretivism. She hitches on the by-now-familiar interplay between individual actors, beliefs, and social contexts. Beliefs shape practices, which in turn influence the social contexts that may be evoked by traditions and ideologies. These beliefs can be accessed through the actors' narratives. As all narratives are incomplete, different and competing narratives operate in relation to the same set of events (2007, 144). To reconstruct the contingent pathways of ideology and tradition, Bevir and Rhodes propagate a combination of ethnographic, historical, and comparative analysis. Their aim is to link microanalysis to aggregate conceptualizations. We see a good bit of this methodological precept in Sullivan's study. After a short history of community leadership in its (British) political-historical context, she draws on different sources of evidence ("academic materials, government documents, findings from individual LGMA evaluations," surveys of local authority officers, and in-depth interviews with a range of actors) to reconstruct the conceptions of leadership that inform the implementation of the LGMA.

On the basis of these materials Sullivan identifies four "interpretations" of community leadership: "as a symbol of change, as a formalization of local government's enabling role, as an expression of citizens' 'voice,' and as an expedient device" (2007, 145). Each of these four articulations is characterized by five elements: "tradition of local government," "narrative of community leadership," "storyline," positive and negative "impact on local government" (ibid.). For example, leadership as "expression of citizen voice" is described as: "community empowerment" (tradition), "devolution" (narrative of community leadership), "better decision making and responsive services" (storyline), "stronger interactions with communities through multiple sites" (positive impact on local government), "challenge to elected members' legitimacy, conflict within communities" (negative impact) (ibid.).

To see how Sullivan builds her interpretations, let's walk through what is probably the best articulated of the four conceptualizations of community leadership: community leadership as the formalization of local government's enabling role. In this formulation of leadership, local government is seen as "shaping actions by others in conjunction with its own activities." Based on her own evaluation of the LGMA, she identifies three core elements of this conception of leadership: (1) "to set a strategic direction and to represent community priorities beyond the locality," (2) "the generation and/or harnessing of sufficient collaborative capacity among local actors to secure 'joined-up' action alongside innovations in taking actions," and (3) "involving citizens in the process of priority identification and delivery" (2007, 149). These three roles are part of a larger British narrative of community governance that Sullivan, drawing upon British scholarship of local government and democracy and her own work on local accountability, describes as follows:

> Local government must evolve to be "fit for purpose" in the 21st century, but contends that its inherent value secures its position as a leader. This value is associated with: the scope and scale of local government and the resulting potential to promote "community well-being" in various sites and at various levels; and the responsibilities contingent on the "democratic" nature of local government, specifically the responsibility to be both inclusive and representative of local views and to be both transparent and accountable in relation to decision making. This protection is rooted in the tradition of local self-government, which considers the protection and promotion of democracy and the delivery of locally appropriate services as equally important. (2007, 149)

Sullivan finds echoes of this tradition in a 1998 white paper from Britain's Department of the Environment, Transport, and the Regions titled "Modern Local Government" and in her evaluation of the LGMA. In the latter, respondents described local government's leadership role as "being in touch with communities" and "developing good relationships between partners" (2007, 149). Beliefs have consequences for people's choice of action, as Bevir and Rhodes argue. Sullivan sees evidence of this when she argues that the government's conception of community leadership in the LGMA "reflects the community governance narrative":

> The 2000 Local Government Act grants local authorities the power to take action to promote economic, social and environmental well-being, combined with a new duty to prepare local community strategies. Developing these community strategies is to be undertaken with partners through another mechanism, the local strategic partnership, and both are to be underpinned by public participation. (2007, 150)

Within local councils the belief in community governance led to organizational changes. The management team was no longer solely organized departmentally, but now also contained "strategic directors" who "work together more corporately" and no longer "within their own directorates and silos" (ibid.).

Finally, and in line with Bevir and Rhodes's emphasis on the inevitable dilemmas and incompleteness that actors working within a tradition face, Sullivan identifies three "unresolved issues" in the institutionalization of the community governance version of local leadership. The first is the ambivalent attitude of central government toward greater autonomy of local councils. The second was a concern among partners that local government leadership would turn into local government dominance. And the third was the disconnection of non-executive members of local councils from governance strategies that involved community participation (2007, 151).

Commentary

Sullivan's analysis of local leadership in British governance carefully draws upon a range of data and convincingly demonstrates her goal to show how "meaning is generated and communicated, and the consequences [that] the transmission of different meanings [have] for the material choices that institutions make" (2007, 158). Sullivan's analysis is also recommendable in its methodological transparency. It is easy to follow how she used her data to arrive at the four interpretations of leadership. But is this what the British approach to interpretivism is all about? At the end of their analysis of New Labour, Bevir and Rhodes describe the goals of their interpretive analysis as follows:

> Neo-liberals portray governance as the uniform outcome of policies, such as marketisation and the new public management, that allegedly are the inevitable result of global economic pressures. In contrast . . . [o]ur decentred theory suggests, first, the outcomes of policies such as marketisation are not uniform but rather reflect regional, national and local circumstances. It suggests, second, that pressures such as state overload are not given as brute facts but constructed as different dilemmas from within various traditions. And it suggests, third, that the policies a state adopts are not necessary responses to given pressures, but rather perceived solutions to one particular conception of these dilemmas, where adopting a set of solutions is a contingent outcome of a political contest. (2003, 139)

This is an elegant and insightful statement of the authors' program of interpreting governance. I am less sure to what extent the applicability of this program has been convincingly demonstrated in the cases they presented, or, for that matter, in Sullivan's analysis of local leadership. If we stick to Sullivan's case, little evidence has been presented in which the microlevel struggles of the relevant actors against the background of their specific circumstances contingently translate into reformulated doctrines or coherent traditions. In fact, the typology of leadership styles is quite similar to frame analysis. A confusing, opaque political phenomenon—local leadership—is organized by the analyst, on the basis of a careful analysis of a wide range of data, into a number of more or less discernable, stable types. Don't get me wrong. I believe that this is an important form of policy analysis, wholly within the classical hermeneutic tradition of clarifying meaning by placing it into a wider social or political context. My point is that this way of interpreting governance falls short of the three-point program that Bevir and Rhodes formulated above. Is this merely because the authors have offered us so far only a first glimpse of the possibilities of their interpretive approach? Or is this another case in which the actual application of the interpretive program lags behind its more developed theoretical underpinning? I don't intend to settle this question here, but I want to point out two problems that, given the authors' own examples, seem to confound the goals of their interpretive program: namely, the ontological fuzziness of the central notion of tradition, and a concomitant ambiguity of the central concept of practice.

In the various statements of their program Bevir and Rhodes again and again emphasize the anti-foundationalism of their interpretive approach. The standard concepts of political science should not be taken at face value, but must instead be seen as the contingent outcomes of the confrontation of people's beliefs and practices with dilemmas and challenges. Traditions are "contingent products" of people's beliefs and actions. Traditions emerge from local reasoning and micro-practices, as Bevir and Rhodes state over and over again. The purpose of this dialectic of individual action and larger belief structures that is at the heart of their concept of tradition is to escape from the alleged determinism of Foucauldian structuralism, and to maintain a healthy dose of agency in the analysis of governance. This is a commendable program, but their anti-foundationalism introduces an ineluctable element of ambiguity into the concept of tradition. On the one hand, traditions are observer-independent entities, or phenomena, out in the world that form the object of study. ("Traditions are contingent products of the ways in which people develop specific beliefs, preferences and actions" [2003, 34].) On the other hand, they are analytical categories that serve as an explanatory tool specifically tailored to the goals of the analyst. ("Political scientists construct traditions in ways appropriate to explaining the particular sets of beliefs and actions in which they are interested" [2003, 33].) In their examples, the authors vacillate between the two. Their analysis of Thatcherism (and of governance, as we saw) is mostly a categorization of the different understandings of the academic literature on the Thatcher reforms according to the four well-known but preconceived political traditions in Britain (Liberal, Tory, Whig, and Socialist). The four "narratives" are not based on any empirical inquiry into the way the Thatcher reforms were experienced by, say, local administrators, professionals at public service agencies, or residents in public housing projects. (See also Finlayson, 2004, 152.) Their analysis of the reforms by New Labour, however, trace the tortuous emergence of joined-up government as the result of labor officials struggling with a series of political dilemmas, policy problems, and the unintended consequences of Thatcherite reforms. I think that the problem is not conceptual (clearly traditions are always living traditions, subject to change and adaptation according to circumstances), but methodological: how does one research changing traditions? The answer would be: by linking micro-practices to larger belief structures, and vice versa. However, the authors' emphasis on narratives as the central analytic unit prevents them from doing just that. Let's look at some examples.

In their analysis of British governance since Thatcher, Bevir and Rhodes in their choice of analytical subject take over, wholesale, the disciplinary agenda of political science. Their focus is on political doctrine and shifting trends in governance and public administration. It is telling, for example, that the "data" for their analysis consist largely of the secondary literature on British political tradition. This has the unfortunate effects of not only bringing preconceived political categories into the analysis, but also uncritically adopting the analytic focus on political doctrine that is one of the hallmarks of the academic literature. But how important is political doctrine, or *a* political doctrine such as New Public Management, to the actors in inner-city Birmingham or in the National Health Service who struggle to get services delivered against a background of financial constraints and conflicting rules from the central office? I intend this as a real, not a rhetorical, question. There is a huge difference between policy as doctrine and policy as implemented. This is obviously a truism that is, alas, generally overlooked in political analysis. It is telling that the question is never even raised by the authors. It is quite likely that National Health Service physicians or local councillors on executive committees feel the impact of New Public Management, but it must be demonstrated how, in what ways. Instead, in Bevir and Rhodes's analysis the importance of the available doctrines is assumed rather than made the object of investigation.

Sullivan, on the other hand, seems to follow a more promising route. She does pay attention to the micro-statements of actors in the field, such as local councillors. However, her approach suffers from an undue reliance on texts. Although she never mentions the text metaphor in her study, she de facto applies it in the way her analysis unfolds. Although she mentions interviews and surveys as among her data sources, her typology of leadership styles is largely based on policy texts. Again, this is important work that does exactly what the hermeneutic approach promises: it clarifies ambiguous political phenomena. Moreover, the advantages of her study over the Bevir and Rhodes study of New Labour is that Sullivan's typology emerges from the data, and we have some guarantee that her leadership types accord with actors' experiences. Yet, what seems missing is a grasp of the real-world experiences of the parties who are involved in local governance. For example, Sullivan mentions that the elected members of local councils had little faith in the usefulness of local strategic partnerships, and, by implication, in the enabling leadership style of which local strategic partnerships were an expression. Does that mean that elected members embraced another leadership style? If so, what were the accompanying beliefs? And what were their micro-experiences that led to this attitude and these beliefs? What does this entail for the enabling leadership style as a discernable type of "tradition"? Is that type perhaps merely a product of policy reports detached from the everyday reality of governing? Or is this an example of the dilemmas that Bevir and Rhodes identify as the drivers of change?

One of the strengths of the Bang and Sørensen paper is that, steeped in careful ethnographic research, it convincingly challenged traditional disciplinary categories. The Everyday Makers seemed to be oblivious of the reach of local officers and city administrators. They operated outside political belief systems. Yet, they were a force in Copenhagen city politics. Politics, as a conceptual category, took on a new meaning, as an integral part of everyday life. Although Bevir and Rhodes are critical of the Bang and Sørensen paper, it does exactly what they exhort us to do: connect individual behavior with the larger context of beliefs in which this behavior is embedded. Perhaps Bang and Sørensen should have foregrounded the particular activist tradition of the Nørrebro district or the participatory tradition in Danish politics that, no doubt, has made the rise of the Everyday Maker possible. But their analysis does exactly what Bevir and Rhodes admonishes the analyst to do: explain from careful attendance to micro-behaviors how new patterns of acting and new belief systems come into being.

The ambiguous status of tradition in Bevir and Rhodes's approach to interpretivism follows from the equally ambiguous relation between action and belief in their work. A tradition, as they define it, is a set of understandings. In other words, traditions are in the head. The suggestion is that therefore they can be changed, if necessary; for example in response to a dilemma. This has the ring of idealism. In chapter 4 we concluded that certain "structural" features of social reality are the emergent property, the unintended consequence, of the (inter-) actions of individual actors. Although they are the outcome of individuals' actions, they are not necessarily willed by those actors. As we concluded in chapter 4, the notion of emergent property does justice to both the supra-individual character of social structures and its origin in individual purpose and action. To policy actors who intervene in the world these "structures" put up resistances. This is a different take than Bevir and Rhodes's notion of dilemmas. They write, "A dilemma arises for an individual or group when a new idea stands in opposition to existing beliefs or practices and so forces reconsideration of existing beliefs and associated tradition" (2006a, 9). Perhaps, I'm inclined to say. Most everyday resistances in the world of public policy do not challenge the actor's belief system. Let's say that we try out a program of involving citizens in community safety. The results are that few people participate and that the white, well-educated people dominate the discussions. Do we jettison our participatory program? No, we adjust it by involving a mediator or providing training to help citizens develop deliberative skills. (The example is taken from Fung, 2004.) Let's assume that we succeed this way in involving disadvantaged citizens. Can we call the program a success? Not necessarily. It turns out that the expectations of the police and the citizens about participation differ. Also, the participating city agencies, because of large organizational problems, are unable to follow up on the citizens' needs. (These examples are taken from my own research on citizen participation.) Do I now abandon my belief in citizen participation? Not so fast. Policy makers now question the choice of neighborhoods for the program. Because crime levels were low, perhaps the urgency was not high enough for participation to succeed. Let's try the experiment in another, high-crime neighborhood.

And so on. And so on. This is an example of the type of "conversation" between intention, design, and the world that ordinary policy making entails. Rarely do policy makers abandon their beliefs wholesale on the basis of the world "talking back." But, one could object, policy makers can be confronted with large shifts in the external environment (a huge economic crisis, a massive terrorist attack, a large wave of immigration) that change the conditions of possibility for their policies. The first objection must be subjected to empirical research. What seems large to an outsider might have a different meaning to the experienced policy maker. (He might find a way to keep the program going at a reduced scale despite the budget reductions.) What is a small and a system-threatening resistance—a dilemma in Bevir and Rhodes's vocabulary—is in the eye of the beholder.

Despite their talk of practices, Bevir and Rhodes focus on political doctrines. Their treatment of New Labour serves as an example. Although their description of the doctrine of New Labour is sophisticated, we don't get an understanding of how this doctrine fared in practice and therefore not of the multiple, conflicting influences that were exerted on New Labour (McAnulla, 2006, 129). For example, although New Labour preaches trust, cooperation in partnerships, stakeholder involvement, and devolution of power to local governments, in practice it often acted in a centralist, dirigiste manner. McAnulla concludes therefore that by disregarding the actual practices of New Labour, Bevir and Rhodes overlook "how both the practice of previous governments and their ideas have both impacted and constrained their successors":

> On gaining power, New Labour was thus conditioned by a variety of structural and discursive factors. It inherited a polity featured by resource inequalities and a centralized structure. Furthermore it was bequeathed a set of institutions imbued (to varying degrees) by neo-liberal, elitist and traditional "public service" discourses. Its interpretation of this context was mediated to an extent by "third way" ideas stressing the need for more decentralization, networks (rather than markets), and trust between partners. The influences of each of these conditions on the *agency* of New Labour can be inferred by an examination of the tensions and paradoxes in the white paper.[21] (McAnulla, 2006, 131)

Despite their repeated allusions to an interventionist vocabulary of practices, Bevir and Rhodes's "theory-in-use" is consistently representational. They are interested in the way political traditions influence beliefs and understandings. Theirs is a largely textual approach to politics. They want their approach to be "fruitful, progressive and open," and to "open up a wide range of new areas and styles of research" (2003, 200). In the way they challenge and open up self-evident ideas among policy makers and academics about governance, they certainly succeed in this aim.

QUESTIONS VERSUS PROBLEMS: THE NECESSARY PLACE OF CAUSAL EXPLANATION IN POLICY ANALYSIS

A final comment on policy hermeneutics. Hermeneutics was in the vanguard of the restructuring of social and political theory (Bernstein, 1976; Fay, 1975; Winch, 1958). The favored rhetorical figure was the antithesis between "bad" positivism and "good" hermeneutics. One couldn't have both in the social sciences. So it was said. As always the rhetoric concealed as much as it revealed. It was great in highlighting the meaning-based nature of social reality and its implications for systematic inquiry. However, with hindsight, the rhetoric was too restrictive and not productive in understanding the everyday nature of social reality. In everyday life we confront problems with a wider and more inclusive heuristic repertoire: describing, counting, storytelling, making value judgments and good guesses, going by our gut feeling, ascribing causality, and—yes—interpreting by situating phenomena in their proper context. Not just one of these but all of the above. It is the intuitive mix that tells us what to do and where to go, and that, sometimes, makes us wiser.

For policy analysis the polarization between causality and interpretation is misleading and near useless. Perhaps it has something to do with the fact that scholars, in academic settings, prefer to deal with questions while practitioners are confronted with problems. What is the difference? A question is a carefully tailored puzzle that can be solved with the concepts and methods the researcher has at his disposal. Usually a question is the result of a backward mapping that runs from a preferred method to a fitting question. A problem always has forward thrust. It engulfs you or hits you in the face. You have control over the first and have barely any over the second. The first is structured, the second resists structuring. The first can be pondered; the second requires urgent action—action that often has irreversible consequences, both for society and for the standing of the decision maker. The policy literature has come up with a number of terms that revolve around this distinction: tame versus wicked problems (Rittel & Webber, 1973), "hard-wiring versus soft-wiring challenges" (Stoker, 2006, 175). Policy makers and practitioners hold the short end of the straw in this distinction. They deal with problems, not questions. As policy analysts aspire to contribute to ameliorating problems, that should be their focus, too—the raw, confusing, thankless urgency as it presents itself to the policy maker.

Some scholars do just that. A few commendable examples: Public education in American cities is a policy-resistant mess. But some cities are more successful than others. Why is that? What can be done about it? (C.N. Stone, et al., 2001) Democracy is at risk in many countries. The number of voters is declining. Public participation is declining. Cynicism toward politicians is boiling over into populism. Why is that? What can be done about it? (Macedo et al., 2005) In the 1980s the number of homeless in American cities exploded. Whole families lived in shelters. Deranged people could be seen at street corners, shouting. Was it deinstitutionalization? Was it the restructuring of inner cities? What can be done about it? (Jencks, 1995). To find your bearings in big, unstructured social problems is always a mix of analysis and practical reasoning. The antithetic rhetoric of hermeneutics acts as a constraint in such cases of real-world policy analysis. It restricts the kinds of problems the analyst is willing to tackle and the analytic methods he prefers to use. To deal with structured questions only risks the yawn of "So what?" I'm not claiming that to reveal the symbolic value of a policy or the multiplicity of what on the surface looks like a monolithic concept is useless. Far from it. There is an undeniable critical element in this "unmasking the partiality of political interpretation" (Bevir & Rhodes, in Glynos & Howarth, 2007, 78). It reveals hidden cognitive constraints, opens up new perspectives, and unleashes creativity. However, analysts who have the stamina to deal with the problems of policy makers tend to stay closer to the world of practice, and keep open the promise of relevance.

The authors I mentioned above all use a wide repertoire of heuristics to hook their analyses in the overwhelming mass of empirical detail that constitutes the problem they address. When they describe and count to get a feel for the size and spread of the problem, they do it with an implicit ceteris paribus clause that presumes that we more or less agree on what school reform, homelessness, or democracy is. Not as a programmatic statement but a practical one. To get a deeper understanding of the issue they then might locate events in their proper context (for example, the different role of business in educational reform in Atlanta than in El Paso [C.N. Stone et al., 2001]) to grasp their particular meaning. To get an answer as to why certain events developed they way they did, they try to find causal relations. Causality? Yes, the antithesis of positivism and interpretivism has obscured the epistemic truism that, both in the social sciences and in everyday life, we regularly and reliably ascribe causality to social phenomena. Meanings describe what something is. But that doesn't tell us *why* something is. For example, when I describe the reasons a patient puts forward to return to the mental hospital, I have provided an intentional explanation of the event. This makes the readmission understandable. However, I have not provided a causal explanation of the rapid increase in readmissions that followed the transformation of mental hospitals into ambulatory care centers. For that I need to provide an explanation in which some condition c is shown to be a necessary and/or sufficient condition for the occurrence of the event *e*. If *e* could have happened without *c*, or vice versa, than *c* did not cause *e* (Elster, 1983, 27; Fay, 1996, 121).[22]

Causal explanations are couched in nonintentional terms. They are not reducible to the self-explanations of individuals, as Glynos and Howarth argue (2007, 86). This explains why causal and intentional explanations are generally seen as complementary. As Fay puts it, causal theories transcend the conceptual and cultural resources of individuals, "employing categories of thought and establishing connections about which these subjects are entirely ignorant" (1996, 123). For example, Lewis and I explained the rise in readmissions following deinstitutionalization as the result of the sudden disappearance of the nontherapeutic functions of the hospital (Wagenaar & Lewis, 1989). This is an explanation that transcends the intentions of individual actors because it proceeds by showing how restricting access to the hospital constrains (and enables) the behavior of other actors (Fay, 1996, 121). The explanation is in terms of the aggregate effects that are generated by the interactions of the many individuals involved and that exceed their individual intention or control.[23] Causal explanation requires that the researcher introduces his own analytic categories. "Self-interpretations" are not enough. We need both to grasp the "buzzing blooming confusion" of real world problems.

NOTES

1. A good example of the "clean-break-with-positivism" trope is the influential book *How Does a Policy Mean?* by Yanow (1996). It is probably not an overstatement to claim that this is one of the books that put the interpretive approach on the agenda in post-empiricist policy analysis. To many people, Yanow's approach to interpretation has become synonymous with interpretive policy analysis proper. The book's argument is cleverly organized around a puzzle: according to any instrumental criterion, such as efficacy or efficiency in reaching the policy's goal, the Israeli policy of creating community centers in new settlements in the 1970s was deemed a failure. Nevertheless, the policy remained well funded for more than twenty years and drew continuing support from a range of political actors in Israel. How could this be? According to traditional, instrumental standards of effectiveness and efficiency, this policy outcome was an anomaly. Yanow's answer to this "anomaly" is that in the context of Israeli society and Israeli politics, the policy had a particular *meaning* for key audiences. Yanow urges the policy analyst to become sensitive to the expressive, symbolic aspect of policy. Not as an add-on to the "real"—read: instrumental, material, power-related—aspects of policy making, but as an intrinsic aspect of each and every act of policy making. These meanings reside in all aspects of a policy; they are not just in the legislative texts that state the policy's intent, but also in the actions of key groups that implement the policy and in artifacts such as agency buildings, their furnishings, and, one could add today, their websites (Yanow, 1996). Policy interpretation is further expatiated in two additional publications by Yanow: a special issue of the journal *Policy Sciences* and a small book on how to conduct policy interpretation. In the introduction to the special issue, Yanow emphasizes that policy analysts must ask not only what a policy means but also *how* it means. That is, analysts must be sensitive to both the substantive content of meaning and to how it is conveyed to the intended audience (Yanow, 1995). She introduces the notion of social constructionism. Most of the things that policy analysts study are socially constructed "in their originating community in an ongoing process of daily re-creation, maintenance, and change. Meanings are never treated independently of the contexts of people doing and saying the things that created those meanings" (1995, 112). Yanow then warns that reality construction is "multiple" and "dynamic": "multiple stakeholders in the policy process engage in constructing and maintaining those images and ideas, as well as in changing them" (ibid.). Methodologically, interpretive policy analysis, according to Yanow, consists of the following elements: (1) identify the artifacts (language, objects, acts) that are the carriers of meaning; (2) identify the interpretive communities relevant to a policy that are the perceivers of this meaning; (3) identify the discourses through which these meanings are communicated; (4) identify any points of conflict that suggest that different groups attach divergent meanings to some aspect of a policy (Yanow, 2000).

2. The importance of Laws's paper resides in his reframing of what is usually seen as a dyadic relationship—between policy and research, or between research and practice—as a triadic relationship. This leads to a different conceptualization, not only of the contribution that social science research can make to policy and practice, but also of the nature and epistemology of research.

3. I return to the role of stories in public policy in chapter 8.

4. Notice the restricted comparison here. Why not see relations as "acting" or as "actions observed"? Winch makes the comparison this way because his aim is to move away from causal analysis in the social sciences. Ideas, like statements, are related logically and internally. By extension, the relation between meanings and the actions constituted by those meanings, and the relationships between actions, are not causal but "logical relations between propositions" (1958, 126). It needs no comment that in the light of the arguments in chapter 4, this is a curiously emaciated rendering of explanation in the social sciences. I will return to this important point at the end of this chapter.

5. Ricoeur's aim is to free social reality and social action from the situation of its origin. Or, differently put, to bring the interpretation of social reality into better accord with the hermeneutics of texts. In good structuralist fashion, method determines ontology here. The analogy for Ricoeur is the difference between, ephemeral, spoken words, which cannot be seen apart from the situation in which they are spoken, and, fixated, written texts that have an autonomous existence by transcending their origins. A systematic, scientific hermeneutics of social reality requires that the analyst move away from everyday meaning (the "immediate meaningfulness of the expressions of life for everyday transactions" [1977, 327]) by objectifying action: "My claim is that action itself, action as meaningful, may become an object of science, without losing its character of meaningfulness, through a kind of objectification similar to the fixation which occurs in writing. By this objectification, action is no longer a transaction to which the discourse of action would still belong. It constitutes a delineated pattern which has to be interpreted according to its inner connections" (1977, 322). For Ricoeur, objectification is the hallmark of a scientific hermeneutics. "The paradigm of text-interpretation" becomes the model for interpretive social science. With social reality objectified into a text, the delineation of meaning remains wholly within the system of textual signs and no longer relies on the interpretation of behavior, gestures, and the like (1977, 328). With his emphasis on meaning deriving from the interplay of textual signs, there are clear echoes of structuralism in Ricoeur's approach.

6. Granted, Yanow's text analogy is meant as a metaphor. (I'm less certain of Ricoeur.) But pressed for time and money in the everyday business of policy analysis, metaphors have a tendency to morph into convenient reality.

7. That relationship is not a simple one, as Taylor argues. It is neither a relationship of correspondence (texts simply describing preexisting actions or feelings), nor a naïve constructionist one where "thinking makes it so" (1985a, 26): "The situation we have here is one in which the vocabulary of a given social dimension is grounded in the shape of a social practice in this dimension; that is, the vocabulary wouldn't make sense, couldn't be applied sensibly, where this range of practices didn't prevail. And yet, this range of practices couldn't exist without the prevalence of this or some related vocabulary" (ibid., 33–34). Taylor finally settles for a dialectical relationship in which structures of meaning are never independent from our interpretation of them (ibid.). This gives rise to his much-quoted aphorism: "Man is a self-interpreting animal" (ibid.). I will return to the tricky relationship between language and social reality in my discussion of social constructivism in chapter 7.

8. Almost identical statements can be found twenty to thirty years later in the work of deLeon (1997) and Fischer (2003a, 2003b). Sobering conclusions indeed, which cry out for a Yanow-Hofmann type of analysis of the symbolic functions of social science in general and policy analysis in particular.

9. "I believe that values are the generalization of our situationally specific purposes." (Rein, 1983a, 87) And: "Facts derive their meaning from the values and purposes that inspire them" (ibid.)

10. Here Rein is inspired by Dewey pragmatist philosophy. The concept of frame draws philosophically on Dewey and Bentley's work *Knowing and the Known,* in particular their insistence on the importance of introducing action as an essential part of the knowing, naming, and thinking process" (Rein, 1983a, 97). In the 1994 book with Don Schön, the connection with Dewey's theory of inquiry is even more explicit (1994, 52). This is not the place to discuss this important and interesting angle to interpretive policy analysis in any detail, but suffice it to say that it has been insufficiently explored and deserves further investigation.

11. As Mary Hawkesworth describes "presupposition theory": "(P)erception depends on a constellation of theoretical presuppositions that structure observation, accrediting particular stimuli as significant and specific configurations as meaningful" (Hawkesworth, 1988, 49).

12. The world of public policy is littered with the ruins of cognitive dissonance. A good contemporary example is the stubborn denial by adherents of the public choice doctrine of the persistent, and often fatal, practical problems in implementing competitive schemes in the public sector. Time and again the initiators' goals are subverted when services become less accessible and more expensive because the promised market fails to materialize (Bobrow & Dryzek, 1987; Self, 1993).

13. Schön and Rein call these "institutional action frames" (1994).

14. The authors refer to Gamson and Modigliani (1989) for more detail on the sampling and coding process and the reliability procedures.

15. We will see the idea of cultural resonance again in Fairclough's concepts of "orders of discourse" and "intertextuality" in chapter 6. The idea is similar: certain perspectives seem self-evident, and gain dominance, because they fit wider cultural themes.

16. This paragraph can be read as a summary of dialogical meaning. I will return to this in chapter 8.

17. As Rein himself states: "Obviously one needs a frame to criticize a frame because we never start *de novo;* all knowledge is linked somehow to purpose" (1983a, 101). However, this statement is added as an afterthought to a description of what frame-critical analysis entails and is not further elaborated.

18. Or, as Bevir and Rhodes put it themselves, they stake out a middle position between hermeneutics and poststructuralism. On the one hand, "We have to redefine tradition in a non-essentialist, decentred manner to aid any lingering sense of objective reason." On the other hand, "While a rejection of the autonomous subject prevents a belief in a neutral or universal reason, the fact of agency enables us to accept local reasoning in a way that Foucault often seems reluctant to do" (2003, 35).

19. I will discuss structuralism and poststructuralism in chapter 6.

20. A good example of this way of thinking is Sabatier's concept of policy belief systems, a more or less stable core in his advocacy coalition framework.

21. This is the influential 1999 white paper *Modernising Government.*

22. This skates over a lot of complications. In addition to determinism, Elster mentions the principles of locality and temporal asymmetry as constitutive of causal explanation (1983, 28–32). In another work Elster discusses the notion, important for the social sciences, of causal mechanisms (Elster, 1999; Glynos & Howarth, 2007). The notion of causal mechanism introduces indeterminacy in causal explanation and thereby uncouples it from its association with prediction.

23. Strictly speaking this explanation of the sudden rise in readmissions is a functional explanation containing a causal explanation in that they are decoupled from intentions. As Elster puts it: "An institution or a behavioural pattern X is explained by its function Y for a group Z if and only if: (1) Y is an effect of X; (2) Y is beneficial for Z; (3) Y is unintended by the actors producing X; (4) Y—or at least the causal relation between X and Y—is unrecognised by the actors in Z; (5) Y maintains X by a causal feedback loop passing through Z" (1983, 57).

6

DISCURSIVE MEANING

MEANING AS THE INTERPLAY OF SIGNS: STRUCTURALISM AND POSTSTRUCTURALISM

Under the heading "Discursive Meaning" I will discuss a number of interpretive approaches that belong to the broad category of discourse analysis. Discourse analysis is anchored in a highly developed linguistic theory, which posits that meaning does not reside in the intentions of actors, but in the structural properties of the text. The tenor of discourse analysis is linguistic. But, as we will see, none in the family of discursive approaches is exclusively focused on language as they all give prominence to practices in the organization of human experience. Perhaps it is more precise to speak of a linguistic ontology than a theory. For, where hermeneutic approaches to policy interpretation used the notion of a text as a generative metaphor (and actual texts as data for interpretive analysis), discursive approaches depart from the much stronger assumption that experience, meaning, and our very notion of reality are determined by language. In a nutshell, one could say that in hermeneutic policy interpretation the world is mediated by language, while in discursive approaches it is produced by it. Producing or "constructing" reality, as the phrase commonly goes in interpretive analysis, is by no means an unproblematic concept, particularly when the claim is put forward that "reality" is constructed through language. The ease and frequency with which the notion of social constructionism is evoked in the interpretive literature has an inverse relationship to its underlying perplexities. In the next chapter I try to unpack some of the difficulties that surround the concept of social construction. In this chapter I momentarily defer these complications to discuss the all-important idea of discourse.

The linguistic theory underlying discursive meaning is known by the dual terms "structuralism" and "poststructuralism." They belong together as Siamese twins because the second is an answer to the shortcomings of the first. Few theories in the social sciences have spawned as much commentary and secondary literature as structuralism/poststructuralism. In the late 1960s and 1970s structuralism/poststructuralism and its two derivative ideas, deconstruction and discourse, swept as a tidal wave over the humanities and social sciences. It happened first in France, but quickly invaded the humanities and social sciences in the Anglo-Saxon world. This overwhelming popularity of what is essentially a rather arcane linguistic theory might seem surprising, but we will see that the analytical implications of structuralism/poststructuralism for our understanding of social and political reality are extensive indeed. It also doesn't hurt the case of structuralism/poststructuralism that, in its sustained attention to social systems and their effects on society, it extends a clear emancipatory and critical promise.[1] And through its formalism it—falsely—projected an image of objective science. Both the analytical implications and the critical promise have been articulated in their most systematic and sophisticated form in the discourse theories of Foucault and Laclau and Mouffe. The British social linguists Norman Fairclough and Ruth Wodak have elaborated a well-developed linguistic version of critical discourse analysis.

Structuralism and poststructuralism have in common that they consider meaning as immanent in language, or more broadly, symbolic systems. Structuralism is associated with the Swiss linguist Ferdinand de Saussure and the French anthropologist Claude Lévi-Strauss. Structuralism holds that the source of experience and meaning is not the individual but the architecture of symbolic-linguistic systems. This claim, and here we encounter one important challenge to mainstream political theory already, flies in the face of two widely held beliefs about human experience, namely that it is the product of the subjective experience of autonomous individuals or that it is the product of underlying a priori causes such as the economy, culture, or a dominating institutional influence such as the church or the state. To situate meaning in linguistic structure is less far-fetched than it may sound at first blush. In fact the basic idea has been suggested by theorists of different stripes who all have grappled with the age-old problem of the relation between language and reality, language and experience, or our well-known conundrum of structure and agency. So what is this basic idea?

In its most dressed-down form the basic structuralist idea is the insight that the meaning of a term is partly or wholly defined by the larger set of related terms. For example, the meaning of the term "mental patient" derives from its place in a system of related terms such as "normality," mental hospital," "psychiatrist," "schizophrenia," "psychosis," "dangerous," and so on. On an intuitive level this is easy to grasp. The basic idea in fact shows considerable similarities to the hermeneutic circle, which holds that the single meaning unit (words, concepts, actions) can only be understood in relation to the whole and vice versa. But this would be mistaken. Hermeneutical meaning is representationist. Words obtain their meaning from their association with ideas, which, ultimately, are themselves coupled with objects in the world. Ideas are the primary system of meaning; language is derivative (Gutting, 2001, 217–18).

In opposition to this, structuralism holds that no meaning or ideas exist prior to a system of signs. As a linguistic ontology, structuralism finds it most elaborate formulation in the work of Saussure. Saussure's ontological aspirations manifest themselves in his proposition that language is a system of signs that express ideas. Signs are bifocal. They unite a sound image (signifier) with a concept (signified) that the signifier designates. The relationship between signifier and signified is purely arbitrary, a convention of the particular language system (so the signified "dog" can be attached to the signifier "dog," "*hond*," "*chien*," "*cane*," etc.). What is revolutionary about this proposition, however, is that Saussure claims that the meaning of the sign does not arise from its pointing to an object in the world, but solely from its relation to other signs within the symbolic system itself. With this he extends the arbitrariness of signs to the very essence of the idea of meaning. The meaning of a term does not arise from it being connected in some way to a preverbal reality or world of ideas. Neither words nor ideas have meaning in themselves (Gutting, 2001, 218). Instead meaning derives from their relationship with other signs in a particular language system.[2]

Saussure extends his structural theory with two additional key principles that elaborate how the single meaning element relates to the whole. The first principle is that language is "form and not substance." This proposition must counter the misunderstanding that a signifier-signified unit acts as a discrete meaning entity. Instead, according to Saussure, the sign cannot be seen apart from the whole system of signs of which it is a part. Language is "a system of interdependent terms in which the value of each term results solely from the simultaneous presence of the others" (Saussure, in Howarth, 2000, 20). To illustrate this point, Saussure uses the analogy of the game of chess. A particular piece, let's say a knight, derives its "value" or "meaning" from the rules of the game and the formal relations it has with the other pieces.[3] Thus, a sign has no meaning outside the symbolic system in which it operates.

Saussure's second principle, that language consists of "differences without positive terms," spells out how signs acquire "value" or meaning. Signs are defined by the contrasts that are inherent in the system of elements that makes up the language. Meaning does not derive from some reality external to the language system, but solely from "conceptual and phonic differences that have issued from the system. The idea of phonic substance that a sign contains is of less importance than the other signs that surround it" (Gutting, 2001, 220; Howarth, 2000, 21). As Howarth summarizes it: "Thus in the formal and relational theory of language that Saussure advocates, the *identity* of any element is a product of the *differences* and *oppositions* established by the elements of the linguistic system" (2000, 22). Despite the considerable criticism that the structuralist conception of language attracted, the relational conception of meaning has survived as a key element of discourse analysis. It is central in the interplay of narrative elements in the analysis of stories, it is prominent in Foucault's concept of "discursive formation" (despite Foucault's qualms about structuralism), and it returns in the idea of relations of difference and equivalence in the critical discourse theory of Laclau and Mouffe. In fact, the idea that meaning resides solely in the play of the differences and consonances of the elements of a symbolic system is the key principle of discursive analysis. It is the shibboleth by which discursive analysis differentiates itself from hermeneutic meaning, which endows objects in the world with representationist meaning that can be accessed by interpreting the verbal or symbolic utterances of individual actors.

It is hard to overestimate the excitement that the structuralist theory of language generated among thinkers in the humanities and the social sciences at the time. Its ideas were "in the air"; its resonances were sensed far and wide. Language as a structured symbolic order came to be seen as the template for all sorts of social and psychological phenomena, such as social relations, kinship structures, religion, or the economy (Lévi-Strauss), and the unconscious (Jacques Lacan). Structuralism promised to reveal the deep structure of society, "the objective laws that govern human activity" (Dreyfus & Rabinow, 1983, xix), and to do this in a rigorous and universal manner.[4] It offered an alternative to humanist approaches to history and social analysis by banishing individual actors to the margins. Structuralism left no role for agency as individual agents were only acting out the hidden structural regularities of the symbolic order they inhabited. Structuralism provided a methodological program. Forget about the individual actor and his subjective experiences. Reveal the large, anonymous symbolic structures that govern individual behavior and consciousness. Describe their internal organization, their emergence, the way they produce social reality. As Paras, one of Foucault's chroniclers, summarizes the prevailing mood of the time:

> Meaning was not the sovereign creation of autonomous subjects. It was the surface effect of a "system" that preceded human existence. This system was to be understood as a set of relations that obtained, and underwent, transformation, independently of the elements that it linked. "Before all human existence, all human thought," Foucault said, "there must already be a knowledge, a system, that we are rediscovering." (2006, 29)

Also, it did not go unnoticed that structuralism contained strong resonances with Marxist theories of society. Both shared the idea of a deep structure that unbeknownst to individual actors determined the latter's activities, beliefs, aspirations, and consciousness. But structuralism reinvigorated Marxist-inspired critical analysis by offering an alternative to its outdated materialistic determinism. Louis Althusser, for example, avoided materialist determinism by projecting a set of structural forces (political, ideological, cultural) that add to the basic economic force in shaping the social "superstructure." Structuralism opened new avenues for the skeptically inclined social analyst. A reinvigorated "hermeneutics of suspicion" had appeared on the scene.

With hindsight Saussurian structuralism provided a remarkably static and self-contained model of language and society, and it didn't take long for its limitations to be articulated by a score of critics, foremost among them the French philosopher Jacques Derrida.[5] To summarize the work of Derrida is a daunting task in itself, not least for his hermetic, elliptical, "poetic" writing style, but more importantly, because it would lead us too far from the subject of this chapter: an exposition of approaches to discursive meaning in policy analysis.[6] Let me therefore summarize what came to be known as the poststructuralist critique of structuralism, under two headings that are pertinent to the subject of this chapter: the opening up of structuralist analysis to the inevitable indeterminacy that comes with language *use,* and the development of a concept of discourse.

Although Saussure did pay attention to language use, he failed to establish a convincing conceptual connection between the structure of the language system, on the one hand, and the give-and-take of language-in-action, on the other hand. Saussure famously distinguished between *langue* and *parole,* or between language as an ordered system of signs with lawlike properties and language as individual acts of speaking. He saw an essential symbolic order, an underlying system of rules, that makes individual language use possible. But Howarth rightly points out that with this underspecification of the relation between *langue* and *parole,* Saussure undercut his own structuralist purposes to "privilege form over substance." For, to make the system of signifiers and signified, of differences and oppositions, work as a means of communicating meaning in everyday situations, Saussure had to surreptitiously smuggle in autonomous free subjects. It is these unattached individual speakers who generate and appreciate the sentences and stories that are made up of the basic building blocks of the formal linguistic order, and hook these onto an intersubjective or material world outside *langue.*[7]

What Saussure failed to see—and Derrida pointed out—was that the system of differences that allegedly generates semantic meaning is not closed but instead contains a remarkable amount of slippage. Differences in the symbolic order do not just sit there waiting to be activated; they must be actively sought out and tested for their relevance or usability in a particular situation at hand. For example, if a child comes running into the house holding his arm and screaming that he has been stung by an animal, we first want to know what kind of animal. After we have established that it was not a bug or a spider, but a snake, we will want to know what kind of snake: the color, pattern, size of the head, and so forth. This small example points to two mechanisms that prove to be crucial in producing meaning through the interplay of differences. First, as Derrida pointed out, every choice of opposition or contrast (bee or spider? insect or snake? brown, narrow snake or broad, striped snake?) implies the deferral of other possible oppositions that might be relevant in other situations. In other words, every act of "meaning-making" rests not only on the selection of a particular pair of differences, but also on the set of deferred oppositions that is *not* selected, and from which it is also differentiated (Howarth, 2000, 41). Second, the reasons for settling for opposition X (brown, narrow snake or broad, striped snake) over Y or Z (bee or spider), is suggested by the particular context-of-use. In other words, to make *langue* workable at all as the precondition for language-in-use, the possibility of contextuality has to be built into it from the very start. And this is accomplished not by importing some prelinguistic order into the formal system of differences, but by acknowledging the essential role of the counterfactuals of deferred possibilities in the production of meaning through the interplay of opposites. Far from being a static, self-contained, and lawlike formal system of symbolic relations, *langue* is wide open to human intention and possibility and as a result rife with novelty and indeterminism.

This opening up of the formal symbolic order of differences and oppositions points toward a theory of discourse that provides an alternative to hermeneutic meaning. The introduction of agency and context in discursive structures makes *langue* essentially incomplete. Agency has the effect of diffusing forever the bonds between signs and meaning in language-in-use. Meanings are actualized in a specific context-in-use, depending on the particular historical circumstances and the specific intentions, challenges, and possibilities that actors face. Yet, the durability of the symbolic order in which actors realize themselves also constrains their horizon. Individuals are not wholly autonomous but at least partly determined by preexisting symbolic-linguistic structures. As we will see, this conceptualization of discourse offers a range of new insights on key issues in political thought, such as power, freedom, governance, state, and public policy.[8] In the hands of Foucault and Laclau and Mouffe this "poststructuralist" conception of discourse as a symbolic structure made up of contrasts and opposites, which simultaneously define the individual agent yet allow for a certain openness to the challenges and dilemmas of everyday reality, will become a powerful tool of social and political analysis. For example, the poststructuralist idea of discourse opens up the possibility of shifting the analytic attention from the implicit meaning of social practices to their effect on individual and society (Dreyfus & Rabinow, 1983, xxvii). It redefines power as dispersed and individuated, while freedom is never unattached but always born out of interaction with power (Moss, 1998, 5). And, government is seen not as the implementation of a priori goals by state actors, but instead as a particular political rationality that operates through the individual conduct and self-images of citizens.[9]

Poststructuralist analysis has entered policy analysis via the fashionable concept of discourse. Similar to narrative (see chapter 8), discourse has seen considerable inflation in circles of interpretive analysts. Discourse is an elusive concept, however, that covers a wide range of ideas and methods. Also, it is difficult to do an adequate discourse analysis of whatever stripe. The concept of discourse applies to sociolinguistic theories of language use out of which emerged the critical discourse analysis of Fairclough. It plays a central role in the work of Foucault in which, as we will see, it has evolving meanings. And discourse is central to the neo-Marxist theories of Laclau and Mouffe, in which it functions to explain positions of political domination and how these are threatened and sustained.

FOUCAULT: POWER, KNOWLEDGE, DISCOURSE

No text on interpretation in policy analysis can ignore Foucault. Not only did he formulate what is probably the most elaborate and sophisticated theory of discourse, but he also suggested many ways of applying this theory to political topics. Although he is perhaps best seen as a historian and philosopher, a large part of his substantive work concerns political topics, such as the development of regimes of power and regulation as exemplified in prisons and mental institutions, or the birth of the modern penal system. Some see him as a political philosopher who has offered startling insights into some of the key issues of political thought (Moss, 1998, 1). In a series of public lectures he delivered at the end of the 1970s at the Collège de France he discussed the emergence of the concept of the state, and in particular its signature political rationality, as we understand it in modern liberal democracies.[10] Perhaps his greatest substantive contribution to political science and the study of governance is in his "positive" theory of power. Instead of seeing power as a negative, repressive force, Foucault depicted power as bringing into being regimes of legitimate knowledge or "truth" and methods of surveillance. This positive, "productive" form of power is no longer considered the sole prerogative of the state. Instead it is dispersed over the professional classes who, in this way, become complicit in governing society. Power exerts its influence through the reciprocity of knowledge and domination. The effect is the politicization of everyday life, the inculcation in the population of a host of internalized practices and ways of speaking that normalize certain categories of behaving and thinking. This insight that knowledge is complicit with power is of course highly pertinent to the discipline of policy analysis, which, after all, has the ambition of improving collective decision making through better knowledge. To my mind, Foucault's ideas on the reciprocity of power and knowledge suggest an ethical stance that I believe is uniquely relevant to the formulation of a critical policy analysis. I will return to this point in the commentary at the end of the section on Foucault.

One way in which Foucault has extended and applied his power concept is in his notion of *governmentality*. The concept connotes both the gradual development of a peculiar, dispersed mode of governing in modern liberal societies that acts through the regulation and self-regulation of individuals and populations, and the expansion of this style of governing to ever more reaches of society. It has long been thought that the term "governmentality" is a neologism that Foucault cooked up to combine the connotation of government (*gouverner*) with that of a particular disposition toward or mentality of governing (*mentalité*).[11] Lemke argues, however, that *gouvernmentalité* is simply the noun of the adjective *gouvernmental*. Foucault put it forward to distinguish his theory of governing from traditional theories of government that centered on state sovereignty (*souveraineté*) (Lemke, 2007, 13). Both of these concepts, the power-knowledge nexus and governmentality, have led to the formulation of a highly interesting and important approach to political analysis by a number of German and Anglo-Saxon scholars such as Lemke, Rose, Miller, and Dean. Given its obvious relevance to interpretive policy analysis, I will discuss the governmentality approach in a separate section.

However, to summarize the relevance of Foucault to interpretive policy analysis is a daunting task. Not only did he publish, in his abbreviated career, a formidable number of books and collections of articles, course notes, speeches, discussions, and interviews of remarkable range, depth, and originality, but he is one of those rare thinkers who are willing to question and drastically reformulate their earlier ideas.[12] In addition, Foucault developed his theoretical statements patiently and painstakingly from detailed empirical studies, which not only makes them difficult to summarize, but also creates the not wholly imaginary risk that any summary will amount to a trivialization of the underlying idea.[13] Also, he ended up with a conception of discourse that is so concerned with the essential dispersion and contingency of social categories that it self-consciously defies and resists all generalizing summaries. And finally, there is an undeniable element of contradiction and inconsistency in Foucault's key concepts. Foucault's critics have jumped on these to point to serious deficiencies in his reasoning, but knowledgeable and sensitive Foucault scholars such as Lemke, Gutting, and Paras point out that perpetual renewal and self-invention are key to understanding Foucault's work.[14] Lemke, for example, argues that it would be premature to try to efface the contradictions and inconsistencies in Foucault's work as they form an intrinsic part of his attempt to question deeply ingrained assumptions about power, government, and the state (Lemke, 1997, 26).[15] I will return to this difficult aspect of Foucault's work in the section below titled "Commentary." It is perhaps for all these reasons that it pays off to become acquainted with the voluminous secondary literature on Foucault. Because every commentator finds his own angle on the rich and elusive corpus of this great French thinker, a *bricolage* of such perspectives helps the reader to grasp its depth and richness. Perhaps Foucault is best appreciated not as a methodical guide to political analysis, but as an exemplar, a continuing source of inspiration, who suggests fruitful and exhilarating ways of inquiry and understanding.

Early Foucault: The Lure of Structuralism—"*Episteme*" and the Death of the Subject

Foucault's work is commonly divided into phases: early, middle, and late; or "archaeological" (1960s), "genealogical" (1970s), and "theory of the subject" (1980s).[16] While such an ordering is less explanatory than requiring an explanation (Lemke, 1997, 29), it will do for purposes of exposition. Because of their immediate relevance for policy analysis, I will concentrate on the archaeological and genealogical aspects of Foucault's work. What does the Foucauldian concept of discourse entail? Foucault always took great pains to declare what he was not, and, indeed, to understand his concept of discourse, it is important to explain what he tried to steer clear of. First, he opposed the deep-seated humanist conception of the autonomous individual who imposes its will on its environment and who gives meaning to everything including its own personality, culture, and history. This idea was rooted in the Enlightenment's ideal of a universal reason that is accessible to every educated person. Concretely, Foucault aimed his structuralist arrows at phenomenological thinkers such as Husserl and Sartre who postulated a transcendental ego that originated in the individual subject as the constitutive origin of being-in-the-world.[17] In less metaphysical terms: individual subjects made their own meaning. Foucault felt that the metaphysical belief in human autonomy and universal reason was seriously misconceived because it overlooked forces that inevitably influenced and distorted individual perception and self-interpretation. As Patton puts it, "He argues that when philosophers invoke 'man' as the basis for their moral and political judgments, they invoke no more than their own or others' concepts of human nature, which are themselves the products of particular historically constituted regimes of truth" (1998, 65). We will later see that Foucault did not oppose the idea of freedom as a pre-condition for politics and ethics, but he opposed an absolutist, transcendental idea of freedom. Foucault saw freedom as necessarily embedded in actual historical conditions (Moss, 1998, 5; Patton, 1998, 73).

On the other hand, Foucault also opposed a hermeneutics of suspicion that locates human self-deception in some overriding, "objective" first cause, such as the economy, the state, or the unconscious, which eludes the individual who is caught up in it. Such large structures are obviously important, but they are not timeless, self-evident causes. Instead they are the product of situated historical developments, innumerable social interactions, and the emergence of shifting intersubjectivities. To sum up, Foucault was deeply suspicious of any approach to social and historical analysis that assumed a foundational or essentialist stance toward social reality. This attitude sprang from an "ethics of individuality" (Allen, 1998, 166) that was extremely sensitive to asymmetries of power and influence and the concomitant foreclosing of human possibility. If there is a common denominator to be found in Foucault's work, it is his relentless challenging of every form of political and social domination in human affairs, particularly the surreptitious and taken-for-granted versions of them (Hoy, 1998, 22).

In his early writings Foucault posited the concept of an *epistème* as a kind of cultural code that governed the thinking and acting of an age. For Foucault there was no such thing as an autonomous subject who had the capacity to act and create individual meaning. Instead, the subject didn't exist as such, but was itself the product of anonymous, preexisting symbolic systems, "silent structures which sustain practices, discourse, perceptual experience . . . , as well as the knowing subject and its objects" (Dreyfus & Rabinow, 1983, 15). As Bevir summarizes this early phase: "Far from individuals constructing *epistèmes* through their rational activity, *epistèmes* define individuals by giving them their concepts, desires, beliefs, and so actions" (Bevir, 1999, 347). Initially Foucault believed that each era was dominated by one, and only one, *epistème*.[18] An *epistème* is not itself knowledge, but a kind of master template that shapes, imprints, the knowledge of the times, and the "epistemic unconscious." In a famous phrase, *epistèmes* create the "conditions of possibility" of the knowledge of an age (Gutting, 2001, 268; Paras, 2006, 23). Foucault conceived of *epistèmes* as sets of structural relations between concepts, which are neither rooted in some natural order nor the product of some grand strategy of a dominating class, but rather are the contingent outcomes of shifts in the relations between concepts and ideas. *Epistèmes* organized (1) the fundamental objects of thought and experience; (2) the nature of the signs in which (1) are expressed (the "deep structure of language"); and (3) the consequences of fundamental objects and the allowable signs for an era's conception of knowledge (Gutting, 2001, 268–69; see also Howarth, 2000, 52–55). For example, the Renaissance *epistème* was "resemblance"; that for the Classical Age "identity and difference." In this epistemic furor subjective meaning was no more than a "surface effect" of these large systems.[19] The individual subject was banned from social and political analysis. What was left were "subject positions" that were created, determined, by *epistèmes.*

Methodologically, structuralist discourse analysis becomes a kind of archaeology. Gutting describes discursive archaeology as follows: "Archaeology emerges as a method of analysis that reveals the intellectual structures that underlie and make possible the entire range of diverse (and often conflicting) concepts, methods and theories characterizing the thought of a given period" (2001, 268).[20] The aim of archaeology is to discover the "rules governing our discursive behavior of which we may well not be aware" (ibid.). As grammatical rules determine which statements are meaningful, and the rules of logic which statements are consistent, so do the rules of discourse determine which statements are "permissible" (ibid.). This is a somewhat ambiguous statement, but from Foucault's examples one gathers that he means "senseful" or "meaningful." For example, in the contemporary discourse of mental disorder, which is organized around the central metaphor of illness, it simply wouldn't make sense to talk of mental disorder in terms of imbalances among the four different humors. It is not that we wouldn't understand such a statement, but it wouldn't have any standing within the institutionalized setting of diagnosing and treating mental disorder. By talking that way, one would disqualify oneself. In good structuralist fashion, the relationship between discursive rules and meaningfulness is quite arbitrary. (There was a time that explaining mental disorder in terms of humors was eminently senseful.) Foucault—the philosopher—calls this the "decline of representation." Ideas have no "ontological thickness." They have no content of their own but only represent the historical, contingent rules that organize a domain of knowledge (Gutting, 2001, 270). More or less by implication this leads to the ethical stance that one can imagine other, better conceptualizations and organizations of a social domain.

Seasoned interpretivists would nod in sympathy with this intellectual program. But we should not downplay Foucault's radicalism here. Archaeology is thoroughly disenchanting. Its aim was no less than to summarily dispense with the thinking, intending, aspiring, striving, creating subject in the history of human endeavor. As Paras puts it:

> The history of knowledge, as observed by the archaeologist, was not the story of the progress of reason; it was certainly not the recounting of a narrative wherein men's thoughts arose and made their impact in the world. The history of knowledge was the unfolding of an anonymous process; a process of the formation and transformation of bodies of *statements* according to isolable rules. Foucault could not emphasize enough that his intended domain was this raw and apparently undifferentiated mass of statements. Attribution was irrelevant. . . . For what needed to be dispensed with was the notion that men's thought was their property, an object of their own creation. . . . [T]he painful truth that needed to be embraced was that men were the wholly interchangeable speakers of *systems of thought* that transcended them. Archaeology did not exist to exalt the voices of those who speak, but to demonstrate that every speaker is a ventriloquist's dummy. (2006, 34–35)

Don't be mistaken. Actors don't choose their systems of thought. Discourse is all. The rules of discourse are not imposed upon otherwise free actors. What they experience as individual agency or personal meaning is dictated, "made possible" by discursive rules. There is no subjective reality outside the rules of discourse.

This is heady stuff. Although Foucault quickly moved on to a more flexible, open-ended, historical version of structuralism, the key notion of hidden epistemic structures, buried in the language conventions of an age, which determined taken-for-granted beliefs and identities, has since lodged deep inside the imagination of social and political analysts. This is the hermeneutics of suspicion writ large! Instead of going out into the field to find reluctant subjects and persuade them to be observed and interviewed, the analyst can now study the archival data of an era and reveal the hidden conditioning underneath. All the thinking, intending, aspiring, striving, creating, and, I should add, negotiating, compromising, deliberating, is no more than froth on the surface of massive discursive systems. But there is light in this cold, dark, impersonal space. Social reality is not what it appears to be. It is not inevitable; it is constructed. To imagine what can be, under the surface of what is, is a critical act in itself.

Let's take stock. How useful is structuralist discourse analysis for interpretive policy analysis? Despite his rhetorical fireworks, from the very beginning, even when he is under the fashionable sway of structuralism, Foucault's version of discourse is much more akin to the openness and contextuality of poststructuralism than to the traditional structuralism of Saussure or Lévi-Strauss. Foucault's poststructuralist affinities show in the fact that his concept of discourse doesn't center on sentences or propositions but on *statements*. The crucial distinguishing element here is the *use* that is made of a linguistic utterance. So, the truth conditions of a particular proposition, even its existence as a stable and meaningful statement, depend upon the context of its use. As Foucault states: "The constancy of the statement, the preservation of its identity through the unique events of the enunciations, its duplications through the identity of the forms is constituted by the functioning of the field of use in which it is placed" (quoted in Dreyfus & Rabinow, 1983, 45).[21]

Foucault opens up the structuralist straitjacket by adding two important elements to his notion of discourse as an "interplay of statements." First, he is not interested in just any type of statement, but—with particular relevance to policy theory—only in "serious statements" (Dreyfus & Rabinow, 1983, 48). Serious statements are a specific class of statements that are understood by hearers as authoritative or true far beyond the immediate context in which they are uttered. This uncoupling of truth from the immediate everyday context is attained because it is recognized that certain statements have serious social consequences and are therefore surrounded by necessary validation procedures, regulation, communities of experts, and so on (ibid.). For example, the statement "You're crazy" is a harmless, perhaps even playful, one when uttered between husband and wife, but has grave consequences when a psychiatrist says it about a patient in the context of an intake procedure in a psychiatric hospital. In other words, certain statements come with generally recognized and accepted truth claims because of their position in a particular institutionalized field of use. Furthermore, Foucault doesn't believe that it is possible to find universal, immutable rules of transformation that link particular statements to other statements, creating meaningful *langues* and *paroles*. Not all rules of transformation are permitted; certain local, contextualized rules in a particular discursive formation define what counts as meaningful and meaningless statements (Dreyfus & Rabinow, 1983, 55). Take notice! Already, at this early stage of his career, Foucault introduces an element of power into the heart of his conceptual machinery. Not only do these validation procedures put forward a hard-to-resist claim to knowledge and authority, but Foucault also asserts—a theme that he will develop in much more depth and detail in his theory of power/knowledge—that ever greater swathes of everyday life are to be subjected to management (Allen, 1998; Dreyfus & Rabinow, 1983, 48).

This description of Foucault's early conception of discourse shows its strengths, weaknesses, and ambiguities. Foucault takes issue with theories of hermeneutic meaning—theories in which meaning is produced and held by identifiable actors, and that aim to uncover the underlying but temporarily obscured meaning of a text or phenomenon. In opposition to this, structuralist meaning is impersonal. Actors do not produce discourse; they are simultaneously its function and its effect (Howarth, 2000, 53). This is where discursive meaning most clearly distinguishes itself from hermeneutic meaning. Where the latter attempts to recover an opaque meaning that underlies apparent reality, Foucault thinks of *both* the appearances and the belief in a deeper, obscured meaning as the product of "organized sets of historical practices which have produced the subject matter of the human sciences" (Dreyfus & Rabinow, 1983, 11).[22] But this is also where different authors see a major inconsistency in Foucault's antihumanist conception of meaning (Bevi 1999; Gutting, 2001, 275–79; Paras, 2006, 52; Taylor, 1986). For if actors only act out the systematicness of discourses, it is hard to see what kind of agency will ever change it. Statements do not change by themselves, actorless. This is not the same as saying that we necessarily need conscious intention as the engine of change. Taylor cites the example of the negative unintended consequences of collective action. No individual subject has willed these unwanted effects, yet the aggregation of their actions brings them into being anyway (1986, 87). In the final chapter I will discuss complexity, in which system states are seen as the emergent effect of the interactions between elements in a system (molecules, neurons, birds, individuals), independent of the state (intention, behavior) of the individual elements themselves (Wagenaar, 2007a). If there is conscious activity in these examples, it is in highly diluted doses. All we need is *some* explanation that ties the state of a system to the actions of subjects.[23] And that thereby restores some, albeit limited, form of influence or agency of individual actors over their social and physical environment.

Another strong point of Foucault's archaeology is its focus on the rules that govern the formation and production of discourse. The focus on rules is methodologically attractive as it provides clear instructions for research to analysts. Meaningful statements, according to Foucault, emerge from a "meaningless field of rule-governed transformations" that make some statements senseful or truthful (Dreyfus & Rabinow, 1983, 79). The task of the analysts consists of identifying and articulating the specific formative rules that constitute the discursive field. However, the concept of rules is a double-edged sword, because it is exactly at this point that ambiguity creeps in. Dreyfus and Rabinow make clear that Foucault gets trapped in his own contradictions here. When he tries to describe the formations that make it possible to talk about madness, for example, he relies fully on the concept of rules, for example "rules that govern different modes of enunciation," or rules that govern "forms of succession and simultaneity" (Dreyfus & Rabinow, 1983, 80–81). But rules don't do the trick of keeping the actor out of the discursive equation. For the question arises whether, and how, actors *follow* these rules in moving about in a discursive field. And, to follow a rule, as we have seen in chapter 4, is itself predicated on a set of practical judgments by concrete actors who possess a modicum of agency (Taylor, 1995c; Wagenaar, 2004). Foucault denies, however, that actors follow rules, because the rules are not in the minds of the actors. (The minds of actors are "subject positions" that are the effect of rules.) But how, then, do these impersonal rules affect actors' activities? According to Dreyfus and Rabinow, Foucault ends up with a pseudo-causal understanding of the working of rules on statements ("statements put into operation sets of rules in accordance with which objects are formed").[24] But this then just shifts the problems surrounding the presumed causality of meaning that bedeviled hermeneutic policy interpretation to the presumed causality of rules. In both cases we cannot decide in which direction the arrow of causality points.

The upshot of this critique is that it is hard to keep subjects out of the analysis of meaning. Because Foucault defines a discursive field as a set of statements, and statements are defined by their use, he surreptitiously brings the subject back in again—via the back door as it were. For, by introducing use, Foucault introduces an element of intention or volition into the heart of his conception of discourse, and no matter how you cut the cake, intentions and volitions are held by actors, even if they are collective. Foucault was certainly aware of this tension in his work, and we have to move on to his later writings to see how he gave more space in his ideas to notions of agency, freedom, and resistance.

Why spend so much time with what is obviously a hyperbolic attempt to write structuralist history?[25] I don't know of any archaeological analyses of public policy.[26] That is hardly surprising. In spite of its strengths and insights, discursive archaeology is a poisoned apple for interpretive policy analysts. Fully dressed, it simply doesn't square with the ethical soul of the discipline: the improvement of undesirable social situations by contributing to better policy making. So why discuss archaeology in the context of policy analysis at all? The answer is that its basic tenets have proven to be immensely influential. Mind you, what stuck in interpretive policy analysis was not the whole archaeological works, but a kind of "structuralism lite": Reveal the hidden rules that shape current ideas, conventions and institutions. Thereby, demonstrate the inherent contingency of these established ideas, conventions and institutions. But hold on to a pre-discursive free subject who has the agency to resist the discursive formation and replace it, in a splendid act of emancipation, with something better. These trappings of discursive meaning have been widely accepted by interpretive analysts. They have become earmarks of social critique. They inform both the poststructuralism of Laclau and Mouffe and the critical discourse analysis of Fairclough.

Middle Foucault: Genealogies of Power/Knowledge

One way to think of the second phase of Foucault's conception of discourse is as an attempt to articulate the functional element that was already implicit in the idea of a *field of use*. From the very beginning Foucault uses the term "practice," but he is quite vague about its meaning, using it as a synonym for the rather noncommittal "activity" or "technique." In his second, genealogical phase, he places "practice" center stage. He also, important for policy analysts, develops his genealogical concept of discourse a propos of a fascinating theory of power and its role in governance. Finally, he reflects on the emergence of the citizen-subject in the modern liberal state.[27]

Foucault's starting point, as always, consists of detailed historical studies, in this case of the emergence of the modern penal system and our collective understanding of sexuality (Foucault, 1979, 1980b). In his attempt to avoid writing "Whig history" (the double bias of writing history from the vantage point of the present, and portraying historical development as a long and linear march that culminates in the present), Foucault ends up with a strongly contingent and perspectivist interpretive position. Abstaining from teleology, "[h]e investigates the unpredictable events that form entities, and stresses the eruption of clashing political forces in key historical junctions as the driving force of history" (Howarth, 2000, 71). True to his earlier, archaeological insight that the categories of historical analysis emerge in the interplay of statements in discourses, Foucault reaches the—logical—conclusion that there is no pre-discursive essence, "nothing absolutely primary," that could be the object of interpretation (Foucault, in Dreyfus & Rabinow, 1983, 107). Interpretations of interpretations are all the analyst may hope to find. Naturally we all do recognize limits on interpretation, but these must then be arbitrarily imposed. Under the influence of Nietzsche, Foucault conjectures that these arbitrary limits must be forcefully imposed on the world: "If history is the violent and surreptitious appropriation of a system of rules, which in itself has no essential meaning, in order to impose a direction, to bend it to a new will, to force its participation in a new game, and to subject it to secondary rules, then the development of humanity is a series of interpretations" (quoted in Dreyfus & Rabinow, 1983, 108). Later he will step away from this stark imagery of violence and domination and soften his conception of power (Foucault, 1983, 219; Allen, 1998, 177), but he never abandons his key insight that history is irrevocably contingent and that changes in its course are determined by conjunctions of power. It is the analyst's task to explain which forces, which "logic of power and domination" (Howarth, 2000, 72), brought certain institutional possibilities into being and foreclosed other historical possibilities (ibid.).

But what then drives these subjugating forces? Foucault's answer is "practices." As Gutting puts it: "Genealogy deals with the connection between non-discursive practices and systems of discourse (bodies of knowledge)" (2001, 278). Genealogy can be seen as a parenthesizing of the core values of reason and rationality. Instead of seeing reason as an autonomous, self-evident system of statements, Foucault introduces the concept of *dispositif* to account for the systems of practices that bring certain social categories and objects into being.[28] *Dispositif* is often translated as apparatus, but it is better thought of as a grid of interpretation. It encompasses both discursive and nondiscursive practices, such as "discourses, institutions, architectural arrangements, regula-tions, laws, administrative measures, scientific statements, philosophical propositions, morality, philanthropy, etc." (Foucault, quoted in Dreyfus & Rabinow, 1983, 121). While this description is suggestive in helping the analyst see where to look for the forces that shape historical devel-opment, as a shorthand it is probably easier to think of *dispositives* as those cultural practices, beliefs, understandings, aspirations, and materials in their particular cultural-historical context that have been instrumental in forming the social and institutional categories that make up our social world. Ordinary individuals react to practical problems that are thrown in their path. In a piecemeal fashion, "without anyone wittingly knowing what they add up to," these practices form "natural," taken-for-granted beliefs, institutions, and ways of managing societal domains (Hacking, 1986, 35). In this sense a *dispositif* represents a thoroughly relational conception of meaning. One recognizes a *dispositif* when one finds "strategies of relations of forces supporting types of knowledge and vice versa." An example might be helpful here.

In a study of the emergence of the contemporary public school system in the middle of the nineteenth century, Hunter employs the concepts and analytical strategies of Foucault's genealogical approach. There are two received views on the formation of the public school system, he states. Liberal educational theory sees the school as the articulation of certain fundamental ethical and political principles such as equality, liberty, and rationality. Marxist theorists see the school as a convenient instrument by which the dominant class is able to impose its interests, in the process conveniently reproducing social inequality (Hunter, 1996, 145). In opposition to these theories, which portray schools as expressing one large underlying principle or force, Hunter suggests that schools should be "seen to emerge not as realizations of underlying principles or developmental laws, but as contingent assemblages put together under blind historical circumstances" (ibid). Echoing Foucault, he characterizes his concern as describing "the detailed organization of the [monitorial] school as a purpose-built pedagogical environment assembled from a mix of physical and moral elements: special architectures; devices for organizing space and time; body techniques; practices of surveillance and supervision; pedagogical relationships; procedures of administration and examination" (ibid.).

Hunter then describes in fascinating detail the elements of the "historical milieu" and "political mentality" out of which the school, as an institution, came forth. There is not the space here to summarize Hunter's meticulously detailed historical analysis. By comparing Britain, Australia, and Prussia, he is able to discern certain similarities in the historical environment of these three states. On the one hand, he describes political objectives and governmental technologies (such as statistical survey and social intervention) of these early modern administrative-territorial states; on the other hand, he describes the institutions and practices of Christian pastoral guidance that were available to the administrative elite at the time. Technologies such as statistical surveys did not so much provide information about particular groups in society as they drew new social-moral boundaries in what was until then an amorphous, and virtually invisible, mass of people. Through the new instrument of social statistics, the working class was created as a new object of political perception and moral action: a population that was the bearer of a series of problematic conducts and capacities (Jones, 1991). In short: problem, relevant and authoritative knowledge, the object of intervention, social technology, guiding ideology, and administrative and pedagogical techniques dialectically influenced and articulated each other, to slowly crystallize into the public school as the liberal, democratic institution that we are all familiar with. Instead of schools being the expression of liberal values, these values grew out of the school system as practical solution to these historical exigencies: "one of the most distinctive characteristics of the modern 'popular' school . . . is that, in adapting the milieu of pastoral guidance to its own uses, State schooling made self-realization into a central disciplinary objective" (Hunter, 1996, 149).

It is important to keep in mind that the concept of *dispositif* is not an abstract, formal analytical scheme (such as an *episteme*). Rather, as the example makes clear, it must be seen as an analytical program. What makes this program attractive to political analysts and policy scholars is that discourse as a genealogical concept is closely tied to a substantive theory of practice, power, and knowledge. In his studies of the penal system, Foucault came to the conclusion that power was exerted in ways that were not adequately captured in political science theories that saw power strictly as a form of domination. Foucault noticed that certain techniques of surveillance, newly emerging scientific disciplines (such as criminology or psychiatry) that "explained" these techniques and provided them with a certain scientific status, and new categories of subjects who were the exclusive object of these new intellectual disciplines, emerged together. According to Foucault, in domains such as the penal system a new kind of power had emerged that, from the point of view of the challenge of the effective governing of liberal democratic states, were more important than the traditional subjugating powers of state and sovereign (Allen, 1998, 165).

This new form of power has a different object, a different goal, and a different site. It is "small power" (as opposed to the "big power" of states and sovereigns that is the object of political science, political philosophy, and the policy sciences for that matter) that operates on bodies instead of territories. These "micro-powers" (the plural is intentional) form an infinitely detailed form of monitoring and supervision whose aim is to control the process of bodily activity (Gutting, 2001, 280).[29] Micro-power power doesn't effectuate itself through mechanisms of coercion, but strives to govern individual conduct by influencing beliefs, values, self-images, and aspirations. Foucault calls this kind of power "discipline," but a surreptitious form of discipline that stealthily inducts people into desired behavior. As Allen puts it, "The point of discipline is not to force people to do what you want, but to make them into the kind of people you want; not to make people do what you want them to do, but to make them want to do it" (1998, 174).[30] The sites where these powers are exerted are no longer the prison or the scaffold, but the everyday locations where people live out their daily lives: schools, households, hospitals, factories, doctors' offices, administrative offices, and armies. Foucault discerned an ever-widening disciplining of societies since the eighteenth century, an increasing demand for the management of ever more areas of everyday life. The aggregate effect was a power that was at once local and global, individualizing and generalizing:

> [A]n instrumental rationality operating locally yet producing effects with the appearance of a global strategy. Despite the absence of a conspiracy or a master plan, discipline has been cut free of its former limitations and spread over broader and broader domains as if in response to the command to discipline the entire social body. (Allen, 1998, 175)

Key to this exertion of micro-power is knowledge about the subjects of power. Foucault indicated his theory with the affix "power/knowledge." With the slash, or backstroke, he wanted to express the intricate relationship between power and knowledge. The backstroke does not indicate sameness. Power is not identical to knowledge. Rather knowledge is implicated in power. In their effectuation in everyday life power and knowledge are reciprocal. How is this reciprocal relationship established? It is important to note that Foucault's ideas about the relationship between power and knowledge were developed as part of his ongoing historical projects. First, his study of the emergence of the modern penal system with its emphasis on disciplining whole populations. Later, his history of sexuality with its focus on the relationship between disciplinary knowledge, self-knowledge and self-monitoring. And finally, in his lectures at the Collège de France, his ideas about governing modern liberal democracies to which he applied the term *gouvernmentalité*. In this context, "the command to discipline the entire social body" in the preceding quote refers to the state as a distinct category that slowly emerges out of concrete practices of governing and the reflections upon these in the works of political philosophers. The power-knowledge nexus was an integral part of these developments. One cannot be understood without the other. Yet, as I will discuss Foucault's theories of governing in the next section, I will focus on the first two aspects of power/knowledge here.

One of the effects of the new forms of disciplining power was the emergence of new professions—psychiatry, medicine, public hygiene, economics—that appropriated the task of managing the body. However, the challenge of managing individuals implied a kind of analytical intimacy that generated knowledge about these individuals, which in turn made the task of management easier again. It is this dialectic between knowledge and management that is at the heart of the power-knowledge nexus:

> The same interventions which produce a docile body also make it possible to compile precise data on individuals and to study them comparatively under controlled conditions. At the same time, this new knowledge enhances the capacity for control. An effective reciprocity develops between the knowledge that discipline produces and the power which it exercises; "the exercise of power itself creates and causes to emerge new objects of knowledge and accumulates new bodies of information," while conversely "knowledge constantly induces effects of power." (Allen, 1998, 175; internal quotations are from Foucault)

As I will show in the next section, the dialectic of power and knowledge is an important heuristic for a genealogical analysis of conventions of belief and understanding in public policy. In his fervor to steer clear of Marxist state-centered analysis, however, Foucault reified the power/knowledge nexus into an ultimately untenable, relativistic theory of "truth-regimes." In Foucault's worldview, truth has no independent epistemic status. It is exhaustively implicated with power. Truth is tied up with—perhaps emerges from—internally coherent, if not monolithic, systems of power/knowledge:

> Truth is a thing of this world; it is produced *only* by virtue of multiple forms of constraint. And it induces regular effects of power. Each society has its régime of truth, its "general politics" of truth: that is, the types of discourse which it accepts and makes function as true; the mechanisms and instances which enable one to distinguish true and false statements, the means by which each is sanctioned; the techniques and procedures accorded value in the acquisition of truth; the status of those who are charged with saying what counts as true. (Foucault, 1980a, 131; italics added)

Truth as a maze without exits. Truth as the exclusive product of the constraining force of power. This truly implies the death of the subject. Clearly, such a conception of power and knowledge strains credulity, and as we will see, in his later writings, Foucault himself backed off from this deterministic, distempered conception of power and truth. He backed off first by clarifying the relation between micro-power and state strategy with the introduction of the concept of *gouvernmentalité* and later by an interest in ethics, resistance, and freedom.

So here we have the three key insights in Foucault's theory of power. First, power is not imposed from above (the subjective will of sovereigns, or the structural forces of capitalism). Instead it must be seen as shaped in and by the everyday relations of individuals with each other and the multiple professional and administrative agencies of modern, liberal society. Power has no owner, but is immanent in everyday conduct. Second, in the practical matrix of governing dispersed populations of individuals, knowledge is simultaneously a product of and a conduit for the exercise of power. In Foucault's universe there is no such thing as neutral, objective, apolitical knowledge. Third, power is not repressive, but instead creates and produces new forms of knowledge, new social categories, new types of relationships, new identities even. As Foucault summarizes these positions:

> [I]t seems to me that the notion of repression is quite inadequate in capturing what is precisely the productive aspect of power. In defining the effects of power as repression, one adopts a purely juridical conception of such power, one identifies power with a law that says no, power is taken above all as carrying the force of prohibition. Now I believe that this is a wholly negative, narrow, skeletal conception of power, one which has been curiously widespread. If power were never anything but repressive, if it never did anything but to say no, do you really think one would be brought to obey it? What makes power hold good, what makes it accepted, is simply the fact that it doesn't only weigh on us as a force, but that it traverses and produces things. It needs to be considered as a productive network which runs through the whole social body. (Foucault, 1980a, 119)

The insights of such disciplines as psychology, pedagogy, management studies, psychiatry, criminology, and policy analysis spring from their practical role as managers of particular societal domains. From this faculty they generate new objects of study, new categories of analysis, new urgencies for public intervention, and new problems for research. Their influence is, however, seldom repressive or totalitarian. Their power derives from their authority, their claims to professionalism, to a "special competence before which we often have little choice but to submit" (Allen, 1998, 177).

This is where the originality of Foucault's remarkable theory of power/knowledge lies. Power is always there. It exerts its influence by acting upon people's actions, either "existing actions or those that may arise in the present or the future" (Foucault, 1983, 220). Power doesn't issue from a single sovereign position, but is dispersed throughout society, exercised in many different relationships. It is not something imposed by an external authority, but functions through internalized ideas, aspirations, norms, and standards (Foucault, 1980b, 94). Power doesn't come from above but from below. It forms and is expressed in countless everyday relationships, which might gel into hegemonic relationships (ibid.).[31] Underlying this concept of power is the basic etymological sense of power as the capacity to become or do things:

> Power in this primary sense is exercised by individuals or collective human bodies when they act upon each other's actions; in other words, to take the simplest case, when the ac-

tions of one affect the field of possible actions of another. In this case, where the actions of A have succeeded in modifying the field of possible actions of B, we can say that A has exercised power over B. "Power over" in this sense will be an inescapable future of any social interaction. (Patton, 1998, 67)

Power in this sense is normatively neutral. It is not necessarily a negative force, a "renunciation of freedom" (Allen, 1998, 177). It doesn't require threats or violence, and it doesn't necessarily need to be monopolized by one institutional entity, such as the state, or psychiatry, or factors of production. It is dependent upon asymmetries of influence, but no functioning society is possible without such asymmetries. They are at the heart of our ability to raise and educate children, to run a business, to settle disputes, to organize complex activities (Allen, 1998). In fact, power as capacity can very well go together with the formulation and enactment of positive ideals or self-fulfillment. Also, power is always exercised between subjects of power "each with their own distinct capacities for action" (Patton, 1998, 68). This means that the exertion of power has unpredictable effects. Subjects always have the capacity to resist. Only in the grossest forms of domination, where asymmetries of power are completely petrified, are the effects of power predictable.[32]

Power as capacity opens up avenues toward a more relaxed notion of freedom in Foucault's theory. One of the most fascinating aspects of Foucault's concept of power in his last writings is the thin line between power, agency, resistance, and freedom. Due to his untimely death, it was up to his commentators to draw out the implications for political theory. One important implication, one that has immediate relevance for interpretive policy analysis, points toward a positive ethics of collective action. Instead of discursive ethics acting as a dystopian hermeneutics of suspicion that unveils the faceless, contingent forces in which we, unbeknownst to ourselves, act out our fate, Foucault provides us with the conceptual tools to analyze the interplay of freedom and subjugation, autonomy and dependency, in the solution of collective problems and the realization of collective goals. I will return to the ethical implications of interpretive policy analysis in the final chapter. Let me just prepare the ground for this later discussion by quoting Allen once more:

> The "problem" that the exercise of power raises is not how to get rid of it, how to free ourselves from power, but how to make the inevitable asymmetries compatible with the greatest personal liberty for subjective individuality. Ethical life requires such liberty, areas of choice where the government of our conduct is up to us. The frontier between ethics and politics is the constantly shifting line between ethical autonomy, or the liberties people can take, and political heteronomy, or the liberties that are taken from them and with them by others. (1998, 177)

One could ask, finally, to what extent this positive notion of power as personal and collective capacity has anything to do with the more conventional, repressive "power as we know it." Perhaps it has drifted too far away from this "basic" meaning of power as nonconsensual influence over others—with its usual imagery of constraint, domination, and human agency (Taylor, 1986, 90)— to be called power at all? I will return to this important question at the end of my discussion of Foucault, but let me here elaborate on Foucault's conception some more. Power as capacity is still power in the sense of "power over" where it enters the functioning of the modern liberal state. One of Foucault's key insights was that the effective functioning of the state has become identified with the positive self-aspirations of its population. Clearly, raw, naked power of the first dimension (Lukes, 1975) is always there, but in our society it has come to be seen as anomaly, an exception, if not an outrage. Power, as Foucault rightly saw, operates by implication. Modern power is internalized. Discipline merges into autonomy; state power into the willingness, if not eagerness, of individuals to subjugate to the needs of the collective, and experience this as an act of free choice.[33] This is not false consciousness all over again. The difference from the traditional Marxist conception of domination is that in the modern liberal state governance, to be effective at all, has no choice but to ally itself with personal liberty and the ever present capacity for resistance that is an inevitable part of it. Power no longer just exerts from centralized, hierarchical agencies, although it does that too. Instead its "site" is composed of the interpersonal relations of the millions of individuals who make up a population, the myriads of personalized forms of power as capacity, which taken together constitute the vast fabric of the modern, dispersed liberal democracy. Power/ knowledge surely contains echoes of false consciousness, but Foucault thoroughly refashioned the Marxist concept; not doing away with its subjugating content, but rearticulating it in such a way that it is more commensurate with the vast landscape of modern liberal governance. He rightly saw that power is not only the effect of the will or interests of a dominating ruling elite, but instead the emergent effect of the beliefs, practices, tactics, doctrines, enthusiasms, and critiques that make up a plural, liberal society.[34]

Let me illustrate the heuristic power of the power/knowledge approach for the analysis of public policy with an example: the regulation of biotechnology, in particular embryonic stem cell research (ESCR) and human cloning, in Israel (Prainsack, 2006). In her study Prainsack addresses the question of why Israel has one of the world's most liberal regulatory regimes of ESCR and cloning, while most other countries have imposed strict regulations on practice and research in these areas. In fact, ESCR and cloning have evolved into one of the most contested moral fields in biotechnology, on a par with euthanasia and abortion. Following the precepts of hermeneutic policy interpretation, she first sets out to seek the answer in Jewish religious teachings. She does indeed see congruencies between the permissive regulatory regime and particular religious principles and strictures (such as that an *ex utero* embryo is not regarded as comparable to an implanted embryo, and in no way equivalent to a fully fledged human being, or the moral imperative in Jewish teaching to improve God's creation). However, as she makes clear, religion is not an exhaustive explanation, and cannot be regarded as the underlying "meaning," of the "permissive" Israeli regulatory regime.

In an analytic move that, as we saw, is typical of discursive analysis along Foucauldian lines, she broadens the subject of analysis, thereby questioning the taken-for-granted boundaries that define her topic. She brings into the analysis related practices and discourses, such as selective family planning policies that distinguish between the Jewish and the Arab populations in Israel, the general discouragement of contraception in combination with generous assisted-reproduction policies, and a "demographic threat" discourse that in strong, warlike similes paints an alarmist picture of the coming demographic demise of Israel as a Jewish state. In such a climate any technology that holds out the promise that it may increase the Jewish birth-rate is likely to find general acceptance. However, because raising the Jewish birth rate is too sensitive a topic to be broadly and openly discussed, Prainsack introduces the concept of self-governing to establish the link between Israeli pro-natalism and the permissive legal situation regarding ESCR and human cloning. She shows that Israeli citizens have internalized the dominant demographic threat discourse and freely engage in family planning practices. To this end they willingly use the reproductive technologies that the state provides them. "Israeli society is obsessed with fertility," one of her spokespeople says, and she goes on to conclude that this "stress on fertility provides a direct correlation between the construction of parenthood and the reproduction of the nation. Through creating individual bodies, individuals not only reproduce themselves, but they simultaneously engage in the reproduction of the collective" (2006, 198). People freely engage in constructive, productive behavior, except that they are not wholly free to choose or invent that behavior because they move about in large discursive formations that influence their actions, beliefs, and aspirations. The individual becomes a subject because he willingly obliges by the practices and goals that are available to him in his culture. As Prainsack puts it, we govern ourselves by establishing truths about ourselves that are in accordance with the truth of the dominant narratives in our societies (ibid.). It is in discourse that power speaks to truth and vice versa.

We should not close our eyes to the fact that there are unresolved—and perhaps irresolvable—ambivalences in Foucault's ideas about power/knowledge and governance. For example, Gordon describes Foucault's distrust of the effects of the increasing spread of governance, and its ancillary belief systems and techniques, over the body of civil society in rather stark language, as a process of increasing domination: "Foucault saw it as a characteristic (and troubling) property of the development of the practice of government in Western societies to tend towards a form of political sovereignty which would be a government of all and each, and whose concerns would be at once to 'totalize' and to 'individualize'" (1991, 3). Similarly, Allen concludes his exemplary essay on Foucault's contribution to political philosophy with an unexpectedly gloomy catalogue of the various "distinctive strategies of political control" that have "corrupted European politics" and that he characterizes as "irrational rationalities" (1998, 189). Yet, neither writer overlooks Foucault's position in his later work that power presupposes free agents, that power can only be called power (and not force or violence) when "it acts upon, and through, an open set of practical and ethical possibilities" (Gordon, 1991, 5). And both authors do not fail to draw the implications for the possibility of a political ethics from this "intransigence of freedom" in the effectuation of power (Foucault, 1983, 221).[35] Before we explore this aspect of Foucault's work any further, however, we need to discuss his ideas about governance and the "rationality of government" that have come to be known under the heading of "governmentality." To this I turn in the next section.

Governmentality, or the Analytics of Government

Exposition

Foucault's later thoughts on discourse, power, and knowledge have exerted a strong influence on political analysts. In the 1990s a wholly new field emerged under the banner of governmentality or "analytics of government" that applied and extended Foucault's ideas to the area of government. In Britain, Australia, France, and Germany researchers applied the governmentality approach to a wide range of subjects. Lemke lists biomedicine and genetics, health policy, organizational sociology, postcolonial theory, risk and insurance, urban planning, criminology, and refugee policies. Particularly in Germany, he says, the number of papers, book chapters, and edited volumes on governmentality is immense (Lemke, 2007, 49–50).

Foucault had introduced the term *governmentality* in a famous lecture before the Collège de France (Foucault, 1991). The lecture was part of a series in 1978 and 1979 in which Foucault applied the genealogical method to some key concepts in political science, concepts such as state, civil society, citizen, and government. As Lemke rightly argues, the governmentality lectures must be seen as an attempt to solve a number of problems in his genealogy of power/knowledge. Foucault was never very clear about the relation between micro-processes of power and the "root" concepts of domination and constraint (and, inversely, resistance) that define the commonsense notions of power. Second, Foucault had trouble conceptualizing state power as more than the result of the micro-processes of "bottom-up" power. Or, differently put, Foucault couldn't distinguish between power and ruling.[36] The focus on government in his lectures at the Collège de France can be seen as an answer to these problems. He was able to distinguish between domination and strategic uses of power. Second, he was able to develop the ambiguous relation between micro- and macro-power (Lemke, 1997, 30–31).

The term "governmentality" depicts a style of governing in which all aspects of public life and individual conduct are in principle subject to regulation. Foucault thinks this style of govern- ing is characteristic of the modern liberal democracies of the Western world. With his theory of governmentality Foucault does not claim that the state has grown to the point that it suffocates civil society. Instead, as Allen points out, Foucault sketches a:

> comprehensive trend towards more resourceful, more intense, more intractable, more fine- grained government; not merely the growth of the state (though there has been that too), but the growth of demands, mechanisms, agencies, and occasions for conducting behaviour, setting options, ordering the field within which people have to choose and act. More and more of everyday life comes under the umbrella of some agency of government, whether of the nation state or some petty local committee, the welfare bureaucracy or the administration of public schools and utilities; whether the requirement is for a license, permit, certificate or credential, or the obligation to meet regulations, standards, ordinances, or codes which, despite a nominal rationale (protecting society or the consumer, say) seem driven mainly by the assumption that there is something scandalous about a possible activity that is not subject to authoritative control. (Allen, 1998, 180)

What Allen beautifully captures in this quote is the apparent contradiction in liberal democra- cies between an ideology of small government and the taken-for-granted presumption that it is perfectly legitimate for government or semi-government agencies to regulate almost every aspect of human conduct. It is Foucault's brilliance to see not only that this contradiction is apparent, but that it is the hallmark of government in modern liberal democracies. With the concept of gov- ernmentality, as we saw earlier, Foucault relates his ideas about governance to his ideas about the positive, generative, "micro" effects of power. Both are part of a vast "history of the present" in which our taken-for-granted categories, institutions, and understandings about politics and gov- ernment are the subject, and in which Foucault traces the peculiar dialectic of ideas and practices of government throughout the ages. Given the purposes of this book, it would go too far in this context to summarize Foucault's signature historiography, but its thrust is the gradual emergence, out of many different, mostly unrelated, challenges, practical solutions, beliefs, explanations, and utopian dreams, of this peculiar style of governing that depends for its efficacy on the simultane- ous acknowledgement of a sphere of civil life that is distinct (and has to be kept distinct) from the political, and the total implication of this sphere in the business of governing. [37]

As an approach to interpretive political research, governmentality is based on a number of basic ideas. Government, at least in the modern liberal society as it has emerged in the Western world since the latter half of the eighteenth century, is no longer identified with the state as the central locus of rule. In their seminal article "Political Power Beyond the State: Problematics of Govern- ment," Rose and Miller take pains to distance themselves from traditional theories of the state. "Many have recognized that the philosophical and constitutional images of the sovereign state are misleading," they write (1992, 176). To give the state, as a territorially defined, institutionally anchored entity, central place in political theory "obscures the characteristics of modern forms of political power" (ibid.). Governing should not be seen as the expression of a monolithic power center or grand ideology, but instead as the accumulation of myriads of micro practices within local programs—such as schools, prisons, welfare agencies, corporations, and disability programs—

that sustain, modify, and even generate what we perceive and experience as the institutions of the state (Bevir, 1999, 352; Foucault, 1991, 102). These regimes of government are made possible because state agencies rely on, and implicate, communities, neighborhoods, private businesses, professionals, and citizens to achieve their ends (Dean, 1999, 70; MacKinnon, 2000). Governing is conceived as "action at a distance," the purpose of which is to create the conditions for the routine functioning of various more or less autonomous social domains (Rose & Miller, 1992, 180). And finally, governing is achieved by inculcating in citizens the need to manage themselves according to widely internalized needs and goals that are congruent with the goals of the state. Self-management is seen as continuous with the regulatory impetus of the state. "Technologies of the self," the alignment of subjectivity with political rule, are a key element in a permanent restructuring and recalibration of techniques of governing (Foucault, 1988; Lemke, 2001).

The governmentality literature has developed into two broad research agendas. The first concerns what Rose and Miller (1992) call "political rationalities." This line of inquiry focuses on the way that programs of government are formulated within broad discourses of collective truth, proper ruling, and moral justification. Concretely, the approach inquires into the conceptualization of governmental power: how government officials determine how best to rule, and what concepts and legitimations they invent and deploy that make subjects governable. Political rationality is both constructionist and performative. It is not just about the information, knowledge, doctrines, and understandings that policy makers mobilize to impose their programs upon society. Political rationality creates the very categories and problems that make up a policy. And it does this programmatically. That is, in a way that the necessary actions, rulings, organizational structures, and policy instruments that allow for the implementation of the policy will logically follow from it (Lemke, 1997, 147). Political rationality, is, in short, about how "government is thought into being" (O'Malley et al., 1997, 502). This is more or less straightforward discourse analysis.

The second line of inquiry, as the preceding alluded to, concerns not the mentalities of government but the technologies through which it tries to achieve its ends, the plethora of techniques that are deployed to put governmental rationalities into effect. Rose and Miller describe these technologies as the "complex of mundane programmes, calculations, techniques, apparatuses, documents and procedures that act on the subjects of governance, to coerce, persuade, cajole, suggest, or goad them to behave in certain preferred ways" (1992, 175). The focus in this line of inquiry is, thus, on how government is *acted* into being. Here the governmentality approach truly distinguishes itself both from more traditional sociological or political science approaches to the study of governance and from a traditional history-of-ideas approach. These dispersed micro-practices then connect and aggregate in complex, only partly intentional ways—the word of choice here is "contingent" (Bevir, 1999, 354)—into formal state projects at the various levels of government (MacKinnon, 2000, 311).[38] Lemke points out that there is no one-to-one correspondence of the mentalities and technologies of government. On the contrary. The purpose of the governmentality approach is precisely to inquire into the inevitable slippage between the two; the unintended consequences and perverse effects that follow every government intervention. But to do this, in good genealogical fashion, with a constructionist focus on the possibilities of being of policy categories and their constitution in the discursive field of a particular policy (Lemke, 1997, 145).

In this dual program the analytic thrust of the governmentality approach is clearly visible. First there is the thoroughly anti-essentialist stance of the governmentality approach. "Our studies of government eschew sociological realism and its burdens of explanation and causation," Rose and Miller state (1992, 177). Instead "political rationalities" not only define the subject matter of government, but they go way beyond that in delineating the legitimate scope of government, its complementarity with institutions and actors in civil society, and the specific nature of the objects of government attention (children, immigrants, criminals, businesses, etc.). There is an unmistakable constructionist quality to this part of the governmentality approach. Political rationalities have a moral and epistemological quality, simultaneously defining and legitimating the world of concerted public action. Methodologically, the categories of analysis are never taken for granted. The aim of the analyst is to show how they came into being in the government reports, expert commentaries, newspaper articles, op-ed pieces, and judicial rulings that surround a policy topic.

Conceptually, this approach is rooted in a reciprocal notion of the relation between knowledge, power, and government. As we saw in chapter 2, in representative democracy experts of many stripes are wedged in between elected officials and administrators managing societal sectors (deLeon, 1997; Manin, 1997). In the governmentality approach this idea is pushed a few notches further by elaborating the power/knowledge equation. What distinguishes political rationalities from policy programs, for example, is that they exert a hegemonic thrust in a particular political field. Knowledge is not "knowledge for knowledge's sake" ("*reines Wissen*" in Lemke's phrase [1997, 147]), but authoritative knowledge; the "serious" statements' of Foucault's earlier work that "take place in a context in which truth and falsity have serious social consequences" (Dreyfus & Rabinow, 1983, 48). Such knowledge cannot be seen apart from its power dimension. Expert knowledge "lays claim" to the sector to be managed or problems to be addressed. It doesn't lightly tolerate any counterclaims to its expertise. This claim to authority is rooted in the alleged scientific character of professional knowledge. "The theories of the social sciences, of economics, of sociology and of psychology, thus provide a kind of *intellectual machinery* for government, in the form of procedures for rendering the world thinkable" (Rose & Miller, 1992, 182; italics in original).[39] Or as Lemke puts it:

> [T]he term [governmentality] pinpoints a specific form of representation; government defines a discursive field in which exercising power is "rationalized." This occurs, among other things, by the delineation of concepts, the specification of objects and borders, the provision of arguments and justifications, etc. (2001, 191)

However, government is not just an arena of ideas and concepts, but also, and perhaps foremost, a field of action, of techniques and routines to execute and implement the goals of government. (I addressed this in chapter 4 and will elaborate on it in chapter 10.) This became clear in the mental health example in chapter 3. Rose describes how, after World War II, a new understanding of mental illness began to take hold within psychiatry. Madness became associated less and less with the florid syndromes that dominated nineteenth- and early twentieth-century psychiatry. Instead, it came to be defined in terms of ill health, personal unhappiness, and social inefficiency, bringing new categories of people within the purview of psychiatry and setting new norms and standards for well-being (Rose, 1986, 52). But Rose emphasizes that, contrary to popular belief, this was the not the result of a reform movement. Underlying this change in understanding were changes in technology: the development of powerful psychotropic medication, forms of ambulant care such as the community mental health center, and the emergence of new types of therapies such as behavior therapy, group therapy, and what Rose calls "therapies of normality." These technologies extend the reach of psychiatry into areas of living where they promise to enhance everyday functional capacities or liberate psychological attributes that have been temporarily blocked (1986, 81). These therapies are not imposed upon unwilling people, but entered into voluntarily with the purpose of improving the quality of life or one's efficacy in the workplace. The result is, in the words of Rose, a "proliferation of sites for the practice of psychiatry." This "psychiatrization of new problems," leads to new ideals of living, new aspirations of the attainable in emotional functioning, new norms of what to expect in self and other, new collective self-understandings.

Technologies of government must not be seen as tools that implement the dreams of rulers. They are not the material expression of power or purpose, although they clearly have power implications. The "serious statements" that I referred to earlier are authoritative not only because of their authors, but also because of their practical implications. The utterances of experts, elected officials, and administrators are not just neutral expressions of how they think that society should be understood; they are stated to be translated into action, into a targeted intervention into the lives of social actors. This does not imply that technologies of government are the product of grand strategies that express the preexisting power differentials or the "natural" interests of the ruling elite. Instead, despite their "rational" underpinnings, government interventions contain a strong element of contingency, of trial and error. Power asymmetries are therefore more an outcome of government technologies than a preconceived result. Government technologies are best seen as a form of tinkering, of thinking on one's feet. A practical, local, situated rationality characterizes public policy. See if something works, and move on to the next program when it doesn't.

This part of governmentality theory takes its cue from Foucault's extremely decentered approach to discourse, in which the discursive and nondiscursive intermingle in complex, unpredictable ways without the guidance of a central manager. In his historiographic work Foucault took pains to describe in abundant detail how actors operating in a particular social field, such as the penal system or psychiatry, continually changed the ways in which they approached practical problems. The significance of these mundane techniques and routines was that, in Foucault's genealogical approach, they always embodied larger social and political forces (Foucault, 1979, 23–24). By stepping back, as it were, one can discern how these micro-physics of power aggregate into larger "strategies" and "dispositions." But there is no grand strategy here, no reform movement by an enlightened elite, no repressive conspiracy. Professionals, administrators, and elected officials design and try out, piecemeal, a solution to a local problem. They are constrained by larger political schemes (rationalities), and run into various resistances. The target group moves along with the new policies, adapting, resisting, making do. Foucault wrote, "This technology is diffuse, rarely formulated in continuous, systematic discourse; it is often made up of bits and pieces; it implements a disparate set of tolls and methods. In spite of the coherence of its results, it is generally no more than a multiform instrumentation" (1979, 26). Over time, the world has changed beyond recognition. These are the sharp breaks that Foucault describes in *Discipline and Punish* and *The Birth of the Clinic* (Hacking, 1986, 29). The aggregate outcome is a new way of managing a societal sector, plus a new understanding of the sector to guide and legitimate our interventions, a drastic reordering of social relations and identities, a transformation of the way we grasp the world. According to Foucault this is power from below. Out of the myriad of practical solutions to everyday problems of managing people and situations emerge larger configurations of ideas and understandings and more durable patterns of influence and power. Power is an emergent property.

This part of the governmentality program has evolved into a sustained engagement—if not obsession—with neoliberal tactics of governing. Neoliberal governments, as the received view goes, no longer intervene directly, by means of specialized, authorized state agencies, but surreptitiously, through the introduction of indirect techniques of guiding individuals. The responsibility for social risks such as illness, unemployment, poverty, and more has shifted from the state to the realm of the family and the individual. Self-care has overtaken solidarity. The heart of neoliberal rationality is the congruence between a moral-responsible and a self-interested subject. In this way, personal well-being and self-fulfillment, on the one hand, and the public interest, on the other hand, coincide. This is micro-power writ large. Governing has become self-governing (Lemke, 2007, 55).

Example of Governmentality

The governmentality literature has generated many fine historical analyses of the transformation of such sectors of liberal government as schools, psychiatric services, accounting, and corporate techniques in local government (Barry et al., 1996; MacKinnon, 2000). However, few analysts have applied the conceptual machinery of governmentality to contemporary topics. A rare example is Cruikshank's book on American social policy, *The Will to Empower: Democratic Citizens and Other Subjects* (1999). As I am interested in the usefulness of governmentality for contemporary policy analysis, I will present Cruikshank's study here.

The topic of Cruikshank's book is the sudden popularity in the 1960s of policies that aim to enhance the self-esteem, the self-awareness, and the democratic participation of the poor. During the Johnson administration, persistent poverty was not just attributed to "objective" causes such as racism, lack of education, a dearth of jobs, or low wages, but also, and perhaps above all, to the powerlessness of the poor. Poverty came to be defined in subjective terms as a "condition of need, helplessness and hopelessness" (Office of Economic Opportunity, in Cruikshank, 1999, 73). The poor must be helped and stimulated to "increase their capacity to deal effectively with their own problems. The Economic Opportunity Act of 1964 made "maximum feasible participation" a key element in its repertoire of programs and policy instruments (ibid.). Community Action Programs were the vehicle for delivering the desired empowerment of the poor. Thus, programs such as Community Action Programs did not seek to help the poor by providing direct services, but by empowering them, by raising self-awareness, by inducing them into democratic participation—in short by acting upon modes of self-governance. Cruikshank frames these policies as "technologies of citizenship," and for her they raise a series of questions regarding the limits of government, the role of the state versus its citizens, and the nature of power in liberal democracies. The book is organized around two questions. First: "What are the problems to which democratic participation is posed as the solution?" And second: "By what means is the capacity, power, consciousness, or subjectivity proper to democratic participation and self-government imbued in citizens?" (1999, 3).

Cruikshank presents her conceptual framework in two main arguments. The first concerns the constitution of citizens by technologies of government. Central in this argument is a distinction between "state" and "governance." The state consists of the "liberal, representative, electoral, administrative, legislative, and judicial institutions and practices articulated within the confines of a liberal constitutional framework." Governance refers to "forms of action and relations of power that aim to guide and shape (rather than force, control or dominate) the actions of others." These latter techniques can be offered as government-sponsored programs, but may not be. They also include initiatives of voluntary organizations or private actors (1999, 4). Cruikshank's argument is that these technologies of citizenship simultaneously enlist and create the capacities of citizens to act on their own. In that sense they are a prime example of Foucault's signature "bio-power" that is both individual and aggregate, both voluntary and coercive: "Technologies of citizenship are voluntary and coercive at the same time; the actions of citizens are regulated, but only after the capacity of citizens to act as a certain kind of citizen is instilled. Democratic citizens, in short, are both the effects and the instruments of liberal governance" (Cruikshank, 1999, 4).

The second argument concerns the methodological maneuver, central to governmentality theory (and discursive analysis in general), to question the categories of analysis. It focuses on the sites where power is exercised and thereby on the nature of power in liberal democracies. We can't simply assume a distinct notion of a state, which exerts power, that is clearly demarcated from civil society, which is subjected to power. Instead, Cruikshank argues:

[T]he political itself is continually transformed and reconstituted at the micro-levels of everyday life where citizens are constituted. If power is ubiquitous, as I assert throughout, then it makes no sense to speak of "the political," "the social," "the private," and "the public" as separate domains. The political cannot be clearly excluded from other domains without excluding some relations of power. (1999, 5)

Power is everywhere, working its effects in the capillaries of society. This makes many of the traditional questions that political science raises about power more or less moot. It "misses the point," according to Cruikshank, to ask yourself why some groups are excluded from politics or from the institutional core of society, or if nonparticipation signals consent or powerlessness. What these questions miss, according to Cruikshank, is the productive effect of power. Power produces the categories and identities that are the subject of policy intervention. And it doesn't do this as part of a plan, let alone as a conspiracy by the political elite, but rather in a haphazard way, as the emerging effect of a series of unrelated administrative interventions. It is at this point that her two key arguments come together in an overarching analytical program:

The citizen is an effect and an instrument of political power rather than simply a partici-pant in politics. The measure of democracy is not the extent to which citizens participate in politics rather than stand back in fear or apathy. That is to mistake power for what it excludes rather than what it produces. The critical question for democratic theory is how citizens are constituted by politics and power. To answer that question, one must recognize the contingency of the political itself. (1999, 5–6)

Cruikshank applies her governmentality program, among other things, to the sudden popularity in the 1970s of policy programs that aimed to empower the poor, the excluded, and the marginal. (She also mentions the self-esteem movement in feminism.) Empowerment was not a program but an "idea in good currency" that united conservatives and liberals; although both groups derived different practical implications from it. The surface logic of empowerment is simple: some groups in society are structurally excluded and therefore lack the means for living a decent life. Instead of providing income support, which only increases the dependency of the poor and maintains the underlying causes of their exclusion, it is better to help them to acquire the capacity (in terms of attitudes, skills, or self-esteem) to govern their own lives and communities and thereby change the conditions of their exclusion. Cruikshank urges the reader to go beyond this surface logic with its simplified dichotomy of the powerful versus the powerless, and pay attention to all the intellectual and administrative work that precedes the idea of empowerment and that establishes its basic conceptual categories. Cruikshank departs from the assumption "that the 'powerless' do not exist as such prior to the application of technologies of citizenship. The 'powerless' are the object and the outcome of the will to empower" (1999, 72). In other words, policy is its own cause, but this time not in a Wildavskian instrumental sense but a Foucauldian constructivist sense. Let's follow Cruikshank in unpacking what this approach to policy analysis entails.

First, she clarifies that it is not her intention to debunk the empowerment movement. Rather, she says, she intends to show that empowerment is a typical instrument or tactic—the phrases are mine—of the "liberal arts of conduct" (1999, 72). Power, and thus empowerment, must be seen in relational terms. First, empowerment programs depend upon theoretical models of the poor, drawn up by experts. In particular the apathy of the poor, their unwillingness to participate in voluntary programs, raised trenchant dilemmas for well-meaning reformers who worked with them. Nonparticipation became both an object of analysis and an object of intervention. In analytical terms the poor were seen as being locked into a culture of poverty that instilled precisely those traits of apathy, lack of initiative, the inability to imagine a future, the need for immediate gratification, the inability to plan, and the unwillingness to participate, that reformers who tried to help them encountered over and over again. In fact, it was the culture of poverty thesis that created "the poor" as a single, coherent category: "before governmental intervention—and I mean that in the broadest sense—'the poor' were disparate, isolated, and often in conflict with one another; they were Appalachian coal miners, urban single mothers, illiterates, unskilled black migrants from the South, southern fundamentalists, the elderly, 'delinquent' youths, and the unemployed" (1999, 86). The culture of poverty thesis was the common denominator that tied all these groups into one political-administrative category: "The notion that the poor share a culture helped create an administrative category of policy analysis out of a vast assortment of divided people whose defining characteristic was said to be their subjective sense of powerlessness" (1999, 77).

This theoretical understanding of the poor suggested another element in the empowerment movement, namely to let the poor speak for themselves. Too often, well-meaning reformers had designed programs that did not speak to the needs of the poor. To really understand the poor, the expertise of the professional had to be continually confronted with the practical expertise of the poor themselves. It became an important element of program design to include the poor. "Planning with and not for the poor" was the slogan (1999, 78). This led to another dilemma of program design. If the goal was to increase the participation of the poor in their community—"maximum feasible participation," as another then-fashionable slogan went—how could this be done without imposing elite intentions upon the poor? The solution was to create local programs, the earlier mentioned Community Action Programs (CAPs), which established cooperative relationships between the poor and public agencies in the communities where the poor lived. As Cruikshank describes it:

> Community Action agencies were clearly designed to govern and administer the War on Poverty but were also, in and of themselves, distinct governmental domains or small publics established "by and for the poor." Though intended to be a public arena for the government of the poor, CAPs were publics not directed by the government but by the voluntary cooperation of all the public and private actors in the "local coalition" fighting the War on Poverty. . . . According to the OEO [Office of Economic Opportunity], "It is a process of building bridges between the poor and non-poor, between government officials and private groups, between professionals and laymen, between agencies which operate related programs, between the poor and the opportunities which could help them become self-sufficient, productive respected citizens. Of great importance is the building of bridges between one poor person and another, so they can share the dignity of self-help in escaping from poverty." (1999, 79)

She then adds, by way of commentary:

> Notice that even the relationships between poor people themselves were to be matters of organization and government; no ties were left untouched. "Self-help" did not mean that autonomous selves got together to help one another, rather self-help meant that the government intervened to create relations of help between selves. (ibid.)

It is for this reason that Cruikshank concludes that empowerment does not mean the creation of social-administrative enclaves where the traditional power relationships in capitalist, liberal democracies are suspended, but that empowerment is itself a relationship of power, a reconfiguration of power, in which power is simultaneously voluntary and coercive (1999, 72).

Commentary

The strong point of the governmentality approach is that it refrains from the usual explanatory tropes in policy research that consider a particular object of analysis (educational policy, crime control, the regulation of biotechnology, the war on poverty) as either "caused" by certain deep principles or forces (class interest, democratic ethos, biology, the inevitable logic of capitalism), or, instead, as the outcome of the will or purpose of a powerful policy elite. Instead, taking Foucault's own work as an exemplar, governmentality studies generally follow a genealogical path. They explain political phenomena as emergent, as more or less "contingent assemblages put together under "blind" historical circumstances (I. Hunter, 1996, 147). Policy programs, and the governmental institutions that carry them, are articulated in the continuous exertion of the myriad mundane social practices that both express and sustain the immediate practical challenges that agents face in their day-to-day life. The "logic" of this emergence lies in the specific historical context that provides to the actors involved both the way they perceive the challenges that confront them, the *mentalité* that shapes and frames their understanding of reality, and the materials and technologies on which they draw to design their practical solutions. In addition, policy is depicted as thoroughly decentered, as shaped and interpreted by a multitude of actors, both from the state and from civil society. In the hands of skilled analysts working in this tradition, this may lead to startling insights that transcend the narrow statism of traditional policy analysis, and allows us a view of what goes on below the surface significance of the world of government. More than any other interpretive approach, studies in the analytics of government tradition explain the absence or presence of particular policies, or the continuation of stubborn controversies, from the linguistic and practical articulation of the basic categories that make up the particular policy.

However, despite the undeniable heuristic value of the genealogical focus, Foucauldian policy analysis in general, and governmentality in particular, suffer from two problems; although, being the ever searching, probing thinker that he is, at the end of his life he even suggested solutions for these. First, the explanatory focus of this approach to interpretive analysis is on how categories and programs of governance, its regimes of power and truth, have come into being and how they were "made authoritative through various social discourses" (Bevir, 1999, 357). The focus is almost always on the *formation* of governance: its categories, its standards of truth and authority, the seeming naturalness of its institutions. Relatively little attention is paid to the actual implementation of government programs, to the technologies of governing in action, and to the effects of the mentalities and technologies once they are set to work in the various domains of civil society. Although the best studies in this genre (Cruikshank, 1999; Prainsack, 2006) show in a general sense how institutions and policies are assembled from exigent materials, few show how agents on the ground accomplish this. As Bevir points out, genealogical studies rarely explore the reasons people had for adopting—or, I would add, resisting—new techniques of governing or new technologies of the self. As he summarizes it, the emphasis in genealogical studies of government is always "on the ways the social world makes the subject, not the ways in which the subject makes the social world" (1999, 357).

Second, genealogy and governmentality lack a well-developed theory of practice. Although practices play a central role in their analytic-conceptual framework, their understanding of practice is curiously emaciated. Practices are never more than mere routines—more or less mechanically applied, rule-driven, endlessly repeated activities. Nowhere in the governmentality literature does one encounter the insight that practice is a distinctive mode of engaging with the world, that it is a creative, generative activity with its own logic, its own demands, its standards of rightness and excellence (Wagenaar & Cook, 2003). The reason for this reductionist view of practices is not difficult to find. Practice implies agency. To use Dewey's vocabulary, practice is a "conversation with the world," in which actors, using practical judgment, act upon the world, and reflect upon the consequences of their action. I think we can all agree: agency sits uneasily in Foucauldian theory. But does that mean that there is no place at all for agency in Foucauldian analysis of governance?

According to many critics the answer is an empathic "No." Dreyfus and Rabinow ascribe to Foucault a conception of power that they describe in stark, machine-related metaphors (for example, as a "machine in which everyone is caught, those who exercise this power as well as those who are subjected to it" [1983, 192]). Bevir highlights the structuring effects of power upon the individual (Foucault's approach "entailed a strong focus on the ways in which individuals are constructed by regimes of power" [Bevir, 1999, 354]). As he forcefully puts it, "Foucault vehemently rejected the idea of an autonomous subject, that is, of the subject as its own foundation, of the subject as capable of having meaningful experiences, reasoning, forming beliefs, and acting outside of a particular social context." And according to Taylor there is a glaring inconsistency in Foucault's idea of genealogical power as all structure and no agency. As he asks rhetorically "'Power' without 'freedom' or 'truth': can there really be an analysis of power which uses the notion of power, and which leaves no place for freedom, or truth?" (1986, 90). Is Foucault really aiming for an actor-less form of analysis, as his critics seem to agree?

As can be expected from a scholar as elusive as Foucault, the answer is ambiguous. There are many passages in his work that point to an almost deterministic understanding of discourse and power. Yet, even in his genealogical phase, his notion of bottom-up power gives a role to think-ing, acting, and deliberating individuals (although their actions are constrained by the cognitive and linguistic frames). Moreover, there have always been two Foucaults: a private one who was a lifelong activist for prison reform and who initially supported the Iranian revolution, only to criticize its excesses and call for resistance against the ayatollahs; and a public one, who ban-ished the individual to the margins of history, and wrote in largely deterministic terms about the conditioning of subjects by vast linguistic-institutional structures.[40] Only toward the end of his life do we see a reconciliation of the private person and the public persona. Foucault did not turn into a political liberal. But in his final years he decisively turned his back on the determinism of his earlier work and promulgated an almost autonomous individual who (*pace* Taylor) exercised the freedom to resist the effects of power on his personal life. He also formulated an ethics that centered on the notion of "care for the self" (Foucault, 1988). It would go too far, at the end of this long section, to discuss at length Foucault's last, "subjective" phase. I want to restrict myself to a few comments that are relevant to our project of an interpretive policy analysis.

In a late essay that appeared as the afterword in the volume by Dreyfus and Rabinow, Foucault discusses the place of the subject in his conception of power. His goal was never the analysis of power per se, he says. Instead his objective was "to create a history of the different modes by which, in our culture, human beings are made subjects" (Foucault, 1983, 208). This is a remarkable state-ment. Not only for its focus on the subject, after several highly acclaimed publications in which structures and practices of power were the center of attention, but in the implicit recognition of pre-discursive subjects: "human beings" on which the tactics and mechanics of power operate.[41] After this turn toward the subject, it comes as no surprise that Foucault turns to resistance against power as a window upon the functioning of power in our society—or "a new economy of power relations," as he calls it (1983, 210). Because of its pertinence to interpretive policy analysis, I quote the relevant passage in full:

I would like to suggest another way to go further towards a new economy of power rela-tions,[42] a way which is more empirical, more directly related to our present situation, and which implies more relations between theory and practice. It consists of taking the forms of resistance against different forms of power as a starting point. To use another metaphor, it consists of using this resistance as a chemical catalyst so as to bring to light power relations, locate their position, find out their points of application and the methods used. Rather than analyzing power from the point of view of its internal rationality, it consists of analyzing power relations through the antagonisms of strategies. (1983, 211)

Foucault continues to enumerate a number of areas where such analysis of resistance could take place. And then in a passage that might be directed straight at policy analysis, he concludes:

As a starting point, let us take a series of oppositions which have developed over the last few years: opposition to the power of men over women, of parents over children, of psychiatry over the mentally ill, of medicine over population, *of administration over the way people live.* (1983, 211; italics added)

Studying resistance is a strategy to understand the multifarious functioning of power in our society. I will skip the obvious questions Foucault's turn toward resistance raises for the issue of ethical subjectivity to take up the question of from what ontological and ethical position the individual is *able* to resist within the Foucauldian power panopticum. This is an important issue that occupied Foucault for most of his final years. My focus will be on the practical and ethical significance of resistance for our project of an interpretive policy analysis.

At first it seems as if Foucault has indeed embraced the humanist-liberal notion of the autono-mous individual in his positing of resistance as an analytical tactic. The following passage, in which he comments on the types of resistance, the struggles, that the analyst could study, seems to suggest as much:

They are struggles which question the status of the individual: on the one hand, they assert the right to be different and they underline everything which makes individuals truly indi-vidual. On the other hand, they attack everything which separates the individual, breaks his links with others, splits up community life, forces the individual back on himself and ties him to his identity in a constraining way. (1983, 211–12)

But very soon, the reader discovers that what Foucault has in mind is not so much a pre-discursive concept of the individual, but something more akin to subject positions:

These struggles are not exactly for or against "individual," but rather they are struggles against the "government of individualization." (1983, 211)

Foucault has never abandoned his concept of disciplining, all-pervasive micro-power. He only tries to integrate a more assertive—and empirically astute—notion of resistance within his theoreti-cal framework. At the end of his career he came to see that freedom and the possibility of resistance are necessary conditions of power (Foucault, 1988, 12). Let's reiterate for a moment. Foucault's project was to formulate a theory of power and governance that is pertinent to contemporary, liberal, mass society with its idolatrizing of individual liberty and democracy. For such a society a conception of power that is rooted in notions of sovereignty and the law is insufficient—not unimportant, just not enough. What Foucault rightly saw is that such dispersed societies require a concomitant decentered notion of power that operates in a similarly decentered way. We have encountered its characteristics. It works through surveillance and persuasion, instead of violence. Its aim is to align productive activities, individual aspirations, personal identity, and modes of discipline. It creates individual identities via so called "subject positions." In its effects it strives to be simultaneously individualizing and totalizing, and it does that by appearing to individuals as natural, self-evident; as a manifestation of truth.

In this conception of micro-power, as we saw, knowledge plays a central role. The type of detailed surveillance that is needed for an effective conditioning of the population requires detailed knowledge of that population. Allen states:

> Discipline produces a docile body, more powerful yet easier to direct and subjugate, and also more calculable and easier to know, a predictable object for the quasi-scientific knowledge of the social or human sciences, which grow up in the same historical moment as the great growth period in the disciplining of European populations. . . . The same interventions which produce a docile body also make it possible to compile precise data on individuals and to study them comparatively under controlled conditions. At the same time, this knowledge enhances the capacity for control. An effective reciprocity develops between the knowledge that discipline produces and the power which it exercises. (1998, 175)

Hence "power/knowledge," with the signature backstroke signifying the reciprocate relation. This is what Foucault has in mind when he elevates resistance as a necessary backdrop for the analysis of power. Not institutions but techniques of power are his target:

> To sum up: the main objective of these struggles is to attack not so much "such or such" an institution of power, or group, or elite, or class, but rather a technique, a form, of power. This form of power applies itself to immediate everyday life which categorizes the individual, marks him by his own individuality, attaches him to his own identity, imposes a law of truth on him which he must recognize and which others have to recognize in him. It is a form of power which makes individuals subjects. (Foucault, 1983, 212)

How does all this add up to a political ethic? First, the concept of power/knowledge brings into question "applied" disciplines like policy analysis (or criminology, psychiatry, pedagogy, education studies, or psychology, for that matter). What these disciplines have in common is their self-ascribed role in assisting the governing elites in managing designated social sectors by producing "truth" about their domain of specialization. Power/knowledge introduces a moment of critical reflexivity into these disciplines (Hoy, 1998, 21). Second, with his focus on resistance Foucault suggests both a strategy and an ethic of critical policy analysis. While a governmentality approach focuses on the analytics of micro-power, its anatomy, its modes of operation, and its effects, resistance introduces a critical ethics. It suggests a focus on the unintended consequences of public policy and acts of everyday resistance as a window upon the hidden assumptions of a policy. Qualitative policy analysis, as I described it in the preceding chapter, is a good example of such a critical approach. What a Foucauldian political ethic adds to qualitative policy analysis is a theoretical elaboration of critique in a decentered field of governance.

Challenging taken-for-granted institutions, opening up everyday forms of domination, is the recurrent theme in a critical, genealogical policy analysis. This critical challenge operates at two levels. First, the purpose of genealogy is to reveal that despite their apparent universal and self-evident character, social institutions are historically contingent. Differently put, genealogy liberates the utopian imagination. Our institutions "as we know them" are not the only solutions to social conduct. New forms of human relation, new possibilities of human interaction, new "truth games," are, in principle, possible (Bernauer & Mahon, 2003, 151; Foucault, 1988, 15; Hoy, 1998, 24). Simply becoming aware of the inessential nature of taken-for-granted practices makes people less certain of these practices, and more open to alternatives (Hoy, 1998, 27).[43]

What does this mean for the analyst? How does he reach "awareness"? After all, he is as much immersed in the *dispositif* of a particular social phenomenon (for example, taken-for-granted, collective understandings of sexuality, poverty, schooling, or Jewishness, to use a few examples we have encountered so far) as the objects of his analysis. In fact, only because the analyst shares cultural understandings and practices with his object of analysis is he able to come up with a common basis of understanding (Dreyfus & Rabinow, 1983, 125). On the other hand, without a certain necessary distance, it would be impossible for the analyst to gain any perspective on his object of analysis and to "see" it at all. The ambiguity that this inevitably leads to is fully brought out in the following quote from Dreyfus and Rabinow, in which they try to capture the nature of Foucauldian "interpretive analytics":

> Interpretive understanding can only be obtained by someone who shares the actor's involve-ment, but distances himself from it. This person must undertake the hard historical work of diagnosing and analyzing the history and organization of current cultural practices. The resulting interpretation is a pragmatically guided reading of the coherence of the practices of the society. It does not claim to correspond either to the everyday meanings shared by the actors or, in any simple sense, to reveal the intrinsic meaning of the practices. This is the sense in which Foucault's method is interpretive but not hermeneutic. (1983, 124)

At a second level, and here we begin to discern the glimmerings of a democratic imagination in Foucault, a critical policy analysis would assist people in resisting the subjugating forces of micro-power. The concept of micro-power dictates that there is no obvious escape from it, for example by appealing to universal principles of justice or liberty, or to a communicative ethics that would make free, unimpeded communication possible. Power is always present in the Foucauldian social cosmology. Critique has to be internal critique. Resistance has to be found within, inside the power/knowledge relations, for "in the modern period, no political issue is more significant than how the person is defined and how one's relationship to one's self is organized" (Bernauer & Mahon, 2003, 154). For Foucault this meant, in the last years of his life, an immersion in Greek codes of self-conduct and early Christian confessional techniques to formulate an "ethics of care for the self" (Paras, 2006). Such a reflection of self-knowledge, on how to behave "correctly" as a free individual in relation to others (Foucault, 1998, 7), could be the only source of resistance to the ubiquitous effects of micro-power. Or as Foucault phrases his political ethic for a pluralist, dispersed society (with a critical nod to Habermas):

> I don't believe there can be a society without relations of power, if you understand them as means by which individuals try to conduct, to determine the behavior of others. The problem is not of trying to dissolve them in the utopia of a perfectly transparent communication, but to give one's self the rules of law, the techniques of management, and also the ethics, the ethos, the practice of self, which would allow these games of power to be played with a minimum of domination. (1988, 18)

Let me end here. We will see in the next section that poststructuralist political theorists will elaborate the democratic angle of a critical political ethic. With all his sophistication about power and governance, democracy gets short shrift in Foucault. And we will see in chapter 8 how a group of theorists and practitioners will formulate another way out of the suffocating maze of micropower: dialogue. Becoming aware of the contingency of social configurations is not enough, their argument goes. We must find ways to supersede our constraints, and to find new, better alternatives. Bridging conflict, and thereby bringing together the combined experiential intelligence of different groups of people is the way to do this.

POSTSTRUCTURALIST POLITICAL THEORY

Poststructuralist political theory is associated with Laclau, Mouffe, Connolly, Howarth, Glynos, Norval and others. Many of these thinkers are associated with the University of Essex in the United Kingdom, which effectively makes it the world capital of poststructuralist political theory.[44] Poststructuralist political theory represents a potentially important source of ideas and insights for policy analysis. I say potentially, because it has so far rarely been put to use in the field of public policy. What it holds out is a focus on identity, discourse, difference, struggle, and power as central forces in politics, a radically pluralistic conception of society, and a critical stance that is rooted in an ethics of pluralism. In poststructuralist political thought the basic ideas about political conflict, identity, and democratic participation are captured in the important concept of *agonistic pluralism.* However, several factors are responsible for the relative unfamiliarity of poststructuralist political theory in the interpretive policy literature.

The first is the exceedingly abstract writing of some of its proponents. Contrary to the work of Foucault, who developed his theories from detailed historical studies of subjects such as mental illness or the penal system, the writings of most poststructuralist political theorists are almost completely devoid of any empirical examples. Laclau and Mouffe, for example, have been rightly criticized for providing an ontology of political discourse but failing to provide a more substantive elaboration of how these large abstract concepts can be put to use in analyzing concrete social and political phenomena (Howarth, 2000, 117). In fact, the main poststructuralist theorists exhibit such a disinterest in substantive social problems that it almost amounts to a form of disdain. I know of few serious attempts to translate the theoretical concepts into workable research strategies. What doesn't help is the abominable writing of some key figures in poststructuralist theory. Laclau and Mouffe in particular have an almost perverse preference for burying the reader under a thick layer of neologisms such as "nodal points," "floating signifiers," "the overdetermination of subject positions," "dislocations, "hegemonic formations," "chains of equivalence," and more. This makes it exceedingly difficult to assess what is new to the theory of political discourse and what is merely a reformulation of ideas found in Foucauldian discourse theory. This abstruse, hermetic style makes it even more difficult to relate the main ideas of poststructuralist political theory to the everyday world of public policy.[45]

A third factor is poststructuralist political theory's origin in (neo-)Marxist theory. It is a fact of academic life that Marxism is scarcely taught in schools of public policy. Policy analysis, as a working discipline, is still submerged in an uncritical liberal, instrumentalist conception of state and society. For most students of public policy the vocabulary of Marxist scholars is utterly alien, and most of them go though their curriculum without any exposure to the basic ideas of Marx, Engels, or important neo-Marxists such as Gramsci and Althusser. Conversely, Marxist or neo-Marxist scholars are barely interested in, if not downright suspicious of, the mundane policy problems that are the staple of public policy curricula. In the writings of Laclau for example, with their almost exclusive focus on popular movements, political institutions hardly play a role (Norval, 2007). Political discourse theory has been put to good use in the analysis of ideology, but most examples refer to a rather doctrinaire literature on radical feminism and racism. Be that as it may, the Marxist heritage of poststructuralist political theory puts it at a somewhat unjust disadvantage in circles of public policy scholars.

As a result, poststructuralist political theory has rarely been applied to the study of public policy. In my experience, students are intrigued by the critical promise they discern in poststructuralist political theory but they have a hard time relating it to their own dissertation projects. We have to turn to a recent book by Glynos and Howarth (2007) to get a taste of the potential usefulness of political discourse theory as a distinct approach to interpretive political analysis.

Which elements in poststructuralist political discourse theory are useful for interpretive policy analysis? I would say the role it accords to conflict and struggle in political analysis, the place it accords to agency and identity in its concept of discourse, and its ethos of agonistic pluralism. The latter is a subject that I will return to in chapter 8 when we discuss dialogical approaches to interpretive policy analysis. Also, poststructuralist political theory is particularly well positioned to deal with policy change. After all, public policy making is all about becoming. It is about trying to change what is seen as problematic or unacceptable and working toward a particular ideal state of affairs. Contrary to Foucault, poststructuralist political theorists place contingency and instability at the heart of social life. This is an improvement over the largely static, ex post facto nature of most policy analysis, which leaves policy dynamics, the irrepressible element of becoming, out of the equation altogether. Let's edge into poststructuralist political theory by first focusing on its notion of discourse.

Discourse

Poststructuralist political theory positions itself as nonessentialist. Passionately so, if we go by, for example, the zeal with which Laclau and Mouffe distance themselves from concepts such as society or social order (1985, 95–96). However, nonessentialism per se is not distinctive of poststructuralist political theory. As we saw, the interpretivism of Bevir and Rhodes, and, of course, Foucault's conception of discourse, also employ a constructivist approach to social theory. Both claim that the objects of political analysis are not given, but emerge out of the practices and interpretations of actors. Similar to these approaches, poststructuralist political theory tries to steer clear of the bugbears of structural determinism and a priori individual subjectivism. What distinguishes the nonessentialism of poststructuralist political theory is its emphasis on difference (and conflict) as the elementary particle of its social-political ontology.[46] Let's illustrate this with the currently fashionable notion of policy networks in the policy literature.

In much writing on this topic policy networks are considered real objects that exist somewhere out there in the policy field of choice. (For example, the network around the projected third runway at Heathrow airport in London, or the one around the construction of and conflict over the *Betuwelijn,* the freight railway through the rural heart of the Netherlands that connects the harbor of Rotterdam with the German export markets.) This common, essentialist understanding of policy networks emphasizes the logic of collective action. Actors in the network are mutually dependent. Differences in interest and position are dealt with by rational dialogue and reasoned consensus (Sørensen and Torfing, 2008). This realist conception of policy networks allows analysts to theorize about their characteristics (open or closed, homogeneous or heterogeneous, durable or fleeting). We can also speculate about managing policy networks, through formulating rules of access or by manipulating the knowledge that is available to participants (Kickert et al., 1997). We can assess to what extent certain networks have achieved their policy goal and their democratic potential, and if necessary intervene through measures of meta-governance (Sørensen, 2006). How does poststructuralist political theory conceive of policy networks? In brief: as the contingent and unstable outcome of the struggle between different groups to assert and maintain themselves and their identities in a perennially contested political field. Or, in more formal theoretical terms, as "subject positions" who are engaged in the "articulation" of their "political subjectivity," resulting in a provisional "articulated discursive totality." Let's unpack this highly coded language by discussing the concept of discourse in poststructuralist political theory.

In developing their conception of discourse, Laclau and Mouffe stay remarkably close to the structuralist, discursive conception of meaning developed by Saussure. In conformity with Saussure's concept of meaning, every element in a discourse is defined relationally. Similar to Foucault in his genealogy, Laclau and Mouffe take language not as a static structure of signs but as language-in-use. As Jørgensen and Phillips, in their admirably clear summary of poststructuralist political theory, put it, "[L]anguage use is a social phenomenon: It is through conventions, negotiations, and conflicts that structures of meaning are fixed and challenged" (2002, 25). This is perhaps a good time to introduce some of Laclau and Mouffe's peculiar terminology.[47] "*Articulation*" is the process of defining—perhaps fixing or settling are better terms—the meaning of certain social phenomena by establishing their relations with other phenomena. The result, a—temporarily—fixed meaning, is called a "*moment.*" Moments are similar to signs in a Saussurian language system. Some "moments" have a more central position in a discursive system and are called "*nodal points.*" Jørgensen and Phillips call "nodal points" "privileged signs around which the other signs are ordered" (2002, 26). Although this sounds reasonable enough, it goes to show the ambiguity that surrounds poststructuralist political theory. Is "mental illness" a "nodal point" in the discourse on deinstitutionalization, or is it simply a "moment"? How do we distinguish between the two? And what good does it do us to distinguish them? Do they anchor certain discourses by grounding them in some alleged ontology, as Connolly argues? Or are they strategic hilltops in the pitched battles for hegemony that surround certain discourses, as Laclau and Mouffe seem to indicate?[48]

However, this is only one side of the poststructuralist conception of discourse. The visible side. The part that sticks above the surface. But meaning in poststructuralist discourse is also defined counterfactually; by what is *not* in the discourse. Every articulated system of moments is reductionist. It closes off the wide, unbounded, giddy universe of *possible* meanings. If we talk of "mental illness" than we cannot very well talk in the same breath of "mental health." The latter term belongs to a different camp. That whole wide field of potential meanings, all the possibilities that the discourse excludes, Laclau and Mouffe call a "field of discursivity" (Jørgensen and Phillips, 2002, 27; Laclau and Mouffe, 1985, 111).[49] Thus the centrality of the principle of difference in poststructuralist discourse. Not only elementary signs are defined in a Saussurian opposition to other signs, but whole discourses. And as no discourse can hope to exhaust all the possibilities in the vast social world, every discourse is at risk of being attacked or invaded or eroded by elements from other discourses. ("Subverted" in the terminology of Laclau and Mouffe.) Thus the centrality of instability or "contingency" in poststructuralist discourse.[50] I will come back to this.

Let's add one more key element to poststructuralist discourse theory. I quote Laclau and Mouffe once again: "Now, in an articulated discursive totality, where every element occupies a differential position—in our terminology, where every element has been reduced to a *moment* in that totality—all identity is relational, and all relations have a necessary character" (1985, 106). A "necessary character"? At first blush this must seem to be an anomaly in a nonessentialist social theory. But, in the context of language use, "necessity" does not refer to fixed positions in a system of differential relations between signs. Rather it must be seen as a stand-in for the self-evident, taken-for-granted way that we experience identity. Seen in this light, the "necessary" character of discursive statements takes on considerable political significance. To an environmentalist or feminist or Christian fundamentalist, their identity appears as given. Its necessity and coherence seems to emanate from some self-evident first principle external to the carrier of the said identity, which itself requires no further explanation. Against this, and to my mind this is one of the most challenging implications of their theoretical position, Laclau and Mouffe (and Connolly) present a thoroughly relational understanding of identity, in which its self-evident character derives not from some a priori ethical or rational principles, but from its position in a wider environment of political positions against which it defines itself.[51] Identity is, by definition, dispersed. Laclau and Mouffe explain this by quoting the linguist Émile Benveniste:

> Whoever says system says arrangement or conformity of parts in a structure which transcends and explains its elements. Everything is so *necessary* in it that modifications of the whole and of the details reciprocally condition one another. The relativity of values is the best proof that they depend closely upon one another in the synchrony of a system which is always being threatened, always being restored. The point is that all are values of opposition and are defined only by their difference. . . . if language is something other than a fortuitous conglomeration of erratic notions and sounds uttered at random, it is because necessity is inherent in its structure as in all structure. (quoted in Laclau & Mouffe, 1985, 106)

To which Laclau and Mouffe add:

> Necessity derives, therefore, not from an underlying intelligible principle but from the regularity of a system of structural positions. *In this sense no relation can be contingent or external, since the identity of its elements would then be specified outside the relation itself.* (1985, 106; italics added.)

Necessity, it turns out, is the ethical core of poststructuralist political theory. To most people their world is self-evident, taken for granted, natural. But it really isn't. What appears natural is really the unintended outcome of an intricately organized set of semantic relations within a system of "signs."

This long quote above nicely illustrates the relational, structuralist, and dispersed character of the categories and objects of social and political analysis. However, this is not the full story of the poststructuralist conception of discourse. Poststructuralist discourse theory distinguishes itself from other theories of discourse by emphasizing—I am inclined to say, relentlessly so—two related features: antagonism and contingency.[52] Taken together, the relational, dispersed, oppositional, and contingent character of discourse makes up the core of poststructuralist political theory. In combination with a remarkably sophisticated theory of political identity, poststructuralist discourse makes up a radical pluralist challenge to the conventional pluralism of American political science (Wenman, 2003a). In the remainder of this section I will discuss both of these features of poststructuralist discourse—antagonism and contingency—and explore some of their implications, such as the inescapable political nature of social relations and the role of power. I will conclude with a discussion of the ethical implications of poststructural political theory. But first I need to make a few brief remarks about identity and its relation to discourse in poststructuralist political theory.

The poststructuralist conception of discourse, as Howarth says, "captures the idea that all objects and actions are meaningful, and that their meaning is conferred by a particular system of significant differences" (2000, 101). This notion of discourse is really a theory of meaning. For example, a nuclear reactor, a community mental health center, or the idea of motherhood derives its specific meaning from its position in a field of "significant" differences (the Three Mile Island incident, a particular understanding of mental illness, or the demographic threat to the state of Israel, respectively). In this sense these "objects" derive their specific identity from their position in this space of distinctions. Identity must be understood here in a broader sense than the common "psycho-sociological" understanding (Wenman, 2003a, 59). The common understanding of identity is part of a larger philosophical category of unity and substance. Identity is that which distinguishes an object from other objects (ibid.).[53]

The particular contribution of the poststructuralist theory of discourse to political theory (and policy analysis) is that it challenges the taken-for-granted understanding of identity that most people hold. As we saw, much of policy analysis operates under strong realist assumptions. A nuclear reactor, a community mental health center, and motherhood are what they are, objects with a set of fixed, recognizable features that can be plugged into analytic projects with widely varying goals. (Reducing dependency on imported oil versus phasing out first generation nuclear reactors. Or reducing teenage pregnancy versus raising the Jewish birth rate in the state of Israel.) Wenman argues that such a fixed, unproblematic notion of identity is at the heart of the conventional political pluralism of Robert Dahl, David Truman, and Arthur Bentley that is the received view in political science and, I should add, policy analysis. The identity of the interest groups that compete for the attention of an arbitrating state are considered settled and given: unions versus employers' organizations; environmentalists versus corporate interests, socialists versus neoliberals. Even the rules of the political game are given. Politics then is defined as the structured competition of interest groups within a democratic parliamentary system. Everything else falls outside the category of politics and belongs to civil society. Thus, politics is an autonomous realm where specialized experts (elected officials, administrators, and policy analysts) arrive at judgments and make decisions on certain prestructured issues and problems.

Conventional pluralism has been criticized "from the inside," but the poststructuralist critique goes much further.[54] It redefines not only the conventional, and widely accepted, notion of pluralism, transforming it from a characteristic of liberal democracy to an ontological feature of *all* societies, but it also challenges the unproblematic character of political identity and thereby the very idea of what constitutes politics. The poststructuralist critique of conventional pluralism centers on the two core ideas of the central role of identity in politics and the constitutive role of difference in establishing identity. Taken together they establish the deep pluralism, which is characteristic of poststructuralist political theory. Let's begin with difference as a precondition for the establishment of identity.

Difference as Social Ontology

The basic idea is simple in its constitution and wide ranging in its implications. Identity, as the conscious entity from which all political desire and action originate, is as much defined by a set of positive identifications with certain ideals, values, beliefs, and action preferences, as by what distinguishes it from a number of rival ideologies and political claims. Or as Connolly puts it, "An identity is established in relation to a series of differences that have become socially recognized. These differences are essential to its being" (1991, 64). For example, my identity as an environmentalist is as much determined by some core beliefs about saving our planet, the contribution of human activity to climate change, and the desirability of a conscious, ecologically friendly lifestyle, as by my resistance to corporate squandering of natural resources, an unthinking consumerist lifestyle that contributes to resource waste and climate change, and dallying governments who are less than forceful in entering and enforcing emission reduction treaties. Or, my identity as a Christian fundamentalist depends to a large extent on my enmity toward atheism and the alleged dissipative tendencies of a culturally permissive society. Poststructuralists like to say that the other, as that which is external and different, is a "necessary condition of self-identity" (Wenman, 2003a, 60).

The latter example shows why poststructuralist theorists see "identity," and not belief or ideology, as both the source and engine of politics. First, the conglomerate of positive and negative identifications makes for a dense, interlocking set of allegiances and preferences that reciprocally keep each other in place. Compromising on one will affect the others. Second, certain beliefs are indispensable to my position. Any compromise on these core beliefs would undermine the integrity of the whole edifice (Connolly, 1991, 7). For example, while I might be willing, as an environmentalist, to negotiate with government officials about the best to way deal with the expansion of Heathrow airport, I will never side with the position of American President Bush's administration on oil drilling in Alaska. The pristine, unspoiled wilderness of Alaska is a key symbol in the environmentalists' fight against climate change and corporate greed. Alaska's wilderness is indispensable to the environmentalist's belief system. By compromising on Alaska, not only would I lose my credibility in the eyes of my fellow environmentalists, but I would also undermine a wide range of beliefs and values that are central to my being an environmentalist. Third, as the example suggests, the beliefs and identifications that make up a particular position have strong affective components. They are jealously guarded against contamination by hostile influences. Interlocking ideas, the indispensability of certain core beliefs, and the affective load of the whole configuration of ideas, beliefs, values, identifications, and action preferences, result in what poststructuralists call an identity. We define ourselves according to certain positions in the ideological landscape. We don't just have environmental beliefs; we *are* environmentalists.

Now, it could be objected that this understanding of identity as defined by difference is a poorer version of the fuller Foucauldian understanding of discourse as made up of the rules, practices, statements, and objects that constitute a particular social field, such as psychiatry, prostitution, or government. I think this is a valid objection. Surely many political self-identities are organized around affirmative and negative identifications. For example, the environmentalist is not just the negative version of the corporate raider or the consumerist, but also embodies positive principles such as justice, solidarity, and good stewardship, and practices such as using public transportation, refraining from frivolous use of airlines, installing proper insulation in the house, eating locally produced crops, and so on. To see such principles and practices as defined only in opposition to their counterparts would be to deny their ability to inspire, motivate, and give meaning to a life consciously lived. It would be to deny the positive, creative aspects of power as Foucault would formulate it.

Yet, the poststructuralists' emphasis on difference highlights two important aspects of difference and identity that remain relatively opaque in Foucault's theory of discourse. First, going beyond identity, poststructuralist political theorists see difference not just as an empirical feature of society (it is that too), but an *ontological* category. It is part of the "deep structure" of politics and community. We cannot assume agreement; not even as an ideal state. Attaining consensus implies overcoming difference. Difference is the condition of possibility of politics. As Norval puts it:

> One cannot . . . presuppose a mutual understanding as Habermas does. Indeed, the *very possibility of commonality* and, hence of political community is what is in dispute in political argumentation and disagreement, and what gets constituted through such argumentation.

. . . The disagreement at the heart of political logic is thus not simply an empirical feature that can be overcome in favor of consensus. It is, indeed, constitutive of that logic, and marker of its presence in democratic regimes. It marks the manner in which both argumentation and political subjectivity are understood. (2007, 42–43; italics in original)

Another way that poststructuralist theorists approach the idea of an ontology of difference is through the notion of contingency in identity formation. Let's discuss contingency by returning once more to the meaning of pluralism. When poststructuralists talk of pluralism, they mean something else than the mere observation that there exists a diversity of opinion, value positions and "conceptions of the good" in liberal societies (Mouffe, 2000, 18). What they mean is that there is not—*and there cannot be*—a common ground (reason, truth, rational choice, the market, or "democracy") that can act as a final arbiter in settling political conflict. Or, to be more precise, whatever common ground is put forward in the name of truth, democracy, rationality, or anything else, obfuscates the work of repression and exclusion that makes dissenting voices invisible and, quite often, unimaginable. Now, this is a provocative and perhaps somewhat mysterious statement that only makes sense if we bring to mind the constructivist nature of political identity. Difference, as we saw above, is a precondition for the (self-)definition of identity. The distinction from others—opponents and adversary groups—is a necessary condition for the existence of my political identity as X or Y. Or, as Connolly puts it, "The definition of difference is a requirement built into the logic of identity, and the construction of otherness is a temptation that readily insinuates itself in to that logic" (1991, 9). The point is that if X defines itself in opposition to Y and vice versa, they don't have recourse to a common ground Z that precedes their respective ensemble of beliefs, values, action preferences, and emotions, to settle their differences.

But how can that be? We all know examples in which even the most bitter opponents can eventually come to agree on a position, an understanding, that forms the kernel of an agreement or a resolution of their conflict.[55] That position or understanding surely represents a common ground that emotion, conviction, prejudice, or obedience to tradition had prevented them from grasping so far. Poststructuralists would answer to this that the example amounts to a misreading of the constitution of political identity. Sure enough, the opponents might, in the end, agree on certain shared principle or procedure, but that sharing is not the discovery of a hitherto hidden presumption that encompasses both their identities. It is the careful and painstaking recognition that *the other's* identity contains elements that, frustratingly, refer to the dangerous world of possibilities that *I* want to exclude. This subversive outside eludes the overly closed definition of my identity, but it contains the kernel of an understanding or rapprochement of the other. Poststructuralists call this the intrinsic contingency of political identity. Contingency should not be seen as "anything goes" here, but as an inescapable ambiguity that lies at the heart of the conglomerate of identification and belief that is political identity. Connolly evokes the Derridean notion of *différance* here, and it is enlightening to follow his argument at this point. With the notion of *différance* Derrida (and with him Mouffe and Connolly, and, as we shall see in the next chapter, Gadamer) attempts to break out of the duality between, on the one hand, a position that ultimately finds recourse in a final principle or procedure to settle political conflict and, on the other hand, a relativism that engulfs the interplay of identity in democratic society. *Différance* springs from the irrepressible fullness of life, the excess of being of which every political position can only be a partial version. The notion of *différance* suggests that we simply cannot keep that abundance of being out of our carefully constructed and guarded political identity. "Every object has inscribed into its very being something other than itself," says Mouffe (2000, 21). And in their theory of discourse Laclau and Mouffe speak of a "surplus of meaning" in society that can never be fully contained within any discourse (1985, 111).

I think there is an element of confusion here. The argument on *différance* works in the abstract but not in the concrete. How do you distinguish between the ontological and the ontic? Between the "genotype" and "phenotype" of politics? Contrary to my genetic metaphor, you can't touch or manipulate the ontological. We don't suffer from policy controversies in the rarefied atmosphere of ontology, but in the cold, harsh light of empirical street brawls. But the thrust of the argument is important: a, necessary, celebration—perhaps it is better to speak of a reminder—of difference as an inescapable feature of politics. Agreement, consensus, is a luxury, obtained with exceeding difficulty. More important, to deny the conflict-ridden character of policy making and to project democratic decision making against the background of consensus has the smell of a ploy. Or as poststructuralist theorists would say: of a hegemonic imposition of consensus as the defining feature of proper democratic process. The effect is a curtailment of democracy; a denial of the wild, rich plurality of experience and belief. And, of the fundamental complexity and unpredictability of large social-technical issues. I will return to complexity and conflict as defining features of politics in chapter 10. I will discuss tactics of dealing with real-world differences in chapter 8.

Contingency

Difference breeds ambiguity. In a very real sense identity is dependent on the very entities that it so fervidly dissociates itself from. What is thought in a discourse or identity always implies what is unthought but present in another discourse or identity (Macdonell, 1986, 47). This is the case both logically and psychologically. Everywhere we turn we discern the dangerous "field of discursivity." Take for example, the evangelical Christian who opposes abortion and suggests sexual abstinence as the solution to unwanted pregnancies. Unthought in this position is the opposite position of sexual libertinism, both as a logical opposite and as very real temptation in one's own life. This kind of difference is inscribed in the very language we use to carve out our position. We may call it abstinence. But abstinence is by definition abstinence *from* something; in this case sexual activity, consummating the call of sexual desire. Through the medium of language the opposite position, that which we try to get away from, is always present, as a shadow, in our subconscious world (Connolly, 1991, 50; Macdonell, 1986). Language always contains traces of *différance*.[56] The result is that elements of this otherness will *always* enter political identity surreptitiously and disrupt its claim to closure. We cannot envision an identity that exists outside the field of differences. It is a logical (and psychological) impossibility. It is for this reason that Connolly consistently uses the double construct "identity/difference" here.

Part of every identity and (as we shall see shortly) discourse, is thus, by necessity, outside the control of its owner. Most poststructuralist writers place great emphasis on this aspect of political identity, and instead of ambiguity they prefer the key concept of *contingency*. Mouffe captures this in the following, characteristically hyperbolic, statement: "Since the constitutive outside is present within the inside as its always real possibility, every identity becomes purely contingent" (2000, 21). And Connolly says, in the same vein, "*Différance* enables disturbs and compromises every system of identity and difference" (Connolly, 1991, 50). Political identity is ambiguous because underneath the surface solidity it works surreptitiously to keep the contrasting other out. Connolly evokes the Catholic imagery of temptation in this respect:

> The definition of difference is a requirement built into the logic of identity, and the construction of otherness is a temptation that readily insinuates itself into that logic—and more than a temptation: a temptation because it is constantly at work and because there may be

political ways to fend it off or reduce its power; more than a temptation because it typically moves below the threshold of conscious reflection and because every attempt to come to terms with it encounters stubborn obstacles built into the logic of identity and the structural imperatives of social organization. (1991, 9)

There is a double message contained within this quote. The first is one of ambiguity and precariousness. The "other" is always there as a possibility; to tempt and disrupt. Identity (or "subject position" in the terms of Laclau and Mouffe) is always an uneasy result of happenstance and local history. Our own rank ordering of what is essential and peripheral to our identity need not be shared by others. No one can foresee all the implications of his position on an issue. To put it in more formal theoretical terms, the "other" is logically implicated in our identity and that means that we have only limited control over its constitution and morphology. By implicating, in its very essence, the existence of the other, political identity is by definition open-ended, vulnerable to the intrusion of alien material. As Laclau and Mouffe put it: "no social identity [is] fully protected from a discursive exterior that deforms it and prevents it becoming fully sutured" (1985, 111; see also Howarth, 2000, 103). Identity (even the most closed and jealously guarded) and discourse (even the most hegemonic and aggressively defended) are inherently open textured (Howarth, 2000, 104). And the very fact that these strategies of protection and fortification largely operate outside the spotlight of conscious awareness makes them even more vulnerable to disruption. Vulnerable not in the sense that a particular political identity is always up for grabs wholesale, but in the sense that every identity contains vicissitudes, internal contradictions, demarcation areas and "temptations" where it can be contested (Connolly, 1991, 174).[57] For example, the environmental activist who has always opposed genetically modified food might find his position seriously challenged in the light of resource scarcity and the attendant price inflation that are the unintended consequence of the use of biofuel. Or the staunch pro-lifer might find his conviction badly shaken in the wake of the brazen abortion clinic shootings in Brookline, Massachusetts (Fowler et al., 2001).

Power and Politics

The second message contained in the Connolly's "temptation" quote is one about freedom and choice: my political identity has come out this way, but it doesn't need to. It could have been otherwise. There are other ways to deal with the identity-difference nexus:

> To come to terms with one's implication in these strategies, one needs to examine established tactics of self-identity, not so much by engaging in self-inquiry into one's deep interior as by exploring the means by which one has become constituted as what one is, by probing the structures that maintain the plausibility of those configurations, and by analyzing from a perspective that problematizes the certainty of one's self-identity the effects these structures and tactics have on others. (1991, 9–10)

Connolly argues for an "ethic of cultivation" that informs an agonistic, pluralistic form of democracy. But before we go there, we need to discuss what such an ethic faces up to. We need to discuss the central role of antagonism and power in sustaining political identity and making it prevail.

Words obtain meaning through struggle. The same word—"liberty," "rights," "natural"—takes on a different meaning depending on the kind of discourse it figures in. In the discourse of liberal democracy, "liberty," "rights," and "natural" are connected with "equality of man" and "human nature." In the conservative discourse the same three words derive their meaning from "inheritance" and "privileges" and the priority of "family" and "hereditary descent." Macdonell, from whom the example comes, rightly concludes that words take up their position in struggle: "The positions, by reference to which words in discourse acquire meanings, are in the end antagonistic" (1986, 51). Ideological positions are inscribed in the words we use to express our identity.[58] Meaning, and in its wake identity, is thus the outcome of the actions we undertake to sustain ourselves in the face of antagonistic positions. Macdonell again: "Meanings are gained or lost through struggles in which what is at stake is ultimately quite a lot more than either words or discourses." Identity is not only relational and differential; it is by necessity the outcome of contestation.[59]

This, to my mind, is the seminal contribution of poststructuralist political theory to political science and policy analysis. This ensemble of interconnected ideas concerning deep pluralism, differential identity, inescapable antagonism, and the political work that is required to sustain identity in the face of opposing identities. This, plus the nonessentialist character of political identity; the insight that no higher principle or idea can escape this self-same interplay of antagonisms and power and can therefore not act to arbitrate political conflict. Let's enter the political nature of identity by focusing on identity work, the continuous effort to keep up the integrity of one's position in the vast field of social and political antagonisms.

When we say that in every identity the antagonistic other is insinuated, it is easy to take this as a useful corrective to conventional political pluralism. Parties with fully constituted identities and interests not only compete to influence executive decisions, but also are compelled to defend themselves against the implications that the other holds for one's own position. This is not what a nonessentialist theory of political identity entails. In such a theory the work of maintaining identity requires that we *constitute* difference, that we construct the other in all his otherness and antagonism. Identity is the result not only of the endless play of differences, but also, and above all perhaps, of the tendency to construct adversaries to consolidate its own self-sameness. As Connolly puts it, "[I]dentity requires difference in order to be, and it converts difference into otherness in order to secure its own self-certainty" (1991, 64). This delineating of the field of political differences is never a neutral or innocent game. The construction of otherness is necessarily couched in a moralistic language. The adversary is not only different, but wrong, blind, inferior, immature, irrational, mad, or evil.[60] This in itself makes identity formation a political endeavor, but the fact that the other will not stand by idly in having him- or herself described as bad, inferior, or immature, and asserts, in the face of this antagonism, his or her right to a positive, respected identity, introduces power into the interplay of difference.

At this point poststructuralist ideas about the ambiguity of identity and the construction of difference come together in a projected drive to stabilize identity by placing its contingent elements outside the reach of public critical reflection. Several concepts all point in the same direction here. Laclau and Mouffe, as we saw, speak of "nodal points" that "partially fix meaning" (1985, 113). Connolly talks of a "spiral of concealment," which originates in a generalized resentment that each identity displays toward that which is new and puzzling, and which results in endowing "some identities with transcendental privileges."[61] And Laclau and Mouffe also give new meaning to the Marxist concept of hegemony as "privileged condensations of meaning" that "underpin and organize social orders" (Howarth, 2000, 110). Different processes are at work here, which, although they all aim at stabilizing precarious and contingent positions, take different routes to doing so. Connolly's resentment is an ethical concept. It purports to describe how, in the field of disagreements that comprises politics, actors will always strive to safeguard their positions by portraying their opponents as morally and intellectually inferior. In this way they deny them a legitimate position within the political and place themselves outside the reach of a critical consciousness.

Hegemony, or "hegemonic formation" (Laclau and Mouffe, 1985, 143), on the other hand, is a political concept. It describes the *political* processes by which positions come to occupy a privileged, dominant position in the vast and dispersed field of differences. In that sense hegemony is a key concept within poststructuralist political theory in explaining how certain positions are able to transcend their particularistic origins and attain a veritable self-evident, universalist status. We will see examples of hegemony at work in the case description at the end of this section. Suffice it to say here that this is yet another example of explaining power differentials and domination without recourse to institutional or teleological a prioris.[62]

Implicit in this description of identity politics in the poststructuralist theory of discourse—and this an important final point to make—is the role of agency. Where in Foucault's theory of discourse the role of agency was ambiguous, Connolly and Laclau and Mouffe all put the willful, purposeful actor center stage without sacrificing the dispersed, discursive nature of discourse and identity. The key concepts here are "subject position" and "articulation." Similar to Foucault, and in line with much twentieth-century philosophy, Laclau and Mouffe dispense with the humanist notion of fully rounded individuals or subjects with an "essential identity" (Howarth, 2000, 108). Instead, actors or subjects position themselves within a discursive structure to occupy a particular "subject position." This subject position then shapes their cognitive-affective horizon and even their experience by the "discursive conditions of possibility" (and impossibility) that are associated with the particular subject position. For example, my position as an environmentalist is not based on a number of detached, a priori values, beliefs, and principles, but is a somewhat open-ended position within a large discursive field of consonances and oppositions around topics such as economics, chemistry, biology, meteorology, the technology of food production, and lifestyle sociology, which shapes the beliefs, statements, and practices that identify me, both to others and myself, as an environmentalist. Within the field of antagonisms and oppositions, poststructuralists argue, the very existence of the other prevents actors from attaining their full identity. Thus, the existence of runaway consumerists or rampant global capitalists will always challenge my position as a self-appointed steward of the natural environment. This then sets into motion the cycle of political positioning and moral appropriation aimed at cementing certain positions and identities, which Laclau and Mouffe call "articulation" (1985, 113).[63]

An Ethos of Pluralism

Two conclusions about the nature of democratic society follow from this nonessentialist understanding of political identity. The first is a reframing of conventional political pluralism into radical or deep pluralism. A pluralism from which there is no escape, and that consists of an infinite landscape of identity and difference. The second is that this is not necessarily a reason for fatalism or despair, but on the contrary one for hope and optimism. Mouffe, Connolly, and Norval have addressed the ethical implications of a poststructuralist conception of politics. I will argue that their positions are exceedingly important for a reformulation of a policy analysis that takes interpretivism seriously. I will briefly discuss their views in this section, and return to them in the final chapter of this book.

We have touched upon the poststructuralist notion of radical pluralism above. It straightforwardly follows from the dispersed, constructionist notion of discourse. When all political positions (identity) are the outcome of the interplay of difference, the implication is twofold. The first is the "impossibility of closure of any identity or structure" (Norval, 2007, 39). The space of human relations stretches out in all directions as an endless, undulating sea of differences and oppositions. But, second, we don't have recourse to a priori principles or beliefs (Christian values, rationality, the market, Western ideals of the Enlightenment) to settle conflict arising from these differences. Not only are such first principles themselves discursively constructed "subject positions," but the appeal to such principles or beliefs as the ultimate self-evident ground for the rightness of my position is itself a willful, an ultimately unilateral, act of power within an open, contingent discursive field. Thus, antagonism, or conflict, is not just an empirical feature of political life, but instead is its ontological "root principle." (See also chapter 10.) Mouffe coins a term, "the political," to describe this political ontology: "By 'the political' I refer to the dimension of antagonism that is inherent in human relations, antagonism that can take many forms and emerge in different types of social relations" (2000, 101).

Clearly people sometimes agree, but within poststructuralist political theory such agreement is looked upon with a modicum of suspicion. Consensus can never be based on some a priori principle that lifts political disagreement above antagonism. Consensus is *also* the outcome of a process of articulation; a "subject position" that is attained by having reached a position or having settled on an identity at the moral exclusion or suppression of other positions or identities. Mouffe even goes as far as calling a "non-coercive consensus" a "conceptual impossibility" (2000, 33).[64] Be that as it may, the importance of this claim is that it raises an important challenge, *namely the moral challenge of how to live and work together in a world of deep and infinite disagreement?* Differently put, what is required is an ethos of pluralism.

The second conclusion is that deep pluralism is not necessarily a reason for fatalism or despair. As Mouffe argues, it is, on the contrary, the denial and repression of the inescapable condition of pluralism that poses the danger, for the insistence on consensus comes at the price of repressing or driving out at least some political voices:

> To negate the ineradicable character of antagonism and to aim at a universal rational consensus—this is the real threat to democracy. Indeed, this can lead to violence being unrecognized and hidden behind appeals to "rationality," as is often the case in liberal thinking which disguises the necessary frontiers and forms of exclusion behind pretences of "neutrality." (2000, 22)

Democratic politics in a pluralist society is grounded in the recognition that no actor can claim to have privileged access to some overriding master principle of social organization.[65] This follows from the discursive nature of identity in which each position, as we saw, harbors, within itself, elements of the very position it opposes; bestowing each political identity with an element of arbitrariness and contingency. Political claims are therefore by definition limited, and recognized, established positions have arrived in that comfortable position through the active exclusion and delegitimization of other positions—in short, through acts of power. Mouffe argues that radically pluralist democracy recognizes the inevitability of power at the heart of the political. "The main question of democratic politics," she argues, "becomes then not how to eliminate power, but how to constitute forms of power which are compatible with democratic values" (2000, 22).

Mouffe's solution is "agonistic pluralism": the transformation of a politics of antagonism into one of agonism. Antagonism she defines as a struggle between enemies (out to eradicate each other). Agonism is a struggle with an adversary, "somebody whose ideas we combat but whose right to defend those ideas we do not put into question" (2000, 102). Mouffe doesn't deny that every democracy, to be viable, requires a minimum allegiance to some key values and "ethico-political principles" such as "liberty" or "equality." However, such principles are themselves an arena of contestation par excellence, so that whatever consensus exists around them can only be a "conflictual consensus" (2000, 103). Such a consensus necessarily excludes some positions (in that sense the consensus is hegemonically constructed), but, as Wenman emphasizes, "the terms of that exclusion are perpetually renegotiated" (2003b, 182). According to Mouffe, this is exactly what agonistic pluralism is, and should be, about: an ongoing confrontation of different conceptions of citizenship.

The general, abstract nature of Mouffe's conception of agonistic pluralism leaves many questions unanswered, such as: How does adversarial confrontation actually transpire? How do we deal with (structural) power differentials? How do particularistic claims and identities acquire more universal, hegemonic, appeal? Connolly's ethos of pluralism focuses more on micro-processes of self-making. Key to Connolly's theory of pluralism, as we have seen, is the anxiety that is produced in established identities by new forms of social identity. Taking his cue from Nietzsche, Connolly speaks of "existential resentment" (1991, 81). As we are living in a world in which new claims and new social identities appear on the scene in ever faster succession, he sees the confusion and anxiety this generates as the central challenge of pluralism (in his rather Manichaean language "the second problem of evil"). To counteract this alleged tendency toward reciprocal existential resentment, he suggests what he variously dubs an ethos of "agonistic respect," an "ethic of cultivation" (1991, xx), or a "generous ethos of engagement" (1991, xxii).

Connolly's ethos of engagement has an individual and a public dimension. Individually it amounts to an attitude of welcoming openness, or as he calls it, "gratitude" toward the irrepressible abundance and fullness of life: "Nontheistic reverence (or gratitude as I now call it) for the abundance of being is the most basic ethical source I confess" (1991, xx). No identity can ever exhaust all the possibilities that life holds in store for us. Instead of considering that a threat, Connolly suggests we value and embrace those so-far-unnoticed possibilities as ever so many sources of creativity and empathy with other forms of life, other identities (1991, 120). It is as much a sentiment as an argument, and, faithful to his discursive, dispersed understanding of the constitution of identity, it is not dictated by some higher or transcendental principle. On the contrary, it emerges from our involvement with the rich variety of our everyday lives:

> You become convinced of (nontheistic gratitude) not merely through argument, but also by tapping into an attachment to the abundance of life that may be there already. Such a faith then becomes infused into the way you receive and inflect arguments. The faith of those who confess nontheistic gratitude is not that it can carry us beyond identity, desire, or self-interest, but that we can draw upon it to fold a larger degree of forbearance and presumptive generosity into our desires, interests, identities, anxieties and negotiating stances. Ethics is not pure, on this reading, floating above desire, sensibility and feeling. Rather, its periodic power and constitutive fragility reflect how it is mixed into the materialities of life. (1991, xxi)

This personal attitude of receptiveness is tempered by "agonistic respect" and "critical responsiveness." This is the public, dialogical dimension of Connolly's pluralist ethos. With these terms he distances himself from Mouffe's notion of an agonistic democracy because "no positive social vision is enunciated and contestation takes priority over every other aspect of politics." Agonistic respect is projected as a strategy to negotiate and include difference and to incorporate them into one's own identity.[66] Agonistic respect is a "civic virtue that allows people to honor different final sources, to cultivate reciprocal respect across difference and to negotiate larger assemblages to set general policies" (somewhat similar to the articulation of hegemonic blocs) (1991, xxvi). There is an undeniable element of realism in this vision of a democratic attitude that is simultaneously agonistic and respectful. While it promulgates an active engagement with public life (as against the more inert and passive tolerance of liberalism that Connolly thinks is insufficient to counteract the dangers of pluralistic resentment), it also recognizes the need for a certain measure of distance and privacy (as in agonism), and at the same time opening oneself up to others and recognizing one's own limits (as in mutual respect) (1991, xxvi).

The final element in Connolly's ethos is an attitude of "critical responsiveness." Where agonistic respect fits a situation in which established groups vie with each other, critical responsiveness fits a situation in which new groups, new identities, try to obtain a place in the political arena. A problem arises when their values, beliefs, and action preferences are so incompatible with those of the established identities that they are automatically considered illegitimate, wrong or worse.[67] In the spirit of an ethos of cultivation, the element of responsiveness signifies an openness and receptiveness to new ways of life, to new ideas and outlooks that may result in a questioning and reorganization of one's own identity. The critical element is an effort to safeguard that the new-comer promises to support, or at least not harm, the spirit of pluralism (1991, xxix).

Finally, for an appraisal of his brand of poststructuralist political theory, it is important to establish that Connolly presents agonistic respect and critical responsiveness as civic virtues. To steer clear of any teleological element or institutional ownership in the articulation of his pluralist ethos, he over and over again emphasizes its contingent nature: "The recurrent need for critical responsiveness exposes the extent to which a positive ethos of political engagement exceeds the reach of any fixed code, austere set of procedures, or settled interpretation of moral universals" (1991, xxix–xxx). Such an individualized ethos of cultivation perhaps fits a globalizing, pluralist world in which allegiances are indeed surprisingly dispersed, and often have to be negotiated on the level of individual relations or neighborhood bonds (Blokland, 2003; Fung, 2004). However, it also negates the issue of what Wenman calls "political obligation" (2003b, 174). With this he means some minimum of binding institutional arrangement that forms the condition of possibility of a functioning democratic pluralism. Or, differently put, that forms the condition of possibility of living together in a world of disagreement. I will turn to the political theory of Norval for a vision of poststructuralist pluralist democratic theory that takes these weaknesses of poststruc-turalist theory into account. But first I will discuss an example of empirical policy analysis from the perspective of poststructuralist political theory.

Case: Airport Governance, Politics, and Protest Networks

I began this section with a realist description of network theory as a contrast case for the exposition of nonessentialist poststructuralist political theory. Griggs and Howarth have provided us with a rare example of poststructuralist policy analysis. Their case is the "emergence, formation and functioning of a protean air transport governance network in the United Kingdom" (2005, 1; 2006). They start their paper with a critique of conventional, realist network theory and the exposition of a poststructuralist alternative. Conventional network theory, they argue, gives short shrift to the democratic potential of network collaboration. There is a subtle chain of biases at work here. It remains rather implicit in Griggs and Howarth's analysis, but it goes somewhat like this: In liberal democracies we make policy in networks to give a voice to the various stakeholders. We do this for reasons of decision-making efficiency, logics of bargaining, and creating democratic legitimacy. Thereby it denies the antagonism and value pluralism that are inherent in any large policy issue, such as air transportation. Controversy is considered an anomaly in the proper functioning of democratic process. The effect is that the critics in the controversy, the antagonists, the opponents of airport growth, are not seen as having the same rightful place in the issue as the proponents. They have less standing. They don't play by the rules. They are not really reasonable. They are, ever so subtly (after all, they sit at the table), and sometimes not so subtly (if you don't get your way, you try to get it in a different network) marginalized. Griggs and Howarth claim that "from our perspective, to deny or circumvent the antagonism and passion which is constitutive of politics poses a potential difficulty for democratic processes, as it runs the risk of fueling and exacerbating the eruption of anti-democratic demands and antagonisms" (2005, 1).

Also, realist network theory denies the sheer complexity and unpredictability of large policy issues. From Griggs and Howarth's case description it becomes obvious that conventional descriptions of what transpires in the air transport network simply negate the overwhelming uncertainty, fragmentation, and sometimes heavy-handed power play that are at work. This raises the question of how valid conventional theories are in explaining the outcomes of these networked policy processes. How valid are they not just in epistemological terms as persuasive representations of the policy-making process in British air transportation, but also, in ethical terms, as critical and "engaged" renditions of the democratic quality of a deeply pluralist policy process?

Against the realist conception of policy networks Griggs and Howarth employ a "genealogical method of investigation [that] requires an account of the political construction and operation of such networks, while simultaneously probing some of the limits and foreclosures involved in their production" (2005, 1). In typical poststructuralist fashion they expand the meaning of politics. They argue:

> [P]olitics cannot be confined to a particular domain of society, nor reduced to a neutral terrain, nor restricted to the practices of a specific agent or group. Instead, it involves acts of power and the construction of antagonisms by actors engaged in hegemonic struggles. The latter involve the drawing of political frontiers that divide "insiders" and "outsiders" through the definition of a "core opposition" between "friend" and "enemy." (2005, 2)

Griggs and Howarth employ the language and logic of the formation of hegemonic blocs here. As I argued above, the logic of hegemony is a central element in poststructuralist political theory. It explains the process of objectification of demands—the process by which, in a dispersed and continually shifting field of identities, initially particularistic demands achieve a broader, more universal appeal, up to the point of appearing self-evident, unchallengeable, and even "natural" (Connolly's ontotheology). One important mechanism through which this process occurs is by forging coalitions of hitherto unrelated groups through a so-called logic of equivalence. This logic can be summarized with the well-known dictum that the enemies of my adversaries are by implication my friends. Or in more formal theoretical language: "[T]he logic of equivalence . . . consists in the dissolution of the particular identities of subjects within a discourse by the creation of purely negative identity that is seen to threaten them" (Howarth, 2000, 106–7; see also Laclau & Mouffe, 1985, 128–29).[68] It describes the well-known phenomenon that in the face of a powerful political opponent that threatens their very existence, a variety of groups are able to shelve their differences and forge a common conception of resistance. In the following passage Griggs and Howarth describe in a poststructuralist vocabulary the hegemonic mechanisms that are at work in the formation of policy networks:

> In our terms therefore, the successful constitution of governance networks will, on the one hand, lead policy actors to seek to cover-over the differences that exist between themselves and others in the policy sub-system. Policy actors will forge popular demands which construct equivalential linkages between previously dispersed social and political demands as they attempt to integrate hostile opponents into governance networks through the negation of existing antagonisms. In fact, in order for social actors to succeed in hegemonizing dif-

ferent groups and sectors around their plans and project, they have to universalize their narrow sectional demands and values, thus promising the symbolic means to unify other identities in a common political project. The construction of these equivalential chains requires the production of empty signifiers, a means of representation, which can serve as points of subjective identification to hold together a diverse set of agencies in a precarious and contingent unity. (2005, 2–3)

Griggs and Howarth criticize an unproblematic notion of interdependence that in conventional network theory is seen as the cement that holds policy networks together. Once actors in a network become aware of their mutual dependence, so the conventional view goes, they are both willing and able to settle their differences through rational dialogue. Instead, the authors argue, mutual dependence is not a given but the (tentative and provisional) outcome of hegemonic processes in the face of the antagonism and power play that ripple through the assemblage of actors. Policy networks are forged through processes of boundary drawing, of keeping allies together and opponents at bay. Policy networks are at heart political. In fact, as the case makes clear, it is not at all certain how the boundaries will be drawn, and if we can speak of networks, as a more or less coherent and integrated group of actors at all. Rather we should perhaps think of networks as chaotic and shifting assemblages of actors, now united, then divided, by strong and weak forces (sharing a common ideal, a temporary strategic alliance against a common foe). Moreover, it is these qualities of policy networks that have to be accounted for in any description of them as being democratic.

Griggs and Howarth focus their analysis on the 2003 white paper *The Future of Air Transport*. First they describe the genealogy of the white paper. They characterize the British aviation policy subsystem as one of "increasing uncertainty" and "fragmented dependencies" (2005, 5). New players entered the policy arena (budget airlines, regional airports), airports were privatized, and a process of continued expansion of air travel ensued. In opposition to these developments, a series of mostly local protest groups had emerged that resisted the expansion of a range of airports. Not only were some of these groups successful (the anti-Heathrow expansion group initially won a judgment over the regulation of night flights in their favor), but, more importantly, they also introduced a series of new arguments and values into the policy debate that challenged the received and expansionist "predict and provide" logic that the government had wielded so far.[69]

Against this background the government launched the consultation process that culminated in the 2003 white paper. The consultation process had all the trappings of the kind of consultation technology that advanced liberal democracies have perfected over the years: commissioning expert background studies, sending out questionnaires to the public, inviting submissions by stakeholders, and staging consultation events throughout the country. There is a powerful subtext here: "This is democracy at work." Habermasian reason reigns. Yet, as the authors make clear, despite the involvement of all major stakeholders, the consultation process was subtly but decisively biased toward the airline industry and its pro-expansion policy. As they state: "[F]ar from a level playing field with access to all, and far from a process of democratic transformation in which actors could converge on a rational consensus through deliberation and exchange, a more profound and classical political struggle between different positioned actors with competing identities and interests was (and is) taking place" (2005, 8).

They relate the structural inequalities in the consultation process to four factors. First, the stakeholders were classified into five different groups: members of the "aviation industry," economic interests (chambers of commerce, trade unions, etc.), surface transport organizations, political stakeholders (county, district and borough councils, MPs, etc.), and a "wider stakeholder group."

The latter category included "national and local environmental groups, consultative committees, airport development opposition groups, and so forth" (2005, 7). Every categorization inevitably involves a decision of where to draw the boundary of inclusion and exclusion. The creation of a category by a government agency means the implicit recognition of the category as part of the official institutional framework of the policy at hand (D. Stone, 1997). The authors don't comment much on it, but in a debate in which the unbridled growth of the aviation industry is pitted against checks on that growth, a categorization of the stakeholders in which the pro-growth groups make up four of the five categories inevitably skews the process toward the pro-growth faction.

Second, Griggs and Howarth mention the technocratic character of the consultation process (even development opposition groups that were "well-versed in the industry and the planning and environmental issues . . . speak of 'being baffled by science' during the consultation process") and the "elitist, managerialist, and top-down character of the interactions during the consultation meetings" (2005, 8). The third factor was the close personal ties that existed between the (Labour) government and "key players advocating growth on behalf of the airline and airport companies." These links were mostly former government officials who had taken lucrative positions as lobbyists for the aviation industry. After listing a series of these connections the authors conclude that "[t]hese personnel and symbolic linkages between the New Labour Government and the civil service, on the one hand, and the aviation industry on the other, highlighted and reinforced the perception of a powerful set of structural and institutional connections between the state and big business" (2005, 9).

Fourth, the authors focus on the political developments outside the consultation process. This is an important factor as the urge of actors to circumvent the consultation process by forging coalitions outside it undercuts the notion of it being an instance of democratic network governance. For example, airport companies, airlines, trade unions, air users, organized business, and the tourism industry forged the Freedom to Fly coalition around the rhetoric of "sustainable growth." In opposition, local airport protest groups and national environmental and conservation lobbies coalesced around the slogan "Demand management." The formation of these rival networks took place *during* the consultation process, which raises questions not only about its political relevancy, but also about the possibility of policy networks to channel or contain these kinds of political antagonisms. The authors describe in great detail "how these rival networks sought to universalize their narrow sectional demands, demonstrating an inclusionary dynamic as they sought to cover-over the differences that existed between themselves and others in the policy sub-system" (2005, 11). This work included the tenuous keeping together of different groups with varied interests, the introduction of new issues in the debate (such as a focus on the considerable subsidies to the airline industry or the demand creation by the government), the formulation of a persuasive vocabulary (responsible growth versus social justice), and the active promotion of a number of highly visible and attractive slogans (sustainable growth versus demand management).

Griggs and Howarth frame these activities as successful instances of hegemonization, in which "logics of equivalence" were evoked to keep coalitions together around "empty signifiers." The result was disastrous for the democratic aspirations of the consultation process—and the "normative project of democratic network governance" in general (2005, 16). "One argument in favor of a move to *democratic* network governance," the authors state, "is that subjects involved in deliberation ought to be open to change and self-transformation—at least in principle—during the process of discussion" (2005, 9). Instead the participants in the air industry controversy were far removed from such a "generous ethics of engagement": "[O]pposed actors tended to grow more apart as the consultation evolved, and engaged in the construction of broader hegemonic projects to prosecute their cases" (ibid.). It comes as no surprise that the white paper came down heavily in favor of the continued growth of the aviation industry: "[A]lthough paying lip service to demands that aviation meets the external costs that it imposes (by abiding, for instance, to the 'polluter pays' principle), the White Paper did not propose any increase in air passenger duty, while controversial matters such as tax on aircraft fuel and control of environmentally damaging emissions such as nitrous oxides and carbon dioxide were left to complex and potentially lengthy negotiations at the EU or international level" (2005, 15). The authors conclude, therefore, that "[t]he consultation exercise may look like an exercise in stakeholder inclusion, but closer analysis discloses in fact new political exclusions and frontiers" (ibid.).

In their final paragraph, Griggs and Howarth attempt to arrive at an explicit formulation of the "ethos" of democratic network governance, to use this as a criterion against which to judge the aviation industry consultation process: "An ideal form of democratic network governance is one in which there is both a maximum inclusion of different groups and interests, compatible with functional decision making, and at the same time the conditions and space for effective challenge and contestation within such networks" (2005, 16). With a reference to Sørensen and Torfing's 2005 paper "Network Governance and Post-Liberal Democracy" (and the evocation of Mouffe's vocabulary of agonistic pluralism), they propose that a successful outcome would be the "establishment of an agonistic form of network governance in which a plurality of actors are included in the policy-making process, extending the scope of political contestation" (ibid.). Against this criterion the authors conclude that "[t]he dynamics of airport governance, the consultation process and subsequent events, reveal . . . potential limits to network governance, demonstrating the constitutive role of the political in the emergence of governance networks" (ibid.)

Griggs and Howarth have offered a stimulating—and badly needed—example of the possibilities of a critical, poststructuralist analysis of a large policy controversy. Their message seems to be that politics functions as a centrifugal force that has the potential to blow up democratic governance networks. In the ensuing debris powerful elites, in conjunction with government, find the space to impose their political will on a struggling opposition. That is probably a fair description of the 2003 British aviation industry consultation process. This is domination *pur sang,* far removed from the subtleties of Foucauldian power/knowledge. Further cases (less controversial, less polarized, and with a less adversarial political culture) should throw light on the generalizability of this conclusion. But even if we accept the conclusions of Griggs and Howarth's analysis, it raises two important further questions. First: How bad is it, anyway, that democratic network governance is intrinsically political? If politics, as the authors conclude, and poststructuralist political theory suggests, is indeed a constitutive force in the shaping of the landscape of policy positions and identities, is it then necessarily a destructive force—as is the impression that this case gives? Are we always hostage to the naked power play of political and business elites, or can politics, under certain structural and ethical conditions, be a constructive, creative force? And second: How do we channel the political dynamics in democratic network governance toward a more agonistic (Mouffe) or cultivating (Connolly) process? I will briefly allude to these questions in the next section, and return to them in chapter 8 and in the final chapter of this book.

Discussion

Let's, by way of summing up, assess the added value of poststructuralist political theory over hermeneutic and Foucauldian discursive policy analysis. Strengths: (1) An awareness of deep difference as well as the prevalence of struggle (plus a commensurate conceptual vocabulary) as defining principles of politics. (2) A well developed ethos of pluralism that functions as a critical standard against which to judge the democratic quality of policy making. Weaknesses: (1) The lack of (or is it lack of interest in by its principal progenitors?) empirical applications of poststructuralist political theory. (2) The relentless impermanence of social and political categories and phenomena (following upon its equally obsessive anti-essentialism), and a concurrent unwillingness to acknowledge the institutional character of many social and political arrangements. (3) The generalist, ineffectual nature of its ethos. I have elaborated upon the benefits in the preceding paragraphs. Let me conclude this section with a brief discussion of some of the weaknesses in poststructuralist political theory.

Its almost exclusively theoretical focus is a serious disadvantage of poststructuralist political theory. If by "theory" we mean explanatory statements that can, in principle, be connected to behavioral indicators, much poststructuralist political theory is not even that; it is ontology. This leads, for example, to unending, disembodied discussions about the amount of contingency versus stability or the possibilities for political change, in the poststructuralist literature—issues that should be settled empirically (Jørgensen and Phillips, 2002, 55). Recently there have been some attempts to distill a research methodology from poststructuralist political theory. Jørgensen and Phillips provide us with a list of concepts they consider useful tools for empirical analysis: nodal points, master signifiers, chains of equivalence, group formation, identity, floating signifiers, antagonism, and hegemony (2002, 50). Apart from the fact that their analysis can hardly be distinguished from Fairclough's critical discourse analysis (see below), their empirical example is of the usual stylized, "precooked" type and cannot be called convincing.

More promising is the 2007 book by Glynos and Howarth, *Logics of Critical Explanation in Social and Political Theory*. It is impossible to do justice to this densely argued, ambitious book in the limited space of these final comments. The authors' aim is to provide a set of concepts that taken together provide a poststructuralist heuristic of analysis. Their key concept is that of a "logic." With "key" I mean that the notion of a logic is meant to capture the nonessentialist, contingent aspect of social categories. Glynos and Howarth define a logic as follows: "The logic of a practice comprises the rules or grammar of the practice, as well as the conditions which make the practice possible" (2007, 136). Markets are an example. Let me quote the authors here:

> Now consider the logic of the market. . . . [T]he meaning of expressions such as the "efficient allocation of resources," "fair price," or "supply and demand" depends on the way we understand the key actors and terms associated with the specific market paradigm we have adopted. There is a clear relational network at stake here, which the concept of a logic must try to capture and name. Crucial in this respect is the way actors themselves interpret their roles and activities. In abstract terms, we can say that a particular market comprises a particular set of rules or grammar that govern the arrangements and meanings that bring together the buyers and sellers of goods and services. Hence the logic of the market comprises a particular set of subject positions (buyers and sellers), objects (commodities and means of exchange) and a system of relations and meanings connecting subjects and objects, as well as certain sorts of institutional parameters (such as a well functioning legal system). However our concept of a logic also aims to capture the conditions that make possible the continued operation of a particular market practice, as well as its potential vulnerabilities. And this involves answering a set of connected questions: What were the conditions under which the institution of this market was made possible? What political struggles preceded its institution? What pressures ensure its maintenance or question its hegemonic status? Logics must also provide the means with which to answer these sorts of questions. (2007, 136–37)

Glynos and Howarth distinguish three logics. Social logics describe a social practice or regime. They capture the peculiar pattern of a domain of social practices, whereby the authors specify that these practices must be understood as following from "the contextualized self-interpretations" of those who engage in the practices (2007, 140). Political logics, on the other hand, focus on how certain regimes have come into being, how they have emerged, and how they have been contested and/or transformed. Political logics focus on processes of collective mobilization, "precipitated by the emergence of the political dimension of social relations such as the construction, defense, and naturalization of new frontiers. But they also include processes which seek to interrupt or break up this process of drawing frontiers" (2007, 141). "Fantasmatic" logics, finally, aim to explain why specific social and political practices and regimes "stick" despite the many contradictions, doubts, failures, and contingencies that characterize them. Fantasmatic logics play a major role in making social and political practices seem natural and taken for granted. On the other hand, they also provide the political idealizations that drive change. Or as Glynos and Howarth put it, "If the function of fantasy in social practices is implicitly to reinforce the natural character of their elements or to actively prevent the emergence of their political dimension, then we could say that the function of fantasy in political practices is to give them *direction* and *energy,* what we earlier referred to as their vector" (2007, 152). This analytical scheme is firmly rooted in a poststructural ontology: "More specifically, social, political, and fantasmatic logics come together to elucidate processes of social change and stabilization within a general theory of hegemony, which presupposes a social field criss-crossed by social antagonisms and the availability of contingent ideological elements—or 'floating signifiers'—that can be articulated by opposed political projects striving to confer meaning on them. Of course, our three logics and their inter-relationships are underpinned by the premises of our poststructuralist ontology—the discursive and contingent nature of all objects and identities, the subject's modes of enjoyment, and so on—which together constitute their conditions of possibility" (ibid.).

The three logics are meant to work together to describe, explain, and criticize the object of analysis. For example, with Glynos and Howarth's analytical scheme we could describe the underlying processes that structure the American mental health services field in the mid-1970s. (The scientific critique of the mental hospital. The rise of psychotropic medication. The patients' rights movement. The fiscal crisis of American states. The rise of nonmedical professions that deal with mental illness.) Their political and fantasmatic logics help us to explain the rise of deinstitutionalization. A vast network of community mental health centers was projected that would provide integrated programs of care to the mental patient close to where he worked and lived, in this way avoiding the debilitating and stigmatizing influence of the large state mental hospital. Finally, both of these logics open up space for a critical engagement with the practices and processes of deinstitutionalization. For example, the mental hospital provided not just care but an array of implicit services (shelter, food, communal relations, respite for the family of the patient) which now must be taken up by the "community" (Wagenaar & Lewis, 1989). We could also probe the deeper social and political logic of the relationship between professional politics and social attitudes toward the mentally ill, as a condition of possibility of the latter's care (Miller & Rose, 1986).

Norval has argued that the emphasis on disagreement as an ontological condition of social and political life has spilled over into the "ontic level," the level of everyday experience (2007, 54). I would add that the same applies to poststructuralist political theory's emphasis on contingency. The two hang together. It is not always easy to infer the precise meaning of their pronouncements, but in their zeal to exorcise Marxist determinism Laclau and Mouffe seem to reject *any* notion of first principles or pre-given objects in the political landscape, and, it seems, any notion of constancy and circumscription. Discursively constructed social objects are almost relentlessly open and dispersed; forever "ambiguous," forever "floating" in an infinitude of discursivity, always "an impossible suture" (1985, 113).[70] This radical anti-essentialism simply flies in the face of common human experience. Worse, it closes off any prospects of a coherent ethos of pluralist democracy.

Experientially, identity is not all exclusion and inconstancy. As an avid amateur cook, I do not profess my love for good food and wine as an act of angry defiance against the fast food industry. It is a positive, substantive identification, and, if anything, out of *that* came a greater awareness of the destructive effects of global food conglomerates. Not the other way around. Not everything is striving and disruption, as not everything is up for grabs all of the time. The flowering of human endeavor requires practical routines and institutional stability. These are the necessary platforms for democratic responsibility (Norval, 2007, 170), creative problem solving, and utopian imagination.[71] We have seen that institutions play an important role in Glynos and Howarth's analytic of logics. Norval elaborates on the confusion around disagreement and difference. What makes her argument interesting is that it opens up a vista upon a more substantive ethos of deep pluralism. Citing Connolly, she portrays democracy as a necessary tension, a "productive ambiguity" between governance and disturbance:

> Since democracy contains the possibility of heightening the experience of contingency, the ethos of democracy is a disruptive and denaturalizing one. However, and this is what needs to be emphasized and developed, an alternative account of democracy must also act as the medium in which general purposes become crystallized and enacted. It is only when democracy maintains the tension between these interdependent antinomies that it can function "as the perfection of politics." (Norval, 2007, 55)

Democracy as eternally poised between stability and disruption, between its own glorification and its own undoing. As Norval argues—following the proto-pragmatist, Ralph Waldo Emerson, and the late pragmatist Stanley Cavell—it is intrinsic to democracy that it will always fall short of its own high standards. Democracy is its own failing.

The intrinsic fallibility of democracy places the individual in a complex ethical position. If we do not embrace a radical rejection of democracy because of its imperfections (regrettably an all-too-common reaction), and if we do not succumb to a worldly wise cynicism, we have no alternative left but to take responsibility and try to repair the imperfections or undo the shortcomings. Democracy constantly has to be rediscovered (Norval, 2007, 175). Following Emerson, Cavell and Norval call this an ethos of perfectionism. According to Norval, Cavell characterizes perfectionism as "aversive thinking, that is, aversion to conformism," concluding that "[w]ithout the ability to criticize and animate our existing institutions, and the imagination to change and challenge them, democratic institutions risk to become fossilized and sclerotic" (ibid.). This has echoes of Connolly's "generous ethos of engagement" and his "critical responsiveness," but with an important added ingredient: positive imagination.

But here poststructuralism's emphasis on dissensus and disagreement kicks in. My conception of how to repair a particular democratic shortcoming is not necessarily similar to yours. My striving for perfection might very well conflict with yours. Yet, I cannot simply ignore you (if I do it will be at my own peril) and act as if you don't exist. In other words: "There is no singular vision of what the good is that is striven for, nor any question of imposing one's own conception of the good onto others. There is also no question of the self being isolated from others" (Norval, 2007, 176). Suspended between agonism and dependency. This is the key ethical challenge of pluralist democracy.

I do not want to expand here on the different ways of dealing with this challenge. Norval develops a fascinating—and significant—argument about the importance of exemplars as guides to our democratic imagination.[72] In chapter 8 I will present various dialogical ways of dealing with agonistic difference. My point here is simply to note that modern poststructuralist thinkers such as Norval, Howarth, and Glynos have come a long way in articulating poststructuralist political theory as a viable approach to a critical analysis of democratic policy making.

CRITICAL DISCOURSE ANALYSIS

To close this chapter on discursive approaches to interpretive policy analysis, I will briefly discuss critical discourse analysis. Critical discourse analysis is associated with the name of Fairclough, the British linguist and social scientist, and it is on his work in particular that I will concentrate here.[73] In a series of books and papers, Fairclough developed the theory and procedure for critical discourse analysis (1992, 2001, 2003). It has many, though not all, of the features of poststructural-ist political theory.[74] Like the latter, critical discourse analysis sees disagreement and struggle as central to social order. This is not coincidental, as critical discourse analysis also has its roots in (neo-)Marxism. In its early formulations, it wears it Marxists genealogy on its sleeve, taking a by and large essentialist position on the primacy of production relations, social class, and ideology. Fairclough assumes that class relations define the nature of society and that class struggle is the engine that drives most social change (2001, 28). However, in his later formulations, particularly in his use of the concept of *social difference,* Fairclough proves himself to be more sensitive to diversity in ideology and to the modern, globalized, media-driven, and governance-mediated nature of modern capitalism (2001, 28, 73; 2003, 32, 40). On the other hand, similar to Laclau and Mouffe, he does conceive of discourse as emanating in a kind of articulatory process with a considerable degree of contingency. As we will see, new positions and identities emerge all the time because people use elements of different discourses in their struggle to grasp initially confusing issues and work out a position for themselves with regard to these. Finally, like Connolly, critical discourse analysis emphasizes the implicit, hidden character of ideology, and the fact that its effectiveness is dependent on its capacity to hide its contingent character to the point that it becomes common sense (2001, 64). In fact, the critical aspect of critical discourse analysis resides in revealing the covert ideological elements in ordinary discourse.

Critical discourse analysis is important to policy analysis because it puts power, conflict, and struggle in the heart of its analytic approach. Similar to Foucault, critical discourse analysis sees covert power claims in our language and practices, which depict our world in a seemingly neutral manner. In addition it offers a sophisticated and well-developed theory of discourse, which, among other things, clearly articulates the relation between text and social practice. It also enables the analyst to trace social change. Finally, it offers a systematic procedure for analyzing texts as windows upon (the struggle between) ideologies and social practices. Well-executed critical discourse analyses are able to reveal the hidden contradictions and tensions that flow from structural power differentials in everyday policy initiatives, as the example that I will present in this section will show.

Discourse and Social Practice

Fairclough defines discourse as "language as social practice determined by social structures" (2001, 14). Folded in to this definition is his program of critical discourse analysis. Let's unpack it by elucidating some of its constituent elements.

In his seminal text, *Language and Social Change,* Fairclough makes a helpful distinction between a textual and a social-theoretical sense of the concept of discourse. The first concerns the analysis of texts and spoken language, as well as the production and interpretation of speech and writing (as in Saussure and social linguistics). The second concerns the constitution of areas of knowledge and social practice (as in Foucault and Laclau and Mouffe). Fairclough states that in his concept of discourse he draws on both of these meanings of discourse. His concept of discourse is therefore:

> [T]hree-dimensional. Any discursive "event" (i.e., any instance of discourse) is seen as being simultaneously a piece of text, an instance of discursive practice, and an instance of social practice. The "text" dimension attends to language analysis of texts. The "discursive practice" dimension, like "interaction" in the "text-and-interaction" view of discourse, specifies the nature of the processes of text production and interpretation, for example which types of discourse (including "discourses" in the more social-theoretical sense) are drawn upon and how they are combined. The "social practice" dimension attends to issues of concern in social analysis such as the institutional and organizational circumstances of the discursive event and how that shapes the nature of the discursive practice, and the constitutive/constructive effects of discourse. (1992, 4)

Underlying this "three-dimensional" conception of discourse analysis lies a sophisticated theory of language as social practice, a theory that provides a far more satisfying answer to the relation between language, text, and social reality than the linguistic reductionism we encountered in the hermeneutic school of policy interpretation. Fairclough explains that the statement "language is a social practice" means three things. First, language and society are not independent entities. Instead their relationship is "internal and dialectical" (I will discuss the meaning of dialectical shortly.): "Language is a part of society; linguistic phenomena *are* social phenomena of a special sort, and social phenomena are (in part) linguistic phenomena" (2001, 19). The qualification "in part" refers to the asymmetrical relationship between language and society. While all linguistic phenomena are social, not all social phenomena are linguistic.

Second, an equally asymmetrical relationship exists between text and discourse. Texts, both written and spoken, are just parts of discourse. The term "discourse" refers to the whole process of social interaction, which gives rise to texts but which also includes processes of production that generate texts and processes of interpretation for which texts (but not only texts [J. Gee, 1990]) are a resource. In life, the process of interpreting slices of social reality involves much more than just texts, and includes resources such as the inflections of spoken language (the prosody of spoken language), the body language of the speaker, the speaker's clothing style, the interpreter's reading of the immediate context of the text, "members' resources" (a term I will explain shortly), and the tacit background knowledge that the interpreter brings to the process of interpretation. Text analysis is therefore, according to Fairclough, only one part of discourse analysis. The aim of discourse analysis is precisely to relate the text under review to the other elements of text production, thereby explaining aspects of the text that were initially obscure or hidden.

Third, members' resources, the implicit and explicit knowledge, appreciations, and expectations that people bring to text interpretation, are socially conditioned. That is, the way that people understand texts, the resources that they bring to the process of interpretation, are dependent on the social and ideological struggles that define a particular society. According to Fairclough, these social conditions relate to three different levels of social organization: the immediate social environment in which the discourse occurs, the level of social institutions, and the level of society as a whole. In his later book *Analysing Discourse* (2003), Fairclough summarizes the dynamic relationship between language and society in Table 6.1.

Social structures (think of an economic order or a particular institutional structure) exert their influence on social actors by defining a set of possibilities. However, the relationship between

Table 6.1

Relationship Between Language and Society

Societal Realm	Linguistic Realm
Social Structures	Language
Social Practices	Orders of Discourse
Social Events	Texts

Source: Adapted from Fairclough, 2003, 24.

the set of structural possibilities and what actually happens, the structure and the actual event, is neither direct nor linear. (We saw a similar loose coupling between aggregate structure and individual behavior in Bevir and Rhodes's discussion of the concept of tradition in chapter 5.) This relationship is mediated by social practices. Social practices, Fairclough states, "can be thought of as ways of controlling the selection of certain structural possibilities and the exclusion of others, and the retention of these selections over time" (2003, 24). For example, in our paper on policy practices, Cook and I describe the modern hub-and-spoke airport as a practice; that is, a patterned ensemble of actions, social relations, (material) artifacts, beliefs, and the concomitant language that originated as a practical answer to the challenge of organizing economically viable air transportation. The hub-and-spoke practice now defines not only the social-economic phenomenon of an airport, but also the myriad of routine everyday activities of airport employees and passengers that keep the airport going (Wagenaar & Cook, 2003).

This tripartite distinction of levels of society is matched by a distinction between levels of discourse. Language as a semiotic system sets broad constraints around what is sayable, acting, similar to social structures, as a set of possibilities. A particular text (let's say a policy document or a newspaper article) is the equivalent of a social event. It is shaped by social structure/language but clearly not in any linear, deterministic way. The linguistic mediating structure is an *"order of discourse."* This concept is pivotal in critical discourse analysis. Fairclough defines it as a "network of social practices in its language aspect." Orders of discourse consist of discourses, styles, and genres (I will define these concepts later), but the important point here is that they "control linguistic variability for particular areas of social life" (2003, 24). Think of orders of discourse as the patterned linguistic expression of institutionalized domains of social activity. Examples are higher education, New Labour, or the drug trade. If we return to the airport example, contemporary airports are an order of discourse. The hub-and-spoke airport has generated, and is carried, by a particular technical vocabulary ("noise contours," "mainport strategy," "minimum connecting time," "maximum transfer time"). The language is inseparable from the activities and relations that comprise the social practice. In that sense linguistic phenomena are social phenomena, as we said above.

That last statement raises the issue of how to conceptualize the relationship between the left hand and right hand column in the table, between society and discourse. Taking pains to avoid both the determinism of institutionalist political theory, and the radical constructivism of poststructuralism, Fairclough sees that relationship as dialectical. "Dialectical" means that although the elements that constitute a relationship can be distinguished, in actual practice they bring each other into being (Lave, 1988). So although the language elements of the airport are clearly not identical to, let's say, a passenger who navigates an airline's website to book a flight, "each in a sense contains or internalizes the other" (Fairclough, 2003, 25). Differently put, the language of the airline website, as embedded in the social practice of the airport, shapes and sustains the activities, social identities, relationships, knowledge, and beliefs of the passengers that are constitutive in both conventional and creative ways.

It is important to note that there are varying degrees of freedom here. Actors exert agency. From the perspective of the actor, practices are, on the one hand, constrained by "a constituted, material reality, with preconstituted 'objects' and preconstituted social subjects" (Fairclough, 1992, 60). On the other hand, actors are not passively subjected to the forces of their environment, but are capable of negotiating, through discourse, their relationship with their immediate and wider environment, resisting or accommodating whatever comes their way.[75] Differently put, Fairclough allows for a considerable amount of agency in his conception of discourse.[76] As the air transportation example of the preceding paragraph demonstrates, they can decide to adjust or resist the behavioral suggestions that emanate from a particular order of discourse. I will return to this issue below.

Wrapping up his description of discourse as a social practice, Fairclough formulates what can be considered a programmatic statement of what critical discourse analysis entails:

> So in seeing language as discourse and as a social practice, one is committing oneself not just to analysing texts, nor just to analysing processes of production and interpretation, but to analysing the relationship between texts, processes, and their social conditions, both the immediate conditions of the situational context and the more remote conditions of institutional and social structures. Or . . . the relationships between *texts, interactions,* and *contexts.* (2001, 21; italics in original)

Power, Ideology, Struggle

Power, ideology, and struggle are central in critical discourse analysis. In a nutshell, Fairclough argues that social interaction, including linguistic interaction, is shaped by all sorts of conventions. These conventions appear to the actors involved as common sense, second nature. Think of the way we behave in a doctor's office, during a lecture, or at the workplace (either as employee or manager in this last example). In these cases we enact fairly clear-cut social roles—or social identities as Connolly would call them—in ways that make us competent members of a particular society. (To get an idea of the extent to which such conventions surreptitiously permeate every aspect of ordinary life, think of the bewilderment we experience when we find ourselves in a different culture.)

Fairclough argues that such conventions are important for a number of reasons. First, they express power differentials in our society. Between a doctor and a patient, or a manager and a worker, clear-cut differences of power and influence exist. Second, these power differentials are mostly hidden or covert. (Even in societies that profess egalitarianism, the doctor, manager, or professor has more influence in shaping social interactions than the patient, employee, or student.) And third, the concealed nature of these power differentials operates through ideology. Ideologies normalize and legitimize power differentials, and one particularly effective way they do this is through language, or better, linguistic practices. For example, we accept it when the office manager tells us to finish a report before the end of the week, although this means working late several evenings. We accept it (despite our muted grumbling), and don't tell him or her off, because we comply with the understanding that he or she has a certain authority over us. We justify our assent when asked because we realize that this is how the workplace hierarchy functions everywhere and that it would hurt our position in the firm if we resisted. As the example shows, in modern society power is exercised discursively. It operates though a plethora of practices and techniques that are all interlinked and expressive of the larger social order (Fairclough, 1992, 55). In fact, the combination of the self-evident, covert nature of power and its anchoring in a dense network of related social practices gives it a hegemonic character. In its most effective, hegemonic, way, power appears to us as the natural order.[77]

For purposes of discourse analysis it is important to distinguish between power *in* and power *behind* discourse (Fairclough, 2001, 36). Power *in* discourse refers to all the small grammatical cues in a text that signal to the reader how to interpret that text. Gee, the sociolinguist, speaks of "contextualization signals," which he defines as indications "as to what the speaker takes the context to be and how the speaker wants the hearer to construct that context (where by 'context' I mean what the speaker assumes the world—including places, people, and their minds—to be like in relation to the current communication)" (J. Gee, 1990, 106). Context also includes signals of how the speaker wants us to see him, "the image or impression he wants to convey" (ibid.). The importance of contextualization signals is that they signal information that is not contained in the text's lexical information. Fairclough gives the example of an exchange between a supervising physician and a group of medical students (2001, 37–38). The grammatical forms in which the physician phrases his questions, the pointed silences at strategic moments, the precise moments in which the physician takes initiative, all contribute to conveying the different roles and identities that structure this situation as a mentor-student relationship. According to Fairclough, many of these contextualization signals have a constraining effect. They mean to shape the contents on what is said or done, the social relations that people enter into, and the subject positions they can occupy (Fairclough, 2001, 39).[78]

However, for power to be truly effective, it also requires power *behind* discourse. A good, and in the context of this book important, example of this particular form of discursive power is the elevation of certain ways of speaking and writing as the generally accepted standard language. The standard language then gets imbued with normative connotations of being civilized, proper, and rational, demonstrating the required level of education, and so on, while all other variants are seen as in some way inferior or falling short, and therefore less legitimate. One often finds this phenomenon in encounters between citizens and government officials or professionals. In such encounters citizens often have a hard time getting their point across because they don't use the "correct" language; "correct" being seen as formal or technical language (think of the patients in Abma's example of a conflict in a mental hospital in chapter 3). More generally, power behind language refers to the capacity to impose a certain discourse type upon the situation at hand. For example, in the above example, the physician has the capacity to impose the format of a mentor-student encounter upon all the participants in the situation (including nurses and patients). But he could also change the definition of the situation, for example by signaling that he prefers a more informal type of interaction.

Power in and power behind discourse obviously merge into each other. One of the most important functions of contextualization cues is that they impose assumptions on the reader of or listener to a text. This is not an inconsequential activity, as the reader or listener has to entertain—although not necessarily to agree with—these assumptions to be able to make sense of the text (2001, 69). For example, if a newspaper report of a citizen meeting states that "the attendance was disappointingly low. Only a few residents of X were willing to enter into a debate with the city's officials about Y," these sentences literally brim with assumptions. The conjunction of low attendance and low motivation suggests an explanation along the lines that citizens are generally not very interested in government affairs.[79] This fits into a number of long-standing objections against participatory democracy in which citizens are depicted as lacking the necessary knowledge, skills, and motivation to engage in solving the complex problems of modern society. The alternative possibility that the meeting was badly organized, or that the format was so unattractive that it wasn't worth spending one's precious time on, are excluded from consideration through the particular way these sentences have been composed.

We grasp the meaning of texts because we share a common background. However, the shared background is not given. As Fairclough observes, "[T]he capacity to exercise social power, domination and hegemony includes the capacity to shape to some significant degree the nature and content of this 'common ground'" (2003, 55). The usual way to shape the common background is by inserting various kinds of assumptions into the text. These are existential assumptions (about what exists), propositional assumptions (about what is, can be, or will be the case) and value assumptions (about what is good, bad, desirable or undesirable). Each of these assumptions is triggered in the reader by the linguistic features of a text. For example, a common way to evoke powerful existential assumptions is by the use of definite articles (the, this, these), the omission of articles (giving the phenomenon a universal factual character), or factive verbs ("causes," "adds," "prevents") (2003, 55–56).

The imposition of assumptions on a text through the manipulation of the shared background knowledge of its audience is an example of the work of power. The better the author can present the assumptional world of the text as common sense, the more effective its ideological message is. Similarly, the more an author is able to suggest that the assumptions in the text are universal, the more he has succeeded in "hegemonizing" its message. In discursive terms, ideology is "common sense in the service of unequal relations of power" (Fairclough, 2001, 70). The way the earlier fictitious newspaper example was formulated, the way that the ideology operates on the reader, surreptitiously suggests a commonsense framework to understand the problem of low citizen attendance in a particular way:

> which helps deflect attention away from an idea which could lead to power relations being questioned and challenged. Ideology is most effective when its workings are least visible. . . . And invisibility is achieved when ideologies are brought to discourse not as explicit elements of the text, but as the background assumptions which on the one hand lead the text producer to "textualize" the world in a particular way, and on the other hand lead the interpreter to interpret the text in a particular way. Texts do not typically spout ideology. They so position the interpreter through their cues that she brings ideologies to the interpretation of texts—and reproduces them in the process! (2001, 71)

It is precisely this disguising of the ideological content of texts to make them seem neutral and natural that is one of the most fundamental effects of ideology (2001, 76).

In line with his conception of dialectic that we encountered above, Fairclough is careful not to present ideology as a monolithic force that reduces people to helpless actors who are subjected to the immutable forces of power and history. In fact, it is precisely the overly deterministic element in Foucault that he criticizes. In contrast to Foucault, Fairclough places diversity, agency, and struggle central in his critical discourse theory. I will briefly discuss each of these.

Following on the distinction between a societal and linguistic realm that Fairclough uses to articulate the intricate relationship between language and society, we can extend this distinction to the place of social diversity in discourse. Echoing poststructuralist notions of identity/ difference, Fairclough uses the notion of *social difference* to refer to the "salience of particular social identities" (2003, 40). The linguistic pendant of social difference is *intertextuality,* another key concept in critical discourse analysis. The intertextuality of a text is "the presence within it of elements of other texts (and therefore potentially other voices than the author's own) which may be related to (dialogued with, assumed, rejected, etc.) in various ways" (2003, 218). As this definition makes clear, intertextuality is not the mere presence of different perspectives in a text, but instead denotes a disposition. The way that difference figures in the text is expressive of the author's attitude toward the other perspective. An example will illustrate this point.

In their paper on airport governance, Griggs and Howarth quote from an article by Brenda Dean, chair of the Freedom to Fly Coalition, in the British newspaper the *Observer* that forcefully argues the need for airport expansion. One of the arguments for adding more runways and terminals to Britain's airports is the risk of losing out to European competitors:

> [T]hese benefits cannot be taken for granted however. Today, many of the UK's airports are straining to cope with this rising demand and lots of us have felt the consequences: it is harder to avoid delays, overcrowding and inconvenience. Congestion causes longer flying times, adds to pollution and prevents growth. Meanwhile Charles de Gaulle in Paris now serves more destinations than Heathrow. In fact while we were labouring through the cumbersome inquiry about a fifth terminal for passengers at two-runway Heathrow airport, the French, Germans and Dutch were busy building the fourth or fifth runways at Paris Charles de Gaulle, Frankfurt and Schiphol. (quoted in Griggs and Howarth, 2005, 14)

This is a classic example of clever rhetorical use of intertextuality. The argument starts with the injunction not to take "these benefits" for granted. The suggestion here is that an unspecified "someone" does indeed take whatever has been achieved in British air transportation for granted. In this manner the author skillfully introduces a second voice whom he can address with his arguments about why complacence in the further development of British air transportation is a bad thing. Notice that in the second sentence this unspecified someone is opposed to "us," with whom the reader easily identifies, who suffers "delays, overcrowding and inconvenience," thereby even further cementing the distinction between "us" (the ordinary British citizen who suffers from the inconveniences of Britain's neglected airports) versus "them" (the complacent other). Notice also how, almost invisibly, a seemingly obvious moral distinction has been attached to the us-versus-them distinction. This happens in the third sentence, where in the form of a factual statement the "obvious" effects of airport congestion are "listed." (Propositional and value assumptions beautifully interact here.) No one can disagree with these "facts." Any critical questions the reader might have with the arguments yet to come are effectively dulled.

In the remainder of this paragraph another perspective is introduced: that of the countries of continental Europe who were busily expanding and improving *their* airports. Fairclough distinguishes between different ways of introducing the voice of the other in the text. These range from more direct to more indirect. Direct citations, for example through a quote (Officials of Schiphol airport said, "...''), are more faithful to the other perspective (2003, 49). Indirect reporting leaves much room for the author of the text to tailor the other's voice to serve his own needs. In the *Observer* article only indirect citation is used. We are not told how many and which destinations Charles de Gaulle serves, only more. The reader cannot judge for himself if a once-a-week flight to Djibouti from Charles de Gaulle is as important as the three daily services to Kennedy Airport from Heathrow. Also important is what is left out here. How do Paris, Frankfurt, and Schiphol rank in number of passengers, for example? Finally, having set up the continental airports as overtaking the British ones, it is an easy step to attribute this to their cooperative governments. While the British governments threw up all sorts of cumbersome, and by implication unnecessary, obstacles to airport expansion, the others were "busy building the fourth or fifth runways." The implication is, of course, that the others don't suffer from "cumbersome inquiries," an implication that, as a Dutch author living in the shadow of Schiphol airport, I can assure the reader is completely and utterly wrong.

The power of intertextuality, thus, rests on the surreptitious shaping of the reader's assumptions (power behind discourse) through the strategic positioning of cues in the text (power in discourse). However, it is precisely this shared background that becomes the battleground for the interplay of power and resistance in discourse. One of the strong points of critical discourse theory is the role it allows for struggle and agency. Fairclough's views of agency emerge in his sympathetic, although critical, discussion of Foucault's concept of discourse. He sees Foucault's work as a major contribution to the view of institutions and subjects as "decentred, as constituted, reproduced and transformed in and through social practice" (1992, 44). However, he criticizes Foucault for his structuralist leaning that "excludes active meaningful agency in any meaningful sense" (1992, 45).[80] The problem he sees is that Foucault lacks a concept of practice. Although Foucault refers to practice, his conception of it is rather anonymous and impersonal, referring to "rules" and "systems." What is needed instead is a conception of practice that refers to "real instances of people doing or saying or writing things" (1992, 57). The relation between rules and practice is never direct and can only be inferred from observing actual instances of it. Summing up:

> [W]hat is missing [in Foucault] is any sense that practice has properties of its own which (i) cannot be reduced to the implementation of structures; (ii) imply that how structures figure in practice cannot be assumed, but has to be determined; and (iii) ultimately help to shape structures. (1992, 58)

Against this, Fairclough poses a concept of discourse that is "polyvalent," meaning open to contestation. Discourse as an ideological practice "naturalizes" certain "significations of the world," but they are never wholly closed: "[T]ypes of discourse may . . . come to be invested in different ways—they may come to be 'reinvested'" (1992, 67). Actors are not helpless in the face of unyielding discursive structures. They can always introduce elements from other "orders of discourse" into a text ("intertextuality") thereby subtly changing the meaning and/or legitimization of the text.

Example: Discourse and Local Democracy

Despite Fairclough's copious conceptual writings on critical discourse analysis, it is remarkably difficult to translate these into clear-cut methods. Part of the problem is a certain ambiguity in the purpose of critical discourse analysis. Is the analyst after hidden biases in the way policy issues are presented in the media or by policy makers? Is he interested in ideology critique? Or is he after the social-linguistic construction of policy problems? A second problem is the sheer wealth of concepts that Fairclough has developed. For the aspiring discourse analyst it is not easy to select those concepts that fit the purpose of his analysis, and then translate these into a coherent, workable method. To give an idea of the possibilities of critical discourse analysis I chose Farrelly's study of area forums as an example (Farrelly, 2006). Farrelly's study is a good illustration of the many creative choices that a critical discourse analyst has to make in the course of his work.

The starting point of Farrelly's research is a simple observation: a large discrepancy exists between the rhetoric of democracy in Britain's Area Forums (as exemplified, for example, in New Labour policy manifestos or the Forums' charter) and their actual practice, between the discourse and the lived experience of democracy (2006, 16). Area Forums were introduced by the Labour Party to renew local government after the party's landslide victory in 1997. They were intended to create opportunities for city councils to communicate directly with citizens on a range of urban issues (2006, 54). Area forums are based on the recognition that "local government is more than efficient service delivery" (2006, 57). And Farrelly quotes a commentator from those days who, in the enthusiastic language of policy reform, states, "The programme is centred around getting 'in touch' with people and strengthening local democracy. . . . The various proposals to enhance participation, public consultation, community leadership and citizenship education, together with the promise of the general power to promote the well-being of their areas, will help to redress the balance of the purpose and place of government" (ibid.). I like this example because it nicely illustrates the starting point of so much policy analysis: a new policy, enthusiastically embraced by its adherents, with unclear goals, which promises more than it will ever be able to deliver. The point is not that the policy falls short of its goals. That is more or less self-evident. Rather, the purpose of analysis must be to show what happens where the rubber hits the road. In other words, to describe and explain, how, in what ways, the policy fails; what impediments and constraints of implementation will give the policy the shape it eventually comes to have on the ground.

Farrelly eventually frames his study as ideology critique (2006, 18). Ideology is taken in Fairclough's meaning as "constructions which 'iron out' contradictions, dilemmas and antagonisms of practices in ways which accord with the interests and projects of domination" (2006, 19). To create a vantage point from which to launch his critique, Farrelly introduces democratic theory. This is a key methodological point in critical discourse analysis that cannot be inferred from the works of the key authors.[81] You need a substantive theory of the topic on which you perform critical discourse analysis. Critical discourse analysis is not a generic method of text analysis.

Farrelly follows Held's well-known book on democratic theory by defining democracy as "collective self-determination that . . . entails a concern for individual self-determination" (Farrelly, 2006, 119; see also Held, 1996). More importantly he puts forward a theory of barriers to fulfilling this ideal of democracy. He enumerates "economic domination, existing political structure, the scale of the political unit, and the contemporary ambiguous relation between national and local government" (2006, 119). After discussing these obstacles Farrelly concludes that democracy is necessarily "limited." He then states his analytic goal as discussing "the ways in which these limitations tend to be glossed over in discourses of democracy which are therefore potential contributors to democratism" (2006, 124). "Democratism" is a neologism that Farrelly introduces to capture the contradictions within the democratic discourse of Area Forums. He defines democratism as: "[T]he ideological appropriation of discourses of democracy into social practices that are fundamentally undemocratic: the recontextualization of the discourse of democracy from practices of collective political self-determination, into practices of social life which are not matters of collective political self-determination" (2006, 22).

As this quote makes clear, practices are central in Farrelly's approach to critical discourse analysis. To my mind this is one of the attractive features of Farrelly's study. Critical discourse analysis is not just the analysis of texts, but rather the analysis of language in the context of action. In a long and detailed description of the setting and course of an Area Forum meeting, for example, Farrelly shows how citizens were effectively shut out from any self-initiated interaction with members of the city council.[82] Methodologically Farrelly emphasizes that good discourse analysis presupposes ethnographic fieldwork:

> The participant observation element of my research gives an important perspective to the analysis of discourses: one cannot assume that the documentary representation of Forums matches the Forums in practice. The discourses could represent Area Forums differently from the way that they were practised, either in the descriptions of Area Forums, or in potential development and contestation of the procedures. (2006, 43)

The concept of practice mediates, as it were, between structure and action. Practices are relatively permanent ways of acting that are simultaneously shaped by institutionalized structures and have the potential to change them (2006, 29).

How then does Farrelly analyze discourse? Key to his approach is the idea of interdiscursivity. This concept points to the contradictions within a discourse and between a particular discourse and its associated practices (2006, 39). Different discourses can appear in the same text. A discourse might also contradict the genre or style that is used in a practice (2006, 95). Farrelly presents a nice example of this kind of interdiscursivity when he quotes the constitution of the Area Forums. On the one hand, the document says that the "purpose of the Area Forum is to provide an open forum to discuss local concerns and issues." Further on, it says, "A period of 30 minutes will be allocated to questions by members of the public." In other words, in one and the same document citizens are represented in an active, participatory and a passive, procedural manner (2006, 96). Farrelly considers this importation of genres and styles that are alien to the core meaning of democracy as self-determination into the discourse of Area Forums, a central feature of democratism: "A second facet of democratism . . . is the colonization of democracy. This is the bringing in of other practices and discourses into what may be considered democratic practice, so that the discourses of democracy are now colonized by non-democratic discourses" (2006, 24). He singles out the discourses of neoliberalism, populism, and managerialism as examples of such democracy-hostile elements. Interdiscursivity, in combination with a sensitivity to practice, allows the analyst to explain the seeming contradiction between the democratic ideal of Area Forums and their much less-democratic implementation.

> Social actors within any practice produce representations of other practices, as well as of their own practice, in the course of their activity within the practice. They "recontextualize" other practices. . . . [T]hat is, they incorporate them into their own practice, and different social actors will represent them differently according to how they are positioned within the practice. . . . [R]epresentations enter and shape social processes and practices. (Fairclough, quoted in Farrelly, 2006, 29–30)

Let me finish this example with short description of a textual analysis. In Farrelly's approach texts are windows upon discourse: "A text can never contain the whole of a discourse; it can only draw upon it partially" (2006, 100). Thus Farrelly searches for discursive contradictions in texts (both written and spoken) and between texts and practices. For his analysis of Area Forums he develops an elaborate analytical scheme that he borrows from the sociolinguist Van Leeuwen. It would far surpass the scope of this example to try to reproduce this scheme. It contains two basic categories, "social actors" and "social actions," each of which can be represented in different ways in a text. For example, the category "social actors" can be assessed along dimensions of "exclusion and inclusion," "suppression" ("In the case of suppression, there is no reference to the social actors in question."), "activation" ("Activation occurs when social actors are represented as the active dynamic forces in an activity."), or "passivation" ("Passivation [occurs] when they are represented as 'undergoing' the activity or as being 'at the receiving end of it.'") (2006, 105–9). In this way Farrelly subjects Area Forum documents and interviews with council members to a fine-grained analysis of their covert meaning, their meaning "between the lines."

Farrelly applies this analytic scheme, for example, to the following short text in the constitutional document of the Area Forums:

In order to give local citizens a greater say in Council Affairs, Area Forums have been created. They involve Councillors for each particular area and are held in public. There are five Area Forums which cover the whole of the Borough of Preston. They are responsible for consulting and liaising with local people about a number of issues, including crime and disorder and community safety, how the council might improve its services, and on policies and strategies which particularly affect the local area.

He concludes that:

The representation of the Social Actors closes down the possibility that this could be a forum that is directly democratic. It does so partly by representing the two categories of state and non-state actors through reference to "local citizens" and "council," and excluding any reference to a collective social actor on the scale of the Area Forums: seeing Area Forums themselves as a social actor, for example. . . . The assumption behind actualizing these categories is that there is only one kind of democracy: the indirect variety. . . . This is potentially ideological in removing direct democracy from view in the context of amending the political space. Having drawn on an indirect democracy discourse, the representation of social actors undermines one view of the democratic element of this relationship. That is to say that the public are not represented as a "public" in a collective sense, but as a group of individuals. As the analysis of Social Actors shows above, the non-state actors "local citizens" are individualized. . . . [T]his representation of a non-collective public cannot be said to prove a liberal model of democracy per se, yet this individualism does match the liberal view of the world which sees politics as the reconciliation of individuals' differing wants, not amongst themselves, but through the intervention of a political class. In representing non-state actors in this way, the discourse assumes a liberal view of the political space. Again, this is potentially ideological in that it does not make a liberal-individualist case for democracy explicitly; therefore this view is more difficult to spot. (2006, 202)

Drawing on the same text, Farrelly then continues to notice that the democratic potential of the Area Forums is undermined by the representation of the public as an adjunct to the forum rather than being an integral part of it. In the two sentences "They involve councilors . . ." and "They are responsible for consulting . . . ," the public is given a secondary role, first through "backgrounding" (in the first of the two sentences) and then through the "juxtaposition of Area Forum and 'local people' as two distinct categories" (in the second sentence). Farrelly then concludes by way of contrast that: "A discourse which saw the public as integral to Forums might be actualised as follows: *Area Forums will provide an opportunity for the public to engage with the Council*" (2006, 203; italics in original).

Finally he spots a "further ideological problem" in the representation of the relation between the national government, the council, and the public of Preston. The passive voice in which the foundation of the Area Forums is rendered ("Area Forums have been created . . .") obscures who, which actors, have been doing the creating:

This powerful collective of social actors, the national government are prominent in the "Constitution" [of the Area Forums], but the constant suppression of them from the text hides the source of the discourse, and of the genre that is being brought into the practice of local democracy. By doing so, it also avoids making more obviously statements that are contradictory to the "greater say" discourse—that in fact the national government has the *greatest* say over local affairs, whilst it is not held to account for them at the ballot box. (2006, 205; italics in original)

NOTES

1. Even more so when it is married to neo-Marxism. I will discuss this other tributary to discourse analysis when I discuss Laclau and Mouffe later in this chapter.

2. As Howarth rightly notes: "This culminates in a *relational* and *differential* conception of language, rather than a realist or essentialist perspective" (2000, 20; italics in original).

3. This analogy is also a nice illustration of the essential arbitrariness of the signifier-signified connection, as the value of the chess piece is defined by the formal rules, not by the material it is made from. Chess pieces can be made from wood, stone, metal, paper, beans, shards of glass, and so forth, and they don't even have to look like knights, towers, kings, or queens.

4. "'Any culture may be looked upon as an ensemble of symbolic systems, in the front rank of which are to be found language, marriage laws, economic relations, art, science, and religion'" (Lévi-Strauss, quoted in Howarth, 2000, 23). Howarth then comments: "He thus seeks to reveal the underlying structures and relationships of human thought and experience that constitute social reality" (ibid.).

5. And of course Foucault. We will discuss his reformulation of structuralism later in this chapter.

6. See Howarth, 2000, chapter 2 for an admirably clear and succinct summary of Derrida's ideas.

7. As Howarth puts it: "Saussure retains the idea of an autonomous subject of language standing outside the linguistic system. His theory revolves around the central role he concedes to language users—human subjects—which pre-exist and are external to the linguistic system and he presets the human speaker as the key agent or mechanism which links the sign to ideas and then finally to 'reality.' His writing is thus replete with references to the 'human mind' and the 'psychological states of speakers'" (2000, 30).

8. This dialectic between structure and agency is also what underlies Bevir and Rhodes's choice of the concept of tradition over discourse.

9. Gutting argues that the main characteristic of poststructuralism—and its main attraction—is the rejection of the belief, or claim, that there is a final truth that social or philosophical analysis is able to reveal. He also believes that this is what in the end did the phenomenology of Sartre and Merleau-Ponty in. Both phenomenology and structuralism suffered from the assumption "that we could attain deep truths about the human situation" (2001, 251).

10. Moss describes this rationality trenchantly as "the modern rationality which demands that everything and everyone be 'managed'" (1998, 3).

11. For example, Allen: "'Governmentality' is a neologism Foucault introduced to combine the idea of *government,* or the power to direct conduct, with the idea of a peculiar *mentality* with which the activity of government has been approached in modern times: the presumption that 'everything' can, should, must be managed, administered, regulated by authority" (Allen, 1998, 179; italics in original). In fact, Foucault explains the emergence of the very notion of the individual in liberal society as simultaneously a free, autonomous subject and the object of the regulatory initiatives of state agencies. As we will see, it is these complementary roles that make possible the peculiar governance regime that characterizes contemporary liberal societies.

12. Lemke's bibliography of Foucault's work contains 220 entries! This did not include the lectures at the Collège de France, which were published later.

It must not be left unstated, though, that reading Foucault is not always undiminished pleasure. His style is elliptical, florid, full of neologisms, and marred by the French predilection for associative word play. But the hard labor of traversing those long stretches of convoluted theorizing is always rewarded with sudden patches of stunning insight or terse, brilliant phrases that open up new horizons of analytic imagination.

13. Hacking has written that "for all the abstract schemes for which Foucault has become famous, he is also the most concrete of writers. He is a fact-lover" (1986, 28).

14. Paras: "[H]ow are we to understand the changeability, the centerlessness of Foucauldian thought? Manifestly, there is no simple answer. Yet we move closer to making sense of the philosopher's trajectory when we recognize that, as a thinker, Foucault was exceedingly *permeable*. He liked to paint himself as an outsider and as one who worked against the grain of his times, and this self-characterization is not without a bit of truth: he shunned institutional commitments, travelled as much as his work allowed, and steered clear of much that was fashionable. As the foregoing chapters have demonstrated, however, Foucault was at every moment of his career highly attuned both to the prevailing intellectual mood and to the needs and expectations of his audience. It was the nature of his philosophical practice to enter a community, to imbibe its concepts, deploy them in powerful and original way—and then move on when the tides changed" (2006, 153). See also Gutting, 2003.

15. Lemke's argument is that (1) Foucault was well aware of the contradictions and inconsistencies in his work, and (2) that critics such as Nancy Fraser, Taylor, or Jürgen Habermas assume the very understandings of power and governance that Foucault tried to escape from.

16. In terms of Foucault's major works: The early, "archaeological" phase includes his books on mental illness and the mental hospital, *The Order of Things* and *The Archaeology of Knowledge.* The middle, genea-logical, phase includes *Discipline and Punish,* the first volume of *The History of Sexuality,* and the volume of interviews and short writings *Power/Knowledge.* The final phase includes volumes 2 and 3 of *The History of Sexuality* and the lectures at the Collège de France, from 1978 on, on *gouvernement,* arts of living, and subject and freedom. However, the multitude of course notes, interviews, and shorter texts that have since been published show much more continuity between the three phases.

17. Paras gives an enlightening and amusing account of the catfight between Foucault and Sartre a propos of the publication of Foucault's structuralist magnum opus *The Order of Things* (2006, 29–38). See also Gutting's account of this famous philosophical brawl. Gutting thinks that Sartre had a point in his critique of Foucault's structuralism (2001, 276–78).

18. This is probably an artifact of the subject of Foucault's book *The Order of Things,* "the entire body of modern human sciences" (Gutting, 2001, 267). Gutting warns that Foucault's work always has a somewhat ad hoc character. One should take into account that Foucault developed his concepts to solve specific historical problems and not necessarily to develop a general social or political theory (Gutting, 2003, 2).

19. Foucault: "'The breaking point was reached the day when Lévi-Strauss for societies and Lacan for the unconscious showed us that *meaning* was in all likelihood nothing but a kind of surface effect, a shimmering, a froth, and that which traversed us deeply, that which was before us, that which upheld us in time and space, was *system*'" (interview with Foucault as quoted in Paras, 2006, 29; italics in original).

20. Paras says that archaeology is not the traditional history of ideas but "the study of the history of the conditions of possibility of ideas" (2006, 33).

21. In fact, statements don't have to be linguistic utterances at all. Maps and pictures can be statements in a particular field of use (Dreyfus & Rabinow, 1983, 45).

22. We will see that Foucault will place this self-reflexivity of discursive meaning at the center of his methodological approach in his later genealogical phase, in which he explains the formations of distinct domains of human consciousness from within social practices.

23. Paras, commenting on "an anonymous and polymorphous will to knowledge" that Foucault posits as the mechanism of archaeological change, says, "Foucault introduces momentum in his system at the expense of an inexplicable teleology" (2006, 52). As Taylor puts it, "It is certainly not the case that all patterns issue from conscious action, but all patterns have to be made intelligible in relation to conscious action" (1986, 88). Gutting claims that Foucault's structuralism is not directed against the notion of individual human be-ings as free agents, but against a particular philosophical conception of man. He adds, however, that the ethical and political subject, "the concern of both Sartre's and Foucault's liberationist activism," falls under the structuralist description of "man" (2001, 277).

24. See also Howarth, who says, "Foucault . . . conflates the idea that rules represent empirical regulari-ties between statements, on the one hand, with prescriptive and causal conceptions of rule-following on the other" (2000, 62).

25. Taylor: "To give an absolute priority to the structure makes exactly as little sense as the equal and opposite error of subjectivism, which gave absolute priority to the action, as a kind of total beginning" (1986, 90).

26. We encountered "archaeological" elements in Hajer's analysis of British environmental politics that I mentioned in chapter 5. Although Hajer emphasizes the framelike and narrative elements in his definition of discourse, in his analysis of the problem of acid rain he also introduces an "institutional context of practices" that shapes the competing discourses/frames. These institutionalized practices, some of which have been in place since the nineteenth century, he describes as "the urban-health bias and urban monitoring system, the politics of consultation and best practicable means, and the science-based policy approach." These institutional rules are so pervasive that they form a common platform of unchallenged assumptions for *both* frames in the acid rain controversy ("traditional pragmatism" and "ecological modernization") (Hajer, 1993, 68).

27. Many theorists attribute Foucault's move toward the more functional analyses of his genealogical phase as an intellectual event: his insight into the inconsistencies of his archaeological project (Dreyfus & Rabinow, 1983. Paras, in his exemplary history of French intellectual life, shows that Foucault became deeply involved in French Marxism. This brought a whole new vocabulary into Foucault's lectures at the Collège de France (power, class, exclusion, culture, history), which signified an analysis of knowledge in terms of their social function (2006, 68–71). Mark Bevir (personal communication) points out that Foucault also adopted the historicism advocated by Marx, and particularly Nietzsche, in his genealogical phase. It underscores my point at the beginning of chapter 4 that the distinction between the three types of meaning,

though analytically useful, is not hardwired into reality. Even a dyed-in-the-wool poststructuralist such as Foucault adopts dialogical, historicist methods, in which actors struggling with challenges and dilemmas against the background of large interpretive frameworks, construct new practices and new cognitive templates to negotiate their changing times.

28. Hoy: "[G]enealogy does not deny rationality as such; instead it investigates rationality not as an abstract theory, but as enmeshed in the background web of concrete practices." And: "The point of Foucault's genealogical historiographies is not to destroy reason, but to remind us that that reason's assumptions of its own necessity and universality may be an illusion that ignores its historical formation in the past, its precariousness in the present, and its fragility in the future" (1998, 24).

29. Foucault uses two other terms for micro-power: "bio-power" and "pastoral power." He uses bio-power "to designate what brought life and its mechanisms into the realm of explicit calculations and made knowledge-power an agent of transformation of human life" (1980b, 143). Pastoral power is the introduction of economy—understood as the wise and diligent care of the father for the household—"into the management of the State" (1991, 92). Both terms are used by Foucault to describe certain changes in the governing of states. I use "micro-power" as a generic term for the ordinary behavioral practices and relations of influence that govern individual conduct.

30. As Lemke puts it, the concept of micro-power differs from traditional power in three ways. First, it distances itself from traditional political analyses that focus on the inter- and intra-institutional power configurations and their underlying instruments of power. Second, instead of an inquiry into power tactics (with its attendant fixation upon failure or success that follows from some predefined function that the power is to fulfill for the actor), the analytical lens shifts to strategies and configurations of power that are situated in a historical discursive field of statements, understandings, and practices. Third, the analysis of micro-power doesn't start with ready-made "objects" (workers, prisoners, mental patients, sexual perverts), that are subjected to all sorts of procedures, but inquires into the practices that bring these "objects" into being, and that form the conditions of possibility of the objects and the procedures to which they are subjected. In short, instead of institution, function, and object, micro-power is about technology, strategy, and constitution (1997, 145–46).

31. Taylor thinks this is the "boldest" aspect of Foucault's theory of power. And in a passage that clarifies the innovative import of Foucault's insight, Taylor explains "that we cannot hope to explain the local 'rapports de forces' in terms of some global relation of dominators and dominated. This is not to say that there may not be identifiable classes or groups of those who are 'on top,' or 'on the bottom' at any given time. But we have to explain this division in terms of the combinations, alignments, mutual effects, oppositions, side-effects, etc., which the micro-contexts of domination produce on each other and with each other. Or, perhaps better, we have to allow for a circular relation, in which the grand alignments, which become concretized in, say, political or military institutions, both result from and have repercussions on the micro-'rapports de forces.' The grand strategies of macro-contexts—state, ruling class, or whatever—form the context in which the micro-relations come to be, modify or reproduce themselves, while reciprocally these provide the soil and point of anchorage for the grand strategies. Thus more than saying that power comes from the bottom, we should say that there is endless relation of reciprocal conditioning between global and micro-contexts" (1986, 85).

32. Although even here one can place question marks. See, for example, the work of James Scott, who shows in great detail the many tactics that the powerless use to redress situations of domination. See also my own work on the unintended use of public policy, in which I show how the beneficiaries of a policy adapt the program to make it fit their own needs (Wagenaar, 1995). Foucault opens up a place for resistance in his theory of productive power: "There are no relations of power without resistance" (1980a, 142). But similar to power, resistance is also dispersed and internal to power: "Just as the network of power relations end by forming a dense web that passes through apparatuses and institutions, without being exactly localized in them, so too the swarm of points of resistance traverses social stratifications and individual unities" (Foucault, 1980b, 96).

33. Again, there are problems here that I will discuss at the end of this section.

34. Patton believes that in his eagerness to avoid a personalized, humanist language, Foucault created many misunderstandings about his concept of power. In his writings of the 1970s he consistently employed a neutral, nonsubjectivist language of bodies, conflicts between force relations, and tactics as the disposition of forces. In his later writings he seemed to revert to the language of agency, but commentators such as Patton and Lemke argue that there is actually more continuity here than meets the eye (Lemke, 1997, 29; Patton, 1998, 66). Foucault attempted to connect a micro-politics of power from below with a strategic notion of power by governing agencies. This dialectic is captured in the concept of "government" (*gouvernement*). We

will see that this concept acts as "hinge" in Foucault's later theories of power. It connects, in one overarching theoretical idea, the activities of states with the self-regulation by individuals of their personal conduct (Lemke, 1997, 31). It ties domination to "subjectivity."

35. For the political-ethical implications of power-freedom, see Gordon, 1991, 6; and Allen, 1998, 177.

36. See, for example, Foucault, *Power/Knowledge* (1980a), 122: "[T]he state is superstructural in relation to a whole series of power networks that invest the body, sexuality, the family, kinship, knowledge, technology, and so forth. True, these networks stand in a conditioning-conditioned relationship to a kind of 'meta-power' which is structured essentially round a certain number of great prohibition functions; but this meta-power with its prohibitions can only take hold and secure its footing where it is rooted in a whole series of multiple and indefinite power relations that supply the basis for the great negative forms of power. That is what I was trying to make apparent in [*Discipline and Punish*]."

37. Foucault projected a gradual change in both the object and modus operandi of government in his favored sequence of Middle Ages, Renaissance, Classical Period, (Liberal) Modern Era. From the disciplining of individual bodies, the object of government became the health and well-being of the population as whole. The modus operandi transmuted from sovereignty, via discipline, to security (Lemke, 1987, 188–94). For those who are interested in Foucault's historiography of government, see first of all his own lecture in Burchell et al. (Foucault, 1991). Lemke, 1997, summarizes and comments on another of Foucault's lectures in the series on governmentality. Excellent summaries of the whole series, and some of the core ideas on pastoral power, reasons of state, and the idea of civil society as a key moment in the development of the liberal conception of governance, are to be found in Gordon (1991) and Allen (1998).

38. Dean, in his overview of the governmentality literature, puts this give-and-take between the governmental and the local as follows: "An analytics of government examines the conditions under which regimes of practices come into being, are maintained and are transformed. In an elementary sense regimes of practices are simply fairly coherent sets of ways of going about doing things. . . . An analytics of a particular regime of practices, at a minimum, seeks to identify the emergence of that regime, examine the multiple sources of the elements that constitute it, and follow the diverse processes and relations by which these elements are assembled into relatively stable forms of organization and institutional practice. It examines how such a regime gives rise to and depends upon particular forms of knowledge and how, as a consequence of this, it becomes the target of various programs of reform and change" (1999, 21). Compare this to the customary "policy instruments" approach in policy analysis, and the analytical superiority of the governmentality approach becomes immediately obvious. Policy instruments, in their effectuation, are never unilateral interventions from a centralized government. Rather they must be seen as relational, interactive, and open-ended, and as working upon target groups who resist, adapt, negotiate, subvert, and put forward their own strategies and practices (Stone, 1997; Wagenaar, 1995).

39. Rose and Miller (1992) don't mention it, but it goes without saying that policy analysis also belongs into this enumeration of knowledge disciplines in the service of governmentality. I will return to this later.

40. Commenting upon Foucault's disappointed reaction to the autocratic turn in the Iranian revolt against the shah, Paras pointedly writes about the gap between the private and public Foucault: "More interesting than his distancing from the excesses of the revolution, however, were the conclusions that Foucault drew from the revolution's outcome. Power is not by nature evil, he observed, but in its functioning, infinite. 'To power,' he reflected, 'one must always oppose unbreakable laws and rights without restriction.' From the perspective of Foucault's philosophical evolution, a statement like this one raises very serious questions. How, we might ask, had the defiant anti-humanist author of *Discipline and Punish* come, in just four years, to formulate a critique of revolutionary violence in the language of political liberalism?" (2006, 77).

41. If we have any doubts about this turn toward the subject, later on Foucault states that "it is not power, but the subject which is the general theme of my research"; and "I have sought to study . . . the way a human being turns him- or herself into a subject" (1983, 208–209).

42. Different from the articulation of rational first principles as conditions of possibility for reasonable discourse. Habermas's way, in other words.

43. This might take time as it can be emotionally painful to let go of cherished beliefs and practices.

44. Of the core group, Norval, Howarth, and Glynos are members of the Department of Government at the University of Essex. Laclau and Connolly are frequent visitors.

45. To be fair, it must be said that the works of Norval, Howarth, and Connolly are accessible and clearly written.

46. This is probably due to its roots in (neo-) Marxist thought: "There is a difference, of no small moment and crucial to grasp, between traditional idealism and Marxist or other philosophies of contradiction, and we

can put it in this way: idealism gives primacy to the idea or logos; Marxism gives primacy to contradiction and struggle. When it comes to the analysis of discourse, what this difference involves is that traditional analyses look for the logic of the discourse, for its meaning in itself, while Marxist and comparable analyses look for the politics of discourses, for their antagonistic relations" (Macdonell, 1986, 70). We will see later how conflict drives the process of meaning creation in poststructuralist political theory.

47. Here is a central, and oft quoted, passage in Laclau and Mouffe's exposition of their theory: "We will call *articulation* any practice establishing a relation among elements such that their identity is modified as a result of the articulatory practice. The structured totality resulting from the articulatory practice, we will call *discourse*. The differential positions, as they appear articulated within a discourse, we will call *moments*. By contrast, we will call *element* any difference that is not discursively articulated" (1985, 105; italics in original).

48. But then the "nodal point" must be sufficiently vague and emptied of meaning that it can function as a projection screen for the contesting doctrinal claims. Laclau calls such empty nodal points "empty signifiers" (Jørgensen and Phillips, 2002, 28).

49. Laclau and Mouffe: "We have referred to 'discourse' as a system of differential entities—that is of moments. But we have just seen that such a system only exists as a partial limitation of a 'surplus of meaning' which subverts it. Being inherent in every discursive situation, this 'surplus' is the necessary terrain for the constitution of every social practice. We will call it the *field of discursivity*." (1985, 111; italics in original). In chapter 8 we will see how the "surplus of reality" is also central to Gadamer's philosophical hermeneutics. However, it is treated very differently there.

50. Jørgensen and Phillips: "[B]ecause a discourse is always constituted in relation to an outside, it is always in danger of being undermined by it, that is, its unity of meaning is in danger of being disrupted by other ways of fixing the meaning of signs. Here the concept of *element* becomes relevant. Elements are signs whose meanings have not yet been fixed; signs that have multiple, potential meanings (i.e. they are *polysemic*)" (2002, 27; italics in original). Undefined signs? I can think of "democracy" as a term with different meanings in different discourses (representative democracy, participatory democracy). Or is this an empty signifier? Perhaps it doesn't matter. The basic idea is that political concepts have different, conflicting meanings, and that these are constantly challenged in political debate. As Deborah Stone (1997) has shown: big concepts (empty signifiers!) such as "equity" and "efficiency" have multiple meanings with wildly different implications for policy intervention. Difference and contestation. Important, but hardly revolutionary insights.

51. Clearly, other theorists, such as Bevir and Rhodes, Foucault, or Fairclough, also operate on a relational understanding of discourse. Yet, in combination with an oppositional definition of what defines discourse or identity, Laclau and Mouffe (and Connolly) emphasize the ineradicable pluralist (and open) nature of politics. This, to me, is the added value poststructuralist political theory brings to policy analysis, over, for example, Bevir and Rhodes–style interpretivism, governmentality, or critical discourse analysis.

52. I use the term "relentless" here because to grasp Laclau and Mouffe's conception of discourse it is important to understand what they distance themselves from. In their case it is the rigid economic determinism of (neo-) Marxism. However, in their zeal to exorcise Marxist determinism (while trying to hold on to the important *critical* thrust of Marxist thought), Laclau and Mouffe reject *any* notion of first principles or pre-given objects in the political landscape, and, it seems, any notion of constancy and circumscription. Discursively constructed social objects are almost obsessively open and dispersed; forever "ambiguous," forever "floating" in an infinitude of discursivity (1985, 113). Even a concept such as society does not represent some transcendental collective ordering principle, a precondition for the play of politics, but is, like any other social object, the result of the endless interplay of differences and consonances (more the first than the latter, as we will see): "The incomplete character of every totality necessarily leads us to abandon, as a terrain of analysis, the premise of '*society*' as a sutured and self-defined totality. 'Society' is not a valid object of discourse" (1985, 111).

53. It must be said that poststructuralist political theory is often ambivalent about its understanding of identity. In most cases, as we will see below, it takes identity in the narrower psychosociological sense of self-identity. People and groups have a particular identity from which their political aspirations and demands originate. What unites this understanding of identity with the broader philosophical understanding is that the first sense of identity is always *about* something, about objects that occupy a central position in psychosociological identity. For example, my identity as someone in favor of the legalization of prostitution centers around my understanding of prostitution as an occupation (albeit an unusual one) that is entered freely by those who engage in it (not denying the possibility and undesirability of forced prostitution), and prostitutes as sex workers. Prostitution abolitionists, on the other hand, see prostitution as by definition coerced (by people or

circumstances), and prostitutes as victims. Is there a neutral, core "object" of prostitution—the exchange of money for sexual services, for example—of which these two "meanings" or "positions" are derivative? That misses the point. In the everyday world of public policy and debate we never refer to prostitution without the "layers" of meaning that surround this social category. To emphasize the monetary transaction metaphor amounts itself to a position in the debate. There is no extra-discursive essence here. (That is something else than saying that there is nothing real here. See chapter 4.) The "objects" of prostitution and prostitute, which are crucial in the constitution of these two political identities, are not given a priori, but are themselves the result of the play of differences.

54. One well-known line of critique of pluralism focuses on its narrow conception of power (Lukes, 1975). A second line of critique focuses on the privileged role of business interests in the allegedly open competition between interests (Hayes, 2006).

55. Gadamer would call that common ground a "fusion of horizons" (see chapter 8).

56. In the next, and final, section of this chapter, I will describe an analytic method, critical discourse analysis, which systematically maps the interplay of contending discourses around particular social issues.

57. Connolly argues that identity is contingent in four different ways. First, and straightforwardly, in terms of the particular gene pool, family setting, education, and so forth. Second, "since the entire complex [of identity traits] is not the product of a single hand or design but formed through a complex history of parental relations, historical events, disparate experiences, and contingent biological endowments, it is highly probable that a variety of tensions, disharmonies, and disjunction reside within this complex of conjunctions." Third, some traits are central to one's identity, others less so. The fourth form of contingency has to do with the relation between actor and society: "Identity is a site of interdependence and strife between incipient formations/presentations of self and intersubjectively constituted modes of identification" (1991, 174–75). As this rather straightforward, mundane catalogue of contingency mechanisms suggests, identity is not, by necessity, fragile. Contingent is not precarious. Ambiguous is not unsubstantial. Connolly again: "Identities, in the ordinary course of events, tend to congeal of their own accord into hard doctrines of truth and falsity, self and otherness, good and evil, rational and irrational, common sense and absurdity. Is it really necessary to seal them over a second time with transcendental proofs? . . . Relativism is an invention of academics who yearn for a type of unity that probably never existed, who worry about an alienation from established culture that seldom finds sufficient opportunity to get off the ground, and who insist that ethical discourse cannot proceed unless it locates its authority in a transcendental command. The invention of relativism as a worry represents an attempt to save the idea of a true identity through negation—as if identity were something easily lost or misplaced. Perhaps it is time to say: stop worrying about relativism, or at the very least, stop acting as if this worry were one everyone must attend to before striving to engage patterns of closure, insistence and exclusion in contemporary patterns of identity" (1991, 173).

58. This is one of the key principles of Fairclough's critical discourse analysis (see later in this chapter).

59. This is also where poststructuralist political theory differs from Foucault's theory of governmentality. As Laclau and Mouffe put it, "To insist on the dispersion of the positions from which 'Man' has been produced, constitutes only a first moment; in a second stage, it is necessary to show the relations of overdetermination and totalization that are established among these" (1985, 117). ("Overdetermination" means that an actor is positioned by several conflicting discourses [Jørgensen & Phillips, 2002, 41].) In other words, genealogical analysis is not enough. The analysts must also trace how certain ideas or positions have come to dominate the political. This, by definition, is an analysis of the role of power in creating social order. I will discuss the role of power in the poststructuralist theory of discourse shortly. Let me just state here that it represents in a way a return to the first and second face of power with agents imposing their will on other agents, although within a discursive framework.

60. In his characteristic theological idiom, Connolly speaks in this respect of the "second problem of evil." (The first problem of evil refers to how to account within a theistic framework for the fact that bad things happen to innocent people.) "The second problem of evil is the evil that flows from the attempt to establish security of identity for any individual or group by defining the other that exposes sore spots in one's identity as evil or irrational" (1991, 8).

61. Connolly uses the Heideggerian neologism "onthotheology" in this context to capture the transcendental, extra-critical nature of the intellectual foundations on which hegemonic identities are grounded: "The ground might be the will of a god revealed in scripture or in the dictates of reason 'given' by that god, or it might be a *telos* in the soul or nature or the body or history or language or the principle of subjectivity. The ground must be treated as knowable, either by God or humanity, either now, in the past, or in the future, and the human link to this ground can be one of faith, intuition, or knowledge. Such theories are

grounded by appeal to a higher command (a law, a will) or an internal predisposition (an intrinsic purpose or potentiality), and they function to provide ontological reassurance to those who draw upon them" (1991, 71–72; italics in original).

62. Norval, for example, describes the genesis of poststructuralist hegemony as follows: "Their [Laclau and Mouffe's] understanding of radical democracy is reached via an elaboration and critique of the concept of hegemony in Marxist theory. Contrary to the dominant understanding in political science of hegemony as domination, Laclau and Mouffe follow Gramsci in his argument that hegemony involves ethical, moral and political leadership. However, while for Gramsci such leadership ultimately has a class core, Laclau and Mouffe untie the concept from its class basis in Marxist theory, and hegemony becomes a form of social relation in which the unity of a political force is constituted through a process of articulation of elements with no necessary class belonging" (2007, 46).

63. Articulation is "every practice that establishes a relation between elements such that the identity of the elements is modified" (Jørgensen & Phillips, 2002, 28).

64. This would be—and is meant to be in Mouffe's hands—the death knell for deliberative democracy, that other political theory that dominated democratic theory since the 1990s. For central to it is the reaching of consensual agreements in an inclusive and noncoercive manner. Indeed Mouffe spends the greater part of her book *The Democratic Paradox,* from which the "conceptual impossibility" quote comes, in criticizing deliberative democracy and its ideal of communicative rationality. Although her arguments are persuasive, they also expose the weak, unprotected flank of poststructuralist political theory. Even if all positions in the political landscape are the result of acts of power, and show traces of what is excluded (Mouffe, 2000, 99), this does not necessarily mean that they are unacceptable or despicable to a large part of the population. I would surmise that an overwhelming majority of people abhors murder or torture and supports solidarity with children or the elderly. Even if these positions are discursively constructed and exclude certain groups, this does not exclude the possibility of arriving at a noncoercive consensus around these issues, even consensus that it would be no great ill to coerce certain people to refrain from murder or torture. Mouffe is right, of course, where it concerns more controversial issues where the divisions are more evenly distributed. But even here, *empirical* work on deliberative democracy and public policy mediation has shown the possibility of reaching noncoercive consensus (Forester, 2009; Fung, 2004; Innes & Booher, 2003; Susskind et al., 1999; Wagenaar, 2007a). It might not always be easy, but it is not impossible. Not all differences are, or turn out to be, after due deliberation, divisive. The problem is that poststructuralists, driven by the logic of a discursive theory of difference, focus exclusively on what divides instead of what binds us. They confuse difference with antagonism.

65. This resonates with a literature that considers complexity an ontological feature of society. Through mechanisms of nonlinear interaction, complexity introduces unpredictability and lack of control in the management of social sectors. One of its implications is that centralized policy making gets quickly overwhelmed by insurmountable problems of failing coordination and lack of relevant knowledge. One of the solutions that have been offered is to open up the policy-making process to a wider range of actors (Axelrod & Cohen, 1999; Wagenaar, 2007a). See also chapter 10.

66. There are again (see also note 56) clear consonances here with Gadamer's notion of a "fusion of horizons" as both a strategy and an outcome of negotiating different perspectives. I will discuss this important concept in chapter 8.

67. In the public policy literature this situation is discussed under the heading of value pluralism. Although it is exceedingly prevalent in public policy, it receives relatively little attention. One reason might be the empiricist research approach that is still widely prevalent in policy analysis. It needs no comment that in empiricism values are not only strictly separate from facts, but also have no cognitive content. For discussions of value pluralism in policy and planning and how to deal with it, see Wagenaar (2002) and Forester (1999b).

68. In the nonessentialist imagery of poststructuralist political theory, the twin terms "logic of equivalence" and "logic of difference" have become key concepts in explaining group formation in radical pluralist settings. The description by Laclau and Mouffe is marred by their hermetic philosophical vocabulary (1985, 127ff.), so I turn to Glynos and Howarth for an explanation. Both "logics" must in the first instance be seen as symbolic or "signifying" logics. Laclau and Mouffe define them therefore in terms of Saussurian linguistics. However, as Glynos and Howarth argue, their analytic utility rests above all in their role as political logics: "Insofar as these signifying logics are instantiated in situations wherein the political dimension of social relations is at the forefront, and in which there is some sort of collective mobilization in play, we could say that they manifest themselves as *political* logics" (2007, 143; italics in original). Both of these political

logics thus provide a conceptual vocabulary that shows how the boundaries between inside and outside are drawn. "[T]he logic of equivalence involves the simplification of signifying space, the logic of difference involves its expansion and complexification. . . . The dimension of equivalence captures the substitutive aspect of the relation by making reference to an 'us-them' axis: two or more elements can be substituted for each other with reference to a common negation or threat. That is to say, they are equivalent not insofar as they share a positive property (though empirically they *may* share something in common), but, crucially, insofar as they have a common enemy. The dimension of difference, by contrast, captures the combinatory or contiguous aspect of the relation, which accounts not simply for differences in identity among elements, but also for keeping elements distinct, separate and autonomous. . . . Logics of equivalence and difference thus emphasize the dynamic process by which political frontiers are constructed, stabilized, strengthened, or weakened" (2007, 144; italics in original). By way of example: a logic of equivalence operates when a suppressed group forgoes its internal differences and bands together under one shared characteristic (being black, gay, women, students, blue-collar workers). A logic of difference is at work when these same groups accentuate their internal differences (black men, black women; affluent blacks, indigent blacks, Democratic blacks, Republican blacks, etc.).

69. In the "predict and provide" logic the state is "understood as simply responding to the demands of the aviation industry" (Griggs and Howarth, 2005, 13).

70. "The critique of structuralism involved a break with this view of a fully constituted structural space; but it also rejected any return to a conception of unities whose demarcation was given, like a nomenclature, by its reference to an object, the resulting conception was of a relational space unable to constitute itself as such—of a field dominated by the desire for a structure that was always finally absent. The sign is the name of a split, of an impossible suture between signified and signifier" (Laclau & Mouffe, 1985, 113).

71. See Norval's important discussion of familiarity, which requires embodied, routine, practices as a precondition of our ability to empathize with and understand other people's emotional states (2007, 172).

72. "In this sense the exemplar acts as a call, as a reminder of another self, and another state of things, capturing both the dissatisfaction discussed earlier, and the possibility of another self, another way of doing things." Exemplars do not act as guidelines, or "best practices." That wouldn't work in an agonistic world. Exemplars give us "access to another realm" (Norval, 2007, 179).

73. Other contributors to critical discourse analysis are Wodak, James Gee, Teun van Dijk, Theo van Leeuwen, and Lilie Chouliaraki.

74. In fact, in his later work Fairclough associates himself with critical realism (Fairclough, 2003).

75. For a policy example, see my paper "Het Onbedoelde Gebruik van Beleid" (The unintended use of public policy). In that paper I give examples of, and explain why, target audiences of a policy program will always transform the program to make it fit their own life-world (Wagenaar, 1995).

76. Notice the similarities with Bevir and Rhodes's version of interpretivism, both in their critique of the alleged determinism of Foucault and in the role they assign to agency (see chapter 5).

77. Think of Connolly's ontotheology. Fairclough also stresses the importance of the cumulative effect of power for its effectiveness in sustaining the social order: "The hidden power of media discourse and the capacity of the capitalist class and other power-holders to exercise this power depends on systematic tendencies in news reporting and other media activities. A single text on its own is quite insignificant: the effects of media power are cumulative, working through the repetition of particular ways of handling causality and agency, particular ways of positioning the reader, and so forth" (2001, 45).

78. For detailed examples of the way that actors employ contextualization cues to shape the meaning of oral narrative, see Wagenaar and Hartendorp (2000) and Wagenaar (2006).

79. Also notice that following up a factual observation with an interpretation in a matter-of-fact style covers up the interpretive character of the second statement.

80. This, as we have seen, is a one-sided view of Foucault.

81. Farrelly, personal communication.

82. Farrelly: "There was no interaction between members of the audience—it was therefore an audience with the presenter and not a Forum in which any deliberation, argument or discussion took place. The questioners raised their hands and were selected by the Chair. He took questions from all who wanted to ask, and allowed second questions only when there were no new questioners. A council member of staff went into the audience with a wireless microphone for the questioner to speak into" (2006, 75). This is indeed not more than tokenism. Consultation in the terminology of Arnstein's famous ladder of citizen participation—giving people a limited voice without any assurance that their ideas will be taken into account (Arnstein, 1969).

7

WHAT DOES IT MEAN TO SAY THAT REALITY IS SOCIALLY CONSTRUCTED?

It sits as a bone in the interpretivist's throat, so it is about time to address the issue head on: Is reality socially constructed? And, if so, in what way? What does "socially constructed" mean? Who is doing the constructing? To what extent is reality construction intentional? "Constructed," and its corresponding term "constituted," are among the most frequently used—better, overused—tropes in the interpretive literature. Why? In chapter 1 I suggested an answer from group psychology. The phrase "socially constructed" functions as a code.[1] You signal to your relevant audience (journal reviewers, book editors, thesis advisers, conference attendees) that you belong to the initiated—"I'm one of you. I know how to use 'constituted' in appropriate ways." That is an interesting but banal observation. It would be more interesting to find out *what* the constructionist code signals.

A somewhat intuitive answer to that question would be that it is a figure of speech, a synecdoche, a stand-in for a vaguely specified moral-philosophical attitude toward political research. Were I to put this implied meaning into words, it would run somewhat as follows: "Many features of the human world, things such as markets, states, taxes, power, or poverty, have the ring of the real. They seem inevitable, but they really are not. Although they are more durable as mere conventions, they are also more malleable and circumstantial than rocks or fire. This plasticity has to do with language. We all know that saying something doesn't really make it so, but somehow the nature of these social objects depends upon the words we use to depict them. In any case, the words we use to depict social objects are more than merely passive representations of what is out there." There is a lot stacked into this statement—philosophically and ethically—so let's try to unpack some of its elements.

First, we need to distinguish between two big claims. One, that reality is constructed, and, two, that it is constructed through language. We have already encountered that second claim, of social reality as a text, or policy as a text. The linguistic is the stronger and less intuitive constructionist claim, so I keep it for last. So let's begin with the weaker claim and ask ourselves what it entails to say that X is constructed.

WHY SOCIAL CONSTRUCTION?

I deliberately ask what constructionist talk *entails*. I do not ask what it *is* (although I will address that question later on the chapter), because one way of getting our fingers behind the phrase "social construction" is to be sensitive to the fact that it is so eagerly used by interpretive analysts. Hacking believes—and I tend to follow him here—that the decisive feature of social constructionist talk is that it is programmatic. It is there for a reason, and that reason is to rouse, to incite, to raise consciousness. The point of using constructionist talk is to be critical of the status quo (1999, 6). I believe that there is an important lesson for the project of an interpretive policy analysis in here, but let's first clarify the critique that is implied by constructionist talk. Hacking elaborates it as follows:

Social constructionists about X tend to hold that: (1) X need not have existed, or need not be at all as it is. X, or X as it is at present, is not determined by the nature of things; it is not inevitable. Very often they go further, and urge that: (2) X is quite bad as it is. (3) We would be much better off if X were done away with, or at least radically transformed. (ibid.)

You can think of 1, 2, and 3 as presuppositions for constructivist talk. Just fill in any of the social categories we have encountered so far—the mentally ill, the poor, welfare, gender, stem cells—and the point of defining social constructionism by its use becomes clear. The minimal condition is 1, but as Hacking points out, it might be rather pointless to declare that some social category is the outcome of some social arrangement. For example, to say that "mind" need not have existed, or need not be at all as it is, that "'[m]ind' is not determined by the nature of things; it is not inevitable" (Coulter, 1979), is a statement of greater import than were we to substitute "football" for "mind." Presupposition 1 with "football" for X is trivial because it is obvious. No one would see the need to argue it. So, for purposes of greater precision, we need another, pre-liminary, precondition, which Hacking states as follows:

(0) In the present state of affairs, X is taken for granted; X appears to be inevitable. (1999, 12)

This is what I meant when I alluded earlier to the "ring of the real." The point is not trivial, because it points to the important distinction between the social construction of reality and the construction of social reality; between an ethical-political program and an ontological theory. As Hacking explains, categories such as "football" (or credit cards, money, marriage vows, mortgages, banks, schools) are:

contractual or institutional objects, and no one doubts that contracts and institutions are the result of historical events and social processes. They are part of what John Searle (1995) calls social reality. His book is titled *The Construction of Social Reality*, and as I explained elsewhere . . . that is not a social construction book at all. (1999, 12)

Hunter's genealogy of the school in the preceding chapter is a good example. While it works as a historiography of the public school as a characteristic institution of Western society, it makes little sense to consider it a constructionist work. No one doubts that the public school is the outcome of an array of social forces. Hunter's purpose was another one: to replace one hypothesis about the emergence of public schools (they are the result of social reform and therefore represent core liberal values) with another, less deterministic, one (in response to a generally but vaguely felt challenge to governing, they are the result of a *bricolage* of social practices and material objects that happened to be available in Prussian society). That second hypothesis is informed by the Foucauldian distaste for the autonomous force of ideology as the mover and shaker of historical change, but that is something else than barnstorming social constructionism. More like solid, ex-emplary social theory, I would say. Hunter titles his piece "Assembling the School." That suggests constructionism, but the construction here is meant in the more neutral sense of "putting together," as in assembling an engine. It is constructing without the implicit critical program.

But what about Foucault's own genealogy of the state? That's a tricky one. I'm inclined to say that the difference with schools is in presuppositions 0 and 2/3. I would venture that most people are more inclined to see the state as an inevitable (beneficial or looming) presence in their lives than schools. While it is possible to imagine a feasible, even flourishing, society without public schools (we could educate our children through homeschooling or at the workplace), it is much more difficult to imagine a feasible, flourishing society without a state (except for some diehard neoliberals). The difference is perhaps along the dimensions of ubiquity and power. Ubiquity would then satisfy presupposition 0, and power presupposition 2/3: although we cannot do without a state altogether, there are many aspects of the state that would make us better off if they were transformed. Yet, in reading Foucault's governmentality studies, I'm left with the impression that a lot of it is social theory in the style of Hunter, to which it would not add much to call it social constructionism. As we saw in the preceding chapter, there is a certain "so what?" quality to statements that subjects or social categories are "constituted" in the micro-practices of power. Yes, I'm willing to accept that empowerment or sexual repression is a social construction, but does that statement satisfy condition 2 and 3? Foucault is less of a revolutionary here than many make him out to be.[2]

My point is not to come up with hard and fast distinctions here. Rather I want to pull apart what is scrambled in much constructionist talk: constructionism as an ontological theory and constructionism as an ethical program along the lines described by Hacking; one that is often adorned with the adjunct "social." Staying close to the sources, I will limit my remarks about philosophical constructionism to the bare minimum.[3] It states that in our dealings with the physical and social world there is no "privileged basis" (H. Putnam, 1983, 155)—not sensations, not facts, not observations, not the direct awareness of inner experience. To put it in a different way: we have no access to a mind-independent world that functions as a point of reference to our descriptions and interpretations of the everyday reality we perceive, experience, and move about in; the reality in which we so assuredly find our bearings. We wouldn't know what such an a priori world—"undescribed, undepicted, unperceived," in the words of the philosopher Goodman (1978, 4)—would look like, because all we know are versions; versions that we put together by assembling, weighing, ordering, deleting, supplementing, and deforming the materials that we encounter (which are themselves fragments of earlier versions) (Goodman, 1978, ch. 1).[4] The things that populate the world we live in, and that we experience as reality (self-consciously without quotations marks here), "do not exist independently of conceptual schemes" (H. Putnam, 1981b, 52).[5] This is the pluralist universe of the two Williams (James and Connolly) of chapter 10, the everyday world that cannot be subsumed under one overarching principle and that will always be full of "litter" (James, 1909 [1996]).

When we use constructionist talk in interpretive texts it is usually not to make a point about ontological constructionism.[6] Most people take for granted that mental hospitals, elections, schools, regulations, or community centers are human artifacts put together in a particular time and place to serve the purposes of a particular community of people. When we use constructionist talk it is usually to challenge a particular version of these social categories, either because we believe that that version is adverse to someone's interest, or, conversely, that the absence of my version is adverse to someone's interest. Mental illness is an example of a category that at some time some people were eager to see disappear or replaced with a different category (mental health) that they felt would increase the well-being of those who were identified as mentally ill. Child abuse is an example of the second, a category that was brought into being because some people felt that it was necessary to raise awareness of a phenomenon (physical cruelty and sexual abuse of children) that was harmful to children, seen as widespread, and not sufficiently acknowledged in our society (Hacking, 1999, ch. 5). I use the abstract term "versions" here, but that does not convey the complex work of assembling, weighing, ordering, deleting, supplementing, and deforming that goes into the construction of these versions. Terms such as "mental illness" or "child abuse" are the outcome of incredibly complex moral political-professional activities. They are shorthand for rich social, historical contexts; for, well . . . worlds. An example will illustrate my point.

"In 1998 Sweden suddenly acquired hundreds of thousands of new perverts," begins a paper on Swedish prostitution policy by American anthropologist Kulick (2005, 205). Surely, the author must mean this in a metaphorical sense. Not so, as the subsequent reading of the paper makes clear. The number, Kulick explains, is an extrapolation of a report, commissioned by the Swedish government, called *Sex in Sweden*. The report discusses the results of a questionnaire on the sexual behavior of Swedish men and women. In one question men were asked if they visited prostitutes: "Have you ever, with money or other remuneration, paid to be together sexually with someone else?" One hundred eighty-seven out of 2,810 respondents answered yes. These 187 men comprised 12.7 percent of the sample. The report extrapolates this figure to claim that one in eight men in Sweden had purchased sexual services (2005, 205).

Now comes the catch. Instead of disappearing in the barrage of numbers in the report, the figure had a huge impact in Sweden. It was widely reported in the press. The report spends thirty pages (more than 10 percent of the text) to discuss this figure. It even appears on billboards throughout the country that show eleven men looking at the viewer with the text: "One man in eight has bought sex. . . . Buying sex is a crime" (2005, 207). Kulick explains his constructionist program early on the paper: "The *Sex in Sweden* survey did not come right out and say that the four hundred thousand men supposed to have paid for sexual services at one time or another were perverts. However, this kind of quantification is one of the processes that is leading to the pathologizing of a new group" (2005, 205). Kulick evokes Foucault to explain the difference between behavior and identity. "In both English and Swedish, words like *client, punter* and *torsk* allude to something a man does—that is exchange money for sexual services. It is not clear that the man's client status has any salience beyond that context. Is the same man still a client when he goes to work the next morning?" (2005, 206). He then explains that in contemporary Sweden this difference between sexuality as behavior and identity has been disappearing in the case of clients. "Clients of prostitutes are making the transition from 'temporary aberrations' to a 'species'" (ibid.). This is a puzzling phenomenon that can only be explained by bringing in the wider context: "What I believe is ultimately at stake in this transition is a much wider phenomenon, namely the entrenchment of an official sexuality, a national sexuality, to which all Swedes should adhere, not because they will be punished if they do not (although, as we will see, they *are* punished if they do not) but because the official sexuality is good sexuality, the morally comprehensible way to go" (ibid.).

The remainder of the paper is a detailed exposition of the development of sexual morals in Sweden, the rather harsh and extensive regulation of a variety of sexual behaviors, the brief period of "sex liberalism" in the early 1960s that gave Sweden its (undeserved) reputation of a country that has lenient attitudes toward sex, the subsequent rise of "state feminism" in Sweden with its unremittingly negative attitudes toward male sexuality, and, "the jewel in the crown," the 1999 criminalization of buyers of sexual services that has by now become one of Sweden's most ardently promoted export products. "The genealogy of the client as a species" must be seen against this cultural background. How did it come about?[7]

Kulick traces the emergence of the client as species through three influential reports. They chart the simultaneous criminalization of prostitution and its clients. In 1981 the first typology of clients appeared in a voluminous report on prostitution. It conveyed the radical feminist message that prostitution degraded all women and should be abolished. Clients were described in the words of prostitutes, but these descriptions were dismissed by the researchers as worthless. They came up with their own two-category typology ("I buy what I want" and "There are no other women"). These categories foregrounded the men's social situation and their motives for seeking out prostitutes. As Kulick comments, "There is no suggestion here that the clients of prostitutes are in any fundamental way abnormal or disturbed. On the contrary, it is stressed repeatedly that they are typical men. The only difference between men who buy sexual services and men who do not is that the former engage in what the report calls a 'pure form of oppressive patriarchal sexuality'" (2005, 214).

In 1984 a book-length treatise on clients appears. It is luridly titled *Sexuality without a Face.* The circumstances of its production are important. The authors are a professor of social work and a student of psychology. The sample consists of sixty-one men who sought treatment for venereal disease and who had answered yes to the question of whether they had ever visited a prostitute (bad sex!). The authors divide the clients into "occasional" and "habitual buyers," with the first making up over 70 percent of the sample. But it is the second group, of habitual buyers, that attracts the authors' attention. Why? Because they have a theory; or doctrine is perhaps the better term here: "Drawing on the ideas of Jung and Marcuse, they [the authors] argue that learning to be a man 'prevents or at least obstructs a genuine encounter with a woman'" (Kulick, 2005, 215). The conclusion about the habitual buyer is not difficult to fathom: "Behind these habitual buyers' actions," the report concludes, "there are not infrequently personal and social problems that ought to be heeded and remedied" (quoted in ibid.). "With those words," Kulick concludes, "the stage is set from a focus on behavior to a focus on personality types" (ibid.).

That focus was provided by a book, *The Sex Buyers,* that appeared in 1996 and that, according to Kulick, is considered in Sweden the definitive statement on clients. "To this day, whenever clients are discussed in the mass media, the book is cited as *the* authoritative text on the topic" (Kulick, 2005, 217; italics in original). The authors are four social workers. Their sample consists of forty men who bought sex at one time or another. The typology now consists of five categories: "The omnivorous consumer," "The relationship avoider," "The supplement buyer," "The relationship seeker," and "The refused." But more important than the evocative labels (or the obvious methodological objections) is the programmatic thrust of the book. The authors explain that "if one wants to understand the male buyer of prostitutes,[8] one has to get behind the myths and the stereotypes and see him both from his personal perspective, his childhood and family situation, and in a societal, historical and cultural perspective" (quoted in Kulick, 2005, 215). This is upping the ante indeed with regard to buying sexual services. Buying sex has graduated from a singular act by inconspicuous men to an onerous psychological disturbance with wide social and even historical ramifications. To get a flavor of the line of reasoning, I quote the entries for the "Relationship Seeker" that Kulick quotes: "'Personality: low self-confidence; has difficulty establishing social contacts. Relationships: few relationships with women; buys sex in between these relationships.' Childhood: 'Disturbed relationship with mother. Cure: Needs therapy and contact with social workers and men's support group 'to provide him with the opportunity to acquire a clearer role as a man'" (2005, 216). Kulick rightly comments that "with this kind of diagnostic typology, there is no longer any possibility of paying for sex without being psychologically disturbed in one way or another" (2005, 217). This conclusion is amply confirmed when the book, with approval, cites experts who claim, "When a person has sex without love, or just sex for the sake of experiencing sex, I see that as a serious psychological defect." Or, "In its compulsive form, buying sex can be characterized as a perversion" (2005, 220).

We need one more necessary step to complete the social construction of the client. One can't possibly make up such a story. So I quote Kulick at length:

> As recently as October 2003 Sweden's largest newspaper, *Dagens Nyheter,* printed a two-part series on a social services organization devoted to reforming men who buy sex. The organization is run by some of the same people who wrote *The Sex Buyers.* In one article in the series, which appeared under the headline "Buying Sex is a Cry for Help," one of the

social workers involved in the project explains that men who buy sex "are also victims." The social worker explains that "many (of these men) suffer from prolonged angst and depression because they were not treated as they should have been as children."

To drive the point home the series included a full-page article titled "Now I Can Stop with the Filth." The article told the story of "Peter," a thirty year old man whom the organization had cured of his "destructive lifestyle" after a year of therapy. Peter's story contains many of the elements that seem to be crystallizing as one type of client childhood. Adopted from an Asian country when he was a few months old, he always felt "different and without roots." The article reports that "seen from the outside, Peter's childhood. . . . was normal and relatively harmonious." But "the family had a secret and shameful problem": Peter's adoptive father drank a lot during the weekends. (2005, 217–218)

Kulick continues to explain that excessive weekend drinking is a national pastime and can therefore hardly be considered deviant in Sweden, and concludes that: "The label appears motivated by the idea that a protoclient's childhood should include some shameful family secret." Peter's mother doesn't escape the blaming game either. Through Peter's self-reports she is described "as a source of Peter's interest in prostitutes and pornography" because she was "both distant and close" and she didn't understand him. In any case "When Peter was fourteen or fifteen years old, he remembers, 'I had thoughts of suicide, and I . . . masturbated a lot.' Eventually, Peter began to consume pornography, which led him to visit strip clubs and, in time, to seek out prostitutes for sex. Feelings of guilt compelled him to phone a men's hotline, which referred him to social workers who rehabilitate clients. Therapy with them enables him to stop buying sex, and he has had only a few 'relapses' into pornography during the past five years." He is now in a stable relationship and has a child, but full rehabilitation cannot be taken for granted. As Peter comments: "For normal people, you know . . . lust and sex go together with love and warm, intimate moments. I hope I can get there one day" (2005, 218–19).

I see the sardonic grin of Foucault. This is normal sex. With a vengeance. A hackneyed expression, but fully justified here.[9]

WHAT IS CONSTRUCTED?

In what way is this social construction? Or perhaps the question is really two related questions: What is socially constructed here? And: Why bother at all? To start with the latter question: one reason why social constructionism makes us queasy is because the whole idea seems uneasily perched on the razor's edge of the real and the fabricated.[10] Seen from a distance, outside of the Swedish context, the sex-buying example has obvious ludicrous aspects. However, it is also "real." Buying sex is not an expression of intimacy, it is destructive for a marital relationship, it is in some instances (although probably relatively few) meant as a degradation of the sex worker, and some forms of prostitution, particularly streetwalking, are harsh and dangerous, far removed from the romantic *Irma la Douce* image that some people hold. There is little virtue in prostitution. The "realness" is even stronger when the constructionist talk concerns mental illness (with its suspected physiological or genetic grounding) or child abuse (Hacking, 1999, ch. 5). What exactly is socially constructed in these three cases? Or to put it more generally: When we say that X is socially constructed, what exactly is it that is constructed?

The most provocative answer would be: a fact of nature. The claim that facts of nature are socially constructed is the basis of the notorious science wars.[11] Sociologists of science who engaged in careful ethnographic study of science laboratories came out with the claim that quarks and thyrotropin-releasing factor (hormone) are social constructions (Latour & Woolgar, 1979; Pickering, 1995). The smoke generated by the subsequent acrimonious debate took away the view of what these authors really meant. In fact they meant nothing more than Goodman's position that quarks and TRF(H) are (1) the result of much careful, guided tinkering with ideas and laboratory equipment, which (2) brings about a powerful version of how a slice of the world is put together, and (3) its persuasiveness is in the descriptions, the operations, and their effects (predicted or unintended) and not in its alleged correspondence with a preconceptualized world.

To grasp where social scientists stand in this, let me introduce an important philosophical concept. The "facts of nature" in the preceding paragraph are called, in philosophical jargon, "natural kinds." It is hard to find a good definition of natural kinds in the relevant literature. They seem to be taken for granted. Hacking describes kinds as a "principle of classification" (1999, 104). Haack defines a natural kind as "a cluster of similarities holding together in a lawful way." She takes pains to go beyond mere similarities here and not to confuse similarity and natural kind. For example, two rabbits are said to be things that belong to a natural kind. But all the square objects on my desk do not belong to the natural kind "square objects on professor's desks" (Haack, 1995, 134).[12] The second has just similarity, the first similarity and lawfulness. Hacking adds to this the helpful remark, in the light of our attempt to grasp social constructionism, that natural kinds are considered "indifferent." That is, "they are not aware of how they are classified, and do not interact with their classification. The canonical examples have been: water, sulphur, horse, tiger, lemon, multiple sclerosis, heat, and the color yellow" (1999, 107).[13]

So, natural kinds are categories of objects that populate the world, the stability of which as categories depends upon some surmised lawfulness that is independent of us, and that therefore do not react to their being categorized.[14] Are these the kinds that social scientists deal with? Yes and no. Some of the categories of social science—sex, race, sexual behavior, mental illness, acid rain, nuclear power, reproductive technologies—come close to being "natural kinds." But even these categories, despite their being rooted in biology or physics and having an air of naturalness or lawfulness or inevitability, are seen as being touched by social diversity. We don't need much convincing to understand that male-female roles or expressions of mental illness vary greatly between cultures, although many of us believe that these are variations on a common (biological, physiological) core. When we deal with "kinds" such as mental institutions, community centers, or child abuse, it is fairly obvious that these are of a different order than natural kinds. The "lawfulness" that holds them together as a category is of human making. The very category is therefore vulnerable to human interpretation.[15]

The idea of using purchased sex in Sweden as my example came to me upon reading Hacking's superb chapter on child abuse as an example of "kind-making." Similar to the child abuse example, the Swedish case is a "powerful idea being molded before our very eyes" (Hacking, 1999, 127). Let's look at some more similarities:

> The immediate reference was battered babies, but the reference was very quickly extended. New connotations were acquired. The idea became embedded in new legislation, incorporated in practices, and changed a wide range of professional activities involving social workers, police, schoolteachers, parents, busybodies. It acquired a new moral weight: child abuse became the worst possible vice. (1999, 125–26)

Change "battered babies" into "men who visit prostitutes" and the quote applies almost verbatim to the Swedish case. What is constructed here is not a single social entity. In fact, the abstract talk of "the social construction of X" is seriously misleading. X is not a singular thing at all. Rather it must be seen as shorthand for a complex "matrix" (Hacking's term) of ideas, values, practices, institutions, professionals, academic research, government agencies, courts, and citizens, the latter acting in various capacities such as parents, spouses, and people with sexual urges. All these "entities" hang together and interact and the changes that ensue this way are subtle, and in a surreptitious way, massive. In the end the ideas, practices, institutions, professionals, academic research, government agencies, courts, and citizens in various capacities are changed and have resulted in a new "world," a new "social matrix." This even applies to self-image, experience, emotion, and personal identity (viz. Peter's confessional testimony), and to the way we perceive and understand our collective past and our future options. Under the influence of the Swedish "discourse" (to bring this term back to the discussion) on prostitution and purchasing sex, Peter has adopted the commensurate behavior, thoughts, feelings, self-evaluations, and aspirations; in other words, the proper "subject position."[16] Similarly, we can maybe imagine a past situation where child abuse was not a recognized problem or fathers took their adolescent sons to a brothel for sexual initiation, but we would conceive of this part of our history as "primitive" or "unenlightened." Children are still battered, men still visit prostitutes (you can call this the underlying reality if you want, but, heeding Putnam, that reality is not preconceptualized either, just differently conceptualized), but we perceive, understand, value, and treat them differently to the extent that the new matrix has crowded out the old one. It's not just that the ideas about child abuse or buying sex change. Or the practices. Or the law. Or our knowledge about the phenomenon. Or even our categorizations, the way we slice up social reality. They obviously do. The point is that all these things change in tandem and interactively. Holistically would be the proper term here. *That* is world making.

To sum up, social constructionism inquires into the way that a complex social setting of ideas, practices, institutions, people, and so forth gradually changes in its entirety. To my mind it is the holistic quality of these changes, the way things hang together on the trajectory of change, that gives us the experience that some slice of reality is being constructed. Particularly so when we perceive the setting from a historical perspective. Contemporary kinds that strike us as natural and self-evident, once were not there. Kinds of the past now seem quaint, incomprehensible, or scandalous. It is no wonder then that social reality strikes us as simultaneously real and malleable. Which element of the real-constructed axis we choose to emphasize is a moral question. If we feel comfortable with the way things are, we emphasize the "realness." If we are critical and strive for change, we like to point out the hidden intentionality of the kinds, the arbitrariness and contingency of their genealogy. Social constructionism is thus bound up, as we concluded before, with an ethical program.

This is what Hacking argued by articulating the presuppositions of social constructionism. He intends them as a gradient of commitment. Taken together they comprise the full critical program, but one need not embrace the full program. One can be content with demonstrating that a phenomenon or kind X emerges in the course of historical processes. (This is what Hunter did for public schools.) But one can also leave the realm of intellectual analysis and engage in radical reform (Hacking, 1999, 19–20). The importance of the gradient is in the more precise articulation of the ethical program that is embedded in social constructionism. We have seen in chapter 4 that the result of policy interpretation is to open up a policy field, to show that different interpretations of a particular policy are possible. Community centers are not just that; they can also be seen as a social ideal that is expressed in the metaphor of a supermarket. Nuclear energy is not just that; it is part of a plurality of worldviews that is made up of ideas about science, the environment, lifestyle, and so forth. Those who engage in policy interpretation engage in mapping the variety of meanings in a policy sector. To open the plurality of the policy world this way is seen to contribute to "increased communication" (Fay, 1975, 82). The following quote by Yanow is illustrative of this stance:

> The last step analytic practice might take could be in the form of negotiation or media-
> tion, in which conflicting interpretations would be identified and explained as such. It is
> an educative process that takes as its goal the fostering of discussion honoring the reality
> of entrenched viewpoints, while nonetheless seeking engaged discourse and debate among
> policy relevant publics. (2000, 21)

Those who engage in social constructionism have a different commitment. Theirs is not to act as a neutral analyst who fosters communication, but to refute, unmask, and reform. Their goal is to reveal the hidden structures that determine our behavior, or the micro-powers that shape our needs, beliefs, and identities. Refuting and unmasking are not the same: "Refuting a thesis works at the level of the thesis itself by showing it to be false. Unmasking undermines a thesis, by displaying its extra-theoretical function" (Hacking, 1999, 56). The extra-theoretical function is usually a reference to the way that the interests of some party have surreptitiously influenced the construction of a phenomenon. In the background there is always the play of power. "Real," subjugating power, not the watered-down, insinuating micro-powers. The point of unmasking, as Hacking says, is "to liberate the oppressed, to show how categories of knowledge are used in power relationships" (1999, 58). The intended effect is to undermine the authority of knowledge. It is the ethical program of governmentality.

DO WE CONSTRUCT WITH LANGUAGE?

One issue needs to be addressed still, as it hovers over the interpretive waters as a dense fog obscuring a clear vision of the issues at stake in interpretive social science: the role of language in constructing social reality. This is not quite the same as the role of language in the social con-struction of reality. The first points to the more basic, fundamental mechanism, or mechanisms, of how language contributes to the conceptual schemes with which we grasp social reality. The second, as we saw, is a moral program. The basic mechanisms may, but need not be, employed in the moral program.

One of the big puzzles in discussing the role of language in social science is to explain its pertinence beyond the rather obvious conclusion that it is hard to see how language can *not* play a role in grasping social reality. If reality comes to us via conceptual schemes, than clearly those schemes depend on language. "'Objects' do not exist independently of conceptual schemes," says Hilary Putnam. "*We* cut up the world into objects when we introduce one or another scheme of description," emphasizing with the italicized "we" that the way the world comes to us is not hardwired, but depends on our ways of organizing the mind-independent reality (1981b, 52). If we take this description seriously, as I do, the conclusion that language plays a role in shaping these "schemes of description" is pretty self-evident. How could it be otherwise?

So why do people get so worked up about language in interpretive social science? I would speculate that an answer to this question consists of two parts. First, the technical claim (language shapes the way we grasp the world) is itself not easy to grasp. Twentieth-century linguistic thought is dominated by the idea that language actively shapes the world. That was not always the case. For many centuries the dominant understanding was that words were labels for things; things that are themselves independently given (Harris, 1988, 9–10). Language is no more than a medium for passively registering an objective reality out there.[17] Then, under the influence of the very different philosophies of Saussure and Wittgenstein, language as a self-contained system of symbols came to occupy central stage in understanding mind and reality. As Harris summarizes it: "Language is no longer regarded as peripheral to our grasp of the world in which we live, but as central to it.

Words are not mere vocal labels or communicational adjuncts superimposed upon an already given order of things. They are collective products of social interaction, essential instruments through which human beings constitute and articulate their world" (1988, ix).[18]

I volunteer two observations at this point. First, few intellectual movements have had such a wide impact on social theory as this reassessment of the role that language plays in the world. I think it is safe to say that none of the human sciences has been unaffected by it. To use the late Donald Schön's words, the active, generative notion of language has become an "idea in good currency." Second, few issues are more muddled than this one. What does it mean that "words constitute and articulate the world"? According to the dictionary, "constitute" (in the active sense) means "to make up; form; compose" and "to make up or form of elements, material, etc." (McKechnie, 1979). The question of how language makes up reality invokes the age-old metaphysical conundrum of the relationship between thought and the world, of whether the world is structured the way we describe it (metaphysical realism) or we impose a structure upon it through our representations and descriptions (nominalism) (Hacking, 1999, 83). "Controversy" is probably a better word than "conundrum," given the fierce polemical tone of the debate. It is one of those philosophical issues about which one is forced to take sides. There is no middle ground. No doubt, some of that fire heats up the language issue in interpretive social science. To wade into this highly technical philosophical issue would only detract us from the goal of this book to throw light on some issues in interpretive policy analysis. (Do we really need ontology to understand the unintended consequences of deinstitutionalization?) However, with regard to the question of how language makes reality, I will develop a line of thought that in its focus on social context and human practice *is* relevant to policy analysis.

Second, and more pertinent to this book, the generative language argument, itself difficult to grasp, burdened with half-digested metaphysical ideas, merges with a moral program that aims to reveal and unmask the alleged biases that are inherent in our self-evident understandings of social reality. In many ways this is an extension of the "Against Inevitability" program that Hacking sees as one of the defining characteristics of social constructionism (1999, 6). If language is both a collective product and an instrument in actively shaping the world, then it is only a short step to the belief that language is the vehicle with which undesired reality can be reformed. If I were to reconstruct the reformist argument it would go somewhat as follows: social reality is seen as made up of language. Language does not just represent reality, it actively shapes it. Language is convention par excellence. *How* we name something is not hardwired into reality. We have choices here. Within broad syntactical bounds we are pretty much free to name something as we see fit.[19] It follows, thus, that social reality is much more malleable than we think. The program could be summarized—admittedly, somewhat schematically—with a fourth constructionist presupposition, the strong constructionist claim:

(4) One important way to reform X is to give it a different name.

I think that the reformist program is mistaken, but I do not want to portray it as silly or trivial. Apart from the fact that its philosophical underpinning is serious and widely accepted, everyday experience may be suggestive here. For example, we all know that metaphor shapes the way we understand the world. The population metaphor in Chock's reading of the congressional debates on immigration in chapter 5 does influence the way we perceive immigrants. And, to stay with this example, the way we address immigrants has a profound influence on the way they are perceived by both the native population and themselves.[20] Changing the designation will help to defuse ethnic tensions. The issue takes on added urgency when we consider the struggles over labels in media reporting. Are we dealing with "terrorists," "insurgents," or "freedom fighters"? Is the West

Bank an "occupied" or a "contested" area? Are the American troops in Iraq a "coalition force" or "occupying troops"? The labels are metonyms for power configurations. So again language hooks into reality in significant, hard-to-ignore, ways.

Finally, we all probably sense that there is something fishy about the Swedish prostitution example. By "fishy" I mean arbitrary, willful, and carrying the suspicion that language played a central role in designating a visit to a prostitute as indicative of a personality disorder. Can it be called a "myth" therefore, as in the "myth of mental illness"? I'm not sure. Mental illness less so than johns, I would surmise. But in both cases language, and the way that language is mobilized in the service of certain power differentials, definitely contributes to shaping our understanding of the categories. Language is generative, and so it is not altogether misguided to make it the spearhead in a reformist program. The problem is, to my mind, that the constructionist literature displays a good deal of confusion about both parts of the language–social reality nexus. It is an area where it is not unusual to encounter radical positions in which social reality seems to be almost wholly reduced to language. (Policy as a text.) It is also one of those topics for which vapid shibboleths, and people repeating the same worn phrases, characterize the literature. So let's see if we can clarify some of the confusion here.

How then does language contribute to the construction of social reality? The first, innocent, claim to stake out is that language is interactive. Language has a social dimension. It is a joint production. *Langue* instead of *parole*. This is an attempt to clarify the language part of the language-construction–social-reality nexus; to get away from the image of language as a static "structure" that represents a homogeneous and stable reality. By emphasizing the communal, interactive character of language, we emphasize its use. To bring the way language is used back into linguistic theory is perhaps the greatest contribution of the twentieth-century language philosophers to our understanding of the relation between language and the world.[21] Use compels us to think of social context and of sense making, the many different ways that people make themselves understood in everyday practical situations.[22] Language, in its sense-making function, is always language-in-use.

With the spotlight on use, we can draw out several other important aspects of the language-reality nexus. Use implies purpose. It is oriented to activity (Potter, 1996, 72). Use suggests use-for. This in turn implies the availability of requirements, some guiding principle that helps us to figure out where to go and what makes sense when we use language in a particular situation. But here the going gets tricky. How are we to imagine such requirements-in-use? The concept of requirements is poised on the interface of language and community and it points therefore in two directions at once: on the one hand, to the practical-moral requirements of a particular community; on the other, to the linguistic requirements of the language. Moreover, such requirements are not formal rules. They are more like the Wittgensteinian rules-in-use I described in chapter 4, hard to articulate but available to every competent user. What we need is a conception of language-in-use that draws out the world-making qualities of language use. A quote from Shotter serves to summarize such an approach to language and reality and provides entry points for further exploration. In contrast to language as "taken-for-granted," a "referential-representational system of coded or meaningful signs," he instead articulates:

> an interest in the contested activity of words in their speaking; that is, in the practicalities of their use as a means or as "tools" in effecting everyday communicative processes, and in particular, in their formative or "shaping" function, and the "resistances" they meet in such processes. Thus the stance I take . . . is that in an everyday process involving a myriad of spontaneous, responsive, practical, unselfconscious, but contested interactions, we unknowingly "shape" or "construct" between ourselves as already mentioned, not only a sense of our

own identities, but also a sense of our own "social worlds." Or, to put it another way, that plane upon which we talk about what we think of as the orderly, accountable, self-evidently knowable and controllable characteristics of both ourselves (as autonomous individual persons) and our world, is constructed upon another, lower plane, in a set of unacknowledged and unintended, disorderly, conversational forms of interaction involving struggles between ourselves and others. (1993, 20)

Let's unpack this vision of language-in-use. The first thing that strikes us in this vocabulary of conversing, shaping, constructing, interacting, and struggling is the image of two planes, an upper and a lower one, upon which language use takes place. The upper linguistic plane is depicted as a realm of outcomes ("the orderly, accountable . . . characteristics of both ourselves . . . and our world"). This is the world that presents itself to us as inevitable and natural. But it is also a construction and that construction takes place through "conversational forms of interaction" on the lower plane. How are we to understand this?

Shotter is what is called a conversation analyst. Without going into the specifics of this linguistic program, I will say that conversation analysts are interested in the way that language-in-use is designed to perform particular actions (Potter, 1996, 62). This seems rather obvious, but as conversation analysts point out, ordinary language use poses several puzzles for linguists. For example, how is it that we experience language, and the way it functions in describing and explaining the world, as relatively stable and coherent? For example, what kind of linguistic work does it require to grasp certain aspects of a situation as uncontroversial "facts"? And, how is it that a relatively small number of descriptive terms is sufficient to move about in a reliable, convincing, and accountable way in a wide variety of situations? For example, the phrase "I love you," depending on the intonation and the rhythmic pattern with which it is uttered, plus the facial expressions and bodily position that accompany it, can signify an earnest declaration of love to a date, a routine expression of affection in an established marital relationship, the closure of a telephone conversation with a daughter who is in college, a desperate attempt to reach an estranged elderly parent, and other things. Or, when I say, "Pick up that book, please," given the particular circumstances at hand, my son will know that of all the books in the house, I am referring to his Latin textbook, which he used in doing his homework and left lying around on the floor. What these examples have in common is that the sensefulness of a word or utterance is dependent on the context of its use (Potter, 1996, 43). This feature of language-in-use is called *indexicality,* and at first blush it seems to point to an irreparable vagueness in language use (Suchman, 1987). However, conversation analysts assert that the intrinsic indeterminacy of language should be seen not as a flaw but as an asset. It allows language users to negotiate the inevitable variety and novelty of everyday reality.[23]

How is indexicality put to good use? To understand this we need to introduce the performative aspect of language. Conversation analysts use the somewhat nonintuitive concept of "reflexivity" here. With this they mean that descriptions are not just about some aspect of the world but are also always doing something. So, when I say to my son, "Pick up that book," I do not merely describe a situation (the messy living room, his Latin book lying on the floor), I am also trying to get him to clean up the mess by asserting my authority as a father. Why is this important? The answer is that it brings us close to the hot core of reality construction. Let me quote Potter at this point:

A simple way of thinking about this [reflexivity] is to consider that people do not use descriptions just for their own sake. Descriptions are performed as parts of actions which are, in turn, embedded in broader sequences of interaction. The notions of reflexivity and indexicality are closely connected. Once you start to treat descriptive utterances as occasioned, you are ceasing to treat them as having a disembodied, abstract relation to some part of the world. Instead you are attending to how they are practically involved with ongoing activities. (1996, 47)

In other words, the situation with the book is not just represented by my utterance; it is evoked, if not brought into being, by it. In a quite literal way the situation with the book is brought about by my concerns with the mess in the living room and my concern with trying to instill some sense of orderliness in my son. Differently put, the situation springs forth from some practical and ethical purposes I have at that moment. I could have decided to just let it be and tolerate a messy house. This "bringing about" is done linguistically by uttering the sentence "Pick up that book, please." In a dense, implicit way the sentence "packages" the situation, as Potter puts it (1996, 48). It hooks onto earlier understandings my son and I have of each other. It suggests some values, such as orderliness, that I hold dear. It sets out a future course of action. It defines our relationship. The upshot is that by uttering this sentence I, interactively and conversationally, create a small slice of reality.

We are zeroing in on the reality-constructing capacities of language. But there is one more concept that I need to introduce at this point. One could object that the wording of my example is exaggerated. Instead of "creating" a slice of reality, I am merely reorganizing a preexisting conceptual world. Surely, this example of "world making" can only be pulled off because we are all familiar with such things as books, messy rooms, disorderly adolescent boys, grumpy fathers, and the like. The answer would be that this is true, but it is precisely the point of constructing reality with language. Remember, conversation analysts are interested in the practical, interactive aspects of language. The reason language enables us to orient ourselves in a situation such as that in the messy room example is precisely its ability to evoke and organize this background of expectations, experience, memories, and know-how. This "background understanding" is the third concept, and as I hope to make clear in this and the next chapter, it is a key concept in knocking the chair from under the realist perspective of knowledge of the world.

Various thinkers have pointed in the direction of a realm of barely articulated, and not completely articulable, understanding that somehow is required for people to be able to talk about and grasp the world as a stable, orderly affair.[24] I will discuss their ideas at greater length in the next chapter, but I just want to mention here both Dewey's and Heidegger's notions of "experience" as a prior stage to knowledge (Dewey, 1916, 2; 1994 [1925]; Safranski, 1998, 94); the concept of "background understanding" as formulated by Wittgenstein and developed by Taylor (1995c, 168); Gadamer's "pre-understanding" (1976); Bourdieu's concept of habitus (1977); Garfinkel's "documentary method of interpretation" (1967, 78); and Shotter's "knowing of the third kind" or "lower plane" of conversational interactions (1993, 18). There are important differences in emphasis among these thinkers, but they are united in the idea that we are embedded in a reservoir of pre-articulated understanding that is partly embodied, partly practical, partly materialized, partly conceptual, and that is activated when we move about in everyday, practical situations such as the messy room example. With "activated" I mean not simply reproduced, but accessed through acting on the situation at hand. It is a form of understanding the locus of which is not in our knowledge or our mind but in our *practices* (Taylor, 1995c, 170). By "activated" I also mean that we do not just, monologically, summon it for purposes of application. Instead, it "announces" itself when the situation calls for it. Then we work upon it, alter, and improve it in the process of acting on a situation and articulating it through the use of language. Eventually it sinks back into this vast realm of background understanding in a transformed, updated way. We converse with our background understanding in a dialogical manner.

Many implications follow from this line of thinking, but I want to restrict myself here to a few points that are pertinent to the issue of language and reality construction. First, the "understanding" in "background understanding" is not only linguistic. Much of this understanding is embodied (for example the kind of understanding that allows us to ride a bike even if we haven't done it in years) and cannot be articulated fully. Other parts of that understanding are material or spatial. These come together when I cook, for example. Not only do I move about in the three-dimensional space of my kitchen in a routine manner, reaching for knives and appliances in a faultless way; I also use the various tools as extensions of my body. Background understanding has emotional components, affective states with roots in biology and cognition. Much of background understanding is institutional. It is about the practical organization of the society we live in. How to master a failing public transportation system. How to avoid the worst rush hour traffic. How to fill out your tax form. Much of this understanding can be put into words, as when we explain to a friend how to negotiate the privatized home care system to obtain care for his elderly mother. But the understanding is above all practical, guided by our personal interests. Large chunks of this background understanding are valuational. Background understanding is about how we feel about certain situations. How we should act in them. How we assess people and institutions. Much of this is so natural and self-evident that it is hard to imagine an alternative. An example is the way we approach people in public spaces. What is proper and common differs starkly between the Scandinavian and the Mediterranean countries. The valuational, embodied, affective, prosodic, and semantic are intertwined here in labyrinthine ways. Even linguistic understanding is not purely linguistic. We all master the art of turn taking in conversations without being able to explain how and why. And we all, unthinkingly, know how to organize a stretch of oral discourse prosodically to convey the meaning we want to convey (J.P. Gee, 1985; Wagenaar, 2006a).[25]

All these examples are an argument against hermeneutic universalism, the position that "there is nothing beneath interpretation which serves as the object of interpretation, since anything alleged to be such is itself an interpretive product" (Shusterman, 1991, 104). From hermeneutic universalism it is only a short stretch to the conviction that everything is language, or at least expressible and analyzable in the medium of language. But the notion of background understanding suggests that there are more ways to converse with the world in a meaningful, intelligent way. In fact, and this is the real message of the thinkers mentioned above, the very ability of conversing in an intelligent way rests on this amalgam of unreflective bodily, valuative "pre-experiences" with their own organization and their own rationale. Language makes few inroads in this realm.

Second, background understanding is holistic. Although it is an open system that stretches out in all directions, synchronically and diachronically, without clear boundaries, its elements hang together. Dewey uses the phrase "saturated with a pervasive quality" (1916, 5). What he wants to convey is that the way we experience a situation as unmistakably being of a certain kind follows from the internal organization of the background understanding. That organization can be corporeal, associational, or thematic (J.P. Gee, 1997), but the point is that we cannot isolate one element at will without interrupting the fabric of experience. Holism has immediate consequences for reality construction. For example, similar signs have different meanings depending on the background understanding upon which they ride. Clients of prostitutes are very different types of men in Sweden than in the Netherlands. One cannot simply equate them. The Swedish client is suffused with background meanings that relate to good and bad sex in the context of the Swedish welfare state, moral stances that suggest what is appropriate and inappropriate with regard to sexual conduct between the sexes. The Dutch client is projected against background understandings that spring forth from Dutch habits, attitudes, and values regarding the sexes and sexual conduct. One could argue that this is true but that there is a common substrate, a core meaning as it were, namely men who pay for sex. But the point is that the core meaning is no meaning at all. When clients are the subject of a Swedish discussion or government report, they are inevitably understood in the light of the Swedish background understanding. To understand them differently would simply make no sense. In philosophical terms: visiting a prostitute in Sweden and in Holland are different "language games," different "life-worlds."[26]

The reverse also holds true. We cannot simply transplant one sign into another system. It has been tried. A Dutch report on prostitution attempted to introduce the Swedish "client" as a person with a personality disorder into the Dutch prostitution debate (Asante and Schaapman, 2005). It failed; at least for the time being. My guess is that in the more relaxed and permissive climate of male-female sexual relations in the Netherlands, this bundle of associations and understandings doesn't make much sense and therefore doesn't make much of an inroad. This suggests that there are limits to reality construction. To turn the Dutch client into a pervert requires a lot more work than simply changing the wording with which we depict him—scientific, professional, valuative work. The kind of work that went into the transformation of the Swedish client from a man buying sexual services to someone with a personality disorder requiring therapy. Just to call them "sex addicts," as the Dutch report did, was an attempt, but a failed one. Perhaps the science wasn't good enough.[27] Or perhaps the juxtaposition of sex with addiction requires a different moral climate. Another linguistic construction, prostitutes as victims, is currently more successful. Again this is not a simple notion. It involves lurid images of trafficked women, the understanding that no sane woman would sell her body if she wasn't impaired in some way, the belief that therefore all prostitution involves some kind of (male) coercion, and authoritative reports—serious statements in Foucault's words—that provide "evidence" for victimhood among prostitutes. If the understanding of the prostitute as a victim becomes generally accepted in the Netherlands and crowds out all other understandings of this profession, than we might also arrive at the client as pervert.

A final remark about the role of language in reality construction: Language itself (apart from its use), as a formal system of signs and meanings, creates drag in world making. We cannot simply agree to change the meaning of a word, because it is part and parcel of an internally related system of contrasts and consonances. This is, in Saussure's terminology, a "*fait de langue.*" Agreeing that from now on we say "personality disorder" when formerly we said "client," doesn't make the old meaning of "client" as "a man buying sex" just disappear. In fact, in order to make sense of the new agreement we presuppose the old meaning (Harris, 1988, 51). For client as pervert to make sense we literally need a new language, a new system of contrasts and consonances by which that term is defined. Clearly languages change, but more slowly than policy enthusiasts perhaps prefer.[28]

So, the upshot is that presupposition 4 of the social constructionist program is not just schematic. It is overly optimistic. There is more to reality construction than just altering the language. Saying it is not making it. Language is important, but changing the language is as much the outcome as the cause of social reform. There is no getting around the long march through the institutions. It also means that the specter of relativism is no more than that: a chimera. As the examples demonstrated, not anything goes. It is not that because all our categories—"worlds" in Goodman's vocabulary—are constructed, that we cannot—and do not—judge the superiority or inferiority of one category or "world" over another. It might be construction all the way down, but it is not, as we have seen, interpretation all the way down. Our "worlds" are not fictions. Against the reservoir of background understanding we judge how much sense a new concept makes. That process of sense making, of assessing the value or rightness of a construction, occurs through intense and heated debate in the context of action. When we intervene we run into "entities" that resist (chapter 4). Confronted with these resistances, confronted with the effects of our actions, diverging positions engage each other. In other words, reality construction requires dialogue. It is to this that I turn in the next chapter.

NOTES

1. Hacking, the philosopher whose wonderfully lucid book *The Social Construction of What?* I make good use of in this chapter, similarly believes that the phrase "social construction" is "both obscure and overused" and functions less to convey content than to signal an allegiance (1999, vii). To illustrate his observation of overuse he presents a hilarious ABC of constructionist titles, ranging from "authorship" to "Zulu nationalism" (1999, 1).

2. By way of commentary to this last, somewhat facetious, statement: Foucault certainly didn't perceive himself as one. He deliberately made himself politically elusive (Lemke, 1997, 27).

3. A serious discussion of philosophical constructionism would go far beyond the confines of this book. The technical difficulties are fierce, but for those who are so inclined, the following are basic, and eminently readable, works: Goodman, 1978; Haack, 1995; Hacking, 1983; H. Putnam, 1981b. For those who want to approach social constructivism from the angle of truth, I recommend Allen, 1993.

4. For those who think that this talk of "worlds" is overdone and front-loads the argument for pluralism, see for example Yanow, who titles one of the chapters of her interpretive textbook "Textwork as World-making" (2000, 86). Clearly that is not an argument (we could both be accused of the sin of excessive imagery), but the phrase "world" is intended to express that we are not indifferent to these "versions." We don't change versions as we change clothes (although that might be a bad example, given how meticulously many people project a particular image through their clothing). We live in our versions as in the only house we know, and when for some reason they start to shift or crumble, it can be cause for great uncertainty and emotional distress. We are invested in our versions, perceptually, morally, spiritually, professionally, and affectively. That is what makes them worlds and not versions.

5. The realist encounter to this position often is: Ah, but then anything goes. The specter of relativism raises its ugly head. Let me quote H. Putnam's rejoinder to this objection: "Internalism [Putnam's term for what I call here ontological constructionism] does not deny that there are experiential *inputs* to knowledge; knowledge is not a story with no constraints except *internal* coherence; but it does deny that there are any inputs *which are not themselves to some extent shaped by our concepts,* by the vocabulary we use to report and describe them, or any inputs *which admit of only one description, independent of all conceptual choices.* Even our description of our own sensations, so dear as a starting point for knowledge to generations of epistemologists, is heavily affected (as are the sensations themselves for that matter) by a host of conceptual choices. The very inputs upon which our knowledge is based are conceptually contaminated; but contaminated inputs are better than none. If contaminated inputs are all we have, still all we have has proved to be quite a bit" (1981b, 54; italics in original). For constructionism at the level of sensations, see Goodman, 1978, ch. 5.

6. Although we might mobilize the ontological argument to make the moral-ethical point of social constructionism. A common rhetorical trope in social constructionist literature is: "See X or Y is not cut in marble. The philosophers also say so. So there is legitimate room for change."

7. Kulick does not pay much attention in the paper to the concept of good sex—read "socially sanctioned sex"—as it emerged in the context of the Swedish welfare state or *folkshem.* Good sex was a generally available linguistic and moral category in prewar Swedish society and even figured in official government reports. It was seen as sex between two consenting young adults in the context of, or preceding, marriage (Dodillet, 2006). Nowadays healthy sex, or *frisk sexualitet,* is still a widely available linguistic-moral category in Sweden, but its contents have shifted to adapt to changing ideas about sexual behavior. It still designates sex between two persons, with consensus and without force, but it includes sex between persons of the same gender. *Frisk sexualitet* is associated with psychological well-being and self-confidence. It opposes to self-destructive behavior and perversion. For example: "*Och fler människor skulle kunna utveckla frisk sexualitet, istället för att söka självdestruktiv verklighetsflykt i perversioner*" (And more people would be able to develop "healthy sexuality," instead of turning to perversions in a self-destructive attempt of escaping reality). And: "*Men det kommer väl dröja ett slag innan kopplingen mellan självkänsla, psykiskt välbefinnande och dess uttryck i frisk sexualitet blir allmängods*" (But it will take a while until the correlation between self-esteem, psychological well-being and its expressions in "healthy sexuality" will become public knowledge) (from www.feminetik.se/diskutera/index.php?sub=4&mid=72546, accessed January 2, 2010; the quotes were kindly translated by Susanne Dodillet). It is interesting to note that the Dutch language

doesn't have a category "good or healthy sex," although coerced sex is of course generally condemned. Widespread acceptance in Sweden of good, healthy sex as a legitimate linguistic category certainly played a role in the condemnation of prostitution.

8. Note the language! Not sex but the whole person. Kulick doesn't comment on it, but since he has lived and worked in Sweden for long stretches of time, his Swedish is impeccable, and I don't suspect a translation error here.

9. It must be noted that many Swedish psychiatrists don't accept the visiting of prostitutes as a symptom of a personality disorder (personal communication, Johannes Fellinger). So even in Sweden reality cannot be constructed at will.

10. Relativism again! See note 5. I will return to this issue later in this chapter.

11. Sokal (1996). See Flyvbjerg (2001, 1–3) for a short and instructive summary of the science wars.

12. H. Putnam points out that similarity is a nondiscriminating criterion, because "everything is similar to everything else in infinitely many respects" (1981b, 64). He gives the example of his typewriter and a coin in his pocket as being similar with regard to being effects of his past action. So to say that a kind is defined by a cluster of similarities is to make certain similarities stand out to define the kind. This means that we make some prior selection, which raises the question on what grounds certain qualities are seen as to constitute "relevant" similarity more than others, which begs the question of why they define a kind, and so on into an infinite regress. For our argument on social constructionism we don't need to follow this path.

13. The issue of natural kinds is important with regard to the problem of induction. When we run into an object that belongs to a natural kind, we have good reasons to assume that the as–of-yet-unobserved objects of that same kind exhibit more or less similar properties. Haack thinks that "the reality of kinds and laws is a necessary condition of successful inductions" (1995, 134).

14. Now, what about Searle's term "intrinsic"? By that he means "features of the world that exist independently of us," or, as he also puts it, "independently of our representations of them" (Searle, 1995, 9). He uses the term to distinguish intrinsic features of the world from those that are "observer-relative," that is, they exist "relative to the intentionality of observers, users, etc." (ibid.). Clearly, there are strong affinities between the notion of natural kinds and Searle's "intrinsic" properties. Searle's project is to formulate an ontology of social reality, and for that he needs to remove from the scene all those elements and objects that are outside the social. Outside intentionality, to be more precise. In other words, his concern is not with kinds but with intentionality. This can be gleaned from the implication that intrinsic properties can easily be brought under some regime of intentionality. For example, iron, wood, and fire are features of a world without human beings (similarities, lawfulness). But when a blacksmith uses the aforementioned three ingredients to forge a knife, he has disciplined them in the creation of an observer-relative object.

15. This is different from the reordering of natural kinds into different categories, an important technique of world making.

16. Hacking calls these "looping effects" (1999, 105). There are clear echoes here with the analytic program of Foucault's genealogy and the governmentality approach to public policy. All three seem to aim at recording and explaining slow, broad, all-encompassing changes in beliefs, understanding, (professional) practices, institutional structures, self-understandings, and personal identity in a particular social-political domain. The difference between social constructionist talk and the other two approaches is in the implicit reformist program of the first. But it is difference of degree, not in kind.

17. The view of language as more or less passively imprinted by external reality is intimately tied up with a particular understanding of truth. We may of course make mistakes in the way we register external reality. But then reality is always there to correct us. Thus, the correspondence theory of truth. Language, ontology, and truth are cut out of the same cloth.

18. This new understanding of the role of language had a long history in the modern philosophers who chipped away at the ontological basis of classical correspondence theory. As Allen summarizes this history: "the chief difference between classical and modern philosophies of truth concerns truth's ontological a priori: a difference in the entity posited as determining, ontologically, the possible existence and content of truth. In modern philosophy, it is not nature or substance, but the self-evident sameness of what is and what is affirmed when a subject is reflectively aware of itself as feeling, thinking, or apparently perceiving one thing and not another which demonstrates, against all skeptical doubt the possibility in principle of a true-making sameness between thought and being. . . . Thus the significance from Descartes to Kant, Husserl, and Moore of subjectivity: a domain where thought and existence are unified; where what is judged and said cannot fail to coincide with what is. With this, the subject moves into the position formerly reserved for nature, and the way is open to Kant's thesis that nature is constituted by the spontaneous auto-affection of subjective

reason" (1993, 31–32). Allen then draws out the implications of the modern understanding of truth for the role of language: "A different understanding of truth's ontological a priori yields a different account of truth in signs. As ancient and modern philosophy agree that utterances owe their truth-value to something that is not itself linguistic or conventional, so they agree in the theme of the secondary sign, but as they differ in what supposedly has to exist if there is truth, so they differ about what to pair against the sign as the original in relation to which it is derived as secondary. . . . Speech is certainly secondary in relation to experience, but the objectivity of experience is itself secondary in relation to the transcendental subjectivity that grounds the existence of truth. The subjective self-presence of experience acquires epistemological priority over the identity and existence of its object, and the sign becomes uniquely secondary in relation to this more originally determinate subjectivity" (1993, 32–33).

19. Even from a narrow linguistic perspective this would be regarded as a simplistic argument. To make sense of language, linguists distinguish no fewer than seven criteria: cohesion, coherence, intentionality, acceptability, informativity, situationality, and intertextuality (de Beaugrande & Dressler, 1981). The labels alone suggest that the sensefulness of language is situated in the interaction between a text and the context of its use. This is the argument I will pursue later on in this section.

20. This is one of the battlegrounds in the current contentious debates about Muslim immigrants in Europe. Although they are exhorted over and over again by public officials to integrate, the non-Muslim population and the (Dutch) media keep referring even to third-generation Muslims as "Turks" or "Moroccans." This results in all sorts of complex counterreactions among these third-generation immigrants, such as a reassertion of religious identity. Language is not without consequences.

21. "Language is not, as the nomenclaturist implies, a set of relations between independently given sounds or marks, on the one hand, and independently given features of the external world, on the other hand. To view language thus is both to isolate words from the linguistic systems to which they belong and, simultaneously, to isolate the language-user from the linguistic community" (Harris, 1988, 17). With different emphases and in different ways, twentieth-century language philosophers as Saussure, Wittgenstein, Austin, and Derrida all tried to get away from an understanding of language as a static system of words or statements that are in some mysterious way connected to objects in the world. Instead they saw language as a practical endeavor, a "medium of action," as Potter puts it (1996, 11).

22. Sense and meaning are not the same. "If meaning is used to designate the potential of a language expression (or other sign) for representing and conveying knowledge (i.e., virtual meaning), then we can use sense to designate the knowledge that actually is conveyed by expressions occurring in a text. Many expressions have several virtual meanings, but under normal conditions, only one sense in a text" (de Beaugrande & Dressler, 1981, 84).

23. This ties in with policy making and analysis. In chapter 10 I will present an "ontology" of policy making in terms of novelty, pluralism, and unpredictability.

24. Think of the rule-following example in chapter 4.

25. See Wagenaar and Hartendorp (2000) and Wagenaar (2006a) for examples of the prosodic organization of everyday discourse in an administrative setting.

26. Saussure would say that in this case "client" might have the same basic meaning in Swedish and Dutch, but wholly different *valeurs*. Harris explains this with the following marvelous example: "Is serving in badminton the same as serving in lawn tennis? Doubtless there are similarities. There must be contact between the racket and the ball/shuttlecock, and the latter must go over the net and so on. But there are also irreconcilable dissimilarities as regards the structure of the two games. For instance, points at badminton can be won only by the server. In Saussurian terms, the value of the service emanates from a different system in the two cases, and hence cannot be the same. Indeed, in neither case can one specify exactly what the value of the service is without explaining the whole conduct if the game in question. The *whole* conduct? Yes: because until someone is in a position to survey the whole of the game there is no assurance that all possible consequences of the service can be correctly assessed" (1988, 45; italics in original).

27. The report claims that there are 600,000 sex addicts living in the Netherlands. It doesn't define sex addiction, and it doesn't even attempt to justify this number methodologically. It simply asserts.

28. Harris cites Saussure: "[I]f stability is a characteristic of languages it is not only because languages are anchored in the community. They are also anchored in time. The two factors are inseparable. Continuity with the past constantly restricts freedom of choice" (quoted in Harris, 1988, 53).

8

DIALOGICAL MEANING

TAKING ORDINARY EXPERIENCE SERIOUSLY

Despite considerable differences in purpose and method, the approaches that fall into the category of dialogical meaning all embrace the following principles:

1. The activity of understanding is grounded in an everyday experience that exceeds our full understanding.
2. Understanding proceeds through dialogue—between actors and between actors and the world—that affects both "parties" involved. Understanding, in other words, is action driven.
3. Understanding/practice take place in emergent time.
4. As a result of 1 through 3, understanding is always imperfect, partial, and incomplete.

At first blush principle 1 doesn't seem like much of a departure from the hermeneutic and discursive approaches to meaning I discussed in the preceding chapters. In fact, as we saw in part 1, *all* interpretive research claims to be based on everyday understanding. This is where it distinguishes itself from the empiricist approaches to social science. This is also the lasting legacy of nineteenth-century phenomenology to the social and human sciences. We use concepts such as, for example, "contracts" as if they were natural kinds, because we have a firm and self-evident grasp of the underlying everyday meanings that support them: agreements, promises, and the ethical obligation to abide by them (Taylor, 1985a). Hermeneutic and discursive meaning take this embedding of meaning in ordinary experience to reveal, systematically and methodically, meanings that are hidden from view. So, what's new in dialogical meaning? What does it add to the other two?

I will argue in this chapter that dialogical meaning is no less than a radical departure from the interpretive approaches we have discussed so far, and that the break is situated in principles 2 through 4. As we will see when we explore the implications of these principles for the activity of understanding, they throw new and unexpected light on the familiar principle 1. If I were to summarize the gist of the rupture with the two other kinds of meaning (and of course traditional empiricist approaches to policy analysis), I would say: dialogical meaning takes the grounding of interpretation in everyday experience seriously—in an epistemological, an ontological, and also, but this is almost by way of implication, an ethical way. It takes it so seriously in fact, that I should add a fifth principle here:

5. No method, theory, special training, or prodigious amount of self-reflection, useful as these may be in many situations, will provide us with the kind of certainty or foundation that scientists or professionals claim to be able to attain.

This is the radical break. To relinquish the aspiration, or perhaps more precisely, the claim that social science puts forward evidently better, more authoritative insights—better, more authoritative, that is, in comparison to the insights of lay people—and live with the consequences. And these consequences—for the pursuit of inquiry, for our ethics, for our professional identity, for our understanding of what a society is, for the very notion of what constitutes knowledge—are wide and deep indeed. Take the self-evident authority of scientific method. Dialogical approaches turn things on their head here. Whatever authority social science may have derives not from superseding everyday experience, but from taking it seriously. From considering it, and the processes by which it emerges in interaction with the world and by which it gets recognized and accepted as right or doubtful, as both the source and the standard of insight into the structure and functioning of the social world. From the realization, in other words, that no matter how hard you try, you cannot break out of ordinary experience. Social scientists are perhaps able to improve upon everyday experience, for example by processing it in more systematic ways, but what constitutes an improvement is not the self-evident outcome of these systematic processings. This itself will have to be assessed and warranted by the criteria and standards of everyday experience. Dialogical meaning has abandoned the pretension that there is a firm foundation. Above all, it professes epistemic modesty.

In the next section I will present some of the philosophical background of the five principles of dialogical meaning. In particular I will discuss *philosophical hermeneutics.*[1] Central in this section is the insight that understanding arises from a situation of engagement, that it is shaped by a particular perspective that we cannot transcend, and that it takes the form of a "conversation" with the object of understanding. I will make use in this section of the insights of some key thinkers in this domain: Dewey, the pragmatist, Taylor, the humanist, and above all, Gadamer, the German sage, who elaborated the vast implications of an approach to understanding that takes everyday experience seriously. Gadamer's work is remarkably subtle and powerful.[2] I will take some time to discuss it because of its significance for our project of an interpretive policy analysis that is both practically and ethically relevant. In his magnum opus, *Truth and Method* (*Wahrheit und Methode*), he takes on one of the largest beasts in modern philosophy, the Brobdingnagian intellectual-ethical complex of institutionalized knowledge-centered, rational epistemology as it has permeated, in known and unknown ways, every aspect of our culture. In the remainder of this chapter I will discuss a number of approaches to policy analysis that are based on the principles of philosophical hermeneutics or dialogical meaning. These are narrative analysis, the late version of frame analysis that came to be known as frame reflection, action research, and public policy mediation.

OVERCOMING METHOD: POLICY ANALYSIS AND PHILOSOPHICAL HERMENEUTICS

Let me begin with an apology. The title of this section is not original. It comes from Taylor's remarkable essay "Overcoming Epistemology" (1995a). The gist of that essay is that epistemology is the product of a number of deeply held anthropological and moral beliefs. Or let me be more precise. What Taylor argues is that epistemology is not merely a formal intellectual justification of scientifically attained knowledge, a particular chapter in philosophy, but instead a moral system that is at the center of our conception of the modern world; a conception that is defined by aspirations to rational individual and collective conduct, with ramifications stretching as far as our conceptions of science, society, politics, and individual and collective self-image. "Overcoming" refers to an awareness of this multitude of deeply rooted, taken-for-granted ramifications. I borrow Taylor's title because I borrow the prophylactic aim of his chapter. Similar to him, and other writers in the dialogical tradition, I try to trace and clarify a series of deeply held, self-evident assumptions about meaning and interpretation.

Ordinary Understanding

In chapter 2 I introduced the notion of *action concepts.* These, as I explained there, are the bricks and mortar of the social sciences. Action concepts are defined by an intrinsic intention. To say that X greeted Y is to ascribe the intention of greeting to X. The intention brings the concept of greeting into being. Without it we would not be able to distinguish greeting from threatening, pointing at, or an involuntary movement of the arm. Following a well-established argument in the philosophy of the social sciences I said that we, as competent, well-socialized citizens, grasp these concepts, and the associated behaviors, in terms of what they *mean* to us. Explaining something with action concepts is engaging not in causal but in intentional explanation. And something is explained intentionally when we are able to specify the future state of affairs that requires the specific action. Now, in philosophical hermeneutics this argument would be seen as a rather impoverished version of what really transpires when we "understand" something. (The quotations marks will become clear shortly.) In everyday life coming to see what someone intends is only one aspect of understanding. In addition to intentions, ordinary understanding involves feelings, expectations, perceptions, preferences, memories, embodiments. As this is a key point in philosophical hermeneutics, let's look at an example.

During dinner in a restaurant, John has been rude to Judy. What does it mean to understand such a situation? First, we have to be aware that what I present in this brief sentence is a conclusion, an end point. Many things transpired *before* I came to this conclusion. If I were to reconstruct this preliminary activity I would begin by saying that most likely we would observe something much more concrete. For example, we might see John rise from the table abruptly without waiting for Judy or handing her her coat, and barge out without holding the door for her. John's behavior strikes us as unusual, as warranting attention, because it violates certain well-established expectations that belong to the realm of male-female interaction in public space. As a consequence, we, as witnesses to this scene, involuntarily are flooded with questions and conjectures. Why does John do this? Did they have a fight? John is known to have a short fuse. But Judy can be a nag. But it is embarrassing to have a fight in public. But what makes you say it was a fight? Didn't I see him answer his cell phone just before the scene erupted? Maybe that's what the fight was about? Or, perhaps he received some disturbing news. Wasn't his father seriously ill? I didn't think that Judy looked hurt. More like startled, I would say. And so on. And so on.

With these questions, conjectures, and assessments we try simultaneously to describe the situation as one that we recognize and to explain it. Perhaps describing and explaining are more or less the same thing. One merges imperceptibly into the other. The process is, as I said, *involuntary.* It kicks in the moment we are confronted with a situation that puzzles us, that we can't quite figure out. It is as if we need to find our bearings. This process of sense making is also *participative.* We become aware of the situation by being an active participant in it, and that is how it acquires meaning. It is also *interactive,* even if we witness this little scene by ourselves. The above sequence of questions and conjectures could be the kind of dialogue we have with ourselves in such a situation. But however we want to characterize our attempts to grasp what transpired between John and Judy, to say that we "know" it seems somehow off the mark.

Perhaps a better way to put our attempts at understanding would be that we try to grasp it. To locate ourselves in the situation at hand. To come to terms with it. The point of such an, admittedly, awkward grappling for words is not a minor one, though. It is to uncouple the concept of knowing in everyday life from the notions of purpose, certainty, closure, and control that are intimately associated with the term "knowing." The everyday knowing that the observers of John and Judy engage in is much more involuntary. It follows its own course, in tune with the situation that is to be grasped. It is part of our being engaged with the situation. It rarely leads to closure, although we might settle with some confidence on the conclusion that John was indeed rude to Judy. It also rarely leads to control, although having concluded that John was rude, we might decide, as good friends of both John and Judy, to go up to him and hold him to account, ask him what was going on, or both. But then our actions will quite likely bring about new information that requires a new round of questioning and conjecturing. The verb "to know" suggests a clearly demarcated moment in a stream of events. "Grasping" or "coming to terms" convey the continuous, never-ending nature of everyday understanding. Everyday knowing evolves as the situation evolves, driven as much by the situation as by our volitional attempts to grasp it. As Gadamer puts it, much understanding "'happens outside our wishes and acts'" (quoted in Grondin, 2003, 19).

How can that be? How can knowing happen outside our wishes and acts? The answer is: knowing, as we are accustomed to understand it from the traditional perspective of science or norms of rationality, is hard to imagine as happening outside our volition. After all, the whole point of knowing something is to deliberately direct the power of our mental faculties and our tried and proven procedures of inquiry and logical reasoning onto a situation to pin it down, as it were, in an unassailable explanation or theory. Within the traditional perspective, to know is the equivalent of the will to know, an imperative that is closely allied with the will to master a particular situation. Knowing as everyday understanding, on the other hand, is seamlessly embedded in the flow of everyday events, to the point that it can hardly be disentangled from it. Everyday understanding is part of being engaged with the world, of acting upon it, of life itself. We live our understanding. As Grondin, one of Gadamer's most astute commentators, puts it:

> If the understanding (and the term is still almost too epistemological) is a matter of event, we do not really know how, nor from where, it comes. It is produced, it rocks and nourishes us, it is the element in which we bathe and which allows us properly to understand ourselves and to share in common experiences. Gadamer draws on the crucial term "experience" in *Truth and Method.* It is not, of course, the experiment which the scientist undertakes in his laboratory, but experience understood in the way meant by Aeschylus (*pathei mathos:* we learn through suffering): experience which strikes us and becomes part of us, more deeply than any syllogism or analytic argument. Our understanding, our experience, are dependent on such a "grounding." The great enticement of modern methodology is to persist in making us forget it. It is like an instrumentalist conception of the understanding which hides its essential unavailability. Fundamentally Gadamer questions this instrumentalism. To understand is not to control, but it is a little like breathing or loving: we do not know what sustains us, nor where the wind which gives us life comes from. But we know that everything depends on it and that we do not control anything. We must be there to know what it is, and to know that it is being rather knowing. (Grondin, 2003, 20)

To be part of being forms the condition of possibility for understanding. We are able to understand at all because the activity of understanding issues forth from, and is embedded in, those ordinary situations, the everyday experiences, such as they evolve around John, Judy, and their audience.[3] Understanding happens.

But, one could argue, granted that understanding is a more or less continuous, unreflective activity, there are situations where one might want to intensify and enrich one's understanding by applying systematic method to it. Think of the psychotherapist who mobilizes his professional technique to arrive at a deep understanding of the patient's predicament. Or the interpretive policy analyst who applies systematic methods of data collection and data analysis to reveal the meaning that a particular policy has for those who are affected by it. In itself there is nothing wrong with this argument. Using systematic method to build upon what we already know about a topic is a sensible way to come to a better understanding. The problem is the implicit, or not so implicit, claim that the application of systematic method leads to more certainty, more stability, more control compared to ordinary understanding. That the method puts a foundation under the understanding thus derived. Or, as often seems to be the implication, that the understanding that is produced by method is somehow removed from the reach of the warrants and standards that we apply to ordinary understanding. In a particularly happy phrase, Taylor calls this process of epistemic colonization the "ontologizing of rational procedure."[4] All these claims about certainty and control are highly dubious because methodical understanding cannot be uncoupled from ordinary understanding and from the context that gives rise to the latter. The work of ordinary understanding, and the challenges that it responds to, keep resonating loudly through methodical understanding. There's no escaping from it. How can this be?

Reality Is Larger Than We Can Grasp

The answer is that understanding, all understanding, even the kind that by the application of systematic method wraps itself in the mantle of knowledge, swims in an ocean of Being.[5] Understanding is not a separate activity, to be switched on when we need it; it is life itself, simultaneously emerging from life and always answerable to its challenges and demands. This kind of understanding always operates from and within a particular setting. The setting—and I use the word here in a more general sense than that of concrete location, more as an only partially perceived set of cultural understandings—functions as the background to our acting and understanding. Acting and understanding are, thus, always confined. In the first instance, it speaks to the situation at hand. It couldn't be otherwise as it originates in a particular, circumscribed social situation. It also emerges from our having a particular involvement with that situation as agents. The situation provides the reason for us to care sufficiently so that we feel compelled to understand. Understanding, in this more universal sense, is, thus, finite and engaged (Hajer & Wagenaar, 2003; Taylor, 1995b, 68). Yet, while understanding is local, its implications are not. When we act in the world, and when we try to understand the effects of our actions, a lot goes on "over and above" our overt intentions and actions that we simply are not aware of.[6] There is always a surplus of meaning in what we do, a plenitude that we can never hope to grasp in its entirety. "With Gadamer, *being* designates what goes beyond the simple thought of subjectivity: what is produced over and above our actions and our knowledge" (Grondin, 2003, 44). In other words, our actions have origins and consequences that we have not foreseen and cannot control. Understanding always involves more than a focusing of intentions. This is a key argument in philosophical hermeneutics—and one of great relevance to policy analysis—so let me draw out some of its implications.

An obvious implication is that understanding is always incomplete. Both in the sense of lacking something and in the sense of being inherently unstable. This double incompleteness entails no less than a radically different approach to what it is to "know" something. To know in the traditional, "epistemological" sense is to attain intellectual control. The sense of control derives from epistemological assumptions about the traditional way of knowing. These assumptions confer a double certainty to inquiry. The inputs to knowledge are representations of external reality. Subsequently, these are upgraded to being knowledge by a formal procedure that enables us to distinguish knowledge from prejudice, emotion, or ideology. The aim of this kind of knowing, as Taylor puts it, is to nail the object of knowing down so that we control it and it can no longer talk back to us (2002, 127). This is the Cartesian ideal of inquiry, which has such a firm hold on our institutions of research and governance (Taylor, 1995b, 63). However, the irreducible surfeit of reality makes this ideal unattainable. What we come to understand will always be partial and provisional, and no amount of method or reflection will change this. Gadamer believes that this ontological given is unacceptable to the scientifically inclined and that (social) science and its corollaries, the professions and applied sciences, are ever so many attempts to deny it. "Throughout, Gadamer seeks to disturb the ease with which we seek to avoid the finitude of human understanding and to make it an issue of method or technique" (Grondin, 2003, 55). As I will argue, irredeemable incompleteness requires not a different method, but a different approach, one that honors the dynamic, interactive, developmental nature of our objects of understanding.

The above can be read as an acknowledgement that the world is larger than we can ever hope to embrace. Yet, that in itself does not provide an argument for renouncing our ideal of certain knowledge and control over carefully circumscribed slices of the world. We can attempt to control the world through obtaining the best possible knowledge of it, while being fully conscious that this will always be an unattainable ideal. The realization of incompleteness does not in itself justify an overhaul of the traditional, disengaged mode of knowing. This argument only works because it treats the irredeemable abundance of reality as scrap, as wastage. The unexplained variance in a regression equation. Something that we will no doubt master when we improve our knowledge and our methods. But such a designation derives wholly from being immersed in the perspective of what is known and controlled; from the variance we have "explained." The surfeit of reality in the world is reasoned away, "avoided," Gadamer would say. But what if we were to take it seriously? How would that affect the way we understand the world?

From this notion of an abundance of reality that we can never aspire to grasp in its entirety, a number of subtle and important ideas with immediate relevance for policy analysis emanate.[7] In the remainder of this section I will attempt to trace a few of them. One line of argument runs from the idea of a surfeit of being to the all-important epistemic notion of *background*. The surfeit of being ("*Zuwachs an Sein*," as Gadamer calls it) is not wastage but instead the source of our engagement as agents. It is not the end but the beginning of understanding. It is from this surfeit that something presents itself as unexpected, different, strange, and in need of an explanation.[8] If John and Judy had just had dinner in the restaurant we wouldn't have given the situation a second thought. But since John walked out abruptly, leaving Judy in the lurch, we, as friends of the couple, feel compelled to reflect on the situation and perhaps to intervene. Reality abundance functions, according to Gadamer, as a statement or message before which we cannot remain indifferent (Grondin, 2003, 42). In this sense, our engagement derives from the always present *Zuwachs an Sein* in every situation. But what does it mean to be engaged, or more precisely, to be an engaged agent?

The first part of the answer is the realization that the plenitude of reality in which we are immersed *precedes* our attempts at understanding. This fullness of being forms the background of expectations, memories, historical events, meanings, understandings, experiences, ideals, norms, embodiments, and unrealized potential against which we act and understand. This background makes our perceptions and our understandings intelligible. It is the source of both the unexpected events that compel us to attend and the configuration of norms and expectations that make certain events stand out as unexpected.[9] We are limited in that we cannot possibly extract ourselves from this background; it is the horizon—in Gadamerian terms—within which we operate. Yet, the background also forms the condition of intelligibility. We are aware of something because there is a largely unarticulated context of attending in place. Our realization that something stands out, that what we perceive is "about" something and not some random noise, is because of the background. This confluence of being immersed in a background and that fact being the condition for our being able to perceive and understand at all, is what is meant by the term "engaged agency" (Taylor, 2002, 68–72).

Objects Are Related to the Observer

A second line of argument brings together the idea of surfeit and the connected ideas of *presentation* and *occasionality*. The latter two ideas refer to the relation between an observing agent and the object or phenomenon he observes. In the Cartesian view the object of observation is unproblematic. It is a given. It simply sits in social or historical space, at an epistemic remove from the observer, waiting to be apprehended by this or that agent who applies some method of observation. The outcome of the act of observing is independent—*must* be independent—of the agent observing. Gadamer problematizes this whole configuration of object, observer, and observing, making its outcome dependent upon the *relation* among these three. First, the object never just sits in space unaffected, impervious, but *presents* itself. Gadamer develops this idea in discussing the way art presents itself to us. In fact, art exists only in its presentation. With this aphorism Gadamer wants to break free from the classical hermeneutic conception of art as a neutral object whose meaning can be discovered by situating it in its proper aesthetic or historic context. So instead of distancing a sculpture as, let's say, mannerist or baroque, Gadamer sensitizes us to the sculpture's current impact upon the observer. The sculpture doesn't exist as a mannerist or baroque sculpture as such, but as something that appeals to us now, in our contemporaneous condition.[10] We see the work because it speaks to something that is important to us in our current situation. So instead of observation being the activity of a detached agent who takes in sovereign objects, Gadamer presents it as a mutual rapprochement. In the act of observing, object and observer accost each other. This is why Grondin summarizes the notion of presentation by saying that it is "simultaneously dialogue and address" (2003, 46). The revolutionary epistemic insight is that an object is perceived because it somehow implicates the observer. Instead of observation hinging on detachment, it implies, on the contrary, an involved, participating agent.

Baroque sculpture might seem far removed from the concerns of public policy, but the idea of presentation is in fact highly relevant to it. Like a work of art, a policy program exists only in the way it presents itself to social agents. Social actors become aware of a policy program because it concerns them. And that concern is not of the armchair type. The policy forces itself upon them, as it were. The policy confronts the agent because it contains an implied or overt challenge to his interests. The meaning of the policy is not in its officially stated purpose but instead in the impact it has on our practical concerns. Policies implicate social actors and it is from this act of implication that we should understand policies. For the social actor there is, in this sense, no getting away from the policy. The agent cannot hold himself aloof. "To participate is not a matter of choice," as Gadamer puts it (quoted in Grondin, 2003, 48).[11]

Does this practical-relational view of observation sets us on the slippery slope of relativism? If objects or phenomena only appear in our field of observation because we have some stake in it, then observation becomes a wholly subjective event. Our observations and understandings will never have any bearing beyond the horizon of our personal interests. We will have returned to the phenomenologist's lived experience as the basic unit of social ontology. But this is not where Gadamer wants us to be, and he introduces the concept of "occasionality" to make his point. With "occasionality" Gadamer brings an element of reference into his theory of observation. If we stick to our example of contemplating a seventeenth-century sculpture, then that sculpture reflects a model, image, set of ideas, or all of these from that particular time and age. Even if we perceive the work because it speaks to our contemporary concerns, it *also* reflects that particular historical reality. The point that Gadamer wants to make here is that we, as observers, cannot simply brush that historical reference aside as irrelevant to our contemporary concerns. Even if we would say, for example, "The mannerist paintings of El Greco are amazing in the way they presage the early expressionism of Van Gogh," we are always aware that El Greco inhabited a different time and world than Van Gogh. As Grondin puts it:

> The reference to the world which is presented is always essential to art. Gadamer calls this reference "occasionality": art always remains linked to the world form which it has arisen. . . . But according to Gadamer, occasionality . . . is still more profound: it is integral to the work itself, which always retains something of the situation from which it is born, even if it is metamorphosed in form. Every work is inscribed in this way in a horizon of life. (2003, 50)

The observation of a work of art is, thus, a balancing act between our personal concerns and the demands of historical reality. One could say that the painting or sculpture also contains a surfeit of reality, an abundance of historical being. We only glimpse a small part of it, but it exerts its influence on us—although usually an only dimly articulated influence. We observe the work of art because it speaks to our personal concerns, yet we cannot completely ignore the historical world in which it originated. That world, however implicitly, will always discipline our observation. The point of the concept of occasionality is that in the act of observation our personal concerns and this historical plenitude come together: "[O]ccasionality, from what can be called a fusion of horizons also implies *our* world in the work of presentation. The meaning of occasionality in the work is always the meaning which the work takes for us, *according to historical considerations*" (Grondin, 2003, 51; first italics in original, second added).

Again, all this is highly relevant to policy analysis. As in observing a work of art, the "presentation" of the object of a policy (a sudden increase in hospital readmissions, the proposed construction of a nuclear reactor, disappointing welfare-to-work rates of single mothers) and the everyday situation that gave rise to these problems are not the same. Policies also contain a surfeit of reality that is suggested by the presentation. And that surfeit often differs in essential respects from what is grasped or represented by the policy maker. For example, a proposal to reduce congestion by introducing road pricing during rush hours, refers to a vast configuration of issues and positions regarding driving habits, government subsidies of public transportation, accessibility of cities and office parks, economic growth, and so on. Even if we become aware of the proposal because we fear higher driving costs, these background issues are there and represent real issues that we can't wish away. In fact, the policy as "presentation" always represents one point of view (that of the policy maker) and is inevitably seen as a threat or opportunity by those who are affected by it. This is the inevitable pluralism in policy—pluralism as the conflict of interests and values. This is why there is no such thing as detached policy analysis. Understanding a policy always involves urgency, implication, and participation. "Occasionality means a work's *demand* for meaning, its *general* attachment to the world, *which is also our own . . .*" (Grondin, 2003, 51; italics in original) To understand is to be involved because the policy requires it.

Dialogue as the Fusion of Horizons

The term "horizon" has popped up several times now and it requires an explanation. It is another key concept in dialogical meaning. On the surface it refers to the by now familiar insight that we always understand the world from a perspective. Gadamer uses it, however, to highlight the radical epistemic claim that is embedded within perspectivism: we cannot understand the world as a detached observer. We are always part of the situation that we try to comprehend. Gadamer takes that in a historical sense. We live and understand in emergent time. More specifically, with the term "horizon" Gadamer introduces "historicity," or the work of history in the activity of understanding.[12]

What does it mean that we cannot grasp the world as detached observers? As we have seen, the disengaged view is not only central to the Cartesian tradition of objective knowledge, but also to classical hermeneutics. In classical hermeneutics the task of the researcher is to clarify meaning that is obscure. To attain this goal he reconstructs the meaning of the phenomenon or text by systematically following proper methods. This presupposes that the observer carefully distinguishes between his own subjective beliefs and the real meaning of the text. He has to efface himself so that the results that he obtains can be said to be independent of himself. Free of any distortions and parochialism that he is likely to bring to the subject. This epistemological stance is supported ontologically by the assumption that meaning resides somewhere out there, detached from the subjective life-world of the interpreter. And finally, the researcher dispatches this task all by himself. He is an outsider, epistemically self-supportive. The whole idea of proper method is about processing carefully obtained inputs in the right way so that they lead to stable, "true" outcomes—that is, insights that grasp the world as it really is (Allen, 1993, 9–10; Taylor, 1995b, 65, 76). This is the "view from nowhere," as Thomas Nagel famously called it.

Gadamer challenges all this. Of course there is distance. Gadamer conceives of distance in historical terms. (That need not be so. Distance can also be cultural. For example, African American single mothers or chronic mental patients versus policy makers. Or religious—biotechnology regulation in Israel. Gadamer chooses to develop his argument around distance in time.) Things come from the past. But, at the same time, as we saw in the preceding paragraphs, we understand things from our own point of view. By trying to understand something we inevitably "add" something of our own to it that we attempt to grasp. As always with Gadamer, there are many things packed into this seemingly simple idea. First, we cannot neutralize history. History is always around us and *in* us. To express this idea Gadamer introduces the term *Wirkungsgeschichte,* or "the work of history." As Grondin explains it, history acts on us in not completely understood ways:

> The notion of work gives us a better idea that history is active in us, works in us or penetrates us, to a greater extent that knowledge can penetrate or suspect. . . . With this concept, Gadamer perhaps best realized his project of going beyond the epistemological and instrumental approach in hermeneutics. The work of history revealed a working of history that is active over and above the historical knowledge we can have. (2003, 92)

In other words, history is part of the excess of reality—the only partly transparent background, which conditions our practical understanding of the world. Understanding is participating in history.

This implies a powerful critique of the ideal of the disengaged observer. The questions we ask about a topic and the answers we give are dependent on the person asking them. Taylor invites us to see the radical implications of this insight. It is one thing to say that we vary the terms of our understanding with the object of understanding. For example, when we study the survival tactics of indigent chronic mental patients in a large American city, we are likely to use different concepts and categories than when we study the governing practices of British civil servants. This is what idiographic (versus nomothetic) knowledge is all about (Taylor, 2002, 130). However, Gadamer in fact extends the idea of idiographic knowledge to the person observing: what *I* perceive and understand will, inevitably, be different from what *you* perceive and understand. And if we add to this, according to Gadamer, that we are locked into our experience (both historical and otherwise), we seem to be in deep trouble. Our own experience or perspective will stand in the way of our understanding other people's experiences or understandings. If we cannot transcend or neutralize our perspective, how can we ever hope to arrive at any knowledge that is worthy of that name at all? Are we to give up the very idea of an objective knowledge that somehow represents the world as it is, and slide into a quagmire of relativism? This would be a fatal misunderstanding of Gadamer.

What Gadamer has done here, in a persuasive manner, is to reveal the everyday basis of understanding that is obscured by the powerful hold that the Cartesian disengaged view has on our institutions of knowledge, science, and governance. Most of the time we are not at a loss in our world. Generally we move about effectively enough without giving it much thought. We are able to grasp other people's points of view, even if these are relatively far removed form our own. Understanding regularly breaks down, but it is not the end of the world. We take it as it is: a situation that can be practically resolved. How do we do it? According to Gadamer, we manage to bridge the gap between perspectives by engaging in *dialogue* with other perspectives.

Let's edge into hermeneutic dialogue by sketching what Gadamer was up to by focusing on the twin concepts of truth and progress. On the one hand, there is the traditional correspondence theory of truth. We have arrived at truth when our observations and explanations faithfully reflect a particular slice of reality. How do we know we struck truth? Because we have carefully followed the precepts of method. There is an added bonus here. When we have arrived at truth, we, automatically as it were, have made progress. To know is perhaps not to predict, but certainly to control—for the better, as the implication goes. Or is it the other way around? Because we crave progress, we need a stable, decisive, correspondence concept of truth to justify it. This is Taylor's "ontologizing of rational procedure." Knowledge, science, method, truth, progress—they are all intertwined.

On the other hand, there is radical perspectivism, as exemplified in its most articulate form by Foucault. As we saw in chapter 6, discursive meaning assumes that we are always locked inside an institutionalized perspective, and that therefore there is no truth to the matter—that is, not in the traditional correspondence sense of the word. Foucault, as we saw, raised the issue of truth very trenchantly, but with him the concept collapsed in configurations of power and strategic relationships in society (Allen, 1993, 151). Truth as a particular power-knowledge configuration can at best be unmasked and opposed—but not overcome, for where would we go? Into the strategic relationships of another power-knowledge configuration? It goes without saying that it does not make much sense to raise the issue of progress here. Indeed, an unspoken but pervasive sense of futility permeates Miller and Rose's analysis of the emergence of the community mental health movement, as we saw in chapter 3. Is it an improvement upon institutionalized care for the mentally ill? The authors warn us not even to ask the question. One set of power/knowledge relations has, contingently, replaced another. That's all there is to it. This seems to be the logical implication of the insight that (1) the precondition of all understanding is to be immersed in a background, a perspective; and (2) that a perspective both enables and obscures understanding. As we are locked into a perspective—particularly when that perspective is linguistically conditioned, as both Foucault and Gadamer assert—how can we ever hope to overcome it? Are we really caught on the horns of the dilemma between realist, disengaged truth/progress, and truth as so intimately bound up with social-political configurations that it doesn't even make sense to raise the issue of progress?

All we have said so far about surfeit of reality, presentation, occasionality, background, and historicism can be seen as a rejection of this dilemma between these two powerful truth versions. It is with the concepts of *dialogue* and *fusion of horizons* that Gadamer tries to avoid the horns of the dilemma. Both capitalize, as everything Gadamer does, on ordinary understanding. Let's begin with dialogue. According to Gadamer, understanding is a universal impulse, not an exception that kicks into gear whenever we run into an obstacle to understanding, and so is dialogue. We engage in understanding/dialogue as much as it happens to us. Dialogue is as much a disposition as an act. It is not foolproof; dialogue breaks down more often than not. But we have little choice. If we are to move about in the everyday world, we need to reach out to and grasp positions different from our own. How, concretely, does this work? We are able to bridge perspectives through:

> the patient identification and undoing of those facets of our implicit understandings that distort the reality of the other. . . . This will happen when we allow ourselves to be challenged, interpellated by what is different in their lives, and this challenge will bring about two connected changes: we will see our peculiarity for the first time, as a formulated fact about us, and not simply a taken-for-granted feature of the human condition as such; and at the same time, we will see the corresponding feature of their life-form undistorted. These two changes are indissolubly linked; you cannot have one without the other. (Taylor, 2002, 132)[13]

This is an admirable description of what happens in dialogue, but it can easily be misconstrued as overly intentional. We set out to engage in a dialogue, we become aware of the limits of our perspective, and we broaden our perspective to embrace the formerly alien point of view of the other. But this is not what Gadamer wants to convey. Remember, his goal is both ontological and practical (another dichotomy he tries to tear down). His purpose is to formulate an ontology of ordinary understanding as a philosophical basis for the human sciences. So, for Gadamer, understanding and dialogue are more possibilities of being than intentional, let alone instrumental, acts. Clearly, at all times we can engage in deliberate acts of systematic interpretation or carefully executed dialogues between contending parties (we will see examples of that in the remainder of this chapter), but Gadamer's point is that these intentional, methodical versions of understanding and dialogue are made possible—that is, they have a chance to succeed at all—because of the underlying process of understanding and dialogue as a mode of being. All this is expressed in Gadamer's key concept of *horizon*.

Gadamer seems to have been very keen on this concept, and according to Taylor it has an inner complexity that we should not lose sight of (Grondin, 2003, 73; Taylor, 2002, 136). It expressed for him not a rigid border, clearly visible from our subjective vantage point, but something more like an orbit in which we live and breathe, which constrains us but also suggests possibilities, that "is always with us and invites us to go further" (Grondin, 2003, 73). In fact, the concept of horizon goes flatly against the idea of an autonomous, independent subjectivity. It is at this point that Gadamer leans on the idea of projection (*Geworfenheit*; literally "being thrown into the world") of his mentor, Heidegger. We find ourselves in a particular configuration of reality, a certain moment in time, a particular state of being, without being fully aware of it and without having full control over it. We are determined by our environment and our history as much as we determine them. In a literal sense of the word, we do not fully know who we are.[14]

The concept of horizon contains a number of important ideas that, taken together, define dialogical meaning. The notion of an engaged, understanding subject living in a setting, and therefore being able to move about purposefully in the world by acting upon it, all come together. In this sense understanding is a universal process. At the same time this universal understanding arises from its own sense of fallibility. This is how Gadamer says it as brilliantly summarized by Grondin:

Understanding also means knowing how to set about something, where we remain implicated because each time it is a matter of a possibility of my being. For Gadamer, the decisive unblocking is there: understanding is no longer an "operation" (which would go the opposite way of the integrated life), but an originating mode of being of life itself. Gadamer says that the understanding no longer indicates a method, but the way of being of the *Dasein*, its essential fluidity. To be a *Dasein*, to be "there," is always to live in a certain understanding, intended in the sense of "being able to set about it," "being good at it." It is clear that it is less a case of an intellectual or mental process than a way of behaving, of an ability to be, in our existence. And understanding always arises from a basis of lack of understanding. I can get out of something by immersing myself in projects of understanding which are so many possibilities of my being in time, because I never completely exist in the present. In forcing the similarity, but only a little, we can say that the *Dasein* is fundamentally an understanding being, but only because, at root it understands nothing at all. All understanding is always only a project, only provisional. It is a "being able to set about it," in a situation that will never be mastered once and for all. (2003, 75)[15]

In understanding we cannot overcome our cultural embeddedness. This is why the idea of a fusion of horizons is so important. The concept carefully balances intending and happening. We do not understand by extending the limits of our perspective to incorporate another agent's point of view. This is important but it is not the full story. It would assume that we have a clear idea of where the line that delineates our horizon is drawn, and that we already possess the vocabulary to take in the other's perspective. Framing understanding in this way still betrays the influence of knowledge as the "scientific grasp of an object." The idea of a fusion of horizons challenges both of these assumptions. It does this by stressing the inherently dialogical character of understanding. Understanding is better seen as coming-to-an-understanding: ongoing, provisional, fallible, always open to revision. We understand when we allow ourselves to be "interpellated" by the other (Taylor, 2002, 141); whether the other be a person, a historical event, a text, or the effects that a policy program has on the world. The result of such understanding is a reframing of our categories, a refashioning of the language we have at our disposal to grasp our world. This has at least two effects. We become aware that what we initially thought was the object of our confusion or misunderstanding needs to be reformulated. We attempted to clarify *our* problem, but the confusion was that we didn't grasp the way that *they* see the problem. We become aware that different parties define problems in different ways.[16] But such insight is not without effect for ourselves. Problem definitions are closely tied into professional or personal identities. They represent ways of mastery, often arrived at with great effort, which we are therefore loath to give up for an uncertain alternative. Understanding, thus, changes us. It inevitably comes, as Taylor puts it, with "identity costs"; the sometimes painful realization of the limitedness of our earlier identity, the letting go of long-cherished beliefs and the subsequent slow process of working through the many, often unexpected, implications this has for our being in the world. Understanding is always also self-understanding.

The Ethics of Understanding

Framing understanding this way reintroduces an ethical moment in hermeneutics that was effectively dispelled by the Cartesian, objectivist aims of classical hermeneutics. Understanding as a fusion of horizons, a concept that is based on our being-in-the-world as engaged agents, collapses the fact-value dichotomy. The corroding agent here is the abandoning of the pursuit of control over knowledge and, by implication, over the object of our understanding. A dialogical notion of understanding implies that we can never have full control over that which we try to understand. This works in two ways. First, I am not fully transparent to myself and, second, I must be willing to open myself up to the other. I always understand the other, the object of my understanding, from the perspective of my horizon, but the latter has itself been formed by my cultural and historical background. Understanding is therefore ontologically fallible:

> What in understanding really comes from "me," and what is taken up from the "past"? Can we really know, with complete assurance? Can understanding be completely transparent to itself? This is why it appears more prudent in Gadamer's eyes to speak of a melting of horizons, of an encounter which mysteriously succeeds. The understanding is more event and effects meaning more than historical or methodological consciousness is prepared to admit. (Grondin, 2003, 59)

We experience that we understand something better than we did before, and we can also agree on it, but we don't quite know how we did it. At the same time, coming-to-an-understanding requires that I am willing to change my assumptions. The dialogical aspect implies that the other and I are willing to "function together" (Taylor, 2002, 128), and that requires mutual openness and respect. The openness that is intrinsic to coming-to-an-understanding implies a moral stance. It is moral because we see the other—again the other can be a person, a text, a historical event, or a policy effect—not in an instrumental way but as someone who, or something that, has something to say to me, something to teach me. The other possesses autonomy and an "independence and voice we must address and by which we ourselves are addressed" (Warnke, 2002, 93). In dialogical meaning ethics is not an add-on; we have no discretionary power over it. It is not something that we can decide either to leave out of the act of understanding or to include as the situation demands. The ethical dimension of understanding is intrinsic to it. This is so because we cannot separate means and ends. I cannot decide to be open to the other and then interpret everything he says from within my own prejudices. The act contradicts the purpose and in such cases I am simply not the person I want to be. The acts necessary to realize the end define both the end and the person engaged in the acts. But also, the understanding that I arrive at through pseudo-openness is of a different kind than when I have truly opened myself up to the other. As Schwandt puts it, "[T]he process [of understanding] itself is implicated in what can be understood, and the process actually transforms one's way of seeing the world in relation to one's self" (2004, 37). Openness and the possibility of self-transformation are constitutive of understanding. That is where the ethical infuses the epistemic.

With the theoretical groundwork in place, I will discuss how philosophical hermeneutics found its way into various approaches to policy analysis. In the next section I will discuss narrative analysis. Then I return to frame analysis, but a thoroughly revamped version of it. In his later work, in collaboration with Schön, Rein shifted the emphasis of frame analysis to reframing and policy design as key processes in resolving policy conflict. We will see that at the heart of reframing sits a conception of dialogue. In the final section of this chapter I will discuss a number of actionable, dialogical approaches to policy analysis such as action research, collaborative planning, and public policy mediation. Action research was much in vogue in the 1960s and 1970s in the wake of the widespread students' revolts in many Western countries. It bore the promise of emancipation of the oppressed and the simultaneous liberation of science from the fetters of positivism. When ideal ran into reality these promises were only partially fulfilled and action research disappeared from view at most campuses. However, underneath the inflated rhetoric, action research harbors some very important lessons about how to conduct research in a dialogical manner. Collaborative planning and public policy mediation can be considered forms of structured dialogue in conflictual settings. We will see that, without falling into the trap of method, many of the ideas of the fusion of horizons can be attained in a structured manner.

NARRATIVE ANALYSIS

The Sudden Popularity of Stories in the Social Sciences

Stories entered the social sciences in the late 1960s. Or perhaps it is better to say: swept over the social sciences. Stories fell in with the tune of the times. Narrative was another vanguard in the restructuring of social and political theory. Stories convincingly tied the social sciences to everyday reasoning. It was one more way to arrive at the well-known phenomenological claim that scientific and everyday reasoning are continuous, that the social sciences cannot but depend on ordinary concepts and arguments. Narrative was thought to close the incompatibility gap and make the social sciences more relevant to their subject.

Until the mid-1970s the interest in narrative was restricted to specialists: historians and linguists. Historians hitched onto narrative as an epistemic category in defense of their discipline against logical positivism. Historical understanding as an autonomous mode of explanation cannot be subsumed under the hypothetico-deductive model. Just as physicists organize brute nature according to theories and laws, so historians impose narratives on unformed streams of events to imbue them with historical meaning (Rouse, 1996, 159; White, 1981). Linguists, mostly of a structuralist-formalist bent, were interested in how narrative structure produces meaning. The Russian linguist Vladimir Propp is the archetypical example. In his influential book *Morphology of the Folktale* (1968 [1928]) he set out to classify Slavic fairy tales according to their component parts and to the way that the parts contributed to the meaning of the tale. Other formalists, such as Mikhail Bakhtin in Russia and émigrés Roman Jakobson and Tzvetan Todorov (in France), continued this work.

One can only speculate how narrative moved from these specialist corners into the mainstream of social theory. The timing of its arrival gives away some of the reasons. Part of the explanation might be the structuralist vogue that also hit literary criticism. Structuralism not only gave central place to texts as windows upon meaning; it also conveyed the universality of the storytelling impulse. The narrative mode was the deep cognitive-cultural structure that moved individual subjects, unbeknownst to themselves. All this was persuasively demonstrated in Labov and Waletzky's landmark study of black vernacular in the ghetto. The seemingly incoherent ramblings of street kids were revealed by the authors to be accomplished, tightly organized narrative renderings of life experiences.[17] In the social scientific consciousness stories moved from quaint folklore to the status of a basic mode of human understanding. Czarniawska provides an instructive quote from Roland Barthes in this respect:

> The narratives of the world are numberless. Narrative is first and foremost a prodigious variety of genres, themselves distributed amongst different substances—as though any material were fit to receive man's stories. . . . [U]nder this almost infinite diversity of forms, narrative is present in every age, in every place, in every society; it begins with the very history of mankind and there nowhere is nor has been a people without narrative. All classes, all human groups, have their narratives . . . caring nothing for the division between good and bad literature, narrative is international, transhistorical, transcultural; it is simply there, like life itself. (Barthes quoted in Czarniawska, 2004, 1)

"Man is a story-telling animal" wrote the British author Swift in one of the better examples of a genre of novelistic writing that self-consciously frames the vicissitudes of its protagonists in their geographical and historical setting in terms of narrative (1983). White, a historian, calls narrative a "human universal" (White, 1981). And Bruner, a psychologist, famously wrote, "There are two modes of cognitive functioning, two modes of thought, each providing distinctive ways of ordering experience, of constructing reality. The two (though complementary) are irreducible to each other" (Bruner [1986, 11] calls them the "logico-scientific" and the narrative mode). There is something exhilarating about the awareness that storytelling is a basic mode of human experience. Once you are made aware of it stories are everywhere. You can't fail to see it. Historical explanation proceeds by imposing plots on archival data (Cronon, 1992; White, 1981). Doctors in hospitals arrive at diagnoses by storytelling, while repairmen negotiate the intricacies of deficient photocopiers by telling war stories (K.M. Hunter, 1991; Orr, 1996). Economists, despite their mathematical grandstanding, are actually spinning tales (McCloskey, 1998). Organizations are repositories of stories that define their origins and their identities (Czarniawska, 2004). Public administrators narratively negotiate the moral dilemmas of their jobs (Wagenaar, 2006a; Wagenaar and Hartendorp, 2000). And some policies are able to outflank others in the political arena because they posses more persuasive narrative qualities (Roe, 1994; Van Eeten, 1997).

But the ubiquity of stories is also their Achilles heel. For if stories are everywhere, what is the point in finding them? Again a quote from Czarniawska proves instructive:

> Many young scholars, fascinated by the presence of stories, proceed to do studies that show this presence. This is not enough; besides it has already been done. . . . A similar phenomenon happened in economics, according to Robert Solow. . . , when the economists were informed (mostly by Deirdre McCloskey . . .) that economics uses metaphors in its writings, the result was a series of studies that Solow summarizes as "Look, Ma, there is a metaphor!" studies. The same thing is taking place in narrative studies: many of them are of the "Look, Ma, there is a narrative!" type. Yet pointing out that science uses stories and metaphors, and so do other types of human activities, cannot be the whole program. The point is: what are the consequences of scientific rhetoric and what are the consequences of storytelling—for those who tell the stories and those who study them? (2004, 41)

Czarniawska has a point. Stories have been oversold in the social sciences in general and policy analysis in particular. In the policy literature the concept of narrative has been inflated beyond recognition. Dubious theories, political exposés, explanatory suppositions, interviews, political doctrine, policy reports—everything is narrative now. Why? I can only speculate. To call something, facilely, a story supposedly gives a mundane text a gloss of deep human meaning. Czarniawska urges us to heed the consequences of storytelling. I prefer to focus on the functions that narrative fulfills in human affairs, or better, in human action.

Stories have functions. They do particular kinds of work, as the planning theorist Forester calls it (1999a, 29), and they do it in a narrative way. That is the central claim of narrative, that it is a distinct mode of knowing. That, by implication, is also the challenge of the narrative analyst: to demonstrate the particular *narrative*—as opposed to logico-deductive, classificatory, or straightforwardly informational—contribution that storytelling makes to a policy, an organization, a decision. This narrative work ranges from the way that storytelling contributes to practical judgment, to the way that policy makers move about in a world of indeterminate outcomes, emerging time, and deep conflict, to the more straightforward representation of political doctrine. What these narrative functions have in common is the insight that stories work relationally. The meaning of a story is not locked up in the constituent elements of the text, but is constructed—actively, dynamically—in a continuous interaction among the storyteller, the elements of the story, his audience, and the environment they share.[18] In this sense stories are dialogues. They operate through a logic of recognition. By telling a story, a situation, initially vague and confused, becomes meaningful because it resembles a situation we recognize and are familiar with. There is more to it, as we will see shortly. Stories are emotive, value laden, open-ended, action oriented, and more. We live in narrative environments, fields of finalized, ongoing, and possible stories. The point is that the burden rests upon the analyst to show how all these tasks and functions are accomplished *narratively.* In the remainder of this section I will first discuss the nature of narrative. Then I will discuss different approaches to narrative analysis, followed by examples. I will close the section with some remarks on the strengths and weaknesses of narrative analysis in policy analysis.

What Is Narrative?

Not everything is a story.[19] Thucydides's report of the Peloponnesian War is a story; the Annals of St. Gallus (White, 1981) are not. The report of the Dutch Parliamentary Committee on Special Investigative Methods is a story; the National Traffic Code is not. *Madame Bovary* is a story; *Finnegan's Wake* is a self-conscious effort to break with the traditional narrative structure of the novel.

A report becomes a story when it possesses certain structural features. In the most general sense we recognize something as a story when a report of some human event presents itself as a more or less unified, coherent whole. This basic insight was established by Aristotle, who postulated that a story depicts a course of action that has a beginning, a middle, and an ending (Aristotle, 1984). The coherence or unity of action follows from the linear sequence that runs from a beginning, in which the protagonist of the story is faced with a challenge or puzzle, via a middle section in which the events develop, to a final section in which the initial challenge is met or puzzle solved. Or as Aristotle calls that last bit, the "reversal of the hero's fate" (1984, 2324).

The unity that is obtained by this ordering of the structural elements of a story is called the story's plot. A plot, to quote White again, is a "structure of relationships by which the events contained in the account are endowed with a meaning by being identified as parts of an integrated whole" (1987, 9). As the term "endowed" suggests, a plot is not something that is given or that is out there, hardwired into nature, but something that is deliberately, willfully imposed by the author. This follows from the nature of the events being described. For example, this sequence:

1.   she received a blow on the head
2.   she developed a bump on the head

is not a story. Items 1 and 2 are compellingly connected through the causal chain between being hit on the head and the inevitable development of tissue swelling. However the following events:

3.   she asked him to clean up after himself
4.   he gave her a blow on the head

are not compellingly connected, as it is not usual, logical, or appropriate to reply to a reasonable request with violence. For this reason the clauses invite us to fill in the blanks (Is this an instance of wife-beating?) that suggests a story. So, for example, the simple chronology of the happenings of the life of a man such as Heracles or Theseus is in itself not a narrative, as it lacks the necessary unity. What someone who is telling a story does is to give the events a point. To create some kind of meaningful cohesion in a situation that doesn't necessarily have that cohesion by itself. Cohesion is attained, according to Aristotle's *Poetics* not just by depicting events as they have happened, but by simultaneously evoking an implied background of what could have happened. (He could have cleaned up his mess instead of hitting her.) With that the story gains a more general significance. By constructing a story the storyteller connects his rendering of events with shared cultural knowledge, with the wider meaning structures of the community. (The story of Heracles or Theseus is located in a framework of virtues and vices, such as heroism or hubris.) He locates his version of events in the more general experiences that the members of a community share with each other, and that they recognize as signifying something meaningful or essential to that particular community. Storytellers, in other words, create plausible, coherent versions of events that have a wider meaning than the actual course of events that occasioned the story.

We can now grasp the deeper implications of this observation for storytelling in real-life situations. In concrete, everyday situations people are constantly faced with the task of not only figuring out what to do, but also of how to account for whatever they did. Stories are a representation of this ongoing process—not after the fact, but *in vivo,* on line. They present an account not only of the actions and the situations that occasioned those actions, but also of the warrants for those actions, in that they convey the message: "For most people this action will do for this particular situation with these particular constraints." Or, conversely: "This action is outrageous in these circumstances." Every storyteller plays with loaded dice. There is considerable evidence that this everyday storytelling is second nature, that it is a routine that even children master, and at a quite early age (Bruner, 1986, 67). Storytelling is what being a competent member of a particular community is about.

Let's try a tentative conclusion: a story suggests a meaningful relation between elements that sequentially follow upon each other in time, but that do not logically or causally entail each other in a compelling manner. This explains why people gravitate toward storytelling in dynamic, emerging, confusing situations: to make sense of events for which the relation between the parts is not immediately obvious. We also use stories in situations in which we know in general outline how things hang together, but that we never get to the bottom of because they are too complex to grasp.[20] In other words, in the kind of dense, evolving situations, full of "litter" and the "incidental, tangential information" that one involuntarily rakes in simply by moving about in an everyday situation, which is the stuff of everyday life—and of policy making, I should add (Connolly, 2005, 73). So we can try a second conclusion: we cannot see stories apart from everyday practical situations. The relationship is reciprocal, if not dialectical. The one brings the other into being. Usually we do not experience confusion and indeterminacy, because we always have a story at hand that makes the situation senseful. But sensefulness is not a given; it is the outcome of the powerful, tacit work of stories. Let's see in a more systematic way how stories do this. I will argue that stories are open-ended, subjective, value laden, and action oriented. The distinction is for analytical reasons. In reality these four features operate with and through each other, as they make up the fabric of life.

Stories are open-ended. A good story deals in possibilities, not certainties. Bruner even believes that this is the most fundamental characteristic of the narrative form (1986, 26). He relies for this insight on the German literary scholar Iser, who sees a narrative text as a reservoir of implicit possibilities and the final story as the outcome of an interaction between the conceivable that lies dormant in the text and the imagination of the reader. Iser sees the major part of the story as de facto unwritten; the reader constructs the meaning of the story from the "textual signals" that are contained in the story and the expectations, memories, experiences, and perspectives that the reader brings to the text. Reading a narrative text is a coproduction of author and reader, and its result, the story as grasped and accepted by the reader or audience, a kind of virtual reality between the text *an sich* and the comprehension of the reader (Iser, 1978).[21] This narrative indeterminacy is clearly visible in the literary masterpieces of the past. The *Oresteia,* for example, is not merely a report of the violent domestic affairs of a noble family in ancient Greece, but above all a literary evocation of universal human themes such as tragic choice, moral accountability, guilt, and the arrogance of power. The enduring value of this tragedy comes from the fact that later generations recognize these themes and are able to project their own dilemmas and unresolved issues onto it.

Storytelling, as a distinct epistemic mode, accords with knowing as coming-to-an-understanding (see the previous section). This is why storytelling is the epistemic strategy of choice in everyday life. The emergent quality and irrepressible pluralism of the world of human affairs rule out the unilateral control that is implicit in knowing as grasp. Stories are meant to be provisional and temporary. And also interactive, dialogical. This is why we don't invest in stories as we would in a scientific theory; we know that stories are makeshift constructions, temporary abodes on a longer journey. The open-endedness of stories fits this picture of conditionality and joint achievement, because it allows teller and audience to adjust the story as the situation evolves. One of the characteristics of everyday reality-as-we-experience-it is that we do not know in advance what information, what detail, will prove to be important and will require attention, and what can safely be ignored. Stories function as scenarios in this "territory of exploration and discovery" (Ellos, 1994, 94). By constructing a story the teller can try out a particular configuration of facts, values, interpretations, and action-preferences. The audience will judge the story's coherence, plausibility, and acceptability. If it fails on any of these counts it will suggest adjustments or suggest a different story altogether.[22]

Stories are subjective. The *Oresteia* may be about enduring themes such as hubris and tragic choice, but the reason that Aeschylus's tragedy has appealed to audiences for more than twenty centuries follows from the fact that the author has rendered those themes through recognizable characters such as Elektra, Orestes, and Agamemnon. Stories are about concrete people, or more precisely, characters. Person and character are not the same, but they figure in stories as counterparts. The epithet "person" points to the fundamentally detailed nature of storytelling. In stories it's the detail that counts. In their study of administrative discretion, Maynard-Moody and Musheno registered the stories of street-level bureaucrats. They observe: "Front-line workers do not think abstractly about the deserving poor: they deal with the blind woman who qualifies for assistance but has a personality disorder that will forever limit her ability to function in society. They do not worry about the policy of zero tolerance for drugs when they ignore the small-scale marijuana dealing of a hardworking day laborer" (2003, 23). Rich, evocative detail is one of the key dimensions on which the narrative mode of knowing distinguishes itself from the "logico-scientific" mode. Why? Because by telling stories we master everyday reality, not by reducing it to a simplified model, but instead by keeping all the balls in the air. By doing justice to the whole *buzzing, blooming confusion* of factual, affective, and moral ambiguities that characterize ordinary life.

As the example of the street-level bureaucrats makes clear, descriptions of concrete people are not just lists of unrelated, distinct features.[23] They are coherent, intelligible portraits. They have an undeniable integrity that goes far beyond a mere enumeration of traits and behaviors. The extent to which the protagonists of a story display these qualities, the extent to which they are lifelike and believable, determines the plausibility and persuasiveness of a story. A story is carried by its characters. It is not entirely clear why stories are intrinsically subjective. One could speculate that the capacity of stories to engage an audience, and to stimulate them to do the interactive interpretive work that is required to fill in the semantic blanks, is dependent upon the possibility for affective identification, either in a positive or a negative way. (Disgust is also a form of affective involvement.) One could also speculate that the subjectivity of stories follows from their naturalistic character. As we saw, stories are structurally isomorphic with ordinary reality. It is characteristic of everyday reality that the large questions, dilemmas, and ambiguities rarely present themselves as abstract issues but almost always in the guise of concrete people, with all their gifts and shortcomings, their sympathies and antipathies, their loyalties and conflicts, their doubts and certainties. It is equally unavoidable that we choose sides in such situations. Our engagement with the small and large issues of everyday life proceeds through our engagement with the people involved. Through them we are also part of the situation. In everyday life as in stories, character and setting are hard to distinguish.[24]

Stories are value laden. The example of Maynard-Moody and Musheno shows that the representation of people in stories is never indifferent. Their typifications of the blind woman and the day laborer are full of cues that suggest how they want us to perceive these people. Also, in recounting frontline workers' stories, it always obvious where their sympathy falls. Characters in stories are moral constructions that indicate our beliefs about how people fit into society (Bruner, 1986, 39). The range of plausible characters suggests the range of legitimate concerns of a society (Bruner, 1986, 39; MacIntyre, 1981). The choice for one type of character or another contains the solution to an underlying personal or collective dilemma. With this we have moved into the realm of moral concern. Characters are positioned in an institutionalized system of relations and obligations. To evoke one is to evoke the other. Our concern with a character when we listen to a story always points to a concern with the larger issues at hand, usually a breach of or threat to the accepted order of obligations and responsibilities. To the moral order, in other words.

Moral positioning is one of the main functions of stories. Stories are about intentions, actions, and their consequences. We think a story plausible if it manages to relate these in a credible and comprehensible manner. In the context of narrative a moral position is not so much an assessment but an explanation of human behavior; a way to understand what concrete people in concrete situations do, have done, or will do (Murdoch, 1985; H. Putnam, 1981a).[25] Constraints are crucial here. Very often we are hardly conscious of our intentions, because the largest part of our activities is routine. But every once in a while we run into an obstacle or limit and the flow of our action is impeded. Our environment does not automatically yield to our intentions and "talks back." At such moments we have to make practical choices, and we have to account for our intentions in relation to the obstacles that we encounter on our path. The philosopher Ruth Anna Putnam has remarked that these obstacles and constraints follow from our actions themselves, from the choices that are inherent in them. Where they conflict we need values to find our bearings (R.A. Putnam 1985).[26]

White speculates that the urge to tell stories arises out of a powerful need for moral closure. As I believe that White's arguments are particularly relevant for policy analysis, I summarize them here in some detail. According to White some sense of legal or social order, however rudimentary, is presupposed for the impetus to tell stories to emerge.[27] One needs to have some idea of a communal order or a shared fate that functions as a source of authority and legitimacy, and the possibility that this order can be threatened by external events or by the actions of its members, for the experience of choice, agency, and urgency to arise in the first place. As White explains:

> Interest in the social system, which is nothing other than a system of human relationships governed by law, creates the possibility of conceiving the kinds of tensions, conflicts,

struggles, and their various resolutions that we are accustomed to find in any representation of reality presenting itself to us as a history. Perhaps, then, the growth and development of historical consciousness which is attended by a concomitant growth and development of narrative capability . . . has something to do with the extent to which the legal system functions as a subject of concern. (1981, 13)

The presence of a social-legal order creates the "norms," the "constraints" (in Ruth Anna Putnam's words) by which someone may conclude that a transgression of a social rule, a discrepancy between norm and reality, has occurred. At such moments the world is experienced as incoherent, out of whack, in need of repair. The moral code that provides it with such a self-evident stability temporarily fails.

In such a situation the imperative arises for a resolution of the conflict, a restoration of the social-moral order. According to White, narrative fulfills that imperative because "the value attached to narrativity in the representation of real events, arises out of a desire to have real events display the coherence, integrity, fullness and closure of an image of life that is and can only be imaginary" (1981, 23). Stories are thus a kind of sleight of hand to present reality as more coherent and more meaningful than it is, and could ever be, in reality. That order is attained by structuring a story in such a way—with a beginning, middle, and end—that the illusion is created that reality has always been governed by an evident moral principle. Differently put, there is a close connection between the moral meaning of a story and its plot, and, thus, its ending. But "illusion" is perhaps a misleading term. It suggests an arbitrariness and contingency that are beside the point of narrative knowing. In the context of practical choice we do not construct stories just for the fun it.[28] As Cronon rightfully observes, stories have an emotional impact: "A good story makes us care about its subject. . . . Historical storytelling helps keep us morally engaged with the world by showing us how to care about it and its origins in ways that had not been done before" (1992, 1352).

It is no exaggeration to say that a story is quite literally constructed backwards. Without some conception of a satisfying ending there would be no story. "The story is inextricably bound to its conclusion," as Cronon states (1992, 1357). The seeming inevitability of the story's conclusion stands for a deep desire for completeness and fullness that the hustle and bustle of everyday reality rarely if ever obtains by itself (White, 1981, 20). This is not an exercise in self-deception but an attempt to create a kind of necessary provisional stability that makes it possible to act on the situation at hand. "Insofar as historical stories can be completed, can be given narrative closure, can be shown to have had a *plot* all along, they give to reality the odor of the *ideal*. This is why the plot of a historical narrative is always an embarrassment and has to be presented as 'found' in the events rather than put there by narrative techniques" (1981, 20; italics in original). This relation among plot, ending, and moral meaning has brought some analysts to conclude that only a limited repertoire of plots is available in a particular culture, and that narrative competence consists of being able, in an unstructured situation, to select a plot that is recognized by a broad audience as senseful and relevant (Cronon, 1992, 1357; D. Stone, 1997). Deborah Stone, for example, suggests that policies are framed according to a few plots: "stymied progress," "change-is-only-an-illusion," "the story of helplessness and control," "conspiracy," "blame-the-victim." The "stymied progress" story, for example, goes as follows: "In the beginning things were terrible. Then things got better, thanks to a certain someone. But now somebody or something is interfering with our hero, so things are going to get terrible again" (D. Stone, 1997, 139). This is the story told by every group that resists regulation. For example, "biotechnology has brought us miracle medicine", according to the biotechnology industry, "but Clinton's planned regulation and price controls threatened the very survival of the nascent industry" (1997, 142). Or, on a more sinister note: The CIA has been doing a great job in fighting terrorism. Banning secret prisons and coercive interrogation threatens to play into the hand of terrorists. Be that as it may, the persuasiveness of a story does not reside in its veracity as a representation of reality. Nature is not narratively structured. Stories are carefully constructed cultural conventions, without which we would be rudderless.

Stories are action oriented. Stories deal with the intentional; with establishing plausible relations among considerations, motives, and interpretations, on the one hand, and actions and behavior, on the other. The credibility of a story is not dependent upon criteria of rightness or truth, but upon plausibility, the ability of the story to establish a convincing connection among intention, action, and effect in a particular situation. The intimate relationship between storytelling and human action runs as a broad theme through the narrative literature. From Aristotle (who considered narrative as *mimeses,* an imitation of human action [1984, 26]), to Bruner (who states that stories construct "landscapes of action" [1986, 14]), narrative is seen as a representation of acting, or rather of the motivations, intentions, and justifications that surround acting.

What exactly is the role of narrative in relation to human action? As we saw, stories emerge in situations in which the everyday moral code falls short and/or the urgency of acting upon the situation at hand is high. Most of the time the two coincide. The usual moral code is found wanting when people are confronted with conflicting demands, in the kind of situations in which values in their effectuations cannot be reconciled. Stories fulfill two functions in such situations: they provide the actor with suggestions for acting, and they give the actor a certain measure of provisional certainty that allows him to act at all. The functions presuppose each other. Several authors (Bruner, 1986; K.M. Hunter, 1991; White, 1981) have drawn attention to the intimate relationship among narrative, certainty, and action.

We find the most developed analysis of this relationship in the work of the policy analyst Roe. The starting point of Roe's analysis is his surprise about the autonomous character of the theories and rationalizations that underlie public policies. The stories that sustain a policy program are highly immune to often rather obvious contesting information:

> Stories commonly used in describing and analyzing policy issues are a force in themselves, and must be considered explicitly in assessing policy options. Further, these stories (called *policy narratives*) often resist change or modification even in the presence of contradicting empirical data, because they continue to underwrite and stabilize the assumptions for decision making in the face of high uncertainty, complexity, and polarization. (1994, 2; italics in original)

Most of us will have little trouble finding examples of the persistent myths that populate the world of public policy. As good example as any is the stubborn belief in privatization, in the idea that public services will be provided more cheaply and better when the delivery system is organized according to market principles. There is actually very little concrete experience or systematic research that supports this story. On the contrary, research and practical experience show that in most areas the quality of services goes down, costs go up, and accountability suffers (Self, 1993). In practice, however, it seems that the more a policy story is discredited, the more policy makers stick to it. Policy stories are coated with Teflon.

How do we account for this seemingly irrational behavior of policy makers? The answer is, as stories are full of suggestions for action, they are indispensable, for policy makers as well as ordinary people. Stories not only enlarge our understanding of the human world, but, even more important in everyday life, they provide actors with the reasons for acting and with intimations about the courses of action that are most adequate in a given situation. Roe calls these "design implications" (1994, 41).

Stories are symbolic representations of human action in practical, concrete situations. They simultaneously functions as explanation, justification, and instruction. A plausible story creates order in a shifting, unpredictable, incoherent environment. It makes past actions understandable and creates the conditions for future action. A good story is an Archimedean point in an otherwise indeterminate world. This is why policy stories are highly resistant against contradictory information. Indeterminacy, unpredictability, conflict, and the imperative to act are the inescapable characteristics of policy making. He who in such situations loses his story, loses his road map. As Roe perceptively remarks, "What displaces a policy narrative . . . is not a negative finding that seems to refute it. Refutation of a decision maker's argument for action doesn't mean that you have taken away her or his perceived need to act" (1994, 40). Experienced policy makers are generally aware of the shortcomings of their standard stories. But they are even more aware that a deficient story is better than no story. For he who in a practical situation, any practical situation, does not have a good story at hand, is condemned to futility.

The Analysis of Narrative

Those who are interested in using narrative in research in public policy face a bewildering variety of approaches. Mishler, whose "Models of Narrative Analysis" presents a very useful typology of narrative analysis, says that narrative analysis is not a distinct discipline, but a "problem-centered area of inquiry." (Mishler, 1995) This explains the diversity of approaches: analysts use narrative to address quite different analytical problems. This perhaps also explains why there is no agreement on a categorization or model of narrative analysis. Czarniawska, for example, adopts a discursive approach to narrative analysis. She uses two categories in her textbook: structuralist and poststructuralist/deconstructionist models. She doesn't define her two approaches, but from the examples we can infer that structural analysis focuses on the way that the elements of a story contribute to its semantic meaning. Poststructuralist analysis, going by the examples again, involves the projection of counterfactuals; trying out different readings of a text. Czarniawska speaks of "interrogating" a text to find out what it does rather than what it says (2004, 88). In other words, it seems that the analyst is interested in the way a story functions in a particular societal context within the framework of a particular moral program. Examples of different readings consist of reversing core elements of the text (insert "female" for "male," for example) to expose the hidden assumptions on which the story operates; examining silences (what is not said); or dismantling common dichotomies as "false distinctions" (2004, 97). So, in addition to focusing on the function of a story, poststructuralist narrative analysis has a programmatic quality. Its purpose is to expose things; to suggest ways that society can be made better.

There are other typologies (Mishler, 1995; Riessman, 1993; Toolan, 2001). Mishler, for example, suggests three broad categories: (1) models that focus on the veracity of what is represented in a story, (2) models that focus on textual coherence and structure, and (3) models that focus on the function of narratives, their contexts and consequences (1995, 90). When I survey the landscape of narrative in policy analysis, this seems like a decent enough typology. Let me give some examples.

Reference and the problem of representation. In this category I group approaches that use narrative analysis in a hermeneutic way. For example, the purpose of many qualitative studies is to summarize a particular processual sequence from a series of individual stories about a particular event. For example, my reconstruction of pathways to the mental hospital is just such an attempt to reconstruct "a told from the telling" (Mishler, 1995, 90). From all the individual stories about how these patients ended up at the hospital, I reconstructed three "master stories" that represented stylized versions of the succession of events that resulted in a rehospitalization. So, the category "Interpersonal Trouble: The Family" suggests the following succession of events: "The patient lives with his family after being released from the hospital. He or she still suffers from symptoms. Families go as far as they can to accommodate the mentally ill family member and his symptoms. However, the symptoms grow worse and worse to the point that the family is so overburdened or downright fearful for their personal safety, that they can't cope anymore. Reluctantly they call the police or they bring the patient to the hospital themselves. They feel both guilty and relieved after this" (Wagenaar, 1987, 211–23).

Another good example is Deborah Stone's notion of a policy plot that we encountered earlier in this section. She organizes the innumerable presentations of policy initiatives in newspapers, television policy reports, op-ed pieces, and other sources into a limited number of story lines. The purpose of this is to reveal the hidden symbolic order of public policy. Policies ride on the back of more or less powerful plots that resonate in the minds of the relevant audience. The persuasiveness of a policy thus has less to do with the strength of its proposals for beneficial action or with its grasp of the facts, but with the particular story line it has appropriated. In fact, *how* facts are presented and how they are related to ameliorative action is determined by the story line, not by some "rational" principle, although elected officials and policy experts will do their utmost to suggest that their presentation of a policy represents the facts as they are. As Stone says:

> Definitions of policy problems usually have a narrative structure; that is, they are stories with a beginning, middle and an end, involving some change or transformation. They have heroes and villains and innocent victims, and they pit the forces of evil against the forces of good. The story line in policy writing is often hidden, but one should not be thwarted by the surface details from searching for the underlying story. Often what appears as conflict over details is really disagreement about the fundamental story. (1997, 138)

Another example is Bevir and Rhodes's political narratives. In their case, stories give meaning to a body of "shared facts" (2006a, 28). If we bring to mind Bevir and Rhodes's analysis of governance in Britain (chapter 5), we will recall that they distinguish four "main narratives," which roughly coincide with the Tory, Liberal, Whig, and Socialist traditions in British politics. So, "narrative" here is another word for "account," "tradition," or even "theory" (ibid.).

Hermeneutic narrative is one of the most common uses of storytelling in policy analysis. Usually the crucial relation with action is more or less implicit. The focus is representing, not so much negotiating, the world of action. In hermeneutic narrative stories are artifacts of analysis. Their purpose is to represent and clarify data. As Bevir and Rhodes put it, "[W]e must compare bundles of narratives, or, if you prefer, theories, in terms of their success in relating various facts to one another by highlighting pertinent similarities and differences, continuities and disjunctions" (2006a, 28). Usually, there is little interest on the part of the analyst in the elements of a story, the interaction of story and audience, or the function of a story in a policy context. There is nothing intrinsically wrong with using stories in a representative way. But when the relationship with action becomes ever more tenuous, there is danger that the term "narrative" is used in an inflated manner. Why use "story" when "account," "theory," or "doctrine" do just as well?

Textual coherence and structure. These models of analysis have their roots in structuralism and sociolinguistics. They focus on "textualization, on narrative strategies that create meaning"

(Mishler, 1995, 103). Their purpose is to demonstrate that the structural elements of a story—however defined—determine its meaning. Understanding thus emerges from the form of the text. "Form and meaning are inseparable" (Mishler, 1995, 106). A good example is the aforesaid study of ghetto children by Labov and Waletzky. Mishler considers this an instance of "recapitulating the told in the telling." However, more recent approaches to these "structural" analyses, such as the analysis of oral narrative and everyday conversation, are much more dialogical. They focus on how actors actively negotiate their environment in sense making (Gee, 1985, 1990; Potter, 1996). The application of oral analysis in policy analysis is rare. My guess is that this is partly because of its relative unfamiliarity among policy researchers, partly because it is exceedingly labor intensive. I believe that oral analysis is potentially an important approach to understanding practical decision making in public policy and public administration; particularly its discretionary, tacit, emergent, and forward-looking aspects. It is a form of microanalysis that elucidates how actors negotiate complex, open-ended, conflictual situations.

I tried my hand at it in my analyses of the oral narratives of welfare officials (Wagenaar, 2006a; Wagenaar and Hartendorp, 2000). For example, the analysis of the story of Joanna, a welfare official who worked with the homeless, revealed the intricate work of practical judgment that goes into administrative discretion. In fact, the whole distinction between rule application and discretion, between rule and setting, collapses in the light of this kind of narrative analysis. Administrative work *is* practical judgment. It involves a careful balancing of incompatible demands, the judging of clients to obtain grounds for acting, the weighing of the effects of one's actions, on both the client and the organization, a constant calculation of personal risk, an ongoing positioning of oneself in one's relevant social environment, a careful calibration of what is right and just in a particular, concrete situation. Rules do figure, of course, but in multiple, unexpected ways: as constraints on doing the right thing, or, conversely, as action channels, as justifications-after-the-fact, as ethical guidelines, as guardians of the organization's integrity. Moreover, as we also saw in chapter 4, rule application requires practical judgment. Much of this work takes place tacitly, behind the scenes, in the workflow of an experienced administrator who acts on the situation at hand. Oral narrative analysis makes this invisible work visible. It lifts it out of the elusive realm of the intuitive into practical judgment as a commonly shared skill. This is a loosely organized, open-ended weaving of narrative elements such as idea units, contextualization signals, themes, genre, and echoes (Gee, 1997). Through these structural elements narrative attains both openness and coherence. Through its loose thematic organization Joanna's story revealed the unfolding of meaning, where meaning is similar to coming to terms with a challenging situation. Oral narrative analysis above all points to the communicative logic of practical judgment. It shows that we are able to understand and to arrive at feasible actions because, and only because, we are an inextricable part of a "community of practice" (Wenger, 1998; see also Maynard-Moody & Musheno, 2003, 22; Wagenaar, 2004, 2006a).

Narrative Functions: contexts and consequences. Narrative approaches in this category focus on the *work* that stories do in a particular political or administrative context. The analyst is less interested in the way that meaning emerges from the interplay of narrative elements. His approach is more general in trying to bring out the story's impact on policy making. "What purposes do they fulfil, and what functions do they serve—for storytellers themselves, their audiences, their larger communities?" Mishler asks (1995, 108). This form of narrative analysis combines hermeneutic purposes (How best to explain the success or failure of a policy in its context?) and dialogical purposes (How do policy makers navigate difficult policy situations?). It is not hard to understand why functional narrative analysis became popular in among policy scholars. For policy analysts they are a "natural." Their open-endedness fits the complex, emerging, indeterminate character of policy making. Their moral focus accords with the pluralism, power differentials, and conflicts that characterize policy making. Their action orientation points toward the imperative to act that looms large over policy makers. A focus on function allows the analysts to bring into the analysis conflict, power, values, and indeterminacy—everything that is ruled out by traditional empiricist theories of knowledge. I will give three examples that demonstrate the range of functional applications.

John Forester: Learning from Practice Stories. In a well-known paper, "Learning from Practice Stories: The Priority of Practical Judgment," John Forester shows how stories work when we consider them in their everyday setting. The story he presents is so familiar, so commonplace that it hardly seems worth paying attention to. But that is precisely the point that Forester wants to make. This is the stuff that gets relegated to the error term in regression equations, but that turns out to be essential in dealing with everyday situations. We sit in on a city planning agency's staff meeting and we witness how, as in countless such meetings in countless such offices all over the world, the difficult, uncertain work of establishing a position and arriving at an acceptable course of action in an unknown, uncertain, conflict-ridden world takes place. We also see how most of that work is done inter alia, between the lines as it were. This is storytelling in action. Caught on the fly.

In the story the planners try to come to terms with the defeat of one of their projects in the city council. The first thing that strikes the reader is that this kind of storytelling is a joint undertaking. The planners build a story together, sometimes supporting each other's statements, sometimes amending or correcting them, asking questions, testing conclusions, probing new directions. What emerges is a "very rich, morally thick, politically engaged, and organizationally practical storytelling" (Forester, 1993, 195). The verb "storytelling" in this quote expresses Forester's intention of demonstrating the active, never-ending activity of sense making in a world of action. Let's see what kind of work storytelling does in a practical setting:

> In planning practice . . . these stories do particular kinds of work: descriptive work of reportage, moral work of constructing character and reputation (of oneself and others); political work of identifying friends and foes, interests and needs, and the play of power in support and opposition; and, most important . . . deliberative work of considering means and ends, values and options, what is relevant and significant, what is possible and what matters altogether. (1993, 195)

Stories organize attention and help in making value judgments. They explore what matters and what is feasible in the situation at hand. Storytelling is a form of practical judgment (Forester, 1999a, 30).

Michel van Eeten: Folktales and the Dike Controversy in the Netherlands. Van Eeten is a student of Roe. He applies Roe's conceptual machinery to a bitter controversy over dike restructuring in the Netherlands. Two big European rivers, the Rhine and the Meuse, flow through the Netherlands and terminate in the North Sea. For many centuries a system of dikes has been maintained along the rivers to protect the surrounding countryside from flooding. However, as the rivers historically offer important means of transportation, many villages and towns have been built close to the rivers. In fact, an intricate, centuries-long fusion of housing construction, dike design, agricultural planning, and nature development has created a unique "culture -landscape" of great beauty, which is referred to by some as the "Dutch Tuscany."

The roots of the controversy lie in the catastrophic flood of February 9 and 10, 1953, in which 1,800 people, mostly in the southwestern part of the Netherlands, drowned and more than 100,000 lost their homes. The disaster was attributed to the neglect of the sea and river dikes, and an overhaul of safety standards was instigated. A new safety standard of 1:3,000, a statistical chance of a flood in 3,000 years, was formulated. Van Eeten explains that the engineers of the *Rijkswaterstaat*, the governmental bureau of engineering, deduce from these norms the necessary level of "outflow," the maximum acceptable high-water mark, and the required dike designs (1997, 39; translations of all quotations from this article are by the author). To abide by the new safety standards, river dikes had to be higher and wider. A first implementation of the new design standards demonstrated their destructive impact on the landscape. In a small river village, Brakel, 180 historic houses were demolished to build a wider dike. As a result, popular opposition to dike improvement geared up and the government decided to install an advisory committee to study the issue. The committee did not succeed in silencing the protests. On the contrary, environmental activists successfully questioned standards and methods and won some legal battles. Dike improvement reached an impasse.

Van Eeten frames the policy controversy around dike improvement in terms of conflicting stories. He argues, following Roe, that the subject of dike improvement is so fraught with uncertainty and complexity that it is actually remarkable that the parties who are involved in the controversy can be so certain of the course of action that needs to be taken. They succeed in this because their position has the structural properties of a story, a story that persuasively suggests how to act (1995, 32). Using Propp's structuralist morphology of the folktale, Van Eeten draws out two conflicting stories from the mass of conflicting argument. Faithful to Propp's imagery, he calls them fairy tales. He dubs Story 1 the "tale of the general versus the partial interest." The story begins with the observation that people living behind the dikes are at risk for a catastrophic flood. Government, the hero in this story, decides to act on the situation to bring these citizens to safety. However, environmentalists place their partial interests above the general interest of safety and thwart the hero's actions. The hero must find ways to defeat the villain, environmentalists, because you can't argue with villains. So the government issues an emergency measure that temporarily suspends appeal procedures. Story 2, a "tale of sustainability versus bureaucratic tunnel vision," reverses the roles of hero and villain. In this version, government is the evil force because it has obstructed dike improvement through a failed attempt to strategically evade the deeper problem. Over the past decades, technical interventions in the natural embankment of the rivers (to facilitate shipping) have decreased its capacity for discharging excess water. Now, the *Rijkswaterstaat* wants to intervene again. Its learning curve is flat. Environmental procedures are not an obstruction of safety, but instead a guarantee of reflective, sensible action.

Van Eeten argues that the controversy issues from what he calls the "moralizing impulse" of the stories. With that he means that stories "transform the technical discussions and arguments about the strengthening of dikes into a story of good and evil." The stories evoke a "narrative universe in which everything is reduced to the intentions of actors" (1995, 38). Van Eeten deplores this narrative reductionism. The stories hold us back from confrontation with the inherent uncertainties that surround dike improvement (1995, 39). Following Roe's instrumentalist thrust, he invites the reader to focus on the arguments themselves with the help of Roe's policy analytic "tool" of stories and counter-stories. In Roe's terminology the controversy becomes one of "narrative imbalance." The environmentalists' account is not an autonomous story, but a point-by-point critique of the "primary" engineering story. The stories hold each other hostage. The main story is weakened by the counter-story, while the counter-story is parasitic upon the main story, but also fails to offer a plausible alternative for action.[29] Again following Roe, Van Eeten argues that a situation of narrative imbalance results in restricted access to information, resources, and decision making arenas for the supporters of the counter-story. They resort therefore to a blanket rejection of the arguments of the dominant story line. He proposes that both parties get equal access to all analytic and decision-making resources. Instead of making the controversy even more intractable, he believes, it will become in fact easier to handle this way. With equal resources narrative reductionism will transform into a "comparison of alternatives with structurally similar argumentations" (1995, 41). This makes it possible to assess and evaluate the different proposals that flow from the conflicting positions. In other words, we must move beyond stories (1995, 39).

Van Eeten's analysis is interesting as he argues, contrary to most narrative analysts, that stories might function negatively in the policy arena. Reducing complex technical arguments to morality tales, he asserts, aggravates the conflicts that are inherent in the dike-improvement issue. We should therefore give central place again to a sober assessment of the technical issues. I don't find the blanket phrase "technical issues" convincing. If he means the reality check of "entities," he has a point (see the final section of chapter 4). But that downplays the "normative leap," to use a felicitous phrase from Rein and Schön, between analysis and action. Technical analyses of the dike issue or its environmental and cultural repercussions are always partial because, to be persuasive, they inevitably leave out important conflicting information. What is left out and what is allowed in are normatively driven. In addition, analysis rarely suggests only one, uncontroversial course of action. Stories are powerful precisely because they fill the normative lacunae in technical analysis. It is hard therefore to see how one can do without stories in situations of policy controversy. As I will argue later in this chapter, the problem does not reside in the stories, but in the absence of constructive dialogue. And there is nothing intrinsic in stories that prohibits dialogue. However, a situation in which dialogue is forestalled results in an impasse of opposing, and quite likely simplified, positions. The task of the analyst is to create a situation of "collaborative dialogue" (Innes & Booher, 2003, 2010) in which the stories of the contending parties become gradually more complex and inclusive to create a joint platform for action.

Cops, Teachers, Counselors: Steven Maynard-Moody and Michael Musheno's narrative analysis of street level bureaucracy. Maynard-Moody and Musheno's book is an exemplary example of functional narrative analysis.[30] In it they develop what amounts to a narrative theory of administrative discretion. The central theme of the book is the inevitable tension between legalism and accommodation, between going by rule and procedure and acting in the spirit of the law by accommodating the particulars of everyday situations and concrete people. The authors argue that rule deviation is not a negative entity, an exception to the rule of law, a dangerous aberration of administrative ethos, to be reined in as much as possible. Instead they discuss the discretion of frontline workers positively, as a necessary and distinct form of practical judgment:

> Our analysis of stories reveals that workers are constantly attentive to who their clients are, acting on their assessments of people's character and identity. Rather than exceptionalism, we find that these moments of special attention arise from the sustained tensions between legal mandates and workers' beliefs about what is fair or the right thing to do. (2003, 13)

As in the example of Joanna, stories are the authors' window upon discretionary judgment. Already in the first chapter they demonstrate the work that stories do. They present a story told by a vocational rehabilitation counselor. The authors call it "A Happy Ending" (2003, 6). It tells of a single mother in a "midwestern city" with a history of mental illness, living "with zero money practically in a real bad part of town" (ibid.), who, against all odds, found a job, but had no transportation to travel to the job. The frontline worker, through some creative accounting and evasion of rules, manages to get the funds together that allows the woman to buy a car. The conclusion of the story is: "Everything worked out beautiful, but if we had gone by the rule book, she would have not gotten the car, she would have not gotten the job. She would have ended up back in the hospital" (2003, 7).

Maynard-Moody and Musheno then explain how the story reveals some "defining, substantive features" of the discretionary judgments of frontline workers. First, the story is a means of character construction. In this instance the story emphasizes the woman's motivation to achieve, her initiative and sense of responsibility, her perseverance in overcoming the debilitating depression that landed her in the mental hospital. The authors describe this character building as "judgments about her essential and defining nature" (2003, 194). Second, the careful construction of the protagonist's character is intertwined with the decision making of the frontline worker. The decisions both reinforce the protagonist's character and are justified by it. Third, and I quote the authors here, "policies, rules, and administration are depicted as barriers to reinforcing judgments about character and identity or as tools for actualizing those judgments" (2003, 7). Rules must often be bent or evaded to assist the worthy protagonist. Fourth, the story shows that frontline workers are highly sensitive to what their co-workers and immediate supervisors think of them. These are the potential allies of the frontline worker, contrary to the higher echelons of management who are seen as out of touch with the everyday realities of frontline work. Finally, the stories reveal that frontline workers unwaveringly focus on the people who are their clients. "They deal with faces," Maynard-Moody and Musheno say:

> The work world of cops, teachers and counsellors is a baffling terrain, dense with laws, rules and procedures; bounded by overlapping hierarchical and agency relationships; and populated with the diverse and often hard to read faces of citizens, clients, supervisors and coworkers. It is a world where identity and moral judgments are bound up with the quotidian work of the state. This is the front line of public service. (2003, 8)

The picture of frontline work that emerges from the authors' analysis of administrators' stories is subtle and complex. Workers are keenly aware that laws, rules, and procedures define their work as well as their identity as professionals. However, they are also aware that, in the face of the unpredictability and complexity of everyday situations, rules often constrain them from helping clients. In fact, as they deal with concrete people, street-level workers "define their work and to a large extent themselves in terms of relationships more than rules" (2003, 20). Maynard-Moody and Musheno continue to frame the dilemmas and complexities of street-level work in terms of what they call "three key relational dynamics." The first is the contradictory relationship with clients. Clients are sources of work satisfaction and accomplishment and of trouble, frustration, anger, and fear. Second, co-workers form the "primary group of belonging." Third, workers define themselves and gain a sense of self-worth and belonging in opposition to what they call "the system," an undifferentiated mix of high-level supervisors, formal laws, elected officials, and the media (2003, 22). Frontline workers are above all pragmatists, "who temper their efforts to do the right thing with a clear understanding of what is possible for individual citizen-clients in the contexts of their everyday lives" (2003, 23). Stories are a key feature of this pragmatist attitude, for "This pragmatism is based on both firsthand experience and wisdom handed down by fellow street-level workers, often in the form of stories" (ibid.).

DIALOGICAL FRAME ANALYSIS

Frame Analysis Revisited: Frame Reflection, Reframing, and Design Rationality

Throughout his long career, Rein has been concerned with policy frames. From the 1990s on we see a shift toward a more action-oriented conception of framing. Or, perhaps it is better to say that he abandoned the representational aspects of framing and developed the action implications that were always central to the frame concept. In the book *Frame Reflection* (Schön & Rein, 1994), he and Schön develop a theory—partly empirical, partly normative—of concerted policy change in a fragmented, decentered policy environment. His work with Laws (2003) traces the dynamic of belief and doubt that leads policy actors to change deeply held beliefs and action preferences. Together these new takes on policy frames make up a remarkably sophisticated theory of policy practice.

In *Frame Reflection* Schön and Rein once more turn to the problem that bedevils professional policy analysis: intractable policy controversies. At the outset of the book, the authors articulate the challenge by distinguishing between disagreements and controversies. Policy disagreements, they write, "refer to disputes in which the parties to contention are able to resolve the questions at the heart of their disputes by examining the facts of the situation. By way of example they refer to how many youths are enrolled in a drug rehabilitation program. These sorts of disputes can be settled by recourse to evidence to which all of the contending parties will agree" (1994, 3). In contrast, policy controversies "are immune to resolution by appeal to fact" (1994, 4). And then, in a sentence that must surely be disheartening to everyone who has set his hopes on the possibility of an authoritative, scientifically based policy analysis, they add: "Disputes of this kind arise around such issues as crime, welfare, abortion, drugs, poverty, mass unemployment, the Third World, the conservation of energy, economic uncertainties, environmental destruction and resource depletion, and the threat of nuclear war" (ibid.). And whatnot, I'm inclined to say.

At first sight Schön and Rein seem to retrace the steps of frame analysis. Policy controversies are rooted in different frames: "Such disputes are resistant to resolution by appeal to facts or reasoned argument because the parties' conflicting frames determine what counts as a fact and what arguments are taken to be relevant and compelling" (1994, 23). Yet in comparison with the work of the 1970s and 1980s, *Frame Reflection* is a very different take on the frame concept. The language of the book is about change, interaction, struggle, adaptation. It frequently talks of shaping situations while being in the situation, transactions with the policy environment, assessing the effects of one's transactions on the world, conversations with the world, reflection-in-action, and the like. The leading question in the book is always: How to act given the constraints of the situation?[31] This is the language—in the vocabulary of chapter 4—of intervention, as opposed to the language of representation that characterized early frame talk. The book's design also speaks to its actionable approach. The argument is developed by presenting three detailed cases of policy controversy, conflict, and change.

Frame Reflection was eagerly anticipated but failed to make a big impact in the field. My guess is that this has something to do with its interventionist program. Representation has hegemonic status in academic talk about public policy. In Foucauldian terms, representation forms a *dispositif*, a system of practices, a grid of interpretation, that brings certain social categories and objects into being. Be that as it may, theory and method reign in policy analysis. In such an intellectual climate practice talk is neither well understood nor much appreciated.

Why do policy actors frame at all? Not just to organize the mass of detail that is a real-world problem. Obviously cognitive organization is important in grasping a social or technical problem, but it is only a surface function of policy frames. Policy actors frame so they know how to act in the situation at hand (Laws & Rein, 2003, 173). Frames are like stories in this respect. They are road maps. Or as Schön and Rein state:

> They select for attention a few salient features and relations from what would otherwise be an overwhelmingly complex reality. They give these elements a coherent organization, and

they describe what is wrong with the present situation in such a way as to set the direction for its future transformation. Through the process of naming and framing, the stories make the "normative leap" from data to recommendations, from fact to values, from "is" to "ought." It is typical of diagnostic-prescriptive stories such as these that they execute the normative leap in such a way as to make it seem graceful, compelling, even obvious. (1994, 26)

A frame is not just a perspective. It is above all an instruction on how to cross the divide between representing and intervening. No amount of theory will ever help us make the normative leap. As Hacking says, when it comes to theory there is no final truth of the matter. Just "a barrage of more or less instructive representations" (1983, 145). Policy makers, public officials, do not have the luxury to remain in the realm of theory for long. Their office compels them to act and to expose themselves to the unforgiving forces of real-world consequences. To have some guidance in that world they hold on to frames. Similar to stories—and Schön and Rein use the terms interchangeably—frames move in a landscape of action.[32]

Here, then, is the central challenge of policy analysis: to grasp the continuous interchange between theory and action, representing and intervening. Analysis without action is sterile; action without analysis, blind. Such a policy analysis is poised on the interface of thought and action. It cannot be just about theory and description—no matter how tempting. It must find ways to meet and incorporate the world of the practitioner; to bridge understanding and purposeful action. The central question for policy analysis is then: does it provide a set of tools—intellectual as well as actionable—that help the analyst travel between these two worlds? In this chapter I argue that dialogue, as both an activity and a concept, is such a "tool," where "tool" must not be understood in a narrow sense, but as simultaneously an ontological category (a condition of possibility for understanding, following Gadamer) and a practical activity (understanding as a fusion of horizons). Dialogue combines thinking and acting. It encompasses both describing and explaining how we understand the world and venture out to meet that world in an active, practical manner. Different scholars give different content to the master concept of dialogue. In Schön and Rein's conception of policy analysis, "design" is central, both as an activity and as a concept. In Laws and Rein it is "reframing." In the literature on planning and mediation it is "collaboration."

One of the strengths of *Frame Reflection* is the face validity of its case descriptions. These are not the usual stylized empirical vignettes to illustrate a theoretical argument. This is policy "as-we-know-it." A decades-long institutional struggle in Germany over early retirement. The initial confusion among policy makers and advocates in Massachusetts over a sudden crisis in homelessness, and the ensuing infighting to design a fitting response. These extended cases have all the trappings of public policy that I will summarize in chapter 10: the uncertainty and lack of control that come with complexity, the fog of emergent time, deep pluralism, and, as the engine that inexorably drives the policy onward on its trajectory, an institutional disposition to act on the part of the actors. Here even the appearance that policy is made by central actors is lost. Instead we see a hopelessly fragmented policy arena; an open field of institutional actors who take each other on or decide to defect when it suits their purpose. The micro-rationalities of individual actors frustrate the macro-rationality of collective problem solving. In this decentered world, policy is driven by practice, which locks the actors into a set course of belief and action:

A distinctive feature of practice is the way it limits and constrains both the thought and action through the development of "sense of reality" in which the natural and the social worlds correspond. This crucial dimension of practice defines what is discussable, what is realistic, what is natural, without the recognition of the arbitrary foundations on which these judgments are based. . . . The taken-for-granted, the self-evident and the unconscious are essential for doing in concrete situations. (Laws & Rein, 2003, 179)

This describes the very conditions that allow officials to act decisively and—most of the time—also effectively insulates them from reflection. This is how, in a decentered policy field, policies stagnate and controversies simmer unresolved, until one or the other of the actors simply decides to walk away from the effort. Practice also explains why policy programs fail to have any effect: the institutional routines that produce them simply fail to speak to the concerns of the target group (see "Qualitative Policy Research" section in chapter 5). Practice explains how perverse consequences emerge. Target groups see their practices frustrated by policy interventions and, in reaction, opportunistically adapt the program to their needs. The result is that programs are used for different purposes than intended by their makers, with concomitant outcomes (Wagenaar, 1995). Incremental change does not always lead to collective good. The myopia of practice prevents "the intelligence of democracy" to flourish. Something else has to happen. Some move that allows the actors to step back from the heat of the battle and reflect on their usual actions.

Laws and Rein summon the French social theorist Bourdieu to set out a line of argument. According to Bourdieu a tension exists between the inherent determinism of practice and its creative potential. We have to make sure that we remain authors of our own actions. That requires that we step back and gain distance from our disposition to act. Gadamer would say that we enter into a dialogue with our own action routines. Through reflective distancing we loosen the hold that practice has on us. We see the situation, and our habitual way of acting in it, in a new light and create the possibility for new modes of action. Laws and Rein call this process "reframing" (2003, 179–80).

Reframing, thus, is reflection-in-action. How does it happen? The Laws and Rein paper gives intriguing suggestions; the Schön and Rein book a theory of policy design. Schön and Rein see their theory as an answer to the limitations of alternative policy theories—rational choice, political contention, and garbage-can theory—which only touch upon restricted parts of the policy process (1994, 83). "In contrast to these models," the authors state:

> We propose a view of policy making as "designing," subject to "design rationality." The design metaphor, we argue, allows us to explain how a policy dialectic may be relatively coherent in spite of its politics of contention and its garbage can quality. Although the dialectic is always conflictual and often disjointed and chaotic, it centers on a relatively constant policy object, such as the social security system in the German story. This constant object serves as an external "memory" of the actors' cumulative moves and anchors the sometimes divergent cycles of policy-making activity. The design metaphor enables us to understand how actors engaging in a symbolic contest that is also a political struggle may nevertheless display policy inquiry characterized by intentionality and intelligence. (1994, 84)

This is a big claim. In the to-ing and fro-ing of policy contestation, the actors nevertheless manage to uphold a modicum of intelligent purpose. Or, as the authors put it themselves in a rhetorical question: "How is it that situated policy controversies lend themselves to pragmatic resolution?" (1994, 165). The authors present a layered theory of policy design. The first layer is the basic configuration of a designer making an object. The authors describe this as a "conversation" between the designer and his intentions with the materials: "The designer is *in* the situation influenced by his appreciation of it at the same time that he shapes it by his thinking and doing" (1994, 166). What does rationality mean in such a design situation?

> The designer's conversation with materials takes the form of seeing/moving/seeing. As the process goes on, the designer sees what he has made, listens (more or less) to back talk from the materials, and thereby constructs new opportunities or problems. Clearly, even in this simple case, design rationality involves reflection—on materials, seeing/moving/seeing, unintended effects, emergent intentions and the form and character of the evolving object. (1994, 167)

This process is guided by a few basic "norms of design rationality." For example, the problem the designer sets for himself, as the object iteratively takes shape, should be adequate to his appreciation of the possibilities and difficulties that are inherent in the materials. The designer's inquiry should incorporate both observed and unintended effects as he reformulates his problem definition, his solutions, and his intentions, "to take fuller account of the observed complexity of the situation and its gradually discovered field of values and interests" (1994, 167).

This is a remarkable description—both empirical and normative—of the way experienced policy makers go about pragmatically solving real-world problems. It is a splendid description also of Gadamerian dialogue; a complex conversation among the designer's intentions, the materials he works on, the effects, both intended and unintended, he observes, back to his original intentions and the materials, and so on, in an ongoing cycle of action-reflection-action. But the design dialogue, in contrast to the Gadamerian dialogue of evolving understanding, is driven more by a pragmatist spirit of acting on the situation at hand.

However, this can only be the beginning of a policy dialogue. As Schön and Rein are quick to observe, policy design is social. Not only is the basic design process always distributed among multiple actors who are engaged, each in his own way, with the evolving policy object, but the actors are also embedded into a larger social-political environment to which they are beholden. Designing is a social process in two ways. The designer is part of a "designing system" made up of a coalition of policy actors. And the designing system "sends it object out into a larger environment." As the authors summarize it: "The social design process now becomes a drama enacted in an arena—an image that captures policy design as well as the collective design of such artifacts as buildings or industrial products" (1994, 168). But how is "design rationality" upheld in a social policy field where interactions are more often than not antagonistic and conflictual? An obvious target is the quality of communication among the policy actors. An open, civilized way of communicating based on mutual respect is clearly preferable over the usual biased and acrimonious bickering. But beware! There is a subtle, but important, shift in language at this point. Where the description of the core design process is mostly empirical, in the case of social design it is almost wholly conditional, as if the authors realize that they had better hedge their bets on social design rationality actually happening. For example, "the members of a designing system *should* seek to arrive at agreements about the problems they are trying to solve. . . . Hence appropriately rational designers strive for reliable communication." And also, "Because policy designing is double designing, the designers' moves *must* meet both the substantive requirements of problem-setting and -solving and the requirements, political and interpersonal, of sustaining the design coalition" (1994, 169–70; italics added). In other words, the "rationality" of the collective design process hangs by slender normative threads.

But there is yet a third layer of design complexity. On top of the design tasks and criteria of rationality that are already in place, we also need to deal with the deep pluralism, the conflicting action frames, of the usual policy situation. Here we are deep into normative territory. Design rationality in the case of frame conflict means among other things that "designers *may* reflect on the changing problematic situation reframing the problem in order to take account of their new understandings." Or: "Members of a designing system *should* reflect on the meanings that underlie policy back talk in order to detect unanticipated design flaws or opportunities" (1994, 171). Or: "Designers *should* reflect on their transactions with the policy environment" (1994, 172; italics added). I think the point is clear. What is left unsaid is how policy makers are not just willing but *able* to transcend the usual interplay of strategic positioning, tactical moves, and hidden agendas that characterizes real-world policy processes. The authors' description of design-in-action has subtly drifted from a descriptive to a normative theory. This is reflected in the case descriptions. With all their accuracy as reports of real-world policy processes, they stretch the notion of "design," with all its associations of purposive, concerted, ameliorative intervention. The outcome in the retirement case is the usual hybrid of intention and happenstance. In the homelessness case one major actor was able, through a more or less fortuitous set of circumstances, to step back from the policy flow and persuade others to try a different course of action.

Example of Dialogical Frame Analysis

Rein's work on frames and frame reflection presents a set of important and intriguing ideas. He is one of the few policy scholars who has consistently focused on the everyday conflictual and action-driven nature of public policy. However, as so often in interpretive policy analysis, he has neglected to develop his concepts into a coherent method for policy analysis. Apart from his own case studies, I know of very few empirical studies that use the notion of action frames as their guiding principle. An exception is a recent study by Forester and Laws on the contested role of facts and scientific knowledge in public policy disputes (Laws & Forester, 2006). The authors distinguish between two kinds of situations. In one, the scientific knowledge is not disputed; the disagreement is about the interpretation of the knowledge or the particular way that it should be interpreted in the case at hand. In the second, more and more common in policy controversies, the scientific knowledge itself is incomplete and unsettled. In this case, as the authors argue, uncertainty is a central feature of the policy domain. One of the many strengths of this paper is the chilling description of the pathologies of the common ways of dealing with this kind of deep uncertainty in policy conflicts. They show how parties in the conflict engage in all sorts of strategic behavior, dig deeper and deeper into their own positions, escalate the conflict almost against their own will, and run circles within their own self-fulfilling expectations. How to escape from this vicious circle of "warring expertise and escalating skepticism"? How to arrive at "design rationality"?

Laws and Forester propose a strategy of "joint fact-finding." Joint fact-finding, they argue, takes place within a broader effort to negotiate commitments to act on shared practical problems, guided by the "procedural commitments of mediation practice." The authors present two cases to develop their argument. The first case concerns the expected disruption of sensitive magnetic resonance imaging equipment by the construction of a metropolitan light rail system near a hospital. The controversy centered on the issue of whether the rail system should go underground or not. A mediator was called in who was able to move the parties from epistemological questions about what we don't know to performative problems of recognizing one's mutual dependence and inquiring about the world together. Quickly the parties discovered that the original question of above or below ground wouldn't make a difference to the expected disruption, and they were able to jointly explore better and less expensive options.

Laws and Forester's second case, the design and siting of a low-level radioactive waste facility, concerns a controversy in which the scientific facts themselves were disputed. Similar to the first case, the participants managed to shape their relationship in such a way that it enabled them to inquire and act together in the face of uncertainty. The story follows the efforts by a citizens' advisory group that was convened by the Maine Low-level Radioactive Waste Authority to understand the scientific consensus on the health effects of exposure to consistent doses of low-level radiation. The citizens' group engaged experts and it gradually became clear that not only were there gaps in the scientific knowledge, but the relationship between science and regulations was exceedingly fallible. In the end the group moved away from epistemological questions of what science didn't know to the practical problem of how to store the waste. They were able to learn about waste storage from the experience of a Canadian waste storage facility that had had to struggle with a nuclear accident, enabling the group to reframe the issue of static waste storage into a more active approach of constant monitoring of waste levels and the health of the environment.

Schön and Rein's theory of frame reflection is an important addition to the repertoire of interpretive analytic approaches. Its strengths are that it takes the conflictual, action-driven, and value-laden nature of policy making serious. In addition it also suggests an intriguing theory of design to capture the pragmatic, purposeful communication that policy makers have with the object of public policy. The associated concept of "design rationality" is meant to indicate that policy making is not all drift, happenstance, and unintended consequences, but is, or can be, subject to collective intelligence and practical judgment. This is what every seasoned observer of politics intuits, but has trouble spelling out. "Intention commingles with interaction," wrote that wry observer of public policy, Wildavsky (1979, 127). But precisely how rationality is upheld in the chaotic give-and-take of everyday politics is mostly left unsaid. Wildavsky believed that rationality is a largely retrospective reflection upon acts and consequences. We rationalize our actions with hindsight, and declare our objectives achieved, or attach objectives after the fact to outcomes obtained (1979, 140). That might be empirically right but it turns public policy into public relations. Schön and Rein are to be commended for having taken on the more difficult task of upholding the stubborn ideal of rationality in the midst of the swirling flow of everyday politics. However, I do not think that they have fully succeeded.

Design is the medium for imposing intention upon interaction. But despite the centrality of design in Schön and Rein's theory, the concept is curiously underdeveloped. The first "layer," the conversation of a designer with his object, is clear enough. But as soon as design moves into the pluralist world of policy contestation, it loses most of its "design rational" characteristics, and becomes an almost purely normative theory. Exactly how contesting actors are to arrive at better solutions in the face of conflict is largely left unsaid. Frame reflection is an ideal. To make that ideal happen in an environment of conflict and acrimony, we need something else, an intervention that truly helps the participants gain the necessary distance to reflect on the situation at hand and arrive at a better solution. Not retrospectively, as Wildavsky has it, but synchronously; in the action. What we need is a theory of design that indicates what deeply divided actors are to do to arrive at practical and consensually accommodating policy outcomes (Forester, 2009, 7). In the next section I will describe a set of approaches that do exactly that: intervene in an ongoing policy process to reflect-in-action for the purpose of designing more productive forms of joint action.

FACILITATING COOPERATION IN POLICY PRACTICE

The approaches I discuss in this final section of this chapter are action research, deliberative and collaborative policy making, and public policy mediation and conflict resolution.[33] What they have in common is that they all take dialogue as the road to understanding. They operate on a number of assumptions. Meaning is constructed in an open-ended, reciprocal, actionable conversation with other parties in a policy situation. It is essential that this dialogue includes the full range of stakeholders. And, stakeholders are sufficiently empowered to have control over both the content and organization of the policy deliberations. These analysts' approach to inquiry is actionable in that they see knowledge emerging out of a process of jointly working on the situation at hand—a process that necessarily includes the analyst. They also reject the dualism between transforming and understanding, living by the famous dictum that the best way to understand something is to try to change it.[34] They are acutely aware of the differences in power and influence that characterize all policy problems. They know, similar to Foucault, that knowledge is a key dimension in these power differentials, and that, therefore, analysts who are in the business of knowledge production are by definition implicated in power imbalances—whether they realize it or not. They do not shy away from conflict, but instead try to see it as an opportunity for learning and growth. All these approaches have in common that they are open-ended, collaborative, participative, inclusive, nonhierarchical, and noninstrumental. They refuse to separate thinking from acting, and see inquiry as a collective problem-solving effort. All attempt to effectuate Lasswell's call for a policy science of democracy.

Action Research

Similar to pragmatist policy analysis, action research is a vibrant but peripheral tradition in the policy sciences. Starting with Kurt Lewin—who coined the term "action research"—in the 1930s, the ideas spread toward the Tavistock Institute and the Norwegian Industrial Democracy Project (Greenwood & Levin, 1998). In a different setting, Freire advocated action research as a means for combining inquiry, education, and empowerment of the poor in Latin America (Horton & Freire, 1990). These ideas have in turn increased the appreciation of the importance of local, layman's knowledge (as opposed to expert knowledge) in policy analysis and planning (Fischer 2000; Forester, 1999a). Strong action research traditions can be found in education (Zeichner, 2006), development studies (Cornwall & Coelho, 2007; Fischer 2000) and planning (Forester, 1999a; Lawson, 2005; Reardon, 2000). In policy analysis in the Western world, action research is exceedingly rare. Although publications such as the *Handbook of Action Research,* edited by Reason and Bradbury (2006), or Greenwood and Levin's *Introduction to Action Research* give various examples of participatory policy analysis, these are the exceptions to the rule. The latter authors even call the place of action research in social science and policy analysis "marginal" (1998, 89).

Action research combines research, transformative action, and participation. Its goal, as Greenwood and Levin describe it, is "to increase the ability of the involved community or organization members to control their own destinies more effectively and to keep improving their capacity to do so" (1998, 6). The dearth of participatory action research in policy analysis is surprising as one of the key characteristics of action research is that it deals with messy problems. For example, the situation in East St. Louis, as described by researchers in the East St. Louis Action Research Project, was a tangle of physical decay, failing city government, corruption, racial discrimination, structural unemployment, industrial decline, environmental pollution, crime, and poverty (Harwood & Zapata, 2007; Lawson, 2005). The willingness of action researchers to take on wicked problems and their refusal to apply reductionist strategies of inquiry follows from some of action research's other characteristics. In a nutshell, action research can be described as follows: (1) It is always situated in real-world contexts in which social problems are experienced and acted upon. (2) It is a form of inquiry where participants and researchers collaborate in an open, reciprocal manner on defining problems, analyzing background conditions, suggesting possible courses of action, reflecting upon the results, and reanalyzing the problem. (3) It is a form of inquiry in which the urge to know is intimately tied to the desire to effectuate change. (4) Success is measured in terms of "workability" and credibility. Results are workable when they lead to a general agreement among participants and researchers that the initial problem is solved or attenuated. Credibility means that the analysis and the outcomes make sense, both to the participants and to outsiders (Greenwood & Levin, 1998, 75–76). (5) Finally, action research has a transformative potential, both on a personal and societal level. Participating in an action research project gives citizens the opportunity to practice democratic skills such as organizing, acquiring knowledge on a specialized topic, presenting ideas and results in public, and resolving conflicts and turning them into possibilities for shared learning. Action research thus has an intrinsic democratic value (Warren, 1992). On a societal level, once citizens have experienced the possibility for self-government that empowerment brings, their relationship to the traditional institutions of government will have changed. As Greenwood and Levin summarize it, "In our perspective, Action Research lies at the very center of human life. It is constituted by a series of communicative actions that take place in dialogical environments created by communities or other organizations for the purpose of the cogeneration of new knowledge, the development and implementation of plans of action and the democratization of society" (1998, 90).

Deliberative Policy Analysis, Collaborative Policy Making, Public Policy Mediation, and Empowered Participatory Governance

Within the term "deliberative policy analysis" I group a number of approaches to collective problem solving, which are characterized by (1) their conscious effort to organize dialogue in situations of policy controversy and prolonged conflict, (2) their practical, hands-on approach to problem solving, and (3) the interpenetration of analysis of and acting on the problem at hand. In our book with this title, Hajer and I argued for a sociological fit between the changing world of governance and a type of policy analysis that would be relevant to such a world. The world of governance we characterized as decentered, radically uncertain, deeply pluralist, and lacking in trust between ruler and ruled (Hajer & Wagenaar, 2003). Policy is often made in between established organizations by civil society actors who define problems in their own way, who do not wait for the state to take the initiative in resolving collective problems, and who do not hesitate to use their legally established powers of obstruction when they feel that their interests are threatened. In a world of decentered governance effectiveness depends upon the ability to establish and maintain constructive working relationships with a large variety of actors (Pierre & Peters, 2000). We then asked ourselves what kind of policy analysis would fit decentered governance. Our answer, not surprisingly, was that it should be interpretive, practice oriented, and deliberative.

Several contributions to the Hajer and Wagenaar book flesh out what deliberative policy analysis might look like practically. Drawing on a rich tradition of communicative planning theory and practice, both Healey et al. and Innes and Booher argue for "collaborative policy making." Healey et al. formulate the challenge that planners and policy makers face in a landscape of decentered governance as follows: "As many now articulate, the challenge is to develop relations between the spheres of civil society, the economy and the state which are less hierarchical and less paternalist, which are sensitive to the needs and aspirations of diverse groups (and especially those who tend to get marginalized) and which have a capacity to learn from diverse knowledge resources" (Healey et al., 2003).

For Innes and Booher this means an approach to solving intractable, contentious problems through collaborative dialogue. They frame collaborative dialogue as a more effective mode of policy making than the traditional bureaucratic, political influence, or social movement models. All of these approaches have their moment in the sun when certain conditions hold. In situations where interests are diverse and conflicting and actors need each other to succeed, collaborative dialogue is the model of choice (2003, 52; 2010, 35). Collaborative dialogue is a process of cooperation for which the following conditions hold: "(1) inclusion of a full range of stakeholders, (2) a task that is meaningful to the participants and that has promise of having a timely impact, (3) participants who set their own ground rules for behavior, agenda setting, making decisions and many other topics, (4) a process that begins with mutual understanding of interests and avoids positional bargaining, (5) a dialogue where all are heard and respected and equally able to participate, (6) a self-organizing process unconstrained by conveners in its time or content and which permits the status quo and all assumptions to be questioned, (7) information that is accessible and fully shared among participants, (8) an understanding that "consensus" is only reached when all interests have been explored and every effort has been made to satisfy these concerns" (Innes, 2004).[35] Innes and Booher stress at all times that these are not abstract conditions but instead the articulation of many years of practical experience with collaborative dialogue. Collaborative dialogue can result in real improvements to the policy system. Drawing on their own experience with the Sacramento Water Forum in California and citing research on consensus building, they list the development of linked identities and shared meanings among stakeholders, and the discovery of new, more adaptive problem solving heuristics which result in "genuine innovations—not just creative ideas, but ideas that get turned into new practices and institutions" (Innes & Booher, 2003, 47–49; see also Innes and Booher, 2010, 10). As Innes concludes that "when a process meeting these conditions is implemented, it can produce joint learning, intellectual, social and political capital, feasible actions, innovative problem solving, shared understanding of issues and other players, capacity to work together, skills in dialogue, and shared heuristics for action" (Innes, 2004, 9) Particularly intriguing, in the light of Gadamer's argument about understanding as departing from a particular perspective, as involving a fusion of horizons, and as bearing some personal risk, is Innes's observation that the effect of engaging in a process of collaborative dialogue can include "new ways for players to understand and reframe their identities in relation to a larger picture and in a way contingent on others' identities" (2004, 8).

Healey et al. frame their view of collaborative planning as a "relational view of institutional capacity" (Healey et al., 2003). The attractiveness of Healey's position is her sensitivity to the wider institutional forces that affect local activity, while at the same time preserving the attention to the "fine grain of interaction" that is characteristic of the collaborative planning tradition. She squarely situates the work of the planner in "complex and dynamic institutional environments, shaped by wider economic, social and environmental forces that structure, but do not determine, specific interactions" (Healey et al., 2003). Drawing on Giddens's structuration theory, among others, the authors develop a relational perspective on institutions, in which institutional designs and deep value systems shape local practices, while the latter continuously instantiate the former. Healey et al. see it as a central task for planners to aid and develop institutional capacity. Institutional capacity "represents a force which is continually emergent, produced in the interactive contexts of its use" (Healey et al., 2003). With this analytic concept the authors summarize the planner's challenge of developing the quality of social relations ("the nature of bonds of trust and norms in the networks of which link people together") and that of the knowledge resources that flow around and through these relations (ibid.).

The notion of social and institutional capital also informs the work on public policy mediation. Podziba, an experienced mediator, describes, for example, how she used a public mediation approach to assist the citizens of Chelsea, Massachusetts, to create a city charter. Chelsea is a small city in the vicinity of Boston with a large minority population mostly made up of Hispanics and Asians. In 1990 the city of Chelsea was placed into receivership by the state because of chronic financial mismanagement and rampant corruption among its city officials. Most citizens had effectively given up on the city government. The mood in the city was one of profound distrust and almost complete disengagement from government. The goal of the charter formulation process was to give the city back to its residents. The case is interesting as an example of public policy mediation because it shows the importance of institutional design as a means of facilitating productive citizen participation in situations of distrust and deep pluralism. The case is too complex to describe here in any detail, but the aim of the mediators was to strengthen democracy by building a public and enhancing social capital. One of the key insights in public policy mediation, and in the other approaches grouped under the heading of deliberative policy analysis, is that dialogue and participation do not necessarily happen spontaneously—particularly not in situations of distrust and antagonism. They can, however, be stimulated by smart, custom-made design of the communicative situation. As Podziba says, "Under conditions of conflict or breakdown of government, a public consensus-building process can be custom designed to fit the existing common public problem and the level of participation required to make a consensual solution implementable" (1998, 17).

Finally, a literature is emerging on empowered participatory governance. Empowered participatory governance is a movement of administrative reform that emphasizes *participation* (ordinary individuals take part in important governance decisions), a *practical orientation* (participatory governance is organized around concrete issues, such as public safety, urban renewal, or land planning), *empowerment* (decisions that follow from participatory processes have real impact on the actions of officials and agencies), and *democratic deliberation* (decisions are made through a "process of structured reasoning in which [actors] offer proposals and arguments to one another)" (Fung, 2004, 4; Fung & Wright, 2003, 16–17). The introduction of empowered participatory governance in situations of traditional hierarchical or market-based governance is fraught with pitfalls and dangers. Often those groups that would benefit most from active inclusion in the governance process are excluded on the basis of ethnicity, language, education, or social skills; participating citizens need to be informed and to acquire the skills necessary to participate in governance processes, citizens need to maintain sufficient motivation to participate, and it is exceedingly difficult for citizens to effectively counteract the formidable agenda-setting power of officials and agencies (Fung, 2004; Wagenaar, 2007a). In addition, participatory governance raises issues of accountability, legitimacy, and efficiency (Stoker, 2006). Similar to public policy mediation, case studies of the introduction of empowered participatory governance emphasize therefore the importance of careful institutional design. However, as such design can hardly be imposed top-down, but has to emerge from the evolving transformation of a traditional administrative configuration into a participatory one, analysts who are involved almost by definition follow principles of action research, working with those involved in reflecting on and designing the situation at hand.

The approaches above contain a number of important lessons. First, despite deep value differences, experience tells us that actors can agree on practical solutions. Interests and solutions are two different things, often confused in multi-stakeholder negotiations. When actors are able to separate them, they open up a deliberative space in which one practical solution can serve diverging interests. Second, collaboration and participation don't just happen when we put a group of stakeholders in one room. Precisely because actors have different interests, come from different worlds, occupy widely different power positions, and bring a history of hurt, injustice, or distrust to the negotiating table, a number of carefully guided activities are required to make productive collaboration happen. Forester argues that we should carefully distinguish among dialogue, debate, and negotiation. *Dialogue* means getting to know the other. It requires that we facilitate conversation so that we are able to listen to the other party.[36] In *debate* the point is to present one's position or solution as convincingly as possible, and to obtain feedback about its flaws and shortcomings. For this we must promote debate and moderate an argument. To get something done, to move beyond the stadium of talk, we must negotiate and mediate proposals for action (Forester, 2009, 6–7).

Third, as the preceding points already implied, actionable policy dialogue in the face of conflict requires careful design. Known by terms such as "mediation" or "facilitative leadership," the contours of such design are becoming clear. It involves:

> (a) assessing stakeholders' options and initial interests, (b) convening representatives of those parties to present their views and data, questions and proposals, (c) enabling parties to engage in joint inquiry and learning, and (d) enabling a process of inventing options and formulating agreements that satisfy at least four specific criteria. (Forester, 2009, 14)

These four criteria—inclusiveness, maximizing mutual gains efficiency, stability, and being technically well informed—comprise "design rationality," the prospect of lifting the outcome of the policy interactions above the lowest common denominator of perennial controversy and strife.

COMMENTARY

The approaches to policy analysis that I have discussed under the heading "Dialogical Meaning" have a number of things in common. They demonstrate the changing relationship between knowledge and action in a practice-oriented discipline such as policy analysis. Faced with messy, evolving social problems, traditional, instrumental approaches to analysis turn out to be either ineffective or irrelevant. The traditional model of calling in an expert to shed light on a case on the basis of general scientific knowledge either doesn't resonate with the actors involved or is unable to move the controversy toward a resolution. Clearly, the problem cannot be solved by striving for better science. The problem is not epistemological but ontological. It has to do with the relation between knowing and acting, and with the place of science in a world of contesting parties and about a deep uncertainty about the future. It is here that Gadamer's fundamental move to frame knowledge in relational terms, as the emergent product of the way that contesting parties manage to work and live together in practical, everyday settings, proves its value. What these approaches all demonstrate—even the most classically hermeneutic of them, narrative analysis—is the intrinsic continuity of knowing and acting. Obtaining knowledge cannot be seen apart from the particular settings in which the need for that knowledge arises, nor apart from the particular relationships among the actors involved. Knowledge is always judged by those involved according to what it contributes to the solution of their concrete, practical problems. Knowledge doesn't make sense outside a context of acting. This ontological reality might sometimes be forgotten in academia, but is quickly driven home, as the examples in this chapter demonstrate, when scientific knowledge is asked to arbitrate in real-world policy controversies. It has been the invaluable contributions of Gadamer, and before him the pragmatist thinkers, Dewey foremost, that have restored this intrinsic continuity between knowing and acting.

Finally, to anchor knowledge in human relations accentuates the close relationship between science and democracy. If effective and relevant knowledge emerges from human relationships, than the quality of such relationships becomes a central issue. This raises questions such as: Who is involved and who is excluded? Or: How can we assure that as broad a spectrum of relevant experiences as possible will inform this particular issue? And also the difficult issue, as Gadamer argued, of how to overcome the limitations of the beliefs, affinities, and understandings that one brings to the encounter. Laws and Forester (2006) cite the philosopher Hilary Putnam, who makes the similar point. Inquiry, he argues, is by nature cooperative. This implies that communities should organize themselves according to democratic standards and ideals. Not because they are good in themselves but "because they are the prerequisites for the application of intelligence to inquiry." This is perhaps the most profound lesson of philosophical hermeneutics: to reframe the ideal of rationality in terms of democracy.

NOTES

1. In the next section of this chapter ("Overcoming Method") I will explain what this term means and where it differs from classical hermeneutics.

2. And not always easy to comprehend. I find affinities in Gadamer with Dewey's elliptical style of writing. Both authors pick up themes and topics only to drop them, seemingly without coming to any closure. After the author discussed a number of other topics, the theme suddenly returns. But it is now richer, informed by what preceded it. The metaphor that comes to mind is that of an ascending spiral. Themes return at higher levels of insight and comprehension. I surmise that this way of writing comes from the task these thinkers set themselves: to combat the whole institutionalized, interlocked, deeply ingrained set of prejudices about knowledge and inquiry in our society. You cannot just refute one; you have to take on the whole matrix of belief and value. But more important, you cannot trust that your reader will accept your argument. He also will perceive your argument from within the same matrix. Getting your point across then means patiently chipping away at the massive structure of rationalist-instrumentalist dogma.

3. Taylor calls this argument concerning possibilities for understanding "the argument for transcendental conditions." He means that critics of the primacy of epistemology all argue for "there being anything like experience or awareness of the world" as an indispensable condition for understanding or knowing. Different critics have construed this awareness in different ways. Heidegger calls it "*Dasein.*" Dilthey, "lived experience." Dewey, "experience." Wittgenstein, "forms of life." And Gadamer, "being" and "*Vorverständnis.*" What these thinkers have in common is an urge to break free of the hermetic space of interlocked assumptions that firmly link instrumental notions of knowledge to modernist conceptions of society and individuality. Taylor in particular has stressed how the traditional understanding of knowledge as disembodied, atomistic, neutral, monological, and the product of formal method, is entrenched in the institutions and practices of modernity: "science, technology, rationalized forms of production, bureaucratic administration, a civilization committed to growth, and the like" (Taylor, 1995b, 76). The quest for instrumental, methodical knowledge has attained the status of a moral ideal. It is part of how we see and understand ourselves (Taylor, 1995a, 6). It needs no comment that policy analysis and the traditional, expert-driven form of policy making that is characteristic of modern liberal democracies are torchbearers for this disembodied, instrumentalist approach to knowledge. What all the thinkers mentioned above share is that they attempt to break out of this space of interlocked assumptions and institutions by positing a tacit, taken-for-granted, only partly conscious, partly explicable realm of experience that precedes, limits, and affords processes of knowing and understanding.

4. "What were seen as the proper procedures of rational thought were read into the very constitution of the mind, made part of its very structure" (Taylor, 1995b, 61).

5. The move toward life as a analytic category represents an important trend in twentieth-century philosophy: "Since Feuerbach and Nietzsche there is a movement in philosophy which prioritizes the category of life over reflection and reason, taking cognitive qualities to be an integral part of life and not uniquely separate qualities. Philosophical attempts to make sense of man and the world from a theoretical and rational standpoint are criticized because philosophical reflection ignores the pre-philosophical thought of the 'life world' and hence does violence to our everyday relationships in the world. We are involved in the world and find our way around in it long before we start to philosophize. In fact the philosophical perspective on life is a distortion depending on forms of thought unrelated to the real character of human relationships in the world" (Law, 2004, 52).

6. This is an ontological argument; not an argument about subjectivity or individual experience. Differently put, I don't have in mind subjective concepts, such as the unconscious or the equally problematic "lived experience." Instead I have in mind a Jamesian form of pluralism; a world that cannot be brought under one overriding principle because there will always be "litter" floating around. A world that derives its particular shape and weave from the myriad of, often fleeting, interconnections that form the complex texture of life (James, 1909 [1996]).

7. See also Law: "[I] argue that the kaleidoscope of impressions and textures I mention above reflects

and refracts a world that in important ways cannot be fully understood as a specific set of determinate processes. This is the crucial point: what is important in the world including its structures is not simply technically complex. That is, events and processes are not simply complex in the sense that they are technically difficult to grasp (though this is certainly often the case). Rather, they are also complex because they necessarily exceed our capacity to know them. . . . the world is not to be understood in general by adopting a methodological version of auditing" (2004, 6). In chapter 10 I will discuss complexity and its implications for policy analysis.

8. In Deweyan terms, a surfeit of reality turns something into a "situation" (Burke, 1994).

9. In the Cartesian tradition of knowing, all this necessary preliminary work is made invisible. That is why knowledge seems disengaged, objective, and universal (see also Taylor, 1995b, 72).

10. That doesn't mean, of course, that the historical, stylistic, or biographical details of the work's origin are of no interest to us at all. In elucidating what it is that appeals to us in contemplating the work, such information might be, and often is, helpful. But notice that we enter the historical world in which the work originated through our contemporary concerns.

11. See my paper on the unintended use of public policy for many practical examples of the way that the targets of a policy adapt it to their life-world. I argue in this paper that unintended use is one of the main causes of perverse policy effects (Wagenaar, 1995).

12. As we will see in chapter 10, Gadamer's ideas on historicity have remarkable affinity with the insights of emerging time and co-evolution as I present these in chapter 10 as essential elements of public policy.

13. Taylor continues: "We can now see how our grasp of the other, construed on the model of coming to an understanding, is doubly party-dependent, varying not only with the object studied but also with the student: with the object studied, because our grasp will have to be true to them in their particular culture, language and way of being. But it will also vary with the student, because the particular language we hammer out in order to achieve our understanding of them will reflect our own march toward this goal. It will reflect the various distortions that we have had to climb out of, the kinds of questions and challenges that they, in their difference, pose to us" (2002, 133).

14. This is all very reminiscent of the related notions of background and what it means to be an engaged agent that we encountered earlier. As we saw, background functions as a context of intelligibility, while "engaged" means that we are made possible as agents because we feel at home in a particular background that enables and limits us. The particular experiences of a particular agent arise within a background and are not intelligible outside it (Taylor, 1995b, 68). Background functions as "unexplicited horizon" (ibid.) and through engaging in practical tasks, it becomes partly articulated. We could say that by trying to understand something or someone we become aware not only of the object or person but also of the slice of background—the horizon—that we inhabit. But, and this is essential, our awareness, both of the other and ourselves, is only partial and provisional. It couldn't be otherwise, because we always need a vantage point from which to articulate what we attend to and what we attend from (Taylor, 1995b, 69).

15. Notice the remarkable concurrence of philosophical hermeneutics with the notion of emerging time as explained in chapter 10. We live in possibilities of being *in* time because we never only inhabit the present. Time always presents itself to us as a historical frame, a set of possibilities, and a continuous, unbroken stream of activities. Time is a horizon in the Gadamerian sense.

16. This insight contains a powerful critique of the popular text analogue in interpretive social science. The argument is actually simple. The metaphor of a text implies that the object of interpretation is delimited. It has a clearly identifiable beginning and end. But that is never the case in history—and also not in policy making. Whatever boundaries we observe are imposed by the interpreter, and spring from an act of demarcation. The assumption of a bounded a priori object inserts a measure of objectivity into the process of interpretation that is wholly unwarranted (Grondin, 2003, 62). Gadamer speaks in this respect of the "philologization" of history (Grondin, 2003, 65). It is yet another attempt to obtain an epistemic foundation where there is none.

17. Labov and Waletzky's paper managed to demonstrate several things at the same time. Not only did the authors convincingly show that language that was judged by middle-class observers as crude and deficient in fact displayed a sophisticated narrative structure that enabled it to organize the personal experience of members of that particular speech community. They also developed a method for distinguishing the basic elements of narrative structure and relating these to the "inferred sequence of events in the experience that is being recapitulated" (Labov and Waletzky, 1967). I dwell on the authors' moral program because with all the critical attention that their structuralist approach subsequently received, it is sometimes forgotten that they used narrative analysis to address a larger social issue. In the spirit of their times Labov and Waletzky approached their question by applying Saussurian structuralism to the analysis of storytelling. Their aim to

is deconstruct stories into their "invariant structural units" (*langue*, in Saussure's terminology) and relate them to a "variety of superficial forms" that represent the actual stories told by the ghetto youth that were the subjects of their research (*parole*). Staying close to Saussure, Labov and Waletzky aim to relate basic narrative elements (such as "free clauses," "restricted clauses," "displacement sets") to the "inferred sequence of events in the experience" (1967, 38). These basic building blocks then combine, in tightly defined structural relations, to form a larger narrative structure (orientation, complication, evaluation, resolution, coda), the function of which is to evaluate or give meaning to the particular slice of experience that the narrator relates.

18. This is a general theme in sociolinguistics. Gumperz, for example, speaks of a "basic relational perspective," with which he indicates that the relations among the elements of spoken language contain the information by which the listener can situate the story in a larger context. Examples of this kind of "relational" aspect of spoken language are tone groupings, timing, pitch rises and falls, pauses, and differences in stress. In other words, while the lexical information gives us the straightforward content of what is being said, it is the music of the language that tells us how to understand it (Gumperz, 1982, 119).

19. This section is based on Wagenaar, 1995.

20. In my study of citizen participation in disadvantaged neighborhoods, I often observed how residents narratively understood the relationship between, for example, urban restructuring and unintended consequences such as crime and physical decay, without being able to specify it in an exact causal manner. I concluded that the openness and ambiguity of these stories must be seen, not as a deficiency, as many professionals would have it, but as a virtue, because of the complexity and constantly evolving nature of the situation on the ground. The stories offered enough temporary stability so that the residents could act on the situation at hand, and have as a baseline to assess the effects of their actions (Wagenaar, 2005). Moreover, as one seasoned urban sociologist was willing to admit, academics who study disadvantaged neighborhoods also have little solid knowledge of causal mechanisms (Reijndorp, 2004).

21. "The literary text activates our own faculties, enabling us to recreate the world it presents. The product of this creative activity is what we might call the virtual dimension of the text, which endows it with its reality. This virtual dimension is not the text itself, nor is it the imagination of the reader: it is the coming together of text and imagination" (Iser, 1978, 279).

22. I have come to believe that everyday knowing operates under a particular narrative morality that is predicated on the open-endedness, provisionality, and interactivity here described. For example, those who insist on sticking to a deficient story (one-sided, not squaring with obvious experience, stubbornly partial) will be negatively characterized as stubborn, prejudiced, or stupid, and eventually be shunned.

23. They are not vignettes such as the characters of Theophrastus.

24. As Bruner puts it, "The inseparability of character, setting and action must be deeply rooted in the nature of narrative thought. It is only with difficulty that one can conceive of each of them in isolation" (1986, 39).

25. As the philosopher Hilary Putnam puts this: "The use of the word 'inconsiderate' seems to me a very fine example of the way in which the fact/value distinction is hopelessly fuzzy in the real world and in the real language. The importance of terms like 'inconsiderate,' 'pert,' 'stubborn,' 'pesky,' etc., in actual moral evaluation has been emphasized by Iris Murdoch in *The Sovereignty of Good*. Even though each of the statements 'John is a very inconsiderate man,' 'John thinks about nobody but himself,' 'John would do practically anything for money' may be simply a true description in the most positivistic sense (and notice 'John would do practically anything for money' does not contain any value term), if one has asserted the conjunction of these three statements it is hardly necessary to add 'John is not a very good person.' When we think of facts and values as independent we typically think of 'facts' as stated in some physicalistic or bureaucratic jargon, and the 'values' being stated in the most abstract value terms, e.g., 'good,' 'bad.' The independence of value from fact is harder to maintain when the facts themselves are of the order of 'inconsiderate,' 'thinks only of himself,' 'would do anything for money'" (1981a, 139).

26. R.A. Putnam: "[O]rdinary men and women, you and I, need values when we are confronted with choices, i.e., when neither instinct, nor deeply ingrained habit, nor internalized values, nor a set of explicit instructions has set us on a road with no exits" (1985, 200).

27. As the quote that follows in the text suggests, White, strictly speaking, restricts this claim to historical narrative, but I believe that it can safely be generalized to all narrative (White, 1981, 13).

28. I do not mean to imply that we never spin tales just for the fun of it. Clearly we do. In fact, telling and listening to a good story in a safe, intimate environment is one of the great delights of life. I confine my statement to situations that matter, situations where stories help us to find our bearings.

29. In fact, in 1995 record high-water levels in the Rhine spurred the regional government of the province

of Gelderland to evacuate more than 100,000 people from the areas adjacent to the river. In the end the dikes held and people returned to their homes. This near flood temporarily weakened the environmentalists' case but did not deal a fatal blow to it.

30. What makes their book exemplary is, among other things, their careful methodology of collecting and analyzing stories.

31. This formulation was suggested to me by David Laws.

32. Schön and Rein don't say much about it (they prefer to talk about values), but the action imperative in public policy explains, to my mind, why most policy prescriptions are based on doctrine, not theory. For an excellent treatise on the distinction between theory and doctrine, and the role of doctrine in public administration, see Hood and Jackson, 1997.

33. A version of this section first appeared in Wagenaar, 2008.

34. The dictum is, of course, from Kurt Lewin (Greenwood & Levin, 1998, 19).

35. The purpose of setting up a collaborative dialogue is to achieve collaborative rationality. Innes and Booher provide the following definition of collaborative rationality: "A process is collaboratively rational to the extent that all the affected interests jointly engage in face to face dialogue, bringing their various perspectives to the table to deliberate on the problems they face together. For the process to be collaboratively rational, all participants must also be fully informed and able to express their views and be listened to, whether they are powerful or not. Techniques must be used to mutually assure the legitimacy, comprehensibility, sincerity and accuracy of what they say. Nothing can be off the table. They have to seek consensus" (2010, 6).

36. On listening in situations of conflict, see Forester, 1989, ch. 7, and Bickford, 1996. Wagenaar, 2007a, shows how ordinary citizens who decided to become politically involved in their neighborhood organize listening by applying principles of, what I call, communicative etiquette.

PART 3

TOWARD A POLICY ANALYSIS
OF DEMOCRACY

Methods and Conclusions

9

STRATEGIES OF INTERPRETIVE POLICY RESEARCH

> *But the difference between facts which are what they are independent of human desire and endeavor and facts which are to some extent what they are because of human interest and purpose, and which alter with alteration in the latter, cannot be got rid of by any methodology.*
> —John Dewey, *The Public and Its Problems*, 1927

FROM METHODS TO HEURISTICS

In this chapter I will discuss how to *do* interpretive policy analysis. Yet, to avoid any misunderstandings right off the bat, this will not be a "methods" chapter in the traditional sense of the word. Instead I will focus on the key concept of *heuristics,* defined here as strategies of discovery in interpretive research.

Let's first deal with the question of methods. In no particular order, I see four compelling reasons why a chapter on interpretive research *methods* in policy analysis would be self-defeating.

First, as this book has made clear, there are many different ways of doing interpretive policy analysis, ranging from finding meaning behind a particular policy, to reconstructing the genealogy of a social institution, engaging in critical discourse analysis, sustaining a policy mediation effort, and to large scale action research on pressing social problems. To do justice to this variety of methodical approaches would go far beyond the confines of a single book, let alone a book chapter. Moreover it would be redundant work. The references in the back of this book, particularly the case examples, give far more detailed and precise descriptions of the various methodical approaches in interpretive policy analysis than I could ever hope to achieve here.

Second, one of the key characteristics of interpretive inquiry is the embeddedness of methods in all the other aspects of doing research. Differently put, it would be difficult—and to my mind, misleading—to single out an object of description called "research methods." Methods cannot be seen apart from finding a good subject, becoming aware of your specific interest in the topic, formulating an interesting question about it, becoming aware of the presuppositions with which you approach your subject, collecting data on your subject, and formulating ideas and concepts that respond to the question. Articulation of one of these elements informs and suggests articulations of the others. They are interlocked, and all move along together, mostly in fits and starts, in a process that is "more spiral in nature than linear and cumulative," more in the nature of an extended improvisation than a well-thought-out-in-advance research strategy (Cerwonka & Malkki, 2007, 17). (I will return to the theme of improvisation later in this chapter.) This improvisational process is *methodical,* in the sense that it is not a trial-and-error affair but instead rests on assumptions and slowly accumulating knowledge and expertise. But to boil it down to the "application" of methods would excise the very heart and soul of it, or more precisely, its heuristic lifeblood. Of course, somewhere in this continuous back and forth, this gradual broadening and deepening of our experience and expertise, are systematic, recurrent activities that we can fruitfully call methods. We interview subjects to collect their stories. Or we register some of their characteristics in a systematic manner to discover how these are distributed in the relevant population. Or we collect texts to reconstruct hidden linguistic patterns that determine how a group is programmed to understand a phenomenon. But why we employ a particular method is always subordinate to the other elements of the process of inquiry.

This interlocking of the elements of the research process in interpretive inquiry is, in my experience, one of the hardest things to convey to students in teaching classes in interpretive policy analysis. There is always the temptation to seek refuge from the self-doubts and deep uncertainty about your project in a fixation on methods. This expresses itself, for example, in the endless conducting of interviews without ever sitting down to analyze them. Or in the foregrounding of a preferred "method" (discourse analysis, for example) without a question to which the method will provide an answer. I see this as the fruitless search for a foundation, some solid ground under your feet. But also as a defense mechanism to avoid the hard and self-confronting work of analysis. (Another such defense mechanism is the shelter that grand theory offers. This expresses itself usually as the endless reading of one more "essential" book on, for example, Foucauldian exegesis or on Derridean deconstruction.) I understand this impulse, and succumb to it myself every now and then (and certainly tumbled into every one of these pitfalls in the past), but in the end it is self-defeating. It is just the postponement of the essential moment in which you have to confront your assumptions with your data and with the body of literature that informs your work, and try to make sense of all three of them. No methods book will be able to help you with this.

Third, public policy, as I have argued, is intrinsically indeterminate, heterogeneous, contested, and action driven. How do we capture these qualities? Whatever research methods we decide to employ have to reflect these generative qualities of our object of inquiry on pain of being misguided, irrelevant, or both. This is the by now familiar problem of fit. Law makes a similar point when he emphasizes the messiness of the social-material world, and the excess of reality in which we move about:

> Parts of the world are caught in our ethnographies, our histories and our statistics. But other parts are not. This is the problem I try to tackle. If much of the world is vague, diffuse or unspecific, slippery, emotional, ephemeral, elusive or indistinct, changes like a kaleidoscope, or doesn't have much like a pattern at all, then where does this leave social science? (2004, 2)

Somehow, the notion of method, with its associations of finality, unilaterality, and intellectual control (Schwandt, 2002; Taylor, 2002), doesn't capture these messy qualities of public policy. Worse, they often lend a false suggestion of certainty and closure to what is inherently and irrevocably a business that is fraught with ambiguities. As Law puts it, methods "distort [the world] into clarity" (2004, 2). But then, how do we avoid this methodological distortion? The answer in the preceding chapter was: dialogue. In this chapter I try to formulate an approach to inquiry that indeed emphasizes the interactive, dialogical character of understanding. I believe that the idea of heuristics will help me to do that.

Fourth, methods purport to function like instructions. That, after all, is their whole idea. They tell you how to go about doing research. But here we run into a huge paradox. The instruction is meant to set the novice on the proper path, yet he only grasps what the method is about after he has found and walked the path himself. The paradox is that instructions are not beginnings, but rather endpoints of a long process of socialization in which instructions are not of much use because the novice doesn't have the body of experience to interpret them properly. Oakeshott captures this effectively by employing the analogy of cooking.

> It might be supposed that an ignorant man, some edible materials, and a cookery book compose together the necessities of a self-moved (or concrete) activity called cooking. But nothing is further from the truth. The cookery book is not an independently generated beginning from which cooking can spring; it is nothing more than an abstract of somebody's knowledge of how to cook: it is the stepchild, not the parent of the activity. (Oakeshott, 1983)

Here is the paradox once more: experienced cooks don't need cookbooks. For inexperienced cooks they are of little use. Similarly, when we talk of methods in the abstract, we are only able to make sense of them because we take our grasp of the *point* of the method for granted. The point is that cooking and doing research are both *practices*. To bring these practices to a successful end, we employ methods (add egg yolks and slowly heat the sauce until it thickens, but prevent the sauce from boiling at all times; conduct an interview with a key informant), but the methods are part of a practical grasp of the activity of preparing a sauce or doing research. This grasp is based on concrete, practical experience with the kind of situation to which the instruction that is embedded in the method refers. Thus, methods, like cookbooks, do not act as instructions, telling the actor what to do. Rather they are repositories of the accrued experience and understanding of a community of people. In that sense they function as signposts in a practical-moral landscape, giving the actor a bearing, suggesting what fruitful and feasible directions to take, and providing standards to assess the direction finally taken.

Variety, embeddedness, messiness, and the paradox of written instruction. Call them challenges to interpretive policy inquiry, or to any form of inquiry for that matter. How then can we access the richness and messiness of public policy and come up with senseful and usable insights? The road I take is one that emphasizes heuristic strategies of inquiry. Methods can—and often are—an important part of these. But, as I said above, only in a subordinate role.[1] The thrust of the process of inquiry is to come up with a set of heuristic strategies that speak to the subject of research, but to do this in a way that they create the conditions for novelty, for surprise. So here is the first heuristic: *Set yourself up for novelty. Organize your research in such a way that you create the conditions for surprise.* What does it take to set yourself up for novelty and surprise? Generally speaking, novelty rarely issues from our own imagination. Granted the rare exception, most people's thoughts and ideas follow reassuringly—or disappointingly, if you prefer—familiar, well-established paths. We have to be prodded into new and unexpected insights by confronting ourselves with reality. Or better, the excess of reality that Gadamer emphasized over and over again. The world contains more variety, more diversity and more surprise than even the most gifted researcher will ever be able to imagine, let alone capture. By opening ourselves up to the infinite richness of the world, we force ourselves to reassess our assumptions, to reframe our experience, and to broaden our understanding. By opening ourselves up to novelty and surprise, we learn. And, as we saw in the preceding chapter, this is a never-ending, ongoing process, a coming-to-an-understanding.

So how do we go about this concretely? How do we move from pious words to concrete activities? What heuristic strategies do we employ? And how do we employ them? I will begin by presenting grounded theory as a core strategy for engaging in a generative dialogue with empirical reality. Grounded theory is often presented as a set of instructions on how to conduct qualitative research. I will argue instead that the reach of grounded theory is much wider than that. I will present it as a heuristic strategy, a general strategy of discovery, which is at the core of every study of an interpretive bend. No matter what other methods of interpretive analysis will be deployed, the key heuristic moment consists of making sense of raw empirical data.[2] This process of sense making always consists of entering into a dialogue between the preconceptions we bring to the study and the empirical data we have collected. Thus, grounded theory. In the sections to follow I will discuss some of the recurrent steps that every researcher has to go through in doing research: formulating a research question, designing the project, getting out in the field to observe and interview, analyzing data, writing up results. These sections come closest to the traditional methods treatise. But, be warned! They are "instructions" only in so far as cookbooks are guides to successful cooking.

GETTING STARTED: FEAR AND SELF-LOATHING IN CHICAGO

In its early phase an interpretive research project is a curious combination of under- and overdetermination. It is underdetermined in that the researcher usually does not have much more than a topic or a field. Some lucky researchers work with an acknowledged policy problem, but many don't even have that. They are interested in a topic: disaster early warning systems, or complexity in urban planning, or innovations in river management, to mention a few that I encountered in my teaching recently. It is overdetermined in that the researcher often approaches this loosely demarcated area with a pet theory—or more likely a metatheory—or with some strong convictions about the field, or both. The student who proposed the early warning project was Chinese and was driven by her indignation at the slow reaction of the Chinese government during the heavy snow storms during the Chinese New Year of 2007 that left many dead and hundreds of thousands of travelers stranded. She strongly felt that the government had failed its citizens. The student who worked on the complexity project was interested in complexity theory (an interest I share with her). But complexity theory is highly abstract, more a perspective than a theory from which one can deduce hypotheses to guide the research (some question if it is a theory at all [Pollit, 2009]), and therefore very difficult to "apply." There is nothing inherently wrong with being overdetermined in this sense. In fact I will even argue that we need our presuppositions to be able to do interesting and productive research at all. (See my discussion of "prejudice" in Gadamer's philosophical hermeneutics in chapter 8. I will get back to this central insight later.) But for inexperienced researchers this early phase, in which the project is still ill defined and seems propped up by some abstract theory or ideological position, can be a source of considerable anxiety, and, when not handled well, lead the project down unproductive paths. Although there are no blueprints for good interpretive policy analysis, there are more and less productive ways to get out of the initial confusion of starting a research project. Let me illustrate my point with a personal example.[3]

In hindsight I was lucky when I started my dissertation project on readmissions to mental hospitals because I hit upon a certified policy problem. The policy problem that I had made the topic of my dissertation was a rapid rise of readmissions to mental hospitals as a result of the deinstitutionalization policies of the 1970s in the United States. I was doubly lucky because, as I explained in chapter 3, my policy problem was the subject of a heated debate between psychiatrists and sociologists about the cause of the problem. I had a Reinian policy controversy by the tail, a deep difference between practitioners that pointed to different courses of action: rebuilding mental institutions versus speeding up the construction of mental health centers. I didn't realize this at the time, but such a controversy between practitioners hands the researcher his research question almost on a silver platter: I was given a dilemma or puzzle (instead of painstakingly having to construct one)—two explanations of the same phenomenon that (seemingly) contradicted each other. One side (psychiatrists) claims that readmissions are caused by insufficient treatment; the other side (taken by sociologically inclined policy scholars) that poverty is the cause of readmissions. Again with hindsight, the explanations don't really contradict each other. Both can be true at the same time, and that was basically what I found. But that is not the point here. A dilemma or puzzle is a wonderful heuristic around which to organize a research project. It allows you to organize the project around one of the horns of the dilemma, and discover whether it holds up against the claims of the other. And this is what I did—intuitively, I must emphasize, without much systematic thought. I pursued the sociological angle of the dilemma for no other reason than that I felt comfortable with it, and discovered that it held up quite well in the face of the empirical material. However I also found that the sociological explanation underestimated the burden on patients and family members of coping with mental illness, and that some of its assumptions, particularly those that had to do with the power of psychiatry, were—well—baloney. But I am now running far ahead of the story. Let's get back to the early stirrings of my project.

I emphasize the qualifier in the opening sentence of the last paragraph ("In hindsight I was lucky") because at the time it didn't feel that way. Like many inexperienced researchers who embark on a large project, I felt out at sea. (And, suddenly living by myself in Chicago to do fieldwork, quite lonely too.) Although I had taken a policy controversy as my topic, I still was confused about my project. But what was my confusion about? Here, an interesting fork in the road to a viable, successful project emerged. On the one hand, I began to have a hunch about how to organize the project in a practical way. The confusion was really about how to understand my topic conceptually, and that confusion was to remain for a while. (We will run into it again when I discuss data analysis.) Again, this is an *ex post facto* reconstruction. At the time the confusion extended to all aspects of my project. But I think that it is useful to distinguish between the conceptual and the practical aspects of a project, or more precisely, between conceptual ambiguity and practical sense, because it helps the researcher to get the project under way. If I were to summarize the importance of this distinction between the conceptual and the practical it would go somewhat like this: *conceptually,* we can expect to be uncertain, confused, and unsettled for quite a while for the simple reason that we embark on a research project because we are unfamiliar with the topic or field and want to learn something new about it. To put it in stark terms: if we knew all the answers, we wouldn't have to do the research. *Practically,* on the other hand, the repertoire of choices is not so large. We have to go into the field, where we observe and interview. We record our findings and begin to analyze them, after which we write up our results. In addition we keep reading about our topic to get a better understanding of it: specialized literature by practitioners, policy makers, governmental agencies, statistical agencies, think tanks, and the like, and the more distant academic literature in which specialists try to frame and conceptualize the field. Out of our immersion in the practical work, our conceptual understanding of the topic gradually deepens, which will then influence the way we organize and go about our reading and fieldwork, and so on, in a continuous spiral. This is how the practical and the conceptual interact, until we notice that at some point, perhaps somewhat to our surprise, we have something original to say about our topic, or that others see us as an expert in the field. The difference between an inexperienced and an experienced researcher is not that the latter's confusion is less than the first's in the early stages of the project, but that he has learned to be tolerant of the conceptual confusion because he knows that it is an inevitable part of any early stage research project, and that the only way out is to diligently do the handwork of reading up and going out into the field.

I have to keep emphasizing that at the time, I didn't see it that way. Although I somehow made the right moves, I kept struggling with getting an intellectual grip on my topic. This combination of practical sense and intellectual confusion is, to my mind, very common with beginning researchers. Many times I have had to say to Ph.D. students who had just embarked on their fieldwork that they were on the right track, the interviews were great, and the project was on course. It didn't feel that way to them. I guess what they wanted to say was that they saw a large gap between what they had to say about their topic, on the one hand, and the writings of the acknowledged experts (in my case Rose, Miller, or, in a later stage, that forbidding Olympian figure, Foucault) on the other. They saw themselves standing on the banks of a wide river and saw the Promised Land on the other side, but didn't see any way to get across.

While I embarked on my interviews and designed the project (my local adviser, Dan Lewis, and I decided to interview those members of a large cohort of patients who were part of a project on the changing state of psychiatric service delivery in Chicago [Lewis et al., 1991] and who were readmitted at the time of my research), I flung about unsystematically, and, I am afraid, somewhat incoherently, in the literature. Obviously, I had read the practitioners' literature, but that became repetitious after a while. I had read the social labeling theorists, but although it satisfied my vaguely emancipist leanings, I was secretly suspicious of its validity. In fact, after the first confrontation with real mental patients in my interviews I radically threw that literature overboard. Labeling simply didn't make sense to me in the face of the impressive symptoms of my first patients. What struck me in those first interviews was that patients displayed thought disorder, reported hallucinations or delusions, and acted decidedly odd, and still had an interesting, coherent story to tell about what it meant to live with psychiatric symptoms in Chicago on a small disability check. But ditching the social labeling literature hardly improved things, because it left me with empty hands altogether. And although I was captured by the literature on the social construction of reality (Berger & Luckmann, 1967) and interpretivist philosophy (Fay, 1975; Taylor, 1985a), I saw no way to connect that abstract metatheory to my topic. What did help me in the end was a paper by Emerson and Messinger on the micro-politics of trouble (1977). It made the essential connection for me between social constructionism and mental illness.

I guess that everybody can tell his or her own particular initiation history. The point I want to make by telling mine is twofold. First, there simply is no linear way to get from your first hunches about your project to the point at which you feel that you don't have to reinvent yourself anew every time you get up in the morning. Early on you simply don't have many criteria by which to judge what is relevant and what is not.[4] The world that you have entered threatens to overwhelm you. And, secretly, you think you're the only one, as everyone else seems, or pretends, to know what he or she is doing. Anxiety and self-doubt are inescapable in this phase of the research. You can't escape it, but you need to make sure that it doesn't overwhelm you. I like the Cerwonka and Malkki book for its, to my mind, realistic depiction of the process of starting up an interpretive research project:

> Because the correspondence illustrates fieldwork in real time as the research process unfolds, we see that the tempo of ethnographic research (like most knowledge production) is not the steady, linear accumulation of more and more insight. Rather, it is characterized by rushes of and lulls in activity and understanding, and it requires constant revisions of insights gained earlier. We see the anxiety and euphoria that accompany the uneven tempo of analytical understanding and systematic research. Thus, the correspondence examines the hermeneutic process as it relates to affective experiences such as doubt, elation, hope, fear, confidence, stress, exhaustion, and projection, further complicating the common idea of a neat boundary between objective and subjective, abstract and concrete knowledge. (2007, 5)

It might fall on deaf ears, but I still want to urge the beginning researcher to see that early phase not as an unpleasant but inevitable part of the research, to be traversed as fast as you can, but positively, as a period of creativity. Yes, you might feel unhinged perhaps, curiously detached from the world in which other people go about exercising their mundane but comforting routines (Cerwonka and Malkki even speak of "a sense of vertigo" in this respect [2007, 80]), but it is also a time of seeing things with fresh eyes, unfettered by earlier investments in ideas, beliefs, doctrines, or career paths. It is a time when you can really immerse yourself in the amazing richness of the new world you have entered. A time when changing ideas and insights are a constant source of creativity. The minor observation, the unexpected event, the oddball idea, might turn out to be the source of your most valuable contributions to the field. The challenge in this phase of the project is, perhaps for emotional or intellectual reasons, not to close yourself off from this richness in the world and in yourself. In the early phase of your project you are *expected* not to know where your project is headed.

My second point is that there are tactics you can use to make your thinking more productive and to prevent yourself from closing yourself off from the abundance of the field. I tend to call them negative and positive heuristics. Negative heuristics are, obviously, things you should avoid; search strategies that lead you away from a productive engagement with your topic. In my experience the most common negative heuristics are a flight into grand theory and the mindless collection of data. Somehow, the emotional vagaries of being out there in the field by yourself (or just the prospect of it) lead some people to find refuge in the safe haven of grand theory. I guess there is something comforting about reading the great thinkers, and, obviously, they can be very inspiring (I hope that this book is a testimony to that), but they also don't really help you in understanding the world of, let's say, mental patients and their families or the world of prostitutes, sex bosses, and administrators who try to keep some minimum of public order in a red light district, to mention two of the projects that I have worked on.

Mindless data collection is somewhat the opposite of the flight into grand theory. Students keep on interviewing and observing, but without a sense of where they are going with all these data. One of the saddest moments in my teaching recently was a workshop in which one of the students presented her work and claimed she had done 120 interviews of 2 to 5 hours each detailing the immigration experiences of a particular ethnic minority, and wanted advice on how to analyze them. After some probing, it turned out that she had no research question and no ready assumptions about her topic. She literally had no idea how to analyze the data.[5] "Someone said that I should read Foucault," she said. "I did that yesterday and it looks relevant to my data." But in such a situation everything looks relevant to the data. As I will argue in the next sections, data collection should proceed hand in hand with data analysis and theory development, the one shaping the other in a dialectical manner. One of the great pitfalls of interpretive research is to collect all one's data first and think about the analysis later.

Let's turn to positive heuristics. I have good experience, both personally and in my teaching, with two heuristics. The first I learned from Deborah Stone. In cases where students who work on a policy study seem to be wedded to a theoretical conviction, she would ask the student: "What is the real-world problem you're working on?" This question turns out to be a remarkably effective stimulus to refocus the student on what I called above the abundance of the field. For students who until then have seen their slice of the field by and large through a theoretical lens, this turns out to be a singularly difficult thing to do. By thinking about the real-world problem the student is in fact asked to imagine what the issues are that the actors in the field struggle with. For one thing it opens up the possibility of formulating problems from the perspective of different actors. For example, in my prostitution study, asking what the real-world problem was urged me to appreciate the complexity of the project. I had sold the project as a study of the implementation of the legalization of sex facilities in the Netherlands. This was fair enough, but it assumed an a priori focus on the world of administrators, police officers, and elected officials. However, the other actors in the field had very different "real-world" problems that directly affected the new law. For example, for the sex bosses the challenge was how to run an economically viable business in the new, regulated environment. On top of that, as I learned quickly, they were threatened by the emergence of the Internet, with more and more prostitutes working independently from behind a website. For the prostitutes the real-world problem was how to maintain a livable wage in an environment where the rents for windows or rooms increased and competition from immigrant women from Eastern Europe was fierce. Even for administrators the problem was much more diverse than mere "implementation." On the one hand, the problem was to make the regulation work; on the other hand, it was to maintain public order. For the police the fight against traffickers dominated their agenda, and obtaining the capacity, in terms of manpower and coordination efforts, for effective enforcement. For the Tax Authority it was the definition of a viable and fair tax regime in an industry that had none of the institutionalization of a regular small business sector. And for prostitution activists the problem was that the promised improved work conditions and labor rights didn't materialize. Also, they were concerned about the ideological onslaught of abolitionism in the European Union that threatened any intelligent discussion of legalization.

A focus on the real-world problem in effect sets the student up for the confrontation of theoretical presuppositions with the richness of the empirical world. As the above example demonstrates, the "real world" of one's research topic is infinitely more complex and surprising than any theoretical category (such as "policy implementation") can capture. At the very least, the research will allow the student to amend the theory, to contribute to it by problematizing some if its assumptions. However, more often than not, immersing oneself in the real-world problems of the actors leads to a reformulation of the original question. For example, years of interviewing scores of actors in the prostitution field has led me to reformulate the original "implementation" question as one of policy effects. I have become impressed with the constant rapid developments in the field, many of which (such as immigration trends) were external to prostitution but affected it strongly; the multitude of unintended consequences; the seeming policy resistance of the issue; and its susceptibility to moral claims with policy makers rushing headlong into new approaches almost solely on the basis of ideological beliefs (Weitzer, 2009). Stone's simple question is a powerful heuristic for challenging initial assumptions and getting the dialogue between theory and data started. It is a call to approach one's topic from a principled, flexible stance. Or, as Cerwonka and Malkki nicely put it:

> [Flexibility] is . . . a principled and reasoned stance. One does not spend years studying field languages, reading the relevant regional or theoretical literatures, and living and talking with people "in the field" simply in order to prove or disprove the hypothesis with which one arrived. The living social context of ethnographic research is expected to transform one's original framing or animating questions. To hold on to the questions posed in one's original grant proposal when the context is continually teaching one how to ask better questions makes little sense in ethnographic field work. This is obvious to most professional sociocultural anthropologists, but it may be useful to underscore for students only beginning their research process. At issue is an improvisational flexibility. (2007, 79)

A second heuristic to help you get started is suggested by Booth, Colomb, and Williams in their wonderful book, *The Craft of Research* (1995). I use it in my teaching and I find that students find it helpful. Early on in the book they describe the steps that someone who begins a research project has to take, as follows: "You must settle on a *topic* specific enough to let you master a reasonable amount of information. . . . Out of that topic, you must develop *questions* that will guide your research and point you towards a *problem* that you intend to solve" (29).

In a number of short, insightful chapters the authors then describe how to move from a topic to an interesting research question against the background of the challenges that the beginning researcher will face. Let's see what Booth et al. have to say about this process.

Most students will have an interest or a topic when they approach the day that they will start their research. When I began my readmission study, I had an interest in social constructionism. I had read the theoretical literature, and in addition some applications in research. I had also taken a course called "Sociology of Mind" with Jeffrey Coulter, the sociologist (whom I quoted in chapter 2). In that course we had to read some of his work on mental illness, which I found fascinating. (I have a background in psychotherapy.) From here to social labeling theories of mental illness seemed only a short step. This is a common starting point for many beginning researchers: a head full of theory and a vaguely defined topic. The beauty of the book by Booth and his collaborators is that they provide you with a few simple steps that will help you to move from that stage to a viable research project. First, you have to narrow down your interest to make it more manageable. How does that work?

The first step is that you have to find a topic that reflects your interest. The good news is that with broad interests the range of topics in which your interest is in play is almost endless. For example, almost any topic will carry a study of social constructionism as Hacking's hilarious ABC of constructionism demonstrates (see chapter 7). In other cases this might be more difficult. It so happens that I encountered two marvelous studies of altruism. Now altruism is as broad and abstract an interest as it gets. You have to find a topic where altruism is at work; engaging in volunteer work, for example. The great British scholar of the welfare state, Titmuss, had the brilliant idea to study altruism through people who donated blood to blood banks (in those days, the 1950s, you weren't paid for that [Titmuss, 1997]). Another example was a psychiatrist I once met—whose name I have forgotten, to my shame—who studied ordinary citizens who, with great danger to themselves, had sheltered Jewish families during World War II in the Netherlands. Both of these topics will allow you to explore the moral and sociological dynamics of altruism. The concrete topic is a window upon the larger interest.

But specifying a topic is not sufficient. You have to take the important step of narrowing down your topic. Booth et al. make an important suggestion here: narrow down your topic by adding "modifying words and phrases" (1995, 38). I have to confess I didn't quite appreciate this step until I began to use the book in teaching and saw how it helped students make that difficult but all-important step from a vague, abstract interest/topic to a more viable research question. Adding "modifying words and phrases," as a perceptive student of mine noticed, amounted really to adding active verbs to the static description of the topic. For example, one of my students had an interest in the development of civil society in post-communist Russia. She had narrowed it down to a topic: the role of foreign and Russian nongovernmental organizations (NGOs) in developing civil society. However, there was an underlying story here. The administration of Prime Minister Putin had enacted laws that severely restricted the activities of foreign NGOs. How to turn this into a research question? The modifying verbs proved helpful. My student phrased her narrow topic as: "The restrictive measures of the Putin administration impede the work of foreign NGOs in Russia." Notice how this statement reads as a claim. That's exactly what it is supposed to be! A good research project is based on one or more claims that you will test against the empirical world. This is the heuristic: *Turn your interest/topic into a claim.* And the way to do that is to add modifying verbs to your topic.

Similar to Stone's sly little question, the heuristic of moving from a topic to a research question by adding qualifying verbs to it, forces you to reflect upon the way that your topic works in the real world. It helps you to leave the world of books and theories behind you for the moment and focus your gaze on the external world. There are NGOs at work in contemporary Russia promoting civil society, but their work is hindered by new laws and regulations issued by an autocratic government that is particularly suspicious of foreign influence and openly expressed critique. What do these NGOs actually do in this hostile climate? Yes, mental illness is perhaps socially constructed (whatever that may mean) but out there patients and their families are struggling to navigate a rapidly changing psychiatric service system. How do they do it? As you see, when you do focus on the outside world the questions come almost automatically. Granted, these are broad, somewhat clumsy questions, but they are a start at least. Booth et al. suggest at this point that you question your topic with the usual *who, what, when, where,* and *how* questions (1995, 39): Which NGOs are at work out there? What is it that they do exactly? How do they adjust to the new restrictions? What is their contribution to Russian civil society? What is their contribution to fostering open democratic debate? With whom do foreign NGOs cooperate in Russia? Who finances foreign NGOs? Which Russian NGOs are at work? How are they financed? How useful is the work of these NGOs really? The list of questions can be very long indeed, but the point is that Booth et al. want you to get a better understanding of what you "do not know or understand about your topic but feel you must" (ibid.). Differently put, they want you to articulate the significance of your narrowed down topic. So for the NGO project the sequence of reasoning could be: "I am studying NGOs in post-communist Russia, because I want to find out what, if any, contribution they can make to civil society under a regime that is hostile to open, democratic debate" Or: "I study how psychiatric patients and their families negotiate the deinstitutionalized psychiatric service system, because I want to find out what effects such large-scale policy changes have on service delivery." From here it is only a short step to a project design that allows you to put your intuitions and claims to the test. The NGO student decided to focus on one Dutch and one Russian NGO. I decided to study readmissions as a concrete way to understand my topic.

The early phase of a research project can be fraught with doubt and anxiety. I guess such feelings are more or less inevitable, but they need not be incapacitating. As I hope to have shown, it can also be a time of freedom and creativity, a moment in your project when you can truly explore the rich possibilities of your topic. When you allow yourself to open up to the world you are going to study, you will be overwhelmed but also thrilled by the variety you will encounter. These impressions will unleash a stream of new insights and ideas. Try using some of the heuristics I discussed to help you organize and develop some of these ideas. Nobody expects you to come up with a fully developed research question in the first two weeks of your project, let alone have answers yet. (If your supervisor does expect this, he or she confuses the finished product for the process.) In fact, as Abbott wisely says, "Indeed, figuring out what the puzzle really is and what the answer ought to look like often happens in parallel with finding the answer itself" (2004, 83). Or, as I, more crudely, say when I try to comfort my students, "It is the dirty little secret of experienced researchers that you only know what your research question is *after* you have done the research." But that initial openness and ambiguity doesn't absolve you from the task of organizing your early hunches and ideas as best as you can into a research topic and research question that will guide the collection and analysis of data and give some assurance that you will in the end have something interesting to say. Early stage research projects are a precarious balance between openness and method, flexibility and purpose, mess and order. The trick, as these two positive heuristics suggested, is to keep both sides of these polarities in the air, as it were. That is, try to be intellectually open while, early on, you let yourself be guided by the empirical world that you have chosen as your research domain. Clearly, you will not know in advance what you are going to say about your research topic, but you will know it will be about the concerns, challenges, and problems of real people in your field of research.

INTERVIEWING

Qualitative interviewing is similar to parenting in that students are supposed to know in advance how to do it well.[6] And, to extend the metaphor, also similar to what we find in parenting, much conflicting advice abounds. For most of us who engage in qualitative/interpretive research, interviews are the main source of data. Or, to put it in more stark terms: deep qualitative interviewing and the systematic analysis of interview data are the core business of interpretive policy analysis.

This statement might strike some, both inside and outside the interpretive camp, as controversial, or as wishful thinking, or just plain wrong. Those who are critical of interpretive approaches generally tend to see them as unsystematic, impressionistic, "soft" ways of doing scientific research. Unstructured, unfocused, qualitative interviews are the epitome of this lack of rigor and order. At best, qualitative interviews will give you a collection of mildly entertaining anecdotes. As I will show shortly, this widespread polemic against interpretive research is based on a fatal misunderstanding of the nature of qualitative interviewing and analysis. Both are systematic, methodical, empirically driven activities that, when done well, set up the conditions for a generative, critical confrontation of theory and the empirical world.[7] Many inside the interpretive camp, particularly those who pursue discursive approaches such as genealogical, critical discourse, or poststructuralist analysis believe that the essence of interpretivism is the analysis of texts. Granted, texts are important, but interviews are often required to give context to the texts, particularly contemporary policy texts. (See Farrelly, 2006, or Paul, 2009, for examples of critical discourse and poststructuralist analysis, respectively, that are fruitfully augmented by interviews.) So, as I have already argued in the preceding section, for those who want to learn something new about their topic of choice, there is no alternative but to go out and expose yourself to the world. In practice that means that you will have to do qualitative interviews.

Given the importance of interviewing for qualitative/interpretive research, it is astonishing that it gets so little attention in academic curricula. Let me summarize my stance on interviewing in three brief programmatic statements:

- A qualitative interview should create the conditions for surprise.
- You should not embark on a course of interviewing if you don't have a clear idea of how to analyze the data. Interviewing and data analysis go hand in hand.
- Interviewing is not about asking questions, but about working with the respondent to produce useful data. To obtain that goal, asking questions is secondary to monitoring the quality of the interview material.

Let me unpack those statements. First, whenever I give an interview workshop, I like to startle the participants by laying out the challenge of a qualitative interview as follows: "You can't ask for what you don't know. So how do you ask for what you don't know?" It pays off to let students think about this Zen-like paradox for a while. I think the statement throws into doubt the students' initial belief that you have a research topic which you "translate" into a set of interview questions, which you subsequently put to your respondent, who will then tell you that you are right or wrong about your topic (hopefully the first). On a deeper level, the statement begins to challenge the deep-seated notion that interviewing is about control: controlling the subject and ultimately controlling the research process. Instead, with my little riddle I hope to open up a horizon of openness and flexibility—by now familiar themes that I import into the "method" of qualitative interviewing.

Second, I urge students to think of qualitative interviewing in terms of backward mapping. The purpose of the research interview is to obtain rich, detailed material that can be used in qualitative, grounded-theory-type analysis. (In fact, I start my interview workshops by practicing grounded theory.) To be able to do grounded analysis, one needs interview protocols of a particular quality. Brief generalized statements or opinions without further explanation, the staple of bad interviews, are utterly useless. Once you have come to appreciate that, you understand the importance of good qualitative interviewing.

That brings us, third, to the interviewing process. From the point of view of the interviewer, I would describe qualitative interviewing as the development and maintenance of three key tasks: establishing a working relationship with the respondent, monitoring the quality of the interview material, and helping the respondent to develop the material.

Establishing a Working Relationship with the Respondent

Robert Weiss frames a qualitative interview as a partnership between the respondent and the interviewer. He then goes on to say that this partnership should be seen as an implicit contract that contains a number of clauses. One states that respondent and interviewer collaborate in producing useful material; useful, that is, in terms of the research goals. Another clause states that the interviewer describes the topic of the interview in the context of the research goals, as clearly as possible to the subject. Then there are a number of ethical clauses, such as one stating that the interviewer will protect the integrity of the respondent (R.S. Weiss, 1995, 65)—not an unimportant stipulation when it comes to interviewing vulnerable populations. To frame the interview as a partnership is important because it introduces an important democratic, or perhaps more precisely, noninstrumental, element in the relationship between researcher and respondent. The term "partnership" in effect communicates to both parties: "We are in this together. We have different functional roles, but we have freely decided to contribute to the research project. We trust each other, and respect each other's specific expertise."

There is a lot to say about the interview partnership, but what is important with regard to interview technique is that the interviewer must be aware that it is largely established in an implicit manner. That is, you always have to try hard to understand how the respondent "reads" you as an interviewer, and if necessary open this up for discussion. For example, the process of establishing a partnership begins at the moment of first contact. How you introduce yourself and your project, or how you are introduced to the respondent, for example, affects the way the relationship gets under way. The same goes for the setting. For my interviews with psychiatric patients, I was introduced by the hospital staff. That meant that I was seen as belonging to the hospital staff, which had certain consequences for what respondents were willing to divulge to me. It took me a lot of hard work to convince the patients that I was an independent researcher without any ties to the hospital staff, and that I would respect their privacy and not communicate anything that was being said to the hospital.[8] To make respondents feel more at ease, and to get a better feel for the circumstances in which they lived, I usually offered to see them in their own house. (Many of the patients I interviewed were already discharged by the time I reached them.) I didn't realize at the time that many patients truly appreciated this gesture, as very few people ever had taken the trouble to visit them in their home, usually an address deep inside the ghetto.

Another implicit way in which the partnership is established is through the type of questions the interviewer asks. Inexperienced interviewers sometimes start the interview with a series of factual questions: "What is your position exactly?" "How long have you been in this organization?" And so on. Sometimes they say they do this to put the respondent at ease with some introductory "small talk." I urge interviewers not to do that. You should know these things in advance, and it communicates to the interviewer that you are after factual, survey-type information. (Or that you are uninformed—even more deadly to a productive working relationship.) Although I don't write out questions—I usually have list of topics at hand that I want to cover—I take great pains to formulate the opening question. Ideally the opening question should give direction to the respondent by indicating the topic that I would like him or her to talk about, and at the same time be sufficiently open so that he or she can enter that topic in his or her own way. For example, the opening question of my readmission study was: "Can you tell me what the circumstances were that led to your most recent readmission?" The question clearly demarcates a topic for the interview (the most recent readmission). The use of the noun "circumstances" asks the respondent to think of the concrete events that resulted in readmission; not an opinion why he or she ended up in the hospital again. And the general nature of the "circumstances" left the field wide open for the respondent to tell his or her particular story. This is what I mean when I say that an interview should create the conditions for surprise.

Monitoring the Quality of the Interview Material

A research interview is not a conversation with a friend. Although there are some similarities (interviewer and respondent may like each other), the "goals" of a conversation between friends and a research interview are completely different. Where the purpose of the first is to confirm and reproduce the friendship, that of the second is to produce useful material for the research project. One doesn't wholly exclude the other, but the role of the "interlocutor" and the course of the "conversation" are wholly different in each case. It is essential for interviewers to constantly be aware of that, particularly as most respondents in an interview situation have little experience with the kind of reactions they are supposed to give, and tend to slip back into a "conversational" style. When I say that monitoring the quality of the material is one of the key tasks of the interviewer, what I mean is to be aware, during the interview, on line as it were, when the respondent's story displays the characteristics of a regular conversation. Let me first explain what I mean by that last statement, and then explain what is expected of a respondent in a research interview and how the interviewer can be helpful in bringing that about.

Regular conversations display the following characteristics. Each one is a singular danger to the quality of the research interview.

Talking in Broad Generalizations

This is such a common feature of regular conversations that we hardly notice it when we talk with a friend. The reason we don't notice it is that we share a context with our conversation partner. So, when our friend, commenting on the situation at work, says, "And it's all because our chef is such a jerk. He simply doesn't have a feel for interpersonal relations," we, as friends, are inclined to nod in agreement. One reason is that we probably have heard other stories about this particular chef. We are likely to have pretty clear picture of what kind of person our friend's chef is, or at least we think we have a pretty clear picture. Another reason may be that we want to communicate support to our friend who is struggling with a difficult situation at work. For a research interview such a statement would be useless. It would be useless because it is a conclusion. It is the endpoint of a long series of events, a richly detailed set of personal experiences, that led our friend to be convinced that her boss is a jerk. In a research interview you want to tap into those experiences, in as detailed a manner as possible. This then allows you in your analysis to reconstruct the situation at work, to gauge what this situation means for your respondent, and to be able to situate your respondent's reaction against a wider background of the activities of colleagues, her own history in dealing with persons of authority, and the like. Let me give an example.

One of the subjects of my readmission study explained that he was fired from his job as a tax officer with the Illinois Internal Revenue Service because "his boss had it in for him." At face value this statement made perfect sense. The subject was a middle-aged male in the grip of the negative symptoms of schizophrenia (unkempt, unwashed, unshaven, with a distinct body odor and a gruff, antisocial manner). (Here I share a context with almost everybody else.) Any department head would have trouble keeping such an employee on the payroll. Yet as interview data the statement was useless. The subject stated a conclusion, the endpoint of a sequence of events that no doubt included others and that eventually resulted in his losing his job. I decided to help my respondent to develop this information and asked him if he could walk me through the process that led to his dismissal. The story that unfolded was in fact the opposite of his conclusion. Coping with the negative symptoms, it became increasingly difficult for the subject to work with clients. On several occasions he treated clients in an impolite, off-putting manner. Nevertheless his colleagues and the department head stuck up for him. Initially they covered up some of his inappropriate behavior. But as his illness progressed, covering up became more and more difficult. When one day he grossly insulted a client who then complained to the agency, the department head had little choice but to let the subject go. In a literal sense, the respondent's conclusion was not wrong: his boss was instrumental in his layoff. However, the meaning of the story was diametrically opposed to the respondent's conclusion. It fit a pattern in which colleagues and department heads go to remarkable lengths to help an employee cope with psychiatric illness to keep him in the job.

Generalized, endpoint talk is very common among policy makers. Somehow many administrators are reluctant to talk about the actual functioning of a policy program. I have no ready explanation for it, but it is a problem for policy analysis as it leaves us without sufficient detail to understand policy process and its effects. Also, this generalized talk is often hard to detect because it masquerades as a series of descriptive, technical statements. Here is an example. The respondent is a citizen who is involved in a participatory initiative to develop anti-crime policies in his neighborhood (Kruiter, van Schijndel, and Wagenaar, 2010). He talks about a program that the city has created to deal with graffiti:

> R: That [the tension between official policy and the residents' desire for creative solutions] is also something that makes it hard for city administrators. On the one hand we are dealing here with a policy program, such as fighting graffiti, which has to operate within an official regulatory framework. On the other hand, within our steering committee we are confronted with the problem of graffiti and we say: how are going to deal with this. Administrators quickly run into what is already given, the regulatory framework, while we think more like, you need as much freedom as possible to deal with it in a different manner. Well, that's when you see that the situation becomes complicated. (Kruiter et al, 2010, 31)

The quote opens and closes with conclusions. Both statements invite further exploration. In between these statements is what appears at first blush to be a description of a situation, but actually amounts to a particular interpretation of the respondent. We don't know if other participants in the steering group, or administrators for that matter, share his understanding of the situation. (In fact, one of the administrators we interviewed expressed a very different reading of the same situation.) So, the upshot is that we need to see the respondent's talk for what it is: not a neutral, technical description of policy program, but a personal *interpretation* of a particular situation. The interpretation might be valid and accurate, but that is not the point. The respondent, in this situation, sees a certain tension, but we don't know what exactly makes him arrive at this conclusion. What looks like a simple description is in fact a highly wrought interpretation that is based on a body of observation and experience. It is the interviewer's task to unpack this interpretation and explore the perceptions and experiences that underlie it.

Stating Good Intentions

This is another common feature of everyday talk. We say things such as: "I decided to quit smoking." Or: "I didn't go to the gym the last couple of months, but now I've decided to go again." We nod in sympathetic agreement when our friends say such things, but as interview material these statements are, again, useless. If this was a research interview, we would want to know what had happened after the respondent had decided to quit smoking or to go to the gym again. We would want to get insight into the inevitable obstacles that accompany the implementation of these good intentions. Let me give an example from the world of public administration.

In the aforementioned study of urban safety and citizen participation, one of our researchers interviewed a city administrator who runs an anti-graffiti program. The administrator describes at some length an initiative in which homeowners and small businesses can sign up for a program in which the city cleans and repairs the façade of their building after it has been defaced by graffiti. The participants only pay a small administrative fee. The administrator ends with the words: "I have to say, it sort of works. But we have reached the point by way of evaluation and conclusion that it isn't good enough yet" (Kruiter et al., 2010, 32). This is a common situation in policy studies. The respondent describes the program and fails to give any detail about how it works in practice. The program description, no matter how detailed, is in fact a statement of good intention. The interviewer's task would be to ask for details of program implementation, participation rates, and policy effects. A good question in this case would be: "Could you give me an example of how the program works?" Or: "What in the way that the program functions now makes you say that it is not good enough yet?"

I guess we talk in good intentions because it is more comforting. Or, in the world of public administration, designing and obtaining funds for a new program absorbs all of the administrator's attention and energy. There are always good reasons that things don't turn out as we intended. Who wants to be reminded of that all the time? But for research purposes, it is precisely these obstacles that we want to learn about. Particularly when we study public policy, where the law of unintended consequences rules with an iron fist.

Expressing Opinion

Most people love to vent opinions in a conversation. We are all familiar with the bore at the party who, uninvited, dishes out his shallow opinions on this or that. Opinions don't require explication. They function as markers that locate the speaker in the social-cultural landscape. John loves to drink pinot noir, thinks that social scientists can learn more from reading Proust than from reading Durkheim, and feels that saving the natural environment is the greatest challenge of mankind. I think we all have a pretty clear image of John after reading these statements. Opinions define us, and that is how they are meant. When friends express opinions, we nod in recognition. We are probably familiar with them anyway, and it would be seen as rude if we challenged them. It becomes monotonous, but for research purposes opinions are worthless. (Except of course when we do an opinion poll. But that is a different type of research altogether.) It doesn't hurt in such instances to underplay the shared context and display an attitude of naïve distance. I often ask people to explain X to me because, I say, "You're the expert. I really like to hear it from you." This is not disingenuous. Even if I'm knowledgeable about the topic on which I interview, there is a lot that I don't know. Respondents can usually give detail or provide an angle on the topic that I haven't encountered yet. In terms of Gadamer's theory of interpretation: I can never hope to master the surfeit of reality. My understanding will always be tentative, provisional.

Distancing

Respondents often talk in what Weiss calls the "generalized present." Instead of saying, "And then I went to my boss and said I said to her . . .," the respondent says, "Well, you go to your boss and you say . . ." I interpret the generalized present as a form of distancing. The respondent indicates that he is not completely engaged with his topic. Whatever the reason for using the generalized present, it leads to generalized statements with little detail. I interpret it as a signal that the respondent is holding back and that the interview is not going well.[9]

Asking Closed Questions

This is a feature of everyday conversation that regards the listener rather than the speaker. A common conversational pattern would alternate snippets of explanation and closed questions. The dysfunctional boss problem again, as discussed by two colleagues:

> A: And then, after we had agreed that we would deliver the report to the commission on April 1, he [the chef] suddenly announced that it must be ready by March 15.
> B: Was he pressured by the board?
> A: Yeah, probably. But it created huge problems for us as we also had to finish the evaluation report for the county by March 15. Why can't that jerk just communicate with us about scheduling?
> B: Maybe he feels he would give in to you then?
> A: Yeah, maybe.

As a piece of everyday conversation between colleagues, this is perfectly satisfying. The two closed questions signal to the speaker that the listener understands the situation and is sympathetic to her plight. The two protagonists in this little morality play obviously share a common context. However, as researchers we would be uncertain as to what the two statements of consent of speaker A mean. Does she also believe that the chef was pressured by the board or has B suggested this to her and now she thinks it a likely explanation? Let's look at a real-world example. It comes from a study of professional practices. The respondent is a police detective who has been investigating a false report of car theft by a woman who is a drug addict. It turns out that the car had been used in a crime:[10]

> Detective: Yeah. You must be able to put yourself in the shoes of the addict. How far would such a person go to get money to cater to her addiction?
> Interviewer: So you might say that if such a person has children than the temptation to commit would be larger than when they don't. I don't know if it works like that?

Detective: Yeah. That could play a role. But to engage in criminal activities to obtain money, that threshold is lower for drug addicted people than for people without drug problems. It not just knowledge of human nature, but also experience. I worked a lot with drug addicts. . . . They are easily persuaded to make their car available.

Interviewer: They are susceptible?

Detective: Yeah, they are susceptible. (Interview transcript provided by M. van Hilten; translation by author)

The first closed question is really a hypothesis offered by the interviewer. The detective summarily accepts the point in order to continue with his general argument about the relationship of drug addiction and criminal proclivities. After the second intervention of the interviewer, the detective simply repeats the interviewer's statement, but we don't know if he believes this himself. The problem with this interview is that the interviewer shares a lot of context with the detective. He has worked for the fraud department of a large insurance company and is familiar with false claims. However, two closed questions in a row effectively kill this part of the interview.[11]

Apart from the problems that closed questions create for the analysis, they have two corrosive effects on the interview. One we saw above. The interviewer's questions interrupt the train of though of the respondent and he gives up. (See also R.S. Weiss's example of an interviewer with an unshakable assumption [1995, 107].) Closed questions are easy to recognize by the answers they generate: usually a short affirmation or negation. When the interviewer persists with asking closed questions, we get the familiar optical pattern of a failed interview: long and frequent "questions" interspersed with brief answers. Closed questions are easy to repair. They can be rephrased as open questions. The first question in the example could be rephrased as: "Can you give examples of the lengths that people went to obtain money?" And the second in a similar way as: "What in your experience makes you say that the threshold is lower for drug addicts?" In both cases we ask for the respondent's concrete observations. The interviewer stays with the respondent but leaves him free to develop the material according to his own experiences.

The second effect is even more pernicious in that it is more dangerous. By asking closed questions the interviewer subtly gets the respondent to say what he, the interviewer, already believes. In the example above the respondent concurs that drug addicts are susceptible. The interviewer could write that up in his report and would even be able to illustrate his "insight" with a quote from the interview. Particularly if he leaves out his own question that initiated the answer, no one would know that he put the words in his respondent's mouth. Many times I have seen the interviewer insert his hypotheses into the interview in this way, as if he wanted direct confirmation from the interviewee of his initial insights. But we test our insights by confronting them, *after the interview,* in the analysis of the empirical material. The analysis is the moment that we do the creative work of interpreting our respondents' observations and experiences. Closed questions are the researcher's royal road to affirming the assumptions with which he entered his research.

Finally, asking open questions is in itself no guarantee for avoiding bias in interviewing. Interviewers can easily load assumptions into the interview through the phrasing of their questions. Asking the parent of a psychiatric patient, "How did you decide to rehospitalize your son?" assumes that the parent made a decision, while it may be that a protracted process of increasingly desperate accommodations preceded the admission. A more open question would be: "What were the events that preceded your son's return to the hospital?" (This example was suggested to me by Charmaz, 1990, 1167.)

Generalizations, good intentions, opinion, and closed questions are all familiar and valued elements of everyday conversation. These conversational techniques affirm relations, solidify friendships, promote cooperation, and in general help us to move along in an imperfect world. They all follow from the circumstance that we share a context with each other. Together they prevent the interviewer from obtaining the kind of rich, detailed stories that are necessary for productive inductive analysis. The problem with these everyday conversational features is that we are all such experienced conversationalists, we are so conditioned to use these features when they are called for, that we hardly notice them when they appear in a research interview. They literally slip by. This is why I call monitoring the quality of the interview material the single most important—and difficult—task of the interviewer. One recognizes the experienced interviewer not by the brilliance of his questions, but by their timing.

Helping the Respondent to Develop the Material

If everyday conversation doesn't give us the material we need, what do we want our respondents to do? The answer is: give a factual report of what he or she has experienced in the field of study. As Weiss puts it: "*In the great majority of research interviews you will want the respondent to provide concrete descriptions of something he or she has witnessed. This includes both scenes and events external to the respondent and the respondent's own thoughts and feelings*" (1995, 66; italics added). The brilliance of Weiss's book is that he recognizes that we have to help the respondent develop his story in this way. It is not that respondents don't want to provide us with concrete, personalized descriptions; but they are as conditioned into the general conversational techniques as we are. So how can we help them? By asking simple questions—at the right moment—that invite the respondent to provide more detail, give examples, and so forth. Weiss gives the following suggestions:

- Suggest to the respondent to develop the situation: What were the circumstances that started it? How did it go on?
- Add detail: Can you give me an example of X? Can we walk through X from when it began to when it ended?
- Identify others who were involved: who else was involved? What did he say or do?
- Identify people who were involved by the respondent: Did you talk with others about it? What did X say or do?
- Ask for inner events: what thoughts/feelings did you have when X happened? (1995, 75–76)

As we see, the questions are precise, yet open. They allow the respondent full freedom to explore his world in his own manner. The concreteness of the questions also allows him to get access to his memory and provide us with a personalized story. And after a while respondents understand what you want and provide detail spontaneously. For example, after I posed my introductory question to the patients in my readmission sample, unfailingly I got a long story in the first person detailing the events of the last readmission. I only needed to ask for concrete examples now and then or prod for a little more concrete detail.

A final observation. Inexperienced interviewers sometimes express reluctance to let the respondent explore his observations and experiences this way because they are afraid they might get richly detailed but irrelevant material. It is often difficult to arrange an interview and you run the risk of blowing your one chance if the respondent goes off on a tangent. Better to follow a strict protocol of questions, then. Underlying this remark is a deep-seated urge to control the interview because it might deviate from the question or theory that animated the project. I don't want to belittle this feeling of anxiety; I have suffered from it myself. But giving in to it kills the interview and, eventually, the project. The answer to this fear is twofold. First, we have some control over the interview through our description of the project to the respondent and our topic list. This way we have broadly demarcated the topic that we want our respondent to talk about. But second, and more important, we don't know in advance what is relevant or not. Relevance is determined *after* the interview, during the analysis. In fact, more often than not I found that my best insights came from material that I had completely missed during the interview. To come back to my opening statement: in a good project the researcher opens himself up for novelty, both in the interview and, subsequently, in the analysis of his interview material. It is time to turn to the latter now.

ANALYZING INTERVIEW DATA: ENGAGING IN A DIALOGUE BETWEEN THEORY AND THE EMPIRICAL WORLD

Most, if not all, students will begin to develop new insights about their research topic while they are interviewing. They see a pattern they were not aware of, they have a hunch about how something might work, or something strikes them although they can't quite put their finger on what it is. These are important creative moments in the research process, and students are well advised to value these early hunches. They inaugurate the analysis of the interview data. If the researcher starts to scrutinize his interview protocol to search for more evidence of his early insight, and possibly develop or amend it, he is in fact engaged in what is known as *grounded theory*. In this section I will discuss grounded theory as a strategy to develop theoretical insights from our empirical data. Or to put it differently, as a generative confrontation of our initial ideas and preconceptions about our project with the body of empirical material that we are collecting.

To my mind, this represents the key moment, the hot core as it were, of qualitative/interpretive research. This is where we initiate the dialogue between our initial perspective on our topic (however inarticulate) and the rich, abundant empirical world that we have entered. As I stated earlier in this chapter, no matter what kind of interpretive research we are involved in, there will be a moment when we have to confront our initial ideas with the empirical world. The empirical world can be interviews, observations, written texts, or even material objects such as buildings. But if we want to avoid merely replicating our original theories, we will have to attend closely to the data and interpret processes or statements within those data (Charmaz, 1990, 1165). Although grounded analysis is part of a larger flexible, emergent, "improvisational" (Cerwonka & Malkki, 2007) process of inquiry and interpretation, in which research design, sampling, data collection, and data analysis weave in and out of one another, qualitative data analysis represents the moment when we test our insights against the world. In qualitative data analysis we open ourselves up the "surfeit of reality" (chapter 8) to which, locked up as we are in our preconceptions, we have had no access so far. This is when empirical precision and "heuristic flexibility" (Cerwonka & Malkki, 2007, 23) go hand in hand, when we constantly adjust our understanding to the particulars of the empirical data. Here is where we extend our early insights into an as yet unknown reality, and hope to learn from the rubs and resistances that this inevitably generates. When the world talks back to us in this manner, it will compel us to refine, change, or sometimes reject our insights. Or, in those wonderful, exhilarating moments, we will suddenly "see" something in our data that we know represents a novel, valuable insight. There simply is no substitute for grounded analysis if we want to arrive at novel insights. Setting up a dialogue between theory and the world is the single most powerful heuristic in interpretive research.

Given the centrality of grounded analysis in qualitative/interpretive research, it is remarkable how little attention it receives in public policy and public administration curricula.[12] I don't know why, really. Perhaps because policy analysis and public administration like to project a "hard," technical, scientific image of themselves. Perhaps because it is seen as a "method" with limited reach, something that maybe works for sociologists, but is too unwieldy and time consuming to be of much use in policy research. Perhaps because grounded theory is seen as a mushy, opaque form of inductive analysis, a fishing expedition in a pond of anecdotal data, far removed from proper scientific reasoning. Perhaps because it is difficult to teach. (I can testify to that.) Perhaps all of the above. In any case, given the misunderstandings about grounded theory, I will begin with short description of its origins, and proceed with a more extended description of some of its key elements.

Grounded Theory as a Heuristic Strategy

In the late 1960s *The Discovery of Grounded Theory,* Glaser and Strauss's pathbreaking book, spearheaded the qualitative revolution in sociology.[13] As is well known among U.S. scholars—and less so among European ones—grounded theory freed qualitative methodology from its status as a lesser kind of research; a somewhat subjective, intuitive, exploratory kind of research that would at best provide hypotheses to be later tested and verified by "real" quantitative research. Grounded theory provided "[s]ystematic inductive guidelines for collecting and analyzing data to build middle-ground theoretical frameworks that explain the collected data" (Charmaz, 2000, 509). It undid the synonymy of theory in sociology with grand theory: large, abstract, and often formalized theoretical statements, deductively arrived at from some a priori, and often untestable, principles, with alleged universal applicability. Instead Glaser and Strauss admonished researchers to enter into dialogue with their data, to develop analytic interpretations early in the research process that would focus data collection that, in turn, would further develop and refine theoretical analysis.

The Discovery of Grounded Theory is not a philosophical treatise on theory, data, and generalizability, but first of all a practical book for the common researcher on how to arrive at credible theories by employing a systematic, methodical approach to designing research studies, sampling, and collecting and analyzing data. In that sense it can—and has—been mistaken for a methods book. However, I believe that the reach of the book is much wider than that. As I argued above, I prefer to see it as an extended set of heuristic strategies—"methods of discovery" in Abbott's words (2004). The heuristic character of grounded theory is best brought out in Glaser and Strauss's repeated emphasis on fit and practicality. It is instructive to recall their original formulation on this: "By 'fit; we mean that the categories must be readily (not forcibly) applicable to and indicated by the data under study; by 'work' we mean that they must be meaningfully relevant to and be able to explain the behavior under study" (1967 [2006], 3). In fact "fit" is a major theme in, if not a rationale for, the book. Over and over again, Glaser and Strauss voice their concern with establishing fit between empirical reality and explanation—and with its absence in much research that begins and ends with an a priori theory.[14]

The benefit of hindsight allows us to see that "fit" is used as a shorthand for a different, better, kind of theory.[15] Grounded theory admonishes researchers to think differently about the nature of social theory, to rethink the goal of (qualitative) social research. Theory is not a final statement about some social phenomenon or activity, but a "strategy for handling data" (ibid.): provisional, open-ended, but always restrained by what the world tells us. "Theory as process," as they call it. Theory as dialogue, I would call it in the idiom of this book. Grounded theory has been taken to task for being overly positivistic (as demonstrated by the objectivist vocabulary of "data" and the naturalistic "fit" of data and theory),[16] but that would be an overly narrow, and unfair, interpretation of what grounded theory is about. Grounded theory presents a strategy of engaging in a dialogue of theory and the world; a strategy that admonishes us over and over again to respect what the world has to tell us. By opening inquiry up to the infinite richness and variety of the world, grounded theory does just what I argued that a strategy of interpretive inquiry should do: create the conditions for novelty and surprise.

Yet, with hindsight, the original formulation of grounded theory as well as its later elaboration and reformulation were not always fully satisfactory to those who engaged in qualitative research. To experienced researchers the almost evangelical insistence to let the data speak, to approach the data without any preconceived notions, simply didn't make sense. The motivation of Glaser and Strauss was clear—to avoid the pitfall of "verifying" a preconceived theory by illustrating it with data. The guiding image of grounded theory was the possibility of systematic inference in which understanding was produced out of empirical materials. In consequence, discussions of grounded theory could emphasize tactics for fostering inference and undervalue the usefulness of approaching the data from already established understandings, concepts, and questions.

To many qualitative researchers these formulations didn't fit with how they experienced the process of qualitative data analysis. That is, if I were to do a qualitative study of the way in which qualitative researchers actually work, I would discover that the initial formulation of grounded theory wasn't quite right. Understanding isn't built up from data; rather, it results from the researcher struggling to understand the meaning of the data and, especially, how they relate to the researcher's questions and preliminary understandings. Qualitative researchers bring to their analysis of data everything they have acquired over the years in terms of experience with the research topic, experience with related topics, and experience with how to write research reports. The researcher not only has theories about his topic—and the richer and more accurate the theories, the better—but also is informed about the field of study within which his particular exploration belongs, and has a practical understanding of what will constitute an illuminating, convincing report. Furthermore he understands how to go about producing a good report that will communicate what he has learned from his study. All these understandings, brought to the analysis of the data, together constitute a combination of scholarship and craft. The more prepared the investigator, the more likely that the qualitative report will be useful.

As we learned in chapter 8, interpretation without at least some initial ideas about the research topic at hand is not conceivable.[17] They are necessary to be able to judge what materials are relevant to the problem and to recognize when materials contribute to an argument or weaken it. Without a prepared mind the analysis of qualitative data is impossible. This does not mean that meaning is inevitably imposed on the data. Rather, it is only in the context of an already existent conceptual framework that meaning can be recognized in the data at all. What I would see as the central issue of qualitative analysis—how best to use the data to further thought—was recognized but not given the importance I would give it.

Coding: Setting Up the Dialogue Between Theory and Data

The analytical steps of grounded theory are well known: coding data, memo writing, and theoretical sampling (Charmaz, 2000, 2006; Glaser & Strauss, 1967 [2006]). By coding a subject's statement or some observation, the researcher elevates this particular instance of empirical reality to a higher level of conceptual abstraction. Coding, thus, involves more than the mere descriptive organization of a mass of data. Good codes tell you something about the data in a way that connects hitherto unconnected instances of the empirical material. A well-chosen, evocative coding label creates a conceptual category that simultaneously describes and explains the data. In the process it also organizes the data by creating conceptual connections of which the researcher was until then unaware. The next step, memo writing, helps the researcher to make sense of the connections and explanatory suggestions that begin to emerge from the data. Memo writing is often a first step toward the integration of categories and properties that have emerged from the data into a broader explanatory theory. Memo writing, again, is more than just taking stock every now and then in the process of coding the data. Instead, it is a key element in the dialogue between data and (emerging) theory in which the researcher "(carries) his thinking to its most logical (grounded in the data, not speculative) conclusions" (Glaser & Strauss, 1967 [2006], 107; see also Charmaz, 2006, chap. 4).

In general terms, data analysis in the context of an interpretive study has two general aims. The first is to move from empirical materials to generalizations. Libraries have been written about generalization. For the moment I simply see it as a description of the data in more general, theoretical terms that put the data in a wider context, that explain the data, or both. The second, and more ambitious, step is to move from empirical materials to model building. The theoretical model will tell us how the phenomenon we have studied works. Although generalization and model building are continuous, I believe that the second is more difficult than the first as it requires much greater versatility with the state of the art in the research field. Building theoretical models is as much a dialogue with the existing literature in a field as a dialogue with the data.

To beginning researchers the precepts of grounded theory can be maddeningly frustrating. Time and again I have witnessed how students—smart and motivated students who were passionate about their research—were at a loss as to how to find an entry into their data. Particularly when I explained and demonstrated the first step of qualitative analysis, the articulation of categories that explain basic units of raw data—and here I prefer the idea of a "meaning unit" to any arbitrary division such as a line or sentence or paragraph of the interview—students were often left bewildered and frustrated. Although they understood and appreciated the explanation, their subsequent reaction made it clear that they simply don't have a clue how to move from the raw data to the evocative, explanatory labels that make sense of the data. Often the reaction was a puzzled: "I don't know how you did that." Students were stuck before they had even begun. For how can you enter into a dialogue with your data if you can't even make the first step to get the dialogue going? In reaction to their frustration students may ascribe a teacher's ability to clarify data as residing in some mysterious, inborn talent that they could never hope to aspire to. Or they may retreat into the defense mechanisms I alluded to earlier: imposing an absolutely unassailable theory on the data, or mindlessly collecting ever more data, thereby postponing the dreaded dialogue of theory and world.

Over the years I have come to take this frustration more and more seriously. I believe that our teaching should take the students' initial bewilderment at coding into account if we want them to learn and enjoy interpretive research. So, what can we tell our students that goes beyond abstract advice? How does the researcher go about coding? As a general attitude my advice would be: trust your intuitions. Value those early insights that came with the interviewing, for example. Often I observe that students simply don't trust their first forays into coding. They see a painful contrast between the finished products of the recognized experts in their field and their own awkward, tentative phrasings. That can't be right, they say. I usually point out that the comparison is wrong. That the experts' first attempts at coding were just as inept, and that the only difference between them and the more experienced researcher is self-confidence and tolerance. When the codes don't come, or don't feel right in the beginning, I don't panic or despair anymore but stay with the data and try out different ways to put my ideas into words. I expect my first attempts to be provisional. I know that my first phrasings will not really capture the meaning and actions in the respondent's statement. Eventually, I have learned, workable codes will come.

What specific advice can we give about coding? The point of coding is to move beyond the data without losing touch with the data. We want to understand the data as part of larger processes (Charmaz, 1990, 1168). One way analysts go about this is to start to interrogate their data by asking, about distinct statements or interview sections: *What is this an instance of?*[18] (R.S. Weiss, 1995, 154). Charmaz advises analysts to answer that question in action terms. I find that advice important:

> Try to see actions in each segment of data rather than applying preexisting categories to the data. Attempt to code with words that reflect action. At first, invoking a language of action rather than of topics may feel strange. Look closely at actions and, to the degree possible, code data as actions. This method of coding curbs our tendencies to make conceptual leaps and to adopt extant theories before we have done the necessary analytic work. (2006, 47–48)

As the last sentence suggests, the importance of coding in action terms is that it helps the analyst to stay close to the respondent's perspective. It will help your theoretical categories to be really grounded in your respondents' experiences and not just your preconceived categories. As Charmaz says, "If you ignore, gloss over, or leap beyond participants' meanings and actions, your grounded theory will likely reflect an outsider's rather than an insider's view" (2006, 49). At the same time, and this is the whole point of coding, by asking ourselves to what larger process or pattern a respondent's statement refers, we lift the statement above the particulars of the respondent's situation. By constructing codes the analyst begins to explain the data. Coding represents the key hermeneutical moment when we begin to grasp the meaning that this particular story has against a wider background. Charmaz again: "By careful attending to coding, you begin weaving two major threads in the fabric of grounded theory: generalizable theoretical statements that transcend specific times and places and contextual analyses of actions and events" (2006, 46). Let me give an example.

In 2007 and 2008 one of my Ph.D. students lived for four months each in disadvantaged neighborhoods in the cities of Antwerp, Dortmund, and Rotterdam to study successful citizen movements. Early in 2008 we started the analysis of the data. The first experience was, to put it mildly, overwhelming. There exists a large but exceedingly abstract literature on participatory democracy, deliberative democracy, and participatory planning. Although this literature has obvious relevance to the project, we wanted to avoid imposing the theoretical categories on our data.[19] However, initially, the data were impenetrable. We were staring at—literally—piles of transcripts, each twenty to thirty pages long, of interviews with residents, community workers, city administrators, police officials, employees of housing corporations, and the like. How to find entry into these data? At some point, after three sessions of fits and starts with codes that somehow didn't feel right, it struck me that each of these citizen movements had a clearly recognizable beginning. Usually the residents were fed up with the bad situation in their neighborhood and decided to organize themselves to do something about it. How to put a term on this? The word that came to mind was "triggered." These initiatives, some already over 10 years old, were all at some point triggered. We settled for "triggering event." In the final report this became "Participation Trigger" (Wagenaar & Specht, 2010).

What we liked about our code was that it described a moment in a participatory citizen movement that was scarcely described in the theoretical literature. Also, our three projects, plus a number of projects in addition to the ones that we were familiar with, had a "triggering event." It could be a violent incident (a murder, Rotterdam), a bad situation that had reached a critical threshold (prostitution and antisocial behavior among local youth, Dortmund), or even a challenge (the construction of a new railway station, Antwerp). What we didn't like was the momentary and impersonal quality of the term "triggering event." It was the residents after all who had acted on a situation they found unacceptable, not some impersonal force. We began to think of "triggers" as dynamic, interpersonal events, extended in time. Not as one-shot events, but as the beginning of a long process in which many different actors were involved. In fact, paying close attention to our data, we saw that triggering events involved a lot of hard work. Here it helped that earlier research had given one of us (Wagenaar) extensive knowledge of the kinds of activities that residents were involved in, such as establishing partnerships with professionals and officials, acquiring necessary skills, dealing with conflict, and establishing themselves in the institutional landscape of the neighborhood and the city. In a quick back-and-forth between the experience we brought to the project and the data, we began to frame triggering events in terms of the different kinds of work that are required to organize a citizen movement. Eventually we came up with the following codes, each of which became a section heading in our report:

- Learning about the problem and its solutions (the morphology of the problem; the range and reach of possible solutions; the landscape of opportunities and constraints);
- Learning about one another; building trust with one another;
- Acquiring the necessary skills; organizing yourself;
- Establishing partnerships; learning about friends and enemies, building trust;
- Creating your niche in institutional space;
- Organizing time;
- Learning to handle conflicts:
- Sustaining motivation (Wagenaar & Specht, 2010; translation by author)

Although the larger, overarching code is abstract and impersonal (yet it did describe real-world events), we had managed to break it down into a series of action codes that described and explained how citizens organize themselves to establish a participatory initiative. Moreover, each of the action codes was phrased in simple, accessible language (no jargon), and was closely tied to experiences of our respondents (Charmaz, 2006, 49).

By articulating categories we link what the respondent has said to the emerging concepts and categories of the report (ibid.). However, although I believe that this is an accurate description of the key analytical moment in qualitative data analysis, it is only a partial description. As we saw in the preceding chapter, it is precisely at this point that Gadamer boldly reformulated the process of hermeneutic explanation in a way that has immediate relevance for the process of grounded analysis. We simply cannot efface ourselves from the process of explaining something that presents itself as opaque. Gadamer's radical epistemological claim was that we cannot understand the world as a detached observer. Inevitably, we approach the topic from within our own cultural and historical consciousness. As we recall, this was not a regrettable compromise for Gadamer, but, on the contrary, a condition for understanding. Understanding, as he explained, is always the gradual, reciprocal influencing of the researcher's position on the one hand, and the nature of the object of explanation on the other. This is where the notion of dialogue enters. The researcher, as I put it in chapter 8, lets himself be "interpellated" by the object of explanation, whereby he gradually comes to see not only the limits of his prior understanding but also possibilities for productively developing it.

In interpretive analysis the researcher is not a camera or voice-recorder who passively registers respondents' statements and behaviors. On the contrary. When a researcher asks about a section of interview data, "What is this an instance of?" he will already have made an implicit prior decision that allows him to demarcate a particular slice of data, a particular unit of information, from the larger body of data. Differently put, he will have asked himself—and answered—the question: "Is what I am reading relevant to my problem?" Initially "the problem" in this formulation is external to the data. To the researcher who is at the start of a project the problem is a given: the puzzle of the spike in readmission statistics, or the liberal regulation of biotechnology in Israel compared to other countries, or the different ways that the problem of acid rain was framed in Britain and the Netherlands, or the unexplained success, in the face of theoretical skepticism, of a number of citizen participation projects.[20] The problem is what he wants to learn about. Obviously, the problem is not unconnected to the data. We collect these data because of the particular question we pursue with our research. The data will begin to inform the problem once analysis gets underway. Part of what interpretive/qualitative data analysis is about is the continuous reformulation of the initial understanding of the problem on the basis of a confrontation with the data.

Preliminary theories tell you what is relevant in the data. Relevance doesn't come with its own tag. Preliminary theories help the analyst to give meaning to the data. Although this position has become popular in post-empiricist social science (usually under the rubric of perspectivism [chapter 2] or constructivism [chapter 7; see also Charmaz, 1990]), Malkki points out that anthropologists have been aware of this for over half a century. Malinowski, writing in the 1930s on land tenure on the Trobriand Islands, and prefiguring Gadamer and the post-empiricists by several decades, wrote, for example:

> The fieldworker in collecting his material has constantly to strive after a clear idea of what he really wants to know; in this case a clear idea of what land tenure really is. And since this idea has gradually to emerge from the evidence before him, he must constantly switch over from observation and accumulated evidence to theoretical moulding, and then back to collecting data again. . . . [Y]our ideas will therefore have to be extremely plastic and adjustable, for your concrete data, of course, cannot be adjusted. . . . Observations are impossible without theory; . . . theories must be formed before you start to observe, but readily dropped or at least remoulded in the course of observation and construction. (Malinowski, 1935, quoted in Cerwonka & Malkki, 2007 172)

When we are involved in grounded analysis we will scan an interview transcript and ask ourselves if the data support, contradict, or develop what we already know. Even if the data corroborate what we already know, they often provide an unanticipated specification of the theory. Even when it doesn't change theory, it becomes enriched. But, more often, the data surprise us because they do not fit our a priori theory. They contradict it, or the theory simply doesn't explain what the respondent says; as happened to me when I dropped social labeling theory as at odds with my observations of mental patients' lives.[21] But, no matter how the data speak to us, they speak to us at all because we bring a preliminary understanding to our analysis of them.

In fact, as the citizen participation example suggests, preliminary understanding extends much further than having an a priori theory that informs our work. All of us who have done extensive research in a particular area will have experienced that we gradually have obtained a deeper understanding of the field that we work in. Signals of such a deeper understanding are that you will find your earlier insights naïve or one-sided, that you are able to situate the statements of research subjects in their proper context, or that you are able to discern nuances, contradictions, and caveats where before you didn't see any. Moving back and forth between the literature and our own and others' research findings, we find that we have a better grasp of the field in that we better understand what is a good, relevant, worthwhile, or promising explanation and what is not.

The code of a "triggering event" immediately "felt" right because I retrospectively recognized it in earlier participation initiatives that I had studied.[22] We will also have experienced that our interviews and observations are getting better because we have a better understanding of what the relevant issues are for our respondents, how they perceive and experience their world, and what challenges it poses to them. In any case, better theories and a deeper practical understanding of the field allow the researcher to enrich the dialogue that he entertains with his data. It is not so much that he will ask better questions about his data, but that he will simply see more in the raw data; the data will yield more insights. In exorcising the specter of crude verificationism, Glaser and Strauss overshot their goal by underestimating the importance of conceptual and experiential preparation of qualitative data analysis. They thereby missed what is obvious to any researcher: practical experience, both with doing and writing qualitative research and with the research topic, enables the researcher to situate his data in a variety of contexts, evoking conceptual categories through comparison of theories and categories from earlier work in sometimes only tangentially related fields. Creative insight cannot be forced, but it can certainly be helped along through preparation and experience.

If this is persuasive at all, how do we avoid imposing our preconceptions on our data? How do we avoid the real danger, not so much of verificationism, but of imposing, in a crude or, more dangerously, in an unnoticed, subtle way (as when we ask closed interview questions) our preliminary assumptions on the data? My answer has two parts: (1) by being respectful to the data and (2) by recognizing that interpretive/qualitative analysis is, in the final analysis, a collective, dialogical enterprise.

Anyone who has immersed himself in a particular social domain, either as a researcher or an interested observer, will have soon experienced that he will have to modify his initial assumptions about the domain and the people who inhabit it. To use a few examples from my own research biography: Mental patients' pathways to psychiatric hospitals in the deinstitutionalized service system of a large American city showed much greater variety than the literature suggested they would (Lewis et al., 1991; Wagenaar, 1987). The way that street-level bureaucrats dealt with difficult cases deviated considerably from the way this was depicted in the literature on street-level bureaucrats and administrative discretion (Wagenaar, 2004, 2006a; Wagenaar & Hartendorp, 2000). The legalization of prostitution facilities in the Netherlands was a much more morally ambiguous affair than what I had learned from policy documents and media reports (Wagenaar, 2006b). In all these cases the world was infinitely more varied, complex, subtle, sophisticated, and equivocal than my preconceptions about it. I might not fully understand what I observed (certainly not initially), and I might not be able to make much sense of it, but I was deeply aware that I was looking at a world that operated differently than I had thought it would.

The lesson is that the theories we bring to an interpretive/qualitative study are always inadequate to the data. That is, the rich, thick descriptions that we obtain through interviewing and extended observation are infinitely more varied and differentiated than any theory we may hold about them. They may add detail to what we already know, they may challenge what we believe, or they may open up a whole new field of inquiry that we were until then unaware of. But the bottom line is that data always suggest new conceptual insights that we hadn't considered before. Insights, we should add, that often have a peculiar "persuasive" quality to them (once you see it couldn't have been otherwise), even if they go against once deeply held assumptions. Charmaz expresses this when, arguing for recording and transcribing interviews instead of working from notes, she says, "Coding full interview transcriptions gives you ideas and understandings that you otherwise miss" (2006, 70). Rich data and thick description force novelty upon us. They surprise us.[23]

LEARNING TO THEORIZE: MEMO WRITING AND DEVELOPING EXPLANATORY THEORIES

Theorizing

The purpose of the dialogue between theory and data that I have described in the preceding section is to formulate explanatory theories. Libraries have been written about the nature of theory in the social sciences. In the spirit of this chapter, I take a pragmatic stance with regard to theory. When I use the somewhat redundant term "explanatory theory" here, I mean *the system of dynamic relationships among elements of our research domain as enacted by our research subjects, which constitutes our research problem.* For example, in the readmissions study an explanatory theory would describe the dynamic relationships among work, income, housing, family relations, friendships, intimate relations, and mental health service consumption that together make up the life of a chronic mental patient. Through these dynamic relationships the readmission behavior of the person is explained, and, on an aggregate level, the surge in readmissions as a result of deinstitutionalization policies.

Several elements of this notion of grounded theory should be noted. First, grounded theory focuses on the *relationships* among elements in the domain of research. With the somewhat awkward term "elements," I intend to avoid the more common "variable." Not only because relationships also hold between people, but also because "variable" suggests a different epistemology, and even ontology—one of singular, preexistent characteristics of the social world, whose relationships are described in a largely statistical manner (Cerwonka & Malkki, 2007, 168–69). In qualitative/interpretive research we are after the way that people and domains in the lives of people interact with each other to produce emergent properties. For example, a particular readmission is explained as the endpoint of a chain of events that roughly leads from the emergence of psychiatric symptoms, to the inability to maintain a job, loss of income, loss of home, dependency on public resources such as a halfway house, subjection to the rules of the house, conflict with the staff, and to institution-initiated readmission. It is not one element in the chain that explains readmission (for example, unemployment), but the way in which all the elements interact. By way of contrast, in traditional empiricist research, as we saw in chapter 3, the readmission would be "explained" as the elevated probability of rehospitalization by virtue of a significant statistical association with one or more of a number of (quantifiable) patient characteristics.

As the example makes clear, a second element is the *dynamic quality* of the explanatory chain. While some or many of the elements of the above explanatory chain were present, the readmissions of other patients in my sample were the outcome of different combinations of events. For example, while some patients ended up in the hospital without the intervention of mental health institutions, in cases where the institution was involved, staff decided to hospitalize the patient for reasons other than a conflict with the staff. This then led me to broaden the explanatory concept "conflict with community institution" to the broader "rule infraction in community institution." Third, the explanations must be cast in terms of the *actions* of people. The importance of formulating our theoretical explanations in terms of our respondents' actions is that it helps us to avoid overly abstract theorizing. It helps us to anchor our theoretical categories in our empirical data at all times. Even more importantly, it is precisely by attending to behaviors that our theories are actually *interpretive* theories. This brings us back to Geertz's famous injunction that "[b]ehaviors must be attended to, and with some exactness, because it is through the flow of behavior—or more precisely social action—that cultural forms find articulation" (1973b, 17). Interpretive theorists explain the actionable chain between actors and policy effects; or, to use a more conceptual language, between structure and agency. And from the descriptions of actions as "public states of affairs" (Coulter, 1979, 41) we infer intentions and meanings, as we saw in chapter 2. Taken together, dynamic relationships among elements of a social domain, which are cast in actionable terms, constitute interpretive theory.

To avoid misunderstanding, "*enacted*" is a broad term. It refers both to verbal and nonverbal behaviors. The readmissions study is an example of the second. Sullivan's study of local leadership, in which she used actors' narratives as the organizing principle, is an example of the first (see chapter 5). Both are examples of what Abbott calls "the semantic view of explanation."[24] In this kind of explanation a phenomenon is translated "from one sphere of analysis to another until a final realm is reached with which we are intuitively satisfied" (2004, 10). Economists translate cooperative or altruistic behavior into individual preferences; anthropologists translate it into culture (2004, 11). Individual preferences or culture are self-evident realms for these two disciplines. Once you arrive at it, you stop looking for other accounts (2004, 8). In the same way, people's behaviors or narratives are self-evident, commonsensical realms for the kind of interpretive explanation that I propagate here. If you are able to reorder the puzzling explosion of readmissions or the complex phenomenon of local leadership into people's behaviors or stories, respectively, you have done your job of clarifying the initially opaque phenomenon.

I will come back to "enacted" however. I deliberately chose it because it is a term that is conceptually counterpoised to "represented." The semantic type of explanation is representational. In the next and final chapter I want to go beyond representation into enacting. Using the dialogical approach to interpretation, I will argue that enacting fits the nature of policy making better. But first I need to wrap up my discussion of strategies of interpretive inquiry by saying a few things about the use of heuristics in analysis. Because whatever type of semantic explanation you chose, the purpose should always be that your theorizing is *generative*. That is, you should be able to say something new and interesting about your topic. Heuristics are a great way to do just that.

Memo Writing

The purpose of grounded theory is to train yourself as a practicing theorist. Charmaz speaks of developing "theoretical sensitivity" (2006, 135). The point of each of these statements is similar: your analysis has to be *generative*. That is, your work has to lead to new theoretical insights of the kind described above. But how do you go about becoming a practicing theorist? One important way is by writing research memos. One of the virtues of Charmaz's book on constructing grounded theory is the strong chapter on memo writing. "Memo-writing constitutes a crucial method in grounded theory because it prompts you to analyze your data and codes early in the research process," she writes (2006, 72). Just as it is smart to start coding early in the interview process, it is equally smart to start writing research memos early in the process of analysis:

> Memos catch your thoughts, capture the comparisons and connections you make, and crystallize questions and directions for you to pursue. Through conversing with yourself while memo-writing, new ideas and insights arise during the act of writing. Putting things down on paper makes the work concrete and manageable—and exciting. (2006, 72)

Memo writing heightens theoretical sensitivity. This, in turn, may direct the researcher toward new, unexplored areas in the data, make him revise his interview schedule, make him explore a new literature, or all of the above. For example, in my study of citizen participation in disadvantaged neighborhoods, I was struck by the frequency and the emotional urgency with which citizens told stories of communicative failure in their interactions with public officials. Often these were stories of officials who promised to return a call or react in a matter of days, and then failed to live up to their promise. Or they told of officials who showed up at a public meeting unprepared or sat through it with obvious lack of interest, checking their smart phones. But there were also disapproving stories of citizens who verbally attacked an official in a personal manner. It seemed to me that some kind of communicative ethics was at work here. This in turn led me to the small but important literature on democratic listening (Bickford, 1996; Forester, 1989), and the wider problem of the dynamics of interaction and collective problem solving in conflictual situations (Susskind et al., 1999). In the report of my study I wrote a chapter on "creating a democratic communicative space," a core challenge of citizen participation (Wagenaar, 2006c). And my current work on citizen participation has a strong focus on the quality of interaction as a condition for collective problem solving. In this I am inspired by the growing literature on negotiation, conflict resolution, and public policy mediation (Forester, 2009). But it all started with a research memo, in which I jotted down instances of failed communication in juxtaposition with the label "communication ethics?"

Research memos challenge taken-for-granted conceptual boundaries. Memos also suggest conceptual connections that the researcher was until then unaware of. They force us to clarify our preliminary understandings and test them against the emerging data. For example, although it was already well documented in the literature that the mental hospital is not just a place for treatment but also a resource for other basic needs such as housing, food, and friendship, the patient interviews made it clear to me that the hospital was only one of a number of resources for survival in the community; resources also included family, friends, work, housing, and community services. Deinstitutionalization had dispersed the implicit functions of the mental hospital throughout the community. The burden of taking care of psychiatric patients was transferred to organizations for ambulant care, families, and the patients themselves (Wagenaar & Lewis, 1989).

For memos to work this way they need to be written spontaneously, without inhibition, without online censorship. Early memos will probably feel crude and awkward. Don't let that deter you from writing and storing them. You can always return to a memo and improve upon it. Eventually, your writing will become more sophisticated, up to the point that your memos become drafts of papers.

Memo writing exemplifies the interplay of theory, design, and data in interpretive/qualitative research. Memo writing demonstrates that in interpretive/qualitative research data do not exist without preliminary understandings, and that theories are formulated and developed through continuous confrontation with empirical data. Memo writing also exemplifies the fact that the quality of our theoretical explanations is at all times dependent upon the ongoing, emerging design and execution of the research project. Although theory, design, and data can be analytically separated, in the practice of research they are intricately related, and—*and this is to my mind a key insight of grounded theory*—the researcher who is at all times aware of this interrelationship in the hundreds of small and large decisions that constitute the progress of a research project is the better researcher. I consider this to be one of the major, and enduring, contributions that the authors of grounded theory have made to the practice of interpretive/qualitative research; namely that, when harnessed to a deep understanding and awareness of their interdependency, the elements of doing interpretive/qualitative research can be made to build upon each other to result in rich, insightful descriptions and sophisticated explanations of social reality. Also, it is this awareness, more than any methodological rules or precepts, that guides our decisions in the ongoing development of the project.[25] This is the message that we should convey to our students.

HEURISTICS IN INTERPRETIVE INQUIRY

How do you arrive at new and interesting insights? How do you avoid such an injunction being a vapid call to action that leaves the student at a loss about what to do to arrive at generative theory? The answer is *heuristics*. Heuristics are strategies of discovery. They enable us to come up with new ideas by looking at our topic from a new angle. The effect is that heuristics challenge our presuppositions, our set ways of approaching our topic. Using heuristics is extremely useful for every researcher, but it is especially to be recommended for inexperienced researchers. Often, I find, they are set in their ways to the point that they get stuck, unable to move the analysis ahead. Probably the reason is that it takes a lot of intellectual effort to come up with a research question that is anchored in the literature. This is all the student has and he or she holds on to it for dear life. To challenge all that hard work risks being left with nothing to hold on to. In such a situation, heuristics are a great way of getting unstuck without questioning everything you have done so far.

I will not summarize Abbott's great little book, *Methods of Discovery: Heuristics for the Social Sciences,* here. I urge every interpretive researcher to read it for himself or herself. It discusses a range of heuristics illustrated with strong, persuasive examples. I restrict myself to a few heuristics that I find useful in my own work and in teaching interpretive inquiry.

For example, the quality of our theoretical explanations is constrained by the range and diversity of our sample. Sampling is always a tricky issue in qualitative research. Few solid guidelines exist, and many researchers use the pragmatic rationale that whatever the number of cases we work with, so long as it is more than a very few, they will provide a basis for a useful report. Yet, when the sample is too small or too homogenous, chances are that some cases, the unusual ones, will escape our attention. In the study of mental patients we might miss the patient who manages to support a family by precariously holding on to a job, although he occasionally has to check in to the hospital. One way to go about sampling is to select enough cases to provide us with an adequate number of instances of the range of our emerging model. So the heuristic is: *sample for relevant diversity— relevant, that is, in the light of your research question.* Glaser and Strauss called this approach to sampling "theoretical sampling" (Charmaz, 2006, chap. 5). The purpose of theoretical sampling is to "maximize differences among comparison groups in accordance with the kind of theory [the researcher] wishes to develop . . . and with the requirements of his emergent theory" (Glaser & Strauss, 1967 [2006], 57). In general, how many people should be interviewed, sites selected, or documents included depends on how much relevant variation in relation to our emerging model there is among our respondents and, also, how much redundancy we want. The more relevant variation, the larger the necessary sample. Also, the more desirable to have redundancy—repeated instances of the same general configurations—the larger the necessary sample.

The problem of course is, as Glaser and Strauss were also aware, that it is difficult to estimate the range of relevant variation in advance. It is useful to try to anticipate what will identify and produce different explanatory configurations and then design a sample that will include different levels of the identifying tag or configuring determinant. Although this sampling for diversity has the benefit of clarity (and enables the researcher to account for what he is planning to do in a grant proposal), nothing guarantees that he has captured the main possibilities or even the right dimensions.[26] This is not necessarily a big problem as you can always check your choices in the analysis phase against what the data will tell you. But this requires that you diligently apply a second important heuristic: *be complete in your coding.* That is, don't skip sections of the interview because they don't make sense or seem irrelevant.

It is here that the injunction to code line by line is important. Although I myself tend to code meaning unit by meaning unit (those can be lines, parts of lines, sentences, or sometimes whole paragraphs), the point of this injunction is that coding must proceed systematically and exhaustively. In fact, as an important heuristic strategy, I usually urge students to pay particular attention to those sections of the protocol that initially do *not* make sense. Quite likely it is in precisely those statements that aspects of our research topic that fall outside our preliminary assumptions will reveal themselves, where the "surfeit of reality" will show itself. Impartial data collection and exhaustive analysis are, thus, not only a matter of research ethos. Leaving out data from the analysis may result in missing important theoretical insights. An example illustrates this point.

As I explained before, in my study of hospital recidivism I reconstructed the path to the mental hospital by extensively interviewing patients, their families, and mental health professionals. The patient interviews covered areas such as work, income, housing, family, friends, intimate relations, and the patient's experiences with mental health service providers. By situating the patients' mental illness in a broader context of poverty in an urban setting, I tried to reframe the received explanation that recidivism resulted from insufficient treatment to an explanation in which the hospital was one resource among several for poor people with psychiatric problems who tried to survive in a large city. During the interviewing many patients spontaneously talked about religious experiences. Many of these stories had a kind of naturalistic, experiential quality. Religion was not an abstract force in these patients' lives; they reported that Jesus actually talked to them, or that they were directly admonished by Jesus to do something or abstain from it. Some were despondent because Jesus had abandoned them. Sometimes these experiences landed these patients in the hospital again. As I couldn't make sense of these stories (they quite self-evidently suggested mental illness to me at the time), and as they were not part of the interview schedule anyway, I ignored them in my data analysis. Much later, I realized that these religious experiences were part of an important underlying principle that I had missed entirely. Religious experiences were to these patients a resource for survival, a means of support, just as family, a job, or a mental health institution was. However, for this destitute, fragile group these resources were a double-edged sword. They carried both benefits and risks. For example, a halfway house provides shelter and is a place to meet friends, but when the patient's behavior becomes a risk for the halfway house, it sees no alternative but to seek the patient's readmission. The importance of the religious experiences is that they brought out the risk element in the balance of resources in much sharper relief than did the other resources. In hindsight, these religious experiences were an important element in a configuration of support and risk in the lives of poor, low-status people who lived in a relation of dependency with various social institutions that they needed for their survival. By ignoring them, I never managed to move beyond partial explanations of my data, and failed to formulate a convincing synthetic theory of hospital recidivism.

In the above example a powerful heuristic is at work: "making a reversal" (Abbott, 2004, 121). What if these patients' resources are not helpful for survival in the community but pose a risk to them? This might at first seem like an outlandish idea. What are resources for if they are not supportive? But it turns out, in fact, to contain an important insight: resources for people who have little or no control over those resources *both* are helpful and pose a risk. The crux is in the level of control. If you are destitute and sick and you are dependent upon mental health providers or your family for your survival, then those providers or your family have the power to restrict access to those resources. And that power translates directly into rule making and the capacity to enforce those rules. The principle applies to other groups as well: patients in general hospitals, welfare recipients, asylum seekers. Making a reversal in fact opened up a whole political micro-economy of resources and dependency that extends to all low-status and/or dependent populations. It also explains how well meant policies can have negative unintended consequences, such as an increase in readmissions. I wish I had thought of it at the time.

Heuristics are great ways to challenge your thinking about your topic, to get unstuck. It pays off to see your topic in terms of analogy, or to ask yourself what happens when you treat what is now a static analysis as a developmental process that is extended in time (Abbott, 2004, 116, 147). The point is that heuristics are not about truth or falseness, but about discovery, finding new ideas (Abbott, 2004, 161). It can be liberating to treat a policy as a text and work out the details of the text analogy, as long as you don't start believing that it *is* a text. Heuristics are a generative engine. They are an effective way to create the conditions for surprise, as one of the leading principles of doing interpretive inquiry. In fact, grounded theory can itself be seen as a powerful heuristic in interpretive research. Engaging in grounded theory forces you to do three things. First, it keeps you focused on data (the world) at all times. It does this by its emphasis on the careful collection of rich, diverse data. It does this by requiring careful, exhaustive coding of these data. Second, it puts your (theoretical) preconceptions to good use. Instead of locking you into your a priori theory, it helps you to set up a dialogue between your theoretical assumptions and the data. As Charmaz nicely puts it, "each preconceived idea has to *earn* its way into the analysis—including your own ideas from previous studies" (2006, 68).

The third strength of grounded theory is its public character. This might not be immediately obvious from texts that explain how grounded theory is to be done. The usual sections on coding and memo writing give the impression of grounded analysis as a somewhat forbidding, solitary enterprise. To me that has always seemed an optical illusion. Grounded theory can fruitfully be seen as a strategy to make the analytic process transparent from the very beginning. Many researchers working in the grounded theory tradition feel comfortable in sharing their insights (codes, memos) in an early stage of the analysis. In this way they test their initial insights against the experience of knowledgeable others, thereby preventing obvious errors, blind spots, or the unrecognized bias of personal preconceptions early on. Nothing prevents the analyst from extending this sharing of insights with the subjects of his research, the practical experts *par excellence*. Grounded theory thus foregrounds dialogue: a dialogue of theory and the empirical world, and a dialogue of the analyst, peers, and possibly subjects.

NOTES

1. Compare Abbott (2004, xi): "What then does it take to have something to say? It takes two things. The first is a puzzle, something about the social world that is odd, unusual, unexpected, or novel. The second is a clever idea that responds to or interprets or solves the puzzle. Everything else—the methods, the literature, the description of data—is really just window dressing. The heart of good work is a puzzle and an idea."

2. By "raw" I do not mean the brute data, untouched by human hand, of empiricism. We are always dealing with "interpretations of interpretations," in Geertz's famous words. By "raw" I simply mean not yet processed by the analytical process to which we subject the data. I want to capture some of the bewilderment and puzzlement that the first confrontation with a slice of empirical reality can evoke in the observer.

3. In this section I try to reconstruct how I experienced my dissertation project at the time I was involved in it, as faithfully as I can remember. But of course it is a reconstruction, subject to all the vagaries and distortions of memory. The benefit is that I can contrast my confused state at the time with later insights. For a wonderful description of the precarious way that an interpretive project unfolds in real time, I urge the reader to look at Cerwonka & Malkki, 2007.

4. This phase reminds me of the early phase of a criminal investigation. There, too, the mass of evidence is overwhelming at first, and what seems relevant at first often isn't, and vice versa. Contrary to what the popular *CSI* television shows depict, the process of inquiry isn't linear either, and is as much determined by happenstance, and personal quirks of the detectives, as by systematic investigation, technical prowess, and personal experience with the field. If we stay with television shows, I urge the reader to watch *The Wire* for a more realistic depiction of the practice of criminal investigation.

5. Clearly, she must have had some ideas about her subject, but I wasn't able to draw them out in the

short space of an encounter during a seminar. As a footnote I should add that this, obviously, is also a case of deficient or absent advice from the student's adviser.

6. This section is based on R.S. Weiss, 1995, and many conversations with him over the years about the art and craft of qualitative interviewing. My purpose in this section is not to summarize or rewrite Weiss's marvelous book—I urge everyone to read it for himself or herself—but to draw out some important principles as I have come to appreciate them in many years of teaching interviewing workshops.

7. I could add that this prejudice about interpretive research also rests on a misapprehension of the implicit interpretive moments in empiricist research.

8. The exception was when they revealed in the course of an interview that they intended to commit suicide or to do serious harm to others. In that case, I had the legal obligation to inform the hospital staff. As all of my respondents were "experienced" patients, they were aware of this legal stipulation.

9. In rare cases the generalized present might be used to protect the respondent from the emotional impact of the material. I once interviewed an ex-prostitute who told me a harrowing story of years of physical abuse by her pimp. She consistently used the generalized present. Initially I kept searching for what I had done wrong until I realized that the only way she could tell her story without becoming overwhelmed by emotion was by creating the distance that is implied by using "you" as the first person singular. In fact, this interview was full of rich detail.

10. To be fair to the interviewer: this is only a brief segment of an otherwise rich and informative interview.

11. Also notice the generalized statement in the detective's story: "But to engage in criminal activities to obtain money, that threshold is lower for drug addicted people than for people without drug problems." The interviewer could have asked for examples to get to the experiential base behind this statement.

12. This might be a peculiarly European phenomenon.

13. I wrote this section in collaboration with my longtime mentor Bob Weiss. It is the fruit of our many discussions about qualitative research, interviewing, and analysis.

14. For example: "This situation [developing grounded theory] is in contrast to the risk of testing a logico-deductive theory, which is dubiously related to the area of behavior it purports to explain, since it was merely thought up on the basis of *a priori* assumptions and a touch of common sense peppered with a few old theoretical speculations made by the erudite. The verifier may find that the speculative theory has nothing to do with his evidence, unless he *forces* a connection" (Glaser and Strauss, 1967 [2006], 29; italics in original). And further on, the authors talk of the "opportunistic use of theories that have dubious fit and working capacity" and relate this to an empirical study "which at its conclusion had a tacked-on explanation taken from a logically deduced theory" (1967 [2006], 4). Or they warn us about "exampling"—research studies that seemingly provide empirical examples for a particular, abstract, a priori theory. Time and again Glaser and Strauss hold a mirror to the research community that shows us the dubious ways researchers, both quantitative and qualitative, handle theory.

15. The following quote leaves no misunderstanding on this point: "Generating theory carries the same benefit as testing theory plus an additional one. . . . A grounded theory can be used as a fuller test of a logico-deductive theory pertaining to the same area by comparison of both theories than an accurate description used to verify a few propositions would provide. Whether or not there is a previous speculative theory, discovery gives us a theory that 'fits or works' in a substantive or formal area (though further testing, clarification, or reformulation is still necessary), since the theory has been derived from data, not deduced from logical assumptions" (Glaser & Strauss, 1967 [2006], 29–30).

16. According to Charmaz grounded theory "marries two contrasting—and competing—traditions in sociology as represented by each of its originators." Glaser would represent Columbia University positivism, and Strauss, Chicago School pragmatism and symbolic interactionism (Charmaz, 2006, 6–7). I talk of "data" myself in this chapter, but not in the empiricist, naturalistic meaning of "sense-datum." Instead I use the term as a shorthand for a much broader notion of "world" or "reality" in the agential sense as I discussed it in the final section of chapter 4: elements of an external reality that affects us without our having much initial control over it.

17. This insistence has been softened in later formulations of grounded theory. See, for example, Charmaz, 2006, 54: "What you see in your data relies in part upon your prior perspectives." And Boyatzis, in his useful little book on qualitative data analysis says: "Knowledge relevant to the arena being examined is crucial as a foundation. . . . For example, it is difficult to perceive and make sense of patterns in Shakespeare without understanding Greek and Roman mythology" (1998, 8). Later he says: "It also helps if the researcher has a grounding or training in the fundamentals and concepts of the fields relevant to the inquiry. This provides

some insight about where to look and what to look for—or more accurately, what to be ready to 'see' (1998, 9–10). Yet, in almost all discussions of grounded theory the bogeyman of "verifying preexisting theory" is paraded. In keeping with a Gadamerian approach to interpretation, I will argue later on that "preexisting theory," when used as a heuristic strategy, can be an important tool for making sense of a field of inquiry.

18. I want to point out that the phrase "distinct statement or interview section" is itself problematic. Glaser and Strauss (and also Charmaz, 2006) recommend doing this interrogation line by line, which strikes me as laborious and often unnecessary. Depending on the goal of the study, it may make sense to take paragraphs as the unit of analysis. Perhaps the answer is to think in terms of "meaning units"—sections of an interview that meaningfully hang together, for example because they cover one coherent topic. In one instance a meaning unit may be a sentence or even a fragment of a sentence; in others it may be a whole paragraph. Below I will argue that analysts discern meaning units on the basis of preliminary assumptions.

19. In fact, one of the main arguments in the research proposal was precisely that the theoretical debate was largely uninformed by empirical data.

20. Notice that in all these cases the researcher has moved beyond a topic to a problem. Perhaps the problem is not well specified, and perhaps he doesn't have a clear research question, yet there is, at a minimum, something of puzzle, something that requires explanation.

21. That doesn't mean that social labeling had been wholly useless. It sensitized me early on in my project to the circumstance that mental illness was not a natural kind, a preconceived category that is hardwired into nature. (As was the position of the psychiatrists in the revolving door debate.) Instead, I came to appreciate the multiple social influences on the course and expression of mental illness. The confrontation with real mental patients and their families convinced me, however, that social labeling was too naive and programmatic a way to frame the complex dialectic between biology and society that is mental illness.

22. Boyatzis speaks of "sensing themes" with which he means recognizing codable moments: "To sense themes or to begin the process of developing codes, researchers must be open to all information. All of their senses should be ready to receive pertinent information" (1998, 9). He also thinks that you can develop this ability to sense themes.

23. Boyatzis adds two insights about coding that I found to be useful; in teaching qualitative data analysis. First, code development doesn't need to be a solitary endeavor. It typically works better when it is done with others (1998, 11). Second, students are often impatient and subsequently disappointed when the good codes don't appear immediately. But Boyatzis rightly emphasizes that you have to immerse yourself in your material, return to it over and over again, to arrive at useful codes (1998, 41).

24. The other two are the pragmatic view and the synthetic view. The pragmatic view of explanation is the famous positivist idea that we know something when we can predict, and intervene in, it. The synthetic view derives from the characteristics of explanation itself. We can be swayed by the sheer beauty of an explanation, for example. The most famous synthetic form of explanation is the well-known covering law model, also associated with positivism.

25. This is hardly a new insight. Hammersley et al., in their excellent discussion of the place of theory in case studies, quote Waller (1934) as saying that "the really great men of sociology had 'no method' in the sense of a fixed procedure. They searched for insight: they went 'by guess and by God,' but they found out things" (2000, 237). Hammersley et al. consider this a very unsatisfactory answer to the question of how causal explanations can be checked (ibid.). This might be, but it also might be that the very problem of "checking causal attributions" relies on an epistemology that doesn't apply very well to what interpretive/ qualitative research does and can do. I will return to this issue later.

26. Glaser and Strauss discuss this question in terms of theoretical saturation, slices of data, and depth of data. However, these strategies do not prevent the possibility of missing entire configurations of explanation.

10

TOWARD AN INTERPRETIVE *POLICY* ANALYSIS

THE ELUSIVE RELATION BETWEEN INTERPRETATION AND PUBLIC POLICY

I confess to an omission. I have failed, so far, to address an issue that sits—uneasily, as we will see—at the center of interpretive policy analysis (IPA), both as a theory and as an actively practiced professional discipline: the relationship between an *interpretive* approach to social inquiry and the analysis of *public policy*. The productive relationship, as the italicized terms suggest, between a methodology of interpretivism and the large, institutionalized endeavor of formulating, implementing, and evaluating public policy. Or, to put the issue as a question: What has IPA to offer to elected officials, administrators, professionals, and citizens over empiricist, technical-rational approaches?

There are attenuating circumstances for my oversight. I have sinned in commission, for curiously enough this topic, although central to the possibilities and limits of the interpretive project in policy analysis, has hardly been addressed by its practitioners. The policy angle in IPA is usually treated as more or less self-evident (as I did so far). Public policy is simply another instance of social science research. But this can't be. Policy analysis, as we saw in chapter 1, is a normative discipline. It operates on the interface of research and practice. Its self-professed goal is to improve policy decisions, or in words from one of the leading policy texts, to "improve," to be "useful," to "critically assess" (Dunn, 2004). And, all policy choices, even the most instrumental ones, rest on value positions. According to the same text, one important aspect of the work of the policy analyst is to explicate those positions. Interpretive social science, as I argued in chapter 1, also harbors a moral program. It wants to reveal hidden assumptions and thereby open up the taken-for-granted manner in which the world appears to us. So in IPA one moral program meets another. Surely this must have consequences for the way the analyst goes about doing his interpretive work.

So what are these consequences? I think they range far and wide, but I select four that cover a fair amount of philosophical and practical ground. First there is the problem of fit. As we saw in chapter 2, interpretive social science claims to be more commensurate with its object of study—social reality—than empiricist social science. That presupposes a theory of the nature of social reality; an ontology of the social world if you prefer. Similarly, if interpretive *policy* analysis is to be more commensurate with the world of public policy, we need an ontology of public policy. Only then can we assess the extent of the fit between the two. Second, there is the normative issue. A good way to approach it is by unpacking what it means to be critical in IPA. Critique is central in different versions of IPA. Think of value-critical policy analysis, critical discourse analysis, or the critical engagement with power in poststructuralist discourse analysis. Naming is claiming here. Going by the examples we have encountered, we get an impression of how critique is enacted in these approaches, but what the critical dimension entails is largely left unspecified. How, in a methodical sense, can the analyst be critical? Are there different ways to be critical in IPA? From what normative vantage point can the analyst be critical? These are questions we need to address when interpretation meets public policy.

Then there is another moral issue: What is IPA good for? What does it offer to those involved in public policy that more rational-technical approaches do not offer? It is not difficult to sense resonances of the first two issues here, but this is a separate issue I think. Some interpretive policy analysts have stated that the specific, unique contribution of IPA to public policy is that it promotes communication between different social actors (Fay, 1975; Yanow, 2000). This goes some way in addressing the issue of contribution, but not far enough, to my mind. What is left unspecified is how such communication should proceed, or under what conditions it is likely to be successful. Also, and perhaps more importantly, what should this enhanced communication be about? Who decides that? A reasonable approach to this question is to frame the contribution of IPA in terms of what it contributes to democracy. This raises a new set of troublesome questions (What is democracy? What is the relation between policy making and democracy?), but these must not detain us from at least raising the issue of democracy and policy analysis. After all, policy making takes place within the institutional framework of the liberal democratic state. Moreover, policy analysis as a distinct discipline came into being as, in the words of Lasswell, a "policy science of democracy."

Fourth, and related to the preceding point, there is the matter of the position of the analysts vis-à-vis his object of analysis. How is the analyst implicated in his object of research? How does his moral position—a necessary condition for discerning anything at all, according to Gadamerian philosophical hermeneutics—translate into methods of data collection, data analysis, and the dissemination of results to various stakeholder groups? How, to put it into plain English, do you work as an academically trained analyst with people who hold different beliefs and values than you do? Or—and this is perhaps a much more dangerous condition—who hold *similar* beliefs and values? Going by the various examples of IPA, with few exceptions, interpretive policy analysts opt for the traditional role of the disinterested observer, who operates on a clear distinction between theory and practice, analysis, and prescription, who has privileged knowledge and who leaves it to the policy maker to use, or not use, the results of his work as he sees fit. This quickly deteriorates into a "policy sciences of the elite" (deLeon, 1997, 67). There are alternatives and we have already met them: action researchers, who argue that analysts should work in close collaboration with the people who are also the "objects" of research, and that the analytic questions must mirror the needs of the public. Or public policy mediators, who actively shape the encounters between conflicting groups to help them resolve their disputes. I will discuss these alternatives to the traditional detached stance later in this chapter, when I talk about the different ways in which IPA can be critical.

THE PERSISTENT PLEA FOR THE FIT BETWEEN POLICY ANALYSIS AND THE POLITICAL

Since Fay, in the mid 1970s, famously argued for the social and political embeddedness of epistemology in policy analysis, the argument has been picked up by other policy scholars who have attempted to break down the conventional wall between social science and political reasoning. Fay built upon ideas put forward by phenomenological and hermeneutic philosophers and developed the by now familiar argument that empiricist social science is incommensurate with the subject matter of the social sciences, and that only an interpretive approach could do justice to the normative and meaningful nature of social reality. In a similar vein, Taylor showed that neutrality in political science is a myth, as every explanatory framework necessarily implies a conception of the good (Taylor, 1985b). In the wake of this "restructuring of social and political theory" (Bernstein,

1976), the emergence of a critical, post-empiricist policy analysis from the mid-1970s on, by scholars such as Rein, Tribe, Fischer, D. Stone, and Forester, was predicated on the conviction that traditional policy analysis failed to address the normative and argumentative dimensions of policy making. Later Dryzek argued that policy analysis, to be relevant to its subject, must address its political setting, the world of public policy, which is characterized by contestation, uncertainty, and intense interaction. Similarly, in the introduction to our book, *Deliberative Policy Analysis* (2003), Hajer and I addressed the normative and sociological challenge to a post-empiricist policy analysis in the following key question: "What kind of policy analysis might be relevant to understanding governance in the emerging network society" (2003, 13)? Our answer to this question is, not surprisingly, that we believe that an interpretive, deliberative approach to policy analysis would be relevant here.

To talk about relevance is, thus, to talk about fit. Yet, on the face of it, fit is a difficult argument. On the substantive level, fit can hardly be called the royal road to insight or relevance. While, for example, there is a prima facie plausibility to couch an analysis of the role of organizations in policy implementation in terms of organizational routines (Allison & Zelikow, 1999), there is no logical or empirical necessity to do it this way. Many creative insights have emerged from borrowing concepts from disciplines far removed from the topic at hand. Organizational decision making has fruitfully been described as a game or a narrative. Conceptual borrowing is a great heuristic (Abbott, 2004). Theoretical concepts may function as allegory or metaphor, illuminating aspects of reality that would otherwise remain obscure. From that perspective, fit would be an obstacle to relevance.

Perhaps the argument for fit refers to something deeper, more enduring, than substantive theory. Perhaps the consonance must be sought at the epistemological or ontological level. The argument that the exclusion of values in empiricist policy analysis precludes a realistic analysis of public policy suggests such a line of reasoning. In the epistemology of empiricism, values have no knowledge content. They are subjective expressions of sentiment. Yet, as everyone can see, values play a central role in politics. Vehement policy battles are waged over different interpretations of the value of equality or liberty (D. Stone, 1997). This is an ontological argument. To give values a place in policy analysis requires a kind of inquiry that makes it possible to have warranted knowledge about them. This is an epistemological argument. One could repeat the argument for the place of meaning in political life.

Yet, even here fit doesn't follow from the observation of the incompatibility of the method and the empirical world that it tries to capture. Game theory is highly empiricist in approach and based on quite strict assumptions about the rationality of individual behavior. Values only play a role as a priori preferences that enter as variables in probability equations. Yet, game theory makes predictions about the outcome of collective decision making, and not all of them are wrong (Scharpf, 1997). Granted, a qualitative or hermeneutic description of the same decision-making process might reveal more and other elements of the empirical world. We might even say that we prefer these approaches because they are more inclusive in that they explain the same phenomena as game theory, plus something additional. But most of the time even that comparison is hard to make. Different theories based on different epistemologies and ontologies illuminate different aspects of reality. They do not challenge one another. They simply coexist.

So Why All the Fuzz About Fit?

So, why all the fuzz about fit then? The argument I develop here is that fit is a nonissue as long as the discussion remains at the level of theory. Or, more precisely, as long as it remains within the realm of *representation.* Fit becomes crucial as soon as we want to make an impact on the world, as soon as we find ourselves in the realm of *intervention.* I introduced this important distinction in chapter 4, where I argued that policy analysis moves about in an environment of *actionable realism.* Actionable realism means that our interventions have consequences that count, that we can't walk away from, that we can only ignore at our own peril. This importunity spills over into the role of representations in policy analysis. We develop images or theories in order to intervene, as Hacking said (1983). Our representations need not be full-fledged scientific theories. Sawing off a piece of wood is based on practical knowledge of wood, saws, and the construction of tables or chairs. But the building of a bridge requires tried and proven knowledge of metallurgy, of stationary mechanics, and so forth. Practical knowledge, know-how, is important here too. How to put things together, and an understanding of the properties of the particular environment in which the bridge is being built, are just as important for the successful completion of the project. Psychotherapy, although supported by a plethora of theories, perhaps requires above all a certain practical knowledge of patients and the conditions for individual change (Lindon, 1991). But whatever kind of knowledge is involved, know-that or know-how, *techné* or *phronesis,* to make the intervention work at all it must be commensurate with the world that is the object of intervention.

Why is this? The argument derives from the affordances that the realities involved impose on us. For bridges and other artifacts, the argument has been made compellingly by Cook, the philosopher:

> A bridge must be understood equally in terms of the functions its design affords, and the properties of its raw materials that afford its design. On the one hand, the form a particular bridge takes can by keyed to the functions of spanning a particular distance, supporting a range of loads, etc. On the other hand, its form needs to be accounted for in terms of what the bridge is made of. A bridge built to serve a specific set of requirements for span and load would look quite different if its raw materials were different (stone would afford one range of design possibilities, steel another). (2008, 262)

Violating the requirements that the combination of purpose, materials, and design impose on the engineers would result in a fatal collapse of the bridge. This is as compelling an argument of fit as I can think of. When we intervene in a world that we do not understand, catastrophic failure is usually not far away. There is a complex argument at work here about (material and social) agency and the real. I also believe that the distinction between representing and intervening has momentous implications for our understanding of the age-old issues and debates that pertain to the relation between knowing and acting. This exceeds the limited space of a concluding chapter. Let me just say that agency comes from outside the realm of representation and that it cannot be reduced to anything within that realm.[1] We can build a model to forecast the weather, or write a poem about spring rain, but those are not the same as getting soaked by a sudden shower upon leaving the house.

What does this imply for policy analysis? Policy analysis purports to be an applied discipline, as we saw. Perhaps it is better to speak of an interventionist discipline. It generates knowledge in the service of purposeful change and collective problem solving. In the language of textbooks the goal of policy analysis is to provide political decision makers with sound, precise, and relevant knowledge to optimize collective decision making in democratic, political settings (Dunn, 2004; Lasswell, 1951). Each element in this description can be and has been challenged, but that is not the point here. The raison d'être of policy analysis, of whatever stripe, is a practical one. It emerges from the urge to alleviate a collectively experienced problem or to bring about a collectively held ideal. That means that policy analysts move about in the realm of intervention. Their work has an undeniable actionable dimension. Policy analysts are precariously balanced on the interface of representing and intervening. Their theories, doctrines, and research outcomes both derive from and contribute to collective problem solving in real-world settings—which is itself a complex assemblage of ideas, convictions, knowledge, technologies, and know-how that hesitantly and tentatively unfolds in real time with real-world consequences (Law, 2004). Within this interventionist setting, the representations that policy analysts generate are either irrelevant (the countless reports that disappear in the proverbial drawer) or have an impact, either a positive or a negative one. In any case the problem of fit is consequential. Partial, incomplete, or wrongheaded understandings of the world from which the impetus for policy research arises will inevitably result in partial, incomplete, wrongheaded, or irrelevant advice and ditto interventions.

Three Generative Properties of Public Policy

So fit is important in applied, interventionist disciplines. But how do we define the world that policy analysis should match? How do we describe the political? As we saw in the opening section, many answers have been suggested to this question. Some sociological (network society), some epistemological (policy making is about values), some philosophical (the human world is about meaning). I do not claim to have a definitive answer. At best a pragmatic one. I argue that the object of policy analysis is characterized by three intrinsic features: complexity, time, and conflict. I think that these three features follow from the actionable, interventionist character of public policy. I also think that from these three properties follow other features, such as the normative and interactive nature of policy making. Is this a return to essentialism? Essentialism has acquired a bad reputation in contemporary social science (Sayer, 2000).[2] Misplaced essentialism, no doubt, easily contaminates acrimonious debates about gender, sexuality, or ethnicity, but it makes sense to approach the concept with an open mind. Complexity, the arrow of time, and pluralism are essential in that they are *generative* properties of policy making. "Generative" means that these properties "determine—or are indispensable for—what [an object] can and cannot do" (Sayer, 2000, 84). They do not necessarily identify or distinguish an object—public policy in our case—in a unique or exhaustive way. Complexity, time, and pluralism characterize any form of human collaboration. But it is safe to say, I believe, that the outcomes of policy making and the process by which it comes about are strongly conditioned by these three features.

I also think that they go beyond more time-bound and contextual characteristics of public policy as described, for example, in my book with Hajer;[3] or more precisely, that the latter characteristics are particularized manifestations of the features I describe here. This is not to say that "the dynamics of trust" or "an awareness of interdependence" (Hajer & Wagenaar, 2003, 11) are less important than complexity, time, and pluralism. In fact, at any particular place or time they could well be more important than the three more "essential" features. By foregrounding complexity, time, and pluralism, I do not want to make a foundationalist claim. These features are not "obvious" or immediately given. I do not place complexity, time, and pluralism outside the ordinary regime of inquiry and confirmation. To say that these features are essential to the policy-making process, and therefore crucial to the issue of fit, is a pragmatic and empirical statement.[4] Its fruitfulness has to be borne out by the results of a policy analysis that takes them seriously.

What makes complexity, time, and pluralism basic? More basic than the emergence of policy networks, for example, or the fragility of trust in government? They are basic because they are *design independent.* By that I mean that everyone who decides to wade into the thicket of collective problem solving will, unfailingly, be touched by one, some, or all of these characteristics. No matter what the intentions of the policy maker, his political affiliations, the nature of the collective problem, the composition of the political agenda, or the structure of the political system are, these are qualities of collective decision making that every policy maker and policy analyst will have to reckon with or ignore at his own risk. A simple example will illustrate what I mean. In chapter 1 I referred to Dunn's discussion of the assessment of the benefits of solutions to industrial pollution. He mentions a recurrent critique of cost-benefit analysis that it doesn't take conflict over preferences into account. In fact, the formulation of the policy choice and the selection of costs and benefits privileges a particular set of values and preferences. As Dunn puts it, assessing the cost-benefit ratio of alternative solutions to industrial pollution already assumes that industrial pollution is the problem. In other words, the application of cost-benefit analysis in a particular situation preempts any political discussion about alternative problem formulations and solutions. Cost-benefit analysis is insensitive to the inherently pluralist, conflictual nature of policy making.

The relation between these "structural" features of the world of politics and human agency is a subtle one. Complexity, time, and pluralism are features that emerge from the past activities of agents, but cannot be reduced to the beliefs and actions of particular individual agents (McAnulla, 2006). So, while agents obviously play a role in the morphology of complexity, time, and pluralism, in the sense that these do not exist independent of them, and while it is agents who have preferences and interests, no single agent or group of agents has a decisive influence over them. The reason for this is that complexity, time, and pluralism have properties of their own, which, while not completely outside the reach of individual agents, cannot be easily influenced by them. For example, while individual policy actors may attempt to condition future events by stating policy goals, these intentional statements have little influence on the chains of unintended consequences that evolve as the inevitable expression of entropy that is inherent to all natural and social systems (Adam, 1990; Prigogine and Stengers, 1985). Similarly, individual actors react in purposeful ways to particular aspects of their environment to influence it according to their needs or aspirations. However, following the laws of complexity, individual agents have little influence over the emergent effects of the thousands of interactions that ensue from their individual actions. So, entropic time and intentional time, or emergent effect and individual action, form two relatively autonomous forces, in which the first circumscribes, constrains, and enables the second (McAnulla, 2006, 122). Differently put, for all practical purposes policy actors operate in a preexisting world that, while not observer independent, is to a considerable extent independent of the *particular designs* that observers impose on that world. Yet, as we will see later in this chapter, intentional statements and individual actions do influence the outcome of complex social systems.

Complexity

There is growing recognition that complexity is a crucial issue for understanding the limits and possibilities of concerted human action (Axelrod and Cohen, 1999; Kiel, 1994; Urry, 2003), and that complexity theory, the eclectic body of knowledge about the functioning of dynamic systems, has important implications for the policy sciences (Kauffman, 1995; Morçöl, 2002; Urry, 2003; Waldrop, 1992). In particular, as some policy analysts have argued, complexity limits traditional strategies of centralized, managerial policy making (Axelrod & Cohen, 1999; Dryzek, 1990; Torgerson, 2003; Wagenaar, 2007a).

What is complexity? A useful definition of complexity is this: "[A] system is complex when there are strong interactions among its elements, so that current events heavily influence the probabilities of many kinds of later events" (Axelrod & Cohen, 1999, 7). From this definition it follows that the core aspect of complexity is the density of the interactions in a system—more so than the number of its parts—although most theorists believe that complexity is caused by a large number of parts and density of interaction among the parts (Cilliers, 2005). Interaction density in turn makes for unpredictability. Because of the large number of connections in a complex system, small effects may reverberate through the system in unforeseen ways adding up to unpredictable, and, in the case of policy systems, unintended outcomes. Small effects may, under certain conditions, magnify into large effects. Similar initial states may, through self-propelling mechanisms of positive and negative feedback, turn into multiple possible outcomes. As a result, indeterminacy and novelty are pervasive in complex dynamic systems (Waldrop, 1992). Complexity thus defies prediction. For our understanding of social systems, and the relevance of the concept of complexity for policy making, I will draw out some important implications from this definition, in the process defining some basic auxiliary concepts.

First, key to understanding complexity is that the whole exhibits properties that are not readily explained by an understanding of the parts (Kauffman, 1995, vii; Waldrop, 1992). Complexity theorists talk in this respect of *emergent properties,* properties of the system that the separate parts do not have and that are produced by the interaction between the parts (Axelrod & Cohen, 1999, 15; Waldrop, 1992, 82). The standard example is liquidity. Liquidity is a property of water—of the ceaseless interaction of millions of molecules, not of a single H_2O molecule. Perhaps, for the purposes of this book, an example from the social world will be more convincing. Local preferences of individual citizens, such as the desire to have ethnically similar neighbors or to be friends with someone from one's own socioeconomic stratum, can lead to a society that is massively segregated along lines of income and ethnic background (Urry, 2003). Neighborhoods and societies exhibit the properties of complex systems.

Complex systems have indeterminate outcomes. This is not merely an obvious statement about unpredictability and the concomitant inability to control the everyday world, but a key property of the morphology of complex systems—a property, moreover, that has decisive implications for public policy. The principle of indeterminacy is in fact the negation of the proven and tried analytic strategy of reductionism. Where reductionism dictates that the analyst reduce everything in the world to a few variables or a few statistical associations that postulate an invariant relationship among these variables, complexity shows, inversely, how a few simple principles can produce the infinitely rich variety and dynamism of the natural and social world (Waldrop, 1992, 153). For example, the basic elements of chess are few and simple (a limited number of board pieces, a few rules), but the number of possible moves and outcomes is almost unlimited.[5] Not only do such systems present themselves to the actors who move about in them as an "immense space of possibilities," but, to bring this insight back to policy terminology, also no realistic hope exists that complex systems will have an optimal or "one best solution." The best that actors can hope for is to find fruitful ways to explore this space of possibilities and look for improvements (Waldrop, 1992, 167).

If we translate this insight about complex systems to public policy, it has momentous implications. It basically means that the usual strategy of bringing expert knowledge to bear on policy situations is flawed, or at the very least, partial. As expert knowledge is primarily aimed at the understanding (and alleged control) of the separate parts of the system (such as labor markets and unemployed workers, food producers and consumers, health care providers and patients, etc.), it threatens to miss the emergent properties of the system entirely.[6] A complex system, on the other hand, cannot be fully understood because the myriad of interactions among its constituent parts can never be captured in full. As a result: "The intra- and intersystem relationships change as a result of self-organization for complex systems. Systemic properties emerge in complex systems as a consequence of such dynamic interactions, and they cannot be reduced to the properties of the system's constituents" (Morçöl, 2002, 150–51). Policy outcomes are an emergent property of complex networks of actors and objects.[7]

Complex systems are constantly evolving in unpredictable ways, but that does not mean that they mutate randomly. Over time it will be seen that most systems will not move through all possible phase states, but center on certain restricted states. These are called *attractors* (Teisman et al., 2009, 139). The simplest example is that of a pendulum. After swinging for a while the pendulum will, through the drag of friction, come to rest at a fixed point in the center. Feedback mechanisms are central to the occurrence of attractors. Again, a simple example is the negative feedback of a central heating system in which the temperature always returns to a particular range specified by the feedback system. But perhaps more important for social systems are positive feedback mechanisms. Positive feedback occurs when a change tendency is reinforced instead of abated, leading the system away from an earlier equilibrium to unspecified, indeterminate states. Urry gives as an example the phenomenon of increasing returns in certain economic systems:

> A social science application of positive feedback can be seen in the economic and sociological analysis of the increasing returns that can occur across a whole industry or activity. This can lay down irreversible path dependence where contingent events set into motion institutional patterns that have long-term deterministic properties. One example would be the way the privately owned steel-and-petroleum car developed in the last decade of the nineteenth century and came to exert an awesome domination over other fuel alternatives, especially steam and electric power that were at the time preferable. The path dependence of the petroleum-based car was established and got "locked" in. (Urry, 2003, 28)

However, the trajectories of *social* systems are not driven by blind forces that are completely outside the grasp of their constituents. In general, through revisions and rearrangements of their building blocks—which are both the result of conscious intervention and the unintended consequences of such interventions—social systems travel on trajectories from one phase to another.[8] In this process actors' images of the future—ideals, perspectives, metaphors, stories—are essential. They are a condition for the system's ability to adapt. All actors, and by extension all complex systems, build models to anticipate the future (Holland, in Waldrop, 1992, 177). In the case of human actors, these models of the future are often based on past experiences that have been transformed into expectations about what so-and-so will say or do. By constantly checking their past and current experience against their image of the future, the actors in a system gain from experience. This process of learning from feedback results in a modifying and rearranging of parts of the system (Holland, in Waldrop, 1992, 146. There are echoes with Schön and Rein's design rationality here). This does not necessarily mean that the system will improve. In fact, just the opposite might happen, as when through selective outmigration a neighborhood ends up in a segregated and dilapidated state (Healey, 2002, 181). On a higher level of organization, however—for example, that of a housing corporation or a city council—this deterioration of the neighborhood will not fit its mental model of the projected effects of urban renewal and will lead to adaptation of the renewal strategy. In any case, it is these models of the future, feedback, and learning that turn complex systems into *adaptive* complex systems.

Finally, complex systems create their own environment. Or, to put it more precisely, complex systems do not develop against the background of a stable environment but they evolve *with* their environments. The principle of *coevolution,* as this is called, contains a deep and subtle principle about complexity with important implications for the policy sciences.[9] First, from the perspective of the actors in a complex system the world is always in flux. As Holland says, "[E]ach agent finds itself in an environment produced by its interactions with the other agents in the system. It is constantly acting and reacting to what the other agents are doing. And because of that essentially nothing in its environment is fixed" (quoted in Waldrop, 1992, 145). Or as Kauffman puts it, "The coevolution of organisms alters both the organisms themselves and the way organisms interact . . . the very process of coevolution itself evolves" (Kauffman, 1995, 208).

"Nothing is fixed" is perhaps too strong when translated to the world of policy making and policy networks (after all, there are such structuring phenomena such as laws, regulations, practices, and institutional inertia). But the essentially interactive nature of policy environments suggests that the possibilities of managing such environments—as opposed to harnessing them—are at best limited. This follows from the implication that complex systems cannot be studied from an external point of view. Knowledge of the system is in principle contextual and participatory. This is not so much a methodological (although it has important methodological implications, as we will see later) as a constitutive principle. The nature of a system is partly defined by the subject. Or, in an observation that has strong relevance to the role of policy makers, "[W]hatever complexity such systems have is a joint property of the system and its interactions with another system, most often an observer and/or controller. . . . 'So just like truth, beauty, good and evil, complexity resides just as much in the eye of the beholder as it does in the structure and behavior of a system itself'" (Casti, 1994, quoted in Morçöl, 2002, 191).

The policy implications of the principle of coevolution are again wide and deep. First, the continuity of system and observer makes our collective images of social systems determined by our point of observation. What we see depends on where we stand. Blondeel, a Belgian urban anthropologist, provides us with an example (Blondeel, 2005, 40–42). On its website the Dutch city of Rotterdam provides descriptive statistics that are disaggregated to the neighborhood level. Statistical indicators about the levels of education and employment show that the *Mathenesserkwartier,* a "low-income neighborhood with a high percentage of ethnic minorities," scores consistently worse than the city average on both indicators.[10] Yet, as Blondeel's observations make clear, many of the residents in this neighborhood are employed in the rich tapestry of semiformal and informal businesses that make up the neighborhood's economy, most of which are not registered by the local Chamber of Commerce and therefore are absent from the official municipal statistics.[11] This economy is also the training ground where many residents receive practical instruction and follow "internships" that are customized to their needs. Far from being a wasteland of unemployment, forced idleness, and absence of education, the neighborhood turns out to have a densely networked economy of small, local businesses and voluntary organizations that contributes strongly to its social cohesion. Second, policy measures that are based on biased images of social systems run the risk of being misguided or irrelevant. Apart from the fact that the official image of the neighborhood and its residents has a stigmatizing effect, policy measures that are based on the official image miss the mark, as Blondeel's observations demonstrate. For example, efforts to improve the general educational level of the population ignore the rich experiential basis of practical training that many residents have obtained through being employed in the semiformal and informal economy of the neighborhood.

To summarize, in this section I have elaborated complexity theory and some of its implications for policy analysis. In particular, indeterminacy because of nonlinear interaction, system states as emergent effects, self-organization, the emergence of attractor states, and coevolution pose serious problems for traditional, centralized policy making. As Morçöl puts it, "Complexity theory depicts a picture of reality that is quite different from the Newtonian picture of reality. It is a complex reality where nonlinear relationships generate partly indeterministic patterns and self-organizing mechanisms create emergent complexity" (2002, 190). The upshot of these basic elements of system complexity, as we have seen, is that the deductive methodology common in the policy sciences whereby analysts attempt to simplify reality by boiling it down to a small number of variables collapses in the face of the behavior of complex systems. System states are not reducible to the characteristics of their constituent parts. Instead the state of a complex system is the emergent, self-reproducing property of the ongoing interaction of the separate parts, whereby small changes in the initial values of some of the characteristics of the system can lead to wholly unpredictable outcomes. Complex systems can in principle not be known in full, and policy makers and analysts cannot hope to be extraneous to the systems in which they intervene.

Time

Public policy is the art of anticipation. It can fairly be described as concerted human action to improve or ameliorate a current state of affairs that is considered problematic or undesirable. Or, in a more utopian vein, as an attempt to attain an ideal or purpose that springs forth from our creative imagination. Also, policies develop in time as plans move into action and begin to generate effects, both foreseen and unforeseen. Public policy, thus, has an intimate relationship to time. Or, perhaps more precisely, policy is immersed in time, straddling past, present, and future, both in imagination and in actual experience. Restlessly, public policy travels the historical trajectory from past to present to future and back, and, as will become clear, generally not in neat linear fashion. Time is a key feature of public policy, and by extension of the analysis of public policy. However, despite this obvious fact, I am aware of very few policy texts in which the role of time in public policy or policy analysis is explicitly discussed. In the policy literature, time is implicit, nonreflected, taken for granted.

How then does time play a role in policy analysis? And, hardly less important, what kind or kinds of time play a role in policy analysis? We get closer to the role of time in policy analysis when we consider the different roles that policy analysis plays in the institutional structure of governance. Generally speaking policy analysis contributes to institutionalized governance in two ways: by clarification or enlightenment and through aid-in-decision-making. Clarification is the oldest and best known of these two and involves all varieties of research for and of the policy process (Lasswell, 1951). For example, an experiment to assess the effects on health care consumption and health outcomes of different insurance packages, a comparative study of labor market participation, or a mathematical model of the drivers of global, energy-related CO_2 emissions, are all examples of policy analysis aimed at clarification. In the words of Carol Weiss, this kind of policy analysis aims at enlightenment (Weiss, 1979, 1980), and interestingly enough, it has been enthusiastically adopted by post-empiricists as an alternative to a more hands-on, "instrumental," "technocratic" image of policy analysis. As Fischer puts it:

> In this view, policy evaluation was seen to play a less technical, more intellectual role. It wasn't so much that evaluators should be expected to discover usable solutions to complex problems; the task was more appropriately understood as supplying information and analytical perspectives that could assist decision makers—albeit more indirectly—in refining their reflection and deliberation about public problems. From this point of view, the conceptualization of a problem was seen to be as important as an innovative solution. (1995, 8)

I think Fischer is right about the importance of conceptual understanding. A model of global, energy-related CO_2 emissions needs to be turned into a persuasive causal-moral story to give it traction among policy makers. We learn then that income per capita and the energy intensity of our technology are the main drivers and not population growth.[12] We can also relate these insights to models of global warming and the implied injunction to reduce our use of carbon fuels, so that we can begin to answer the questions: What is happening? And: What to do about it? But from the "albeit more indirectly" in Fischer's quote I infer about policy enlightenment a) that its relation to policy action is tenuous (more about that later), and b) that its time orientation is implicit. Transformation is expected to occur, but how and when remains unstated.

One could say that the enlightenment function of policy analysis looks predominantly backward. Aid-in-decision–making, on the other hand, deliberately looks forward. Analysis directly seizes upon an immanent policy decision with the aim, through systematic analysis, of improving its outcome. Early examples are the well-known techniques of decision analysis, linear programming, Markov-models, queuing models, and cost-benefit analysis (Stokey & Zeckhauser, 1978).[13] Current examples include model building, scenario formulation, and risk analysis. First-generation aids-in-decision-making proceeded by formulating policy goals, specifying alternative courses of action, predicting the consequences, and valuing the outcomes of the alternatives. The final decision is a self-evident outcome of the analytic process (1978, 5). Current aids operate on a deeper understanding of the dynamic complexity of most natural-social phenomena, and instead of deriving the "one best decision" try to answer more general forward-looking questions such as: What is necessary? And, what is possible? In both cases analysis boils down to creating a model. Models are purposeful, simplified renditions of the world. The model can be descriptive or prescriptive. In the first case it "predicts how some variables will respond to changes in the system" (1978, 14). For example, the model that described global, energy-related CO_2 emissions was based on three decades of observations, and then projected the trends three decades into the future. The projections were calculated under three different scenarios, each based on different assumptions about key parameters such as climate sensitivity or future or marginal mitigation costs. Prescriptive models suggest "procedures for choosing among alternative actions, given the decision makers' preferences among the outcomes" (ibid.). As these examples show, assumptions about (future) time are explicit in aid-in-decision-making. The models of global warming usually project trends under different scenarios. Markov models are probabilistic models of the way the agents in a system will behave in the future. The discounting in cost-benefit analysis is a direct attempt to incorporate the unidirectional effects of inflation on the value of investments (an example of entropy) into the calculations of current costs.[14]

Enlightenment and aid-in-decision-making constitute the two institutional roles of policy analysis. One looks backward, hoping that diagnostic reflection will aid in a better anticipation of the future (Wildavsky's retrospective rationality). The other looks forward, hoping that extending trends will result in a better grasp on the future. Both try to decrease the uncertainty of acting into an unknown future. Together they signify that policy analysis operates in a perennial, uneasy, and not very well understood tension among past, present, and future time. Let us try to unravel some of the issues at stake.

Ordinarily, people have a remarkably flexible, multidimensional sense of time. According to the circumstances, time in everyday life can be unidirectional, irreversible, cyclical, accelerating, decelerating or coming to a complete standstill, stretching out into the past (historical time), stretching out into the future (intentional time), or nested (in which the past and the future are folded into the present). In opposition to this, the time that is implicit in policy analysis is one-dimensional clock time. Clock, or natural, time is usually opposed to experiential, or social, time, and is described as "purely quantitative, shorn of qualitative variation" (Sorokin & Merton, quoted in Adam, 1990, 150). Unlike experiential time, clock time is characterized by invariance and quantity. Clock time is a derivative of Newtonian time. In Newtonian physics time is seen as a quantity: "invariant, infinitely divisible into space-like units, measurable in length and express-ible as number" (Adam, 1990, 50). Clock time marches onward from the past through the present into the future in a relentless rhythm. The ultimate expressions of Newtonian time are clocks. Like all mechanical devices, clocks are realizations of Newtonian laws, and as such they represent the above-mentioned time principles such as invariance, equal intervals, and extension (see also Adam, 1990, 53). But perhaps more importantly clocks are seen as the graphic expression of "the arrow of time," the trajectory extending from the past into the future that is the expression of the quantifiable time of Newtonian physics. The movement of the hands on the clock thus comes to stand for the inexorable motion of absolute time.

Commenting on the dual dimensions of time, Connolly observes that clock time encourages you to think of the past, present, and future as separate and discrete (Connolly, 2005, 99). At first blush this cutting up of the flow of time into discrete units makes ultimate sense. Now I'm work-ing at my computer. In two hours I will be picked up by a colleague to drive to an appointment together in the town of Leiden. This evening a friend will come over for dinner. Clock time helps us to organize our lives and our activities in time and space. And so it is with policy making. In October 2000, the Dutch parliament passed a law that legalized sex facilities in the Netherlands. Two years later most Dutch municipalities had a licensing and monitoring system in place. Currently Dutch authorities and representatives of the prostitution sector are debating further regulation to fight trafficking. The past is related to the present, and extends further into an anticipated future. Prostitution policy is neatly organized along the dimension of time.

Or is it? Two rather apparent observations cloud this simple unidirectional time scheme. First, those involved in prostitution policy disagree about its origins. Some describe the law as the outcome of a progressive feminist discourse on prostitution and the sexual autonomy of women, tempered by an awareness of trafficking (Outshoorn, 2004). Others see the law as the regrettable outcome of naïve do-gooders who exposed vulnerable women to the base objectives of clients and sex bosses, and making the Netherlands a haven for traffickers in women. Brought back to our conception of time: disagreement suggests that the past is tied to our beliefs, understandings, and intentions. Or rather, the past is not an invariant slice of history, but is based on how we read the present. As Oakeshott puts it, the "present determines what particular past shall be sought, and the relationship between this present and its past is contingent" (1983, 9). So instead of an orderly succession of past and present, in Dutch prostitution policy—and in any policy for that matter—the present extends into the past as the past into the present, both affecting each other in unforeseen ways.

Second, what retrospectively is seen as past was once prospectively considered future. Or, dif-ferently put, the future doesn't follow from the present as it appears to do from the vantage point of the present. With hindsight, things look much more determined and linear than they once were. The progress of time tends to bleach contingency out of history. Take the introduction of the licensing scheme that followed the legalization of sex facilities. The creation of licensing and monitoring schemes by municipalities was written into the law. In this respect the creation of these schemes is a simple example of policy implementation. Shortly after the legalization I studied the creation of a licensing system in The Hague (Wagenaar, 2006b). At the time the creation of this scheme was not a done deal at all. In fact, brothel owners resisted it and engaged in protracted fights with city officials, both parties taking each other to court several times. In the end, thanks to the deliberative skills of an enlightened police official, a licensing system was created that was underwritten by city officials and brothel owners. However, subsequent developments made this accomplishment look somewhat like a Pyrrhic victory. In advance of their entry into the European Union (EU), visa requirements for Bulgarians and Romanians were relaxed in the summer of 2003. The result was a sharp increase of economic immigrants. The men were recruited as illegal workers in the agricultural industry; many of the women often ended up in prostitution. However, as the law stipulated that all women from non-EU countries who worked in prostitution were by definition illegal, licensed sex facilities were off-limits to them. Many ended up on the street, particularly the designated street-walking area that The Hague had created for drug-addicted prostitutes. By the end of 2003, the number of women in the designated street-walking area had more than tripled, and anecdotal evidence suggested that many of the young Eastern European women who worked there were in the hands of pimps and traffickers.

This story contains a number of lessons about policy and time. Time develops contingently. How things will work out is essentially undetermined. Time is not a geometrical line with the past, present, and future sequentially arranged as beads on a thread. Such a spatial image of time is highly misleading.[15] It suggests that the future already exists. But a preexistent future is an impossibility. We can imagine the future but we cannot access it. The only way it opens itself up to us is through becoming (Čapek, 1971). Prospectively, before the future has solidified into the past, situations are brimming with potential, or with uncertainty, the dark side of potentiality. Possibility can unfold in many different directions, depending upon the obstacles and resistances it bumps into and the subsequent actions and reactions of the actors involved. The present is brought into being not through planning, extrapolation, or control, but by winging it, by improvising on the spot; by a heady brew of judgment, orientation, and acting on the situation at hand; and by a "dialectic of resistance and accommodation," as Pickering calls it (1995, xi; Wagenaar & Cook, 2003). Policy makers anchor their policies into diagnoses of the past and anticipations of the future. Problem statements and goal formulation mask the twisting and turning, the happenstance and fortuity with which policies unfold in time.

The deeper problem with the preponderance of clock time in our collectively held images of policy making is a confusion between two dimensions of time: succession and becoming (Jacques, 1982). Succession is reconstruction. It consists of the projection of events on a time line that extends in time-space. Succession is closely related to Newtonian clock time: invariant, universal, forward-moving, discrete. We need succession to orient ourselves in time-space. It is the ultimate organizer of our experience and perception. As Connolly puts it, succession, or clock time, "organizes experience in the interests of potential modes of action" (2005, 98). Succession is, thus, the medium of design. It is the symbolic representation of the plans we have for the world.

But succession must be seen for what it is, a projection, a reconstruction, a symbolic representation that is unrelated to the becoming that is emerging time. While succession or clock time is expressed in terms of nouns such as bits, events, periods, and discrete units, emerging time is expressed in the present participle: flowing, becoming, streaming, unfolding. Again, images may deceive us here. Emergent time should not be seen as a continuously moving, autonomous stream of a primordial natural-biological process, independent from our strivings and endeavors, in which we are immersed and which carries us along helplessly. Emerging time is not the time of biorhythms, which, as a kind of natural essence, underlie the social time of memory, foresight, and symbolic representation (Adam, 1990, 70). Emerging time includes both biological and social time. Emerging time cannot be seen apart from our activities and the way we orient ourselves in the landscape of action. Emerging time is not time flowing but the unfolding of actions and the experience of change and novelty that accompanies it. Our actions are not *in* time. Time is not an "empty and inert receptacle, additionally filled up by concrete changes and events." Or as Čapek, whose words these are, continues, "In other words, there is no distinction between the duration itself and its content. Psychological events are not *in* time, since they in their ceaseless emergence *constitute true time itself*" (1971, 9; italics in original). Acting *is* time.

Čapek summarizes here a conception of time as duration (or *durée*, as developed by the philosopher Henri Bergson) that is highly relevant to an understanding of policy making. Bergson's *durée* emphasizes becoming and novelty. Time is a "*continuous emergence of novelty* and can never be conceived as a mere rearrangement of permanent and pre-existing units. It never barely *is,* it always *becomes*" (Čapek, 1971, 90; italics in original). In *durée* the past does not exist separately from the present but is an integral part of it. The past survives in the present as the novelty of the present is created by the very act of becoming (Čapek, 1971, 130).[16] Past, present, and future are part of one ongoing, flowing mental field that is brought into being and maintained by our wishes, desires, intentions, expectations, and memories (Jacques, 1982, 83). Time as becoming is, by its nature, always incomplete, "being always a *fait accomplissant* and never a *fait accompli*" (ibid.)— a fact about the everyday reality of policy making that is expressed by Wildavsky in his famous insight that most policy making is its own cause (Wildavsky, 1979). Perhaps even more pertinent to policy making is the insight that emerging time is predicated upon our active engagement with the world. By acting upon the world we set in motion those chains of action and back talk that "constitute true time itself." Emerging time is coterminous with practice.

It is in its identity with practice that emerging time touches upon two of the other design-independent features of policy making: complexity and pluralism. The key that unites all three is the inevitable slippage that results from practical engagement. When we act upon the world to set some wrong right or to attain some imagined good, we intervene in a complex system. These perturbations set in motion trajectories of interactions, the consequences of which far exceed our ability to comprehend and control. And as Connolly says, "The result is an uneven trajectory of development that can be rendered intelligible retrospectively, though not predicted" (2005, 83). In other words, time as lived experience requires our participation, yet it exceeds it (Connolly, 2005, 103).[17] Systems change, develop, and move along, only partially knowable, hardly controllable, and barely predictable. This, as we will see shortly, amounts to a pluralist view of the universe; an acknowledgement that some parts of the world, some connections and combinations, will always exceed our intellectual and practical grasp.[18] As I said earlier, the stable, linear world of clock time, where the present is causally or intentionally related to the past and pointing toward a reassuring future, is a powerful tool for organizing the continuous flow of emerging time. To use a metaphor, clock time functions as a map or narrative of emerging time, and can be used to navigate the flow of experience in the interest of a particular ideal or intention. But just as maps are always partial renditions of real landscapes, so clock time is never more than an impoverished form of the richness and layering of emerging time. Again, there is nothing inherently wrong with that except when policy makers confuse their static maps with dynamic, ongoing becoming.

Policy making occupies an unusual position here. Self-advertised as the craft of collective problem solving it is, as we saw earlier, intently focused upon the past and the future. Moreover, policy making, and in its wake policy analysis, project a promise of control. In policy analysis control is knowledge, explanation, enlightenment. But all these are, by their nature, after the fact, and for that reason only tentatively related to the eternal becoming of emerging time. As Connolly puts it, himself quoting Bergson:

> Sure, after the fact you and I might "explain" the whole process, or fit the story into a familiar narrative scheme. Quantitative explanation or deep, authoritative interpretation, the two options competing unevenly for hegemony in the human sciences. Each is relatively easy to do. . . . But "it is always possible to take the latest phase of renovation, define it by a concept, and say that the others contained a greater or less quantity of what the concept

includes, that therefore they all led up to the renovation. But things assume this form only in retrospect: the changes were qualitative and not quantitative; they defied all anticipation." (2005, 109)

Alternatively, policy makers and analysts can find recourse in an imagined future, in the utopian, unanswerable realm of projected trends and ideals. For example: Under different scenarios of economic growth, temperature change will be between 3 and 5°C in the next hundred years. If we don't invest in renewable energy sources fast, the control and mitigation costs will be prohibitive. Or: A prolonged stay in a mental institution has deleterious effects on the patient. Ambulant care in the community will emancipate mental patients. Or: By legalizing sex facilities we will be able to separate "good" prostitution from its criminal side effects and improve working conditions for sex workers. Similar to explanations, policy goals aim at control, but both flounder on the irrepressible novelty of emerging time. The "qualitative changes" in the last example point toward the unexpected, unpredictable combinations and recombinations that emerge from the waves of interactions in complex systems.

We can continue, but the point is made, I hope. Policies are projections of intentions or explanations of past events. And although both are important as guideposts for acting, they bear only a tentative relationship to the everyday practice of policy making. In a friendly vein we can say that explanation and intention are necessary to temporarily stabilize a world in flux to allow us to act on it in an intelligent way with insufficient knowledge. From this perspective, both are necessary forms of reflection. In a more cynical vein, explanation and intention are manifestations of denial, of the suppression of anxiety from the awareness that the world of public policy is one of deep uncertainty and our interventions unleash chains of unintended consequences that threaten to overwhelm the policy maker. That is not to say that we are helpless before the irrepressible novelty of becoming. What the theory of practice teaches us is that we can participate in becoming, we can rely on our experience and know-how to engage in the kind of guided improvisation that helps us to negotiate the situation at hand (Pickering, 1995; Wagenaar & Cook, 2003). Differently put, practice helps us to navigate a pluralistic universe. It is to pluralism in public policy that I will turn now.

Policy Pluralism

The term "pluralism" refers to an ontology, a moral theory, and a political philosophy. Perhaps above all, it suggests that, at the risk of inconsistency, the three cannot be seen as separate domains. Our beliefs about the architecture of the natural and social world spill into our ethical beliefs, which in turn inform our understanding of what politics is about, and vice versa. When you accept diversity and incompatibility in one realm, you cannot very well deny it in other realms. The world in which we move about, our values and passions, and our propensity for collective problem solving are like a suite of rooms with the connecting doors wide open.

Although ontological, ethical, and political pluralism set different emphases, their relevance for public policy is inescapable. Pluralism shatters any hope for unitary solutions in policy making. With "unitary solutions" I refer, for example, to those decision-making algorithms whose economic logic results in "the one best solution" (Stokey & Zeckhauser, 1978), rigorous "evidence-based" studies whose purported scientific authority cannot but sway policy makers, or interpretive studies that reveal the "real" interpretation of a policy phenomenon. Pluralism suggests that the world refuses to be organized under one overriding external principle, whether it is a scientific epistemology, a universal moral principle, or a rational politics beyond power and doctrine.

Ontological Pluralism

Ontological pluralism depicts a world that is intrinsically incoherent and open-ended. Clearly the world is governed by regularities, but a) these do not exhaust the whole diversity of the natural and social world, and b) they are anthropocentric (Connolly, 2005, 73). That is, whatever regularities we discern are not hardwired into the world out there but the result of an ongoing interaction between our interests in the world and the resistances it puts up to our meddling and intruding. "Natural" regularities precariously balance between convenience and affordance.[19] One reason the world always eludes us is that it is permanently in flux. Complexity theory taught us that systems are intrinsically dynamic. They permutate into unforeseen and unpredictable states because of the interaction of its component parts. Even when systems self-organize into a state of dynamic equilibrium, it is always vulnerable to new permutations because of external shocks to the system. The notion of duration, as emerging time, taught us about the centrality of becoming and novelty. In the unceasing flow of duration, stable states are moments of retrospective reprieve that help us to find our bearings in a developing universe and to recalibrate our intentions and goals. Taken together, complexity and duration make the world fundamentally indeterminate. What is clear, true, or obvious now may not be so tomorrow.

In discussing James's *A Pluralistic Universe,* Connolly draws out an aspect of ontological pluralism that is highly relevant to the shape and direction of an interpretive policy analysis. Connolly muses on a remark by James that the world is filled with "litter." We have encountered this term before. Litter refers to spillage, debris, things left over—objects that have no place in whatever organization we prefer to impose upon the world. But *why* does this ontological litter remain? Why does it resist being stored away in a natural or social law, a master narrative, or a policy utopia? Connolly's answer, surprisingly, points in the direction of tacit background knowledge. Litter remains because:

> There are always subterranean energies, volatilities and flows that exceed our formal characterizations of being. These elements either exceed the whole, if you treat the whole as the gathering of everything that exists, or they show the whole to be more than rational, smooth or intelligible in the last instance, if you define the whole as everything that exists and subsists. (2005, 73)

Connolly then proceeds to quote James on indeterminism.

> Indeterminism . . . says that the parts have a certain amount of loose play on one another, so that the laying down of one of them does not necessarily determine what the other shall be. . . . Indeterminism . . . denies the world to be one unbending unit of fact. It says that there is a certain ultimate pluralism in it. . . . To that view actualities seem to float in a larger sea of possibilities from out of which they are chosen. (James, quoted in Connolly, 2005, 88)

And then, in a language that echoes complexity and emerging time, Connolly comments:

> This "loose play" between elements is the medium of "indeterminism," or better, *emergent causation* in nature. In a process of emergent causation the novel concatenation of disparate elements on occasion issues in something new, which could not have been predicted before it came into being and may set the stage for other unpredictable emergents in the future. Emergent causation participates in creative evolution rather than mechanical evolution. . . .

The loose play referred to by James operates in nonhuman nature as well as human-centered processes. The word "chosen" seems to point to a series of affinities and resonances between human and nonhuman processes. James does not invest agency entirely in humans while divesting it altogether from nonhuman processes. Chemicals, minerals, and electrical currents enter into the composition of our being. These elements carry an energetic element of loose play in them; and our own experiences of complex decision making, choice, will, experimentation, and the like may be imbued with selective *affinities* to those primordial processes. Certainly the loose play in the former processes preceded and conditioned it in us. It is because of the loose energy in nature that we may feel a host of affinities and connections to the larger world in which we are set. Such feelings occur at different levels of awareness and degrees of complexity, depending upon the affinities in question. The rationalist division of the world into "subjects" and "objects" represses such affinities insulating our consciousness from the world that courses through, over, and around us. . . . The lines of difference between human beings and the rest of nature now become multiple rather than singular, and distributive rather than categorical. Each difference now comes equipped with a corollary connection. Our capacities to think, feel, see, smell, choose, deliberate, speak, and innovate are prefigured in other sectors of the world; and some of these capacities in us are exceeded elsewhere. Since ethical life, for James, is more a matter of inspiration and attraction than command and obedience, the point is to encourage this feeling of interspecies connection across a broad array of differences. (2005, 88–89)[20]

In a pluralistic world of novelty and possibility, things are not only connected causally, but also, and perhaps more pertinently for our ability to act effectively and appropriately in an indeterminate environment, through affinities, echoes, associations, correspondences and resonances. Many of these we are only dimly aware of, while others jump to our attention; but glimpsed or not these accordances affect us in multiple unseen, subliminal ways. The result, as Connolly explains, is that the border between ourselves and the world is much more porous as we tend to believe. In fact, pluralism suggests that we are continuous with the world. The world is as much in us as we are in the world; a theme that was articulated both in Dewey's famous dictum that we don't live in but by means of an environment (Burke, 1994; Dewey [1938] 1991), and Taylor's notion of background knowledge as a precondition for appropriate action (Taylor, 1995c).

Value Pluralism

Values were the proverbial camel's nose in the tent of rational, empiricist policy analysis. Early critics, such as Rein, Tribe, and Fischer all argued that rational policy analysis either was unable to deal with the role of values in political decision making, or, more pernicious, obscured the hidden value positions in instrumentalist procedures of policy analysis under a veil of rationality or economic efficiency. The problem was seen as one of methods and epistemology. Policy empiricists adhered to the positivist dogma of value noncognitivism, better known as the fact-value dichotomy. Values were seen as expressions of feeling, and therefore devoid of any cognitive content. Value statements could therefore not be subjected to scientific procedures to verify their truth content. Obviously this was not an innocent distinction. As Hawkesworth rightly observed, the fact-value dichotomy serves as a crucial boundary marker, a regulative ideal that demarcates science from nonscience (Hawkesworth, 1988). The very soul of rational policy analysis hinged on its alleged value neutrality. To let values inside the tent was tantamount to fatally compromising the whole rationalist project. There would be nothing to distinguish policy analysis from politics as usual, biased, distorted, and swayed by passions and prejudice.

The philosophical critique was bolstered by methodological innovation. Values in public policy could become the subject of reasoned analysis through techniques such as frame critical analysis (Rein, 1976, 1983a); practical reason (Fischer, 1980; Hawkesworth, 1988); normative evaluation (assessing policy goals as to their compatibility with current social arrangements, Fischer, 1995); value identification (explicating the values that inform a particular policy); or a more general probing of the theoretical presuppositions that make up policy claims (Hawkesworth, 1988). These are important additions to the conceptual and methodological tool kit of policy analysis, but with few exceptions, these early critics of empiricist policy analysis have failed to address what is surely one of the key characteristics of values, namely that they ineluctably and irredeemably clash.[21]

Moral theory, like public policy, is about conceptions of the good life. Moral or value pluralism postulates that a good life requires the realization of different values that in their practical consequences, inevitably, conflict or exclude each other (Kekes, 1993, 11). For example, in most countries national health policy strives to attain high-quality health care that is both affordable and accessible for all. In their practical realization, the drive for high quality and for optimal accessibility conflict with the containment of costs. Similarly, introducing national ceilings for health care outlays reduces accessibility by creating waiting lists. Value pluralism describes the condition in which conceptions of desirable social states are plural *and* in which the realization of these conceptions mutually exclude each other. As the moral philosopher Kekes puts it, "Pluralists are committed . . . to the view that the conceptions of a good life and the values on whose realization good lives depend are plural and conditional. These conceptions and values, however, are often related in such a way, according to the pluralists, that the realization of one excludes the realization of the other" (1993, 21). "Conditional" in this phrase means that no value or moral code exists that is sufficiently authoritative to always override other values in case of conflict. Instead, pluralists assert, every value or combination of values may be defeated by some other value or combination of values that, in the specific context, is more important (1993, 20).

Genuine value conflict presents itself to the individual as a situation with no obvious way out. The alternatives can be so compelling, necessary, or binding that the forgoing of any one of them is experienced as a genuine loss (Berlin, 1997, 11). Or, on the contrary, the alternatives that present themselves to the actor can all be so repulsive that the forced choice of one amounts to a sense of irreparable damage (Stocker, 1990). There is nothing exotic about this. Loss and dirty hands are an unavoidable part of the policy-making process, as every seasoned politician knows. What makes these conflicts intractable is the circumstance that the values involved are both incompatible and incommensurable. These are complex concepts and for the purpose of understanding serious value conflict in public policy making we need to be clear about their meaning.

Incompatibility arises when "some values are so related as to make living according to one totally or proportionally exclude living according to the other" (Kekes, 1993, 55). The incompatibility derives not from any external source (lack of knowledge, deficient organization, bad planning), but from qualities intrinsic to the values themselves or to human nature. One can't pretend to be a dedicated father yet spend sixteen hours a day, seven days a week, at the office. Commitment to our children and blind ambition cannot be reconciled. These are incompatible values because each implies the denial or negation of the other and because of the biological fact that human organisms need at the very minimum five hours of sustained sleep.

Incommensurability arises when no common denominator or overriding value exists to which we can reduce the conflicting claims. Lukes states it most succinctly: "The key idea, then, is that there is no single currency or scale on which conflicting values can be measured, and that where a conflict occurs no rationally compelling appeal can be made to some value that will resolve it" (1991, 12).[22] Incommensurability of values is widespread in everyday life and not necessarily a matter of much concern. It arises when people express widely different tastes in, for example, music (Bach versus the Beatles) or interior decorating (Biedermeier versus Bauhaus). We live with it by leaving each other in peace and not forcing the issue. In public policy, incommensurability is usually a more serious matter. The choices involved are comprehensive in that they affect large portions of the life of a person or community (Raz, 1986, 32). For example, the fact that we experience an acute sense of loss when we are forced to demolish a centuries-old river landscape to fortify dikes (Van Eeten, 1997) flows from the incommensurability of safety against floods and natural beauty. A sure signal that some conflict is the result of the incommensurability of the values involved is the aforesaid experience of loss. It is not only that the actual choice between the conflicting claims, even by compromising on one or both, entails an irredeemable sense of loss, but that even inactivity would evoke the experience of loss as it is the situation itself that is tragic.[23] Being confronted for the first time with incommensurable values is what we have come to call the loss of innocence, and is seen as an inevitable, even required element of maturation, both in private and professional life.

Political Pluralism

Value pluralism arises when values are both incompatible and incommensurable. This makes it highly pertinent to policy making. Most policy issues center on situations that involve irreconcilable goals. Do we expand the airport to stimulate economic growth, or do we heed the warnings of environmentalists about noise and air pollution? Do we restrict legal rights of citizens to be able to better prosecute Islamist extremists or do we leave those rights alone and make ourselves potentially more vulnerable to terrorist attacks? Do we emancipate mental patients by giving them all the civil rights of other citizens or do we make it easier to hospitalize them? Do we keep rent control in place and maintain a stock of affordable housing or do we liberalize rents and provide just returns to owners of real estate? In all these cases major values—economic growth versus environmental integrity; justice versus safety; freedom versus safety; positive liberty versus negative liberty—conflict because in their realization they point to courses of action and consequences that exclude each other, or there are no standards or higher-order values that can arbitrate between the claims of each policy alternative, or both. We can clinch the case by saying, for example, that economic growth, safety from terrorism, the freedom of patients to live as they choose, and the freedom of property owners to obtain a fair return on their property override the other options, but that doesn't make the claim of the other option go away. In fact, there will be reasonable people who argue that noise and air pollution are serious matters and that the supply of low-cost flights or tax breaks on kerosene or a consumerist lifestyle create an unnecessary demand for air traffic (Griggs & Howarth, 2006). Or, some will argue that the freedom to live one's life as one pleases is a great good, but that some mental patients have a hard time sustaining themselves in the community or pose a danger to others so that they and the community would be better off if we could hospitalize them, against their will if necessary. In such cases it is difficult to find an easy way out. No compromise, appeal to higher-order values or fixation on desired outcomes, or conversely, no denial of the conflict by reducing it to mere emotions or passions, will make it go away. There simply is no common ground in these cases from which to arbitrate rationally between the conflicting values. Conflict in such situations seems unavoidable.

   Political pluralism acknowledges the unavoidability and ubiquity of conflict in the realm of politics. Conflict cannot be wished or reasoned away because of the incompatibility and incommensurability of the values involved. It is this fact that prevents one overriding value or combination of values to settle the conflict. As Kekes puts it:

For it seems that the claim that any particular value should always override any incompatible or incommensurable value that may conflict with it is bound to be arbitrary. On what grounds could any value be regarded as invariably overriding if the values it is supposed to override are so utterly unlike as to exclude the possibility of comparison between it and them? (1993, 22)

Although political pluralism issues from value pluralism, it distinguishes itself by its emphasis on conflict, power, and the functioning of political and administrative institutions. One could say that political pluralism is value pluralism as it expresses itself in the real world of politics and collective problem solving.

Similar to the other pluralisms, political pluralism has to make its case against powerful monist propensities. One such propensity is the claim of ruling elites in liberal democracies that their regime is based on consensus and general agreement. They claim that since they have been democratically elected, the majority of the people agree with their political program and ideological presuppositions. There are some people who disagree, but they are a minority and, for all practical purposes, have less standing. Election results are the hard evidence of the legitimacy and rightness of the elite's position. Otherwise the adversaries would have won. Another monist proclivity in politics is the deep-seated ideal that for all societal problems rational or scientific analysis will be able to dissolve the original, underlying conflict. Rationalism in politics usually amounts to obfuscating the underlying values that are at stake. A plea for a rational approach to this or that problem generally means that one value, usually economic efficiency, or one interest, usually that of the business community, surreptitiously drives the policy solution. A third monist tendency is the belief in a common political culture. Governments of leftist, centrist, or rightist signature may come and go, people may exhibit widely different lifestyles, but we are all united by a common set of values, a *Leitkultur,* a language, a shared history, and trust in the adjudicating power of a set of democratic procedures to resolve societal conflict.

Value pluralism is an ethical theory and consequently it moves in the rarefied realm of abstract philosophical argument. Political pluralism deals with the everyday world of politics. Political scientists and students of public administration prefer to portray that world as one of consensus and reasonableness, and in many cases it is, but there is another side to it.[24] The world of politics is ruled by power differentials. Deception, discrimination, manipulation, and double-crossing are common means to clinch political conflicts. People get duped, hurt, and marginalized, or are denied their rightful claim. Power can be seen as yet another engine of monism. Power either forces the issue by brute domination or, more subtly and more commonly in the liberal democracies in which most of us live, by organizing some positions out of the spectrum of legitimate, feasible, reasonable, or even imaginable options (Foucault, 1980a; Lukes, 1975). Covert or latent power is a particularly effective means to cover up real and potential conflict. The active ingredient is the denial of standing to a particular group or position. Standing is denied because the group is said to lack core values, to speak the wrong language, or to lack necessary skills or attitudes, or because their desires would imperil "obvious" values or benefits, they don't play by the rules, and so on. The intended effect is, through the exertion of overt or covert power, to circumscribe a domain in which a consensus of interest and values is established and one value position goes unchallenged (Mouffe, 2000).[25]

DOES INTERPRETIVE POLICY ANALYSIS FIT PUBLIC POLICY?

The incompatibility theorem has hovered over the social sciences since the early days of phenomenology, now more than a century ago. It states that a social science that is true to its subject,

Table 10.1

Fit of Empiricist and Interpretive Policy Analysis to the World of Public Policy

| | Contribution to Policy Making | | | | | |
	Complexity	Time	Pluralism	Action-orientation	Enlightenment	Aid-to-Action
EPA	−	+	−	+ / −	+	+ / −
IPA-herm	+ / −	+	+	+ / −	+	+
IPA-disc	+	−	+	−	+	−
IPA-dial	+	+	+	+	+	+

the life-world of everyday human beings, must be able to elucidate what is characteristic of that world, namely that it is meaningful, intentional, and value laden. The conclusion from the preceding section is that that is not nearly enough. A policy analysis that fits its subject should not only do justice to schemes of meaning and intention, but on top of that it should take complexity, time, and pluralism into account. That's a tall order. It is not enough to just state that policy analysis must be interpretive and normative, but it must also be able to throw light on the effects that complexity, time, and pluralism have on the process and outcomes of public policy. And it must also be action-able. That is, it must be sensitive and relevant to the policy maker's imperative to act on the situation at hand. It must be able to assist in navigating policies into emerging time and steering them between the shoals of irredeemable value conflict. In the remainder of this chapter I will explore what action-orientation, complexity, emergent time, and policy pluralism mean for interpretive policy analysis (IPA). I will first consider the traditional roles of policy analysis—enlightenment and aid-in-action—and see how the two major approaches, empiricist policy analysis (EPA) and IPA, hold up against the demands of our policy ontology. I will then discuss the three remaining issues in the relation between IPA and institutionalized public policy: the notion of critique, the nature of good communication, and the stance of the analyst.

As a first cut to the problem of fit I have summarized in Table 10.1 the contributions of different approaches to policy analysis.

Let me walk through the table. Not surprisingly, all approaches have a contribution to make to understanding the complexity of policy problems. EPA, particularly in its modern versions, is strong in obtaining facts, in particular by estimating how a phenomenon behaves over time or how a subset of data is distributed in the wider population: trends in readmission rates, growth in the number of airline passengers, changes in global temperature, attitudes toward paid work among low-income single mothers. It can do much more than that. By building models or sketching scenarios, it can formulate meaningful narratives (in numbers and images) of how variables hang together or how a problem might evolve in future time. This is not a mean feat. Problem analysis starts with getting the facts right. EPA is much less strong on capturing the dynamics of complexity. Because it is exclusively representational, it runs into epistemic limits in capturing the myriad of ongoing interactions that lead to emergent outcomes.

The problem, of course, is that the facts are often controversial. Facts are always "facts"—the quotation marks indicating the assumptions, biases, and power differentiations that enter into the selection and shaping of the categories that we single out for presentation and analysis. (Or the surreptitious influence of research method on outcome, as we saw in the quantitative readmission study in chapter 3.) "Industrial pollution" is a societal problem, and thus a statistical category, because it implicitly assumes driving habits and a particular infrastructure biased toward the automotive society, to follow Dunn's example from chapter 1. This is where IPA comes in. Hermeneutic IPA is strong on amplifying the voice of the policy targets; the meaning that a problem has for different audiences. Hospital readmissions are not just a mechanical by-product of a restructuring of services to the mentally ill, but above all, an answer by the actors in this field—patients, families, service providers, police—to the challenges of dealing with chronic mental illness in a big city with fragmented services for mental patients. Articulating that voice is an important counterweight to the professionalist, elitist bias in implementing, understanding, and depicting deinstitutionalization policies. Hermeneutic IPA captures system dynamics, but in an impressionistic narrative manner (Wagenaar, 2007a, 26–27). The "but" suggests second best, but that is not what I intend. The stories of policy audiences depict the actionable, interactive struggling with a social issue. In that sense they balance representation and intervention: we obtain stories of the way actors intervene in the world, their lived, everyday world. Those are rich stories of change full of the incidental, tangential information that bring out the interrelational dynamics of moving about in an uncertain, complex world. Narrative complexity is, as I will show, a first step toward the pragmatic, actionable, emergent navigating of complexity that is often all we have. I will return to this point later in this chapter.

Discursive IPA fulfills a similar enlightening and critical role, though in different manner. Discursive IPA is strong on "denaturalizing" the taken for granted, the deep assumptions that we breathe unknowingly like air. The mental hospital transforms because the concept of mental illness has widened (and is now called "mental health"), while surveillance techniques have shifted from external to self-regulation. This is a worldwide sea change in our collective attitude toward mental illness, with profound implications for the institutionalization of care for the mentally ill. Dialogical IPA has a limited, but important, contribution to make to complexity. It is more distant and less action oriented because it relies more on the analytical skills, and concomitant critical distance, of the discursive analyst. Discursive analysis is by definition ex post facto—a reinterpretation of events that we have held self-evident for so long. Its promise for the future is the somewhat implicit emancipatory promise that things could have been different. A better, more enlightened, more equal world organized around ethically more acceptable moral first principles. But most of the time it is not more than that: a promise, because the institutional forces that keep the deep assumptions in place are not easily dislodged. Needless to say, both hermeneutic and discursive IPA, by amplifying weak voices and unearthing deep assumptions, contribute greatly to grasping the inherently pluralistic nature of the policy world.

Dialogical IPA is strong on complexity because of its interactive, evolving, and pragmatic character. In their famous article "Beyond Backyard Environmentalism," Sabel and his collaborators show how intricate environmental problems, such as the pollution of the Chesapeake Bay estuary, are cleared up through the interactions of farmers, environmental activists, government agencies, and administrators (1999). The case is an archetypical example of the Deweyan interventionist problem solving that also inspired Schön and Rein's policy design: a conjecture is put forward and rejected by the resistances of observable facts, which suggest another conjecture, and so on until the initial problem is simultaneously reformulated and nailed down, at least provisionally. What makes the case fascinating is that the whole process is dispersed, involving many people, often adversaries, in different locations. The authors see it as an example of democratic deliberation. Dialogical IPA is equally strong on the time and pluralism dimensions. It captures the evolving nature of the estuary problem and brings different perspectives on the issue together.

Public policy proceeds under the imperative to act. The upshot is that what is a constraint for purely representational versions of IPA—hermeneutic and discursive—is an affordance in the case of dialogical versions of IPA. The actionable, pragmatic, situated nature of dialogical IPA makes it able to cope with complexity, time, and deep value differences. While the evolving nature of dynamic complex systems is impossible to model in any accurate, useful manner, people have been dealing pragmatically with complex situations for centuries. Complex systems, physical, biological, and certainly human, self-organize and evolve without there being very clearly defined problems for the agents to struggle with, and without a clearly circumscribed criterion of fitness or reward to decide in advance who might win or lose out. This adaptive acting in the face of complexity without full or even any clear understanding of the situation at hand is what Axelrod and Cohen call "harnessing complexity." As they describe it, "Harnessing complexity involves acting sensibly without fully understanding how the world works" (1999, 45). The same goes for deep value differences. It is a widely shared observation that people who disagree on general principles are very well able to agree on practical recommendations in concrete cases (Forester, 2009, 6; Jonsen & Toulmin, 1990, 18–19). Pragmatic strategies of accommodating complexity, emerging time, and deep value differences are obviously not foolproof. The point is a different one. An actionable, dialogical approach sets the conditions for practical judgment; it makes room for the play of wisdom in public affairs. This, ultimately, is the decisive difference between representation and dialogue, between method and heuristic. I will return to this.

Is dialogical IPA therefore the optimal form of policy analysis that allows us to discard the other variants? Clearly not. We represent to intervene, and our interventions lead to better, more inclusive, representations. The actors in the estuary case relied throughout their interactive problem solving on EPA and, more implicitly, hermeneutic IPA. They formulated performance targets that specified the reduction of nutrient loadings and developed a monitoring regime. They developed and adjusted images of the water quality of the bay, formulated narratives of governance, and creatively employed these in what the authors call "a grab bag of regulatory techniques, legal instruments, and voluntary measures" (Sabel et al., 1999). The somewhat banal conclusion is that all forms of policy analysis are complementary, not necessarily in one and the same study or project, but in the sense that each has something unique to contribute, something that is not reducible to one of the other variants, to policy analysis—or more precisely, as I will argue shortly, to democratic policy analysis. This is an obvious conclusion, but it doesn't hurt to reaffirm it in the polemical environment of IPA. Empiricist and interpretive policy analysis are both necessary in describing, diagnosing, and solving complex, future-oriented, pluralistic policy problems. Let me elaborate on the various contributions by successively discussing two remaining issues: the critical nature of IPA, and its contribution to democracy.

IN WHAT WAYS IS INTERPRETIVE POLICY ANALYSIS CRITICAL?

I think it is fair to say that critique comprises a large part of the allure of IPA. But what does being critical mean if it is to go beyond the by now oft-repeated claim that it is different from traditional EPA? In what way are the different approaches to IPA critical? Let me unpack the claim of critique in this section.

Perusal of the dictionary results in some surprising notions of the adjective "critical." If I restrict myself to meanings relevant to policy analysis, "critical" can be "inclined to judge severely and find fault," but also the almost opposite "characterized by careful, exact evaluation and judgment" (as in "a critical reading"). In a different vein "critical" can mean "[f]orming or having the nature of a turning point; crucial or decisive" (as in "*a critical point in the campaign*"), or, more pointedly and more relevant to the complexity of policy systems, as a tipping point, as "relating to the value of a measurement, such as temperature, at which an abrupt change in a quality, property, or state occurs" (as in "*a critical temperature of water is 100°C, its boiling point at standard atmospheric pressure*"). Also there is "critical" as "relating to a medical crisis" (as in "*an illness at the critical stage*"). A nice meaning of "critical" in the context of policy analysis is "indispensable; essential" (as in "*a critical element of the plan*"). And, also relevant to policy analysis is, finally, "critical" in the meaning of "being in or verging on a state of crisis or emergency" ("*a critical shortage of food*") or "fraught with danger or risk; perilous" (www.thefreedictionary.com/critical). Thus, being critical means many things, and not surprisingly it is not difficult to recognize them in the various approaches to policy analysis. EPA, for example, can be critical in the sense of "careful evaluation" and of pointing out "critical turning points." The act of collecting reliable data about the size of a problem or the way it develops over time is in important ways a critical act. (Particularly when the data show the problem to be much smaller or larger than popular sentiment suggests.) Here we encounter a deeper meaning of "critical"—one underlying many of the dictionary meanings quoted above—which is "lifting the veil of ignorance." This is what enlightenment is all about, after all: being given information, being informed or instructed on a topic, obtaining intellectual insight. Collecting data often makes us aware that there is a problem. (Not surprisingly, as the author otherwise wouldn't have taken the trouble to collect them in the first place. All presentations of "data" project an argument.) Most people, including elected officials and administrators, simply lack the time, resources, or wherewithal to be informed on everything. No one but the most dedicated specialist has enough of an overview of the data to make them cohere into global temperature trends, for example. And, I should add, to do that in a "critical" manner by applying good judgment about the quality of the data.

What about IPA? Hermeneutic IPA is critical in the last-mentioned sense of confronting one's assumptions about the world with the resistances that the world presents to a policy intervention. The difference from EPA is in the type of "data." In the case of hermeneutic IPA they are meanings; the meanings of the people who are affected by the policy intervention. When policy makers create incentives to induce single mothers to get off welfare and find paid work, this policy intervention, or policy "instrument," is based on an image, a set of assumptions, about single mothers ("hard to motivate," "preferring welfare over work," "promiscuous, hedonist lifestyle," "trapped in a culture of poverty," etc.). Most of the time these are assumptions of one, elite, group about another, more marginal, group with whom it has little or no contact. Having one's sacred, taken-for-granted assumptions knocked over by the confrontation with a thick description of the lived world of the target group, is thus an elementary act of critique and enlightenment. (And it fosters democracy too, as I will discuss in the next section.) Another important way in which hermeneutic IPA is critical is in disassembling what is assumed to be coherent. Leadership in local government turns out, on closer inspection, to have at least four different meanings, each of which drive policy interventions. Attitudes toward nuclear power are really a fragmented field of "frames," each with its own coherent set of beliefs, values, images, and action-preferences. Policy makers hate this work of willful fragmentation. It undermines their quest for unity and control. But its importance is that it acknowledges the complexity and pluralism of policy problems, features that everyone who intervenes in the world does well to respect, as we saw earlier in this chapter.

The importance of EPA and hermeneutic IPA lies in their emphasis on fieldwork. The importance of fieldwork is its ability to confront deeply held beliefs about the world. Good, patient fieldwork creates the conditions for learning new things. Not just "facts," but the explanations and conceptualizations that make sense of the "facts." Compared to fieldwork, theory leaves less space for learning. This is the deeper meaning of Austin's famous quote that facts are richer than diction.[26] You can't get more critical than this.

Both camps often overlook how well EPA and hermeneutic IPA work together in critically illuminating a complex policy problem. Again, an obvious point that needs occasional re-affirmation.

A good example is the recent report of the American Political Science Association's Standing Committee on Civic Education and Engagement. The title says it all: *Democracy at Risk: How Political Choices Undermine Citizen Participation, and What We Can Do About It* (Macedo et al., 2005). The authors argue that American democracy is threatened by a series of internal trends. Citizens turn away from politics, are cynical about politicians, and participate less often in civic associations. The risk, as the authors state, is to "the health and survival of our shared political order" (2005, 1). This is a big topic that displays all the trappings of public policy: great complexity, deep fissures of income, ethnicity, and political opinion, and considerable uncertainty regarding adequate courses of action. The authors carefully build their case, drawing on a "rich set of research traditions" that highlights the relationship between political participation and a wide range of personal, demographic, and institutional variables (2005, 3). In subsequent chapters they bring a wealth of survey studies to bear on such questions as whether voter turnout in presidential and congressional elections is stable or has declined. (It has been more or less stable at a rather low level since the 1960s, but it should have increased on the basis of the rising level of education in that period [Macedo et al., 2005, 23].) They also consider whether smaller units of government are related to higher levels of participation. (They are, but problems of scale and diversity mediate the effects of size on civic engagement in important ways [2005, 70].) And they look at whether participation in civic associations is really declining, as Putnam famously asserts. (The authors work around the issue somewhat by focusing on volunteer work and the nonprofit sector. Participation in volunteer work seems to "buck the trend" [2005, 118].)

However, the report is not just a collection of data and statistical associations; it presents an argument, and an important one at that. To make this happen the authors mix interpretive elements into their empiricist stew. How do they do it? First, and most importantly, they state their argument from the very beginning. The problem, as they see it, is that declining levels of civic engagement are surprising because Americans have become better educated and wealthier since roughly the 1970s. Both are strong predictors of civic and political participation. "So," the authors ask:

> why are Americans turning away from politics and civic life? More important, what, if anything, can we do about it? Do we know enough to diagnose the cause and cast light on possible remedies? Our aim here is not simply to join the chorus of those who chronicle civic decline. Nor is it to cast blame on Americans for being poor citizens. Rather our aim is constructive. We believe America can do better by improving the design of institutions and policies that govern our civic and political life. Our central argument is that the levels and distribution of civic activity are themselves political artifacts. Whether consciously intended or not, the design of our current political institutions and practices turns citizens off. (2005, 2)

Democratic participation, civic engagement, is good, the authors argue, because it enhances the quality and legitimacy of democratic government, while it also enriches the life of individual citizens (Macedo et al., 2005, 4). Yet civic participation has declined, not so much because of personal reasons, but because the design of political institutions discourages more active political involvement of citizens (Macedo et al., 2005, 119; see also Mathews, 1999). The argument is the usual hybrid of the empirical and the normative that we so often encounter in policy analysis. Think of the global warming problem, regulation of cloning, services for the chronically mentally ill, leadership in local governance—to mention a few examples from this book. What makes this report valuable as an exercise in policy analysis is that the authors never lose sight of their normative position. The analysis is guided by their values regarding democratic participation, not according to the empiricists' fear that the empirical analysis is distorted or biased by the normative position of the authors, but in the interpretive sense that values suffuse the data with meaning. The normative "*problematique*" of the authors helps them to tell a meaningful story, a story, moreover, that is simultaneously enlightening and critical. Let's illustrate this important point by looking more closely at an example.

An enduring issue in democratic research revolves around the relationship between town size and civic engagement. The evidence seems to point toward an inverse relationship: smaller units of government invite more political participation (Macedo et al., 2005, 70; Oliver, 2000).[27] However, before we start to eulogize small town life, the authors point out that the effects of place on civic life are more complex than these relatively straightforward regression studies suggest. First, there is the dilemma of scale. Certain important public issues, such as redistributive policies, immigration policies, policies "with broad and unconfined benefits," are better dealt with at a higher level than that of the small town. The authors approvingly quote the political scientist Grant McConnell, who says, "A political order composed exclusively of small constituencies, whether drawn on lines of geography, function, or other dimensions, would exclude a variety of genuine values of real concern to the members of society" (quoted in Macedo et al., 2005, 71). Redistributive taxation imposed by small communities may indeed create incentives for the well-off to exit and the worse-off to enter (ibid.). In fact, this is exactly the position of proponents of public choice in metropolitan governance. In their view exit is an important form of political participation, in that citizens votes with their feet to select from among the jurisdictions available the community that best satisfies their particular preference for the public goods offered. The authors are quick to point out, however, that (1) the marketplace approach to metropolitan governance leads to segmentation along lines of class and ethnicity, and (2) that it offers an impoverished vision of civic life (2005, 76). Voting with one's feet represents an unwillingness to engage in public debate, an avoidance of civic engagement. After all, the heart of democratic participation is precisely the willingness and ability to engage in debate with people who hold different views. To sum up: a skilled and careful combination of empirical and interpretive analysis, in combination with normative reasoning, results in an insightful and incisive analysis of the problem of democratic participation in contemporary society. There is another word for this blend of analytic faculties: judgment or wisdom. I mentioned it before. I will return to it later.

Discursive approaches to IPA are the most overtly critical. They wear it on their sleeve. Critique is their selling point. What they have in common is their ability to reveal hidden power differentials. Underneath that critical claim lie the third and fourth faces of power (Digeser, 1992; Lukes, 1975). Both, in slightly different ways, describe the naturalization of power in taken-for-granted beliefs, language conventions, and everyday practices that surreptitiously shape our norms for self-understanding. The mission of discursive IPA is to make these covert traces of power in language and institutions visible. The positive ethical claim is that this act of critical revelation suggests alternative ways of living together. In able hands this is a potent program of policy analytics, as we have seen. A genealogical analysis of a policy domain, when done well, gives the distinct impression of "seeing below the surface," of putting contemporary controversies into perspective against a deeper historical context. A governmentality approach to policy analysis decenters the state into numerous dispersed civil and administrative micro-practices that aggregate into what we call a "policy." Or it articulates the cognitive structures that shape and legitimize what is possible, and even thinkable, in a particular policy domain. Both are sobering enterprises. Both should put a check on dreams of heroic policy making. From the perspective of policy making as an interventionist activity, the limitation of the discursive approach, as we have seen in chapter 6, is its lack of agency. What works as an intellectual exercise works much less as a constructive contribution to concerted collective action. Or, to put it differently, the positive ethics of an analyt-ics of governance approach or critical discourse analysis is weakly developed. Much discursive analysis starts with an a priori ethical claim (usually the subordination of a particular social group), but that leaves the analysis vulnerable to a "so what?" reaction. ("I agree that women, African Americans, Muslim immigrants, are discriminated against. What are we going to do about it?") The critical task of elected officials and administrators is to improve societal conditions that are seen as wrong or dysfunctional. Even if such officials possess the intellectual and moral space to accept the cognitive-linguistic structures that constrain a social domain (and many do), they still want to know what can be done within these constraints. (Or, for the lone brave soul: how to act to break out of the cultural-cognitive fetters and chart a new course.) They simply can't do without agency. Much ordinary policy making is reactive, routine drudgery: acting without understanding. Discursive IPA, however, is often the reverse: understanding without implications for acting.

Dialogical approaches add a different dimension to the critical challenge of IPA: participation. Take fact finding, the strong point of EPA and hermeneutic IPA. As we saw, getting the facts right is a key aspect of policy analysis, but in dialogical IPA the essential contextuality and contesta-tion of facts is taken into account right off the bat. In collaborative planning, action research, or public policy mediation, it is recognized that facts never speak for themselves; different parties attach different values to different constellations of facts. One important phase of dialogical IPA consists of getting to know each other, of gaining mutual understanding (Forester, 2009, 14–15). This is a process that goes far beyond "getting the facts right." Gaining mutual understanding, as Forester makes clear, usually takes place in deeply contested situations. Mutual understanding is therefore above all an act of appreciation, of recognizing and acknowledging the other, even, or especially, when the other holds beliefs or has interests that widely differ from yours or that you consider threatening to your worldview or lifestyle. Gaining mutual understanding also involves appreciating the emotional investment of the other in his position, but not uncritically, and always without denying one's own position. This is hard, emotionally taxing, work. The critical aspect of gaining mutual understanding is that it confronts the beliefs we hold about the other, the motivations we, unreflecting, ascribe to him or her, with a more accurate understanding. Mutual understanding is the willingness and capacity to learn about and from each other. This is no mean feat, for as Connolly has rightly pointed, out our ascriptions of difference are intimately connected with, or more precisely, critical to, our most cherished self-understandings. Critical listening in contested situations not only involves learning about others but also about ourselves. The one does not go without the other: the taken-for-granted assumptions with which we approach the world, how we confuse solutions with interests, what our interests really are in the face of the other, and what we have in common with the other. Or, to put it differently, in learning about ourselves in the process of learning about the other, we find out what binds in addition to what divides us.

Dialogical analysis is also critical in its orientation to the future. Critique tends to be stuck in the present. Forester equates critique with complaint, and says that "[c]omplaint . . . tells us what's wrong—unjust, racist, manipulated, sexist and so on—but tells us nothing new about how the world can be otherwise, how we can change the world, resist injustice, do justice" (2009, 19). That seems overstated to me. There is always a promise of utopia in critique, but mostly implicit, embedded in the implied negation of the exposed injustice. Forester is right in that dialogical IPA (mediation, in his account) aims to make explicit what is desirable and possible. And not just in an abstract, idealized manner, but concretely, here and now, in the face of real-world institutional and personal obstacles (Forester, 2006, 129).[28] This requires, among other things, that we take pluralism seriously. Dialogue is more than advocacy. While advocacy sides with one party (in the name of justice, fairness, equality), dialogical IPA remains in touch with all parties. Its purpose is pragmatic: to attain workable accommodations in a conflicted world. This is not a relinquishing of our ideals, or a cowardly giving-in to the demands of the other, but a recognition of the legitimacy of the other's position, our mutual dependencies, or both. This requires also that the analyst is a skillful designer of dialogical and participatory situations. This is a practical but important task, for the design of a meeting shapes the conditions of possibility for the parties to participate and actually listen to each other (Forester, 2009; Fung, 2004; Innes and Booher, 2003; Podziba, 1998; Susskind et al., 1999).

INTERPRETIVE POLICY ANALYSIS AND DEMOCRACY

I want to conclude this chapter, and this book, with a question that goes to the heart and soul of interpretive policy analysis: to what extent does IPA contribute to democracy? A lot has been written about the relationship between policy analysis (of the mainstream, empiricist, variety) and democracy, much of it critical (deLeon, 1997; Dryzek, 1989; Torgerson, 2003). The standard argument is one of discontent. Although the contribution to promoting and protecting democracy is written into Lasswell's founding charter of policy analysis, little has come of it in practice.[29] So, to explain this fall from grace of mainstream professional policy analysis and articulate what IPA has to contribute to democracy over and above the traditional approach, let's take a closer look at the relationship between policy analysis and democracy.

Let's first agree that, for various reasons, this relationship is exceedingly complex. First, policy analysis and democracy are not just a set of ideas and values but also, and above all, a collection of institutional practices and vested routines. Also, democratic policy analysis has to operate in the real world of politics: complex, suspended in emerging time, conflictual, and action oriented. And finally, allegiance to a democratically ordered society is just one of the pillars of policy analysis. It must also contribute to the betterment of society; its insights and conclusions must contribute to the solution or amelioration of pressing public problems. A policy analysis that is only inclusionary and not effective would amount to no more than an empty ritual. Even in its most modest instrumental definition, policy analysis aspires to improve public policy (Dunn, 2004, 2).[30] But in a more general formulation, policy analysis aspires to rationality as "the capacity to solve the collective problems confronting a polity" (Dryzek, 1989, 99). In other words, it won't do to criticize and reformulate policy analysis at a theoretical level only. That's the relatively easy part. The difficult challenge is this: whatever formulations of policy analysis we can come up with that combine democratic legitimacy with efficacy must withstand the cruel test of politics in the real world. We will see that most of the democratic critique of policy analysis is of the first, theoretical, kind. The reformulations—most of them along participatory lines—are well developed but rest, by way of empirical illustration, on a limited number of examples. I do not claim to present a fully developed, empirically tested alternative to instrumentalist, empiricist policy analysis here. Not only does the short space of a section in a concluding chapter not allow that, but, more importantly, such an alternative has not been articulated by anybody so far as I know. The only thing I can aspire to is to sketch out the direction where such an alternative formulation of a democratic policy analysis for the real world would lead us.

In the wake of the philosophical "restructuring" of policy analysis in the 1970s and 1980s, the late 1980s and early 1990s witnessed a spate of *democratic* critique of traditional policy analysis. A number of policy scholars (Dryzek, Durning, Torgerson, Stone, deLeon) began to address the contribution of policy analysis to democracy. The general thrust of the democratic critique of policy analysis concerned its intellectual roots and its professional practices. Intellectually, policy analysis is said to be beholden to microeconomics and positivism (deLeon, 1994, 1997; Dryzek,

1989; D. Stone, 1997). The first-mentioned intellectual debt applies in particular to Anglo-Saxon policy analysis. Stone rightly observes that the microeconomic model of policy analysis has its roots in a concomitant liberal worldview that sees society in terms of individualism, competition, and the maximization of self-interest (Stone, 1997, 33). That probably explains why this form of policy analysis made fewer inroads in continental Europe, where the prevailing model of society was couched in terms of solidarity, security, and equality. Although the core economic value of efficiency ("in terms of the allocation of scarce resources to welfare-generating policies" [Dryzek, 1989, 101]) has been widely adopted in most European countries (in particular in the wake of the public choice revolution in public administration), economics-inspired tools such as cost-benefit analysis and operations research were not widely applied in the European governance context.[31] In European public administration, efficiency merged with general notions of rational decision making and empiricist ideals of social science into a more diffuse, instrumental, expert-driven understanding of rational policy making and analysis. General rational tools such as program evaluation and evidence-based policy making, in combination with corporate management techniques, became the distinguishing mark of the rational policy maker. A preoccupation with method (with promises of rigor and precision) was that of the academic policy analyst.

The professed goal of most European policy analysis is what Dunn calls "descriptive" and "normative" analysis. Descriptive analysis is explanatory. (See also, Dryzek, 1989, 101.) Its aim is "to establish the approximate validity of causal inferences relating policies to their presumed outcomes" (Dunn, 2004, 14). A quasi-experiment about the effects of police patrolling on the prevalence of crime or a study of the distribution of welfare careers in the population of welfare recipients are examples of this type of explanatory policy analysis. Normative analysis "tests normative and descriptive decision theories" (Dunn, 2004, 14). An evaluation study of welfare-to-work programs would qualify as normative analysis (Balder, 2007). However, the institutional position of many policy analysts results in a different, vulgarized, form of normative analysis. Most policy analysts work inside large government bureaucracies, in for-profit think thanks or research agencies, or within universities but with close ties to government officials. Their research is paid for by government money. They form a professional class of experts whose task it is to advise the government. They identify with the ruling elite they advise and often have close ties to key figures in the administration. In such a set-up, officials and analysts share important values, beliefs, problem definitions, and a horizon of acceptable problem solutions. The result is a rather crude kind of normative analysis, in which the prescriptive link that connects guiding values with policy outcomes is not held to a critical test, but instead normative policies are pushed and legitimized with a veneer of scientific rationality. Affirmation, not critique, is the name of the game.[32] In this way various public sector reforms such as the public choice and new public management revolution in health care, public transportation, and energy have been promoted on the basis of dubious evidence by academically affiliated policy experts (Self, 1993).[33]

The problem with mainstream policy analysis, whether in its microeconomic Anglo-Saxon or descriptive, normative European guise, is that it has profound antidemocratic implications *in practice*. Dryzek summarizes them for us: It preempts political debate with the imposition of narrow value judgments such as economic efficiency. It treats ends as fixed prior to contemplation of a problem and conceives of politics in terms of technological fixes by experts. It reinforces hierarchical (and, I would add, managerial) notions of control of human beings, and affirms the (ideological) status quo (1989, 101). By stressing "in practice" I mean to say that these baneful effects are not willfully imposed on society by a sinister elite, but instead are the almost innocuous, but inevitable, by-products of "the day-to-day production of analysis" (Dryzek, 1989, 102). In other words, the Fourth Face of Power again.

A reasonable objection to this argument would be that it is exaggerated and therefore unfair. If we leave the inevitable excesses aside, the large majority of public officials and experts in the liberal democracies of the West are reasonable and well-intentioned and wholeheartedly subscribe to the principles of democracy. Point taken, but it raises the important question: What democracy? The term "democracy" covers an incredibly wide range of ideals, beliefs, practices, and procedures (Held, 1996), so it is important that we are clear what kind of democracy we have in mind when we criticize mainstream policy analysis. To articulate an alternative to mainstream policy analysis (and to make our critique stick), we first need to address the underlying question: What is democracy?

Clearly, we cannot even begin to do justice to one of the most prolific chapters in political theory. So let me, for purposes of discussion, boil this vast question down to one seminal principle: political equality. Call it a minimal norm. Whatever theoretical or institutional form of democracy one prefers, limited or expanded, if it doesn't include some normative and institutional allegiance to the principle that "every individual potentially affected by a decision should have an equal opportunity to affect the decision" (Warren, 2002, 678), it cannot properly be designated as democracy. Warren immediately concedes that in today's liberal democracies the principle of political equality is usually restricted to voting. Considerations of scale, complexity, differentiation, and excessive pluralism allegedly impose considerable restrictions on a fuller, more participatory rendering of the principle of the maximization of rule by and for the people (Warren, 2002, 679). In addition, a combination of widespread voter apathy and the domination of the public debate by vast administrative and corporate bureaucracies would certainly seem to have dimmed the prospects for the more inclusive forms of democracy that are embedded in the ideal of political equality. Yet, as Warren argues, this kind of democratic realism is very much a self-reinforcing set of arguments and observations that conceals the fact that democratic expectations are indeed growing within contemporary liberal democracies.[34]

First, what appears as voter apathy is really voter disaffection (Mathews, 1999; Warren, 2002). Citizens have not turned away from politics and government but from politics and government in their common liberal democratic form. Citizens expect a different kind of politics: more responsive, more accountable, less cynical, with better performance and less incompetence and graft (Boyte, 2004; Mathews, 1999; Warren, 2002, 681). Citizens feel "displaced" and "driven out by a professional political class" as Mathews puts it (1999, 15). Second, in today's fragmented, decentered field of governance with its multitude of organizations and actors, collective problem solving is no longer the sole prerogative of the state. Corporate actors, NGOs, professionals, and citizen associations "replace, displace, or work in concert with state powers" (Warren, 2002, 682; see also Hajer & Wagenaar, 2003). Contemporary democratic theorists conclude from this that the traditional distinction between representation and participation is eroding. For example, reading through Warren's account of the enhanced democratic representation that is required in today's complex, differentiated, fragmented field of governance, one can only conclude that it shows remarkable similarities, in terms of the necessary skills and organizational forms, with democratic participation. (For similar arguments, see also Castiglione & Warren, 2005; Pitkin, 1967; Plotke, 1997; Saward, 2006.) As Saward states, representative claims are no longer the prerogative of democratically elected officials but are put forward by a multitude of actors, ranging from NGOs to celebrities. Moreover, and perhaps more importantly, each claim is assessed and if necessary challenged, by groups who amend or resist the political identity that is bestowed upon them by the representative (2006). Or, analysis of collective problem solving in complex urban environments shows that the efforts of governments standing alone fall far short of the mark. In the contemporary urban environment "[p]ublic policy impacts (and therefore public policies) depend on complementary actions from nongovernmental sources" (C.N. Stone, 2005, 311).

The upshot of these developments in democratic theory is that democracy is no longer seen as something that stands apart from governance. Democracy is no longer an ideational and institutional background against which the (instrumental) business of governing takes place. In many, but certainly not all, policy domains, democracy is now seen as an intrinsic characteristic of governance.[35] Contemporary understandings of governance, "in all its ambiguities, untidiness, and contradiction" (De Souza Briggs, 2008, ix) are intimately linked up with notions of democratic legitimacy. For large classes of collective problems—wicked, complex, nonroutine problems with a large potential for contingent side-effects—states simply don't have the wherewithal to design and put through effective solutions. In such cases the challenge is to bring together and sustain over considerable periods of time coalitions of stakeholders, including grassroots involvement (De Souza Briggs, 2008; Stoker, 1995; Stone et al., 2001, 315).[36] And, although the state plays an important role in such coalitions, more often than not the impetus for the formation of such civic coalitions rests outside the sphere of government. Differently put, in decentered settings democratic inclusion has become intrinsic to effective governance. In fact, effective governance and public administration in complex, fragmented policy environments is seen to rest on three pillars: democratic legitimacy ("meaningful and consequential participation in public life" (De Souza Briggs, 2008, 34), effectiveness (getting things done; having an impact; transcending "talk, talk, talk" (De Souza Briggs, 2008, 9; Forester, 2009) and accountability ("the need to rethink accountability relationships in the context of community leadership" (Stoker, 2002, 38; 2006). In practice that means that democracy today, to return to our initial question, consists of highly pluralistic and fluid ensembles of actors organized around concrete societal problems, often uncomfortably positioned in relation to the traditional institutional structures of liberal representative democracy. It is within these complex and shifting environments of democratic governance that contemporary policy analysis functions.

What does this mean for the democratic prospects of policy analysis and in particular IPA? The early critics of the anti-democratic implications of mainstream policy analysis agreed on some form of participatory policy analysis as an alternative to technocratic, instrumentalist policy analysis (deLeon, 1997; Dryzek, 1989; Torgerson, 1986). With the exception of urban planning, in the late 1980s participatory policy analysis (PPA) was more an ideal than a reality in professional policy analysis, so calls for PPA necessarily were largely programmatic. The blueprint for PPA contained elements of inclusive participation in free and open deliberations about collective problems, the transformation of the detached expert-adviser into a facilitator of public deliberation, and the introduction of an "interpretative or hermeneutic paradigm of inquiry" (deLeon, 1997, 111; Dryzek, 1989; Torgerson, 1986, 41). How these were to be integrated into an everyday, professional disciplinary practice of policy analysis was left unspecified, however. As so often, developments in the real world of policy making overtook these discussions among professionals. Faced with a severe legitimation crisis and overwhelmed by global trends in immigration, climate change, and economic restructuring, policy makers, stakeholders, and citizens feverishly sought for answers to fight such structural collective problems as poverty, ethnic integration, the deterioration of inner cities, a crumbling school system, environmental degradation, and crime and antisocial behavior. Partly driven by administrative trends toward decentralization and privatization, partly by the emergence of new, autonomous players in the field of governance, the result is the highly decentered form of governance that I described above.[37] Within this world of decentered governance PPA, or, as I will argue, IPA, is no longer an ideal but a dire necessity.

In many ways IPA, and by this I mean something broader than the early articulations of

PPA, is ideally positioned to contribute to decentered governance. First, the less state-centered, more pluralistic governance environment opens up more opportunities for IPA in all its different manifestations. Not only have policy analysts a much broader repertoire of analytic approaches at their disposal, they are also no longer beholden to one designated client, government agencies. For example, to confront the assumptions of a particular policy by showing how it affects the life-world of a particular marginal group is, in the decentered world of governance, an act of democratic inclusion. The interpretive analyst in fact amplifies the voice of an otherwise excluded group. It is a relatively easy next step for the analyst to try to persuade public authorities to include the excluded group in public deliberations about better policies (Wagenaar & Specht, 2010). Similarly, analysts can offer their services to groups other than public authorities, such as NGOs or citizen groups. A good example of the latter is the activities of Residents4Regeneration (R4R). R4R is a movement of citizen associations throughout Europe assisted by a small group of advisers and academics, who assemble, exchange knowledge, and organize for action for the purpose of neighborhood revitalization (www.r4r-europe.com). In R4R we see many elements of the democratic potential of IPA in the new constellation of governance. While R4R is organized by citizens for citizens, the role of the advisers and academics consists of facilitating (at meetings of the Resident University,[38] youth conferences, exchange visits for citizen activists, doing research (qualitative, ethnographic research into the nature of and conditions for successful bottom-up citizen participation [Wagenaar & Specht, 2010]); and disseminating experience, practical knowledge, and research results.

Decentered governance has opened up the discipline for the influx of important practical and intellectual developments outside the direct sphere of professional policy analysis. In our collection Deliberative Policy Analysis, Hajer and I brought developments in democratic political theory, collaborative planning, public policy mediation, and discourse and practice theory into policy studies (Hajer & Wagenaar, 2003). In our introductory essay we propose a deliberative policy analysis that is interpretive and practice oriented. It is easy to read the hermeneutic, critical-discursive, and dialogical forms of IPA into our proposal for a deliberative policy analysis. Similarly, collaborative planning and public policy mediation are rapidly making inroads in contemporary policy analysis. Key scholars in these traditions such as Forester, Healey, Innes, and Podziba are frequent guests at conferences on IPA and act as advisers on research projects on multi-stakeholder governance (www.nicis.nl/nicis). Even more important, their seminal works are assigned to curricula on policy analysis, where, at least in Europe, a new generation of policy scholars is being formed who are as familiar with qualitative policy research and discourse analysis as they are with multiple regression techniques and pseudo-experimental research designs. Although it would go too far to describe IPA as a fully developed and accepted form of professional policy analysis, it has progressed beyond the "dim" apparition on the horizon of professional policy research that Torgerson witnessed in 1986 (1986, 39). Under the influence of the rapid changes in the field of governance, IPA has evolved into a powerful and vital alternative to mainstream analysis.

CONCLUSION

The incompatibility theorem has hovered over the social sciences since the early days of phenomenology, now more than a century ago. It states, as we saw, that a social science that is true to its subject, the life-world of everyday human beings, must be able to elucidate what is characteristic of that world, namely that it is meaningful, intentional, value laden, and action driven. We cannot hope to understand social phenomena unless we are able to situate that understanding in categories of human action (Bernstein, 1976 154). Applying the impossibility theorem to policy analysis,

I reformulated it in terms of fit. A policy analysis that is true to its subject, the world of politics and collective problem solving, should accord to that subject. There is much discussion about what it is exactly that characterizes the world of politics and collective decision making, with some descriptions being rather impressionistic (policy making is political), and others steeped in sociological imagery (policy is currently made in networks). I suggested that we will get closer to our goal of outlining a relevant policy analysis when we take the action-oriented character of policy making seriously. Public officials live under the imperative to act on a situation that is considered unacceptable or in need of improvement. By implication policy analysis also attains an actionable character; it stands in the service of those whose task it is to act on the situation at hand and do that in a legitimate and effective manner. This then confronts policy analysts with three characteristics of the world of policy making that every public official has to reckon with. They must be reckoned with because they capture something essential—essential in the sense that they determine the limits and possibilities of policy making. For this reason I call them design independent; no matter what our plans and intentions for a particular slice of the world are, we will always run into complexity, the flow of emerging time, and the various forms of pluralism.

So, the conclusion of this book is that a policy analysis that fits its subject should not only do justice to schemes of meaning and intention, but on top of that it should be action oriented, and take complexity, time, and pluralism into account. That's a tall order. It is not enough to state that policy analysis must be interpretive and normative; it must also be able to throw light on the effects that complexity, time, and pluralism have on the process and outcomes of public policy. It must be able to assist in navigating policies into the fog of emerging time and steering them between the shoals of irredeemable value conflict. That these are not merely theoretical categories is amply proven by the recent developments in the field of governance that I have described. In most policy domains contemporary governance is now a shifting, uneasy alliance of stakeholders who are grouped around concrete societal problems, often uncomfortably positioned in relation to the traditional institutional structures of liberal representative democracy. In this concluding section I will briefly discuss this second part of the compatibility equation. I will elaborate the notion of fit in two ways: as dealing with the limits on policy making and with the creative, productive possibilities these limits hold out.

Complexity, time, and pluralism set limits to policy making. In a shorthand kind of way, these limits can be described as limits to understanding, limits to designing the good life, and limits to organizing the good life. Taken together, all three result in constraints on the capacity to control collective problem solving. The indeterminacy that follows from the cascading interactions in a loosely coupled complex system and the constant emergence of novelty in "the twists and swerves in the flow of time" (Connolly, 2005, 110) make it hard to understand and predict what is going on while we are in the middle of it. Anticipation is difficult if not impossible, and whatever understanding we have of the situation at hand is imposed on the situation retrospectively. The inevitable conflict among the values we deem essential for our conception of the good life make it hard to realize that ideal. The incompatibility and incommensurability of values can be denied or acknowledged. In the first case policy makers rally behind one value (equality, economic efficiency, safety) that they declare overriding, and worry about the negative unintended consequences of their policies later. In the second case the policy design reflects the tensions among multiple key values but feels like a lame compromise, and policy makers experience a sense of loss and fear public disapproval. Finally, the realities of asymmetrical power relations and conflicts of interest in our political institutions make it difficult to effectuate and implement whatever compromise in good living we have arrived at. Again we see two types of reactions. Those affected by policy decisions that they consider antithetical to their interests will resist them as much as they can.

Alternatively, when a despised policy cannot be averted the affected parties will "play the system" by using the policy in such a way that it is more conducive to their own interests and practices (Wagenaar, 1995).

However, acknowledging complexity, time, and pluralism is not synonymous with fatalism. Although choices can be tragic, and the wise policy maker is attuned to a sense of the tragic, in the final analysis value conflict can be a source of novelty, discovery, and creativity. People make effective, creative, and feasible choices all the time in situations where understanding is limited and design is thwarted by irredeemable conflict. Indeterminacy and pluralism wreak havoc on policy strategies that aim at control and centralization, but there are many strategies for dealing with situations of limited understanding and deep value conflict. So, how then do policy makers and administrators deal with complexity, emerging time, and pluralism in ordinary circumstances?

To arrive at judgments policy makers employ different strategies. Key, as we have seen, is the experiential, hands-on knowledge that is embedded in *practices*. What makes practices pertinent to indeterminism, dynamic change, and pluralism is their contextuality and emerging character. Context is a relational term; it signifies both the active, ongoing relationship that an actor maintains between himself and his environment, and the fact that this relationship is driven by the particular intentions and understandings of the individual as they emanate from the task that he engages in. Instead of passively reacting to the constraints of a particular context, the term "setting" denotes that the actor purposively seeks out those elements of his environment that are relevant to the task at hand. In this sense the actor "negotiates" his environment by actively designing accommodations to the resistances he encounters.[39] (See Schön and Rein's "design rationality.") This negotiating is largely habitual, routine, and second nature, but at the same time open and improvisational and guided by purpose. In this sense, practice is always *situated,* meaning that the actor and his setting mutually bring each other into being in the course of participating in a particular practice, and *action-driven*, that is, "carried in patterns of appropriate action" (Taylor, 1995b, 51).

But practice is a blanket term. Under its auspices many subtle, hard-to-perceive, hard-to-describe skills and activities occur that we deal with every day. We engage in practical judgment (Beiner, 1983), in which we display a greater or lesser degree of wisdom (Sternberg, 1990). We employ self-knowledge in reflection (Velleman, 1989), and we explore the possibilities of life and negotiate the unknown future by various forms of moral imagination (Kekes, 1993; Warnock, 1976). We gain a better understanding of problems and imagine possibilities for resolution by engaging in intensive interaction with our colleagues and peers. Through the mutual disclosure of interests we not only learn about what we really want, but also build solutions that accommodate instead of compromise (Forester, 2009, 24). We attempt to deal with unavoidable conflict by deliberating, negotiating, and engaging in various forms of conflict resolution (Forester, 1999a, 2009; Innes, 2003; Kekes, 1993; Susskind et al., 1999).

What these skills and activities have in common is that they project a policy analysis that is a form of becoming, a kind of guided improvisation. This kind of policy analysis, that I have called IPA, does not fixate the future by stipulating policy goals, but treats goals as intentions, as a form of imagining. This kind of policy analysis is open-ended, attentive to the emergent effects of unforeseen and unpredictable interaction effects in complex social systems. In this sense it recognizes time as the development of action, encompassing past experience and future imagination in its attempt to negotiate the evolving nature of the present. It uses the inevitable partiality of a point of view not as a form of distortion and bias to be avoided, but as the starting point for dialogue and joint exploration (Gadamer, 1989; Innes & Booher, 2003, 2010; Taylor, 2002). It deals with political pluralism through agonistic respect, critical responsiveness, and democratic listening (Bickford, 1996; Connolly, 2005; Mouffe 2000). IPA is hermeneutic, participatory, and dialogical; it involves professionals and stakeholders in the definition of problems, the cogeneration of relevant knowledge, and the interpretation of experience (Greenwood & Levin, 1998). Its aim is not certain knowledge and the exorcism of bias and political conflict from the policy-making process, but instead the return of the political to policy making. *Interpretive policy analysis* is concrete, interactive, hermeneutic, pragmatic, personal, and action oriented. It aims as much at good results as at proper procedure. But what counts as a result is not the definitive resolution of a conflict, but the temporary stabilization of a situation that is unhinged or threatens to become so. In the final analysis *interpretive policy analysis,* in all its manifestations, is a powerful affirmation of Lasswell's ideal of the policy science of democracy.

NOTES

1. Compare Pickering, 1995, 6: "Much of everyday life, I would say, has this character of coping with material agency, agency that comes at us from outside the human realm and that cannot be reduced to anything within that realm." See also Hacking, 1983, 146: "We shall count as real what we can use to intervene in the world to affect something else, or what the world can use to affect us."

2. Essentialism in philosophy attempts to distinguish the crucial from the merely accidental. "Essentialism is generally taken to be the doctrine that objects have certain properties which make them one kind of a thing rather than any other" (Sayer, 2000, 82). Essentialism is often confused with reductionism, but those features that are deemed to be crucial for the thing to be what it is are not its only features, and certainly not its only important features. Essentialism is also often confused with foundationalism. That is, the features that are considered crucial are thought to be so certain or true that they are deemed obvious or "transparent," as requiring no explanation outside the ordinary regime of inquiry and confirmation. Sayer, who has written a useful and clarifying chapter on essentialism in the social sciences, believes that the concept is made to do too much. Generally it is used in a generative and identifying way, and the two are not necessarily compatible. Policy is conditioned by complexity, time, and pluralism, but we cannot very well use these features to distinguish it from other collective activities. Sometimes the two functions do coincide. Sayer comes up with the example of the capital-labor relation as the essence of capitalism, both in a generative and a distinguishing sense. But capitalism has other essential features, such as industrialism, which do not distinguish it from socialism, for example. Finally, Sayer makes the useful statement that referring to essential characteristics is not the same as asserting sameness. I have already argued that it might very well be the nonessential features that are most important in understanding a phenomenon. What we should be concerned about, according to Sayer, is mistaken claims of homogeneity. "We should be concerned about assertions of non-existent commonalities or denials of significant differences, and equally about assertions of insignificant differences and/ or denials of significant commonalities" (2000, 83). Racism, Sayer adds, involves both kinds of error.

3. Or other policy texts, for that matter. I am thinking here of the traditional policy stages model that organizes many textbooks in policy analysis, or a differentiation in policy aspects. I consider these as aspects that are imposed by the analyst, and that are therefore design dependent.

4. For this reason I refrain from calling complexity, time, and pluralism a policy ontology. The term ontology refers to the categorical preconditions for the existence of objects and the possibility of their investigation. (See also Glynos & Howarth, 2007, 163.) Moreover, the term "ontology" has a ring of the foundational. As I argued above, complexity, time, and pluralism are not preconditions of existence of public policy, but features that condition its limits and possibilities. Moreover, I do not claim that these three exhaust the generative properties of policy making. For example, policy making is, by definition, an interventionist, performative activity. Yet, most policy analysis is representational in that it seeks to produce knowledge that maps or mirrors the world as it "really is" (Pickering, 1995, 5). Obviously one can faithfully describe an intervention; however, sticking with our quest for fit and relevance, it could well be argued that an alternative, performative description of policy making, as agents doing things in real time, opens up another, more actionable understanding of public policy, that is more true to its interventionist nature. However, such an undertaking would go well beyond the aims of this book.

5. Waldrop provides an estimate that there are 10^{120} possible moves in chess, and adds that it is "a number so vast [as] to defy all metaphor" (1992, 151).

6. In some policy areas analysts begin to exhibit an understanding of the emergent properties of the policy system as something above and beyond the properties of the individual parts. For example, the food

sector is now regularly framed as a chain, in which problems in one part of the chain can have disastrous consequences higher up in the chain. Similarly, among some scholars and policy makers the Dutch disability law is regarded as complex system of employers, employees, administrators, certifying physicians, overseers, and others, whose interactions add up to undesired outcomes that are extremely resistant to policy intervention.

7. For this reason, experts who deal with dynamic, integrated systems, such as climate change or urban development, usually build models or formulate scenarios. The understanding is that the models do not so much predict (therefore the number of variables and interactions is too large), but function as heuristics in public discussions about the nature of the problem and the shape of possible solutions. One needs models or scenarios as aids for judgment and learning. I will return to this point in discussing time.

8. The term "trajectory" is from Strauss (1993). It denotes both a development of something from A to B, plus the (at least partially) contingent nature of that development.

9. The concept of coevolution has been introduced in complexity theory to deal with the circumstance that complex systems evolve without a central planner who directs the system toward a preconceived goal. In fact, complex systems, physical, biological, and social, self-organize and evolve without there being very clearly defined problems for the agents to struggle with, and without a clearly circumscribed criterion of fitness or reward to decide in advance who might win or lose out. As Axelrod and Cohen put it, "Harnessing complexity involves acting sensibly without fully understanding how the world works" (1999, 45). Coevolution answers to this that agents evolve and system states emerge because everyone is constantly adapting to everyone else. Agents and systems evolve because they form each other's environment, effectively dissolving the age-old dichotomy between actor and context.

10. With the quotation marks I want to indicate the problem of language as one expression of the continuity of system and observer. The quoted phrase is typical of the way that neighborhoods such as the *Mathenesserkwartier* are described in the public sphere. The whole point of the example, and of Blondeel's study, is to show that underneath this official image, a different neighborhood exists that can be accessed with ethnographic observation. Blondeel himself speaks of "strong" and "weak facts."

11. Blondeel observes an "informal economy of temporary and made-to-order subcontracting for example in connection with the car business on the *Mathenessserdijk*. The same goes for the furniture industry, for the packaging industry, and the supply of parts for regular retail businesses. It is important that we do not neglect these networks when we talk about social cohesion" (2005, 49).

12. The information on the model of global, energy-related CO_2 emissions in this section comes from Peake and Smith, 2009.

13. Any direct advice from consultants to political decision makers falls under this category, but I am reluctant to discuss this large element of institutionalized policy analysis because of its weak analytic base.

14. Take the opening sentences of the chapter "Valuation of Future Consequences: Discounting" in Stokey and Zeckhauser: "Many decisions made today will have repercussions next year and in the years thereafter. Some decisions will have effects that stretch for decades" (1978, 159).

15. See also Adam, 1990, 153: "The Newtonian-Cartesian understanding [of time] causes yet another difficulty. Elias insists that we need to understand time as an immense synthesis rather than an abstraction. However, the conceptual tools that are being used to understand this synthesis are, as we have seen, based on an understanding of reality that abstracts bits, particles, aspects, units, events, or periods in order to understand them. It is becoming obvious that the wrong conceptual tools are being used to if we seek to grasp and theorise synthesis, qualitative rhythmicity, intensity and a causal relationships with the aid of Newtonian and Cartesian assumptions."

16. There are clear echoes here of Gadamer's notion of the fusion of horizons.

17. More echoes of Gadamer, this time of his central idea of the surfeit of reality.

18. Yet, at the same time, it is these barely understood preliminary affinities and intuitions that enable us to act at all, and to engage in the patterned, contextualized stream of activities that we call "practice." I will return to practice, and the way it is embedded in an unarticulated reservoir of background knowledge, in the next section, on pluralism and in the conclusion of this chapter.

19. There is an inner complexity to this statement that I do not have the space to go into here. Let me just say that I want to steer clear of both subjectivism and naïve realism. See Pickering (1995) for an actionable depiction of objective knowledge that subtly balances subjective purpose and material agency.

20. The resonances with Gadamer's surfeit of reality are obvious.

21. The obvious exceptions are Rein in his analysis of the conflicting frames that structure a policy controversy, and D. Stone, who builds her conception of policy analysis around the public deliberation over

conflicting interpretations of core values such equality or efficiency (Rein, 1983a; Schön & Rein, 1994; D. Stone, 1997).

22. For a more extended and formal treatment of incommensurability, see Kekes (1993) and Raz (1986). Raz defines incommensurability as a breakdown of transitivity: "Two valuable options are incommensurable if (1) neither is better than the other, and (2) there is (or could be) another option which is better than one but is not better than the other" (1986, 325). One of the main reasons for such a failure of transitivity is an "incomplete definition of the contribution of criteria to a value." That is, the criteria that make up the value of the options are so numerous, and in addition are themselves evaluations, that we are unable to arrive at any stable and definitive ranking. This in turn makes it impossible to compare such a complex option with another, usually equally complex option, be they the relative merits of great writers or the rightness of two great values.

23. Loss as a concomitant of tragic choices has been described by several authors on value conflict; a particularly eloquent description comes from Kekes: "The sense of loss, therefore, is a frequent experience in our lives. It need not be due to having made a choice that we come to regret. For we can feel that we have lost something important even if we are convinced that we have made the right choice and that we would make it again if we had to. If the loss is accompanied by regret, the regret is about life's being such as to exclude the realization of all the values we prize" (1993, 54). See also Hampshire (1983), Stocker (1990), and Berlin (1997).

24. A rare exception is Adams and Balfour, 2009

25. For an example that is as impressive as it is disturbing, and in which all of these power mechanisms are in play, see Porter (2009). Porter has interviewed residents who were relocated because of the organization of large sporting events.

26. The full quote is: "[H]owever well equipped our language, it can never be forearmed against all possible cases that may arise and call for description: fact is richer than diction" (Austin, 1979, 195). The quote was kindly suggested to me by John Forester.

27. While the statistics point in the same direction, the explanation of these numbers is, as always, more speculative. People participate in smaller towns, it has been suggested, because they know each other, because they feel that they can make a difference, or because residents of smaller places are more likely to trust each other (Macedo et al., 2005, 70).

28. "In applied settings, in the face of complex projects and policy and project disputes, planners' interviews, we will see, need to reach far beyond traditional survey research interviews, and far beyond even ethnographic interviews, in part because planners must try not only to explain, not only to understand, but also to imagine, clarify, and refine–actually design!–future action. So they must try both to probe and to organize possibilities and thus too, profoundly, in revealing those possibilities, they work to organize hope" (Forester, 2006, 129).

29. Upon careful reading one must admit that Lasswell hedges his bets on the prospect of a democratic policy analysis. Although throughout his work he speaks of a "policy sciences of democracy" and indicates some of its elements, he sees the emergence of a policy science in the service of democracy as at best a possibility: "It is *probable* that the policy-science orientation in the United States will be directed toward providing the knowledge needed to improve the practice of democracy" (1951, 15; italics added). Lasswell's is above all a programmatic statement that later generations have to develop and effectuate.

30. I don't mean this pejoratively, but in relation to Lasswell's more grandiose claims for policy analysis as a beacon of enlightened human progress.

31. Economic modeling is a different story. At least in my own country, the Netherlands, this form of policy analysis has been elevated to the dominant analytic approach by the national agencies that monitor and evaluate, often ex-ante, the economic policies of national governments.

32. This type of everyday, mainstream policy analysis is what Torgerson calls the second face of policy analysis, which he characterizes as follows: "While claiming an allegiance to reason, conventional policy analysis not only serves particular interests, but also reinforces the order and ideology of the established political world" (1986, 38).

33. The repeated complaint that the policy sciences are of marginal use to policy makers and that they lack a coherent body of theory on which to base policy recommendations (deLeon, 1997; Fischer, 2003a) are beside the point. The usefulness of policy analysts to public officials is not so much in the results of scientific research as in the legitimization that "scientific" research provides to government policy.

34. For a superb treatment of the emergence of "democratic realism," and its self-referential nature, see Westbrook (1991), chapter 9.

35. The exceptions to this observation are national security, foreign and economic policy, and in Europe, much EU policy. In these domains policy is still largely determined by a small, centralized elite of policy makers.

36. The key concept here is "civic capacity." Discussing the case of school reform, C.N. Stone et al. state: "Civic capacity concerns the extent to which different sectors of the community–business, parents, educators, state and local officeholders, nonprofits, and others–act in concert around matters of community-wide import. It involves mobilization—that is, bringing different sectors together but also developing a shared plan of action" (2001, 596).

37. The notion of decenteredness goes beyond the surface meaning that collective decision making is distributed over a wide array of actors and sites in contemporary governance. It does not merely denote the dispersion of collective decision making throughout society, or the functional differentiation of mutually dependent and complementary actors in policy networks, but rather the contingent construction of meaning by actors who face all sorts of challenges and dilemmas (Bevir, 2003, 209). A decentered approach to governance gives a wide berth to agency as it thinks of institutions, societal problems, policy networks and democracy as created and sustained by actors who, operating within large societal frames (Rein, 1983; Schön and Rein, 1993) or traditions (Bevir and Rhodes, 2003, 2006) struggle with dilemmas and dislocations. To be able to observe, understand and explain decentered governance we, thus, need an interpretive methodology.

38. This is a virtual university that "emerges" every time the citizen associations meet in one of the member countries to address a particular issue, such as "opportunities for inner city youth," or "disadvantaged neighborhoods and the press."

39. Compare Wenger (1998): "I intend the term *negotiation* to convey a flavour of continuous interaction, of gradual achievement, and of give-and-take." See Pickering (1995) for the dialectic of resistance and accommodation that he sees as central to practice.

REFERENCES

Abbott, A. (2004). *Methods of Discovery: Heuristics for the Social Sciences*. New York: W.W. Norton.

Abma, T. (1997). "Machtige Verhalen: Over de Rol van Verhalen ter Continuering en Verandering van de Professionele Praktijk in een Psychiatrisch Ziekenhuis" (Powerful stories: About the role of stories in the maintenance and change of professional practice in a mental hospital). *Beleid & Maatschappij* 24(1): 21–32.

———. (1999). "Introduction: Narrative perspectives on Program Evaluation." In *Telling Tales: On Evaluation and Narrative*, ed. T. Abma. Stamford, CT: JAI Press, 1–29.

Adam, B. (1990). *Time and Social Theory*. Cambridge: Polity Press.

Adams, G.B., and D.L. Balfour. (2009). *Unmasking Administrative Evil*. 3d ed. Armonk, NY: M.E. Sharpe.

Allen, B. (1993). *Truth in Philosophy*. Cambridge, MA: Harvard University Press.

———. (1998). "Foucault and Modern Political Philosophy." In *The Later Foucault: Politics and Philosophy*, ed. J. Moss. Thousand Oaks, CA: Sage Publications, 164–98.

Allison, G., and P. Zelikow. (1999). *Essence of Decision: Explaining the Cuban Missile Crisis*. New York: Longman.

Archer, M.S. (1995). *Realist Social Theory: The Morphogenetic Approach*. Cambridge: Cambridge University Press.

Aristotle. (1984). *Poetics*. Vol. 2 of *The Complete Works of Aristotle: The Revised Oxford Translation*, ed. J. Barnes. Princeton, NJ: Princeton University Press, 2316–41.

Arnstein, S. R. (1969). "A Ladder of Citizen Participation." *Journal of the American Institute of Planners*. 35(4): 216–24.

Asante, A., and K. Schaapman. (2005). *Het Onzichtbare Zichtbaar Gemaakt: Prostitutie in Amsterdam Anno 2005* (The invisible made visible: Prostitution in Amsterdam anno 2005). Amsterdam: Partij van de Arbeid.

Austin, J.L. (1979). *Philosophical Papers*, ed. J.O. Urmson and G.J. Warnock. 3d ed. Oxford, UK: Clarendon Press.

Axelrod, R., and M.D. Cohen. (1999). *Harnessing Complexity: Organizational Implications of a Scientific Frontier*. New York: Free Press.

Balder, C. (2007). "De betekenis van bijstand: Een Kwalitatief Onderzoek onder Bijstandscliënten en Medewerkers van de Sociale Dienst van de Gemeente Leiden" (The meaning of welfare. A qualitative study among welfare recipients and caseworkers of the welfare office of the City of Leiden). Unpublished report, Leiden, NL.

Bang, H.P., and E. Sørensen. (1999). "The Everyday Maker: A New Challenge to Democratic Governance." *Administrative Theory and Praxis* 21(3): 325–41.

Barry, A., T. Osborne, and N. Rose (eds.). (1996). *Foucault and Political Reason: Liberalism, Neo-Liberalism and Rationalities of Government*. London: Routledge.

Becker, H.S. (1996). "The Epistemology of Qualitative Research." In *Ethnography and Human Development: Context and Meaning in Social Inquiry*, ed. R. Jessor, A. Colby, and R.A. Shweder. Chicago, IL: University of Chicago Press, 53–71.

Beiner, R. (1983). *Political Judgment*. London: Methuen.

Berger, P.L., and T. Luckmann. (1967). *The Social Construction of Reality: A Treatise in the Sociology of Knowledge*. Anchor Books.

Berlin, I. (1997). *The Proper Study of Mankind: An Anthology of Essays*. London: Chatto and Windus.

Bernauer, J., and M. Mahon. (2003). "Michel Foucault's Ethical Imagination." In *The Cambridge Companion to Foucault*, ed. G. Gutting. Cambridge: Cambridge University Press, 149–75.

Bernstein, R.J. (1976). *The Restructuring of Social and Political Theory*. Philadelphia: University of Pennsylvania Press.

Bevir, M. (1999). "Foucault, Power, and Institutions." *Political Studies* 47: 345–59.

———. (2003). "A Decentred Theory of Governance." In *Governance as Social and Political Communication,* ed. H.P. Bang. Manchester, UK: Manchester University Press, 200–22.

———. (2006). "How Narrative Explains." In *Interpretation and Method. Empirical Research Methods and the Empirical Turn*, ed. D. Yanow and P. Schwartz-Shea. Armonk, NY: M.E. Sharpe, 281–91.

Bevir, M., and R.A.W. Rhodes. (2002). "Interpretive Theory." In *Theory and Methods in Political Science*, ed. D. Marsh and G. Stoker. 2d ed. New York: Palgrave Macmillan: 131–53.

———. (2003). *Interpreting British Governance*. London: Routledge.

———. (2004). "Interpreting British Governance." *The British Journal of Politics and International Relations* 6(2): 130–36.

———. (2006a). *Governance Stories*. Milton Park, UK: Routledge.

———. (2006b). "Interpretive Approaches to British Governance and Politics." *British Politics* 1(1): 84–112.

Bickford, S. (1996). *The Dissonance of Democracy: Listening, Conflict, and Citizenship*. Ithaca, NY: Cornell University Press.

Bleicher, J. (1980). *Contemporary Hermeneutics: Heremeneutics as Method, Philosophy and Critique*. London: Routledge and Kegan Paul.

Blokland, T. (2003). *Urban Bonds*. Cambridge, UK: Polity Press.

Blondeel, P. (2005). "Reading and (Re)writing the City: the Use of the *Habitus*. Concept in Urban Research and Development." Paper presented at the conference "Doing, Thinking Feeling Home: The Mental Geography of Residential Environments," October 14–15, 2005. Delft, The Netherlands.

Bobrow, D.B., and J.S. Dryzek. (1987). *Policy Analysis by Design*. Pittsburgh, PA: University of Pittsburgh Press.

Bohman, J.F. (1996). *Public Deliberation: Pluralism, Complexity, and Democracy*. Cambridge, MA: MIT Press.

Bohman, J.F. et al. (1991). "Introduction: The Interpretive Turn." In *The Interpretive Turn: Philosophy, Science, Culture*, ed. D.R. Hiley, J.F. Bohman, and R. Shusterman. Ithaca, NY: Cornell University Press, 1–17.

Booth, W., G. Colomb, and J. Williams. (1995). *The Craft of Research*. 3d ed. Chicago: University of Chicago Press.

Bourdieu, P. (1977). *Outline of a Theory of Practice*. Cambridge, UK: Cambridge University Press.

Boyatzis, R.E. (1998). *Transforming Qualitative Information: Thematic Analysis and Code Development*. Thousand Oaks, CA: Sage Publications.

Boyte, H.C. (2004). *Everyday Politics: Reconnecting Citizens and Public Life*. Philadelphia: University of Pennsylvania Press.

Bruner, J. (1986). *Actual Minds, Possible Worlds*. Cambridge, MA: Harvard University Press.

Burke, T. (1994). *Dewey's New Logic: A Reply to Russell*. Chicago, IL: University of Chicago Press.

Cabinet Office. (1999). *Professional Policymaking for the 21st Century*. London: The Cabinet Office.

Čapek, M. (1971). *Bergson and Modern Physics*. Dordrecht, NL: D. Reidel.

Cartwright, N. (1983). *How the Laws of Physics Lie*. Oxford, UK: Oxford University Press.

Castiglione, D., and Warren. M. (2005). "Rethinking Representation. Seven Theoretical Issues." Paper presented at the Midwestern Political Science Association Annual Conference, Chicago, April 2005.

Cerwonka, A., and L.H. Malkki. (2007). *Improvising Theory: Process and Temporality in Ethnographic Fieldwork*. Chicago, IL: University of Chicago Press.

Charmaz, K. (1990). "'Discovering' Chronic Illness: Using Grounded Theory." *Social Science and Medicine* 30(11): 1161–72.

———. (2000). "Grounded Theory Methodology: Objectivist and Constructivist Qualitative Methods." In *Handbook of Qualitative Research*, ed. N. K. Denzin and Y. Lincoln. 2d ed. Thousand Oaks, CA: Sage Publications, 509–35.

———. (2006). *Constructing Grounded Theory: A Practical Guide Through Qualitative Analysis*. Thousand Oaks, CA: Sage Publications.

Chock, P.P. (1995). "Ambiguity in Policy Discourse: Congressional Talk About Immigration." *Policy Sciences* 28(2): 165–84.

Cilliers, P. (2005). "Complexity, Deconstruction and Relativism." *Theory, Culture & Society* 22(5): 255–67.

Cohen, S., and A.T. Scull (eds.). (1983). *Social Control and the State*. New York: St. Martin's Press.

Connolly, W.E. (1991). *Identity/Difference: Democratic Negotiations of Political Paradox*. Minneapolis: University of Minnesota Press.

———. (2005). *Pluralism*. Durham, NC: Duke University Press.

Cook, S.D.N. (2008). "Design and Responsibility: The Interdependence of Natural, Artifactual, and Human Systems." In *Philosophy and Design: From Engineering to Architecture*, ed. P. E. Vermaas, P. Kroes, A. Light, and S. A. Moore. Delft, NL: Springer, 259–73.

Cornwall, A., and V.S. Coelho (eds.). (2007). *Spaces for Change. The Politics of Citizen Participation in New Democratic Arenas*. London: Zed Books.

Coulter, J. (1979). "Transparency of Mind: The Availability of Subjective Phenomena." In *The Social Construction of Mind: Studies in Ethnomethodology and Linguistic Philosophy*, ed. J. Coulter. Totowa, NJ: Rowman and Littlefield.

Cronon, W. (1992). "A Place for Stories: Nature, History and Narrative." *Journal of American History* 78(4): 1347–76.

Cruikshank, B. (1999). *The Will to Empower: Democratic Citizens and Other Subjects*. Ithaca, NY: Cornell University Press.

Czarniawska, B. (2004). *Narratives in Social Science Research*. Thousand Oaks, CA: Sage Publications.

Dallmayr, F.R., and T.A. McCarthy. (1977). "Introduction: The Crisis of Understanding." In *Understanding and Social Inquiry*, ed. F.R. Dallmayr and T.A. McCarthy. Notre Dame, IN: University of Notre Dame Press, 1–14.

Danziger, S., and A.C. Lin (eds.). (2000). *Coping with Poverty: The Social Contexts of Neighborhood, Work, and Family in the African-American Community*. Ann Arbor: University of Michigan Press.

Dean, M. (1999). *Governmentality: Power and Rule in Modern Society*. Thousand Oaks, CA: Sage Publications.

de Beaugrande, R-A., and W.U. Dressler. (1981). *Introduction to Text Linguistics*. Harlow, Essex, UK: Longman.

deLeon, P. (1997). *Democracy and the Policy Sciences*. Albany: State University of New York Press.

De Souza Briggs, X. (2008). *Democracy as Problem Solving: Civic Capacity Across the Globe*. Cambridge, MA: MIT Press.

Dewey, J. (1916). *Essays in Experimental Logic*. New York: Dover Publications.

———. (1994 [1925]). *Experience and Nature*. Chicago: Open Court.

———. (1991 [1938]). *Logic: The Theory of Inquiry*. Carbondale: Southern Illinois University Press.

Dewey, J., and A. F. Bentley. (1949). *Knowing and the Known*. Westport, CT: Greenwood Press.

Digeser, P. (1992). "The Fourth Face of Power." *Journal of Politics* 54: 977–1007.

Dodillet, S. (2006). "Prostitutionspolitik in Deutschland und Schweden. Zum Ideologischen Hintergrund von Sexarbeit und Sexkaufverbot" (Prostitution policy in Germany and Sweden: On the ideological background to sex work and client criminalization). In *Verhandlungen im Zwielicht—Momente der Prostitution in Geschichte und Gegenwart* (Negotiations in the twilight—Moments of prostitution in the past and present), ed. S. Grenz and M. Lücke. Bielefeld, Germany: transcript Verlag, 95–112.

Dreyfus, H.L., and P. Rabinow. (1983). *Michel Foucault: Beyond Structuralism and Hermeneutics*. Chicago, IL: University of Chicago Press.

Dryzek, J.S. (1982). "Policy Analysis as a Hermeneutic Activity." *Policy Sciences* 14: 309–29.

———. (1989). "Policy Sciences of Democracy." *Polity* 22(1): 97–118.

———. (1990). *Discursive Democracy: Politics, Policy, and Political Science*. Cambridge: Cambridge University Press.

Dunn, W.N. (2004). *Public Policy Analysis: An Introduction*. Upper Saddle River, NJ: Pearson Prentice Hall.

Dunne, J. (1993). *Back to the Rough Ground: "Phronesis" and "Techne" in Modern Philosophy and in Aristotle*. Notre Dame, IN: University of Notre Dame Press.

Ellos, W.J. (1994). *Narrative Ethics*. Brookfield, VT: Ashgate.

Elster, J. (1983). *Explaining Technical Change*. Cambridge: Cambridge University Press.

———. (1999). *Alchemies of the Mind: Rationality and the Emotions*. Cambridge: Cambridge University Press.

Emerson, R., and S. Messinger. (1977). "The Micro-Politics of Trouble." *Social Problems* 25(2): 121–34.

Estroff, S.E. (1981). *Making It Crazy: An Ethnography of Psychiatric Clients in an American Community.* Berkeley: University of California Press.

Fairclough, N. (1992). *Discourse and Social Change.* Cambridge, UK: Polity Press.

———. (2001). *Language and Power.* Harlow, UK: Pearson Education.

———. (2003). *Analysing Discourse: Textual Analysis for Social Research.* Milton Park: Routledge.

Farrelly, M.J. (2006). "Discourse and Local Democracy: A Critical Discourse Analysis Case Study of Area Forums in Preston." Ph.D. diss., Lancaster, UK: Lancaster University.

Fay, B. (1975). *Social Theory and Political Practice.* London: George Allen and Unwin.

———. (1996). *Contemporary Philosophy of Social Science.* Malden, MA: Blackwell.

Finlayson, A. (2004). "Meaning and Politics: Assessing Bevir and Rhodes." *British Journal of Politics & International Relations* 6(2): 149–56.

Fischer, F. (1980). *Politics, Values, and Public Policy: The Problem of Methodology.* Boulder, CO: Westview Press.

———. (1995). *Evaluating Public Policy.* Chicago, IL: Nelson-Hall.

———. (2000). *Citizens, Experts, and the Environment: the Politics of Local Knowledge.* Durham, NC: Duke University Press.

———. (2003a). "Beyond Empiricism: Policy Analysis as Deliberative Practice." In *Deliberative Policy Analysis: Understanding Governance in the Network Society*, ed. M. Hajer and H. Wagenaar. Cambridge: Cambridge University Press, 209–27.

———. (2003b). *Reframing Public Policy. Discursive Politics and Deliberative Practices.* Oxford, UK: Oxford University Press.

Fischer, F., G.J. Miller, and M.S. Sidney. (2007). *Handbook of Public Policy Analysis.* London: CRC Press.

Flick, U. (2003). "Constructivism." In *A Companion to Qualitative Research*, ed. E. von Kardorff, U. Flick, and I. Steinke. Thousand Oaks, CA: Sage Publications, 88–95.

Flyvbjerg, B. (2001). *Making Social Science Matter: Why Social Inquiry Fails and How It Can Succeed Again.* Cambridge: Cambridge University Press.

Forester, J. (1989). *Planning in the Face of Power.* Berkeley: University of California Press.

———. (1993). "Learning from Practice Stories: The Priority of Practical Judgment." In *The Argumentative Turn in Policy Analysis and Planning,* ed. F. Fischer and J. Forester. Durham, NC: Duke University Press.

———. (1999a). *The Deliberative Practitioner: Encouraging Participatory Planning Processes.* Cambridge, MA: MIT Press.

———. (1999b). "Dealing with Deep Value Differences." In *The Consensus Building Handbook,* ed. L. Susskind, S. McKearnan, and J. Thomas-Larmer. Thousand Oaks, CA: Sage Publications, 463–94.

———. (2006). "Policy Analysis as Critical Listening." *The Oxford Handbook of Public Policy,* ed. M. Moran, M. Rein, and R. E. Goodin. Oxford, UK: Oxford University Press, 124–52.

———. (2009). *Dealing with Differences: Dramas of Mediating Public Disputes.* Oxford: Oxford University Press.

Foucault, M. (1979). *Discipline and Punish: The Birth of the Prison.* New York: Vintage Books.

———. (1980a). *Power/Knowledge: Selected Interviews and Other Writings.* New York: Pantheon Books.

———. (1980b). *An Introduction.* Vol. 1 of *The History of Sexuality.* New York: Vintage Books.

———. (1983). "The Subject and Power." In *Michel Foucault: Beyond Structuralism and Hermeneutics,* H.L. Dreyfus and P. Rabinow (1983), 208–26.

———. (1988). "The Ethic of Care for the Self as a Practice of Freedom" (interview translated by J.D. Gauthier). In *The Final Foucault,* ed. J.B. Bernauer and D. Rasmussen. Cambridge, MA: MIT Press, 1–20.

———. (1991). "Governmentality." In *The Foucault Effect: Studies in Governmentality,* ed. G. Burchell, C. Gordon, and P. Miller. Chicago, IL: University of Chicago Press, 87–104.

Fowler, A. et al. (2001). "Talking with the Enemy." *Boston Globe,* January 28.

Fung, A. (2004). *Empowered Participation: Reinventing Urban Democracy.* Princeton, NJ: Princeton University Press.

Fung, A., and E.O. Wright (eds.). (2003). *Deepening Democracy. Institutional Innovations in Empowered Participatory Governance. The Real Utopias Project IV.* London: Verso.

Gadamer, H.-G. (1976). *Philosophical Hermeneutics.* Berkeley: University of California Press.

———. (1989). *Truth and Method.* New York: Seabury Press.

Gamson, W.A., and A. Modigliani. (1989). "Media Discourse and Public Opinion on Nuclear Power: A Constructionist Approach." *American Journal of Sociology* 95(1): 1–37.

Garfinkel, H. (1967). *Studies in Ethnomethodology*. Englewood Cliffs, NJ: Prentice-Hall.

Garland, D. (2002). *The Culture of Control: Crime and Social Order in Contemporary Society*. Chicago, IL: University of Chicago Press.

Gee, J.P. (1985). "The Narrativization of Experience in the Oral Style." *Journal of Education* 167(1): 9–36.

———. (1990). *Social Linguistics and Literacies: Ideology in Discourses*. Basingstoke, UK: Falmer Press.

———. (1997). "Thematized Echoes." *Journal of Narrative and Life History* 7(1–4): 189–97.

Geertz, C. (1973a). "Deep Play: Notes on the Balinese Cockfight." In *The Interpretation of Cultures: Selected Essays*. New York: Basic Books, 412–54.

———. (1973b). "Thick Description: Toward an Interpretive Theory of Culture." In *The Interpretation of Cultures: Selected Essays*. New York: Basic Books, 3–32.

———. (1983). *Local Knowledge: Further Essays in Interpretive Anthropology*. New York: Basic Books.

Gerodetti, N. (2006). "Eugenic Family Politics and Social Democrats: 'Positive' Eugenics and Marriage Advice Bureaus." *Journal of Historical Sociology* 19(3): 217–44.

Gibbons, M.T. (1987). "Introduction: The Politics of Interpretation." In *Interpreting Politics*, ed. M.T. Gibbons. Oxford: Blackwell, 1–32.

Glaser, B.G., and A.L. Strauss (1967 [2006]). *The Discovery of Grounded Theory: Strategies for Qualitative Research*. Chicago, IL: Aldine.

Glynos, J., and D. Howarth. (2007). *Logics of Critical Explanation in Social and Political Theory*. Milton Park, UK: Routledge.

Goffman, E. (1961). *Asylums: Essays on the Social Situation of Mental Patients and other Inmates*. Garden City, NY: Anchor Books.

Goodman, N. (1978). *Ways of Worldmaking*. Indianapolis, IN: Hackett.

Gordon, C. (1991). "Governmental Rationality: An Introduction." In *The Foucault Effect: Studies in Governmentality*, ed. G. Burchell, C. Gordon, and P. Miller. Chicago, IL: University of Chicago Press, 1–52.

Gorman, R.A. (1976). "Phenomenology, Social Science, and Radicalism: The View from Existence." *Politics & Society* 4(4): 491–513.

Greenwood, D., and M. Levin. (1998). *Introduction to Action Research: Social Research for Social Change*. Thousand Oaks, CA: Sage Publications.

Griggs, S., and D. Howarth. (2005). "Bringing Government Back In: Problematizing Aviation Policy and Practice in the United Kingdom." Unpublished paper.

———. (2006). "Networks of Popular Resistance against Airport Expansion." In *Democratic Network Governance in Europe*, ed. M. Marcussen and J. Torfing. London: Palgrave, 66–88.

Grob, G.N. (1983). *Mental Illness and American Society, 1875–1940*. Princeton, NJ: Princeton University Press.

Grondin, J. (1994). *Introduction to Philosophical Hermeneutics*. New Haven, CT: Yale University Press.

———. (2003). *The Philosophy of Gadamer*. Chesham, UK: Acumen.

Guignon, C.B. (1991). "Pragmatism or Hermeneutics? Epistemology after Foundationalism." In *The Interpretive Turn: Philosophy, Science, Culture*, ed. D.R. Hiley, J. Bohman, and R. Shusterman. Ithaca, NY: Cornell University Press, 81–102.

Gumperz, J.J. (1982). *Discourse Strategies*. Cambridge: Cambridge University Press.

Gusfield, J.R. (1984). *The Culture of Public Problems: Drinking-Driving and the Symbolic Order*. Chicago, IL: University of Chicago Press.

Gutting, G. (2001). *French Philosophy in the Twentieth Century*. Cambridge: Cambridge University Press.

———. (2003). "Introduction: Michel Foucault: A User's Manual." In *The Cambridge Companion to Foucault*, ed. G. Gutting. Cambridge: Cambridge University Press, 1–29.

Haack, S. (1995). *Evidence and Inquiry: Towards Reconstruction in Epistemology*. Oxford: Blackwell.

Hacking, I. (1983). *Representing and Intervening: Introductory Topics in the Philosophy of Natural Science*. Cambridge: Cambridge University Press.

———. (1986). "The Archaeology of Foucault." In *Foucault: A Critical Reader*, ed. D.C. Hoy. Oxford: Blackwell, 27–41.

———. (1999). *The Social Construction of What?* Cambridge, MA: Harvard University Press.

Hajer, M. (1993). "Discourse Coalitions and the Institutionalization of Practice: The Case of Acid Rain in Britain." In *The Argumentative Turn in Policy Analysis and Planning,* ed. F. Fischer and J. Forester. Durham, NC: Duke University Press, 43–76.

———. (1995). *The Politics of Environmental Discourse: Ecological Modernization and the Policy Process.* Oxford, UK: Oxford University Press.

Hajer, M., and H. Wagenaar (eds.). (2003). *Deliberative Policy Analysis: Understanding Governance in the Network Society.* Cambridge: Cambridge University Press. Editors' introduction, 1–33.

Hammersley, M., R. Gomm, and P. Foster. (2000). "Case Study and Theory." In *Case Study Method,* ed. R. Gomm, M. Hammersley, and P. Foster. Thousand Oaks, CA: Sage Publications, 234–59.

Hampshire, S. (1983). *Morality and Conflict.* Cambridge, MA: Harvard University Press.

Haket, V. (2007). "Veranderende verhalen in het Strafrecht. De Ontwikkeling van Verhalen over Verkrachting in het Strafproces" (Changing stories in the criminal law. The evolution of stories of rape in the criminal court proceedings). Ph.D. diss., Leiden: Leiden University.

Harris, R. (1988). *Language, Saussure and Wittgenstein: How to Play Games with Words.* London: Routledge.

Harwood, S.A., and M. Zapata. (2007). "Creating Space for Hermeneutics in Practice: Using Visual Tools to Understand Community Narratives about the Future." *Critical Policy Analysis* 1(4): 371–89.

Hawkesworth, M.E. (1988). *Theoretical Issues in Policy Analysis.* Albany: State University of New York Press.

Hayes, M.T. (2006). *Incrementalism and Public Policy.* Lanham, MD: University Press of America.

Healey, P. (2002). "On Creating the 'City' as a Collective Resource." *Urban Studies* 39(10): 1777–92.

Healey, P., C. de Magalhaes, A. Madanipour, and J. Pendlebury. (2003). "Place, Identity and Local Politics: Analysing Initiatives in Local Governance." In *Deliberative Policy Analysis: Understanding Governance in the Network Society,* ed. M. Hajer and H. Wagenaar. Cambridge, UK: Cambridge University Press, 60–88.

Held, D. (1996). *Models of Democracy.* 2d ed. Cambridge, UK: Polity Press.

Hitzler, R., and T.S. Eberle. (2004). "Phenomenological Life-World Analysis." In *A Companion to Qualitative Research,* ed. E. von Kardorff, U. Flick, and I. Steinke. Thousand Oaks, CA: Sage Publications, 67–72.

Hofmann, J. (1995). "Implicit Theories in Policy Discourse: An Inquiry into the Interpretations of Reality in German Technology Policy." *Policy Sciences* 28(2): 127–48.

Hood, C., and M. Jackson. (1991). *Administrative Argument.* Brookfield, VT: Dartmouth.

Horton, M., and P. Freire. (1990). *We Make the Road by Walking: Conversations on Education and Social Change.* ed. B. Bell, J. Gaventa and J. Peters. Philadelphia, PA: Temple University Press.

Howarth, D. (2000). *Discourse.* Ballmoor, UK: Open University Press.

Hoy, D.C. (1998). "Foucault and Critical Theory." In *The Later Foucault: Politics and Philosophy,* ed. J. Moss. Thousand Oaks, CA: Sage Publications, 18–32.

Hunter, I. (1996). "Assembling the School." In *Foucault and Political Reason: Liberalism, Neo-Liberalism and Rationalities of Government,* ed. A. Barry, T. Osborne, and N. Rose. London: UCL Press, 143–67.

Hunter, K.M. (1991). *Doctors' Stories: The Narrative Structure of Medical Knowledge.* Princeton, NJ: Princeton University Press.

Innes, J.E. (2004). "Consensus Building: Clarifications for the Critics." *Planning Theory* 3(1): 5–20.

Innes, J.E., and D.E. Booher. (2003). "Collaborative Policymaking: Governance Through Dialogue." In *Deliberative Policy Analysis: Understanding Governance in the Network Society,* ed. M. Hajer and H. Wagenaar. Cambridge: Cambridge University Press, 33–60.

———. (2010). *Planning with Complexity. An Introduction to Collaborative Rationality for Public Policy.* Milton Park, UK: Routledge.

Iser, W. (1978). *The Act of Reading.* Baltimore, MD: Johns Hopkins University Press.

Jacques, E. (1982). *The Form of Time.* London: Heinemann.

James, W. (1909 [1996]). *A Pluralistic Universe.* Lincoln: University of Nebraska Press.

Janowitz, M. (1978). *The Last Half-Century: Societal Change and Politics in America.* Chicago, IL: University of Chicago Press.

Jencks, C. (1995). *The Homeless.* Cambridge, MA: Harvard University Press.

Jones, G.S. (1991). *Outcast London. A Study in the Relationship Between Classes in Victorian Society.* Harlowe, UK: Penguin Books.

Jonsen, A.R., and S. Toulmin. (1990). *The Abuse of Casuistry: A History of Moral Reasoning.* Berkeley: University of California Press.

Jørgensen, M., and L. Phillips. (2002). *Discourse Analysis as Theory and Method.* Thousand Oaks, CA: Sage Publications.

Kagan, R. A. (1978). *Regulatory Justice. Implementing a Wage-Price Freeze.* New York: Russell Sage Foundation.

Kalil, A. et al. (2000). "Mother, Worker, Welfare Recipient: Welfare Reform and the Multiple Roles of Low-Income Women." In *Coping with Poverty· The Social Contexts of Neighborhood, Work and Family in the African-American Community,* ed. S. Danziger and A.C. Lin. Ann Arbor: University of Michigan Press, 201–24.

Kauffman, S. (1995). *At Home in the Universe: The Search for Laws of Self-Organization and Complexity.* London: Viking.

Kekes, J. (1993). *The Morality of Pluralism.* Princeton, NJ: Princeton University Press.

Kickert, W. et al. (eds.). (1997). *Managing Complex Networks: Strategies for the Public Sector.* Thousand Oaks, CA: Sage Publications.

Kiel, L.D. (1994). *Managing Chaos and Complexity: A New Paradigm for Managing Change, Innovation, and Organizational Renewal.* San Francisco, CA: Jossey-Bass.

Kingdon, J.W. (2002). *Agendas, Alternatives and Public Policies.* New York: Longman.

Kruiter, H., M. Van Schijndel, and H. Wagenaar. (2010). *Bewonersparticipatie en Veiligheid. Tussen Droom en Daad . . . in een Complexe Bestuurlijke Context* (Citizen participation and safety. Policy challenges in a complex urban environment). Leiden, NL: Universiteit Leiden, Campus Den Haag.

Kulick, D. (2005). "Four Hundred Thousand Swedish Perverts." *GLQ: A Journal of Lesbian and Gay Studies* 11(2): 205–35.

Labov, W., and J. Waletzky. (1967). "Narrative Analysis: Oral Versions of Personal Experience." In *Essays on the Verbal and Visual Arts: Proceedings of the 1966 Annual Spring Meeting of the American Ethnological Society,* ed. J. Helm. Seattle: University of Washington Press, 12–44.

Laclau, E., and C. Mouffe. (1985). *Hegemony and Socialist Strategy: Towards a Radical Democratic Politics.* London: Verso.

Lasswell, H.D. (1951). "The Policy Orientation." In *The Policy Sciences: Recent Developments in Scope and Method,* ed. D. Lerner and H.D. Lasswell. Stanford, CA: Stanford University Press, 3–15.

Latour, B., and S. Woolgar. (1979). *Laboratory Life: The Social Construction of Scientific Facts.* Thousand Oaks, CA: Sage Publications.

Lave, J. (1988). *Cognition in Practice: Mind, Mathematics and Culture in Everyday Life.* Cambridge: Cambridge University Press.

Law, J. (2004). *After Method: Mess in Social Science Research.* London: Routledge.

Laws, D. (2007). "The Divided Profession: The Interplay of Research, Policy and Practice." *Policy and Society* 26(4): 39–66.

Laws, D., and J. Forester. (2006). "Learning in Practice: Public Policy Mediation." *Critical Policy Analysis* 1(4): 342–71.

Laws, D., and M. Rein. (2003). "Reframing Practice." In *Deliberative Policy Analysis: Understanding Governance in the Network Society,* ed. M. Hajer and H. Wagenaar. Cambridge: Cambridge University Press, 172–208.

Lawson, L. (2005). "Dialogue Through Design: The East St. Louis Neighborhood Design Workshop and South End Neighborhood Plan." *Landscape Journal* 24(2): 157–71.

Lemke, T. (1997). *Eine Kritik der Politischen Vernunft. Foucaults Analyse der Modernen Gouvernementalität* (A Critique of Political Reason: Foucault's Analysis of Modern Governmentality). Hamburg: Argument Verlag.

———. (2001). "The Birth of Bio-Politics: Michel Foucault's Lecture at the Collége de France on Neo-Liberal Governmentality." *Economy & Society* 30(2): 190–206.

———. (2007). "Neoliberalismus, Staat und Selbsttechnologien. Ein Kritischer Überblick über die Governmentality Studies" (Neoliberalism, state, and technologies of the self. A critical overview of governmentality studies). In *Gouvernementalität und Biopolitik* (Governmentality and biopolitics). Wiesbaden: VS Verlag für Sozialwissenschaften, 47–65.

Lewis, D. et al. (1991). *Worlds of the Mentally Ill: How Deinstitutionalization Works in the City.* Carbondale: Southern Illinois University Press.

Lewis, D.A., and R. Hugi. (1981). "Therapeutic Stations and the Chronically Mentally Ill." *Social Service Review* 55(2): 206–20.

Liebow, E. (1967 [2003]). *Tally's Corner: A Study of Negro Streetcorner Men.* Lanham, MD: Rowman and Littefield.

Lin, A.C. (2000). "Interpretive Research for Public Policy." In *Coping with Poverty: The Social Contexts of Neighborhood, Work, and Family in the African-American Community,* ed. S. Danziger and A.C. Lin. Ann Arbor: University of Michigan Press, 1–27.

Lindon, J.A. (1991). "Does Technique Require Theory?" *Bulletin of the Menninger Clinic* 55(1): 1–22.

Ludwig, A.M., and F. Farrelly. (1966). "The Code of Chronicity." *Archives of General Psychiatry* 15(6): 562–68.

Lukes, S. (1975). *Power: A Radical View*. London: Macmillan.

———. (1991). *Moral Conflict and Politics*. Oxford, UK: Clarendon Press.

Macdonell, D. (1986). *Theories of Discourse*. Oxford: Blackwell.

Macedo, S. et al. (2005). *Democracy at Risk: How Political Choices Undermine Citizen Participation, and What We Can Do About It*. Washington, DC: Brookings Institution Press.

MacIntyre, A. (1981). *After Virtue: A Study in Moral Theory*. Notre Dame, IN: University of Notre Dame Press.

MacKinnon, D. (2000). "Managerialism, Governmentality, and the State: A Neo-Foucauldian Approach to Local Economic Governance." *Political Geography* 19: 293–314.

Manin, B. (1997). *The Principles of Representative Government*. Cambridge: Cambridge University Press.

Mathews, D. (1999). *Politics for People: Finding a Responsible Public Voice*. 2d ed. Urbana: University of Illinois Press.

Maynard-Moody, S., and M. Musheno. (2003). *Cops, Teachers, Counselors: Stories from the Front Lines of Public Service*. Ann Arbor: University of Michigan Press.

Mayrl, W.W. (1977). "Ethnomethodology: Sociology Without Society?" In *Understanding and Social Inquiry*, ed. F.R. Dallmayr and T.A. McCarthy. Notre Dame, IN: University of Notre Dame Press, 262–80.

McAnulla, S. (2006). "Challenging the New Interpretivist Approach: Towards a Critical Realist Alternative." *British Politics* 1(1): 113–39.

McCloskey, D. (1998). *The Rhetoric of Economics*. Madison: University of Wisconsin Press.

McKechnie, J.L. (ed.). (1979). *Webster's New Twentieth Century Dictionary*. New York: Simon and Schuster.

Merton, R.K. (1936). "The Unanticipated Consequences of Purposive Social Action." *American Sociological Review* 1: 894–904.

Miller, P. (1986). "Critiques of Psychiatry and Critical Sociologies of Madness." In *The Power of Psychiatry*, ed. P. Miller and N. Rose. Cambridge: Polity Press, 12–42.

Miller, P., and N. Rose (eds.). (1986). *The Power of Psychiatry*. Cambridge: Polity Press.

Mishler, E.G. (1995). "Models of Narrative Analysis: A Typology." *Journal of Narrative and Life History* 5(2): 87–124.

Morçöl, G. (2002). *A New Mind for Policy Analysis: Toward a Post-Newtonian and Postpositivist Epistemology and Methodology*. Westport, CT: Praeger.

Moss, J. (1998). "Introduction: The Later Foucault." In *The Later Foucault: Politics and Philosophy*, ed. J. Moss. Thousand Oaks, CA: Sage Publications, 1–17.

Mottier, V. (2008). "Eugenics, Politics and the State: Social Democracy and the Swiss 'Gardening State.'" *Studies in History and Philosophy of Science Part C: Studies in History and Philosophy of Biomedical Sciences* 39(2): 263–69.

Mouffe, C. (2000). *The Democratic Paradox*. London: Verso.

Murdoch, I. (1985). *The Sovereignty of Good*. London: Routledge.

Newman, J. (2001). *Modernising Governance: New Labour, Policy and Society*. Thousand Oaks, CA: Sage Publications.

Norval, A.J. (2007). *Aversive Democracy: Inheritance and Originality in the Democratic Tradition*. Cambridge: Cambridge University Press.

Oakeshott, M. (1983). *On History and Other Essays*. Totowa, NJ: Barnes and Noble Books.

Oliver, J.E. (2000). "City Size and Civic Involvement in Metropolitan America." *American Political Science Review* 94(2): 361–73.

O'Malley, P., L. Weir, and C. Shearing. (1997). "Governmentality, Criticism and Politics." *Economy and Society* 26 (4): 501–17.

Orr, J.E. (1996). *Talking About Machines: An Ethnography of a Modern Job*. Ithaca, NY: Cornell University Press.

Outshoorn, J. (2004). "Voluntary and Forced Prostitution: The 'Realistic' Approach of the Netherlands." In *The Politics of Prostitution: Women's Movements, Democratic States and the Globalisation of Sex Commerce*. ed. J. Outshoor. Cambridge, UK: Cambridge University Press, 185–205.

Paras, E. (2006). *Foucault 2.0: Beyond Power and Knowledge*. New York: Other Press.

Patton, P. (1998). "Foucault's Subject of Power." In *The Later Foucault: Politics and Philosophy*, ed. J. Moss. Thousand Oaks, CA: Sage Publications, 64–77.

Paul, K.T. (2009). "Food Safety: A Matter of Taste? Food Safety Policy in England, Germany, The Nether-lands, and at the Level of the European Union." Ph.D. diss., Amsterdam, The Netherlands.

Peake, S., and J. Smith. (2009). *Climate Change: From Science to Sustainability*. Oxford, UK: Oxford University Press.

Pickering, A. (1995). *The Mangle of Practice: Time, Agency, and Science*. Chicago, IL: University of Chicago Press.

Pierre, J., and B.G. Peters. (2000). *Governance, Politics and the State*. New York: St. Martin's Press.

Pitkin, H.F. (1967). *The Concept of Representation*. Berkeley: University of California Press.

Piven, F.F., and R.A. Cloward. (1971). *Regulating the Poor: The Functions of Public Welfare*. New York: Pantheon Books.

Plotke, D. (1997). "Representation Is Democracy." *Constellations* 4(1): 19–34.

Podziba, S. (1998). *Social Capital Formation, Public Building, and Public Mediation: The Chelsea Charter Consensus Process*. Dayton, OH: Kettering Foundation.

Polanyi, M. (1958). *Personal Knowledge: Towards a Post-Critical Philosophy*. Chicago, IL: University of Chicago Press.

Pollit, C. (2009). "Complexity Theory and Evolutionary Public Administration." In *Managing Complex Governance Systems. Dynamics, Self-Organization and Coevolution in Public Investments*, ed. G. Teis-man, A. van Buuren, and L. Gerrits. Milton Park, UK: Routledge: 213–31.

Porter, L. (2009). "Planning Displacement: The Real Legacy of Major Sporting Events." *Planning Theory and Practice* 10(3); 395–418.

Potter, J. (1996). *Representing Reality: Discourse, Rhetoric and Social Construction*. Thousand Oaks, CA: Sage Publications.

Prainsack, B. (2006). "Negotiating Life: The Regulation of Embryonic Stem Cell Research and Human Cloning in Israel." *Social Studies of Science* 36(2): 173–205.

Prigogine, I., and I. Stengers. (1985). *Order out of Chaos: Man's New Dialogue with Nature*. London: Fontana Press.

Propp, V. (1968 [1928]). *Morphology of the Folktale*. 2d ed. Austin: University of Texas Press.

Prus, R. (1996). *Symbolic Interaction and Ethnographic Research*. Albany: State University of New York Press.

Putnam, H. (1981a). "Fact and Value." In *Reason, Truth and History*. Cambridge: Cambridge University Press, 127–49.

———. (1981b). "Two Philosophical Perspectives." In *Reason, Truth and History*. Cambridge: Cambridge University Press, 49–74.

———. (1983). "Reflections on Goodman's *Ways of Worldmaking*." In *Realism and Reason. Philosophical Papers*. Volume 3. Cambridge, UK: Cambridge University Press, 155–70.

Putnam, R.A. (1985). "Creating Facts and Values." *Philosophy* 60(2): 187–204.

Raz, J. (1986). *The Morality of Freedom*. Oxford: Clarendon Press.

Reardon, K.M. (2000). "An Experiential Approach to Creating an Effective Community-University Part-nership: The East St. Louis Action Research Project." *Cityscape: A Journal of Policy Development and Research* 5(1): 59–74.

Reason, P., and H. Bradbury (eds.). (2006). *Handbook of Action Research. The Concise Paperback Edition*. Thousand Oaks, CA: Sage Publications.

Reichertz, J. (2004). "Objective Hermeneutics and Hermeneutic Sociology of Knowledge." In *A Compan-ion to Qualitative Research*, ed. E. von Kardorff, U. Flick, and I. Steinke. Thousand Oaks, CA: Sage Publications, 290–96.

Reijndorp, A. (2004). *Stadswijk: Stedenbouw en Dagelijks Leven* (Neighborhood: Metropolitan development and everyday life). Rotterdam: NAi Uitgevers.

Rein, M. (1976). *Social Science and Public Policy*. Harmondsworth, UK: Penguin Books.

———. (1983a). "Value-Critical Policy Analysis." In *Ethics, the Social Sciences, and Policy Analysis*, ed. D. Callahan and B. Jennings. New York: Plenum Press, 83–112.

———. (1983b). "Action Frames and Problem Setting." In *Social Policy: Issues of Choice and Change*. Armonk, NY: M.E. Sharpe, 221–34.

———. (1983c). *Social Policy. Issues of Choice and Change*. Armonk, NY: M.E. Sharpe.

Ricoeur, P. (1977). "The Model of the Text: Meaningful Action Considered as a Text." In *Understanding and Social Inquiry*, ed. F.R. Dallmayr and T.A. McCarthy. Notre Dame, IN: University of Notre Dame Press, 316–35.

Riessman, C.K. (1993). *Narrative Analysis*. Thousand Oaks, CA: Sage Publications.

Risser, J. (1997). *Hermeneutics and the Voice of the Other*. Albany: State University of New York Press.

Rittel, H.W., and M. Webber. (1973). "Dilemmas in a General Theory of Planning." *Policy Sciences* 4(2): 155–69.

Roe, E. (1994). *Narrative Policy Analysis: Theory and Practice*. Durham, NC: Duke University Press.

Rose, N. (1986). "Psychiatry: the Discipline of Mental Health." *The Power of Psychiatry,* ed. P. Miller and N. Rose. Cambridge, UK: Polity, 43–84.

Rose, N., and P. Miller. (1992). "Political Power Beyond the State: Problematics of Government." *British Journal of Sociology* 43(2): 173–205.

Rosenhan, D.L. (1973). "On Being Sane in Insane Places." *Science* 179: 250–58.

Roth, P.A. (1991). "Interpretation as Explanation." In *The Interpretive Turn: Philosophy, Science, Culture*, ed. D.R. Hiley, J. Bohman, and R. Shusterman. Ithaca, NY: Cornell University Press, 179–97.

Rothman, D.J. (1971). *The Discovery of the Asylum: Social Order and Disorder in the New Republic*. Boston: Little, Brown.

Rouse, J. (1991). "Interpretation in Natural and Human Science." In *The Interpretive Turn: Philosophy, Science, Culture*, ed. D.R. Hiley, J. Bohman, and R. Shusterman. Ithaca, NY: Cornell University Press, 42–59.

———. (1996). *Engaging Science: How to Understand Its Practices Philosophically*. Ithaca, NY: Cornell University Press.

Sabel, C., A. Fung, and B. Karkkainen. (1999). "Beyond Backyard Environmentalism: How Communities Are Quietly Refashioning Environmental Regulation." *Boston Review* (October/November).

Safranski, R. (1998). *Martin Heidegger: Between Good and Evil*. Cambridge, MA: Harvard University Press.

Saward, M. (2006). "The Representative Claim." *Contemporary Political Theory* 5: 297–318.

Sayer, A. (2000). *Realism and Social Science*. Thousand Oaks, CA: Sage Publications.

Scharpf, F.W. (1997). *Games Real Actors Play: Actor-Centered Institutionalism in Policy Research*. Boulder, CO: Westview Press.

Schön, D.A., and M. Rein. (1994). *Frame Reflection: Toward the Resolution of Intractable Policy Controversies*. New York: Basic Books.

Schwandt, T.A. (1997). "Evaluation as Practical Hermeneutics." *Evaluation* 3(1): 69–83.

———. (2000). "Three Epistemological Stances for Qualitative Inquiry: Interpretivism, Hermeneutics, and Social Constructivism." In *Handbook of Qualitative Research*, ed. N.K. Denzin and Y.S. Lincoln. Thousand Oaks, CA: Sage Publications, 189–215.

———. (2002). *Evaluation Practice Reconsidered*. New York: Peter Lang.

———. (2004). "Hermeneutics: A Poetics of Inquiry Versus a Methodology for Research." In *Educational Research: Difference and Diversity*, ed. H. Piper and I. Stronach. Aldershot, UK: Ashgate, 31–44.

Scott, W.R. (2007). *Institutions and Organizations: Ideas and Interests*. Thousand Oaks, CA: Sage Publications.

Scull, A.T. (1979). *Museums of Madness: The Social Organization of Madness in Nineteenth-Century England*. New York: St. Martin's Press.

Searle, J.R. (1995). *The Construction of Social Reality*. New York: Free Press.

Self, P. (1993). *Government by the Market? The Politics of Public Choice*. London: Macmillan.

Shotter, J. (1993). *Conversational Realities: Constructing Life Through Language*. Thousand Oaks, CA: Sage Publications.

Shusterman, R. (1991). "Beneath Interpretation." In *The Interpretive Turn: Philosophy, Science, Culture*, ed. D.R. Hiley, J. Bohman, and R. Shusterman. Ithaca, NY: Cornell University Press, 102–28.

Sieber, S.D. (1981). *Fatal Remedies: The Ironies of Social Intervention*. New York: Plenum.

Soeffner, H.-G. (2004). "Social Scientific Hermeneutics." In *A Companion to Qualitative Research*, ed. E. von Kardorff, U. Flick, and I. Steinke. Thousand Oaks, CA: Sage Publications, 95–101.

Sokal, A.D. (1996). "Transgressing the Boundaries: Toward a Transformative Hermeneutics of Quantum Gravity." *Social Text* 14(1): 217–52.

Sørensen, E. (2006). "Metagovernance: The Changing Role of Politicians in Processes of Democratic Governance." *American Review of Public Administration* 36(1): 98–114.

Sørensen, E., and J. Torfing. (2005). "Network Governance and Post-Liberal Democracy." *Administrative Theory and Praxis* 27(2): 197–237.

Sørensen, E., and J. Torfing (eds.). (2008). *Theories of Democratic Network Governance*. Basingstoke, UK: Palgrave Macmillan.

Stanton, A.H., and M.S. Schwartz. (1954). *The Mental Hospital: A Study of Institutional Participation in Psychiatric Illness and Treatment.* New York: Basic Books.

Stocker, M. (1990). *Plural and Conflicting Values.* Oxford: Clarendon Press.

Stoker, G. (1995). "Regime Theory and Urban Politics." In *Theories of Urban Politics*, ed. D. Judge, G. Stoker and H. Wolman. Thousand Oaks, CA: Sage Publications, 54–72.

———. (2002). "International Trends in Local Government Transformation." In *Democratising Local Government: The South African Experiment*, ed. S. Parnell, E. Pieterse, M. Swilling, and D. Wooldridge. Cape Town, SA: University of Cape Town Press, 31–40.

———. (2006). "Public Value Management. A New Narrative for Networked Governance?" *American Review of Public Administration* 36(1): 41–57.

Stokey, E., and R. Zeckhauser. (1978). *A Primer for Policy Analysis.* New York: W.W. Norton.

Stone, C.N. (2005). "Looking Back to Look Forward: Reflections on Urban Regime Analysis." *Urban Affairs Review* 40(3): 309–41.

Stone, C.N. et al. (2001). *Building Civic Capacity: The Politics of Reforming Urban Schools.* Lawrence: University Press of Kansas.

Stone, D. (1997). *Policy Paradox: The Art of Political Decision Making.* New York: W.W. Norton.

Strauss, A.L. (1993). *Continual Permutations of Action.* Hawthorne, NY: Aldine de Gruyter.

Sternberg, R.J. (ed.). (1990). *Wisdom: Its Nature, Origins, and Development.* Cambridge, UK: Cambridge University Press.

Suchman, L.A. (1987). *Plans and Situated Actions: The Problem of Human-Machine Communication.* Cambridge: Cambridge University Press.

Sullivan, H. (2007). "Interpreting Community Leadership." *Policy and Politics* 35(1): 141–62.

Sullivan, H., and C. Skelcher. (2002). *Working Across Boundaries: Collaboration in Public Services.* Basingstoke, UK: Palgrave Macmillan.

Susskind, L. et al. (eds.). (1999). *The Consensus Building Handbook: A Comprehensive Guide to Reaching Agreement.* Thousand Oaks, CA: Sage Publications.

Swift, G. (1983). *Waterland.* London: Heinemann.

Szasz, T. (1984). *The Myth of Mental Illness: Foundations of a Theory of Personal Conduct.* Harper Perennial.

Taylor, C. (1985a). "Interpretation and the Sciences of Man." In *Philosophy and the Human Sciences: Philosophical Papers 2.* Cambridge: Cambridge University Press, 15–58.

———. (1985b [1967]). "Neutrality in Political Science." In *Philosophy and the Human Sciences: Philosophical Papers 2.* Cambridge: Cambridge University Press, 58–91.

———. (1986). "Foucault on Freedom and Truth." In *Foucault: A Critical Reader*, ed. D.C. Hoy. Oxford: Blackwell, 69–103.

———. (1991). "The Dialogical Self." In *The Interpretive Turn: Philosophy, Science and Culture.* ed. J. Bohman, D. Hiley, and R. Shusterman. Ithaca, NY: Cornell University Press, 304–14.

———. (1995a). "Overcoming Epistemology." In *Philosophical Arguments.* Cambridge, MA: Harvard University Press, 1–19.

———. (1995b). "Lichtung or Lebensform: Parallels Between Heidegger and Wittgenstein." In *Philosophical Arguments.* Cambridge, MA: Harvard University Press, 61–79.

———. (1995c). "To Follow a Rule." In *Philosophical Arguments.* Cambridge, MA: Harvard University Press, 165–81.

———. (2002). "Gadamer on the Human Sciences." In *The Cambridge Companion to Gadamer*, ed. R.J. Dostal. Cambridge: Cambridge University Press, 126–42.

Teisman, G., A. van Buuren, and L. Gerrits (eds.). (2009). *Managing Complex Governance Systems. Dynamics, Self-Organization and Coevolution in Public Investments.* Milton Park, UK: Routledge.

This, Hervé. (2007). *Kitchen Mysteries: Revealing the Science of Cooking.* New York: Columbia University Press.

Thomas, D. (1979). *Naturalism and Social Science: A Post-Empiricist Philosophy of Social Science.* Cambridge: Cambridge University Press.

Throgmorton, J.A. (1993). "Survey Research as Rhetorical Trope: Electric Power Planning Arguments in Chicago." In *The Argumentative Turn in Policy Analysis and Planning,* ed. F. Fischer and J. Forester. Durham, NC: Duke University Press, 117–45.

Titmuss, R.M. (1997). *The Gift Relationship: From Human Blood to Social Policy,* ed. A. Oakly and J. Ashton. New York: New Press.

Toolan, M. (2001). *Narrative: A Critical Linguistic Introduction.* London: Routledge.

Torgerson, D. (1986). "Between Knowledge and Politics. Three Faces of Policy Analysis." *Policy Sciences* 19(1): 33–59.

———. (1995). "Policy Analysis and Public Life: The Restoration of Phronesis?" In *Political Science in History: Research Programs and Political Traditions,* ed. J. Farr, J.S. Dryzek, and S.T. Leonard. Cambridge: Cambridge University Press, 225–51.

———. (2003). "Democracy Through Policy Discourse." In *Deliberative Policy Analysis: Understanding Governance in the Network Society,* ed. M. Hajer and H. Wagenaar. Cambridge: Cambridge University Press.

Tribe, L. (1972). "Policy Science: Analysis or Ideology." *Philosophy and Public Affairs* 2: 66–110.

Urry, J. (2003). *Global Complexity.* Cambridge: Polity Press.

Van Eeten, M. (1997). "Sprookjes in Rivierenland: Beleidsverhalen over Wateroverlast en Dijkversterking" (Fairy tales in Riverland: Policy stories about floods and dike improvement). *Beleid en Maatschappij* 24(1): 32–43.

Velleman, D.J. (1989). *Practical Reflection.* Princeton, NJ: Princeton University Press.

Vinzant, J.C., and L. Crothers. (1998). *Street-Level Leadership: Discretion and Legitimacy in Front-Line Public Service.* Washington, DC: Georgetown University Press.

Von Wright, G.H. (1971). *Explanation and Understanding.* Ithaca, NY: Cornell University Press.

Wagenaar, H. (1987). "Virtual Institutions: Community Relations and Hospital Recidivism in the Life of the Mental Patient." Ph.D. diss., Department of Urban Studies, Massachusetts Institute of Technology.

———. (1995). "Het onbedoelde gebruik van beleid" (The unintended use of public policy). In *Het Bedrijf van de Verzorgingsstaat: Naar Nieuwe Verhoudingen tussen Staat, Markt en Burger* (The business of welfare: New relationships between state, market and citizen), ed. L. Aarts, P. de Jong, R. van der Veen, and H. Wagenaar. Amsterdam: Meppel Boom.

———. (1999). "Value Pluralism in Administrative Practice." *Administrative Theory and Praxis* 21(4): 441–54.

———. (2002). "Value Pluralism in Public Administration: Two Perspectives on Administrative Morality." In *Rethinking Administrative Theory: The Challenge of the New Century,* ed. J.S. Jun. Westport, CT: Praeger, 105–30.

———. (2004). "'Knowing' the Rules: Administrative Work as Practice." *Public Administration Review* 64(November/December): 643–56.

———. (2005). *Stadswijken, Complexiteit en Burgerbestuur* (Neigborhoods, complexity and citizen participation). Den Haag: XPIN.

———. (2006a). "Bureaucratic Order and Personal Order: The Narrative Analysis of Administrative Practice." *Nederlandse Geografische Studies* 344: 43–63.

———. (2006b). "Democracy and Prostitution: Deliberating the Legalization of Brothels in The Netherlands." *Administration & Society* 38(3): 198–235.

———. (2007a). "Governance, Complexity, and Democratic Participation: How Citizens and Public Officials Harness the Complexities of Neighborhood Decline." *American Review of Public Administration* 37(1): 17–50.

———. (2007b). "Interpretation and Intention in Policy Analysis." In *Handbook of Public Policy Analysis: Theory, Politics and Methods,* ed. F. Fischer, G.J. Miller, and M.S. Sidney. London: CRC Press, 429–43.

———. (2008). "Introduction: Dialogical Meaning in Policy Analysis." *Critical Policy Analysis* 1(4): 311–34.

Wagenaar, H., and S.D.N. Cook. (2003). "Understanding Policy Practices: Action, Dialectic and Deliberation in Policy Analysis." In *Deliberative Policy Analysis: Understanding Governance in the Network Society,* ed. M. Hajer and H. Wagenaar. Cambridge: Cambridge University Press, 139–71.

Wagenaar, H., and R. Hartendorp. (2000). "Oedipus in the Welfare Office: Practice, Discourse and Identity in Public Administration." In *Government Institutions: Effects, Changes, and Normative Foundations,* ed. H. Wagenaar. Dordrecht, NL: Springer, 147–78.

Wagenaar, H., and D. Lewis. (1989). "Ironies of Inclusion: Social Class and Deinstitutionalization." *Journal of Health Politics, Policy and Law* 14(3): 503–22.

Wagenaar, H., and M. Specht. (2010). *Geëngageerd Bewonerschap: Burgerparticipatie in Drie Europese Steden* (Engaged residents: Citizen participation in three European cities). The Hague: Nicis Institute.

Waldrop, M.M. (1992). *Complexity: The Emerging Science at the Edge of Order and Chaos.* New York: Simon and Schuster.

Warnke, G. (2002). "Hermeneutics, Ethics and Politics." In *The Cambridge Companion to Gadamer*, ed. R.J. Dostal. Cambridge: Cambridge University Press, 79–101.

Warnock, M. (1976). *Imagination*. London: Faber & Faber.

Warren, M. (1992). "Democratic Theory and Self-Transformation." *American Political Science Review* 86(1): 8–23.

———. (2002). "What Can Democratic Participation Mean Today?" *Political Theory* 30(5): 677–701.

Weiss, C.H. (1979). "The Many Meanings of Research Utilization." *Public Administration Review* 39: 426–31.

———. (1980). "Knowledge Creep and Decision Accretion." *Knowledge: Creation, Diffusion, Utilization* 1: 381–404.

Weiss, R.S. (1995). *Learning from Strangers: The Art and Method of Qualitative Interview Studies*. New York: Free Press.

Weiss, R.S., and M. Rein. (1970). "The Evaluation of Broad-Aim Programs: Experimental Design, Its Difficulties, and an Alternative." *Administrative Science Quarterly* (March): 97–109.

Weitzer, R. (2009). "Legalizing Prostitution: Morality Politics in Western Australia." *British Journal of Criminology* 49(1): 88–105.

Wenger, E. (1996). "Communities of Practice: The Social Fabric of a Learning Organization." *Healthcare Forum* 39(4): 20–28.

———. (1998). *Communities of Practice: Learning, Meaning, and Identity*. Cambridge: Cambridge University Press.

Wenman, M.A. (2003a). "What Is Politics? The Approach of Radical Pluralism." *Politics* 23(1): 57–65.

———. (2003b). "'Agonistic Pluralism' and Three Archetypical Forms of Politics." *Contemporary Political Theory* 2(2): 165–86.

Westbrook, R.D. (1991). *John Dewey and American Democracy*. Ithaca, NY: Cornell University Press.

White, H. (1981). "The Value of Narrativity in the Representation of Reality." In *On Narrative*, ed. W.J.T. Mitchell. Chicago: University of Chicago Press.

Whyte, W.F. (1943 [1993]). *Street Corner Society: The Social Structure of an Italian Slum*. Chicago, IL: University of Chicago Press.

Wildavsky, A. (1979). *Speaking Truth to Power: The Art and Craft of Policy Analysis*. Boston: Little, Brown.

Winch, P. (1958). *The Idea of a Social Science and Its Relation to Philosophy*. London: Routledge and Kegan Paul.

Wiseman, J.P. (1979). *Stations of the Lost: The Treatment of Skid Row Alcoholics*. Chicago, IL: University of Chicago Press.

Wittgenstein, L. 1974. *Philosophical Investigations*, trans. G.E.M. Anscombe. Oxford, UK: Basil Blackwell.

Yanow, D. (1995). "Editorial: Practices of Policy Interpretation." *Policy Sciences* 28(2): 111–26.

———. (1996). *How Does a Policy Mean? Interpreting Policy and Organizational Action*. Washington, DC: Georgetown University Press.

———. (2000). *Conducting Interpretive Policy Analysis*. Thousand Oaks, CA: Sage Publications.

Zeichner, K. (2006). "Educational Action Research." In *Handbook of Action Research: The Concise Paperback Edition*, ed. P. Reason and H. Bradbury. Thousand Oaks, CA: Sage Publications, 273–84.

INDEX

ABOUT THE AUTHOR

Hendrik Wagenaar is an associate professor of public policy at the Department of Public Administration at Leiden University. He is also Research Director of the Centre for Governance Studies-Urban at the Hague Campus of Leiden University. He publishes in the area of urban governance, citizen participation, prostitution policy, administrative practice, complexity theory, and interpretive policy analysis. His recent publications include *Deliberative Policy Analysis: Understanding Governance in the Network Society* (Cambridge University Press, 2003) (with Maarten Hajer). His article "Governance, Complexity, and Democratic Participation: How Citizens and Public Officials Harness the Complexities of Neighbourhood Decline" won the best article award in the 2007 volume of the *American Review of Public Administration.*